COMPUTERS
Concepts and Uses

COMPUTERS
Concepts and Uses
Second Edition

MARY SUMNER

Southern Illinois University at Edwardsville

Prentice Hall, Englewood Cliffs, New Jersey 07632

Editorial/production supervision: *Pamela Wilder*
Cover and interior design: *A Good Thing, Inc.*
Manufacturing buyer: *Barbara Kittle*
Photo research: *Teri Stratford*
Photo editor: *Lorinda Morris-Nantz*

```
            Library of Congress Cataloging-in-Publication Data


Sumner, Mary.
    Computers : concepts and uses / Mary Sumner. -- 2nd ed.
      p.   cm.
    Includes index.
    ISBN 0-13-163446-1
    1. Computers.  2. Electronic data processing.  I. Title.
  QA76.5.S8943 1988
  004--dc19                                              87-33414
                                                         CIP
```

© 1988, 1985 by Prentice-Hall Inc.
A Division of Simon & Schuster
Englewood Cliffs, New Jersey 07632

Printed in the United States of America
10 9 8 7 6 5 4 3 2 1

ISBN 0-13-163446-1

Prentice-Hall International (UK) Limited, *London*
Prentice-Hall of Australia Pty. Limited, *Sydney*
Prentice-Hall Canada Inc., *Toronto*
Prentice-Hall Hispanoamericana, S.A., *Mexico*
Prentice-Hall of India Private Limited, *New Delhi*
Prentice-Hall of Japan, Inc., *Tokyo*
Prentice-Hall of Southeast Asia Pte. Ltd., *Singapore*
Editora Prentice-Hall do Brasil, Ltda., *Rio de Janeiro*

Chapter Opening Photo Credits

Chapter 1 Courtesy of Landmark Graphics / *Chapter 2* Reprinted from *Popular Mechanics.* Copyright 1975 Ziff Communications Company / *Chapter 3* © Chuck O'Rear / *Chapter 4* Photo Courtesy of NCR Corporation / *Chapter 5* Courtesy of Sperry Corporation / *Chapter 6* Courtesy of IBM Corporation / *Chapter 7* WordPerfect Corporation / *Chapter 8* Courtesy of Javelin Software / *Chapter 9* Courtesy of GE Calma Company, Milpitas, PA / *Chapter 10* Westinghouse Information Services / *Chapter 11* Courtesy of GTE Corporation, Stamford, Connecticut / *Chapter 12* Courtesy of Index Technology Corporation / *Chapter 13* Courtesy of Atari, Incorporated / *Chapter 14* Blair Seitz/Photo Researchers, Inc. / *Chapter 15* Gary Gladstone / *Chapter 16* © Hank Morgan/Photo Researchers, Inc. / *Chapter 17 Clockwise from top left:* BLAISE PASCAL, photo courtesy of IBM Corp.; LADY ADA AUGUSTA LOVELACE, The Bettmann Archive, Inc.; HANS HOLLERITH, photo courtesy of IBM Corp.; JOHN VON NEUMANN, The Bettmann Archive, Inc.; JOHN KEMENY and THOMAS KURTZ, Hawthorne/Olson—Darmouth College; COMMANDER GRACE M. HOPPER, Ret., U.S. Navy photo; STEVE JOBS, AP/Wide World Photos; STEVE WOZNIAK, courtesy of Apple Computer, Inc.; MITCH KAPOR, Lotus Development Corp.; *center,* WILLIAM GATES, Microsoft Corporation.

Contents

Chapter 5   Auxiliary Storage and File Processing   107

Chapter 6   Systems Software   135

Chapter 14   Programming Languages   377

Chapter 15   Management Information Systems   413

Chapter 16   Decision Support Systems and Artificial Intelligence   461

Chapter 17   Careers in Data Processing   495

Appendix A   Representing Data Within the Computer   511

Appendix B   Introduction to BASIC Programming   521

Glossary   607

Index   619

Preface

Many of us use or come in contact with computers and information systems on a day-to-day basis. Point-of-sale scanners are used at supermarkets at the checkout counter. Computer-based systems process our airline tickets and hotel reservations. When we call a mailorder company, information about our order is usually keyed into and processed by a computer system. An understanding of computer-based information systems, the technologies that support information processing, and emerging technologies such as microcomputers and office automation systems is important for every individual in our society.

Objectives

The primary objective of this text is to present the fundamental concepts of computers and computer-based information systems to you in a clear and interesting way. Basic concepts such as computer operations, the central processing unit, auxiliary storage, and input and output are presented in the context of numerous application examples so that you can see how technology is being used. The tools of computing, such as microcomputer-based spreadsheet, data base, and word processing software packages, are explained in detail. You will also learn about the process of information systems design and about new tools such as artificial intelligence and decision support systems.

Major Distinguishing Features

One of the major features distinguishing the second edition of *Computers: Concepts and Uses* from its previous edition is its extensive coverage of microcomputer-based application software. You will learn about the characteristics and uses of microcomputer-based spreadsheet, data base, and word processing software in three new chapters in the text. An additional chapter on computer graphics and desktop publishing is also included. You can learn how to use MS-DOS utilities in a special section of the operating systems chapter.

You may want to acquire a supplementary text to gain hands-on experience using software packages designed to support these applications. The software accompanying this supplementary text includes educational versions of the TWIN spreadsheet program and the DBASE III Plus data base program. You will have a choice of either WordPerfect or WordStar for word processing.

Another new feature of the text is a new chapter on decision support systems, artificial intelligence, and robotics. You will learn about how managers use decision support systems, how an expert system works, and

how robotics technology is being used in the manufacturing environment. Comprehensive coverage of data base management systems has been made possible by including material on microcomputer data base management in addition to material on large computer data base management.

The content of all of the existing chapters has been augmented with the use of up-to-date highlights on new technologies and applications in various environments. In the auxiliary storage chapter, you will learn about the uses of CD-ROM as well as how to take care of floppy disks. In the chapter on operating systems, where you will learn about MS-DOS, OS/2, and the UNIX operating system, a highlight explains some of the more common MS-DOS utilities. PC bulletin boards and local area networks are new topics covered in the data communications chapter, and a highlight details "Pitfalls to Avoid in Implementing a LAN." New material in the systems analysis and design, program design, and programming languages chapters describes computer-assisted software development tools, fourth-generation languages, and natural-language programs. The final chapter on careers discusses emerging job opportunities in the data processing field and strategies for finding a job.

Another feature of the second edition is the use of Focus sections—reprints from periodicals such as *Business Week, Information Week,* and *Forbes.* "Next: Computers with Ears," "Pushing Computers Closer to the Ultimate Speed Limit," and "Software's Old Man Is 30" are examples of these special sections. These reprints provide timely and interesting news stories, case studies, and biographies of important people in the computer field. They also provide up-to-date material about practical issues and technology trends.

In addition to new chapters, updated content coverage, and Focus sections, much of the material from the first edition has been reworked, consolidated, and reinforced with new ideas. For example, you will see that the first edition's two chapters on computer operations and the CPU have been consolidated into one chapter. Input and output concepts are also covered in one chapter instead of two. The consolidation of material has made it possible to include much of the new material. The result is a text with many new topics and examples as well as a foundation in basic concepts and applications.

Teaching and Learning Aids

The text includes many devices to support teaching and to encourage learning. Each chapter has performance objectives, which will help you to understand learning outcomes. Key terms are introduced throughout each chapter, and major points are summarized at the end of each chapter. End-of-chapter exercises include short answer type review questions as well as discussion questions enabling you to apply concepts. Application exercises are included for such topics as drawing a flowchart and drawing a data flow diagram.

The BASIC Appendix has been completely revised for use in a microcomputer setting. As in the previous edition, the BASIC Appendix includes

detailed coverage of programming syntax and logic and numerous programming projects. Since BASIC programming is still an important component of many introductory data processing courses, this material is an important resource.

Supporting Material

The supplementary material for this text includes an instructor's manual, a test item file, a study guide, and color transparencies. All of these materials have been completely revised to support the second edition. The study guide provides many additional short answer questions and exercises.

A supplementary microcomputer software text including instruction in TWIN, a spreadsheet program, DBASE III Plus, a data base program, and word processing programs, will be available to users of *Computers: Concepts and Uses*. You may purchase educational versions of TWIN, DBASE III Plus, and either WordPerfect or WordStar along with this supplementary microcomputer text for an economical rate. Using these materials will give you an opportunity to gain valuable hands-on experience using spreadsheet, data base, and word processing programs. The supplementary text and software can also be used for future reference and in other courses.

Acknowledgments

The development of the second edition would not have been possible without the efforts of many dedicated professionals at Prentice Hall. I would like to thank Joyce Perkins, the development editor who was largely responsible for the success of this second edition. Her hard work and insight into how to integrate new material with previous material was very important to this project. I also want to thank Dennis Hogan, the executive editor who initiated the project several years ago and who has demonstrated a major commitment to its success ever since. His ongoing support, his many excellent ideas, and his insight into market needs have been critical to the development of this manuscript.

The end product would not have been feasible without the hard work of many others, including production editor Pamela Wilder; art director Florence Silverman; director of photo research Lorinda Morris-Nantz and researcher Teri Stratford; and marketing director Gary June. All of these people have provided good ideas and invaluable support.

The development of this manuscript was supported by the efforts of experienced educators and writers. I am grateful to Michael B. Murphy for the outstanding revision of the BASIC Appendix. Daphne Swabey, Peter Fuhrman, and Gregory Buck all deserve thanks for their work on the microcomputer software chapters.

The text would not have been possible without the feedback received from many reviewers during its development. Changes suggested by them were incorporated into the text during the development process and significantly improved the final product. These reviewers follow:

- Huann-Ming Chung—Pembroke State University
- Lillie Gail LeFevre—Florida Community College
- Charles G. Davidson—Milwaukee Area Technical College
- Shannon Scanlon—Henry Ford Community College

The reviewers for the first edition were:
- Lincoln Andrews—Miami-Dade Community College, North
- Robert Behling—Bryant College
- Virginia B. Bender—William Rainey Harper College
- Herbert Bomzer—Central Michigan University
- George Brabb—Illinois State University
- Wayne Brown—Vanderbilt University
- William E. Burrows—University of Washington
- W. Maxine Buxman—Central Connecticut State College
- Lance Eliot—California State University—Dominguez Hills
- Irv Englander—Bentley College
- David Ferbrache—Eastern Connecticut State College
- Richard Fleming—North Lake College
- George C. Fowler—Texas A & M University
- Jon Fults—Cerritos College
- George Gintowt—William Rainey Harper College
- Seth Hock—Columbus Technical Institute
- Stanley P. Honacki—Moraine Valley Community College
- Herman P. Hoplin—Syracuse University
- Donnavae Hughes—North Harris County College
- Richard Kerns—East Carolina University
- Eldon Li—California Polytechnic State University
- Bijan Mashaw—Central Michigan University
- Richard E. Matson—Schoolcraft College
- Michael Michaelson—Palomar College
- John J. Neuhauser—Boston College
- Edward L. Nock—DeVry Institute
- Atalh Omidi—New York Institute of Technology
- Jerry T. Peters—Lambuth College
- Deniel Petrosko—College of Lake County
- Gary R. Reeves—University of South Carolina at Columbia
- Ernst Rilki—William Rainey Harper College
- Fred L. Scott—Broward Community College
- Robert D. Smith—Kent State University
- Rod B. Southworth—Laramie County Community College
- Ronald J. Teichman—Pennsylvania State University
- Robert C. Tesch, Sr.—University of North Carolina at Greensboro
- Eileen Wrigley—Community College of Allegheny County

Mary Sumner
Southern Illinois University at Edwardsville

COMPUTERS
Concepts and Uses

Introduction to Computing

Carl Willis turns from the computer screen and reaches for the phone, pushes a button and says, "Ronnie, I just saved you ten million bucks. It isn't any good where we got the sample, but to the right below a downslope is a big one, and the little one'll drain into it." Carl drills oil wells in Texas. In this financially risky business, Carl and his partners can lose millions any time he fails to strike an oil deposit or strikes one too small to be profitable. But Carl has found a new way to reduce his risks, and he keeps it on his desk. He uses a Landmark Graphics Corp. computer system that creates three-dimensional images when data from underground soundings —seismic surveys—are loaded into it. The computer tells Carl where the oil is and whether there's enough of it to make sinking a well pay off.

Elaine Leaf says into the phone, "I'm going to put you on hold a minute. Let's see what we can find out," and turns to her computer. She takes a compact disk out of its cover, sets it up and hits a few buttons on the computer keyboard. "Their dividend is nothing, but they have paid one for the last three quarters. Wait a minute—there's a note here that they made an announcement yesterday . . . let's see what they said. . . . Oh, nice! They just got a three million dollar contract from Campbell foods. You could either try it for six months or think of it as a real long-term investment. Plant genetic technology has a lot of potential, and if they hit on anything, one of the big companies may buy them out."

Elaine is an investment advisor in Cleveland. After five years at a big brokerage firm, Elaine decided to go into business for herself. Out on her own, Elaine liked having her own clients and making decisions independently, but she missed all the information resources she had had at the brokerage house. Last month Elaine subscribed to Datext, a data service that provides her with information about 10,000 publicly held companies. Elaine can get a huge amount of information about a company from compact disks that work with her personal computer. If she wants a stock's current trading price, she can make a selection from the choices listed on her computer monitor, and the computer automatically dials her telephone to hook into the Dow Jones News/Retrieval service, an on-line data base. Within seconds, ticker-tape data about current stock transactions on the major exchanges are moving across the screen. Datext accesses other on-line data bases, too, and each month, Elaine is sent a CD disk of update information.

Exploring for oil and managing financial investments are as different as two careers can be. Still, Carl and Elaine enjoy the benefits of a technology that makes each one more productive: computer data processing. Computers make it possible to store and retrieve huge amounts of data, to perform

Warehouse-based Computer System

Courtesy of National Css, a company of the Dun and Bradstreet Corp.

calculations on data unimaginably fast, and to convert data into amazing visual and audible forms.

A computer simulation of the topography of Saturn is so astonishing that we all notice it. But even more astonishing is the way computers have changed everyday activities and the speed with which this computer revolution occurred. In only a generation, computers have evolved from football-field-size monsters reserved for government and business applications to typewriter-size machines in football locker rooms, offices, and homes as well as in government buildings and businesses large and small. Let's relive a bit of not very ancient history. . . .

A Day Without Computers

It is early September 1956, and Mary Bensky has her hands full. Three days a week and one evening she takes courses toward her BA degree at the university. She works part time as a clerk as well, verifying sales from a dozen branches of a chain of clothing stores. Today is one of her days at the office. On her desk is a hand-operated adding machine. For each sales slip,

she verifies the subtotal and then the total including sales tax and calculates the commission due the salesperson. Then she adds up weekly sales for each store and each salesperson. Again and again, Mary punches the numbers on the adding machine, pulls the crank for a total, and tears off the tape and staples it to each store's bundle of sales slips.

At noon Mary runs out to deposit her weekly pay in the bank. She takes the cash out of the pay envelope and gives it, a deposit slip, and her bank book to the teller. The teller enters $32.50 in Mary's bank book and in the bank ledger, looks in the card file drawer to verify the account number, and hands back the bank book.

Mary stops next at the library, where the librarian checks Mary's two books back in by crossing out the return date on the paper slip tucked in the cardboard pocket glued inside the front cover of the book. The librarian then checks both titles off the record of borrowed books.

After work Mary goes to the university gym and gets in line to register for the afternoon section of one of her courses. When she finally gets to the head of the line, the section is filled. At the other end of the gym, a student updates the list of class sections, touring the registration tables every 15 minutes and then revising the blackboard. Mary finds another afternoon section and gets in line, hoping that it won't close before she can register.

On to the bookstore. She tells the clerk what books she needs and waits while he searches for them. Eventually he comes back with two of the three texts. As for the third, the clerk cannot tell whether it is in stock, on order, or in transit. "Come back next week," he advises. "We should have it by then."

Today

A generation later finds Mary's son Rob studying at the same university. He works part time in a pharmacy, where he is learning to use the store's system for computerized control of the prescription process. At a keyboard Rob enters data customers have filled in on standardized forms. Along with their names, addresses, and birth dates, they list their allergies, other health and medical information, and whatever medications they take. When a customer presents a new prescription to be filled, the computer alerts the pharmacist if the new drug might interact badly with the customer's other medication or if a prescription might adversely affect some other health condition.

The bank is closed by the time Rob finishes work, so he deposits his $159.95 paycheck in an automated teller machine that is open 24 hours a day. He programs the machine to put $50 in his savings account, return $35 in cash to him, and deposit the rest in his checking account. The machine pops out a card listing the various transactions so Rob will have a record of them.

Rob returns his library books at the book drop; the librarian will check them in, running a light pen over the bar code sticker on each book, when

A Pharmacy's Computer
System

the library opens in the morning. A computer will automatically record that the books are again available.

When Rob registers for classes, at the keyboard of a computer terminal he enters numbers for the section of Business Statistics he prefers. SORRY, SECTION 127 IS CLOSED appears on the screen, followed by the names of two other business courses that meet at the same time as section 127. The screen tells Rob to type OTHER if he wants to know what Business Statistics sections are still open.

Within 15 minutes Rob has registered for all his courses, arranging his schedule to fit in with his job. He types BOOK on the keyboard, and on the screen the titles of each course's required textbooks appear. Rob types COPY, and the printer connected to the terminal prints out the list of books. When Rob gives this list to the clerk at the bookstore, she types commands into another terminal that tells her the location of each book. One of them is on order; the other two are in stock. Their cost, including tax, is automatically entered in the sales terminal. The figures will be added to Rob's consolidated quarterly statement of charges issued by the bursar's office.

What Is Data Processing and Why Do We Need It?

When Mary added the clothing stores' sales figures, computing the tax and commissions, she was processing **data,** the sales transactions figures and facts she worked with. When all the data had been manipulated into a

meaningful form—weekly records by store and by clerk—they became **information.** Information of this kind was available for managers of the clothing chain to make decisions about reordering or discontinuing merchandise, about prices to charge or discounts to offer. The managers also used this information to review the performance of sales people and store managers. In the **manual data processing** environment of the 1950s, time lags were unavoidable between ordering and sales and between sales and performance reviews.

In contrast, managers today have nearly immediate access to sales information through the use of **electronic** or **computer data processing.** Sales clerks and cashiers in each branch store enter sales data on a point-of-sale terminal that records and stores the data. Terminals in all branches are linked to a computer in the company's main office. The computer-based system can organize the data in a variety of ways. Today's sales managers can press a few keys on a terminal and have access to the data just entered by a sales clerk in a branch store. A manager can review the sales for the day for each store and each salesperson. A store's cumulative sales for the year can be compared with those made in the same period in any preceding year. The manager can know how many navy blue, pin-striped, double-breasted suits imported from England are left in the warehouse—by size—by retrieving that information from the system. That manager can communicate with store managers about their stock and their personnel without having to ask each one individually for all the details; the details are as close as the computer terminal.

Terminals and the other devices that go with them, such as printers, keyboards, modems, and other equipment are computer **hardware.** The instructions, or **programs,** for operating that hardware are known as **software.** A **computer system** consists of a connected set of hardware along with the software that makes it work.

When data are manipulated or processed, they are combined and converted into forms that make them usable for decision making. The usable form of data is called **information.**

What exactly does "computers process data" mean? Computers actually can perform only a limited number of tasks. They can do simple arithmetic problems, such as adding, subtracting, multiplying, dividing, and finding square roots or percentages. They can compare data and reorganize, or **sort,** it. They can **store** data and make it available on demand, or

When sales clerks enter sales data at a branch store, sales managers can access the data almost instantly.

Tim Davis—Photo Researchers, Inc.

FIGURE 1.1

retrieve it. And, most important, they can do these things at rates as high as millions of operations per second. (See Figure 1.1.) Computer systems can arrange data in visual forms—from printouts of columns of numbers to 3-D special effects for films. Systems can convert data into audible forms—from the voice at the check-out counter to electronic music needing neither players or instruments. Computer applications are exciting and varied.

Computer Applications in Today's World

Computers are so well-integrated into daily life that they are often completely invisible. Computer systems track airplane parts produced in three different parts of the world and make sure that what is needed at the point of assembly is manufactured and on hand in the right quantities.

Distribution and transport of goods, too, is expedited electronically. In North America, goods travel almost exclusively by train and truck as they make their way from supplier to manufacturer to customer. Electronic systems can keep track of trains on sidings in Wyoming, and they can trace parcel-delivery trucks on side streets in New York City. In fact, cars may soon come equipped with a small computer system that will let a driver program a destination and then be warned—by the computer—if the car gets off course.

Computers have entirely changed the operations of banks and the securities markets. Consumer deposits and withdrawals, once possible only during "banker's hours" from 9:00 to 3:00, now can be conducted around the clock, at automated tellers in banks, in stores, in bowling alleys, and on street corners. Securities trading, too, has changed radically since the

Computer systems help Federal Express monitor deliveries.

computerization of the major stock exchanges. The volume of trading has skyrocketed because transactions are executed and confirmed and all the paperwork is handled by computers, permitting greater volume. Computers have also been instrumental in creating something called program trading, in which traders use computers to monitor specific market behavior, chart a course of action, and advise how best to follow it.

In the service industries, although a person may still grill your hamburger at Burger King, a computer is likely to screen your data sheet at an employment agency. The robotics industry also sees an important segment of its future in service-industry applications. Gas-station robots may pump gas and home-care robots may lend help to the elderly.

Here are some other areas where computers have enabled new procedures, products, and possibilities.

Manufacturing and Design

Computers are getting at least some of the credit for helping some old-line manufacturing industries to become competitive again in the late 1980s. Ford Motor Company, for example, owes its surging sales primarily to the Taurus and Sable lines. Not only did computer-assisted design (CAD) develop the streamlined look of the car, but robots do 98 percent of the welding on them. Right now, General Electric is working on a new expert system that—entirely within the computer—will test out car designs and analyze the information to determine whether a particular design can be manufactured efficiently.

The automotive industry will probably be one of the first in which a product is designed and tested entirely within the computer and then its specifications translated to production lines that are themselves run by computers and robots. But good old Heinz catsup will probably get there first. Food manufacturers, among the most package-conscious of producers, use computer simulation to design new packages and to test their effectiveness. Package designers can test designs—again, entirely within the computer—not just for how well they contain a food product but for how safely and economically they ship, how secure they are on store shelves, and how appealing consumers are likely to find them.

7

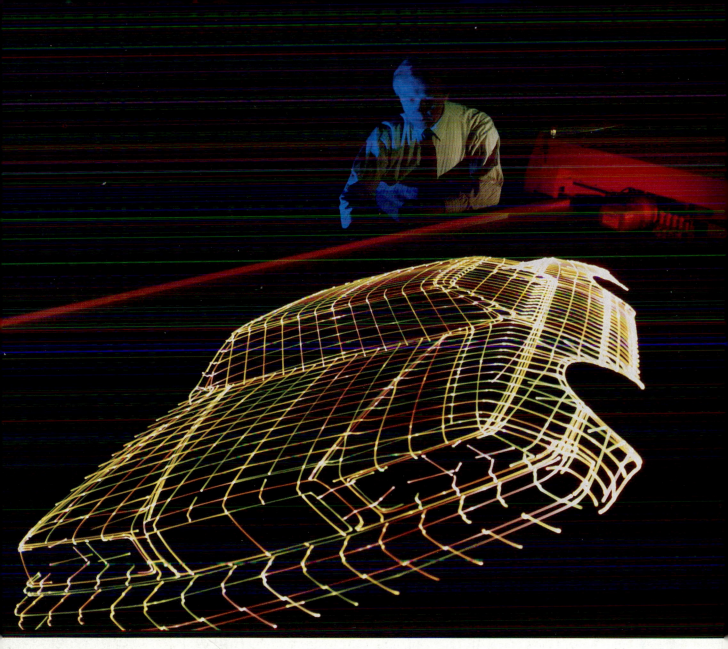

CAD Screen of Ford's Taurus/Sable Line (page 8)   A Robot-run Section of a Taurus/Sable Assembly Line (page 9)

Photos courtesy of Ford Motor Co.

Two related industries that had practically disappeared from the United States are back and thriving, thanks to computerization. In the textile and clothing industries, computerization has helped U.S. manufacturers recapture their long-lost reputation for speed, efficiency, and economy. Computerized textile inventories get fabrics to manufacturers and into cutting rooms, CAD/CAM (computer-assisted design/computer-assisted manufacturing) networks get designs drawn and made up, and information networks link mills, shippers, manufacturers, and sellers in a way that competitors outside North America cannot match.

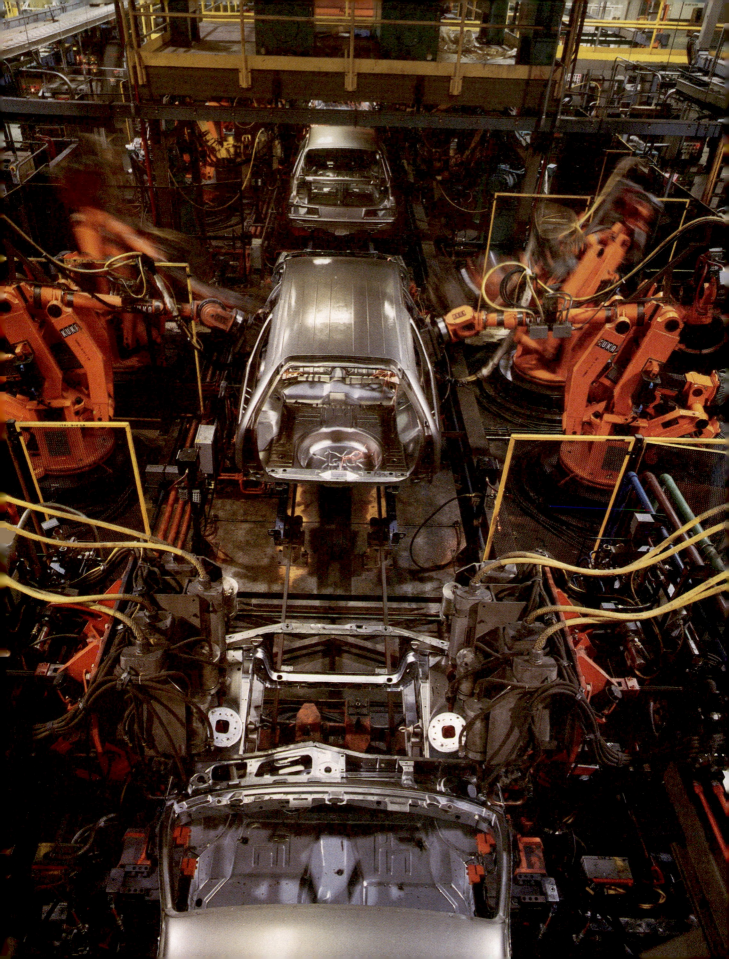

Textile Design at the Computer

Courtesy of IBM Corp.

Retailing

If the pharmacy of the not-too-distant future has a robot behind the counter filling prescriptions, supermarkets today are already testing computer-driven systems to cut time and costs. One electronic system has customers checking out their own groceries by passing them over a price-reading electronic beam. After a store employee bags the groceries (and checks the item list—to prevent shoplifting), customers pay for their purchases at a central location. These processes speed up checkouts and reduce the numbers of employees needed for that function.

Supermarkets are also testing video display terminals that give recipes and suggest appropriate wines to accompany them or that give cooking demonstrations and then print out the recipes. Finally, in the super supermarket, another computer can take electronic note of what you buy and pop out money-saving coupons for related items.

Video display terminals in supermarkets dispense recipes—and sometimes show demonstrations of how to prepare them.

Hank Morgan

Health, Medicine, and Research

Computers are helping to improve delivery of health services, they're aiding medical research, and they're enhancing the quality of life for people with physical disabilities. A Florida dentist, for example, is using a Macintosh, so-called "dental" software, and a digitizer to translate from a patient's X rays the probable outcome of oral surgery. For all kinds of plastic surgery, computer simulations show prospective patients how the results are likely to look. More important, simulations help surgeons to predict conditions likely to be found once surgery begins and to plan step-by-step approaches for reconstructive surgery that requires many operations.

People with speech disabilities have two computer-oriented approaches to improvement. One computer speech-therapy system shows on a monitor the syllables a speech-impaired person is to practice. Electronic sensors at the person's nose and throat translate the sounds to a computer that then displays how the tongue should be positioned to make the sound correctly. Another system, used in helping deaf persons to speak clearly,

Computer Simulation of Tornado Formation

National Center for Atmospheric Research/National Science Foundation

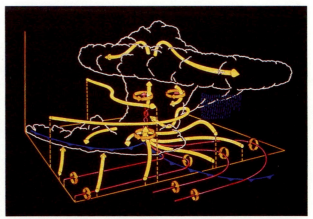
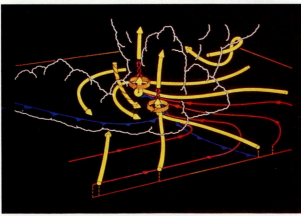
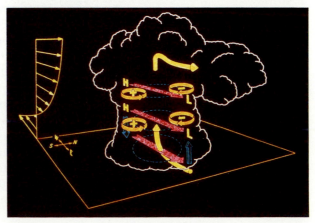

shows a computerized pattern of a correctly pronounced word on the monitor. Students can then practice the word, watching the pattern each pronunciation makes on the screen until the student's pattern looks like that of the speech therapist.

One of the more astonishing medical applications of computerization is robot-performed brain surgery. Certain parts of extremely delicate operations can be handled better by robots, whose hands never shake and whose eyes never blink, than by human brain surgeons.

In the laboratory, supercomputers are used to simulate natural processes, such as the development of tornadoes and wind shear, that can't be tested as well under real conditions as they are in simulations. When wind shear began to be implicated in airplane crashes, computer simulation helped analysts to discover that it is associated with a much broader range of weather conditions than had originally been believed. Other phenomena cannot be tested at all except by computer simulation. What scientists understand about black holes, the theoretical outcome of an exploding star's collapse, comes from supercomputer simulation.

Government

From the largest federal agency to the smallest local administrative office, computers are used to organize information and improve services. Computers save money and time, help to solve crimes and find lost people, plan budgets, keep track of registered voters, and more. Also, as the largest supporter of research, the government "owns" enormous quantities of useful data. It has decided to make available to industry a free data base, Textran, which summarizes the results of government agricultural and biological research, primarily. Textran's level of detail is useful for industrial purposes, but it's not specific enough to prevent the government from patenting processes and even products the original research develops.

Education

Computers are fixtures in many schoolrooms, and computer-assisted instruction (CAI) is commonplace for drills and repetitive learning tasks in elementary schools. But more exciting computer applications are beginning to suggest that the computer's early promise as a revolutionary educational tool will be realized. It may soon be possible for a personal computer system to play a Beethoven sonata, for example, from a CD disk that will also deliver instructor's lecture on it, and then the system will transfer the student's questions back to the instructor via electronic mail. The electronic university already exists, making undergraduate and graduate degree programs available to people unable to go to school on campus. And the Jack Nicklaus Academy in Orlando, Florida, uses a computer to help students learn how to make their golf swings as much as possible like a "perfect swing," which was itself—you guessed it—determined from a computer simulation!

Computers and You

No matter what career you choose, no matter where you live, your future will involve computers and computing. An important place in that future belongs to people who can interpret computer-generated information, who can operate computers, who can design software to teach computers new tasks, and who can help others put software and hardware together into productive computer applications. People will be needed to sell the machines and to repair them. Engineers will be needed to design new and better computer systems and applications. Teachers will be needed to help impart all this computer-related knowledge and to help people learn to

The future is bright for people who can interpret computer-generated information.

Photo courtesy of Ford Motor Co.

perform all these computer-related jobs. Even if you do not ultimately work directly in the computer field, the technology and its effects will be part of your life—at school, in the workplace, and at home.

Summary and Key Terms

1. Computers enable people to get, keep, and **process** vast quantities of **data** quickly, converting data into **information.** Computers have changed the way we do things in every area of life. Less than 30 years ago, manual data processing was the rule. Information was often slow in coming and obsolete once obtained. Today, **business applications** make it possible for people to spend more time being productive and less time waiting for the information they need.

2. Data can be **stored** in a computer system, ready for **retrieval** at some later time. Data can also be **transferred** from one place to another, one person to another. Data are often made available to users through **terminals,** which are part of the **hardware** of the system. The instructions for how the hardware is to operate are called **software.**

3. We live in an "age of information." We are deluged with a mass of continually changing information. This can create greater flexibility, efficiency, and complexity in our lives.

4. Computer applications are many and varied. They have become essential in manufacturing, transportation, retailing, and virtually every business area. Banking and investment industries cannot do without computers.

5. Computers are making significant contributions to medical care, government, law, education, and scientific research.

6. Your future will involve computers, no matter what your career. They will affect you in school, at work, and at home.

Review and Discussion Questions

1. Briefly describe how each of the following computer-based information systems benefits the users in each situation. Explain how each of these procedures would have been accomplished without the use of a computer system:

   a. Ordering supplies for hospitals.
   American Hospital Supply Corporation enables purchasing agents in hospitals to use computer terminals to enter orders and to check inventory levels of various items. These orders are transmitted immediately to American Hospital Supply's order department, which in turn gives its customers, the hospitals, immediate information about prices and delivery dates.

   b. Tracking freight on the railroad.
   The Union Pacific Railroad has a computerized dispatching system which keeps track of every freight car on the line and makes sure that cars are fully utilized. Customers of the railroad can get information on their railroad cars, including their location and planned delivery dates for shipments.

   c. Producing the best flight plans for the airlines.
   Computers are at work evaluating possible flight plans. Given information on passenger load and cargo, the computer can pick the best altitude and route for each flight. Computerized flight plans are designed to assure safety and to minimize fuel costs.

   d. Subscribing to newspapers via computer.
   Today personal computer owners can subscribe to newspapers such as *The Wall Street Journal* by dialing up an external data network which provides an issue in electronic form on a timely basis.

   e. Paying your bills electronically.
   Home banking services are offered by several commercial banks in Boston. Personal computer owners can obtain access to their checking account balances, pay their bills, and receive information

on banking services by dialing up the banks' computers.

f. Selling insurance electronically.

A number of major insurance companies have equipped their sales agents with personal computers. These sales agents can use their PC's to dial up the home office computer to create new policies, to update existing policyholder information, and to obtain policy information for their customers. Word processing software can be used to send sales letters to insurance prospects as well.

2. Describe computer-based information systems which you may have come in contact with in each of the following places:

a. At the grocery store.

b. At school.

c. At the library.

d. At a doctor's office.

e. At home.

3. Give three reasons why it is important to learn about computers and their applications today.

HOW TO "READ" FM TUNER SPECIFICATIONS

Popular Electronics

WORLD'S LARGEST-SELLING ELECTRONICS MAGAZINE   JANUARY 1975/75¢

PROJECT BREAKTHROUGH!

World's First Minicomputer Kit to Rival Commercial Models...
"ALTAIR 8800"   SAVE OVER $1000

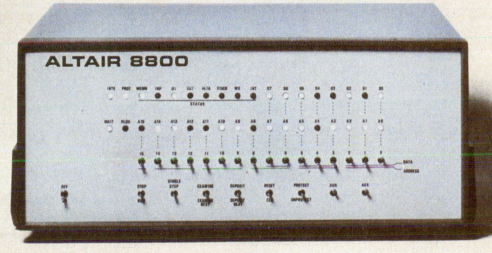

ALSO IN THIS ISSUE:

- An Under–$90 Scientific Calculator Project
  - CCD's—TV Camera Tube Successor?
  - Thyristor–Controlled Photoflashers

TEST REPORTS:

Technics 200 Speaker System
Pioneer RT-1011 Open-Reel Recorder
Tram Diamond-40 CB AM Transceiver
Edmund Scientific "Kirlian" Photo Kit
Hewlett-Packard 5381 Frequency Counter

The Evolution of Computers

2

Chapter Objectives

After studying this chapter, you should be able to

1. Identify major early developments in computing, such as Babbage's invention of the analytical machine.

2. Describe the emergence of the first electronic digital computers, such as the Mark I and the ENIAC, and the development of the stored-program concept by von Neumann.

3. Describe characteristics of computing technology distinguishing among the four generations of machines.

4. Explain the impact of technology, such as the invention of the microprocessor, chip technologies, and language developments, on computing and its applications.

The U.S. Census was first computerized in 1890, using a punched-card tabulating and sorting machine invented by Herman Hollerith. With Hollerith's machine, the 1890 Census took just four years to tabulate, an improvement over the 1880 Census, which was not published until 1887! But most important, Hollerith's invention marked the birth of what we now call data processing.

Computing and tabulating, however, did not begin—or end—with this invention. Pascal, Leibniz, and Babbage had already helped to make computation easier by automating parts of the counting process. If Hollerith can be viewed as providing the first input system, it was they who provided the first machinery. John Napier, the inventor of logarithms, and George Boole, among others, provided the theories of math and logic that made the science of computer programming possible.

By the 20th century, the stage had been set for the emergence of modern computers. World War II created an urgent need for new data-processing methods. Aircraft and ballistics designers required fast and efficient solutions to complex equations, and vast quantities of statistics had to be processed. Large, complicated machines were developed to meet such military needs in Germany, England, and the United States. These were the first of the modern computers. In this chapter we will follow the exciting developments in computer technology that have brought us from the first digital computers to microcomputers in many homes and offices to supercomputers that make animated films or design products and run the production processes that take them from computer screen to store shelf.

The Early History of Computing

People have been *"computing"* throughout history, probably since they first learned how to count with pebbles (the word *calculus* comes from the Latin word for "stone"). People living in the ancient civilization of the Tigris-Euphrates Valley about 5000 years ago used a fire-hardened clay board with grooves in which pebbles could be moved easily from one side to the other. This technique was also known in the Far East, where both the Chinese and the Japanese adopted and modified it. The abacus—which uses movable beads strung on wires above and below a crossbar—is thought to have originated in China about 2600 B.C. The Japanese had a similar device, called the *soroban*. These inventions are still in use today.

Better techniques for keeping records by hand, along with specialized calculating devices, continued to be developed throughout the centuries.

Pascal

In 1642 Blaise Pascal (1623–1662) invented the pascaline, an automatic desktop machine that could add and subtract. Made of brass and about the size of a cigar box, Pascal's calculator consisted of a set of toothed wheels, or gears. Each wheel had the numbers 0 through 9 engraved on it, one number for each tooth of the wheel. The user could add or subtract by turning the wheels. When one wheel made a complete revolution, it caused

An Abacus

The Bettmann Archive, Inc.

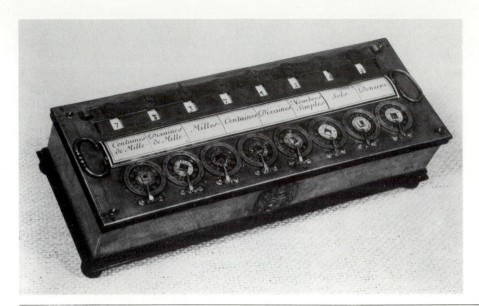

The Pascaline ''Calculator''

Photo courtesy of IBM Corp.

the wheel to the left of it to make one tenth of a revolution. In this way the machine kept a total of the numbers counted, which were displayed through a glass ''window'' at the top of the box.

Pascal's automatic counting machine, a remarkable achievement, still had a few drawbacks: It could only add and subtract, not multiply and divide, and the results were not always accurate because the gears often got stuck between two digit positions. In the business world it was a complete failure.

Leibniz

In 1671 the German philosopher Gottfried Wilhelm von Leibniz (1646–1716) developed the ''stepped reckoner.'' In this device Leibniz overcame the defects of Pascal's toothed gears. A desktop calculator like the pascaline, the stepped reckoner could add and subtract automatically. It could also multiply and divide by using repeated additions and subtractions.

Although many models of Leibniz's machine were used in his day, his later designs for improved calculating devices could not be produced commercially: Precision machine tooling to make identical metal parts did not exist in the 17th century.

Babbage

Charles Babbage (1791–1871), an English mathematician, was responsible for the next step in the evolution of computers. Babbage, professor of mathematics at Cambridge University, had a reputation for a quick temper that earned him the nickname ''the irascible genius.'' True to his nature, he became annoyed by the mathematical errors he was constantly finding in printed navigational and astronomical tables. He hit on the idea that those

tables might be more accurately calculated by machines. The "difference engine," which he invented in 1822, was designed specifically to compute polynomials (the sum of two or more positive terms, such as $x^2 + x + 41$).

Babbage next went to work on what he called an "analytical engine." A dramatic improvement over his one-task computer; the analytical engine was a kind of *general-purpose computer* designed to solve any arithmetic problem. In fact, it had most of the elements present in today's digital computer systems: a "mill," or *processing unit,* which manipulated data according to certain rules; a "store," or *memory,* which held information; data recorded on *punched cards,* or *input;* and automatic printing of computations, or *output.* A logical set of instructions led the user to subdivide calculations into steps performed in a sequence—in other words, a program—that could be changed.

Babbage got the idea of using punched cards to feed instructions into his huge machine from an invention by Joseph Marie Jacquard, a French inventor (1752–1834). In 1801 Jacquard used cards with holes punched in them to activate rods that raised and lowered threads on a weaving machine. A sequence of Jacquard cards produced a pattern in the woven cloth; each sequence of cards (each program, in other words) produced a different pattern.

Babbage's analytical engine was very complicated and required thousands of gears, levers, and belts all working together in fine-tuned precision. Although he worked on it obsessively until his death in 1871, Babbage never completed his wonderful machine.

Lady Ada Augusta Lovelace

Lady Ada Augusta Lovelace (1815–1852), daughter of the poet Lord Byron, was an admirer of Babbage and his work. She became his close friend and public supporter. Lady Ada has been called the first programmer. She discovered some of the key elements of programming and program design. For example, she figured out that the same set of punched cards could be reused to repeat certain instructions. Today we call these instructions in a program "loops" and "subroutines."

Babbage's Engine

Photo courtesy of IBM Corp.

Hollerith and the American Census

Pascal, Leibniz, and Babbage were spurred to invent new computing devices because they were impatient with the way things were being done in their day. The lack of efficiency in counting the United States Census in 1880 similarly inspired major new computing developments. Several thousand people and 7½ years were required to count (manually) its results. By the time it was done it was almost time for the 1890 Census! Dr. Herman Hollerith (1860–1929), a mechanical engineer and statistician, was hired by the Census Bureau to help solve the problem. He suggested the use of punched cards to record census data. (Hollerith said that this idea occurred to him when he saw a train conductor hand-punch tickets to record passengers' destinations.)

After trying a few other formats, Hollerith designed cards the size of a dollar bill that had 288 locations where holes could be punched. The rows and columns of holes in Hollerith's punched cards represented numerals and population characteristics, such as sex and race and whether an individual was native or foreign born. People throughout the nation entered local data by punching holes in the cards, which were then sent on for tabulation.

To handle these cards, Hollerith built an electric machine that could tabulate them at the rate of 50 to 75 a minute. The machine contained metal pins that "read" each of the 288 locations in each card. Wherever holes had been punched a pin would pass through the card, making contact with mercury-filled cups and completing an electric circuit. Each time a circuit was closed, a counting mechanism in the machine was activated. In this way the different items (age, sex, etc.) contained on the cards were tabulated at the same time.

By the time the next census was being planned, punched cards had permanently changed the nature of the counting process. Hollerith knew that he had come up with a money-making invention. In 1896 he set up the Tabulating Machine Company, which manufactured both the machines and the cards. After many mergers and name changes, Hollerith's company eventually became part of IBM.

George Boole

Meanwhile, another 19th-century mathematician, George Boole (1815–1864), had introduced a theory of logic that was to prove very important to the development of electronic computers. In what is now known as Boolean algebra, Boole reduced logic to two-valued *binary notation*. In binary notation, only the values 1 and 0 are used to express numbers. By stringing enough 1s and 0s together, any number can be expressed—and with Boolean algebra, the numbers can also be operated on logically. Binary notation turned out to be virtually made to order for electronic components, which can be either on (the equivalent of 1) or off (the equivalent of 0). All these inventions paved the way for the birth of the electronic digital computer.

The Birth of the Electronic Digital Computer

The Mark I

In 1937 Howard H. Aiken started developing a computer at Harvard University. Aiken wanted to combine a punched-card input method with contemporary electrical and mechanical technology. In 1944, after half a million dollars in funding from IBM, Aiken and four IBM engineers completed the Mark I, also known as the IBM Automatic Sequence Controlled Calculator.

The Mark I was 50 feet long and 8 feet high. Its thousands of moving parts were controlled by electric current. It took Mark I approximately 4½ seconds to multiply two 23-digit numbers. The Mark I fed raw data on punched paper tape into a "mill," where the calculations, supervised by a set of logical instructions, were performed.

The Atanasoff-Berry Computer

Dr. John V. Atanasoff, a physicist at Iowa State College, made an important contribution to the continuing development of computers, although he rarely gets credit for it. In 1939, Atanasoff, assisted by a graduate student named Clifford Berry, built the first electronic digital computer, called the ABC or Atanasoff-Berry Computer. Atanasoff's machine was the first entirely electronic computer, using vacuum tubes rather than electromechanical relays. The vacuum tubes functioned as switches and were able to close circuits much more rapidly than electromechanical parts, which meant that calculations could be done faster.

Atanasoff's pioneering machine was never taken seriously. It was ahead of its time in using advanced electronics but behind its time in being limited to a single purpose.

ENIAC

The Electronic Numerical Integrator and Computer (ENIAC) was developed by John W. Mauchly and John Presper Eckert, Jr., at the University of Pennsylvania. Mauchly and Eckert had already been discussing the feasibility of developing an electronic computer when the U.S. Army's Ballistic Research laboratories came to them with the problem of computing new trajectory tables for use in World War II. The armed forces needed to know the firing ranges and paths of different types of artillery in different geographical settings (from the deserts of North Africa to the forests of France) from every conceivable angle. Calculating a single trajectory involved numerous trigonometric equations, which usually took one person with an automatic calculator about 12 hours. A complete firing table required the calculation of as many as 3000 trajectories.

Vacuum Tubes for ENIAC,
which Used 18,000 of Them

Photo courtesy of IBM Corp.

With $400,000 provided by the Ballistic Research laboratories, Eckert serving as project manager and Mauchly as technical consultant, the electronic-computer project got under way in April 1943. In 1946, 200,000 work hours later, ENIAC was finished, too late to contribute to the war effort but in plenty of time to set new records for calculating speed.

Because it was electronic and more powerful than anything yet built, the ENIAC could do an unprecedented 5000 additions per second. In half a minute it could solve a problem that usually took the desktop adding machines of that day 20 hours. On its trial run, ENIAC solved in just 2 hours a problem that would have taken a physicist 100 years to work through! In fact, ENIAC was so fast that it could calculate a trajectory faster than the projectile itself could travel over the same trajectory. As you can see, the greatest asset of modern computers—their speed—was first experienced with ENIAC.

The new computer had its limits, however. It contained more than 18,000 vacuum tubes; it needed a huge amount of electric power to run. Although ENIAC weighed some thirty tons and occupied the entire basement of the University of Pennsylvania's Moore School of Electrical Engineering, it could store only 20 numbers of 10 digits each. Its operations were controlled by programs that required manual rewiring, so a change from one program to another was a major task. In fact, a program change meant rewiring some 40 interconnected control panels, which took days. ENIAC's calculating speed was offset to some extent when the time lost in rewiring the machine was taken into account.

The Stored-Program Concept

Hungarian-born mathematician John von Neumann found the solution to this problem: the **stored program.** With a stored program, the instructions for the computer are coded as numbers and stored inside the machine. The machine's operating instructions are placed, or stored, in the same memory as the data to be processed, and they are written in the same binary notation. The basic operations that the machine can perform are built into its circuitry; each operation is given a number; and the stored program can

call for any operation by its number. Stored programs thus give computers great flexibility. The EDVAC (Electronic Discrete Variable Automatic Computer), which Von Neumann helped invent, was the first computer to use the stored-program concept. Completed in 1949, it was operating by 1951.

Von Neumann also recognized how important it was for computers to use binary notation, since the binary system corresponded to the "on" or "off" nature of electronic components. Since EDVAC, all computers have been designed to use binary notation.

The First Generation of Computers (1951–1958)

Eckert and Mauchly turned out to be shrewd entrepreneurs as well as scientists. Their Eckert-Mauchly Computer Corporation set out to make the public aware that computers existed and could be used for other than academic or military purposes. In 1950 they sold their company to the Remington Rand Corporation (later Sperry Rand and, today, with Burroughs, Unisys Corp.), which built UNIVAC I and delivered it to the Census Bureau in 1951. There would, however, be more UNIVAC I's. UNIVAC I became the first commercially available computer.

Certain characteristics of UNIVAC I were typical of what has become known as the first generation of computers:

1. Binary notation was used instead of decimal notation. All instructions and information were stored in the computer as 1s and 0s, which correspond to the electronic conditions "on" and "off."

2. The computers were entirely electronic; they had no moving parts. They used vacuum tubes, not mechanical gears or electromechanical relays, as switching devices.

3. Programs could be stored. This made it possible for general-purpose computers to perform a variety of tasks without the cumbersome rewiring earlier computers had required.

The UNIVAC

Sperry Corporation

The different "generations" in computer history correspond to key breakthroughs in electronics. Vacuum tubes provided the electronic power of the first computer generation, as they had been doing for radios for many years. But vacuum tubes had some major drawbacks. They took several minutes to warm up, and when they were completely warmed up they became quite hot. (So do vacuum-tube radios after playing for a while.) Early computers, with thousands of vacuum tubes, filled entire rooms and required an enormous amount of electric current to run. The enormous heat that was produced had to be dissipated by expensive air-conditioning systems. In addition, vacuum tubes were unreliable; the mean time between tube failures (MTBF) in ENIAC was 12 hours.

As a result, the 1950s witnessed a great deal of experimentation with different types of memory systems. The system called magnetic-core memory proved to be the most useful. It was used in UNIVAC II and became the industry standard in the second generation of computers.

The Second Generation of Computers (1959–1964)

The technology that signaled the arrival of the second generation of computers was the manufacture of a tiny, deceptively simple device called a **transistor.** It was invented by three physicists at the Bell Telephone Laboratories in 1948, and it would replace the bulky vacuum tubes then used in radios, television sets, and computers.

Transistors had several advantages over 200-times larger vacuum tubes. Less costly to manufacture, they were ready to go to work more quickly, and they had far fewer failures. Transistors also provided much more power than vacuum tubes did, yet they gave off nowhere near the amount of heat and drew a very small amount of electricity.

Second-generation machines brought another innovation—magnetic-core memory for internal storage. A magnetic core is a tiny ring of ferromagnetic material only a few hundredths of an inch in diameter; thousands—sometimes millions—of these rings were strung on very thin wires to build a computer memory. Because cores were far smaller than vacuum tubes, internal storage capacity became greater even though the overall size of second-generation computers was much smaller.

During the early 1960s, magnetic tape and disks began to be widely used for auxiliary storage. Magnetic disks made possible another revolutionary development—**direct access.** It was now possible for the computer to go directly to any specific item of data stored anywhere on a disk, instead of having to read from the beginning of a file until a specific item could be located.

Computers and Supercomputers

Transistors and relatively low-cost magnetic-core memories made it possible to build smaller, more powerful computers. At the same time, faster,

more efficient input devices (like card readers) and output devices (like printers) were developed.

The second generation also brought the first supercomputers. Much more powerful than other computers, supercomputers were designed to do calculations many times faster than any other machine available at the time, and to do more of them. One of the earliest of these supercomputers was the CDC 6600. As an example of the speed of this computer class, the CDC 6600 could perform over 3 million operations per second. Government agencies and very large business organizations were the customers that needed and could afford this amount of power.

Because second-generation computers were cheaper, more compact, and could handle a greater variety of data processing tasks more rapidly, they appealed to an expanding business clientele. In fact, the earliest transistorized computers were medium-speed, business-oriented systems. The awe that had been inspired by computers in their early years began to fade. The idea that people who weren't necessarily computer experts could use these machines gained popularity. Many changes still had to take place before this notion could become a reality. By 1957, however, the yearly computer market was already exceeding $1 billion.

New Languages

At the same time that computer manufacturers were developing business-oriented machines, they were also trying to devise humanlike programming languages that would be suited to business purposes. The government became concerned about the fact that there would soon be a number of different computer languages, each designed for a particular purpose. Therefore, in 1959 the office of the Secretary of Defense brought together major manufacturers and users of data processing equipment to discuss the need for a standardized programming language. The Conference On DAta SYstems Languages (CODASYL) was formed and, some time later, it came

The CDC 6600

Courtesy of Control Data Corporation Historical Archive

up with a standardized, business-oriented language called COBOL (COmmon Business-Oriented Language).

Not every computer manufacturer was thrilled about adopting COBOL as the standard language. However, the U.S. government announced that it would not purchase or lease computing equipment from any manufacturer unless a COBOL language compiler was available. This "no COBOL, no sales" (to the government) approach removed any remaining resistance.

The late 1950s and early 1960s saw a "software explosion"; one programming language after another was developed. In 1963, FORTRAN IV (FORmula TRANslation) was standardized as a language particularly suited to scientific and engineering applications. ALGOL (ALGOrithmic Language) was developed at about the same time to deal with specifically algebraic functions.

These and other high-level languages helped make programming easier and therefore accessible to nonspecialists as well as specialists. Thus, at the same time that transistors and magnetic-core memory made computers smaller and more powerful than ever, the advances in symbolic programming languages made the power of computers more readily accessible, further extending the potential of the still "new" machines.

The Third Generation of Computers (1965–1970)

The next significant electronics advance for computers was the integrated circuit, which moved them into the third generation. The integrated circuit had what had been the separate parts of an electronic circuit etched on a single small piece of silicon, or **chip.** As the name implies, a chip was small indeed. When the chip arrived, it reduced even further the size of computers while increasing their speed. Computers could now perform operations in nanoseconds, or billionths of a second.

A major development in the third generation came with the introduction of the IBM Series 360 computers in the mid-1960s. This series incorporated a number of structural advances. It could do many more operations at one time than could earlier computers. Thousands of 360s were sold to businesses, and many features of that series were accepted as standards by other manufacturers.

Another development that changed the way people used computers was time-sharing, a feature of some IBM 360 models. Time-sharing made it possible for several people to use computer resources simultaneously. A time-shared computer allows many users, each working at a separate input/output terminal, to use it at the same time.

The Minicomputer

In 1965 the Digital Equipment Corporation (DEC) introduced the first minicomputer, smaller and less expensive than the large computers. Even small businesses could afford minis. Now that more than one user could

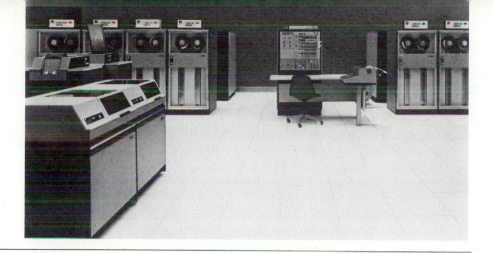

IBM's 360 Series

Photo courtesy of IBM Corp.

access computer power at the same time and different machines could even "talk" to each other, people began to find more and more uses for computers.

Because the design of third-generation computers was so different from that of second-generation computers, most of the second-generation software—that is, the computers use to perform specific tasks—was incompatible with the new machines. Much software had to be rewritten and many programmers had to be retrained. A range of new, English-based programming languages was developed for use with these more accessible machines.

New operating-systems software also had to be developed during this period. (Simply put, operating systems are programs that supervise the flow of work through the machine and between the machine and its input/output devices.) The need for new operating-systems software was clear, but its development lagged behind the development of new hardware.

The demand for application software (specific programs for specific business purposes) began to grow. Because commercially available software often had to be modified to fit a user's exact needs, large organizations began to maintain their own programming staffs. A sizable software industry emerged and flourished alongside, but separate from, hardware development and production. New techniques, such as structured programming, were devised to improve software quality. We will look much more closely at software—both systems software and application software—in Chapters 6–9.

The Fourth Generation

Following the first three generations, developments in the computer field took off so fast that the lines dividing subsequent generations can be hard to define. Some people maintain that we have already passed through the fourth, fifth, even the sixth generation. Although people may disagree about what generation we are in, everyone agrees about the next important electronic advance, large-scale integration.

LSI, VLSI, and the Microprocessor

Large-scale integration, or **LSI,** refers to the compression of large numbers of integrated circuits, or transistors, on a single silicon chip. This technology permitted truly incredible numbers of transistors to be placed on chips: 5,000 for the works of a digital watch; 20,000 for a pocket calculator. **Very large-scale integration, VLSI,** placed more than a million circuits on a single sliver of silicon.

With so many circuits on a chip, it was only a matter of time before someone got the idea that one chip could contain all the circuits necessary to perform the basic functions of an entire computer. The person who first put this idea into action, in 1969, was M. E. (Ted) Hoff, Jr., a young engineer with the newly formed Intel Corporation. Hoff used LSI to put the computer's "brain," the central processing unit, on a single chip, creating a microprocessor.

Microprocessors are, in effect, general purpose computers that can be programmed to do any number of tasks, from running a watch to guiding a missile. Companies in a variety of fields rushed to take advantage of the

Microprocessors

Commodore Computer Systems

Computer Translation

By the year 2000, James G. Carbonell, director of Carnegie-Mellon University's new Center for Machine Translation, believes that a computer system will have begun to break down language barriers. CMU's goal is to develop a system for translating the international phone conversations of people speaking different languages. When you want to wheel and deal with your business contacts in Japan, for example, it won't matter anymore that you don't speak Japanese. The Carnegie-Mellon system will be able to change what you say into text; put that text into words, phrases, and sentences of another language; and then convert it back to speech. Via phone lines hooked into the computer system, all this will take place instantly, as you speak. Phone calls are the target application for this developing innovation, but it could be used in any number of other translation settings as well. Contributors to the funding of the Center for Machine Translation include Japanese, American, and European backers.

Source: "Say Sayonara to Long-Distance Language Barriers," *Business Week,* July 14, 1986, p. 73.

microprocessor's power, putting them in blood-chemistry analyzers, telephone systems, and microwave ovens. Microprocessors power artificial limbs, automobile transmissions, and robots. They make it possible for cash registers to total bills and for pacemakers to regulate heartbeats. They set thermostats, record telephone calls, tune radios, amplify rock music, and record and read fingerprints on plastic identification cards. Microprocessors have entered all areas of our lives.

Microcomputers

Microprocessors were also the first step in the development of the **microcomputer.** The first microcomputer, the Altair 8800, was offered in kit form. Users had to build and program these computers themselves, as well as to build peripheral equipment such as monitors. In 1977, Stephen Wozniak and Steven Jobs introduced the Apple, and Radio Shack introduced the TRS-80. These micros had a central processing unit (CPU), a monitor, an operating system, and a programming language in one assembled package. Version II of the Apple became the fastest selling microcomputer and took the lion's share of the micro market, especially in schools.

In 1981, IBM introduced the IBM PC, which used a refined 8080 chip, the 8088. The IBM PC rapidly became the leader in the microcomputer market, and it became the computer of choice in the business world. Because businesses bought the IBM PC in large volume, it became the industry standard. Very quickly, PC "clones" appeared. These were microcomputers compatible with the IBM PCs but less expensive and sometimes with more features.

The PC DOS operating system became the microcomputer standard as well, which encouraged programmers to develop commercial software products. William Gates and Paul Allen started what was to become a billion dollar company, Microsoft, marketing BASIC (see below) and PC DOS as well as the MS DOS software that the clones ran on. Dan Bricklin created VisiCalc, the first electronic spreadsheet, which recalculated data arranged in columns and rows whenever the numbers were changed. Mitch

Kapor developed Lotus 1–2–3, a more powerful spreadsheet than VisiCalc, that integrated data base and graphic capabilities. Word processing programs made the preparation of documents easier and easier.

BASIC—The Language of the Microcomputer   The popularity of the microcomputer depended not just on the speed and size advantages created by microprocessors. Also partly responsible was BASIC, a programming language created in 1964 by two professors at Dartmouth College, John Kemeny and Thomas Kurtz. Kemeny made computer use an integral part of the mathematics curriculum at Dartmouth and, with his colleague Kurtz, devised a simplified computer language, BASIC, so that students who were not specializing in computer studies could still learn to use and program the machines. BASIC is interactive; that is, it lets the computer respond

Intel's 80286 Chip

Courtesy Intel Corporation

Thinking Machines

As we know, computers have memories and can solve problems, but they can't really think. That is, no machine has the capacity to reason and learn as we humans do. They can't learn to recognize a particular person, for example, from an angle they've never seen before the way even a baby can. They can't make anything but yes-no decisions or solve problems based on fuzzy or incomplete information. And they certainly can't independently figure out how to solve problems without specific instructions from human programmers. Or can they? Computer scientists researching the possibilities of artificial intelligence are bringing all these limitations into question, as they create computers that approximate the way humans think.

The latest "thinking machines" are known as neural-net computers. The idea is based on understanding how human brains function to give us what we know as intelligence. Limited though this understanding is, it has already given computer scientists some remarkable results. In the brain, when one neuron is stimulated, it "fires," or stimulates a network of other neurons. Those neurons, in turn, excite others so that one signal instantly spreads over a large area of the brain. There are probably some 10 billion neurons in the brain; the number of links between them is 1,000 times that many.

Computers designed in the traditional way work very differently from human brains. The basic idea, developed by John von Neumann in the 1940s, is to have physically separate memory and processor within the computer and one link so that they can communicate. The processor must wait for information to be retrieved from memory each time it needs to perform some function.

Neural-net computers, as their name suggests, work more like our brains. In this new design, the computer has many processors, all linked with each other in a large number of combinations. TRW Inc. has developed a neural-net computer with 250,000 processors joined by 5.5 million connections, and Robert Hecht-Nielsen, director of the company's Artificial Intelligence Center says that the company has already designed systems that have 100 million processing elements. Even neural-net computers built on a much smaller scale can perform in startingly intelligent ways. Terence J. Sejnowski of Johns Hopkins University together with Geoffrey E. Hinton and Scott E. Fahlman of Carnegie-Mellon and IBM's Scott E. Kirkpatrick created a neural-net computer with 200 linked processing elements. The machine has the potential to teach itself to read aloud, to recognize images, and to change speech into text.

Other examples of neural-net computers that are already in operation include TRW's machine developed for the Pentagon's DARPA—Defense Advanced Research Projects Agency—to aid a conventional computer in recognizing images. But the company believes that this computer could also be used to make quality inspections in factory settings.

directly and immediately to the input of the user, and it uses standard English code words. Kemeny helped other New England colleges and secondary schools establish computers in their curriculums, and that is how BASIC began to spread. When microprocessors made it possible to produce small, relatively low-cost personal computers, a group of young, enthusiastic, BASIC-literate people already knew how useful computer technology could be. Also, Microsoft marketed BASIC, so it was widely available as the microcomputer trend grew.

In 1984, IBM introduced the AT microcomputer, which used the Intel 80286 chip. This machine was much faster and had a more powerful CPU

California Institute of Technology and AT&T Bell Laboratories have developed a neural-net computer that can solve what is known as the "traveling salesman problem," or determine the shortest route between a number of cities, much faster than a conventional computer. That's because in order for a traditional computer to solve the problem, it would make a list of the cities and the distances between them, then compare all the possible combinations. With ten cities, the number of possible combinations is 181,440; for 30 cities, there are one trillion billion possible combinations. With such a large number of possibilities, even a large mainframe gets bogged down and takes about a full hour to come up with a solution. Using a network of 100 processors arranged in a grid, Bell Labs and Cal Tech's machine's columns of processors each selected one city, arriving at a final solution through communication between the processors. All this was achieved in a matter of .1 second.

At London's Imperial College, Igor Aleksander's computer, Wisard, can recognize patterns of him from any perspective. Having been presented with a number of pictures of him in the past, Wisard has retained a kind of pieced-together image. The machine has "learned" what Aleksander looks like, even from angles it has never been exposed to, just as a baby can recognize familiar people, despite changes in their appearances. Conventional computers, on the other hand, cannot recognize images unless there is an exact match between the image and one stored in its memory or unless it has been programmed to recognize some of the image's distinguishing features.

A number of researchers have worked with the neural-net's capacity to provide correct solutions based on incomplete information. Cal Tech's John J. Hopfield has put lists of words into his system's memory, then presented just part of a word on one of the lists to prompt the computer to recall a full set. Even when Hopfield scrambles the clue by rearranging the letters in the wrong order, the system corrects his mistake and produces the right response. In a similar test, James A. Anderson at Brown University has stored data on a number of diseases and their treatments in his neural-net computer. When the system receives information on even an unfamiliar diagnosis, it can suggest the correct treatments.

One other difference between these new machines and conventional computers is that neural-net computers can come up with a good answer, while conventional computers only present perfect solutions. But experts agree that in situations where speed is critical, a good answer will do just fine.

Source: Otis Port, "Computers That Come Awfully Close to Thinking," *Business Week,* June 2, 1986, pp. 92–96.

than the original PC, could address more memory, had greater disk capacity, and at approximately $6,000 put the power of a low-end minicomputer into a desktop unit.

Apple introduced the Macintosh in 1984, too. Based on Motorola's 68000 32-bit chip, the Mac was more powerful than the IBM AT and was incompatible with it and its programs. The Mac's processor produced excellent graphics, a feature IBM didn't match for years. The Mac also used icons—diagrams rather than words to show machine and program functions—pulldown menus, and the electronic "mouse." The mouse, a small electronic device developed at Xerox's Palo Alto research facility, lets

IBM's Personal System/2
Model 30

Photo courtesy of IBM Corp.

a user point to any spot on a monitor and press a button to choose a desired function. These capabilities made the Mac very user-friendly (easy to use without special training in computers), a reputation it still has.

In 1987 IBM introduced the Personal System/2, a new line of hardware and software designed to interact with other IBM computers, both mainframes and PCs. The new features include larger amounts of memory, hard disks as optional or standard equipment, and, in the most powerful model, the 80386 microprocessor, a very fast 32-bit chip. Increased graphics capabilities are meant to make IBM more competitive in an area that Mac clearly dominated in the 1980s. The Personal System/2 can be run with the PC DOS operating system, but IBM is also providing a new operating system to take advantage of the machines multitasking capabilities. IBM's new PS entries also emphasize connectivity. In today's computer environments, networking and communication among users, machines, and other parts of computer systems, once the province of mainframes and minicomputers, is an increasingly important attribute of microcomputers.

Portable laptop microcomputers have the power of desktop models plus the convenience of smaller size and self-contained power sources. Average laptop models weigh between 9 and 12 pounds. Typically, laptops have 3.5-inch disk drives, ROM-based programs, internal modems, and printer ports. One tradeoff for the small size and low power requirements of laptops is that their monitors have limited display capability.

Mainframes and Minicomputers

LSI and VLSI started a mainframe and minicomputer trend that continues with every advance in chip technologies: more memory, smaller size, and lower cost than third-generation machines. Affordable mainframes and minis from IBM and DEC and other manufacturers, such as the IBM 3090

34

and System 36 and DEC's VAX series, have introduced the use of computers in many new areas. Rapid technological developments are blurring the distinctions between mainframes and minicomputers.

Supercomputers

VSLI can pack more than 500 billion circuits into a 1-cubic-foot space, making truly astonishing supercomputers possible. Today's most powerful computers have huge memory capacity and the capability to perform millions of instructions per second. They cost from $5 million to more than $17 million and may require a year to install and program. Seymour Cray is one of the pioneer producers of these machines in the United States. Japan is the other important source of supercomputers. Cray's company's supercomputers tested designs for the America's Cup-winning yacht Stars & Stripes. In a way, the 1987 race engaged supercomputers as well as sailing vessels: Bracknell, a British subsidiary of Cray, was involved in the supercomputer-assisted design of the Australian yacht Kookaburra III.

Fourth-Generation Languages

Fourth-generation languages—4GLs or VHLLs, for very high-level languages—were first developed in the mid-1970s. These languages allow the user to concentrate on what to accomplish rather than on how to

A Laptop Computer

Photo courtesy of IBM Corp.

CAD Screens of Hull Design
with a Cray Supercomputer

Courtesy of Cray Research Inc.

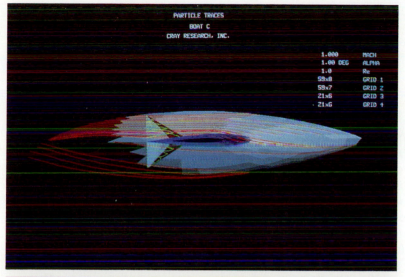

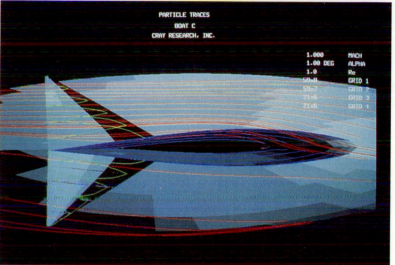

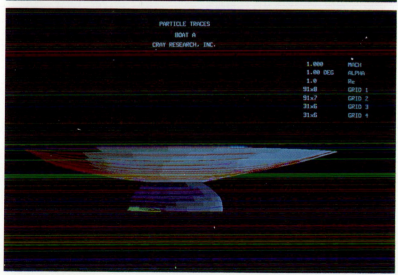

accomplish it. Using statements very much like English-language statements, novices can learn enough of a 4GL quickly to begin to get useful output. However, some users believe that once the demands on a 4GL become complex, these languages are less efficient than older ones that take longer to learn. They also require much more CPU memory than third-generation languages.

One classification scheme categorizes 4GLs as end-user-oriented languages, DBMS-oriented languages, or 4GL-like tools. End-user-oriented languages—such as IDMS, SQL, Ramis II, and Nomad 2—run on mainframes and interface with databases. DBMS-oriented languages are designed to work with specific databases; examples include Ideal, Natural, and Inquire. Gener/OL, ADA, and Focus.5 are 4GL-like tools, used to generate menus and applications programs. ADA is a 4GL developed by the U.S. Department of Defense for military applications.

Artificial Intelligence, Robotics, Desktop Publishing

Essentially new areas of computer research and development since the end of the third generation, artificial intelligence (AI), robotics, and the associated areas of expert systems and decision support systems are the subject of Chapter 16. Desktop publishing, a computer-based technology that is revolutionizing the production of documents inside and outside the business world, is discussed in Chapter 9.

Looking Into the Future

As it has been in the past, technology will be the driving force of the future. Speed will be enhanced by super-conducting Josephson junctions, which operate 1,000 times faster than semiconductor chips currently in use. With LISP chips packaging an entire AI system on one chip, AI processes will become more widely used. Bipolar circuits that can operate in normal environments without requiring special cooling will make supercomputers easier to maintain. Memory chips will hold four megabytes or more of storage, and with new chip technologies it will be possible to make individual circuits less than one micron wide.

Manufacturers will use work stations that can design and test product prototypes entirely within the computer, make independent "best-case" choices, and then transmit manufacturing specifications directly to the robot-run production lines of an automated plant. Artificial intelligence systems will diagnose medical ills, control weapon systems, and solve ever more complex problems. Supercomputers will use processing techniques that split problems into segments that can be solved simultaneously. In this way, larger problems will be solved faster. Perhaps even biochips that use biological cells to store information and perform logic functions will be able to repair living tissues.

A LISP Chip

Photo courtesy of Texas Instruments

Table 2.1   Time Line: Important 20th-Century Dates in Computer Development

Year	Event
1943	The ENIAC project begins at the University of Pennsylvania.
1944	The Harvard Mark I is demonstrated. EDVAC concepts are developed. John von Neumann, J. Presper Eckert, and John Mauchly describe the stored-program concept in the proposal for EDVAC.
1946	ENIAC begins operating at the Moore School at the University of Pennsylvania. John von Neumann publishes a paper describing the stored-program concept.
1948	Bell Labs develops the transistor that initiated the second generation of computers.
1951	Remington Rand delivers the first UNIVAC to the U.S. Bureau of the Census.
1956	Thomas J. Watson, Sr., of IBM dies.
1957	Digital Equipment Corporation is founded.
1958	Jack Kilby at Texas Instruments develops the integrated circuit.
1959	Robert Noyce develops the process to create circuits on silicon.
1960	Noyce and Gordon Moore found Intel Corporation.
1963	DEC's PDP-1, the first minicomputer, is introduced.
1964	The IBM 360 is introduced.
1970	S. E. Greenfield develops a processor on one chip.
1971	The first microprocessor—the Intel 4004—is announced.
1972	Intel introduces the 8000 series of microprocessors.
1973	The courts declare John Atanasoff the inventor of the electronic digital computer.
1974	Bill Gates and Paul Allen found Microsoft Corporation.
1975	The MTS Altair appears on the cover of Popular Electronics. Steve Jobs and Steve Wozniak show the home-built computer that will become the Apple I to enthusiasts of the Homebrew Computer Club.
1976	The Apple I goes into production.
1977	The Apple II goes on the market. The TRS-80 Model 1 is introduced.
1979	VisiCalc is introduced.
1980	The Apple III is introduced.
1981	The IBM PC is introduced.
1983	Lotus 1-2-3 is introduced.
1984	Apple introduces the Macintosh.
1985	The Cray 2 Super Computer is introduced.
1986	IBM puts into commercial production the first 1 megabyte RAM chip.
1987	IBM introduces the Personal System/2 line of computers.

Adapted from *Microcomputers: Practices and Procedures* by Dennis P. Curtin and Leslie R. Porter, Prentice-Hall, 1986.

Optical Processing Could Leave Today's Supercomputers in the Dust

Pushing
Computers Closer
to the Ultimate
Speed Limit

"You can still say it's impractical, but you can't say it's impossible anymore." Alan Huang, head of a year-old research effort at AT&T Bell Laboratories, is talking about his passion: optical computers. The idea of building blindingly fast machines that compute with light pulses instead of electrical signals has been controversial for two decades—and the prevailing view is still one of skepticism.

But Huang reckons that several recent breakthroughs will change minds. In early June, Bell Labs unveiled the first rudimentary computer chip containing multiple optical switches, or transistors. Huang gleefully predicts that Bell Labs will have a full-fledged optical computer prototype by 1990. Although that timetable seems ambitious even to other proponents—who typically target the mid-to-late 1990s—related announcements of major progress in optical-switch technology have been pouring from research labs worldwide, including those at GTE, Xerox, Sweden's Ericsson, Tokyo Institute of Technology, and Scotland's Heriot-Watt University.

Codes and Bombs The reason for the excitement is that optical computers promise speeds thousands, even millions of times faster than today's speediest supercomputers. The most optimistic estimates for the switching time of familiar silicon transistors is 50 picoseconds, or close to a trillion switches a second. But a conventional supercomputer will probably never run that fast. Since electrons travel through copper wires at only a fraction of the speed of light, the system has to wait for signals to arrive from other chips. Bell Labs thinks it already has an idea of how to make optical transistors with switching times as fast as 50 femtoseconds, or quadrillionths of a second, and 1 femtosecond is the ultimate goal. And light rips through optical fibers at almost the speed of light.

At such fantastic speeds, computers could open the doors to new scientific insights that would give users a commanding edge in engineering everything from new materials to aircraft that would fly circles around existing planes. These computers could be crucial to cracking now-unbreakable codes and designing superior nuclear weapons—the purpose for which supercomputers were originally conceived. And they could be the cornerstone of President Reagan's Star Wars missile shield. Optical computers, says Air Force Lieutenant Colonel David R. Audley, program manager for battle management systems at the Strategic Defense Initiative, "could revolutionize the way we think about computing, much as the semiconductor chip revolutionized electronics 30 years ago."

Not surprisingly, the main booster of optical computers—which could cost up to $100 million to build because virtually all of the technology has to be developed from scratch—is the Defense Dept. The SDI, through its Innovative Science Technology (IST) directorate, supports research in optical computers at a dozen universities, from Caltech and Georgia Tech to MIT and Stanford, plus several research institutes. Add in separate contracts with other labs, such as Carnegie Mellon University's Optical Data Processing Center, and Star Wars backs the bulk of university research on optical computers. The fiscal 1986 budget for optical computing doubled to $3 million and IST has asked for $5 million for next year, not including funds for two more research groups in the planning stage.

Melting Point The granddaddy of industrial consortiums is the Optical Circuit Cooperative, formed three years ago at the University of Arizona. It is now supported by a dozen companies, including Boeing, Du Pont, IBM, and TRW. To ensure that Europe won't be left out of the revolution in optical computing, the European Commission last year set up a project that involves scientists from West Germany, Italy, France, Britain and Belgium. The newest co-op is in Japan. On June 3, a baker's dozen of the country's electronics giants, including NEC, Matsushita, Hitachi, and Fujitsu pooled resources with funding from the powerful Ministry of International Trade & Industry to launch a 10-year effort to develop so-called optoelectronic chips.

Although Bell Lab's chip is crude by today's silicon standards—it contains all four switching elements—it proves that microswitches for directing laser-light pulses can be ganged together. Until now, many critics charged that optical switches would need so much power and generate so much heat that a large optical computer would be in danger of melting. The Bell Labs device requires no more power than a silicon circuit.

Son of SEED Other laboratories are bringing in more evidence that optics can be practical for computers. Just as Bell Labs announced its breakthrough, researchers at Heriot-Watt University demonstrated a crude optical-computer circuit. It is patched together from discrete optical switches—just one per chip—but it can perform elemental computer-logic operations.

Still, a commercial optical computer is a long way off. The optical transistors in the Bell Labs integrated circuit (IC), for example, are 200 microns across, roughly 100 times the size of their silicon counterparts. But the AT&T scientists say they can shrink the switches, dubbed with Electro-optic Effect Devices (SEEDs), to 20 microns or less. "This is just the first step," says Huang. "Son of SEED and other developments are coming."

Even if optical switches never catch onto the ever-shrinking silicon chip, the potential power of optical computers is astounding. James A. Ionson, head of Bell, predicts that 10 years hence an optical computer packing the power of 2,000 Cray X-MPs will fit in a suitcase. The reason that so much power can be crammed into so little space: Laser beams don't cause short circuits when they cross paths. That makes it easier to engineer compact systems with so-called passively parallel architectures—computers that attack problems by processing multiple streams of data at the same time. David A. B. Miller, who designed the Bell Labs IC, says a single optical chip covered with 10-micron SEEDs could handle the traffic from all 5 billion inhabitants of the earth talking simultaneously on telephones.

Beams and Umbrellas With parallel processing in mind, some researchers are already working on tricky ways to deliver light-wave signals to millions of switches simultaneously. At Texas Instruments Inc., for instance, Dean R. Collins, director of the systems components laboratory, has developed a tiny chip covered with 10,000 miniature mirrors, each capable of being tilted independently at various angles. Because each can shift direction a million times a second, the entire array can handle 10 million signals per second—10 times the capacity of today's supercomputers. And by making the mirrors smaller, TI says that in five years it could boost capacity to a trillion signals per second. Called PAP, for photonic array processor, the chip is the missing element in optical computation, says Collins. "We can generate light, and we can detect it—but how do we manipulate it?"

Holograms might provide a comparable communications link, according to Larry A. Bergman, a technical staff member at the Jet Propulsion Laboratory

in Pasasdena, Calif. A holographic lens could direct multiple light beams to the same spot without losing the identity of each signal. Such a "switch," a prototype of which is being developed on the University of California's San Diego campus, would allow two or more parallel processors in a computer simultaneously to retrieve separate bits of information stored on the same chip, eliminating the bottleneck inherent in so-called shared memory systems.

Despite all the hoopla, no one is writing off electronic computers for the foreseeable future. For one thing, the optical chips being developed by TI and JPL could give regular computers a new lease on life by speeding communications between conventional ICs. But in the long run, optics researchers are confident that optical computers will have no peer for certain applications, especially for processing visual information and routing calls on a phone system that relies increasingly on fiber optics. For Huang's group at Bell Labs, "this is an incredibly exciting time," he says. "I've told management I'm going to buy a refrigerator for the lab, because 2 of my 11 people already have sleeping bags in the lab."

By Otis Port in New York, with bureau reports. Reprinted from *Business Week,* July 28, 1986.

Summary and Key Terms

1. In 1937 Howard Aiken began developing the Mark I computer at Harvard University. The Mark I used punched paper tape to input data. This computer was not limited to one particular type of function.

2. Vacuum tubes, used in the Atanasoff-Berry Computer (ABC), worked faster than the electromechanical relays that the Mark I used. The tubes functioned as switches that opened and closed circuits and made the ABC an entirely electronic computer.

3. ENIAC could perform different functions because its operations were controlled by different programs. The major problem with this electronic computer was that changing a program required rewiring control panels, which took up too much time.

4. The **stored-program concept** allows for internal storage of programs by coding the programs as numbers in the circuitry of the memory. The operating instructions are written in binary notation and are called up, when needed, by number. No rewiring of circuitry is necessary.

5. **Binary notation,** vacuum tubes, and stored programs are features of the machines in the **first generation of computers.** The computers of this age were very large. Also, their vacuum tubes took time to warm up and emitted great amounts of heat. A tremendous amount of electricity was needed to run electric current through the tubes, and the tubes had to be replaced very often.

6. The **second generation of computers** is earmarked by the development of transistors and magnetic-core memory. **Transistors** replaced vacuum tubes as switches for electric current. They were smaller, less costly, more reliable, had more power, and produced far less heat. **Magnetic-core memory** was an internal storage development. A magentic core is a tiny ferromagnetic ring that can be charged by electric current. Auxiliary storage advanced in the form of magnetic tape and disks. A feature of magnetic disks is direct access. With **direct access** the computer can go precisely to the location of the data on the

disk without having to go through previous data. Computers in the second generation were smaller, faster, and stored greater amounts of data.

7. **Supercomputers** were developed during the second generation. They were more powerful in that they could do more calculations at a faster rate. One of the supercomputers, the CDC 6600 could do over 3 million operations per second. These computers were, and are, very expensive.

8. Integrated circuits and microprocessors were electronic advancements of the **third generation of computers. Integrated circuits** allowed computer designers to place separate parts of electronic circuits on a single silicon microprocessor chip. A **microprocessor** chip could contain a number of transistors and their connections. Access time in the computer was now measured in billionths of a second.

9. The concept of **time-sharing** was also developed at this time. Time-sharing allows several people working at separate input/output stations to use the computer at the same time.

10. **Minicomputers** expanded the horizons of the computer industry to small-business and individual users. They were smaller, less costly, and used English-like languages.

11. The third generation of computers caused chages in the computer industry. New operating-systems software—programs that control the flow of work completely through the computer—was needed. Applications software, software used for a specific purpose, had to be developed to suit different users' needs.

12. The **fourth generation** is marked by **large-scale integration (LSI),** the ability to place large numbers of integrated circuits or transistors on a single silicon chip. Using **very large-scale integration (VLSI),** as many as 500,000 transistors can be placed on a single chip.

13. In a **microprocessor,** large-scale integration is used to put all the necessary circuits and transistors for a whole computer on a single chip. These microprocessors make possible a general-purpose computer called the **microcomputer** or personal computer. The microcomputer is a compact, relatively affordable, easy-to-use machine. It uses **BASIC,** an English-like language, and is **interactive**—it responds directly and immediately to the input of a user. **Random access memory,** a feature of microcomputers, allows data in a memory location to be accessed without referring to other memory locations.

14. **Fourth-generation languages,** or **4GL,** use English-language-type statements, are easy to start using, and require large amounts of memory.

Review Questions

Fill-in

1. Von Neumann is credited with the development of the _____ concept.

2. The _____, the first commercial computer, was delivered to the Census Bureau in 1951.

3. The electronic technology supporting second-generation computer systems was _____.

4. The electronic technology supporting first-generation computer systems was _____.

5. A computer on a chip is called a _____.
6. The programming language that was designed for business applications was _____.
7. The first English-like programming language, developed at Dartmouth College, was _____.
8. The electronic technology supporting third-generation computer systems was _____.
9. The _____ supported the fourth generation of computers, which features microcomputers.

Matching

a. integrated circuit
b. machine language
c. M. E. Hoff
d. Aiken
e. vacuum tube
f. Mauchly and Eckert
g. transistor
h. Babbage
i. time-sharing
j. binary
k. RAM

_____ 1. invented the analytical engine
_____ 2. characteristic of second-generation computers
_____ 3. responsible for the development of the ENIAC
_____ 4. language that the computer understands
_____ 5. refers to the ability to directly access any storage location in memory
_____ 6. concept permitting many users to share the resources of the computer system
_____ 7. characteristic of third-generation computer systems
_____ 8. responsible for the development of the Mark I.
_____ 9. invented the microprocessor
_____ 10. number system that is the basis for computer operations

Discussion Questions

1. Briefly explain these major developments in electronic technology and how they affected the growth of computer systems:
   a. vacuum tube
   b. transistor
   c. integrated circuit
   d. LSI and VLSI
   e. microprocessor
2. Name at least two major characteristics of each of the following computer systems:
   a. first-generation computer systems
   b. second-generation computer systems
   c. third-generation computer systems

3. Why were each of the following developments important in the history of computer systems?
   a. stored-program concept
   b. binary number system
4. Explain what is meant by:
   a. electronic digital computer
   b. supercomputer
   c. minicomputer
   d. microcomputer
5. Explain what is meant by the democratization of computers and give several reasons why you feel that this democratization has occurred.

Basic Computer Operations and the CPU

3

Chapter Objectives

After studying this chapter, you should be able to

1. Understand basic computer operations, including input/output operations, arithmetic operations, and logical operations.

2. Describe computer procedures for updating, sorting, and summarizing records.

3. Describe the components of the central processing unit (CPU), including the control unit, the arithmetic/logic unit, and main memory.

4. Understand how main memory is organized.

5. Understand the basic operations of the CPU, including how an instruction is decoded and executed.

Ann and Bill Giardini own a medium-sized distributorship for art and hobby supplies. In the warehouse they store paste and paintbrushes, crayons and canvases, various kinds and colors of paper, even easels and drawing tables. Their customers include art-supply stores and entire school districts as well as individual artists and craftspeople.

The Giardinis keep customer records on index cards in a file box on the counter. This record-keeping system worked five years ago, when they had only 50 customers. But now, with almost 450 customers, their records are never up-to-date. Ann thinks they might increase business with mail order promotions. She'd like to send flyers on new products to customers who might be interested, but she hasn't had time to go through the cards in order to target customers appropriate for specific products.

Inventory presents other difficulties. Some of the more than 5000 items the distributorship offers sit for months in the warehouse. Yet Bill knows from experience that when a big order comes in, he often needs to back-order half the items the customer wants. Which stock items sell quickly, which slowly? He wishes he knew!

Still, business is growing. The number of orders has climbed in five years from 25 a week to 50 a day. Sometimes there is a lot of paperwork, such as checking to see whether the customer has an outstanding balance or reordering supplies to replenish inventory. The manual procedures the Giardinis use to process orders just aren't fast enough to keep up with the increase in their business.

These frustrating problems lead to losses of sales and income. If orders

aren't filled promptly, customers find other suppliers. Excessive stock sitting in the warehouse represents an investment that is not bringing in any return. Out-of-date information on customers means some promotions fall flat. Following up on overdue accounts is barely possible because the clerical system is so overloaded. Ann and Bill Giardini know they can increase profits by making the distributorship more efficient. But short of hiring a small army of clerks, how can they accomplish that?

As millions of business people know, computer systems can help people to control these situations and solve these problems. In this chapter we will take a closer look at the work computer systems perform —computer operations—and at the brain of the computer—the central processing unit, or CPU.

What Do Computers Do?

The most general description of what computers do is that they manipulate **data**—raw facts—turning the data into **information** usable by people. Suppose the Giardinis need a list that shows the names of all their customers and the total annual dollar amount of each customer's purchases. A computer can easily provide a list like that, but first the computer system must have entered into it data—also known as **input**—about customer names and purchase amounts. The computer can then analyze and organize—or **process** the data following instructions it gets from a **program.** The information that results is available as **output.** What *does* a computer do? A computer performs **automated,** or **electronic, data processing.** It manipulates data to achieve some result.

For now, you can think of data at three different levels of complexity. From simplest to most complex, these levels are field, record, and file:

- A **field** is a basic unit of data, such as a customer number, a name, an address, or dates of sales or amounts of sales.
- A **record** is a collection of related fields, such as all the data on a customer card, including the number, the name, the address, the dates of sales, and the amounts of sales.
- A **file** is a collection of related records, such as all the data about all the Giardinis' customers. A file is the basic organizing unit for data gathered for some kind of processing.

In Chapter 10 you will learn about a fourth level—the most complex—a data base.

Data entered into a computer are called **input.** A computer can **process data** from a **file** according to instructions called a **program. Output** results from the processing of data. With this basic information, you are ready to look at the components of a computer system.

The Components of a Computer System

A computer system takes in and stores data, manipulates those data in various ways specified by a program, and makes the results of its data processing available in some form. As Figure 3.1 shows, a computer system consists of input devices, output devices, auxiliary storage devices, and a CPU.

Input and Output Devices

Whether they "read" data from bar codes on product labels or use a typewriter-style keyboard to etch codes on magnetic tape, **input devices** enter data into computer systems. Common to all input devices is this function: they convert data into a form the computer can use and transmit the converted data to the CPU.

   Output devices reverse the process. Whatever results the computer is programmed to deliver are transmitted from the CPU to output devices. These devices translate data from the form used in the computer back into a form that people can understand. In Chapter 4 you will learn in detail about both the media and the devices used in input and output operations.

Storage Devices

The CPU contains some storage capacity, called **main memory** (see Figure 3.1). Main memory may be called *main storage, working storage, working memory,* or *primary storage,* but all these terms refer to the place where the data and instructions needed for processing are held. Only a limited amount of data and instructions can fit into main memory at one time. To hold the excess data and instructions, **auxiliary storage** is required. Magnetic disks and magnetic tape are the media used for auxiliary storage (see Figure 3.2). When needed, the data and instructions in auxiliary storage can be read into main memory. Obtaining data from auxiliary storage, because it involves additional input and output operations—takes somewhat more time than obtaining data contained in main memory.

The CPU

The CPU (central processing unit) is the part of the computer that actually handles and processes data. As Figure 3.1 shows, the CPU has three distinct functional parts:

1. An **arithmetic/logic unit** performs calculations and logical operations on data.
2. **Main memory** holds input data as well as program instructions on how to process the data.

FIGURE 3.1
Components of a Computer System

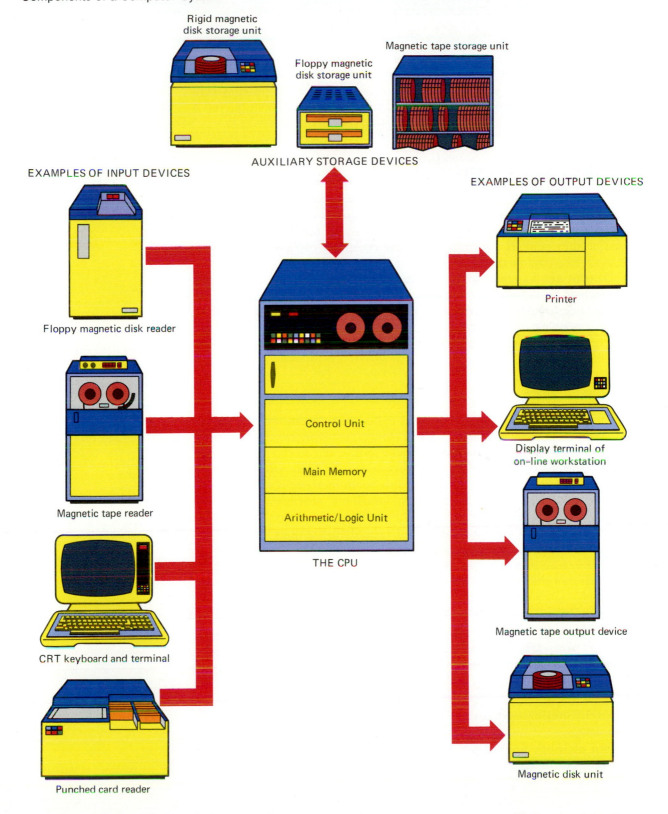

Rigid magnetic disk storage unit

Floppy magnetic disk storage unit

Magnetic tape storage unit

AUXILIARY STORAGE DEVICES

EXAMPLES OF INPUT DEVICES

Floppy magnetic disk reader

Magnetic tape reader

CRT keyboard and terminal

Punched card reader

Control Unit

Main Memory

Arithmetic/Logic Unit

THE CPU

EXAMPLES OF OUTPUT DEVICES

Printer

Display terminal of on-line workstation

Magnetic tape output device

Magnetic disk unit

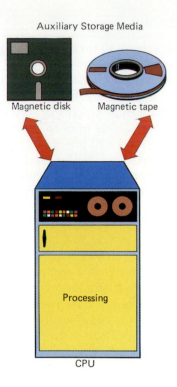

Auxiliary Storage Media

Magnetic disk   Magnetic tape

Processing

CPU

FIGURE 3.2
The CPU and Auxiliary
Storage Units

3. The **control unit** guides the transfer of data and instructions to and from main memory and to and from auxiliary storage and the input/output devices.

You will learn about the CPU in more detail later in this chapter.

The Computer's Basic Operations

Computer systems can do a variety of things particularly applicable to business users:

1. Input/output operations
2. Basic arithmetic computations and logical operations
3. Storing and retrieving information
4. Sorting data or information
5. Summarizing information

As you will see, all five functions can help the Giardinis run their art and hobby supplies distributorship.

Input/Output Operations

One of the jobs computers spend a lot of time doing for businesses does not involve computing at all: the digestion of input and the production of reports or other output. Computers do input/output operations at a much slower pace than they can calculate because in most cases input/output devices are mechanical as well as electronic; the electronic activities must sometimes wait for the mechanical ones to catch up.

For instance, a printer must still physically move and space the paper it prints on; the electronically driven typing element must wait for the paper to be brought into position on every line. Although input/output operations are the slowest thing that a computer can do, computers still perform them far faster than people can.

Assume that Ann and Bill Giardini install a computer system. They can improve their business management just by using the computer system for input/output operations. Information about each customer is keyed in at a computer terminal and recorded on a computer-readable storage medium such as a disk. In this way the customer records are turned into a form the computer can work with. When a new customer places an order, a new record is created. Whenever a complete list of customers is needed, the computer can read all the information from input recorded on disk and produce a printed list of this information as output (see Figure 3.3).

A customer list is only one type of simple printed output useful to the Giardinis. Others are lists of items and quantities on inventory, customer credit records, and lists of overdue accounts. A computer system can also print on special forms. Ordering and billing can be automatic functions,

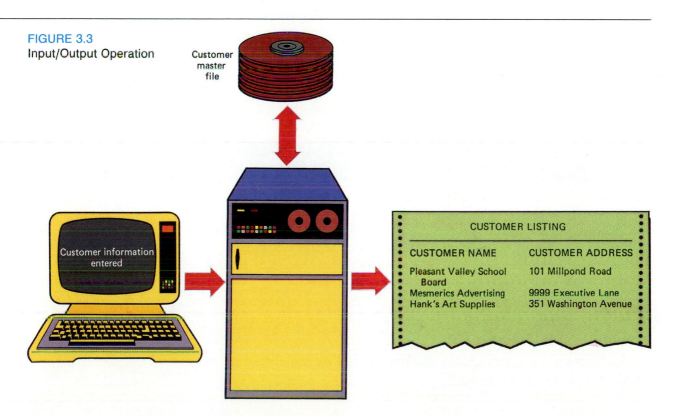

FIGURE 3.3
Input/Output Operation

Customer master file

Customer information entered

CUSTOMER LISTING

CUSTOMER NAME	CUSTOMER ADDRESS
Pleasant Valley School Board	101 Millpond Road
Mesmerics Advertising	9999 Executive Lane
Hank's Art Supplies	351 Washington Avenue

with the computer even putting names and addresses on the billing envelopes. All the Giardinis have to do is put the bills in the envelopes and mail them.

Basic Arithmetic Computations and Logical Operations

In addition to their input and output functions, computers compute. That is, they can add, subtract, multiply, and divide. Let's say that the Giardinis decide to print their bills by computer. To print bills on preprinted order forms, the computer needs to know who is being billed (customer names and addresses), what items customers have ordered, and the quantities and prices of these items. What the computer does *not* require as input is the total dollar amount of each order, the sales tax for the order, or the total of the order including sales tax. It can calculate these.

The computer has a record for each customer to be billed, a printout of which looks like this:

Cust. No.	Cust. Name	Customer Address	1st Item	Price	Qty.	2nd Item	Price	Qty.	3rd Item	Price	Qty.
00031	Pleasant Valley School Board	101 Millpond Road	3950	$79.95	83	2164	$.04	5000	5311	$8.50	10
20335	Mesmerics Advertising	9999 Executive Lane	1010	$402.80	1						
01482	Hank's Art Supplies	351 Washington Avenue	3946	$19.95	20	0051	$.82	75			

The computer can multiply the quantity of each item ordered by the price (83 × $79.95 = $6635.85 for item number 3950 on the printout). The computer can total these amounts for each customer. And it can calculate the prevailing rate of sales tax. In other words, given basic information, and under the guidance of a program, the computer can complete the bills.

The computer can also compare one value with another value and take alternative actions based on the outcome of the comparison. In other words, it can perform logical operations. For instance, the Giardinis' policy is that quantity orders are discounted according to the following schedule:

Quantity	Discount
if 1–9	None
10–99	10%
100–999	15%
1000–9999	20%
10,000 or more	25%

When it calculates bills, the computer can compare the quantity of each item ordered with the values in the discount schedule. The results of that comparison (for example, that 83 is greater than or equal to 10 and less than or equal to 99) indicate what discount the computer should apply to the price (10% for item number 3950). The computer then does exactly that, calculating the discount, subtracting that amount from the full price, and indicating the discounted price.

Storing and Retreiving Information

We've seen that a computer can digest input to produce output in a specified form, can make calculations along the way, and can follow logical decision-making rules. Another important task that computers perform efficiently is to store information in a compact form and then retrieve and use it later.

Data stored in a computer system's auxiliary storage are in computer-readable form, ready to be input for processing at any time. Such storage takes far less physical space than card files or similar paper records. Stored data can be on magnetic disks or magnetic tape, which can be kept on a shelf or in a cabinet between uses. Auxiliary storage keeps information not needed at the moment from cluttering up main memory, but that information is "on call" whenever it is needed. Information that may be wanted on only a moment's notice is usually stored in auxiliary storage so that it can be retrieved whenever the computer is running.

The Giardinis' computer system includes a terminal at which people can get information that the computer keeps in auxiliary storage. Ann wants to know whether the local school board payment is overdue. Although the computer prepares a biweekly list of overdue accounts, the school board might have paid its bill since the last printout was issued. Ann wants to make sure before she bills again.

She enters the school board's customer number at the terminal. This number is the "key" identifying this particular customer. She also indicates that the particular file she wants to use is the overdue-accounts file. The computer locates this file in auxiliary storage and then reads it until it finds the record matching the key Ann gave. Then the computer displays the contents of the record on the terminal screen as in the figure at the top of page 53.

The fact that the record still exists on the file indicates that the school board has not yet paid, for the computer deletes records from the overdue-accounts file the moment payment is received. The computer can also select accounts that are 30, 60, or 90 days overdue and generate different letters to the customers in each category.

The computer has done a lot, but it cannot tell Ann whether to turn the account over to a collection agency or to wait a few more weeks hoping to get a check in the mail. Nor can it tell whom to telephone on the school board. Computer systems create astonishingly efficient ways to process, store, and retrieve information, but only humans can decide what to do with that information.

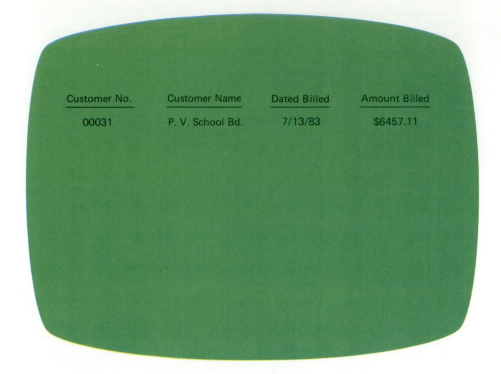

Customer No.	Customer Name	Dated Billed	Amount Billed
00031	P. V. School Bd.	7/13/83	$6457.11

Sorting Data

Have you ever had to prepare a reference list for a term paper or draw up a list of words or names and then alphabetize the items? Easy enough when there are only a few items, alphabetizing is a tedious task when there are hundreds of items. Alphabetizing is a form of sorting, and computers are often called upon to sort.

Bill Giardini wants a list of sales categorized by customer. He knows that the local school board is a big customer, but he suspects that he has other customers who make enough small purchases to qualify as big customers too. To find out, he needs a listing of customers ranked by sales amount.

The computer can read the file and reorder or sort the information by sales amount. Sorts can be done in two different sequences that would be helpful to Bill's purposes: ascending order, which starts with the lowest value and progresses to the highest; and descending order, which starts with the highest value and progresses to the lowest. Bill just specifies for the (appropriately programmed) computer which field to sort on—total sales in this case—and the computer does the rest. Figure 3.4 illustrates a customer file before and after a descending-order sort. (In it, customer numbers and addresses have been omitted to simplify the customer records.)

Summarizing Information

Much of the data-processing output generated in business applications helps people make decisions. Such output often summarizes a situation so

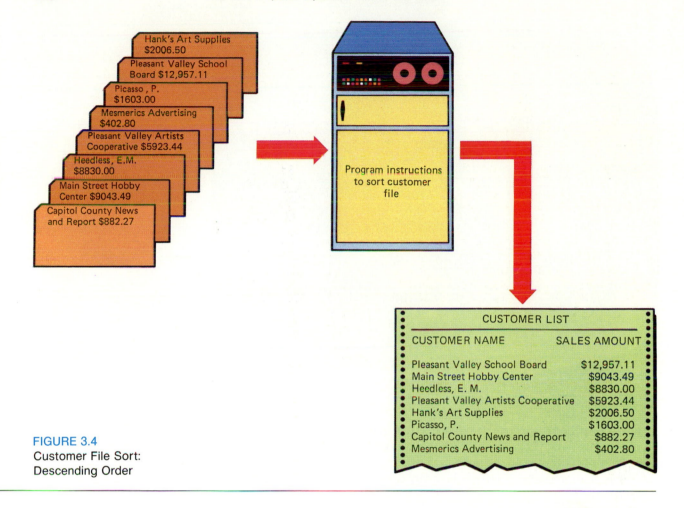

Hank's Art Supplies
$2006.50

Pleasant Valley School
Board $12,957.11

Picasso , P.
$1603.00

Mesmerics Advertising
$402.80

Pleasant Valley Artists
Cooperative $5923.44

Heedless, E.M.
$8830.00

Main Street Hobby
Center $9043.49

Capitol County News
and Report $882.27

Program instructions
to sort customer
file

CUSTOMER LIST

CUSTOMER NAME	SALES AMOUNT
Pleasant Valley School Board	$12,957.11
Main Street Hobby Center	$9043.49
Heedless, E. M.	$8830.00
Pleasant Valley Artists Cooperative	$5923.44
Hank's Art Supplies	$2006.50
Picasso, P.	$1603.00
Capitol County News and Report	$882.27
Mesmerics Advertising	$402.80

FIGURE 3.4
Customer File Sort:
Descending Order

that decision makers can focus on essentials as they come to their decisions. Information that helps decision-making processes is as important to small businesses, like the Giardinis', as it is to corporate information-management systems. For example, once the computer sorts the customer file by total sales, the Giardinis can spot some useful information that lets them get a feeling for important trends.

They want to find out how much business sales of oil paints account for. Before summarizing the oil-paint information, they have to find it. One source is the billing file, which lists item stock numbers. All item numbers between 1000 and 1999 correspond to oil paints. Each time the computer finds such an item number, it can add it to a running total of sales for that item. Once all records of the file have been processed in this way, the computer can print out the total volume of sales of oil paints. (See Figure 3.5)

You can probably think of variations and refinements of this example yourself. It might be also be useful, for example, to have subtotals for the different types of oil paints sold, sorted in descending order by sales amount. If the computer calculates a figure for total sales, it becomes possible to determine what proportion of business sales of oil paints

FIGURE 3.5
Summarizing Data

Item Number	Sales Transaction Amount
1123	134
1123	233
1124	100
1124	50
1124	890
1130	765
2344	666
2344	100
2355	900
2366	400
2366	700

Sorted Input File

Magnetic Disk

Item Number | Sales Transaction Amount

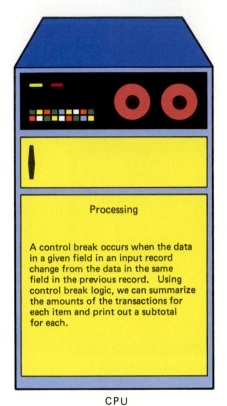

Processing

A control break occurs when the data in a given field in an input record change from the data in the same field in the previous record. Using control break logic, we can summarize the amounts of the transactions for each item and print out a subtotal for each.

CPU

Summarized Sales Report	
Item	Sales Transaction Amount
1123	134
1123	233
Total	367
1124	100
1124	50
1124	890
Total	1040
1130	765
Total	765
Grand Total	2172

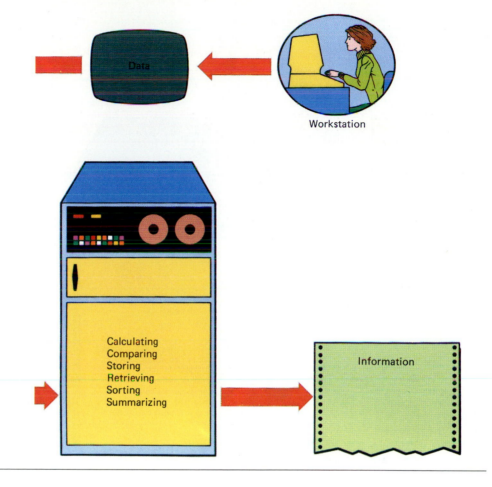

Workstation

Calculating
Comparing
Storing
Retrieving
Sorting
Summarizing

Information

FIGURE 3.6
Summary of Data
Processing Operations

represents. Summarized data make it possible to draw comparisons and analyze results. Computer users can then put the information to practical use.

Reviewing Data Processing Operations

Figure 3.6 summarizes the activities involved in computer data processing. Usually the output comes in the form of reports. You can think of a data-processing system as a production system that takes in data as the raw materials and converts them into the product—information in the form of a report.

Types of Processing Alternatives

In business situations, basic computer operations are used in varied forms. When a data processing system is designed to handle routine processing of data such as orders, inventories, payroll, and accounts receivable, these

functions are known as business applications. The word *application* simply refers to the purposeful use of a computer. In some applications —inventory control, for example—inputs should be made to the system as soon as possible after a transaction (data items that are input for a business application are called **transactions**) takes place, and outputs must be received promptly. In other applications—payroll, for example—a number of transactions can be accumulated for processing at the same time. These two different business applications require two different modes of processing data:

1. In batch processing, the computer processes all input for an application at one point in time to produce the desired output. Input data might be collected periodically, but it is processed all at once. (The payroll application would use batch processing.)
2. In an on-line or interactive system, the computer accesses and updates individual items of data on request. Outputs include the data items that are retrieved for examination on demand, updated data items, and summary reports that can be produced whenever needed. (The inventory application would use some type of on-line system.)

Batch Processing

As the word *batch* implies, batch transactions are done all at once. If all transactions for a customer file are saved for a week or two, and then submitted in a group to the computer to update the customer file, that is a batch processing application. The application can be repeated with new transactions anytime—two days later or two months later—but each time, all the processing is done right then to produce the output.

On-line Inquiry

Inquiry means using a terminal to check data that the computer maintains on auxiliary storage. For instance, when you walk into a bank and use a terminal in the bank's lobby to check your account balance, you make an on-line inquiry. You may have made similar inquiries about airline reservations, course registration, or credit checking in a store. With an on-line inquiry, a number is entered at the terminal (your bank account number, the airline flight number, or whatever), which the computer uses as a key to search for a record in a file on an auxiliary storage device. (A security code may also be requested, to help make sure that the person asking for the information is entitled to do so.) When the computer finds the record, it displays the data requested on the terminal screen. Figure 3.7 shows this process.

On-line Inquiry with Update in Batch

Economics may dictate that updating be done in batch mode rather than on-line mode. For instance, when a bank teller keys the information about your deposit or withdrawal into a terminal, the computer treats this as a

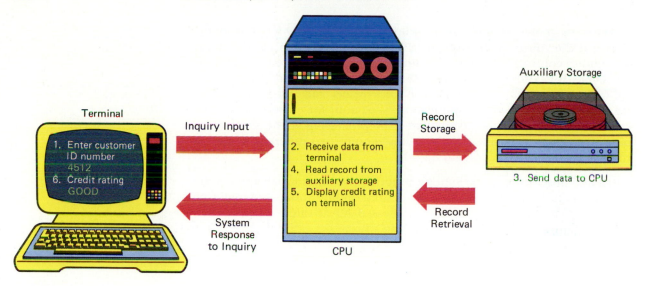

FIGURE 3.7
An Example of On-line Inquiry

transaction. It can be placed on a transaction file at the bank's central computer center. Then, at night, the transaction file can be run against the customer account file to update all customer accounts in batch mode.

An advantage of doing the actual processing in batch rather than on-line mode is that it frees the computer for other work. Batch processing can take place in off-peak hours. For some applications—such as the direct entry of the number of hours worked from various locations in a large factory—an advantage is that data can be entered near the workplace, saving travel time; work hours could be accumulated on a central file and then batch-processed every Thursday night, to produce the next day's paychecks.

On-line Inquiry with Immediate Update

In on-line inquiry with immediate update, the file accessed by the computer in response to an inquiry can be supplied with update data immediately. Airline reservations are the best example of on-line inquiry with immediate update. When someone reserves a seat on a flight, the data for that flight are modified on the spot to indicate that one less seat is available. An airline must constantly have current information about the availability of seats.

Inside the "Black Box"

In data processing jargon, a computer is frequently referred to as a "black box." The term implies that what takes place inside is hidden from view; we can only see what goes in and what comes out. So far, though, we have

looked into the black box to see the different operations the computer employs to carry out its functions: input/output operations; basic arithmetic computations and logical operations; and operations for storing and retrieving information, sorting information, and summarizing information.

By now you should have a good general impression of what a computer does. In the rest of this chapter, let's look deeper into the black box to see in more detail the internal features that enable a computer to perform its calculations and other operations. In other words, through a study of the CPU, we will learn *how* a computer does what it does.

Components of the CPU

A computer's CPU has three components: a control unit, an arithmetic/logic unit (or ALU), and main memory (see Figure 3.8).

The **control unit** is the supervising component. It interprets instructions provided by the computer program held in main memory. As the program instructions are followed, the control unit directs the flow of information and data, controlling input and output devices, routing data between the ALU and main memory, and telling the ALU which operations to perform.

The **arithmetic/logic unit** (**ALU**) performs arithmetic calculations and logical operations, such as comparisons.

Main memory can be thought of as an electronic filing cabinet. It holds data and instructions coming from input devices and the ALU. When data and instructions are required for computer operations, they are called from main memory by the control unit. After processing, data are sent back to main memory from where they can be routed to output devices. Main memory holds only those instructions and data needed for the series of operations the computer is currently executing. (Additional data and instructions can be held in auxiliary storage, outside the CPU. Auxiliary storage is discussed in Chapter 5.)

Characteristics of Main Memory

Main memory is a computer's internal, electronic storage system for programs and data. It has these characteristics:

1. Each specific location in main memory is designated by a number called its **address.**
2. Each address in main memory can hold either of two kinds of information:
   a. a piece of data or
   b. an instruction to the computer from a program.
3. The contents of each address in main memory have been translated into a group of bits (or **b**inary di**g**its——0s or 1s); this group is generally called a **word.**

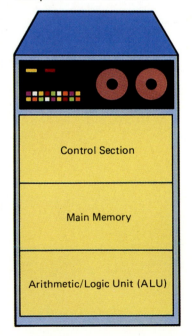

FIGURE 3.8
Components of the CPU

Control Section

Main Memory

Arithmetic/Logic Unit (ALU)

4. A computer program specifies the address to which a word is sent, and a word placed in an address in main memory will remain there until it is changed.

5. When a new word is sent to an address that already holds a piece of data or an instruction, the new word replaces the original contents of that address. The original contents are destroyed.

Main memory has a capability described as **read/write memory.** This means that information can be written into (or transferred into) a specific

How Chips Are Made

Developments in the technology for making semiconductor chips are advancing as fast as the industry as a whole. Understandably, the placing of electronic components on these tiny pieces of silicon is a highly exacting business that requires a great deal of precision machinery. More than 60 kinds of equipment are involved in the making of a chip, in addition to very careful handling by people. The entire process takes up to six weeks. Manufacturers aim at making the chips as small as possible. Spaces between their electronic components can be as narrow as 2.5 microns, or one twentieth the diameter of a human hair.

Chips begin as parts of larger wafers of crystalline silicon. Each future chip must have an outline or pattern on it that shows where its electronic components belong. To create this small map, the silicon is first coated with a substance that raises or lowers its ability to conduct electricity. A film is then placed over this conducting material, which make the wafer sensitive to light. Then, using a device known as a photoaligner, the parts of the wafer that correspond to electronic components are kept covered, while the spaces between them are exposed to light. When the film is developed, the unexposed areas form an outline for the chip's transistors, capacitors, and other components. Very complex chips have many such patterns layered on top of one another.

The next step is to test the wafers to check that their processing has succeeded to this point. They are then cut into smaller pieces, or chips. These are placed into ceramic or plastic casings and connected by gold wires.

As you might expect, there are many ways in which chips can end up defective. If the elements are too close together, for example, they can come in contact with one another and cause short circuits. This happens when the image created by the photoaligner is not sharp enough. Also, if layers don't match up perfectly, connections will be faulty. In the late seventies, GCA Corp. of Bedford, Massachusetts, made a critical breakthrough in chip-making by developing a photoalignment machine known as a stepper. Earlier photoaligners had exposed entire wafers in one shot, while the stepper exposes just one chip at a time, adjusting its focus for each one as it steps from chip to chip. This individualized photoalignment cut down considerably on the possibility that focus could be blurred and that layers of exposure could end up misaligned. As a result, the stepper increases the chip yield of each silicon wafer by about 300 percent. The introduction of the stepper heated up competition in chip manufacturing in the early eighties as companies tried to become the fastest producers of highly desirable steppers. As competition reached the boiling point, there were even accusations by American companies that the Japanese had stolen their stepper designs.

Source: Bro Uttal, "Japan's Latest Assault on Chipmaking," *Fortune,* September 3, 1984, pp. 76–81.

storage address and that, when needed, the information can be *read* from (or retrieved from) that address.

Each word held in main memory can be directly retrieved from its address independent of the order in which the words are stored. This capability is known as **random access memory (RAM)**. The time required to read out the contents or to write information into a randomly selected address in memory is called **access time.** Access time differs in two kinds of storage technologies—magnetic-core memory and semiconductor memory.

Cheaper Chips Mean More Memory

While semiconductor chips are small and powerful, they are also expensive. Up to now, the main use for them has been to hold the information the computer needs to operate its main memory. So traditionally large-memory computer systems have relied on disk drives to supplement their main memories. Supercomputers, for example, use disk drives for the enormous memories that are needed to allow them to perform their complex tasks. As it works, a supercomputer has to switch back and forth between its very fast main memory, composed of semiconductors, and its slower disk drives. Recently the price of semiconductors has been dropping fast, though, which is causing a few computer scientists to think about changing the way computers are designed.

The larger a computer's memory, the more it can do. With that in mind, Richard J. Lipton, computer science professor, and Hector Garcia-Molina, both of Princeton University, are working on a minicomputer that behaves like a supercomputer. Instead of relying on a disk drive for the computer's memory, Lipton and Garcia-Molina have used lots of chips. This makes the computer a lot smaller and faster than it would be with a hard drive. As the price of chips continues to drop, the scientists expect the gap between the price of a disk drive and the price of a chip memory to continue to grow dramatically smaller. For example, today the cost of one megabyte of chip memory is ten times that of disk memory. By 1990, industry experts predict, semiconductor memory will be just two-thirds more expensive than disk memory. Lipton and Garcia-Molina predict that computer makers will soon be using chips where large memory is needed, producing more powerful machines in a manner that not so long ago was unimaginable.

Now the Princeton team is involved in a new project. Their latest machine will have a gigabyte of memory—that's the capacity to hold one billion characters—and Lipton says it will be able to solve problems that a $5 million supercomputer can't. Even better, the machine will cost $500,000.

There are a number of applications in which such massive memory would be extremely beneficial. Take airline reservations systems. At the moment, they can handle several hundred thousand transactions per second, while a bigger memory might increase the number by as much as ten times. Bank computer systems would also be greatly enhanced by such a massive memory. Supercomputers would also become faster machines because they would be able to do away with their disk drives. Lipton predicts that in the nineties, computers will compete not on the basis of speed or the power of their operating systems, but rather the most critical feature will be how much memory they have.

Source: Steve Dickman, "Giving Computers an Elephant's Memory," *Business Week,* September 1, 1986, p. 50.

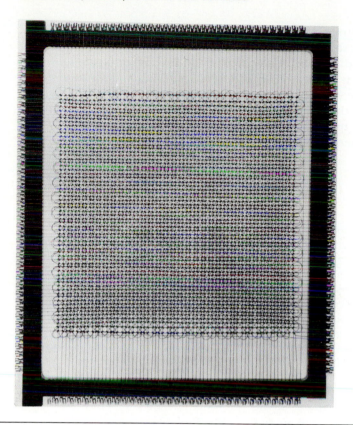

Magnetic Core Memory

Courtesy of IBM Corp.

Magnetic-Core Memory **Magnetic-core memory** uses electrical currents to move tiny metal rings into "on" or "off" positions based on bits. The "on" position is equivalent to the binary value 1, and the "off" position is equivalent to the binary value 0. Even though each ring is only a few hundredths of an inch in diameter, magnetic-core memory is big and slow compared to today's most common memory technology, semiconductor memory.

Semiconductor Memory Most modern computers contain semiconductor random-access memories. Transistors (tiny electric switches) generate electric currents to turn each circuit "on" or "off." As in magnetic-core memory, these "on" and "off" states are represented by the binary digits 1 and 0. The circuits in semiconductor memory are used as signals to represent information.

In semiconductor memory, the transitors and the circuits needed both for storage and for writing and reading data within the computer system are packed close together on tiny chips of silicon crystal. (Silicon is a semiconducting material refined from quartz rock.) Tiny wires link the components of a chip to form the heart of a modern computer. A chip only one-eighth of an inch square can contain 30,000 transistors and is capable of performing hundreds of thousands of calculations per second. Such a chip contains all the CPU components described earlier in this chapter. Wires made of gold or aluminum, which are connected to exterior plugs,

carry electric currents into and out of the chip. Semiconductor memory has much shorter access times than magnetic-core memory. The major problem with semiconductor memory is that it is **volatile,** meaning that it loses its contents if the electric current is removed. Magnetic-core memory, on the other hand, is **nonvolatile.**

Semiconductor random-access memories are classified according to their storage capacity. Memories supported by chips containing only a few transistors are referred to simply as **integrated-circuit memories (ICs)**. A chip that contains thousands of transistors is manufactured by means of a technology known as **large-scale integration (LSI)**. The technology used to pack as many as 100,000 transistors onto a single memory chip is called **very large-scale integration (VLSI)**. In the class of computers using microprocessors, microcomputers, the electronic content of the entire computer is constructed on a single chip smaller than a penny or a human fingernail. A microcomputer's microprocessor is a single integrated circuit containing both the ALU and the control unit. A mainframe's CPU, on the other hand, consists of a series of integrated circuits much more sophisticated than the microprocessor.

Beyond the 64K Chip   In the early 1980s, the 64K chip was the major building block of RAM (random access memory) in personal computers. RAM could be expanded in increments of 64K by using multiple chips for 128K, 256K, and 512K RAM. A 64K chip is roughly equivalent to 64,000 bits, and a 256K chip to 256,000 bits. Recently, announcements have heralded the introduction of megabit chips moving to personal computers. A megabit chip is equivalent to 1,000,000 bits of RAM memory.

The megabit chip quadruples the amount of RAM available to users of personal computers. The benefits of additional RAM include the capability ·to store larger documents and spreadsheets, the ability to run multiple applications, and the ability to lessen manufacturing costs. It will be cheaper to install megabit chips than an equivalent nine or ten smaller chips for RAM. The major benefit of increased memory, however, will be

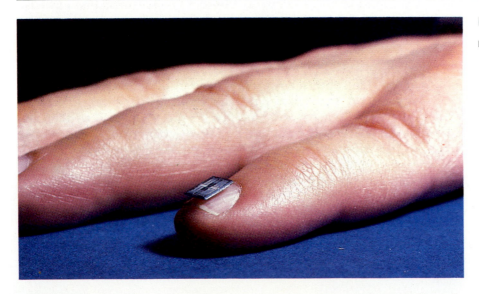

Microprocessor

Raytheon Corp.

the increased power and capability of applications run on personal computers.

Read-Only Memories   Main memory is random-access memory, allowing any piece of stored information to be directly retrieved, regardless of the order in which it is stored. Some CPUs, however, have storage areas in which instructions can be written into storage locations only once. These instructions can be repeatedly read whenever needed but cannot be changed. This storage is referred to as **read-only memory** (**ROM**). In a microcomputer, a ROM is a memory chip containing instructions that have been permanently stored during the manufacturing process.

Some ROM chips make it possible for a computer user to custom design instructions by adding a few specialized functions. Thus, frequently used operations can be built into the machine by putting them on these **programmable read-only memory chips** (**PROMs**). Once all their microcircuits have been programmed in this way, PROMs cannot receive any new information. Building these functions into a machine allows specific tasks to be performed in a fraction of the time required if the same tasks had to be programmed using software.

Another kind of control chip, however, can be erased and reprogrammed: **erasable and programmable read-only memory chips** (**EPROMs**). They typically need to be removed from the CPU and exposed to ultraviolet light to erase previous instructions before the new ones can be entered on them. EPROMs are electrically erasable, simplifying the procedure.

Capacity of Main Memory

Bits   Recall that the instructions and data held in main memory are represented by the two digits of the binary numbering system, or **bits,** 0 and 1. These two digits correspond to the "off" and "on" states of the electronic switches in main storage.

Bytes   A grouping of bits is known as a **byte.** In most computers, a byte is composed of eight bits, but some systems are designed so that a byte holds some other quantity of bits. Usually each byte represents a single unit of data, such as a letter or an integer.

Words   In many computers, however, each address in main memory holds a fixed number of bytes (or characters), and the groups of bytes held in each storage address is called a **word.** Since each word is assigned an address, information is stored and retrieved as words rather than as individual characters. This approach is referred to as **fixed word-length storage.** In each type of computer, a word contains a designated number of bytes. (Figure 3.9 illustrates 8-bit, 16-bit, and 32-bit computers.)

In some computers, each address in main memory can reference only one byte. For example, a sequence of characters such as *Mary* would fill four storage addresses, and *$2* would require two storage addresses. Since each byte is assigned an address, information is stored and retrieved as individual characters. This approach is called **variable word-length storage.**

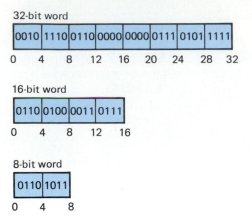

FIGURE 3.9
8-bit, 16-bit, and 32-bit
Computers

Classifying Memory Capacity

The memory capacity of a computer is expressed in the number of storage
addresses contained in main memory. This capacity is usually expressed by
using the letter *K* preceded by a number, such as 8K. *K* stands for *kilo,*
which means 1000. Thus you would expect 8K memory to have 8000
addresses. However, in computer electronics, K actually represents 1024
units (2^{10}, or 2 to the tenth power). The size of a given computer's
memory—that is, how many bytes will be contained per storage address
and how many addresses will be contained in its main memory—is
determined by the individual manufacturer.

When we consider memory capacity, it is clear why memories employ-
ing electronic chips now dominate the computer market. On tiny chips,
electronic charges have less distance to travel during processing. This
means that the CPU can store and retrieve information in much less time,
and that information can be processed at correspondingly higher speeds.
The number of bits that can be stored on a chip continues to expand rapidly,
so that the cost per bit of storage has been steadily declining.

Operations of the CPU

Much of what the CPU does takes place in **registers,** temporary storage
areas for data and instructions within the CPU. A register can receive
information, hold it, and transfer it very quickly. Five registers are discussed
here: the instruction register, the instruction address register, the memory
address register, the data register, and the accumulator. They are illustrated
in Figure 3.10.

Instructions in a computer program must be executed in the order
given, and the control unit is responsible for ensuring that the proper order
is followed. Crucial to that process are the instruction register and the
instruction address register.

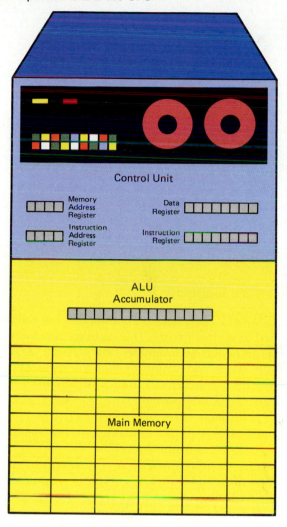

FIGURE 3.10

Five Registers in the CPU

Registers are temporary storage areas for information required during the operation of the CPU.

The **instruction register** holds the instruction currently being executed. The **instruction address register** holds the address of the *next* instruction to be executed. The **memory address register** holds the address of the data on which the current instruction is being performed. When data are retrieved from the address specified in the memory address register, they are transferred into the data register.

When a piece of data has been retrieved, it is held in the **data register.** The data register receives from memory data that will be used in calculations or logical operations performed by the ALU. When those operations are completed, the data register receives the resulting data and sends them to storage.

The accumulator, a register in the ALU, holds data resulting from an operation performed by the ALU. For example, in an addition program, the first value to be added is placed in the accumulator. Then a second value might be transferred from an address in main memory into the accumulator. There it would be added to the value already contained in the accumulator, and the resulting sum would replace the previous value in the accumulator.

Memory Boards

Instruction Fetch, Decoding, and Execution

The CPU functions by repeatedly carrying out three steps: fetching, decoding, and execution of instructions. Remember that the instruction address register holds the address of the next instruction to be executed. The address in the instruction address register is transferred to the memory address register and the number in the instruction address register is then increased by 1, so that the instruction address register will continue to hold the address of the next instruction to be executed. The control unit reads the contents of the memory address register and fetches the computer word from the address specified. That word is channeled into the data register and from there is transferred into the instruction register.

The second step in processing is **instruction decoding.** Before the contents of the instruction register can be executed, the control unit must interpret—that is, decode—the instruction. The control unit analyzes the

67

operation code (recall that the operation code tells the computer which operation is to be performed) specified by the instruction and relays the operation to the ALU. The address portion of the instruction is relayed to the memory address register. This address gives the address of the data on which the instruction will be performed.

The third step is **instruction execution.** The ALU performs the specified operation upon the data. The address of the data is specified in the memory address register. For example, in an *add* instruction, the address portion of the instruction is routed to the memory address register, and the data located at that address are transferred to the data register. Then the data register and the accumulator are added together and the sum is held in the accumulator.

Some instructions may, as part of their function, change the contents of the·instruction address register. When this happens, the control unit is instructed to "jump" to an address that does not follow in sequential order and read next the instruction contained in that address.

Instruction Execution

How is an instruction executed? Consider a sample instruction that is written as eight hexadecimal digits. (The hexadecimal numbering system is used as a shorthand for writing computer instructions, and each hexadecimal digit represents four binary digits inside the computer.) Since each hexadecimal digit is made up of 4 bits, our sample instruction takes up 32 bits in storage.

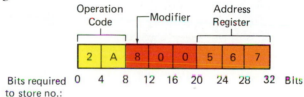

We can analyze the instruction. The first two digits are the *operation code.* In this case, the operation code is 2A, which for this illustration we are assuming is an *add* instruction.

The third digit is a **modifier.** It tells the control unit which register will be used to hold the values used in this particular operation. In this example, the accumulator—register 8—will be used.

For this illustration, the fourth and fifth digits are simply place holders and will not be used.

The last three digits specify the contents of the *address register.* This tells the control unit which address holds the data to be used in this operation. Here, the data held in storage address 567 are to be added to the data already contained in the acccumulator. Let's execute this instruction.

- The operation code is 2A, *add.*
- The address register is 567. The control unit will retrieve from main storage the data stored at address 567.
- The modifier is 8. Register 8 is being used as the accumulator. We will add the value stored in address 567 to the value already held in register 8.

Figure 3.11 illustrates how the CPU executes an instruction.

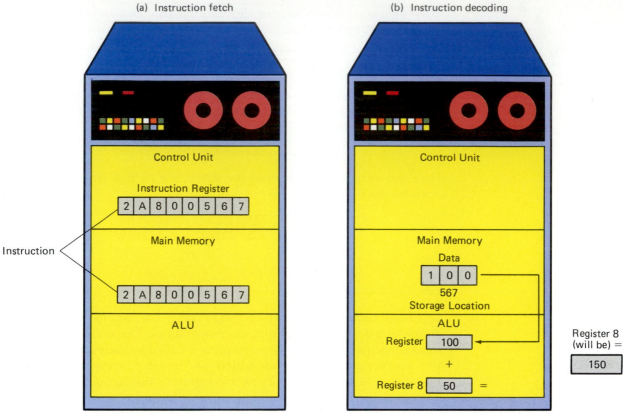

FIGURE 3.11 How the CPU Executes an Instruction

Executing a Series of Instructions

Let's see how the computer would execute a series of instructions. The computer in this example is designed to use the following operation codes:

Operation Code	Meaning
18	Load accumulator
2A	Add to accumulator
20	Store
2B	Subtract from accumulator
20	Store

Here the instruction means to load the contents of address 14D into the accumulator (register 2).

Here the instruction is to add the contents of address 30C to the data already stored in the accumulator (register 2).

Here the instruction is to store the resulting sum (which is already held in the accumulator) in address 684.

Here the instruction is to subtract the contents of address 876 from the accumulator (register 2).

Here the instruction is to store the difference (which is now held in the accumulator) in address 144.

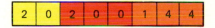

An Instruction Set

Our illustration used only five operation codes, but most modern computers are designed to execute hundreds of operations. The set of all the operations a machine is capable of performing is called its **instruction set.** Since the instruction set specifies which operations a computer is able to perform, it is necessary to know a computer's instruction set in order to write programs for it.

Succeeding at the Impossible

UI Team Creates Chips that Stun Computer World

MOSCOW [Idaho]—The computer Gary Maki built fits on your fingernail and solves 1 billion problems a second.

Skeptics said no one—let alone a dozen engineers and mathematicians in a University of Idaho basement—could build a computer so small and powerful.

Some still doubt its existence.

But ask NASA scientists about it and they will say Maki's Microelectronics Research Center may be the best-kept secret of the computer age.

The five tiny computer chips that Maki is on contract to produce for NASA will replace more than 2,000 chips running 30 times slower, said Warner Miller, NASA's technical adviser on the $800,000 job.

The five chips will help the National Aeronautics and Space Administration beam error-free facts, figures, and photographs from earth-orbiting satellites through lightning storms and space dust to tracking stations on the ground.

Their offspring, also likely to be produced by Maki, will help NASA cool infrared cameras used to study the origin of the universe and astronauts who repair equipment outside the safety of space laboratories.

"They have, literally, done what every other scientist said was impossible," Miller said. "I've gotten more out of a handful of people at the University of Idaho than out of all of Rockwell International."

Miller will lead a delegation of NASA scientists to UI in March to pick up the last two high-speed chips. Already, he said, he is looking forward to the expression on his colleagues' faces when they see Maki's workroom.

Tucked into the basement of the university's old engineering building, the microelectronics lab is a hodgepodge of old classroom tables, water pipes, electrical wires and more than $1.2 million worth of computers.

The walls are bare. The space is cramped. The light is dim.

But the atmosphere is charged and morale is high. This is, Maki said, the new frontier.

Maki, who came to Moscow in 1969 fresh out of the University of Missouri's electrical engineering school, likes the idea of pitting his unassuming environs against the shiny snobbery of the Silicon Valley.

"When a big research lab in California says it can't be done, our ears perk up," he said. "We thrive on the challenge of designing custom computers that do the impossible."

Maki, 40, credits his success to a team of co-workers "not driven by selfish ambitions, but by an interest in working for the common good."

With a group this small and assignments this big, brilliance has to be the norm, said Gary Gapp. As campus coordinator for Hewlett-Packard in Boise, Gapp has provided Maki with the equipment he needs at the price he needs.

To date, Maki can account for more than $1 million worth of computers donated to his research center by H-P.

'There's nothing glamorous about Maki's setup," Gapp said. "But there's something very, very brilliant about it. The people he has brought to Moscow are highly motivated and deeply committed."

Maki, who Gapp said could triple his salary at the high-tech corporation of his choice, is the idea man and the mathematics wizard. He also is one of only three faculty members ever awarded a UI presidential citation.

Maki's right-hand man since 1979, when NASA took a gamble and sent Maki home from a summer job with a $17,000 contract, has been Pat Owsley, an assistant professor of electrical engineering.

In the years since, Maki has skimmed the best off of Gould-AMI in Pocatello—including engineers Sterling Whitaker and Kelly Cameron, layout technician John Canaris and circuit design specialist John Shovic.

On campus, an eager cadre of electrical engineering faculty and graduate students kick in their best bets.

Two students, Carrie Claflin and Jay McDougal, were lead engineers for the final two computer chips, now being manufactured at H-P's plant in Corvallis, Ore.

UI faculty members John Purviance, Joseph Feeley, Damu Radhakrishnan and Howard Demuth fill out the roster of specialists—a roster Maki said several universities have offered to hire as a multimillion-dollar package.

"Maki's people are a gold mine," Gapp said. "They have had their hands in the field. They know what it takes to get jobs done—and they get it done a lot faster than the big boys bogged down in bureaucracy out in industry.

"The chips they've produced have astounded some people, NASA included. Some people still don't believe they exist.

"But I know they do. I've seen them work. They go beyond the bounds of technology."

Robert Lord, chairman of Washington State University's Computer Science Department, said Maki's chip design is important if computers are to evolve—ever smaller, ever faster.

"That's how we progress," Lord said. "The computers we buy this year are 20 percent faster than last year's. You can't sustain growth like that

Gary Maki: "When a big research lab in California says it
can't be done, our ears perk
up."

without guys like Maki."

The UI chip, Lord said, "is very, very fast because it is tailored to do a specific job."

WSU's IBM computer, the most advanced on the market, solves 50 million problems a second—compared with Maki's 1 billion a second.

But Lord cautioned that the UI chip does but one job—error correction —and his bigger, slower computer does many jobs.

"Maki's chip won't do a thing for the computer I have right now," he said. "But it sure could speed things up in the future. If you want to build a faster computer, the first thing you need is faster error correction."

Maki said he has turned down offers from other schools because of the delay such a move would cost his work—and because UI came through with $100,000 each of the past two years so he could hire more microelectronics technicians.

To date, Maki said, taxpayers have not put a penny into the lab. The university's contributions came out of other research contracts. At least one new faculty job was financed by H-P.

"We're here becaue we're interested in personal growth and because Moscow is a nice place to live," Shovic said. "We do the research we want to do, not what some company wants us to do."

The birth of UI's Microelectronics Research Center dates to Maki's first summer fellowship at Goddard Space Flight Center near Washington, D.C., in 1979.

"My first 10 years here," he said, "I went out to private companies each summer and tried to match my research interests with their needs—with no success.

"As soon as I hooked up with NASA, though, things clicked. They had technical needs with no solutions. I liked that and I liked their willingness to take a gamble on an unknown."

It took Maki and Owsley nearly three years to come up with a new way of thinking that got them past the impossible and into the possible.

First came the mathematics and design theory for the tiny chips, which measure a quarter of an inch on a side. Then came at least eight months of design work per chip. Then countless months of computer checks.

"Everything must be perfect before we send a chip to the foundry," Shovic said. "You can't spend $30,000 for a chip and then find a design flaw."

What makes perfection so astounding, Shovic said, is that each chip contains 165,000 transistors represented by 1.5 million rectangles—all of which must be drawn by one of the center's four layout technicians.

"Each rectangle must be in the right place or the chip will not work," he said. "The process is very, very complex. Luckily, our layout people are very, very good."

Each high-speed chip to be delivered to NASA can find and correct errors on the equivalent of 5,000 pages of typewritten text per second. That means 100 pages could leave a space lab completely in error and would be correct by the time they reached earth.

Shovic likens the process to a game in which skiers are sent up a mountain on a chairlift and told to remember one number apiece.

"Say the wind starts gusting and the chairs start swaying," he said. "Some people get scared and forget their numbers. If our computer chip is running the show, every error will be corrected instantaneously."

For NASA, that means an end to the garbled transmissions caused by noise in space and weather disturbances in the earth's atmosphere, Miller said.

It means error-free transmissions from deep space, where spacecraft such as Voyager rely on a mere 100 watts of electricity to transmit data millions of miles.

Miller said NASA has asked Congress for $2.5 million the space agency wants to give Maki to build a "space refrigerator" that will cool infrared detectors looking back in time.

"If Gary can keep our cameras cool for long periods of time and with great precision—and I think he can—we can study the remnants of the Big Bang, the explosion that created the universe 15 billion years ago," he said.

Other NASA scientists, Miller said, want Maki to improve the communications backpacks that astronauts wear during space walks—another multi-million-dollar job.

A third group based at Goddard is working on a new generation of super computers and needs Maki's know-how to achieve the speed required, Miller said.

That sort of opportunity, Maki said, is what keeps his troops going—that and the work of Richard Callahan, director of the Idaho Research Foundation and the UI administrator responsible for marketing on-campus research.

"We are lucky that people like Gary Maki came here initially," Callahan said. "But it will take more than luck to keep them here. Candidly, there is no guarantee they will stay."

Callahan said he will do his part to avoid the brain drain by selling Maki's designs to private industry and channeling a percentage of the royalties and license fees back to the designers.

"Our region has a responsibility when it sees talent like this to do whatever it can to encourage the activity to stay in the area," he said. "Technology means new business. It means contracts that turn around many times in the local economy."

Callahan doesn't like to talk about his plans for Maki's inventions, but

said the same technology could be valuable for any communications outlet —telephones, stereos, radios and television sets, for example.

UI has applied for a patent on the chip design. The computer industry, Callahan said, is highly competitive, and even academicians such as Maki must guard their work against piracy.

Maki also is working on a single chip that would replace the five he made for NASA. That chip, he said, could wind up in desk-top computers. That's all he will say, though, for fear of losing his competitive edge to industry.

Maki and Purviance do like to tell taxpayers—and have asked UI President Richard Gibb to include their pitch in his presentation to state legislators—that their work produces better-trained graduates.

The stars of UI's electrical engineering program have gone to job interviews in which they knew more about new technologies than the engineers asking the questions, Maki said.

H-P's Gapp agreed.

"Gary Maki's team has produced students who are able to contribute at the moment they start in industry," he said.

H-P recruits dozens of UI graduates each year, Gapp said, as do other big names in the computer industry.

What Maki wants now is for the big names to look to UI for contracts and computer designs—and to give his humble surroundings a healthy measure of respect.

"The biggest computers in the world perform between 10 million and 100 million operations a second," he said. "Our computer does 1 billion operations a second and is physically much smaller.

"The applications beyond error correction are endless. But we've got to let people know what we can do. A lot of them don't even know where Idaho is, much less what Idaho does."

Source: "Succeeding at the Impossible" by Sherry Devlin. Copyright © 1987, The Spokesman-Review and Spokane Chronicle. Spokane, Washington.

Summary and Key Terms

1. *Data* are facts or representations of facts. They are the raw material from which information is processed. As used by a computer system, data are usually organized into three levels of complexity: field, record, and file.
2. Data processing is the manipulation of data to achieve a desired result.
3. The components of a data-processing system include input devices, output devices, auxiliary storage devices, and the central processing unit (CPU).
4. From a business user's point of view, the possible functions of a computer are input/output operations, basic arithmetic computations and logical operations, storing and retrieving information, sorting information, and summarizing information.
5. Data processing should provide *information,* which is data in a form that can be used for decision making. An application means the use of a computer for a specific task. A business application is the use of a computer to handle routine processing of an organization's data.
6. Input data items to a business application are called transactions. A transaction can be a sales record, a name and address change, a time card, a bank deposit

slip, or many other items. Output data from a business application can include management reports, paychecks, correspondence, and mailing labels. Transactions are used to update master records.

7. Two basic processing alternatives are available for business applications. On-line processing handles input when it arises. Batch processing handles all input for the application at once. On-line inquiry with update in batch combines both processing modes.

8. The CPU has three major components:
   - The *control unit* directs and coordinates the operations of the central processing unit and regulates the flow of instructions and data during processing.
   - Main memory holds data and instructions. After processing has taken place, it holds the resulting data.
   - The *arithmetic/logic unit* performs the calculations and logical operations necessary for processing data.

9. Within main memory each storage location is assigned an address. In most computers, the contents of each address is called a word. The storage of words can either be by fixed word-length or variable word-length. A word can be a piece of *data* to be used in calculations or which has resulted from some calculation, or an *instruction*.

10. An instruction specifies how the data are to be processed. A series of instructions is a program. Each instruction must specify the kind of operation to be performed and the address of the data to be used in the operation. The set of all the operations a computer is capable of performing is its instruction set. Once a computer's instruction set is known, programs can be written for it.

11. A capability of main memory is random-access memory (RAM): each word in main memory can be directly retrieved from its address, independently of the order in which the words are stored. The time required to read out the contents or write information into a randomly selected address in memory is called access time. ROM (read-only memory) is the type of memory in which instructions are written into storage locations that cannot be changed.

12. Main memory is either magnetic-core memory or semiconductor memory.

13. The capacity of a computer's memory is expressed in the number of storage addresses in main memory. This capacity is usually described by using the letter K, which represents the number 1024.

14. Data are represented internally in the computer by using the two *bi*nary digi*ts* (*bits*) 0 and 1. A grouping of bits is known as a byte.

15. Registers are temporary storage places inside the computer used for routing data and instructions during processing. Registers can receive, hold and transfer information quickly.

16. The CPU functions by repeating three kinds of instructions: *fetching, instruction decoding,* and *instruction executing*.

Review Questions

Fill-in

1. _____ is the collection, processing, and distribution of facts and figures to achieve a desired result.

2. When data are read into the computer system and printed out in roughly the same format, this type of operation is known as _____.

3. Examples of output devices are _____ and _____.

4. The internal storage unit of the central processing unit is known as _____.

5. The _____ unit of the computer is responsible for such operations as addition, subtraction, multiplication, and division.

6. When a bank teller uses a terminal to access a customer record to determine an account balance, this is known as an _____ application.

7. _____ serves as traffic manager of the computer system, directing and coordinating computer operations.

8. An _____ is a computer word which specifies how data is to be processed.

9. _____ is the portion of the instruction that defines the specific operation to be performed by the computer.

10. _____ is the kind of memory from which data or program instructions can be directly retrieved from any given address.

Matching

Listed are five examples of computer operations. Fill in the letter representing the appropriate computer operation supporting each of these applications.

a. input/output operations

b. arithmetic operations

c. storing/retrieving

d. sorting

e. summarizing

_____ 1. Calculate discounts on orders.

_____ 2. Produce a listing of students in alphabetical order.

_____ 3. Generate a mailing list of employee names and addresses from an employee master file.

_____ 4. Obtain access to a customer's credit status, using a terminal.

_____ 5. Provide subtotals of total sales, by region, for a specific product line.

Discussion Questions

1. Describe which of the following processing modes would be most appropriate to support each of the following applications and explain the reasons for your choice:

   a. batch

   b. on-line with batch update

   c. on-line with immediate update

   _____ 1. a payroll system

   _____ 2. a hotel reservations system

   _____ 3. a point-of-sale retailing system for sales order entry and inventory updating at a major retail store, such as Sears.

   _____ 4. a banking system which records deposits and withdrawals to customer checking accounts.

2. Assume that a computer uses a 32-bit machine language instruction format described in the text.
   a. Write the bit positions (0, 4, 8, 12, 16, etc.) in the diagram below.
   b. Write an instruction that would cause the computer to perform the following *add* operation, using these guidelines:
      (1) Place the op code for *add* (8A) in its proper position.
      (2) Complete the rest of the instruction to cause the computer to add the data in working storage location 614 to the contents of the accumulator, which is register 3.
      (3) Place zeros in the remaining portions of the instruction.

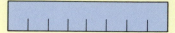

4

Input and Output Methods and Devices

Chapter Objectives

After studying this chapter, you should be able to

1. Identify common methods of system input and output.

2. Understand the uses of direct keying devices, source-data automation systems, and such input technologies as voice recognition and touch-sense.

3. Recognize the characteristics and

applications of impact and nonimpact printers.

4. Identify uses for computer-output microfilm and the value of computer-assisted retrieval.

5. Understand the applications of various output technologies and their uses in information systems.

Jerry Bragg sells motorcycle parts. A year ago, Jerry ran a six-person operation, but now business has tripled and he's hired four more employees. A computer system made the difference in Jerry's operation, but not, as you might think, by helping him keep track of inventory or bill customers. Jerry's business grew because he became a desktop publisher.

Jerry issues a mail-order catalog that used to take eight months from the time he began compiling it to the time it was typeset, printed, and ready to send out. That meant he was limited to easily available inventory that he could either keep on hand or order quickly in large quantities. He couldn't afford to list unusual items available only in small quantities because too often by the time the catalog came out the special items had been sold to walk-in customers.

Jerry knew that if he could get the catalog out faster, he could sell a lot of "time-sensitive" products. A computer system based on an Apple computer let him do just that, combining words and pictures in page formats made up by the computer and special "desktop publishing" software. The catalog project that used to take eight months can be accomplished in a week now, and that one improvement in service has translated into a healthy jump in business.

In addition to projects like the catalog, desktop publishing makes it possible to produce proposals, newsletters, letterheads, and other documents without having to use a commercial typesetting system. The Apple Macintosh, combined with the Apple LaserWriter printer and Aldus Corporation's PageMaker software, created the desktop publishing market.

79

In this computer system, data are input at the keyboard; output is available on the monitor screen and as hard copy from the printer.

Photo courtesy of Hewlett Packard

Desktop publishing, covered in detail in Chapter 9, is one of the latest expressions of the fundamental purpose of computer systems: data entry, data processing, and information output in a form people can use. This chapter focuses on the two ends of the process, input and output.

The term **input** refers to data ready for entry into a computer processing system. *Input* is also used to name the process by which data are entered into the system. Many input methods and devices are available for computer systems, but they all have a single purpose: translating data into the electronic code the particular system uses. **Output** can be defined as information or data transferred from a computer to a user. Not many years ago, *output* was synonymous with *printout,* but today many forms of output are available, a development that is easy to understand when you consider how much the group of users for computer output has grown.

Input Devices

A remarkable variety of data-entry, or input, devices can take data prepared by and for human beings and make them understandable to a CPU:

1. Key-driven devices. Several input methods require an operator to read the source data and strike a keyboard. Keypunch machines record data on punched cards; key-to-tape machines enter data on magnetic tape;

key-to-disk machines record data on magnetic disks. With all key-driven devices, accessory devices such as card readers and tape or disk drives are needed to enter the coded data into the computer.

2. Source-data automation. With this input method data are "read" directly into the computer by means of magnetic-ink character recognition (MICR) or optical character recognition (OCR). In these technologies the data must be in machine-readable form to begin with.

3. On-line entry. Data can be directly entered into a computer through the keyboard of a terminal that is connected (on-line) to the computer system.

Off-line Input Devices

Off-line means that the data are recorded on a computer-readable medium, such as magnetic tapes or magnetic disks, before entering the computer itself. From these media the data are transferred in batches into the CPU for processing. Off-line key-driven input units were the earliest input devices; with the development of faster, more efficient means of input, their use has become more limited.

Keypunch Systems   The keypunch machine, rarely used now, was once the most common input device. Figure 4.1 shows a punched card of the kind used in a keypunch system. A well-known example of a keypunch system is that of workers inserting punched cards into a time clock in order to check into and check out of a job. As another example, data on cards attached to furniture or major appliances can be used by wholesalers and retailers to report the location of an item to its manufacturer.

Key-to-Disk Systems   A **key-to-disk** work station consists of a keyboard for entering data and a CRT screen to display data and other information, such as directions to guide the operator. Figure 4.2 depicts the flow of information in a key-to-disk system. In addition to massive storage capacity

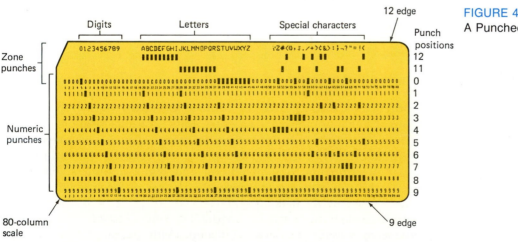

FIGURE 4.1.
A Punched Card

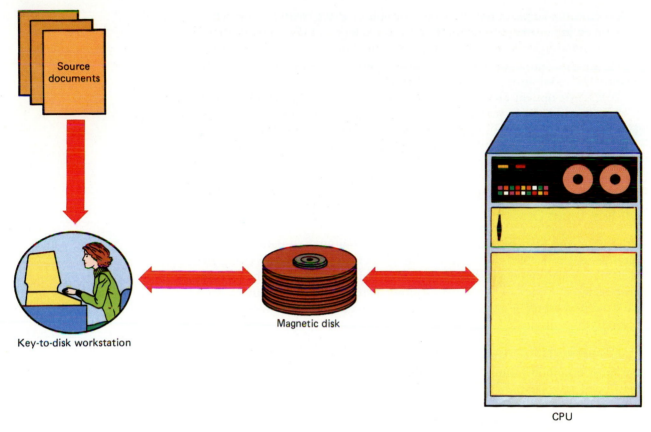

FIGURE 4.2.
A Key-to-Disk Input System

and random-access capability, editing and control functions can be programmed into the data recorder. The system can maintain production statistics and batch totals as data are entered. The recorder can be programmed to record or verify data. It can also search for information previously stored on disks. Data recorded off-line on disk can be physically transported to the computer center. To work more rapidly, the key-to-disk recorder can be put on-line to transmit data directly to the CPU.

Distributed Data Entry

Distributed data entry (DDE) or **remote job entry (RJE)** refers to the setting up of single or multiple data-entry units at various locations. The use of distributed data entry is expanding, as many organizations move input functions out of their centralized data-processing center and install them in individual departments, branch offices, and regional outlets. For many businesses, this practice permits more efficient use of the staff and decreases the time required for data entry.

Data recorded on magnetic media are often stored in a location convenient to where the data originated. With the flexibility of most

modern input systems, either the storage media can be physically transported to the company's central processing center or the stored information can be transmitted on-line from the data-entry points to the central computer system. Figure 4.3 illustrates the flow of information in a distributed data-entry system.

The increased use of microcomputers has encouraged the distribution of data-entry functions. Moving the actual processing power as well as data entry out into departments and branch offices sometimes provides for the most efficient use of personnel and equipment. Processed information can then be submitted to corporate headquarters in ready-to-use form.

The specific data-entry needs and practices of every organization are different. In making decisions about an input system, the various company locations as well as the knowledge, feelings, and attitudes of the personnel must be considered.

On-line Input Devices

Input Terminals Terminals are on-line devices that can be used to enter data into the computer system and also to receive processed data as output. **On-line** means that the terminal is linked directly to the computer. Thus, data can be sent directly to the CPU for processing, and do not need to be interpreted by a reader first. Because of their greater efficiency and speed in entering data, terminals have in many cases replaced off-line key-driven input devices. A terminal consists of a typewriterlike keyboard, which is used for data entry, and a **cathode ray tube (CRT) screen,** which looks

FIGURE 4.3.
A Distributed Data-Entry System

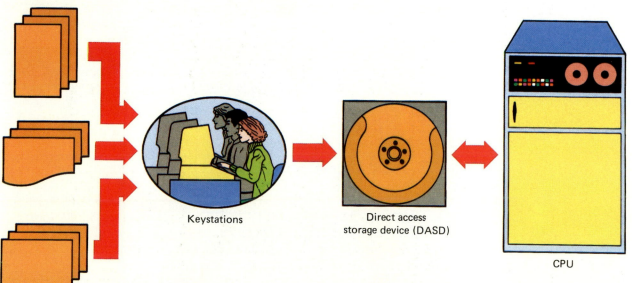

Source documents

Keystations

Direct access
storage device (DASD)

CPU

much like a television screen and can display both the data being input and the processed information that is the system's output.

Dumb Terminals   **Dumb terminals** are input devices used only to input data and instructions into the computer and to receive the processed information from the computer. A dumb terminal consists of a display screen, a keyboard for data entry, and a communication link to the CPU. Dumb terminals display information just as it is received; data need not be entered in any predetermined format. When a dumb terminal is used for entering data, the CPU must perform all data editing, checking for errors, and processing of input, as well as the assigning of format to output, and file updating.

Intelligent Terminals   **Intelligent terminals** incorporate microprocessors along with the display screen, keyboard, and the communication link to the

FIGURE 4.4.
Abilities of Dumb and
Intelligent Terminals

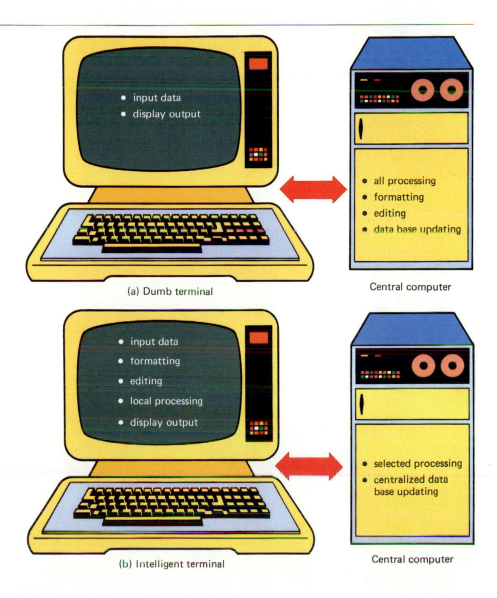

- input data
- display output

- all processing
- formatting
- editing
- data base updating

(a) Dumb terminal

Central computer

- input data
- formatting
- editing
- local processing
- display output

- selected processing
- centralized data base updating

(b) Intelligent terminal

Central computer

CPU. Thus they have the ability to edit, manipulate, store, and process data at the data-entry site. Intelligent terminals can increase data-entry efficiency by performing many preprocessing functions. This relieves the CPU of many routine operations and reduces the amount of time the CPU must spend communicating with the terminal. In addition, the trend is away from just intelligent terminals to intelligent work stations, which can do certain activities entirely by themselves without involving the host computer. Figure 4.4 compares the capabilities of dumb and intelligent terminals.

Direct-Keying Devices

Direct-keying devices are connected directly to the computer system. Thus, data entered at a terminal keyboard can go directly to the CPU. The familiar **Touch-tone telephone** is one type of direct-keying device. It can be used for entering numeric data into a computer system. When Touch-tone phones serve as terminals, an electric translation device is needed to interpret the unique tone produced by each telephone key. The translator converts the tones into computer-readable code and enters the coded data onto tape.

Another common direct-keying device is the automated teller machine. After inserting a plastic card that contains a magnetic strip with the machine-readable account number, a banking customer keys into the machine a personal identification number. For security reasons, that number is known only to that individual customer. Because the teller machine is directly linked to the central computer, the account numbers entered by card and keying can be compared to files in the computer's direct-access memory. Thus the CPU can instantly discover whether the customer's numbers are valid. If they are, the customer can used the teller machine to make deposits or withdrawals, transfer funds between accounts, or check the account balance.

Electronic funds transfer (EFT) is a somewhat more complex direct-keying process. In an EFT system customers can pay bills directly, thus eliminating a great deal of paperwork. The same system will automatically credit a salary check to an employee's bank account.

Here's how EFT works: say that someone has decided to buy jogging shoes. She gives the sales clerk a plastic bank credit card. The clerk inserts the card in an electronic key-type "cash" register and rings up the athletic supply shop's account number. This information is now on-line to the shop's bank, which transmits it to the customer's bank as well. The central computer at her bank verifies that she has $34.95 in her account and debits her account for that amount. It then tells the central computer of the store's bank that $34.95 has been transferred to the store's account. With a signal from the store's bank to the in-store terminal, the transaction is completed. It's easy to see why EFT is expected to lead to a cashless and even checkless society.

Source-Data Automation

Source-data automation describes various means of inputting data directly from source material. In these methods a scanning device is used to

On-Line Transactions

On-line transaction processing is becoming a major market for the computer industry. In retail stores, customers presenting credit cards to pay for a purchase can complete their transactions almost instantly. J.C. Penney Co., for example, uses on-line systems in its stores nationwide. In any of its retail outlets, Penney's salespeople scan the bar codes on customers' credit cards with optical scanning wands and key in the amount of each purchase. At the company's data center, located in Columbus, Ohio, transactions in California or Connecticut or at any of Penney's retail stores come in via either satellite or land lines. The system compares the amount of each customer's purchase with the account's credit limit, deducts the current sale from the amount of allotted credit, and okays the purchase. Such an on-line transaction is complete in less than ten seconds. Some of the areas in which large computers are an important part of business are retail stores, banks, brokerage houses, airlines, and factories.

In the 1960s, airlines were the first to use transaction systems, which depend on large computers to store and process large amounts of data very quickly. Banks' automatic teller machines were another early use for this kind of system. These two areas may not see many major changes in computer equipment in the near future, as banks and airlines don't see any immediate need to change their existing systems. But this type of system continues to expand into new areas of application. A major opportunity for growth, experts say, will be expanded use of transaction processing systems in retail stores.

"read" raw data and convert it into computer code. Source-data automation methods eliminate the intermediate step of hand keying, which is a source of frequent errors. The three major technologies used in source-data automation are mark sensing, magnetic-ink character recognition (MICR), and optical character recognition (OCR).

Mark Sensing The optical reader used in **mark sensing** can detect the presence of any writing (as long as the mark is dark) but not the shape of a character. Mark sensing is often used for scoring multiple-choice or true-false tests, or for recording grades or attendance. Mark sensing has often served as a computer input device for surveys, censuses, compilations, and billing. Information is gathered by asking respondents to make heavy pencil or ballpoint-pen marks in preprinted positions on a specially designed form. Each position on the form has been assigned a meaning. For example, a mark might represent a "yes" or a "no" in a questionnaire or a specified letter or digit on a multiple-choice test.

Mark sensing offers clear advantages for certain applications. The only equipment required for gathering input is a pencil or other writing instrument and the specially designed forms. Because of their simple recognition logic, mark-sensing readers are much less expensive than devices designed to read characters. When used as a turnaround document —for example, when respondents are asked to fill out and return a questionnaire—a mark-sensing form requires no editing or verifying because preprinted sections have already been verified and the data filled in are the original replies given by a respondent.

Magnetic-Ink Character Recognition **Magnetic-ink character recognition (MICR)** readers can read and interpret a single line of information

Lucky Stores, with 300 supermarkets in California, is installing terminals in its stores that will allow customers to pay for their groceries by using their ATM cards. Gas stations around the country are beginning to install similar systems. At Lockheed-Georgia, a division of Lockheed Corp., a transaction processing system keeps track of what jobs each worker is busy with at all times. This involves some 600,000 transactions a day, and the company plans to expand use of the system to include records of parts and orders. Brokerage houses are another area in which the use of transaction processing systems will expand. Today transactions in this business tend to happen around the clock, and computers that can track market transactions full time are an attractive prospect.

Computer and software companies are engaged in competition for business in this growing area of the industry. On the hardware side, many companies are devleeping no-fault systems, or those that resist crashing. For businesses in which hardware is already in use, updated software is the emphasis. Another area of development focuses on making the system cheaper to use. Today each transaction costs between five and 20 cents to complete. Experts believe that in the near future, costs could drop as low as a penny per transaction.

Source: John W. Wilson, " 'On-Line' Systems Sweep the Computer World," *Business Week,* July 14, 1986, pp. 64–65.

Ski-lift tickets are available as an on-line transaction.

Photo courtesy of Diebold, Inc.

---

printed in a special ink that contains magnetic particles. This technology is used primarily by banks.

Bank checks are preprinted with a line of characters at the bottom to identify both the customer and the bank. This information is printed on a standard type font with the special magnetic ink. This standard font ·contains only fourteen characters—the ten decimal digits plus four special control symbols (see Figure 4.5).

When a check is cashed, the first bank to process it enters the amount of the check by using a key-driven machine called an **encoder.** To assist the bank's accounting process, the encoder also accumulates a total of the amounts of all the checks being processed in the batch. After the check amount is thus encoded, each check is processed on a **reader/sorter,** which interprets the information on the check, then groups the checks according to the banks on which they are drawn. Checks written on other banks are forwarded for collection, and checks written by the bank's own customers are sorted by account number. The reader/sorter also creates a file on tape or disk to be used for preparing monthly statements for each bank customer.

MICR is a reliable method for processing documents that must be frequently handled. A major advantage is that smudges or stray ink marks will not cause interpretation errors. Also, since numbers are visibly printed on the document, the character can easily be visually verified. By requiring that only preprinted checks be used for drawing funds, the MICR system helps guard against fraudulent check writing.

Optical Character Recognition   **Optical character recognition (OCR)** input devices read characters optically rather than magnetically. Thus, the data to be input using this method can be printed in ordinary dark ink. *Page*

FIGURE 4.5.
MICR Fonts
Digits and symbols of (a) the CMC-7 MICR font used by the European banking community. and (b) the E-13B MICR font adopted by the American Banking Association.

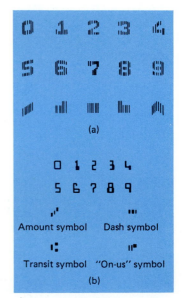

FIGURE 4.6.
OCR-A, The ANSI Standard
OCR Character Set

Source: Courtesy American National
Standards Institute

readers are OCR devices that can read a wider variety of characters and documents. They are able to interpret a typewritten page, an adding-machine tape, or a computer printout. Some are even able to read hand-printed characters. OCR allows the use of a much larger character than is possible with MICR. A standard OCR type font, called OCR-A, has been adopted for use in the United States (see Figure 4.6).

A Business Application of OCR   Typically, the use of an OCR device to enter orders and report sales has been found to save time and money. In one cosmetics company, sales representatvies used to send each order by mail to the order department. There the form was checked to see that it was correctly filled out. It was then sent to the keypunch department. Orders were seldom processed on the day they were received. Or, if sales representatives telephoned their orders to the order department, telephone conversations sometimes lasted as long as two hours or more.

Then the company gave all its sales reps hand-held, battery-powered portable computers that could receive and store the data they used to write on the order form. Now orders are entered when the sales representative optically scans a bar-coded form listing items and quantities. All orders are automatically transmitted to the central data-processing department every day.

Using this OCR device, the company has speeded order processing by seven to ten days; saved money on postage, telephone bills, and keypunch data-entry costs; and eliminated duplicate orders that postal-service delays often made necessary. In addition, sales data are known immediately, and supervisors can closely follow each sales rep's performance. The sales staff can promise delivery to customers more confidently, since the uncertainty

Supermarket POS Terminals and the UPC Bar Code

The time and expense involved in making and attaching OCR-readable labels at each individual store can be eliminated when sales data are placed directly on the product package by the manufacturer. This requires a uniform standard code that can be read by equipment used in any store. Problems of developing a standard code were discussed at length by representatives of grocery manufacturers and supermarket chains. They formed the Universal Grocery Code Council and developed a standard **bar code** for labeling products sold in supermarkets. This code is known as the Universal Product Code (UPC).

The advantage of the UPC to the supermarket industry is clear: There is a significant reduction in data-entry error made by checkout clerks. It also enables grocery manufactuers to code and label items at the same time, saving retailers that extra step of coding. Using the UPC system, it is more economical to post prices on the shelves where goods are selected than to mark prices on each item individually. Price changes can be entered into the central computer system, and do not have to be made on every package. But consumer groups have protested the absence of individual pricing. Some states require current prices to be posted on the supermarket shelf or in some other obvious location.

A **controller** in each store is the link between the system's central processor and all the terminals in that store. When a terminal reads an item's

caused by postal-service delivery and keypunching errors has been eliminated.

Point-of-Sale Terminals   Many retail businesses now use **point-of-sale (POS) terminals.** These are input/output devices linked to a computer system and used in the place of conventional cash registers. The POS terminal is, in fact, an electronic cash register. Its components include a numerical keyboard, some special function keys, a display that guides the checkout clerk step by step through the sales transaction and indicates any input errors, a cash drawer, a printer for customer receipts, and a sales journal roll. You can see all these components for yourself the next time you go to the supermarket.

Information about each sales transaction can be input through the keyboard or machine-read by a scanner. The latter may involve either of two kinds of optical reader devices. In some POS terminals, the sales clerk passes a miniature hand-held scanner over the label of each item; these scanners are designed to read either bar-coded data or an OCR font. Other POS terminals, often found in supermarkets, have a slot-type scanner mounted on the package conveyor at the checkout counter. These use laser beams to read the bar code on each packaged item.

The POS terminal is used to input data at the time and place of the sales transaction. It also performs arithmetic functions—figuring price extensions, totaling sales, and calculating sales tax, fees, discounts, and markdowns. Clerks can handle customers more efficiently. The computer system can keep verifying customer identities and checking credit ratings. The POS system collects sales data for each store, processes information for management reports, and analyzes overall store operations.

bar code, it contacts the store controller, which in turn consults a file maintained by the company's central processor. One file maintained by the central processor contains the price and description for each item in the store's inventory. Another file contains customer account and credit authorization information. This file is consulted by the controller when the checkout operator requests check validation through a terminal. The controller returns information about the items' description and price to be printed on the customer receipt.

The supermarket POS terminal improves service to customers, increases checkout speed, and provides more reliable sales information. The time, number of personnel, and amount of paperwork required to facilitate each sales transaction is significantly reduced. The receipt issued by the terminal is an accurate purchase record for each customer. Each day's sales and other operational information is immediately available to managers. The terminal automatically records inventory data. Buyers can promptly reorder, and thus keep popular items in stock while reducing inventory of slower-moving goods. The system can also calculate and furnish a variety of long-term summary reports to summarize store operations and project future needs and profits. This enables managers to make better decisions about the company's operations.

New Technologies for Data Entry

In today's business environment, information needs are increasing and data entry is decentralized. New methods to enter more data more rapidly and more easily are being sought. Voice input, for example, requires only the words spoken by the user. Other newly emerging technologies include electronic surfaces that are able to interpret characters hand-printed on them, surfaces that are sensitive to touch, and devices that can electronically select items displayed on a screen without using a keyboard.

Voice Input and Speech Recognition

Computer recognition of the human voice is one of the most promising new data-entry possibilities. To understand how **voice-input technology** works, we must first review two different technologies, analog and digital systems.

As we have seen, most contemporary computers are based on **digital technology.** That is, they respond to the "on" "off" pulses of electricity that can be represented by the binary digits "1" and "0." Analog-computer technology, on the other hand, responds to infinite variations in electrical current or voltage. Analog tehcnology need not be electrically powered; some familiar analog devices are a standard "face" clock and a blood-pressure gauge.

The earliest computers were **analog computers,** which functioned on the basis of electrical voltages. Calculations were performed by adding, subtracting, multiplying, and dividing voltages. Analog computers were fast, but their level of accuracy and reliability presented problems. Digital computers are more accurate than analog computers.

Voice waves can be directly converted to electrical waves and thus lend themselves easily to analog-computer technology. Therefore, voice input

Voice Input

Photo courtesy of Texas Instruments

presents technical problems of conversion of analog voice signals into digital code.

This is generally accomplished by subdividing the analog signal (the human speaking voice) into a series of small units. These units represent samples of the sound wave taken at regular intervals. Each sample is assigned a digital value based on the voltage of the sound wave at that interval. The result is a sequence of digital units of information representing the human voice that can then be stored, edited, indexed, or transmitted by the computer system.

Voice Mail   The recording of voice input in digitized form provides the basis for an important application of voice-input technology—voice mail. Voice mail is similar to a telephone answering machine message. The technologies are, however, radically different, and voice mail lends itself to a much wider range of uses.

The message is recorded on a disk and can be accessed at any point; unlike a tape recording, it need not be approached sequentially. This feature allows the receiver to listen to selective parts of a message, to replay parts at will, or to skip messages entirely until a later time.

It is possible to send voice mail to multiple recipients and also to forward it to third parties. In addition, the widespread availability of the telephone creates, in effect, a voice-mail terminal in every office, home, or telephone booth. Some systems have what is called a dial-out feature: The system dials the telephone number of each recipient and plays the recorded message. The recipient then hears several options for responding to the message. In other systems the recipient can call in to a "mailbox" to receive voice-mail messages. Closed systems have been designed for internal company use and have been employed widely as an alternative to written memos or individual calls to multiple recipients.

Speech Recognition   **Speech-recognition technology** allows the computer not only to record voice input but to actually understand speech as well. This requires an additional step after the analog-to-digital converter has translated spoken sound waves into binary code: The computer must compare these digital values with the digital values of word patterns already stored in its memory. Thus the computer must already contain a large vocabulary of digitized syllables. In order to recognize a new spoken word, it must match the digitized sound to the digitized syllables that it already "knows" and "understands."

The conversion of sound to digital form requires a relatively large amount of memory space. For this reason, the size of a computer's stored vocabulary is usually fairly small, in most cases only a few hundred words. Thus a computer's ability to understand speech is limited by the size of its memory. In practice, this means that a speaker must talk from a restricted vocabulary. If the computer is to be used for data entry in a single application—inventory or orders, perhaps—this would not necessarily be a problem. In fact, in such applications it might even be an advantage, ensuring uniform wording by all workers. In inventory control and quality control, voice data entry drastically reduces data-entry costs, improves data quality, and increases the productivity of inventory clerks and inspectors.

Substantive developments in speech recognition are yet to come. At present, only words or short phrases can be understood. The technology is not yet sophisticated enough for a computer to understand continuous speech. Moreover, most voice-recognition devices in use today are speaker dependent. This means they are trained to understand only one user's voice. Some speaker-independent devices do exist and are designed to recognize the voices of many operators.

Speaker-dependent systems have been used as security devices by banks in handling the electronic transfer of funds. By matching the speaker's voice over the telephone with a recorded voiceprint, financial institutions are able to detect fraudulent transactions.

Other Input Devices

Innovations in interactive computer input devices enable users to communicate directly with the computer system by writing on or by touching an electronic surface.

Light Pens
One such device is the **light pen.** The computer user can point with this electronic mechanism, about the size and shape of a regular

Input Devices
Clockwise from top left: Touch panel, mouse, light pen, keyboard

Photo courtesy of Hewlett Packard

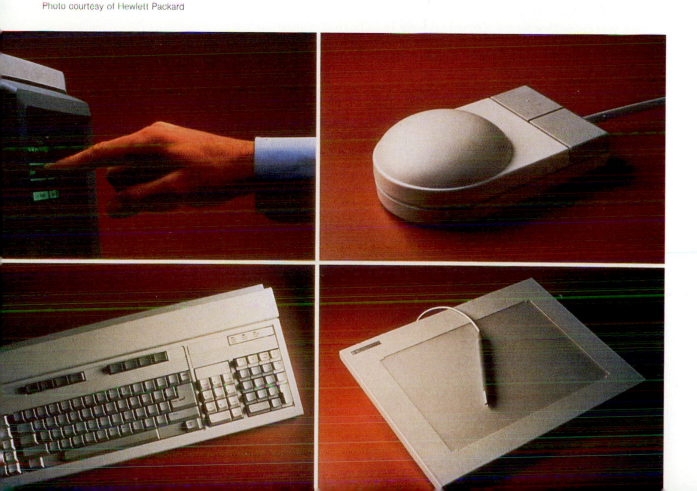

pen, to an item displayed on the CRT screen. When held near the screen, the light pen sends a signal to the display unit. The computer can identify the specific location to which the pen is pointing, and determine the item selected by the user.

Touch Panels   The **touch panel** offers a similar technique for selecting items displayed on the CRT screen. The touch panel is a piece of plastic covered with a touch-sensitive surface that is mounted on the face of the display screen. When the user touches the screen's surface, the computer is able to identify the specific location, thus recognizing the command or other item the user is selecting, and receiving it as input.

Joysticks   The **joystick,** which first became known as a means of manipulating items in computer games, has potential uses in the business world as well. A small stick protruding from a box, the joystick can be pushed in any direction. When released, it returns to its original position. A small cursor displayed on the CRT screen moves in response to a user's manipulation of the joystick. Usually the angle at which the stick is moved determines the cursor's rate of movement. When the user presses a button, the item indicated by the cursor's position enters the computer.

The Mouse   Microcomputer systems like the Apple Macintosh are designed for use by people who have no technical training in computer commands or procedures. A user can sit down for the first time with these computers and, within minutes, be entering commands and data into the system and receiving the needed information.

A key feature of these systems is illustrated on the CRT screen. A picture (called an **icon**) of a wastebasket, for example, may represent the disposal of information, making it unnecessary to use the term *delete*. A picture of a clipboard may indicate temporary storage, and a file folder may stand for data in a file.

These microcomputer systems include a display screen, a keyboard for entering numbers and text, and a hand-held pointer device called a **mouse.** The mouse is a plastic box, about the size of a television remote-control unit, with a button on top and a cable linked to the computer. When the mouse is moved across the desk, an electronic ball on its underside causes an arrow (or cursor) to move in a corresponding direction on the CRT screen. The arrow is used to quickly select the graphs, numbers, words, or pictures needed for the task at hand. The functions for a given program are clearly and simply displayed across the top of the screen, and the user can quickly use the mouse to select and send a command to the computer.

Printed Output

Computer output can be converted into printed form by a great variety of printers. There are two categories of printers, impact and nonimpact. The difference between them is simply whether the paper actually comes in

contact with a type element in order to print (impact), or whether the print is created by some other means (nonimpact).

Impact Printers

The first printers to be developed were **impact printers** and these are still the workhorses of most computer centers. With impact printers, type elements push an inked ribbon against the paper to produce the printed output (see Figure 4.7).

Serial printers print one character at a time, like a typewriter (in fact, some electric typewriters can be hooked up to microcomputers as output devices). Line printers print a whole line at a time, advance the paper, and then print the next line. Serial printers, which are used by most microcomputers, generally give a better print quality than line printers. A good serial printer will produce output whose quality is equal to that of a well-typed letter. Line printers are by far the most common type of printer used in computer centers. They are considerably faster than serial printers.

The technology behind impact printers—both serial and line—has continued to develop. Impact printers have become faster over the years, as well as taking a variety of forms. There are six main kinds of impact printers, classified by the kind of print element they use: type-bar printers, "golf-

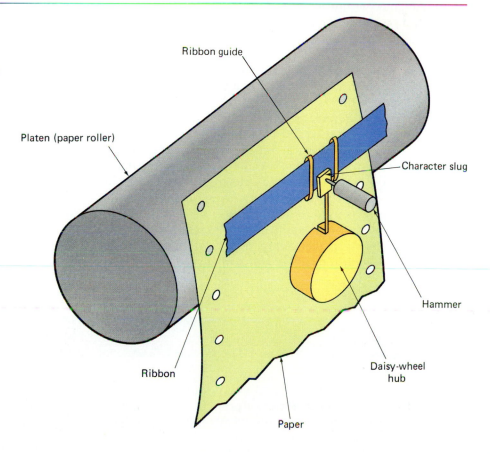

FIGURE 4.7.
How an Impact Printer Works

The mechanical arrangement of a daisy-wheel print element.

Ribbon guide

Platen (paper roller)

Character slug

Hammer

Ribbon

Daisy-wheel hub

Paper

ball'' printers, daisy-wheel printers, drum printers (see Figure 4.8), chain and train printers (see Figure 4.9), and dot-matrix printers.

Dot-matrix printers use a number of small rods to "construct" each character from rows and columns of dots (the *matrix*). Figure 4.10 shows how dots can be used to represent different characters. In order to print a given character, it is necessary to strike the corresponding configuration of rods; however, no type element has to be shifted. The more dots included in the matrix, the sharper will be the appearance of the resulting print. Dot-matrix printers are very common in microcomputer-based systems.

Nonimpact Printers

Nonimpact printers are those that do not contact the paper with a type element in order to print. These, too, may be either serial or line printers. In addition, nonimpact printers introduce a new category—the **page printer,** which prints a whole page at a time.

Nonimpact printers vary considerably in speed, but most are faster than impact printers and produce better quality print as well. Many nonimpact printers require specially treated paper and are expensive both to purchase and to maintain. Some nonimpact printers offer more output possibilities than impact printers—for example, the ability to use more than one color, to combine graphics and text, and to print on objects like tin cans as well as on paper.

FIGURE 4.8.
(1) Drum printhead with type characters on outside. (2) Paper, which does not move. (3) Inked ribbon. (4) Print hammers equal in number to the print positions on a line.

FIGURE 4.9.
Chain-Type Mechanism of the IBM 1403, Model 2 Line Printer

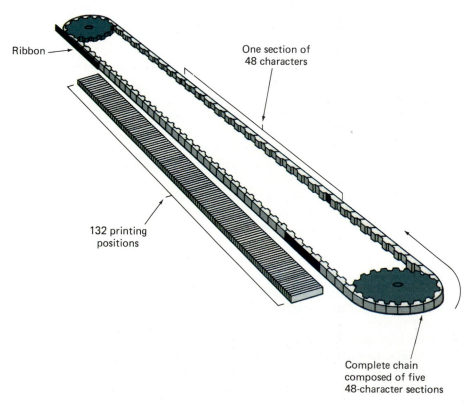

Ribbon

One section of 48 characters

132 printing positions

Complete chain composed of five 48-character sections

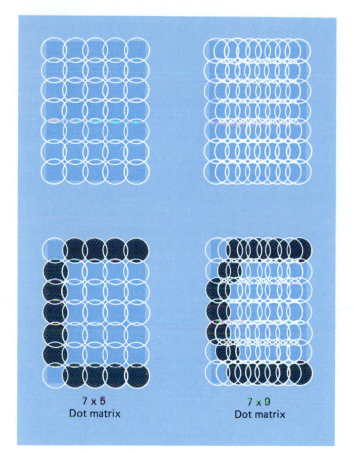

7 x 5
Dot matrix

7 x 9
Dot matrix

FIGURE 4.10.
The representation of letters by a dot matrix. Note that when there are more dots in the matrix, the dots overlap, thus producing a character with more definition.

There are four main types of nonimpact printers, classified by the type of technology they employ. One characteristic that all have in common is that characters are constructed from dots, as shown in Figure 4.10. The more dots per inch a printer is capable of, the finer the print quality. In high-quality nonimpact print, the characters will not appear to be made up of dots unless they are viewed under a magnifying lens. The four categories of nonimpact printers are thermal printers, electrostatic printers, laser printers, and ink-jet printers.

Thermal printers use a number of small heating elements to construct each character from dots. Special heat-sensitive paper turns black where the elements heat it, producing the printed characters. The output from thermal printers looks dotlike rather than typewriterlike, and these slow serial printers are the least expensive of the nonimpact printers.

Electrostatic printers use small pins that charge with electricity a treated paper in spots that correspond to letters or graphics. After being "charged," the paper is passed through a toner solution, which sticks to the charged spots to produce the printed output. Some electrostatic printers produce high-quality print; others produce print that appears like finely dotted lines. Electrostatic printers can be either line or page printers.

The process used by **laser printers** is similar to that of office copying machines. The key difference is that instead of working photographically

from a printed page, the printer creates the image with a laser beam. Laser printers produce high-quality output from text or data generated from a word- or data-processing system using the media of magnetic cassettes, cards, or diskettes. These printers can take text received from a data-processing or word-processing system in one format (for example, text keyed in at 80 characters per line in 12-pitch type) and print it out in another (40 characters per line in 16-pitch type). They also have the ability to integrate undigitized hard copy originals with already stored and digitized text and graphics.

There are numerous applications and uses for laser printers in the modern office. They can be used as remote output devices, sending or receiving data electronically over certain voice-grade switched lines or privately leased lines to and from other computer systems. This communication capability allows them to distribute documents from a centralized location to a network of decentralized locations. It also allows them to send and receive electronic mail to and from a maintained list of mailboxes of other printers. Many printers can store up to 1000 pages of incoming documents within their electronic mailboxes until users request printouts. They can also store forms (including logos, signatures, and graphics), generate them automatically, update them when necessary, and transmit them from machine to machine. Their graphics-reproducing ability makes them the printer used in desktop publishing systems.

Ink-jet printers use an array of tiny nozzles to spray ink that forms printed images onto a page or an object. In this complex technology, the ink is broken into droplets, which are charged by electrodes corresponding to the character or graphic form desired. Then the droplets are directed to the appropriate place on the paper or other print medium. Ink-jet printers can use different nozzles for different colors and can print on almost anything that will accept ink, such as packages or even fruit. They produce high-quality output except at peak speed, and they can be serial, line, or page printers.

Table 4.1 summarizes the characteristics of impact and nonimpact printers. As you can see, the two types of printers differ substantially, just as the kinds of printers within each category vary. Which printer is right for a given data-processing system obviously depends on many factors.

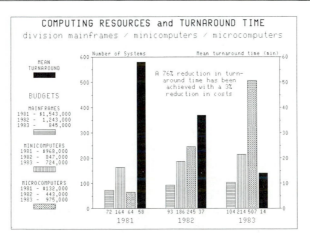

Laser Printer and Output

Qume Corp.

Table 4.1   Some Characteristics of Impact Versus Nonimpact Printers

	Impact Printers	Nonimpact Printers
Techniques used	Type bar Golf ball Daisy wheel Drum Chain or train	Thermal Electrostatic Laser Ink jet
Mode	Serial or line	Serial, line, or page
Speed	Up to 3000 lines per minute	Up to 45,000 lines per minute
Print Quality	High quality for serial, lower quality for line	High quality for all but thermal and some electrostatic
Print Fonts and Graphics	Fixed or interchangeable print fonts, no graphics	Interchangeable print fonts, graphics
Multiple Copies	Up to 6, which must be collated	No multiple copies
Paper Requirements	Regular Paper	Regular paper for laser and ink jet, special paper for thermal and electrostatic
Noise Level	Noisy	Quiet

Plotters

Plotters produce hard copy output by drawing graphs, maps, charts, and pictures on any sort of paper. Though earlier plotters were frustratingly slow and produced ragged zigzag output, today they produce much higher resolution output, are faster, and have more capabilities. In addition, some plotters have their own control units. This makes it possible for a computer to generate the data to be plotted on magnetic tape and then go about its other business while the tape is fed off-line to the plotting system to produce the graphic output.

Microfilm and Microfiche Output

In sufficient quantities, paper can virtually strangle a business operation. It can become very difficult to know what documents are current and who is or is not allowed to see what. Desks and even windowsills are littered, and file drawers overflow. Computers have made this problem worse with high-speed printers and multiple-copy printouts. But while computers compound the problem, they also offer a solution: Put it on microfilm or microfiche. Microfilm is 16-, 35-, or 105-millimeter photographic film that records data in greatly reduced size. Anything that can be photographed can be put on microfilm. If you have ever examined old copies of *The New York*

Times in a library for a term paper, you probably viewed them on microfilm. Our focus here, however, is not on reproducing existing documents on microfilm but on placing *computer output* on microfilm. Documents on microfilm occupy about 1 percent of the space taken by the originals, which, of course, suggests a solution to some paper-overflow problems. In addition, computer output can be recorded on microfiche, a sheet of microfilm usually 4 inches by 6 inches that can store as many as 270 pages. Both microfilm and microfiche can be read using special viewing stations that are similar to still projectors.

Computer-Output Microfilm (COM)

Computer-output microfilm (COM) is produced as shown in Figure 4.11. Computer-generated data, text, and images to be microfilmed are output on magnetic tape. The tape is input to an off-line microfilm recorder to create the microfilm. The output can then be stored in cabinets that are specially designed for microfilm, and viewed at microfilm viewing stations.

Computer-Assisted Retrieval (CAR)

Storing data on microfilm is fine as far as saving space goes, but we also need to *use* the data. In libraries, if you want to look at an article in an 1890 edition of *The New York Times,* you most likely have to write the date on a form and give it to a librarian, who wil retrieve the roll of microfilm containing that edition. Then you must mount the microfilm on a reader and

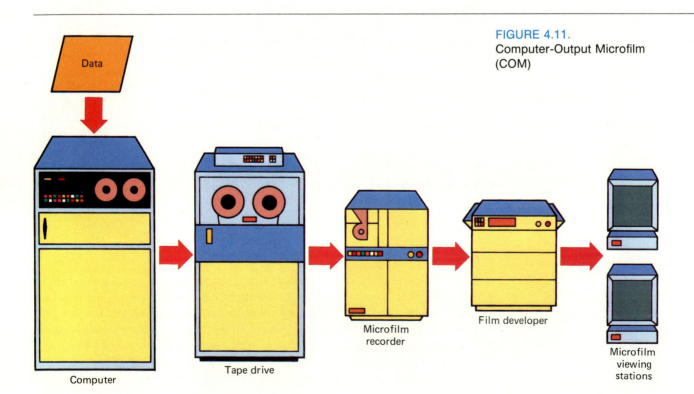

FIGURE 4.11.
Computer-Output Microfilm
(COM)

Data

Computer

Tape drive

Microfilm
recorder

Film developer

Microfilm
viewing
stations

spin through the reel manually, stopping often to see what date you have reached, until you find the issue you want and then the page you want.

Computer-assisted retrieval (CAR) automates some of these steps. To find a document, you key in keyword descriptors or an identifying number at a terminal. In response, the terminal displays the microfilm retrieval index for the document. This index will enable you to physically identify the correct roll of microfilm, which you can then mount on a reader. Next you key in the microfilm retrieval index at the reader, which will locate the document you want and display it. As you can see, the process is not completely automated, but the computer does help significantly in locating the information. CAR also offers you the option of getting a printed copy of the data displayed on the microfilm reader.

COM and CAR on the Job

Microfilm or microfiche output and computer-assisted retrieval are most suitable for applications that require a quick response. For example, to find out a customer's current account balance in a bank when the customer is standing at the teller's window waiting to make a withdrawal, on-line inquiry systems using alphanumeric display terminals cannot be surpassed. Also, lists, reports, catalogs, and the like are more easily managed and stored on microfilm or microfiche.

For instance, The Toy Place stocks thousands of different items. Every year the firm prints out a complete list of all of those items, together with current information about each of them. Such a list would be useful to store managers, enabling them to see what they have and to compare the items they have with new items offered by manufacturers' sales representatives. Such a ''catalog'' of merchandise might be placed on microfilm using COM and viewed using CAR. For one thing, this would make it easier to send a copy of the new catalog (which would occupy only a roll or two of microfilm) to each store in the chain; also, only one copy would be needed at the main office—not a thick volume on each person's desk. COM/CAR technology is also frequently used for:

- Computer-generated bibliographies and directories
- Bank and credit statements
- Insurance company records
- Archival copies of customer lists
- Parts catalogs
- Police files
- Accounts-payable and receivable records
- Library records

The key point about microfilm output is that for high-volume applications it is both cheaper and more manageable than printouts. Making data more manageable means that those who need the data can get at a specific item quickly, which is a significant aid in decision making. E.I. DuPont de Nemours and Company found that in one department alone—its Polymers Products Department—over 900 reports were generated monthly, yielding a 25-foot-high pile of paper. By going to COM. the department was able to

save money and storage space and make the information more readily accessible to those who used it in their work.*

Voice Output

Have technological developments reached the point at which a computer can actually *speak* words to us? Yes, with one qualification. With currently available voice-output technology, computers can indeed speak to us. *What* they say, however, remains for us to program. Here's how the process works:

1. A system analyst determines what the computer's vocabulary should be for a given application.
2. A person records these words in a recording studio.
3. The words are then translated into the digital signals that a computer can understand, and are stored in a computer file.
4. To produce voice output, the computer application program first determines what the computer should "say" for the particular situation at hand.
5. The program then retrieves the appropriate words from its memory and transmits them to the audio-response output device, which "speaks" them over audio equipment.

Although the earliest voice output sounded "robotic," today's systems produce better-quality sounds. The rhythm and emphasis of complete sentences remain slightly mechanical—but only slightly.

The devices that deliver voice response do so either directly to a person at a "talking terminal" or indirectly over a telephone. In addition, they can be custom tailored by the manufacturer for an application or range of applications specified by the customer. Audio output devices can be acquired "off the shelf," as can most of the other output devices we have discussed.

Selection of System Output

We have reviewed a wide range of computer output technologies in this chapter. Which one is right for a given application? The one that provides us with the benefits we want and at the same time does so most cost-effectively. Table 4.2 summarizes the different computer output technologies, the advantages of each, and their applications. An understanding of user needs is the key to providing the right form of output. Efforts should be devoted to analyzing these needs before investing in expensive equipment that may not be right for the job.

*From "COM & Printout Services Add New Dimensions to Business Data," *Information & Records Management,* 16 (8), August 1982, p. 36.

Table 4.2   Summary of Computer Output Devices

Output Technology	Advantages/Benefits	Applications
Impact Printers	Long record as "workhorse" (reliability); carbon copies	Routine computer-generated reports and listings, invoice forms, paychecks, word processing
Nonimpact Printers	Top speed, wide range of output formats, colors, graphics, cost-saving when preparing copy for final reports	High-volume output, high-quality finished reports, electronic publishing
Alphanumeric Terminals	Rapid, targeted retrieval of data	On-line applications such as hotel and airline reservations, banking and securities transactions, order entry, inventory update
Graphics Terminals	Condensed, readily understandable output	Management summaries, aid to developing graphics for presentations
Plotters	Hard-copy graphics output	Applications are more common in engineering and science than in business, maps, graphs
Microfilm output	Easy access to data, reduced volume of paper to be stored	High-volume "archival" applications such as customer billing records, parts inventories, personnel records, police files
Voice Output	Makes by-telephone computer applications possible, offers computer access to the blind	Applications requiring short, formalized output such as order entry, credit checking, stock quotations, emergency repair instructions

Next: Computers with Ears

James and Janet Baker, Dragon Systems

If the word-processing revolution threatens to render you obsolete, a mote in the dustbin of office history, do not despair. If you can speak, you may yet survive, thanks to James and Janet Baker, proprietors of Dragon Systems Inc., a small software-research firm in Newton, Massachusetts.

This husband-and-wife enterprise aims to introduce the first natural-language speech-recognition package for a personal computer. If they succeed, you will be able to simply dictate to your computer and watch your words appear magically on the screen.

Most speech-recognition researchers say this is at least five years away, if not 10. But according to Janet, Dragon's president, a speech-transcription program with a vocabulary of at least 10,000 words will hit the market by year's end. The entire package—desktop computer, modifications, and software—will cost $10,000 to $15,000. The system will be limited, requiring a speaker to pause after each word. But it will still be faster than writing in longhand.

Janet, 39, and James, 41, both earned doctorates in computer science at Carnegie-Mellon University and worked together at IBM's Watson Research Center for several years. They launched their business in 1982 and have since shared all the work, from research to administration.

James, Dragon's CEO, is a mathematician and an expert in stochastic processing—a branch of science that analyzes systems governed by probability. When a speech-recognition system "hears" a word it is unsure of, it must quickly calculate the most probable choice. The challenge is to design programs that are ever faster, more efficient, and cost-effective. Eventually, James says, speech will replace the keyboard as the standard way to create text.

Starting out in biophysics, Janet became interested in how biological systems process information. "While knowledge of how humans or other organisms receive or send signals is pretty low," she says, "we do not dismiss the potential of that knowledge. And we have profited by incorporating some of those ideas." For example, research on how neurons in the ear process sound signals has led to more effective speech-recognition systems.

James says that teaching a computer to take dictation is an enormous computational task. "You need knowledge of the language, of the syntactic structure of sentences, of semantics, and of the way things fit into paragraphs. We try to do all those things efficiently on a PC." Emphasis on computational efficiency sets the Bakers apart. While some private and university research teams have developed experimental speech-recognition systems beyond the capabilities of Dragon's, those systems also require hundreds of thousands of dollars' worth of hardware.

Researchers in speech recognition tend to favor one methodology or another. The Bakers refuse to commit Dragon to any one approach. "We're willing to try virtually anything," Janet says. "We are consciously integrating ideas of all kinds." This open-mindedness, she adds, has been a major factor in the company's success—it has been profitable from the start.

Dragon operates by licensing its technology. IBM, for instance, uses Dragon technology in three speech-recognition products. Apricot Ltd. of Birmingham, England, uses Dragon techniques in the Apricot, the world's first portable computer with voice activation as a standard feature.

The Bakers have carefully limited the size of Dragon's research staff —currently 13 full-time technical people. "Almost all major technical achievements were carried out by small groups," Janet notes. "Our field is highly interdisciplinary, which means you have to communicate very effectively. And there are natural bounds to how many people you can communicate closely with."

Perhaps the key to Dragon's future is the Bakers' firm belief that speech recognition can really work. "We don't want our technology sitting around as a laboratory curiosity," says Janet. "We want to get it out where people can actually use it."

Source: Alex Kozlov, *Science Digest,* September 1986.

Summary and Key Terms

1. **Input** is the process of entering data into the computer system and translating it into the coded electronic patterns recognized by the computer. A wide variety of devices can be used to accomplish this task.

2. **Control units** and **data channels** link input/output devices to the CPU and make it possible for the CPU to continue operating while data are being entered.

3. **Off-line key-driven devices** record data on computer-readable media such as punched cards. These were among the earliest computer input devices. Today magnetic disks offer still more flexible and efficient storage capabilities following **key-to-disk** input.

4. **Input terminals** have keyboards for entering data and **CRT screens** to display information. These are on-line devices that transmit information directly into the computer system. They are now the most commonly used input devices in offices. In **distributed data entry,** input can take place at the dispersed locations where the data originate.

5. **Optical character recognition (OCR)** devices scan written or printed material, either alphanumeric characters or **bar codes.** These data are then digitized and read into the computer system. **Mark-sensing** devices can only "read" solid dark areas, like the filled-in answer boxes on questionnaires. **Magnetic-ink character recognition (MICR)** requires that the data to be read be printed in magnetic ink.

6. **Electronic funds transfer (EFT)** reduces the flow of paper—bills, checks, receipts—in financial transactions.

7. New data-entry technologies, such as **voice input** and **interactive input devices,** help ease the data-entry bottleneck. They make possible the use of computers by individuals at every level of business organization.

8. **Output** is data that are transferred from a computer to a user or storage device in any medium. Output that is directly used by people (that is, in other words, the end product of a data processing system) is produced by printers, terminals, plotters, microfilm devices, and voice-response devices.

9. Printed output can be produced by impact or nonimpact printers. **Impact printers** include **type-bar, golf-ball, daisy-wheel, drum, chain, train,** and **dot-matrix printers. Nonimpact printers** include **thermal, electrostatic, laser,** and **ink-jet printers. Plotters** produce certain kinds of **graphic output.**

10. **Serial printers** (impact or nonimpact) print one character at a time; **line printers** (impact or nonimpact) print one line at a time; and page printers (nonimpact only) print one page at a time. Nonimpact printers produce better-quality output, can produce output in several colors, are more flexible in output format, and are notably faster than impact printers.

11. The use of microfilm output can reduce the volume of paper in a business while permitting fairly easy access to data. **Computer-output microfilm (COM)** and **computer-assisted retrieval (CAR)** are best suited to applications that use a large volume of data.

12. **Voice output** is delivered at "talking terminals" or over the telephone. Suitable for applications in which the output required is brief, voice output makes data for order entry and credit checking readily available.

Review Questions

Fill-in

1. The _____ handles input/output operations independently of the CPU.

2. The _____ for a particular input device handles such functions as validity checking and code conversion.

3. A terminal with some built-in processing functions is called an _____ terminal.

4. An _____ enables text or data to be optically scanned and automatically stored on computer-readable storage media.

5. Using an _____, a customer can withdraw or deposit cash in a checking account.

6. _____ characters on bank checks are used to identify customers and bank information.

7. The type of terminal which is used to enter sales-transaction data at local store sites is called a _____.

8. The uniform product coding scheme used in many supermarkets is known as the _____.

9. _____ is a technology which makes it possible to transmit voice messages to multiple recipients.

10. _____ works by the comparison of digitized speech patterns with digital values stored in the computer's internal memory.

Matching

Identify which of the following output alternatives would be most appropriate for each of these applications, and explain the reasons for your choice:

Choose from:

_____ a. impact printer

_____ b. nonimpact printer

_____ c. graphics terminal

_____ d. CRT terminal

_____ e. plotter

_____ f. computer-output microfilm

Applications:

_____ 1. Information summarizing sales, by product line, this year versus last year.

_____ 2. Data on customers' credit status.

_____ 3. Data on quantity on hand of various inventory items.

_____ 4. Sales-order records for the past two years for a particular customer.

_____ 5. Information on mortgage loan balances.

_____ 6. Letters requiring carbon copies.

_____ 7. Information depicting sales and profitability trends, by division, or a major company.

_____ 8. Departmental general-ledger data.

_____ 9. Text for the in-house company newsletter.

Discussion Questions

1. Explain how you would improve upon the current approach used to input student registration data at this university:

   At registration, students with a proposed schedule of courses, which has been approved by their advisor, are given punched cards for each course in which they register. With these punched cards, they are able to complete registration, including being billed for tuition based upon courses in which they enroll.

   Then, during the first week of class, students give a punched card to each of the instructors in the courses in which they are enrolled. The instructors take the stack of punched cards they have accumulated from students in their classes and give them to data processing, which uses them to prepare the class rosters and to update student registration data.

2. Explain the advantages and disadvantages of each of the following input approaches that could be used by a computer dating service.

   Option 1: When applicants come in, they are asked to complete a detailed application form specifying their likes and dislikes, their interests, and other personal characteristics. Then, these data are keypunched and input into the computer system using a card reader.

   Option 2: Applicants complete a mark-sense questionnaire by blackening the spaces representing their desired answers. Then these data are input into the computer system using a scanning device.

3. Describe how an electronic printing system, such as a laser printer, can save money in each of the following applications:

   a. Printing out word processing-generated letters and merging them with names and addresses from a computer-generated data file.

   b. Automatically generating purchase requisitions, along with purchase-order data.

   c. Printing out computer-generated general-ledger data which needs to be formatted in 8½-by-11 inch pages.

4. Much of the information that is stored in the computer can be retrieved using a CRT terminal or a microcomputer terminal. With the increased availability of information in electronic form, the prediction is that there may be less need for hard-copy output, leading to the "paperless" office. Explain why you either agree or disagree with this prediction. Do you see any evidence of the "paperless" office in your life?

5. List some applications for the following technologies:

   a. Voice output.

   b. Desktop publishing

   c. Computer-assisted retrieval.

Auxiliary Storage and File Processing

Chapter Objectives

After studying this chapter you should be able to

1. Understand the characteristics of floppy disks, hard disks, and CD-ROM disks as used in microcomputer systems.

2. Understand the characteristics and purposes of magnetic tape and magnetic disks as used in large computer systems.

3. Understand the differences between direct and sequential access.

4. Understand the reasons for selecting specific auxiliary storage media.

The LOW DISK message flickered in the upper corner of the computer screen. "Oh great, just what I need—one more disk to store for this book." Rita Patel is a writer, and when she first began to use a computer, she was delighted to be able to keep on a single floppy disk material that would have filled sheet after sheet of typing paper. But for the book she is working on now, what with her research notes and several drafts, Rita already has two notebooks of disks, including backups.

When she went back to the dealer who sold her the computer, Rita found out that it's probably time for her to graduate to a hard disk. Her machine doesn't come equipped with a hard disk, so if Rita makes the decision to buy a hard disk, the dealer will attach it to the inside of the processor unit, as he would do if she bought an extra memory board. Once she has copied onto the hard disk all the files she has on floppy disks, Rita will have the whole book in one place, and she'll be able to go between Chapter 1 and Chapter 15 without changing disks, with no more than a few keystrokes.

What Is Auxiliary Storage?

Auxiliary storage is one of the key issues for computer users, whether the computer is a personal computer used by one person for limited applications or a large computer used by many people for multiple applications. As

you learned in Chapter 3, main memory stores the data and programs a computer is using for an application in progress. Main memory is limited in size and may not be able to hold all the data needed for a specific application. Main memory is also volatile. When a microcomputer is turned off, for example, the programs and data stored in main memory are not retained. Computers require a cheaper, larger, longer lasting storage medium than main memory. As a group, such media are called **auxiliary storage.**

Storage Technologies in Microcomputers

The two primary storage technologies for microcomputers were mentioned at the start of this chapter: floppy disks and hard, or Winchester, disks. A new storage technology is optical storage. These three technologies are direct-access storage media. **Direct-access media** allow a computer user to get to a record stored anywhere in a file without having to start at the beginning and proceed sequentially until the desired data are located.

Floppy Disks

Floppy or flexible disks are used for storage on most small computers. They come in diameters of 8, 5¼, and 3½ inches. Most commonly used now are the 5¼-inch floppies. Made of flexible Mylar plastic, floppy disks were introduced in the mid-1970s as a cheaper and easier-to-transport alternative

Floppy Disks

Courtesy of BASF Systems Corp.

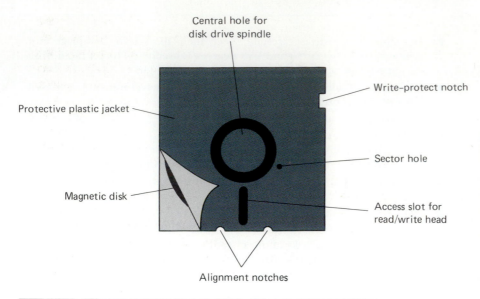

Central hole for
disk drive spindle

Write–protect notch

Protective plastic jacket

Sector hole

Magnetic disk

Access slot for
read/write head

Alignment notches

FIGURE 5.1
Floppy Disk Diagram
In use, the magnetic part of a
floppy disk spins inside the
jacket and is written or read
through the access slot.
Alignment notches help to
keep the disk oriented precisely. When the write-protect
notch is covered, a disk can
be read but not written.

to regular-sized disks. Microcomputers became popular soon thereafter and
adopted floppy disks as virtually their own. (See Figure 5.1.)

A diskette is composed of tracks onto which data are written in
magnetic bit patterns. Most diskettes have 40 tracks per side, with tracks 0
to 39 on one side and tracks 40 to 79 on the other. Floppy disks are divided
into sectors. A sector is the amount of data that can be read from or written
to a track of a disk at one time. When a diskette is formatted, the software
defines the number of sectors on each track and the number of bytes per
sector, commonly nine sectors per side and 512 bytes per sector.

To be read, a diskette must first be inserted into a disk drive. A
read/write head positions itself over the correct sector and track and rests
on the surface of the rotating disk. **Access time** refers to the time it takes
for the read/write head to position itself and to retrieve the data that have
been requested. The retrieved data are then transferred to main memory.

Diskettes have different capacities. Data can be recorded on and read
from one side only of a single-sided diskette but from both sides of a
double-sided diskette. The density of a diskette affects how much data can
be stored as measured by bits per inch (bpi). A double-density diskette
stores data twice as close together as a single-density diskette.

Advantages and Disadvantages   Just as the cost of floppy disks is low, so
is their storage capacity and speed. It would be quite possible, for instance,
to have a medium-size file spread over three floppy disks just to store
information about 1000 customers. To process such a file, it would be
necessary to change disks continually. Another disadvantage is that to
process more than one file at a time, disks have to be endlessly catalogued,
retrieved, inserted into the drive, removed from the drive, refiled, and so
on, indefinitely. Each handling step takes time and effort.

Still, floppy disks were developed as a low-cost storage medium with a
high degree of portability, and these advantages are important in many
situations. People who work on different computers in different places

Taking Care of Floppy Disks

- ■ DO store floppy disks carefully. Keep them in a clean, dry place at a temperature between 50 and 150 degrees Fahrenheit. Protect them from extreme temperature variations. Stand them on edge.
- ■ DO handle a floppy disk by its plastic jacket, and never touch the exposed parts of the recording surface.
- ■ DO take care when you put a floppy disk into and take it out of the disk drive.
- ■ DO open the door of the disk drive (or release its closing lever) if you are going to leave a disk in for more than an hour without using it.
- ■ DO make backup copies of important disks; store the backups and the originals in different places.
- ■ DO write out disk labels before you put them on the disks. If you have to write on a label on the disk, use a felt-tipped pen and write lightly.
- ■ DON'T store or use disks in direct sunlight, near sources of heat, or near magnets. (Radios and TVs, electric motors, answering machines, and other equipment containing magnets. A safe distance is at least 2 feet away.)
- ■ DON'T eat, drink, or smoke near disks.
- ■ DON'T bend or fold disks.
- ■ DON'T use paperclips or rubber bands on disks.
- ■ DON'T insert or remove a disk when the red light on the disk drive is lit.

Source: Adapted from "Storage Media" by Datapro Research Corporation, Delran, NJ, © 1985; and from *Microcomputers: Software and Applications* by Dennis P. Curtin and Leslie R. Porter. © 1986 by Prentice-Hall.

—students who use computers both at home and at school, for example —need floppy disks. Floppy disks are also completely satisfactory for people who use computers for a number of limited applications—such as students and home-computer users, who are unlikely to need to store large amounts of data for very long times.

Floppy disks are handled more than other storge media, and they may be exposed to a greater range of environments. The box explains some of the *Do*s and *Don't*s of caring for floppy disks. Because the read/write head rests on the surface of the diskette, normal wear eventually harms the ability of the floppy to hold data. In this respect, floppy disks are rather short-lived. Also, despite their great advantages of low cost and portability, floppy disks tend to handcuff the processing potential of microcomputers. Fortunately, as Rita Patel discovered, there is an alternative—the hard disk.

Winchester Disks

Winchester disks, or **hard disks,** are considerably different from floppy disks. First, they are more expensive than floppies, and, unlike floppies, they ordinarily cannot be removed from the inside of the processing unit.

What the nonremovable hard disk offers is greater storage capacity and faster access times. A small hard disk can store about 5 million bytes or

A Winchester Disk

Microscience International Corp.

megabytes (MB), equivalent to about 2500 typewritten pages. Compare that to a floppy disk's range of 160,000 to 650,000 bytes, which equals 80 to 320 pages. Data can be read from a hard disk to the computer or written from the computer to the hard disk approximately 20 times faster than with a floppy. Hard disks come in 5¼-, 8-, and 14-inch diameters.

A hard disk is made of metal rather than plastic. Its access head is much closer than a floppy's to the disk surface (only a few ten-thousandths of an inch). The hard disk is not flexible, and usually it is not removable, so it isn't ordinarily exposed to damaging environments or foreign objects, such as dust. Consequently, a hard disk can be engineered to greater precision than a floppy disk. The closer location of the head means access speed can be more rapid because data can be packed more tightly on the disk. It is possible with a hard disk to access the same disk from more than one terminal attached to the same small computer at the same time.

In summary, for applications that require a lot of storage, quick access to data, and/or switching back and forth among files, a hard disk is the faster, more reliable alternative. In the long run, even though hard disks cost between $1500 and $2000, they may also prove to be the cheaper alternative.

Hard disks and floppy disks are two kinds of magnetic disk storage. The technical characteristics of magnetic disk storage are described in a later section, Storage Technologies for Large Computer Systems.

How a Hard Disk Works

A hard disk consists of an aluminum disk or platter covered with a thin ironoxide coating. (See the diagram below.) Its read/write head hovers about 20 micro-inches above the disk surface as it rotates at about 3300 to 3600 revolutions per minute. The read/write head creates and reads magnetic fields on the surface of the disk.

Each track on a hard disk starts at one particular radius, called the index position. From here, a track is divided into equal arcs, or sectors, which is the smallest unit of data a disk catalogs and retrieves. There are usually 32 sectors of 256 bytes each or 16 sectors of 512 bytes each.

A disk must be formatted before it can be used. This means that the controller for the hard-disk creates a set of track/sector addresses by marking tracks and sector boundaries on the disk and storing the information in a data dictionary on the disk itself.

When the computer issues a request for data, the disk controller checks the data dictionary to see where the data are located. The dictionary specifies the track and sector where the data begin and tells how many tracks and sectors they are stored on. Then the head actuator moves the head to the proper track to start reading the data. (See the diagram at the left.)

The process of writing data to disk is similar. The data dictionary specifies the tracks and sectors available for receiving data. When called upon to write data to the disk, the controller checks the dictionary for a large enough area

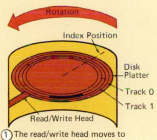

① The read/write head moves to the proper track

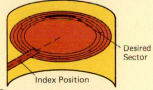

② It detects the index position

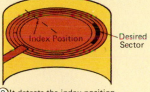

③ When the index position is detected, the disk controller starts reading data

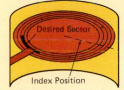

④ When the desired sector is under the read/write head, the controller begins transmitting data

Reading Data from a Disk

© Valerie Lewis. Used by permission

A Removable Hard-Disk Cartridge

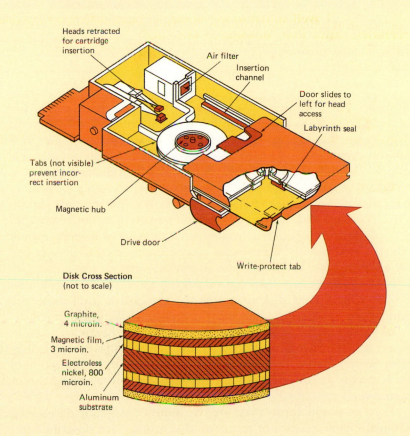

Disk Cross Section (not to scale)

and then moves the head to the proper track. The controller also enters the newly written data's names and address in the disk's data dictionary.

Hard disks can be fixed or removable. A fixed hard disk is permanently sealed into a compartment along with its read/write heads. This sealed environment prevents contamination from dust particles and grease. Removable hard disk cartridges are housed in an airtight plastic container, which also helps to prevent contamination. The read/write heads gain access to the disk through a door that slides open only when the cartridge is latched into the drive (see below).

Source: Figures and text adapted from David Powell, "How a Hard Disk Works," *Popular Computing*, May, 1984, pp. 120–122. Used with permission.

CD–ROM

CD–ROM stands for compact disk read-only memory. This optical storage medium can hold huge amounts of data, including data in the forms of text, sound, and graphics. A CD–ROM disk, which looks like a compact disk for sound reproduction, can store up to 550 megabytes of data, which is the equivalent of 1200 floppy disks or about 150,000 printed pages. CD–ROM disks are read in hardware units that can be attached to computers—from micros to mainframes.

CD–ROM is well suited to the storage of large data bases, catalogues, directories, parts lists, newspaper files, and the like. Currently, many on-line data bases, such as the Dun and Bradstreet Million Dollar Directory, are available to users via on-line access with by-the-minute or -hour costs for connect time. As any private user of an on-line data base knows, connect time adds up quickly. Instead, users can purchase entire data bases on a

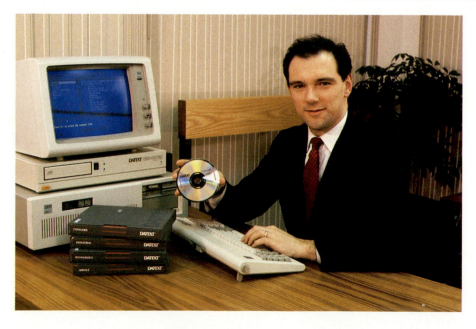

A CD-ROM Disk

This CD-ROM disk holds vast amounts of financial data accessible with the CD-ROM unit that the monitor stands on.

Datext, Inc.

CD-ROM disk and use a CD–ROM player to access these data. For example, a lawyer preparing a brief could have access to legal precedents on a PC screen via a CD–ROM disk.

CD–ROM will not necessarily replace large on-line data bases. Rather, this technology will enable users to buy certain data bases for personal or in-house use, similar to maintaining a personal or in-house library. External on-line data bases will also be important, especially for time-sensitive data like stock market transaction prices or often-updated data like newspaper files.

CD–ROM technology uses metal-coated, clear plastic platters onto which a laser burns digital information. The disk resembles a continuous spiral composed of small, circular indentations, or pits, moulded onto one side. Once the disk is inserted into a disk drive, a low-power laser reads information from the tiny pits stamped into the disk.

Two disadvantages of CD–ROM are that the average access time is slower than that of a floppy or hard disk drive and that the user cannot write

Applications of CD–ROM

In the business world, applications of CD–ROM are just beginning to emerge. Companies like automotive and aerospace firms need to distribute parts catalogs including information on thousands of parts to numerous maintenance locations. Until now, it was necessary to use printed catalogs or microfiche. With a CD–ROM system, a parts clerk can type in a simple request and pull up a page with required information. Graphics capabilities can make it possible to see an image of the part along with the description.

Policies and procedures manuals, sent out by financial institutions, are also good candidates for CD–ROM.

Technical documentation for telecommunications equipment is currently being tested using a prototype CD–ROM system by Northern Telecom. This information will enable customers to reprogram switches to meet dynamic, changing needs.

In still another application, Statistics Canada, the agency responsible for collecting and maintaining enormous data bases on facts and figures on Canadian economic life, is designing a bibliographic system using CD–ROM. This bibliographic system will simply tell the user where the data is and how to get it. Keyword searches are possible using retrieval software. Later on, the actual data may be housed using CD–ROM as well.

Lotus Development, the firm responsible for developing software for financial analysis, is now turning to CD–ROM to deliver massive databases to the financial services industry. Each week Lotus Development's One Source service distributes a CD–ROM disk that contains more than 300 million items of financial data.

Using this data base, a user can retrieve 20 years of sales data for two companies and create a comparative graph, all in about two seconds. Essentially, this service is bringing mainframe-style financial databases to the desktop.

The benefits of CD–ROM are made clear by these examples. CD–ROM offers compact storage of encyclopedic data bases, quick information retrieval, and minimization of paperwork. Charges incurred by downloading mainframe-based data are offset, and information is readily accessible because users don't have to wait for data to be printed out.

Source: CD–ROM Special Report, *PC World,* April, 1987.

any information out to a CD–ROM disk. However, CD–ROM's tremendous storage potential is creating a market for its encyclopedic data bases among users of personal computers.

Optical Storage

CD–ROM is an example of optical storage—technologies that use lasers to record and play back data. Extensive research into optical storage is going on right now, for audio and graphic images can be recorded, as well as text. The principle of optical storage is that any of these kinds of data are converted to digital codes to be retrieved by laser beam. Optical storage systems require absolute precision of all their parts in order to play back high-quality data. Also, many of these technologies are read only, like CD–ROM. However, recordable optical disks for computer use have been produced in limited numbers, called DRAW (direct read after write) and WORM (write once, read mainly). Among others, 3-M Corporation, IBM, and AT&T are currently developing optical storage media.

Storage Technologies in Large Computer Systems

The principle storage media for large computer systems are magnetic disks (the floppy disks and hard disks used in microcomputer systems are magnetic) and magnetic tape.

Magnetic Tape

Magnetic tape comes in reels or cassettes and is similar to sound-recording tape. Data are written onto the tape and read from the tape as it passes the read/write head of a tape drive. The different ways data can be recorded on

Magnetic Tape Reels

Courtesy of BASF Systems Corp.

Magnetic Tape Cassette

Courtesy of 3M

and read from magnetic tape depend on the number of tracks, the density, and the blocking factor of the tape.

Tracks   Data are recorded on magnetic tape in the form of magnetic spots. The presence of these magnetic spots represents "on" bits, and their absence represents "off" bits. The combination of bits in a vertical column defines a character which conforms with a code the computer can understand.

The magnetic tape on which data are recorded has either seven or nine tracks. *Nine-track tape* handles characters in the EBCDIC code, which uses eight bits to represent a single character. Eight of the tracks on a nine-track tape correspond to these bits; the ninth track is the parity or check bit. The parity bit is used to assure the validity of the data. In even parity, the number of "on" or "1" bits always adds up to an even number. If data are coded in even parity, the check bit is turned either on or off to make the total number of bits representing a character add up to an even number. One way of checking the validity of input data is to make sure that each character is either in *even* or in *odd parity*. See Appendix A for further explanation.

Seven-track tape handles characters in a different, older code. BCD, or binary-coded decimal, requires only six bits to represent a character, and six of the tracks on a seven-track tape correspond to these bits; the seventh track is the parity or check bit (see Appendix A). Figure 5.2 shows how the

FIGURE 5.2

Representation of the Characters A, B, and C on 9-Track and 7-Track Tape.
Vertical lines represent 1-bits. Blanks represent 0-bits

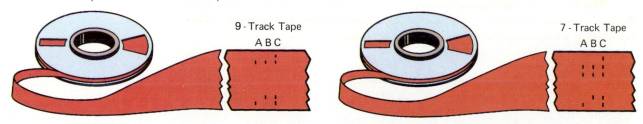

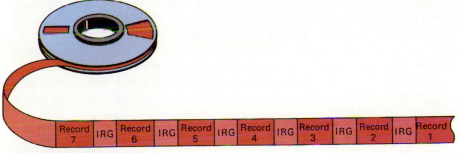

Unblocked records (a)

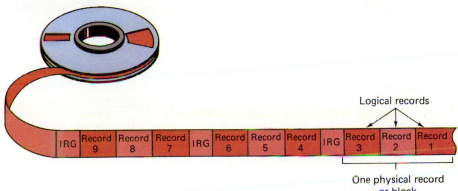

Logical records

One physical record
or block

Blocked records (b)

FIGURE 5.3
Unblocked (a) and Blocked
(b) Records

bits are recorded on a segment of nine-track and seven-track tape for the characters A, B, and C.

Density The density of a magnetic tape is the number of characters or bytes per inch (bpi) that the tape accommodates. Data can be recorded on tape in different densities. Some typical tape densities are 800, 1600, and 6250 bpi. Obviously, the higher the density, the more data a tape can contain. High-density tape units also read and write tapes faster, but are more expensive to purchase.

Blocking Factors Data records stored on tape are stored in order, one after another. The records contained on a magnetic tape are separated by interrecord gaps (IRGs), as shown in Figure 5.3a. The IRGs indicate where one record ends and another begins. The IRGs take up additional space on a tape.

Blocking is the grouping of several records (known in this context as *logical records*) together into one block (called a *physical record*). This technique eliminates the IRG between records within a block. Between blocks, a gap is still necessary, but there are fewer of these, and thus more data can be stored on the tape. Furthermore, since there is a brief start and stop of the physical tape media after each IRG, reading and writing can proceed more rapidly when records are blocked. Figure 5.3 shows blocked records on a tape.

The blocking factor is the number of logical records per physical record. In Figure 5.3b, the blocking factor is 3. The higher the blocking factor, the less wasted space a tape contains; however, the higher the blocking factor, the more working storage must be devoted to data that are read in. This is because the data are read in in one block at a time. Therefore, the larger the block (that is, the higher the blocking factor), the more data can be read into working storage at one time and the more space the data will occupy.

Magnetic Disk

The majority of storage devices used in computer centers are magnetic disks. Magnetic disks accommodate **direct-access files,** which means that records can be accessed directly and without searching sequentially from the beginning of the file for the desired record. This is the reason that magnetic disks are known as **direct access storage** devices, or DASDs (pronounced "daz-dee").

A Magnetic Disk (during manufacture)

Courtesy of Sperry Corporation

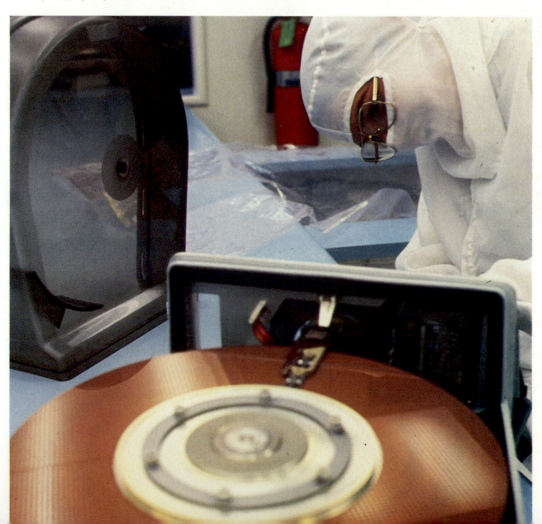

Disk Pack

Courtesy of Control Data Corporation

Magnetic disks can be fixed or removable. An increasing number of DASDs use magnetic disks that cannot be removed; for instance, the IBM 3370 uses several units, each containing six nonremovable disks. The contemporary trend is away from removable disks and toward nonremovable disks, which are more reliable and less costly.

A magnetic disk pack looks like a stack of long-playing phonograph records, and the analogy does not end there. Just as the arm of a phonograph advances across the record as the record plays, so does an "arm" of a DASD move back and forth over the disk surface to find a data location. Since a magnetic disk has a stack of recording surfaces, however, it also has a number of access arms, one for each surface. Figure 5.4 shows a magnetic disk with its access arms.

Every disk location where data can be recorded has an address. When a computer program wants to read or write data, it refers to this direct address, and the appropriate access arm goes to that location for the read or write operation.

An important feature of a direct access storage device is **overwriting,** which means that a record can be read from direct access storage into the computer's main storage, updated there by a computer program, and then written back into the original direct access storage location. Data can be changed efficiently and be immediately available for further use. The record

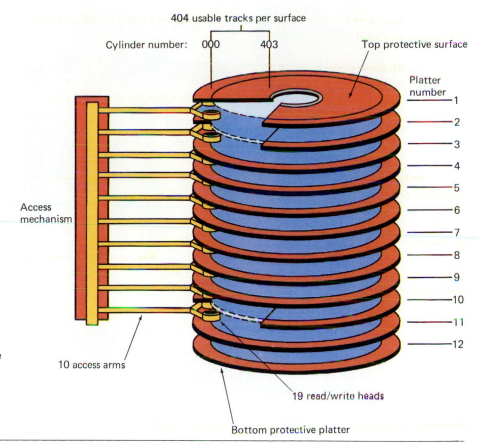

404 usable tracks per surface

Cylinder number: 000 403

Top protective surface

Platter number
1
2
3
4
5
6
7
8
9
10
11
12

Access mechanism

10 access arms

19 read/write heads

Bottom protective platter

FIGURE 5.4

Schematic Representation of IBM 3330–1 Disk Storage and IBM 3336–1 Disk Pack

Source: Adapted from Tyler Welburn, *Advanced Structural COBOL* p. 34. Used by permission of IBM Corporation

with the original values, in other words, is lost. Procedures are available, however, for keeping track of the original information if a mistake is made, such as logging the "before" and "after" version of all changed records in another file.

Overwriting is not possible on sequential files; a program that reads a magnetic tape for input has to write another complete tape for output —even if only one or two records on the tape were changed.

Files for Storing Data

From Characters to Files

As discussed in Chapter 3, data are the raw facts presented to the computer for processing. When data are used by a computer system, they are organized into several different levels, or hierarchies. This makes it easier to process and store the data.

The first level of data is the **character.** A character is a number (such as 1), a letter such as A), or a special symbol (such as $). Although the character is a basic unit of data, by itself a character does not mean much.

At the next level is the **field.** A field is a group of characters that means something as a unit. For example, "212" is a telephone area code, "Perez" is a name, and "$7,004,917" is some lucky person's bank-account balance. Fields are identified by a name ("area code," "last name," or "current balance," as in our examples).

Next in the hierarchy is the **record,** a collection of related fields. To understand records better, imagine that a computer training center uses a computer for business purposes. One such application is processing employee records. An example is shown in Figure 5.5. The name for each field of the record is given above the field.

An important feature of a record is its **key,** the field that identifies each record in order to differentiate it from other records. For instance, the key in Figure 5.5 is the employee number field. Since no two employees can have the same employee number, this key provides a unique identifier for the record.

The next higher level in the data hierarchy, a **file,** is a collection of related records. Each record in a file repeats the same fields, but with different data. For instance, the employee file might consist of sixty records; each record would start out with the particular employee's number, followed by the employee's name, followed by the other information about that employee, as shown in Figure 5.5. (There is actually one higher level in the data hierarchy, the *data base,* covered in later chapters.)

Fixed- and Variable-Length Records

Records can be either fixed length or variable length.

■ In a **fixed-length record,** every occurrence of the record has each of the fields present, and a given field is the same length from record to record. This means that each occurrence of a record in a file is the same—or a fixed—length.

FIGURE 5.5
Examples of Character, Field, Record and File

Employee Number	Employee Name	Department	Job Title	Date Hired	Salary
00001	Hartrock, P.	Administration	Director	4/1/78	$45,000
00002	Keys, Ken	Administration	Typist	10/22/84	$13,500
00003	Ohm, Vivian	Building Maint.	Electrician	7/13/70	$18,725
00005	Sauberkeit, Sam	Building Maint.	Cleaning Person	5/16/83	$11,000
00006	Caution, B.	Counseling	Student Advisor	8/8/75	$24,500
00011	Flurry, Larson	Administration	Asst. Director	4/2/78	$31,300

A FIELD → (00005)
A RECORD → (00003 row)
A CHARACTER → (1 in 00011)
A FILE → (entire table)

■ In a **variable-length record,** every occurrence of the record need not have each of the fields present, and a given field need not be the same length from record to record. This means that each occurrence of a record in a file is not the same—or is a variable—length.

Figure 5.5 showed a file of fixed-length records. Each record had each of the six fields present; and the length of a field did not vary from one record to the next. For instance, the employee-name field was 15 characters long regardless of how long the name was. This meant that the director's first name (Phineas) had to be abbreviated (P.) to fit. The same applied to the department and job-title fields.

Figure 5.6 shows an example of variable-length records. The figure shows a student records file for our computer-center example. Here, instead of abbreviating course names they are spelled out in full, followed by the grade the student received in the course. In this case the field length varies. More significantly, *the number of fields* present in a record can vary, since the longer a student is in the center, the more courses he or she has taken. For each course completed, a course and grade field is simply added on to that student's record.

In practice, fixed-length records are easier to work with. More work is required to keep track of variable-length records at every stage of their processing.

Sequential Files

A **sequential file** is a file containing records ordered in some predetermined sequence. (Usually, the records are ordered in ascending or descending sequence based on a key. A key is the field that identifies each record in order to differentiate it from other records. Keys will turn out to be very important in our later discussion of the design and processing of files.) Both Figures 5.5 and 5.6 are examples of sequential files. In order to get records into ascending order by the value of their keys, the records are sorted using a computer program. Then the file is ready to be processed by other programs.

To get at the record for J Miller in Figure 5.6, the computer program would have to read the records for MA Sanchez and PB Macmillan first, since those records occur first in the file. To get at the record for CB Hong in Figure 5.6, the computer program would have to read all of the records in

FIGURE 5.6
File of Variable-Length Records

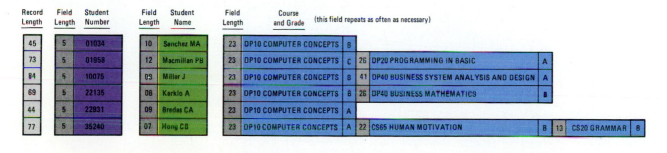

Record Length	Field Length	Student Number	Field Length	Student Name	Field Length	Course and Grade (this field repeats as often as necessary)								
45	5	01034	10	Sanchez MA	23	DP10 COMPUTER CONCEPTS	B							
73	5	01958	12	Macmillan PB	23	DP10 COMPUTER CONCEPTS	C	26	DP20 PROGRAMMING IN BASIC	A				
84	5	10075	03	Miller J	23	DP10 COMPUTER CONCEPTS	B	41	DP40 BUSINESS SYSTEM ANALYSIS AND DESIGN	A				
69	5	22135	08	Kerklo A	23	DP10 COMPUTER CONCEPTS	B	26	DP40 BUSINESS MATHEMATICS	B				
44	5	22931	09	Bredas CA	23	DP10 COMPUTER CONCEPTS	A							
77	5	35240	07	Hong CB	23	DP10 COMPUTER CONCEPTS	A	22	CS65 HUMAN MOTIVATION	B	13	CS20 GRAMMAR	B

the file before it found the one it was after. And as you have probably already observed, this need to read a (variable) number of records in a file before finding the record sought is the drawback of sequential files. Sequential files are often stored on magnetic tape, but they can also be stored on magnetic disk. In the next section, we will learn about how sequential files are processed.

Sequential File Processing

In a business context, the typical use of a sequential file is in applications that require two files. One (sequential) file contains data that must be updated, based on transactions read from another (sequential) file. Figure 5.7 gives a graphic view of such two-file processing. In this section we will look at an add/change/delete application that follows this figure.

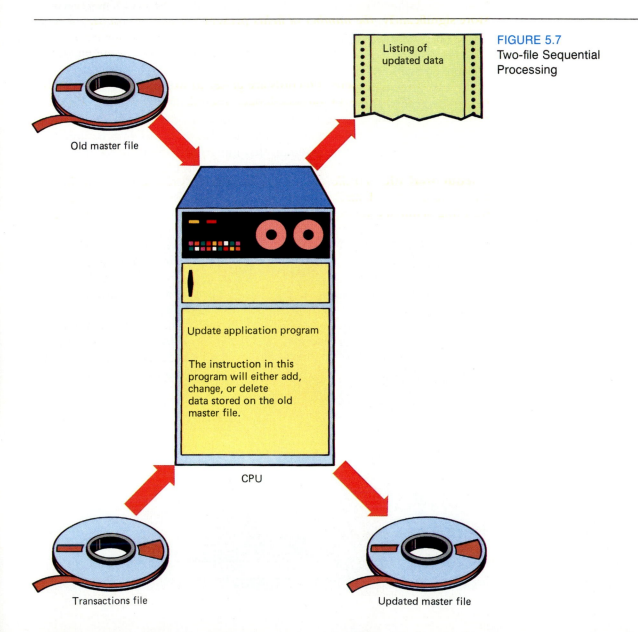

Old master file

Listing of updated data

FIGURE 5.7
Two-file Sequential Processing

Update application program

The instruction in this program will either add, change, or delete data stored on the old master file.

CPU

Transactions file

Updated master file

The computer training center has a fixed-length employee record, as shown earlier in Figure 5.5. The file contains one record for each employee of the center. Every so often employees resign or are fired, new employees are hired, and people receive raises and their salaries change. The appropriate fields on the employee master file then need to be updated.

The add/change/delete records are recorded on a transactions file, along with a code for each transaction indicating whether it is an add (A), delete (D), or change (C). The application program reads the (old) master file and the transaction file in *sequential order* until it finds a matching key. When it finds a match, it performs the requested operation. The output to the new master file reflects the change.

Figure 5.8 shows how the process works with real data. The old master file contains the data shown in Figure 5.5. Another sequential file, containing update transactions, contains a change (a raise) for the director, a change (a name change, because she got married) for the student advisor, a deletion (he resigned) for the assistant director, and an addition (she was hired) for the new assistant director.

First the program reads record 00001 from the old master file. Then the program reads update transaction 00001 from the transactions file. Since these employee number keys match, the program updates the data contained in the record and writes it to the new master file.

Next the program reads record 00002 from the old master file and record 00006 from the transactions file. There is no match, and the difference in keys tells the program that more old master-file records must be read to "catch up" with the transaction record. Accordingly, the program writes record 00002 unchanged to the new master file, reads

FIGURE 5.8
An Add/Change/Delete
Application

OLD MASTER FILE

00001	Hartrock, P.	Administration	Director	$45,000
00002	Keys, Ken	Administration	Typist	$13,500
00003	Ohm, Vivian	Building Maint.	Electrician	$18,725
00005	Sauberkeit, Sam	Building Maint.	Cleaning Person	$11,000
00006	Caution, B.	Counseling	Student Advisor	$24,500
00011	Flurry, Larson	Administration	Asst. Director	$31,300

TRANSACTIONS FILE

00001	Hartrock, P.	Administration	Director	$49,500 C
00006	Sullivan, B.	Counseling	Student Advisor	$24,500 C
00011	Flurry, Larson	Administration	Asst. Director	$31,300 D
00012	Goodkind, E.	Administration	Asst. Director	$30,000 A

CODE

NEW MASTER FILE

00001	Hartrock, P.	Administration	Director	$49,500
00002	Keys, Ken	Administration	Typist	$13,500
00003	Ohm, Vivian	Building Maint.	Electrician	$18,725
00005	Sauberkeit, Sam	Building Maint.	Cleaning Person	$11,000
00006	Sullivan, B.	Counseling	Student Advisor	$24,500
00012	Goodkind, E.	Administration	Asst. Director	$30,000

record 00003 from the old master file and writes it unchanged to the new master file, and does the same thing for record 00005.

When the program reads old master-file record 00006, it finally has a match for transaction record 00006. Since this is a change, the program writes the changed record to the new master file. Next the program reads record 00011 and transaction 00011, which match. Since the transaction is a delete, the program does not write record 00011 to the new master file. The program would read more records from the old master file, but there are none; however, there is another transaction, 00012, which the program reads and, since it is an addition, writes to the new master file.

The contents of the new master file are shown at the bottom of Figure 5.8. The significant thing to note in this example is that *all* of the processing was done sequentially: the reading of the old master file, the reading of the transactions file, and also the *writing* of the new master file.

Direct-Access Files

It is possible to go straight (or fairly straight) to the data we want in a file. Going "directly" to data in this way is what *direct access* is all about. **Direct-access files** are files from which data can be read, and to which data can be written, by placing the read/write mechanism directly at the location for this data. The term **random access,** means the same thing. Direct- or random-access files are stored on magnetic disk, including the floppy disks used in microcomputer systems.

Processing Direct-Access Files

There are two basic ways of retrieving data stored in a direct access file. First, we can go there directly. Every record in the file must have a key that corresponds to a particular storage location. For instance, if we request student record 22136, "22" might indicate that it is on cylinder 22, "13" that it is on track 13 within the cylinder, and "6" that it is the sixth record on the track. So just specifying this key would enable the DASD to directly locate this record.

However, this method often does not work. Our key of 22136 was a student number, and it might also happen by coincidence to be a disk address. If we really used the student numbers, we would run into problems, either because we came up with nonexistent addresses or because we wasted a lot of space (which translates to greater access time) skipping around from one key to the next. For instance, the numbers 22131 through 22139 allow nine records within a track, when the track might really have room for thirty; the rest would be wasted. Or more commonly, we might have a key that, with the best of intentions, bore no resemblance to a disk address. These problems bring us to the second way of getting at data in a direct-access file: hashing.

Hashing   Sometimes called **randomization,** hashing is used to transform a key into a disk address using a type of formula (called a transformation formula). In this way we can convert virtually any record key into a disk address (location) that corresponds to the physical format of the disk.

Here is one common hashing technique: We can divide the record key by the largest prime number that is greater than the number of records in the file. (A prime number is a number that can be evenly divided only by itself and the number 1.) The *remainder* of the division can then be used as the record address.

For example, let's say our student course records file is 1995 records in length. The largest prime number greater than 1995 is 1999. Now, let's say we want to calculate the address for student 35240 (from Figure 5.6). We divide 35240 by 1999. This gives us 17 with a remainder of 63. The remainder, 63, then becomes the relative physical file address where the record can be found. The '63' is not the physical disk address of the record but is the relative location of the record in the file. This computation is performed when the record is first written in the file, and by every program thereafter that needs to read the record.

Figure 5.9 shows an example of where the records of a direct-access file end up in terms of record addresses using a hashing calculation. Now you

FIGURE 5.9
How Hashing Works

Record key	3521
Number of records in file	95
Prime number	97

In hashing we divide the number of the record key (3521) by the nearest prime number which is greater than the number of records in the file. (The number 97 is the prime number nearest to and greater than 95, the number of records in this file.) In this way we can determine the relative location in the file where this record will be stored. When 3521 is divided by 97, the remainder will give us the relative location:

$$
\begin{array}{r}
36 \\
97 \overline{)\,3521} \\
2910 \\
\hline
611 \\
582 \\
\hline
\end{array}
$$

29 is the remainder.

Thus, 29 is the relative location in the file where record number 3521 will be stored.

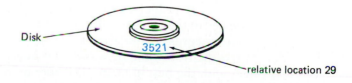

Disk

3521

relative location 29

can appreciate why "random access" is used synonymously with "direct access": The location of records on a file using a transformation formula as in hashing produces addresses at random. It must be added, however, that since we know the formula, we also know where the records are; this is vital for later processing of these same records.

A disadvantage of hashing is that records may get distributed in an uneven, scattered fashion on the disk, since they will land wherever the conversions place them. Disk storage space is therefore not used as efficiently as in a sequential file. The tradeoff, however, is speed of access.

Another drawback of hashing is that the same disk address might be created for more than one record. When this happens, all records, if any, after the first with the same address are "bumped" to an overflow area. This slows access speed somewhat in the case of the overflow records: First the access arm has to go to the address calculated, and then it is directed to the overflow area, which is a second movement. In practice, it is not a good idea to have more than 20 percent of the records of a file stored in the overflow area, since this begins to slow access time substantially.

Indexed Sequential Files

The **indexed sequential access** method is used to retrieve data from files stored on magnetic disk. With this technique, indexes are used to divide a sequential file into segments. You can find a record more quickly because you can go directly to the segment that contains it, without having to go through other, irrelevant data along the way.

Here's how it works. Imagine that you are after a book in a library. One way to find it would be to search all the shelves, examining each and every title along the way (the sequential-access method). Given the quantity of books that a library contains, this would be absurd. Instead, you use the card catalog to find the call number that gives the approximate shelf location of the book you want. Then you go to that shelf and, after scanning only a few titles, find your book.

Searching the card catalog to find a book in a library is exactly like using the indexed sequential access method to find a record on a sequential file. A separate file is created that contains only an index to the data file. The index has an entry that is the lowest key for every segment of records in the data file. If we decided when designing the file that segments would be 50 records long, and the file contains 40,000 records, then the index would contain 800 records. When a program sought a particular record, it would read through the index file sequentially until it found a key that is near the location of the record sought. Then the program would go straight to that segment of records on the direct-access device and read through those records until it found the record it was after.

An example of indexed sequential file organization is given in Figure 5.10.

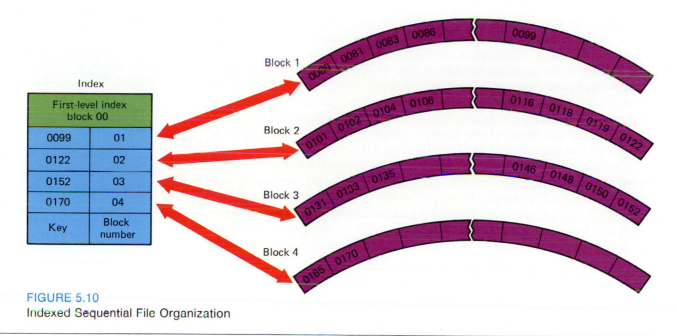

FIGURE 5.10
Indexed Sequential File Organization

Storage Considerations for Magnetic Tape

Magnetic tape is the best storage medium to use for applications with the following characteristics:

- **Timing.** Transactions or changes to a file that can be saved until a future, preset time before being processed work best on magnetic tape. (On the other hand, applications that require immediate processing of individual transactions, such as airline reservations, would be more suited to a disk storage medium.)

- **Backup.** When updating a file that's originally on magnetic tape, the program reads the old file and the transaction file and writes a new file based on the two input files. In this way, the original file still exists. (When updating on disk, you rewrite records to the new master file on the same disk. In this case, a backup copy of the old master file is retained on tape.)

- **High Volume.** An application program that needs to read and update a large proportion of the records contained in a file is best stored on magnetic tape.

Storage Consideratons for Magnetic Disks

Storage on magnetic disk should be used with applications that have the following characteristics:

- **Interrogation.** DASDs should be used when a user needs to obtain a specific response to a specific inquiry. For example, in an inventory-control application a user might ask, "What is the quantity on hand of inventory item number 998834?" Having this information stored on disk will enable the user to find this information more efficiently than if it were stored on magnetic tape.

- **Low Volume.** When an application program needs to read a small proportion of the records contained in a file, then the use of a disk storage medium is preferable. This avoids the necessity of reading sequentially a lot of records that are not of concern.

- **Real-Time Updating.** "Real time" means that data must be changed quickly enough to be reused in an ongoing process. In an application context, this means that updating must take place as soon as possible after a transaction occurs, because the updated data will affect future transactions. The classic example of real-time updating is an on-line airline reservations system, which enables users to find out the current status of all seats on all flights at all times.

Now that IBM Is Adopting the Microfloppy, It Could Become the Industry Standard

Big Disk, Little Disk: The Coming War in Floppies

When Columbia Records Inc. brought out the 33⅓ rpm record in 1948, it rocked the industry. Instead of five minutes of scratchy music from a brittle shellac surface, it promised 25 minutes of high-fidelity sound on a sturdy vinyl disk.

In the early 1980s, Sony Corp. tried to make the same kind of splash by improving the floppy disk, the plastic platter used for storing personal computer data. It developed a 3½-in. floppy that not only was more reliable than the conventional 5¼-in. disk but also could store more data. Nobody cared. Even after Apple Computer Inc. used the Sony disk on its Macintosh in 1984, the other computer makers stuck with the 5¼-in. version International Business Machines Corp. used. Only IBM could force the switch.

Now, IBM is using its clout. Its portable PC Convertible, introduced on Apr. 2, is the company's first major product to use 3½-in. floppies. As IBM adds new PC models, it is expected to make the "microfloppy" disks standard —and competitors are likely to follow its lead. Although 3½-in. floppies accounted for only 2% of 372 million disks sold in the U.S. last year, market researcher Dataquest Inc. predicts that by 1990 they will outsell 5¼-in. floppies. That's even though the original floppy is used on more than 9 million business computers.

A vocal minority claims the 3½-in. version can't overtake the 5¼-in. floppy. Says Rod Canion, president of Compaq Computer Corp., the No. 1 maker of IBM-compatible PCs: "The momentum of the 5¼-in. drive may be too much. The advantages of the 3¼-in. drive don't overcome the disadvantages of changing."

New Headaches The biggest obstacle is getting computer owners and software suppliers to convert. If an IBM PC owner wants to use the new floppies, or if he buys a Convertible and wants to use data recorded on 5¼-in. disks, he has to buy a 3½-in. disk drive and a new version of the IBM

operating-system software that has programs for transferring data from one type of floppy to another. IBM's 3½-in. disk-drive add-on for its PCs lists for $395. The software is $95.

For software companies, the issue is inventory. Major suppliers say they will put out programs on 3½-in. floppies, but they're unsure about how many 5¼-in. and 3½-in. versions to produce. Softsel Computer Products Inc., the largest U.S. software wholesaler, is wary about the inventory headaches. Says David S. Wagman, co-chairman of Softsel: "The last thing we need is duplication."

Whatever angst the microfloppy causes consumers and software companies, diskmakers are betting that the shift will take place—and offer them fresh opportunities. The 5¼-in. floppies have become a commodity product, and severe price cutting has led to a two-year shakeout and consolidation among its makers. The survivors have been efficient manufacturers with brand-name recognition and extensive distribution: Maxell, 3M, Xidex, and Eastman Kodak lead the market with about 11% each.

U.S. companies may not be the prime beneficiaries of the changeover, however. Maxell Corp., a subsidiary of Hitachi Ltd., is the only Japanese company in the top four now. But other Japanese manufacturers are gearing up—especially in microfloppies. Some 92% of 3½-in. floppies sold worldwide last year came from Japan-based companies, according to Magnetic Media Information Service, a market researcher. In Japan, where 3½-in. disks have been more widely used, there's a three-way tie among Sony, Maxell, and Fuji.

The U.S. market for microfloppies "hasn't developed as quickly as the Japanese wanted," says Stephan T. Haymann of the New England Consulting Group. They assumed that Macintosh would sell faster and that IBM would switch to microfloppies sooner. To move inventories, the Japanese have halved the wholesale price of a 3½-in. disk in the past two years, to around $1.40. Dataquest analyst Robert R. Gaskin says that could drop to 60¢ by 1990.

"Mean Thing"   Keeping up with price cuts in the microfloppy business will be harder than it has been in 5¼-in. disks. Small manufacturers who used simple machinery or cheap labor to make 5¼-in. floppies won't be able to do so with microfloppies. A 3½-in. disk has a two-part plastic case, a metal hub, and a spring-loaded shutter, all of which must be carefully assembled. A machine that makes 40 microfloppies a minute costs about $5 million. "The 3½-in. floppy is a very mean thing to manufacture and requires massive investment in automation," says Magnetic Media President Laurence B. Lueck. "That will separate the men from the boys."

U.S. suppliers aren't discouraged. With deep price cuts, "Sony is attempting to hold down the number of companies competing in 3½-in. disks," says Richard T. Bourns, president of Eastman Kodak Co.'s Verbatim Corp. subsidiary. "But we put in [3½-in.] capacity early, and we'll be a major player." Verbatim, which once had 25% of the U.S. floppy market, sold out to Kodak in 1985 after price-cutting caused heavy losses. Now it counts on heavy automation, a Mexican plant, and joint ventures in Japan and Brazil to keep up. Also, under Kodak's brand name, Verbatim is expanding distribution from computer and office supply stores into mass-merchandisers.

Other suppliers also want to cash in on household names. Despite its slow start in 5¼-in. floppies, Polaroid Corp. is gearing up for 3½-in. disks. "The market eventually will be comprised of major manufacturers with brand names," says Shakeel Mozaffar, Polaroid's marketing director for computer data-recording products. "We aim to be one."

So does 3M Co. The St. Paul (Minn.) company already has used its Scotch and 3M trademarks to gain a top position in the 5¼-in. floppy market and is

eager to expand its share with 3½-in. floppies. "We've already made the investment," says William T. Monahan, commercial markets director of 3M's Magnetic Media Div. Analysts, however, suspect 3M's investment in the floppy business has produced little profit. The company won't comment, but it recently cited declining floppy-disk and videocassette prices as a reason for a 55% slide in operating earnings for its Electronics & Information Technologies Sector in 1985.

Playing It Safe   Xidex Corp., which catapulted to a leading market share by merging with Dysan Corp. last year, remains wary of the new market. It makes 3½-in. disks, but it isn't betting too heavily on them. "The 5¼ is so well established," says Executive Vice-President Bert L. Zaccaria. "I don't see it being displaced."

Some industry watchers feel the current 3½-in. floppy itself could be eclipsed. "By the time [the 3½] erodes the 5¼ market, there may be other products that are really exciting," says Raymond R. Shook, engineering vice-president of Memorex Media Products, a division of Burroughs Corp.'s Office & Media Products Group. Some possibilities: 3½-in. floppies that store 2 million or 4 million characters of data per disk—three or six times what the IBM 3½-in. disk holds. And, Shook says, ultimately there may be storage on optical disks—a relative of the compact audio disk that is now making Columbia's LP obsolete.

Source: Geoff Lewis, "Information Processing," *Business Week*, May 5, 1986, pp. 111-12.

Summary and Key Terms

1. **Auxiliary storage** or **secondary storage** contains data that cannot be kept in working storage due to size limitations. The principal secondary storage devices for microcomputers are **floppy disks** and **hard disks. CD–ROM disks** store large data bases. The principal secondary storage devices for large computer systems are **magnetic tape** and **magnetic disks.**

2. Magnetic tape has tracks on which the data are recorded. Tapes have different densities. Density refers to the number of bytes per inch (bpi) that the tape can hold. Interrecord gaps (IRGs) are the spaces that separate singular (logical) records from each other on tape. Blocking is a more efficient way to use space on the magnetic tape. Several *logical records* are grouped together to form what is called a *physical record.* With blocked records only the physical records are separated by interrecord gaps, therefore less storage space is used.

3. The majority of **direct access storage devices** (DASDs) are magnetic disks. A magnetic disk pack consists of a number of recording surfaces. For each recording surface there is an access arm. The access arm uses assigned addresses to locate data on a disk.

4. The concentric paths on magnetic disks are called **tracks.** A magnetic disk drive uses its access arms to reach the data on the tracks. A cylinder consists of all the tracks that the access arm can reach in one position. DASDs use a feature called **overwrite;** records are written in changed form back to the storage locations they were read from.

5. Data on auxiliary storage are arranged in a hierarchy, or by levels. The different levels of data (low to high) are: **character, field, record,** and **file.** An important feature of a record is its **key,** which differentiates it from other records. Records can be fixed or variable in their length.

6. **Sequential files** contain records stored in some order. Most sequential files are stored on magnetic tape. Sequential file applications typically require two files, one containing data that must be updated, based on transactions read from the other. Output is a new sequential file containing the updated data. Sequential files must be processed in sequence—there is no way to reach a record at some point in the file without reading all of the records prior to it.

7. **Direct-access files** are files from which data can be read, and to which data can be written, by placing the read/write mechanism directly at the location for this data. **Hashing** or **randomization** is a method used to organize data in which a key is transformed into a disk address. Hashing allows for greater speed of access but it does not use space as efficiently as a sequential file does.

8. An **indexed sequential file** divides a sequential file into segments. A separate file then contains an index to the segments of the file. Programs need not read the entire indexed sequential file, but can consult the index first, and go to the relevant segment, saving processing time. Indexed sequential files use direct-access storage devices.

Review Questions

Fill-in

1. The type of storage that is able to hold input for processing or output that has been processed is known as _____.
2. A _____ is a collection of related data fields.
3. A group of characters that means something as a unit is called a _____.
4. A _____ is a collection of related records.
5. In a _____, each record in a file has the same fields present.
6. The process of grouping several logical records together to form one physical record is known as _____.
7. The _____ is the number of logical records grouped together to make a physical record.
8. The type of file in which records are ordered in sequence is known as a _____.
9. When records are stored in an _____, you obtain access to a particular record by searching through an index first.
10. The type of storage media which makes it possible to locate the address of a record without searching through all the records from the beginning of the file in sequence is _____.

Multiple Choice

____ 1. The method used to transform a record key to a physical disk address, using a pre-defined formula, is:
   a. direct access

    b. hashing
    c. blocking
    d. indexing

____ 2. A type of removable disk storage device that is used with microcomputers:
    a. hard disk
    b. mass storage unit
    c. floppy disk
    d CD–ROM

____ 3. A new storage technology, which is capable of storing voice, data, text, or video images, and which cannot be altered once data have already been recorded on it, is:
    a. magnetic disk
    b. floppy disk
    c. CD–ROM
    d. thin film media

____ 4. When some of the records in a file have a different number of fields, these records are known as:
    a. fixed-length records
    b. blocked records
    c. variable-length records
    d. indexed records

____ 5. A _____ divides physical records from each other in a magnetic tape file.
    a. track
    b. block
    c. interrecord gap
    d. key

Discussion Questions

1. Explain why a greater blocking factor makes reading tape files more efficient. What factors need to be taken into consideration in determining the appropriate blocking factor?

2. Given each of these application requirements, identify what type of storage medium—magnetic tape, magnetic disk, or floppy disk—would be most appropriate for storing each of the following files. Explain the reasons for your choice.
    a. An inventory master file which is updated daily to reflect sales order transactions (these transactions update approximately 10% of the inventory master records daily).
    b. A backup copy of a mortgage loan file.
    c. A central master file of hotel reservations which is used by reservations agents making inquiries and updates based upon customer requests.
    d. A masterfile of 1000 real estate records with approximately 500 characters in each record created and mainained by a local real estate agency; these records contain information about the characteristics of residential properties, including address, schools, utilities, services, price, and dimensions, and are used by agents to locate appropriate offerings for prospective buyers.

3. Which *microcomputer storage media* (floppy disk or hard disk) would be most appropriate in each of these situations:
    a. Storing a file of patient records for a dentist's office (300 records at 200 characters per record) in a situation where no growth is anticipated over the next 2–5 years.
    b. Storing multiple files, consisting of invoice records, customer records, and inventory records; some applications requiring processing multiple files.
    c. Storing text files, consisting of short letters and 10- to 15-page reports requiring multiple revisions.
    d. Storing a master file of engineering specifications consisting of 300 pages of text. Copies of the file are created and edited in order to compose proposals for specific projects.

4. Identify some applications in which the following storage media would be appropriate.
    a. CD–ROM
    b. hard disk

Systems Software

6

Chapter Objectives

After studying this chapter, you should be able to

1. Understand how an operating system works.

2. Name important operating systems for microcomputers and large computers.

3. Understand the operating system's role in single tasking, multitasking, multiuser, and time sharing environments.

Tom had just finished setting up his new computer and could hardly wait to use it. He inserted the word processing diskette into drive A and turned the computer on. A red light came on at drive A, and then a message appeared on the screen:

```
Non-System disk or disk error
Replace and strike any key when ready
```

He tried again, but the same thing happened. Tom was stumped. The clerk had told him that everything was ready to go. After reading a few of the manuals he finally came across the word "system." But he couldn't find an adequate explanation except something about making a disk bootable. He finally decided to phone the store.

"Before you can use any application program you have to load the operating system into the computer," the manager said. "An operating system is a set of programs written for a particular type of computer hardware system that makes it easy for you to operate the computer. It also makes sure that all application software written for that particular operating system works with your particular computer. Look, I can at least explain to you over the phone how to make a bootable disk so your word processor will work. Here's what you do. . . ."

More and more, computers are complex machines designed to be used by people who have little or no knowledge about how the machine actually functions. Microcomputer users, especially, want to use a computer and applications software such as a word processor to make the task of writing easier. They don't necessarily want to know how a computer operates or how the application software interacts with the computer hardware. As Tom quickly found out, **operating system software** is the component of a computer system that takes care of such things. It consists of a series of programs that manage the hardware and improve the use and the perfor-

mance of a computing system. Operating systems software includes the operating system, utility programs, and programs that aid in the creation or use of application software.

What Are Operating Systems, and What Do They Do?

All computers, from large mainframes to microcomputers, use an operating system. The operating system manages the operation of the computer hardware either through direct commands given by the user or through commands given by the application software. As Figure 6.1 indicates, an operating system insulates the user from the hardware. Users communicate with the operating system in a manner it understands, but users need not be concerned with how the operating system interacts with the hardware of a particular computer system. The operating system also greatly improves a computer's operating efficiency. It can manage its own operations at its own speed without the need for human intervention. Before operating systems were used, computers sat idle most of the time. Human operators loaded data for processing, flipped switches to call printers and disk storage to perform their tasks, scheduled programs for execution, and cleared memory. Today's operating systems perform these tasks automatically.

An **operating system** is a collection of programs that allows a computer to supervise its own internal operations. It automatically calls in

FIGURE 6.1
The operating system insulates the user from the computer hardware.

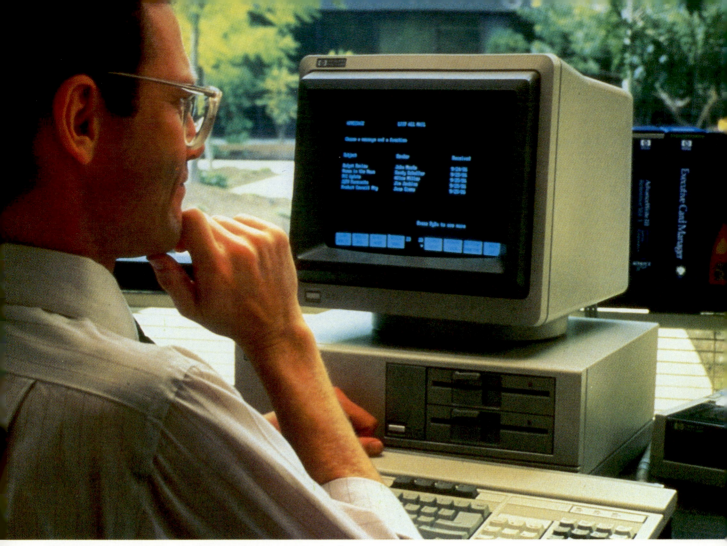

Single-tasking operating systems perform one job at a time.

Courtesy of Hewlett-Packard

language translators and application programs from disk, and sends data from disk storage to printers or to other storage devices for continuous throughput of jobs. It is the function of the operating system to manage the computer's resources as efficiently and effectively as possible.

There are two basic types of operating systems: single tasking and multitasking. With **single tasking** operating systems, one task can be performed at a time. **Multitasking** operating systems share the CPU among programs or users, with each having access to the CPU in turn.

Developing an operating system for mini and mainframe computers is a complex and costly process. Computer manufacturers must design their operating system software to work specifically with their own line of computer equipment. In the early days of the microcomputer industry, each manufacturer developed its own operating system. However, with the increasing popularity of the IBM PC or compatible computers, there has been considerable standardization in operating systems software. Some of the more common operating systems are shown in the box on page 139.

Multitasking operating systems permit more than one job at a time to take place.

Courtesy of Honeywell

Control and Service Functions of the Operating System

An operating system supervises the control functions and the service functions of a computer system (see Figure 6.2). **Control programs** monitor the operation of the computer system and perform tasks such as data input/output, program scheduling, and job management. Control programs also provide a communication link between the computer system and the user or programmer. Finally, control programs also execute the second type of operating system program, service programs. **Service programs** are used to prepare and execute application programs.

AKA

Both control and service functions are controlled by a **supervisor** program, also known as the monitor or executive. This program is loaded into memory and executed when the computer is first turned on. Part of the supervisor program consists of short routines known as resident programs. They perform common tasks and because they are always loaded in memory are readily available for use. Less frequently used routines known as transient programs are kept as separate programs on disk. These are called by the supervisor when needed by the user or the application program and are loaded into main memory for execution.

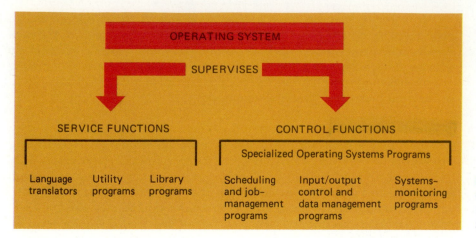

FIGURE 6.2
Control and Service
Functions of the Operating
System

The operating system performs some functions automatically, such as clearing memory and allocating main memory. However, specific jobs such as running a payroll program or updating inventory files require specific instructions. These instructions are communicated to the supervisor through a small program written in a **job-control language.** The programmer specifies the beginning of a job, the specific program to be executed, the actual work to be done, and the input/output devices required. The **job-control program** then translates the job-control statements in the source program into machine language for execution. If no job-control program precedes the application program, the operating system uses default options that specify a standard method of handling data input, processing and output.

Input and Output Management   Using a computer involves three procedures: input, processing, and output. For example, a typical microcomputer system will have a keyboard, a monitor, a printer, and two floppy disks connected to it. An operating system's **input/output (I/O) manager,** also known as a device manager, must have the ability to link different kinds of devices to the computer. It must also be able to distinguish among more than one device of the same kind. A printer, for instance, might have a 132-character line and operate at a slow speed, while a CRT will have an 80-character line and operate at a much higher speed. Similarly, the device manager must be able to separately identify both disk drives.

PC–DOS	The IBM PC operating system	**Types of Operating Systems**
MS–DOS	The operating system used on IBM compatible computers	
UNIX	A multiuser, mutitasking operating system used primarily on minicomputers but also used with microcomputers and some mainframes.	
CP/M	A once-popular 8-bit microcomputer operating system	
VAX/VMS	The operating system for DEC's VAX minicomputers	
MVS, OS/VS, VM	IBM mainframe operating systems	

To solve these problems, the operating system stores information in main memory on the characteristics as well as name and address for each device. When you want to work with a file, you specify the file name, along with the device where it is located. Based on this information, the operating system determines the address and characteristics of the device and opens a connection between it and main memory.

Program Execution

Scheduling and job-management programs belong to the operating system and are used in program execution. **Scheduling programs** identify the priority assigned to the running of a program either by the programmer or the user. Then they assign computer resources such as the CPU and input/output devices as they become available.

Job-management programs control the computer resources used during program execution as well as the resources needed to load, process, and end jobs. When the scheduling program decides that computer resources are available, the job management program transfers control to the CPU, and program execution begins. It then checks for various kinds of information. For example, it checks that information is available about location of input data or that the printer is equipped with special forms when required.

Job control programs also have an error handling task. They check for nonexistent data, program instruction errors, and equipment malfunctions. When the job-management program detects such errors, it either causes the program to stop executing or sends out an error message so that the computer user can intervene.

Memory Management

The operating system must manage memory to prevent two major problems: It must make sure that an application program does not access areas of main memory that the operating system has used to store information about files and devices, and it must make sure that the application program doesn't accidentally alter the running operating system code. A second function of memory management is that the operating system must be able to provide more memory than is actually physically available for large programs.

There are several ways to solve the first problems. The memory manager component of the operating system usually incorporates some feature that makes it impossible for the application program to access areas of memory reserved for the operating system. The simplest way to do this is to check every memory address the application program attempts to use. If the address is within the area reserved for the operating system then it aborts the program. Alternatively, the operating system can prohibit access to those portions of memory reserved for it, either by having separate hardware addressing, or by having a read-only memory (ROM) which the user cannot change. This last solution is sometimes used in microcomputers.

Often a program requires more memory than is available. With computers that can run only one program at a time, the solution is to use an overlay structure. If a program needs 30,000 bytes of memory to run but the machine only has 20,000 bytes available, the memory manager can execute the program by calling in successive chunks as needed.

Large computer systems, which run more than one program at a time, must be able to manage memory by allocating it to programs as required and ensure that the programs in memory remain separate from each other. We will discuss multiprogramming and concurrent processing later in this chapter.

Operating systems also have service programs involving language translation and utilities. They help the programmer create and run application programs. For example, a so-called source program is written in a **high-level language** such as BASIC, COBOL, or FORTRAN, which uses English-like words to make programming easier. Because a computer cannot execute a program in a high-level language, the operating system supplies a **translator program** that translates each program step into machine language.

One type of translator program is called a compiler. A **compiler** translates each step in the high-level-language source program into machine language. In addition, the compiler produces a listing of the original source program as well as a listing of any errors or diagnostic messages. These messages usually indicate either improper use of the language or typing errors made during the input of the source program. If a source program contains serious errors, it probably will not compile. The source program must then be corrected, a process known as **debugging.** Sometimes, warning messages simply indicate source program errors that are not serious enough to prevent the machine from executing the program.

Microcomputer Operating Systems

Most microcomputers today use a **single-tasking operating system,** which means that only one CPU-controlled task can go on at a time. If you are using a word processor to write a report, for example, nothing else can be happening on the computer at the same time. Although most microcomputer users do not find this as a major restriction, there are times when it becomes a problem. For example, when you are printing out a long document, your computer performs a minor control function—sending data from the computer to the printer. If your document is long and your printer is slow, the computer can be tied up for a long time.

Single-tasking operating systems for microcomputers may soon be a thing of the past. The new so-called super microcomputers with the Intel 80386 microprocessor are able to address huge amounts of memory and are very fast in their operation. The UNIX operating system, discussed in the following section, could be used with these new super microcomputers for multitasking and for time sharing between a number of users. A new version of the MS-DOS/PC-DOS operating system is also currently being developed for these machines.

Now let's look at some popular microcomputer operating systems before looking at one of them—MS-DOS—in more detail.

Types of Microcomputer Operating Systems

Of the many microcomptuer operating systems in use today, the most popular ones are AppleDOS/ProDOS, MS-DOS, UNIX, and the Macintosh operating system.

AppleDOS/ProDOS

Apple DOS was designed as a simple disk operating system when Apple introduced its first disk drives in 1978. **ProDOS,** an updated version of AppleDOS, allows use of a hard disk and other microcomputer system components (known as **peripherals**), and speeds up some operations. Because of the many applications programs available for Apple computers, particularly for home and educational use, AppleDOS and ProDOS will be used for some time.

MS-DOS/PC-DOS

When IBM approached Microsoft Corporation, well-known for its BASIC Interpreter, to develop a disk operating system for its line of PCs, there was not enough time to develop an operating system from scratch. So Microsoft bought an operating system in 1981 from Seattle Computer Products, refined it, and licensed it to IBM under the name of PC-DOS for use with its PC computers. Microsoft also licensed it to a number of computer manufacturers that produced IBM-compatible computers and renamed it MS-DOS. With the IBM stamp of approval, the operating system became entrenched in the microcomputer world.

Like most microcomputers, this Apple has a single-tasking operating system.

Courtesy of Apple Computer Inc.

MS–DOS/PC–DOS is similar to the once-common 8-bit operating system that preceded it, CPM. However, MS–DOS/PC–DOS commands are more logical and its error handling is better than CPM's. It particularly helps the hard disk user by providing a hierarchical directory system for creation of subdirectories to keep files separated for easier use. Nevertheless, it is still not a particularly easy or user-friendly system. You must become quite familiar with it before you can use its full power. DOS requires users to give instructions directly to the operating system, which means users must know the commands and how to apply them.

UNIX   UNIX was developed at AT&T's Bell Laboratories in 1971 by Ken Thompson and Dennis Ritchie, as an operating system for a DEC minicomputer. During the 1970s, UNIX was highly promoted by AT&T, which gave free copies to many colleges and universities where students and faculty became familiar with its use. In the early 1980s, a substantial price reduction further contributed to its greater use. It is a complex operating system, with time-sharing and multiuser capabilities and many other features. It contains more than 200 utility programs that can be used by programmers to perform useful functions, so a programmer does not have to completely develop these routines for individual application programs. UNIX is written in a high-level language, known as C, and it is not dependent on a particular microprocessor. Although originally developed for a minicomputer, today it runs on mainframes as well as microcomputers.

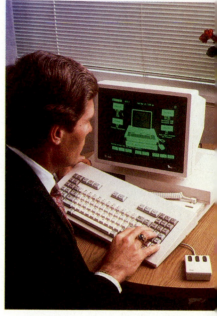

This microcomputer uses the UNIX operating system.

Courtesy of UNIX

UNIX has extensive file manipulation utilities, which allow you to channel or "pipe" one file directly to another, where it can be processed as input while the first program is still working on the original file. This capability can significantly increase data-processing, for a number of tasks can be completed in one operation instead of each task having to be completed before the next one can be started.

Although UNIX appears to have a bright future, some problems accompany its use at the present time. It is not particularly easy to learn. It also lacks security features that are important to business users on multiuser systems. Some of the features that have been developed are not standardized, even though the heart of the system is virtually identical on all systems. Also, with the exception of scientific and engineering applications, relatively little business software is available to run under the UNIX system. Still, UNIX permits the use of the same software by microcomputers and large computers, and it supports communications networks and data bases, capabilities that will be needed for applications in the 1990s.

The OS/2 Operating System   The OS/2 operating system was introduced for IBM's PS/2 line of computers in 1987. Although these machines are compatible with DOS and application software created for DOS, the OS/2 system in effect supersedes DOS and will permit multitasking, high-resolution graphics, and other features beyond the capabilities of DOS. The Standard Edition of OS/2 will support the workstation level, and the Extended Edition will provide data base management, communications, and end-user interface features that will, it is claimed, create connectivity between the PS/2 workstation and the range of IBM hardware. As a result, users of PS/2 workstations will be able to invoke with equal ease applica-

tions on remote IBM equipment or a spreadsheet program stored on a floppy disk.

The OS/2 extended edition's end-user interface is based on Microsoft Windows, which permits the simultaneous loading and screen display of several application programs and the ability to move easily back and forth among them. OS/2 provides access to a full video graphics array, high-resolution color graphics, and interfaces to host graphics.

OS/2 fits into IBM's broader concept of System Application Architecture (SAA), which has four elements, including a common menu-based interface to a full range of IBM systems; a common programming interface (to COBOL, FORTRAN, C, SQL, and other languages); common communications support (to mainframes, laser printers, local area networks, or LANs, and other networks); and an interface to a set of common applications (initially focusing in on IBM's mainframe-based office automation software).

OS/2 is seen not only as a local PC-based operating system but as a capability making it possible to link PC-based workstations to communications networks, host computers, LANs, and high-speed laser printing facilities.

Macintosh A significant difference between other operating systems and the one used in the Apple Macintosh computers is that the latter is intended to be user friendly. There is no long list of commands to get to know. A mouse is used to move a pointer on the screen to available options. When the user clicks a button on the mouse, pulldown menus on the screen make additional commands available. A file is opened, for example, by pointing at that particular option on the screen. This process makes learning how to operate the Macintosh very easy.

How Do Microcomputer Operating Systems Work?

The amount of memory occupied by microcomputer operating systems varies depending on the operating system used. Early microcomputers had very little memory, so operating systems had to be small and consequently were limited in their functions. Today, operating systems can occupy as much as 128K, although 40K to 60K is normal.

The **supervisor program,** or **executive,** is the heart of the operating system. It contains the instructions that communicate with the user, cause input/output operations to occur, and generally control the operation of the computer.

To get a better idea of what makes a microcomputer operating system work, let's first look at its five generic components: input/output, file handling, memory managing, executive, and boot loader.

I/O Component The **I/O (input/output) component** directs the movement of data within the system. It keeps track of the various hardware devices, such as disk drives, keyboard, monitor, and printers, connected to the system. Together with the executive component, the I/O component coordinates all transfers of data between the hardware devices in the microcomputer system, thus permitting each device to send and receive data from the various devices.

File Component   The **file component** packs data into groups and records these groups in a **file.** It also keeps track of the location of files on the disk and retrieves information from files when requested. It records and writes a disk **directory** containing the file names and their locations. When you change a disk, the file component must read the new disk's directory to find out where the files are located on the disks.

Memory Component   The **memory component** allocates the microcomputer's RAM (random access memory) to the application software programs and/or data loaded to perform a specific task. It also recovers memory by loading new software programs and/or data into the main memory location of old programs and data no longer needed. RAM managed by the memory component is **volatile.** That is, everything in main memory is erased when power is turned off. Anything that has to be reused must therefore be put into auxiliary storage—saved to disk—before the system is turned off.

Executive Component   The **executive component** controls the entire operating system. It directs the various functions and makes sure that the correct programs are executed. The executive interprets the commands entered at the keyboard and acts as the interface between the user input and the other generic components of the operating system. For example, when you request a program, the executive directs the appropriate operating system component to locate the program requested. Then it copies the program into a work space in main memory and begins execution of the program's instructions.

Boot Loader   The **boot loader** helps load the rest of the operating system into main memory on ''boot-up.'' The boot loader resides on the *bootable storage medium*—the outer track of the diskette or hard drive and contains enough information to access the booted media and find other components of the system.

MS-DOS Operating System Files

To perform the functions of the five generic components discussed above, MS-DOS uses four system programs: MSDOS.SYS, IO.SYS, COMMAND.COM, and MSDOS boot loader. MSDOS.SYS is the director of the system. It provides the interface for application programs and performs all disk and file management activities. It sends commands to IO.SYS, which issues specific instructions for work to be done and selects specific hardware components to do it.

The COMMAND.COM program performs the executive or supervisory functions. It acts as the interface between user and other components of the operating system by interpreting the commands entered at the keyboard. It consists of two parts, the resident and the transient portion. The **resident** portion always remains in memory and loads programs, handles device errors, and allows the user to interrupt programs through the CTRL–BREAK keys. The **transient** portion includes all the resident commands, such as DIR, PATH, BREAK, CLS, and batch processor. A utility or application

Using a Few MS–DOS Utilities

DATE & TIME (resident)   After the computer is first booted, the time and current date can be set or changed using these two commands. This information is entered on a disk's directory to show when a program or data file was created or modified.

DIR (resident)   The directory program displays on the monitor screen a listing of the files contained on a particular disk. It's a good idea to print out the directory for any important disk for a fast, easy record of that disk's contents.

DELETE or DEL (resident)   DEL is used to erase one or more files from a disk. If you type

DEL B:TEST.1

the file on drive B called TEST.1 will be removed.

RENAME or REN (resident)   The rename command is used to rename a file. After renaming a file, the new name appears in the directory and any reference to the old file is gone.

COPY (resident)   With the COPY program you can copy one or more files to another disk without destroying the files that exist on the target disk.

TYPE (resident)   The TYPE command allows you to display the contents of a text file on the screen. It will only display files with printable characters. Command files (.COM and .EXE) and system files (.SYS) cannot be displayed.

FORMAT (transient)   Before data can be copied onto a floppy disk, it has to be formatted with the operating system that it will operate under. Every operating system handles disk formatting in a different manner.

The formatting program partitions the disk into 40 tracks of 9 sectors each. (Each sector can hold 512K of data, so a normal 5-¼-inch disk can hold 368,640 bytes of data.) It also creates a file allocation table to keep track of which sectors belong to which files, because a file can extend over many sectors. Finally, it creates a directory area where file information is stored for the user. Reformatting clears the file allocation table on the disk as well as the

program that requires more memory than is available may overwrite the transient portion of COMMAND.COM, which must then be reloaded after the current program completes its task.

The fourth program, the MSDOS boot loader, is not a file. It is a program recorded on the first track of the formatted disk that helps to load other system components from disk to memory during boot-up. It also contains specific instructions about hardware components and is hardware dependent.

Using MS–DOS   Remember Tom, who was stumped by the "Non-system disk" message? He soon found out that meant no operating system was on the disk that could be loaded in memory. With a bootable disk, loading the operating system takes only several seconds. The A > prompt appears on the screen and signifies that the operating system is ready to accept any valid commands to load utility or application programs to perform other tasks.

One of the first commands Tom might give is to read the directory of the disk in drive A. When he types DIR at the A > prompt, the resident

directory information. This process makes all previously stored data recoverable only with special programs.

During the formatting process, this program will also check the recording surface of the disk for flaws, and it makes such areas inaccessible to the operating system so no data will be copied to it. After the formatting process is completed, the operating system can also be copied to the disk, either by specifying this when first entering the format command or with a special program called SYS.COM. Copying the operating system to the disk makes the disk bootable. A disk does not have to be bootable if it is to be used only for storing data.

DISKCOPY (transient)   This program is used to transfer the entire contents of one disk to another, and it formats the target disk before the contents of the new disk are copied to it. The DISKCOPY utility program is useful for making duplicates of other disks such as backing up information.

CHKDSK (transient)   The CHKDSK program (check disk) displays file and disk information as well as how much space remains available on the disk.

EDLIN (transient)   The editor is a utility program that you can use to create programs or text documents. For example, under MS–DOS, when you type EDLIN at the system prompt, the editor program will load into memory. Then it asks you for the name of the program or document that you want to create. You can now type a memo, letter, or report. When you have finished entering information on the screen, the appropriate command will store the file onto the disk.

BAT (resident)   Batch files are special command files you can create for executing several instructions with one batch command. You can use an editor to create a batch command file with the extension of .BAT (e.g. COPY.BAT). When you type the name of the file without the extension, the operating system looks for it and, once found, executes the individual commands contained within. This procedure can save time and a lot of typing. It also makes the use of the computer easier for people with little knowledge in operating microcomputers, for they have to remember only a single command.

directory program already in memory as part of COMMAND.COM will instantly display a list of files on the monitor. A printout of a directory is shown in Figure 6.3.

Tom might now want to do some file management, which includes formatting disks so new files can be stored on them, deleting files from a disk, and copying files from one disk to another. To **format** a diskette and make it bootable, Tom must use a transient utility program called FORMAT.COM. Tom must therefore make sure that he has a disk with the format utility program in drive A. Then he can give the operating system the following command:

```
A> FORMAT/S
```

Remember, A > is the system prompt. The /S indicates to the operating system that after the disk is formatted, the system should be transferred to it.

```
A>dir

Volume in drive A has no label
Directory of   A:\

COMMAND   COM     15957    11-10-83    12:03p
LE        EXE    186448     6-01-85    12:00p
EDMSGS    TAB     20395     6-01-85    12:00p
HELPMSGS  TAB     43311     6-01-85    12:00p
PRINTER   PR        363    12-19-84     4:27p
PAN1091   PR       4095     3-26-86     1:48a
MODE      COM      5386    10-10-84     7:21p
FORMAT    COM      7536     8-21-85    11:53p
DEFAULT   BIN       512     5-25-87     2:27p
)LEPWP    DDR      1024     6-22-86     8:08p
INITIALD  DIR       512    12-13-86    11:54p
STANDARD  DOC      6144     6-22-86     8:08p
        12 File(s)        39936 bytes free
```

FIGURE 6.3
A Printed-Out Directory

Once the command is given (by typing FORMAT/S and then hitting the ENTER key), the red light in the drive comes on to indicate that the read/write head of the drive is searching the disk's directory to see if FORMAT.COM is there. Seconds later, a message appears on the screen telling Tom to insert a new disk into drive B and hit the ENTER key. For approximately a minute there will be a barely audible series of soft clicks as the 40 tracks on a normal 360K diskette are formatted. When the red light in drive A goes out, the formatting process is completed and the system files have been copied to the new disk. The newly formatted, bootable disk will have approximately 320K bytes of storage left.

Tom can now **copy** other program files to the disk. For example, he can make a working copy of his word processor so that he can put the disk in drive A and have the computer automatically boot the system and bring up his word-processing program when he turns the computer on. The word processing manual will specify how to do this.

All these procedures are part of a set of programs known as **system utilities.** Utilities programs make computer operations possible or easier. They are simple, single-task programs that allow a user to format disks, copy disks, copy and rename files, sort data, and list a disk's directory. Some MS-DOS utilities are described in more detail in the box.

Once the application program is installed on a working disk, Tom can use it. He will have to enter the name of the main program after the systems prompt to load and execute it. The application program will then take over and, together with the operating system, call up other programs to perform various functions either automatically or in response to Tom's requests. For example, if Tom wants to check a document for spelling errors, the main program calls in a separate program through the operating system to perform the spelling check.

When Tom has finished with the word processor, he exits the application program as specified in the manual. This process gives control back to the operating system and to the program COMMAND.COM, which again shows the system prompt.

Large Computer Operating Systems

Operating systems on large computers perform many of the same functions as operating systems on microcomputers. However, they are larger and more complex, for operating systems in large computers allow multitasking and multiprogramming, also known as concurrent processing.

Multiprogramming and Time-Sharing

A **multiprogramming** system differs from a single-user system in that it has the ability to handle many programs at one time, with all of them usually at different stages of execution. The main advantage of multiprogramming is that a user doesn't have to wait until the computer finishes running all other programs. Furthermore, a multiprogramming system can increase data *throughput* (throughput is the average number of jobs a computer can process in a given time period). That means computer resources are used much more effectively than they are in single-user systems.

In a typical multiprogramming system with dozens of programs running concurrently, the operating system switches from program to program quickly, executing small portions of each program at a time. Although each user may feel he or she has the undivided attention of the computer, that is not the case; only one program can control the system's CPU at a given moment.

The switch from one program to another is accomplished through **interrupts.** Whenever a major change happens in a program, such as the request for a new record from a data base stored on disk, the operating system issues an interrupt. This process temporarily suspends operation of the program, turns it over to another part of the computer, and moves on to the next program that is ready to resume program execution. Once the previous program has completed the task that caused the interrupt, the operating system will put that program back into the **queue,** or string of programs waiting to resume operation when the CPU is available. Multiprogramming is used primarily for batch programs such as payroll, accounts receivable, and inventory updating.

Time-sharing means that more than one user can access the system even while other programs are running. When a new user requires access to the system, an interrupt will suspend a currently running program and look after the request of the new user. All programs and users have a priority rating known to the operating system. A higher priority user can interrupt a lower priority user at any time.

Large computer operating systems support multiuser and multiprogramming functions.

Courtesy of Shell Oil Company

The multiuser environment allows a number of users to share a single mini or mainframe computer connected to individual terminals. Each terminal will look and act to the user like an independent computer, sharing the operating system and software of the host. Multiuser environments allow expensive equipment, such as printers, hard disks, and plotters, to be shared among many users. The operating system acknowledges when a new user signs on to the system through an ID number and a password. Then the CPU is made available to process data for each user. Although each user accesses the CPU for only a fraction of a second, the CPU's high processing speed makes it appear to individual users that the computer is theirs alone. As the number of users increases on the system, however, the **response time**—the time that elapses between a typed request to the computer and the computer's reply—may increase, making the system appear slow and cumbersome.

In a time-sharing system, the computer is under the control of the operating system, which allocates the time slice to individual users. The operating system may give priority to some users, who would then get access to the system more often, which improves service. For example, a

computer may be used for several tasks, including accounting, on-line inventory management, and credit checking. Since a credit check must be accomplished quickly, it is given priority over the other two tasks. Thus, an inventory update will be interrupted if a user wishes to check a customer's credit standing. Once the computer provides that information, it will return to the interrupted lower priority task.

Operating System Functions

Earlier in the chapter we discussed in general terms the various control and service functions of a computer operating system. These functions are also performed in large computer systems, but to support multiprogramming and multiusers, these operating systems must be considerably more complex. Let's take a closer look at the operation of large computer systems to see how they work.

Process Management   A **process** is a program—operating system or application—either ready to run or running. For the application program to do a job, and for the operating system to help it, some kind of communication between processes must take place. The major goal of process management is to make sure that processes don't get in the way of one another and that they do what they are supposed to do when they are supposed to do it.

In a multiprogramming system, programs can be in various states: running, ready, or waiting. **Running** simply means a process is in control of the computer; **ready** means a process will run as soon as it receives a so-called *wake-up call;* and **wait** means a process can't do any work until a certain event takes place. Many programs can be in the ready state, each waiting for the supervisor to give it a turn at the computer. At the same time, many can be in the wait state, needing a computation to finish or a called subroutine to complete or a record to be read, before they can continue.

Figure 6.4 is a flowchart demonstrating how and why processes move from state to state. There are three cooperating processes: the problem program, the supervisor, and the file manager. Let's trace them through the stages of a request to read in a record for the problem program. The problem program begins the sequence in control of the system. The supervisor and file manager are in a ready state, waiting to do any requested activity. The problem program finds it cannot continue processing until it receives a record, so it issues a wake-up call to the supervisor (see 1 in Figure 6.4) and moves from the running state to the wait state. The supervisor moves from ready to running, examines the information supplied with the call, and sends the information, along with the wake-up call (see 2 in the flowchart), to the file manager. Then the supervisor goes into a wait state, while the file manager moves from ready to running and fills the request.

After filling the request, the file manager issues a wake-up call to the supervisor (3) and returns to the ready state. The supervisor moves from wait to running (it does not go into a ready state, since it doesn't have to select itself as the next program to run), sees that the problem program's

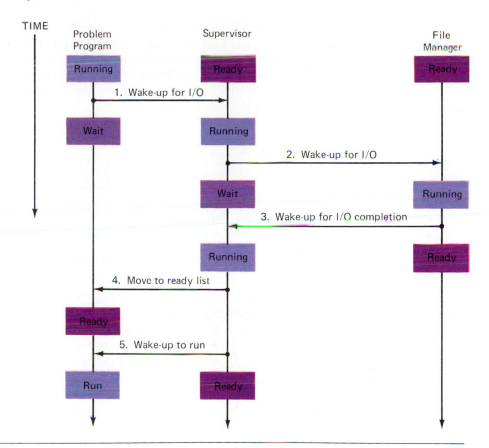

FIGURE 6.4
The Dynamics of Ready,
Running, and Wait States in
a Multiprogramming System

pending request is completed, and moves the problem program from the wait list to the ready list (4). When it is the turn of the problem program to have the CPU as a resource (that is, when it reaches the top of the ready list), the supervisor issues a wake-up call (5), and the problem program continues its activity.

In a single-user system, the problem program is always either running or waiting; there is no ready state. Once the supervisor has completed a request, the problem program moves immediately to the running state. The reason for the additional ready state in a multiprogramming system is that the supervisor has a criterion for selecting what programs will run next. It can ignore all programs in the wait state, since they are unable to continue; this capability increases throughput.

I/O Management   Some functions performed by large operating systems overlap the areas of file management and device management. These functions are accompanied by supporting hardware. The major goal of these operating system functions and the hardware is to maximize throughput. We loosely group these functions and the supporting hardware under the heading of input/output management.

Spooling   The term **spooling** means that peripheral (I/O) devices can do work while the CPU is doing work. Spooling allows the computer system to be used more effectively.

The importance of process management can be seen by looking at the classic operating-system problem caused by inadequate communication between processes: deadlock. **Deadlock** is defined as a situation in which two or more processes are blocking each other in such a way that no process can finish its designated activity. For example, two processes are running, and each of them needs two devices—printer 1 and disk 2—to complete its activities. Process A has control of printer 1 and requests disk 2 from the supervisor. Process B has disk 2 and requests printer 1. *Each process is in a wait state, and will remain there forever.* Neither process can relinquish its device until it gets the other device and completes its task. Situations where deadlock occurs are resolved by the operating system. This is achieved by process-to-process communication, so that processes competing for a resource can signal to each other either that the resource is busy or that it is free.

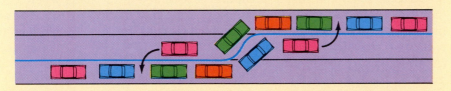

The Importance of Process Management

Traffic Deadlock
Imagine two adjoining left-turn lanes in the center of a road, where the traffic has formed in such a way that the lead car in each lane is blocked from turning. Neither lane can move because each is blocking the other.

Another situation illustrating the importance of process management is one in which multiple users are involved. In a multiprogramming environment no two users should be able to gain access to the same file concurrently unless they just want to read the file. If two users could simultaneously *change* a file, the following scenario might occur:

Tom opens a file.
Susan opens to the same file.
Tom reads the first record.
Susan reads the first record.
Tom changes the first record.
Susan changes the first record.

If Tom reads the record after Susan has changed it and Tom is using the same file concurrently, Tom will not be handling the most up-to-date data that includes Susan's changes. The same can happen to Susan.

Clearly no file should be allocated to a user while another user might be changing that file's contents. When a file is allocated, the operating system must make sure it is not allocated elsewhere at the *same* time, unless the users just want to read it.

Early computer systems often ran programs to create a specific output, such as a series of daily reports. A program read records from an input file, formatted them, and printed them. The speed of the whole system was limited to the printer speed; in other words, the system was I/O bound. In effect, the whole value of a computer—its ability to handle a lot of data quickly—was sacrificed, because it spent 10 percent of its time handling data and 90 percent of its time waiting for the printer to print a line.

In a multiprogramming system, this problem becomes critical, especially because many users are waiting for the resource. The first and simplest solution is to include in the operating system a program that writes

the reports to a high speed file (disk or tape) designed to look like a print file. As far as the operating system is concerned, it is writing to a printer, except that printing to disk is 1000 times faster than a mechanical printer. Thus, during heavy use, the system is not limited to a slow-speed device.

Then, during off-peak hours, a second program is started whose job is to dump the "printed" files from the high-speed device to the mechanical "real" printer. Note that this solution does not increase overall system speed, because printing is still limited to the speed of the printer. But it does increase the overall amount of work done and increases throughput during busy hours.

Multitasking   The drawback to spooling is that users have to wait—often a full day—to get the printed material they want. So a further refinement was invented. A small and simple computer is attached to the disks where the files are stored and prints the output at the same time the large central processor continues with its operations (see Figure 6.5). This simple computer is called a front-end processor, and its overall functions are referred to as front-end processing.

FIGURE 6.5
Multitasking System with Small Front-End Processor in Addition to Main CPU

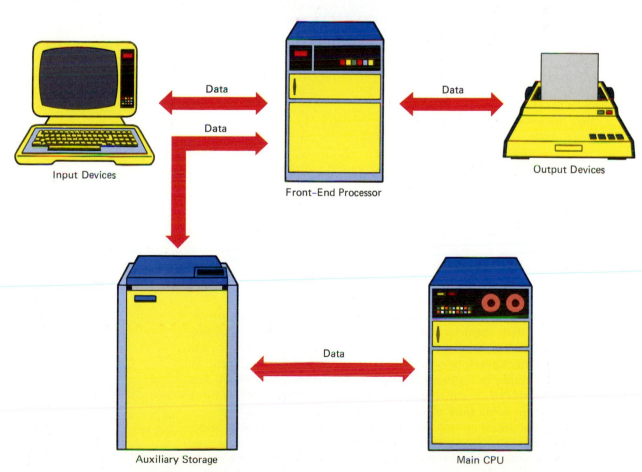

Input Devices

Data

Data

Front–End Processor

Data

Output Devices

Data

Auxiliary Storage

Main CPU

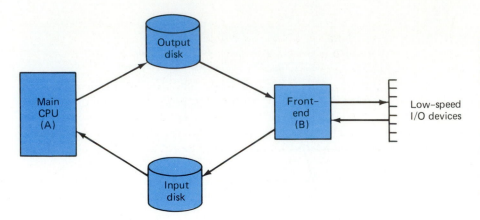

FIGURE 6.6

Processor A, the main CPU, manages programs, taking their input from the input disk and writing their output to the output disk.
Processor B, a simple computer, is a *front-end processor* that handles the transfer of files between the input and output disks and the low-speed devices.

As Figure 6.6 shows, this process can also be used to handle input from low-speed devices. This solution allows all of the low-speed I/O devices to work at their own speeds while the central processor keeps itself fully occupied handling problem programs.

This combination of activities in an operating system—the ability to handle related processes simultaneously by devoting separate processors to separate parts of a task—is known as **multitasking.** In some large systems, these output processors are called **channels.** They work concurrently with the main CPU, but they do not work totally independently. For a channel to operate, the supervisor must issue a channel command (such as START I/O) accompanied by the necessary information (such as memory location for input or output, device name, file name). The operating system must then not touch that area of memory until it receives a signal that the work is complete. Once again, communication between concurrent processes is necessary for successfully completing this operation.

Device Management   Both single-user and multiprogramming systems handle device management in much the same way. There may be more devices, and more kinds of devices, attached to a large system, but it is still the operating system's main job to distinguish among different types of devices and to know the characteristics of each one. The operating system must know where a device is (what channel it is attached to and what its address is on that channel), what kind of device is attached, and how long it takes to transfer data from that device (its **data transfer speed**). If a new device or new channel is attached, the operating system must be told all this information so it can talk to the device appropriately.

In order to increase throughput, multitasking is used extensively in large systems. We have seen how it works between a channel and a CPU, but Figure 6.7 carries the process one step further. We have linked a third processor, called a control unit, to the channel. A control unit is a processor that handles only multiple devices of the same type. Figure 6.7 illustrates a CPU with two channels. Channel A handles many low-speed devices and channel B handles two control units. One control unit handles tape drives, while the other handles disk drives. This configuration not only leaves the CPU free for managing the problem program, but it allows the channels to operate faster because all they need to do is transfer the data to and from

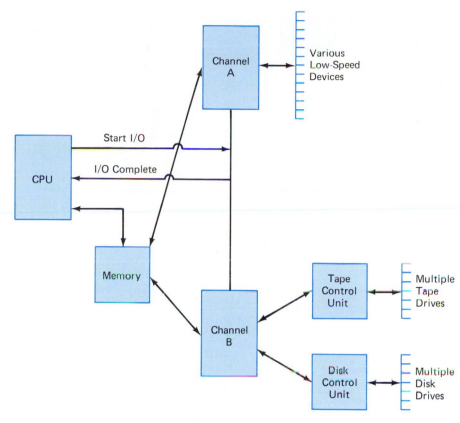

FIGURE 6.7
Multitasking and Device Management.

The control units manage multiple devices of the same type. The channel forwards the necessary information from the CPU, and the control units perform the read and write activities, while CPU and channels perform other activities. Note that the channels and the CPU access memory independently, which speeds up the data transfer process.

memory. Specific file hookups are handled either by the control units or by yet another processor that is built into the storage devices.

Memory Management   The final major concern of a multiprogramming system we will examine is the management of memory. Four major issues must be dealt with:

1. Handling multiple users
2. Maximizing throughput
3. Protecting users from one another
4. Dealing with programs that exceed the physical amount of available memory

Since the mid-1960s, operating systems have been written that tried to solve these issues. Fixed partitions, variable partitions, and virtual memory are three important solution schemes.

Fixed Partitions   Early multiprogramming systems tried to handle multiple users with a simple scheme for allocating memory: The system ran a fixed number of programs, and each user got a **fixed partition** for his or her program. Figure 6.8 shows how this scheme worked on a system with 250,000 bytes of memory, of which the first 50,000 were allocated to the operating system. With such a scheme, we can run four programs at a time,

FIGURE 6.8
Fixed Partition Memory Allocation

Memory Address

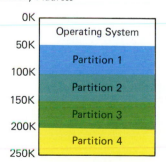

each running in its own partition. Since no user can be a so-called core hog, because no user can have more than 50,000 bytes of memory, throughput will be increased. Programs that are larger than the available memory can be run by using the same kind of overlay structure that we saw was used in single user systems. Finally, we can protect one user's partition from another's by letting no programs generate a program greater than 50,000. These are not difficult problems, and the scheme is certainly an improvement over the single-user system.

But the fixed-partition scheme has disadvantages. First, only 4 programs can run at a time, unless we decrease the partition size. If we do that—suppose we want to run 40 programs—each program can have only 5000 bytes of memory. However, the smaller (and more numerous) partitions increase the amount of work the operating system has to do to keep track of all the users and also increases the probability of overlays. Also, if we retain the partitions at 50,000 bytes, many small programs (which perhaps need only 5000 bytes to run) will use memory inefficiently, since 90 percent of their allocation will go unused.

Variable Partitions   The next type of operating system to be tried was based on the idea of **variable partitions.** It allocated memory by allowing a variable number of variable-sized partitions. For example, suppose we have the same 250,000 bytes of memory and run three programs of different sizes. Program A is 100,000 bytes long, B is 30,000 bytes long, and C is 20,000 bytes long. The programs are loaded in turn, and memory is allocated as indicated in Figure 6.9a. Now suppose program D, which needs 80,000 bytes of memory, requests that amount of space. It can't run because there is not enough memory available (only 50,000 bytes) for it. Even if program C finishes and uses less memory than was allocated to it, D still cannot run because the only remaining available portion is 70,000 bytes. If B finishes, a total of 80,000 bytes is available, but D still cannot run because the available memory is "fragmented" (Figure 6.9b).

Allocating memory on the basis of variable partitions overcomes some of the drawbacks of the fixed-partition scheme. Programs use only the amount of memory they need, and more users can have access to the system than in a fixed-partition scheme. Overall efficiency is thereby increased.

Virtual Memory   The **virtual memory** management scheme is presently the most common way of implementing memory management in large systems. To help you understand how this scheme works, here is a simple analogy.

Imagine a mailroom with 10 pigeonhole boxes, each of which has an address (Figure 6.10a). Clearly, only 10 people can have mail addressed to them, but suppose that 25 people want to have their own mailbox. This situation is similar to a program needing more address space than the system has memory. There are two simple solutions to the problem: We can add more mailboxes or we can implement a virtual address scheme. Since we can't afford more mailboxes, we will play with the addresses. Every mailbox will have a two-part alphanumeric address (a number and a letter). The first part will be a digit (0 to 9) and will indicate the physical location of the mailbox. The second part (the letter *A, B,* or *C*) will represent a logical address. We now have 30 logical addresses for 10 physical mailboxes (see

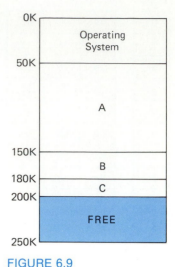

FIGURE 6.9
Variable Partition
(a) Initial allocation of partitions in a variable-sized memory management scheme.

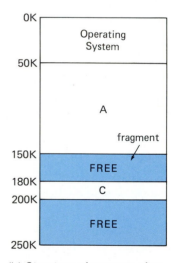

(b) Structure of memory after B finishes. Although there are 80,000 bytes of memory available, a program of that size can't run because the memory areas are noncontiguous, or "fragmented."

0
1
2
3
4
5
6
7
8
9

0A	0B	0C
1A	1B	1C
2A	2B	2C
3A	3B	3C
4A	4B	4C
5A	5B	5C
6A	6B	6C
7A	7B	7C
8A	8B	8C
9A	9B	9C

FIGURE 6.10

Virtual Address Scheme

(a) Ten physical mailboxes. (b) Thirty virtual mailboxes.

1	2	3	4	5
6	7	8	9	10
11	12	13	14	15
16	17	18	19	20

FIGURE 6.11

Virtual Memory Scheme

(a) 4000-byte memory mapped into 20 200-byte frames.

1	2	3	4	5
6	7	8	9	10
11	12	13	14	15
16	17	18	19	20
21	22	23	24	25
26	27	28	29	30
31	32	33	34	35
36	37	38	39	40

(b) 8000-byte program mapped into 40 200-byte pages.

Figure 6.10b). In effect, we have 30 mailboxes. We have created a more effective way to use our limited mailbox resource. There is, of course, a disadvantage: Every user must now sort through all the mail in one physical mailbox to find his or her own mail.

A virtual memory scheme follows a similar principle. It allows us to treat physical memory address space as if it were larger than it is (that is, we "virtually" have all the memory we want). Suppose we have an 8000-byte program and only 4000 bytes of memory to run it in. If we divide the 4000 bytes of memory into a series of 200-byte sections (these are called **frames**), we will have 20 frames (mailboxes) available to use (see Figure 6.11a).

Now let us divide our program on the same principle but call the 200-byte sections **pages** (Figure 6.11b). It is clear that if we implement a routine that translates the page number into a frame number, we can run the whole program in one single frame in memory simply by running it one page at a time. When all the instructions in page 25 are executed, the operating system can bring page 26 in—either to the frame that page 25 currently occupies or to a free frame elsewhere in memory—and continue execution. What the virtual memory system does, in effect, is create many small partitions and divide programs into very small portions.

A well-designed virtual memory system is good for most multiprogramming applications. The only ones that suffer are those that are "time critical" and need instantaneous response from the computer, for they very often must wait for pages to be brought in, in order to continue their activity. In general, a virtual memory management scheme is invisible to the application program. As in all multiprogramming systems, the management scheme tends to slow down what a single user is trying to do in order to increase overall use of the resource.

Utility Programs for Larger Computer Systems

Many of the utility programs for microcomputers are duplicated for large computer systems. But there are some that are required by large systems on a regular basis while executing programs and processing data. For example, a **sort** program is used to sort data into a sequence for updating files. A **merge** utility program then merges the sorted transaction files into an updated master file. Other utility programs are called by main programs to perform specialized mathematical calculations such as calculating square roots.

File handling utilities convert files from one form to another, such as from disk to tape or to another disk, or from disk to printer. A **spooling** program will transfer data from disk to printer while the CPU is occupied with the processing of other data.

A frequently used utility program on large computer system is a **backup** program. While microcomputer users often neglect this function, in large systems backing up data is a regular function carried out many times each day. Master files after processing must be backed up to other disks, or more often to tape, for storage at places away from the computer center.

Choosing to buy into IBM's Personal System/2 line is not merely a decision of hardware and software. It is a choice to follow IBM's connectivity philosophy for the future. IBM's announcements may force MIS managers to rethink the direction computing will take in their organizations during the next 20 years.

IBM's OS/2 environment introduced for its PS/2 line is part of a broader IBM software scenario that includes applications on hosts and mid-range systems and IBM System Application Architecture. OS/2 was designed as the workstation-level component of this scheme, with IBM's data base management, communications and end-user interface features reflected in offerings throughout the firm's product line. . . .

IBM's PS/2 line is not just a personal computer, and OS/2 is not just a personal computer operating system. Granted, these products provide multitasking, Intel Corp. 80286 protected mode, windows, high-resolution graphics and numerous other PC features, but IBM designed this principal PC product line to form an integral part of the firm's broader product scenario.

The extent to which the OS/2 operating environment is integrated into the full IBM scenario is striking. In particular, OS/2 Extended Edition, as a set of bundled capabilities, does not suppose a user may want to pick and choose his features; for the extra $470, you get connectivity to virtually the entire IBM product line, a commitment to an SQL-based relational data base management system (DMBS) and the core of an end-user interface that will ultimately provide transparent access to every facility of every system in an IBM network. It is rather like a workstation integration Solutionpac, a comprehensive set of "load-and-go" features.

IBM obviously put a lot of planning into its latest move, whose origins can be traced to 1983, when IBM started putting together a global software infrastructure designed to form the core of its large end-user solutions well into the 21st century. Some of these capabilities have been implemented, some are due soon and some are still in IBM programming laboratories.

These capabilities include a complex of relational DMBS reflected in OS/2 Extended Edition's Database Manager; a multiformat communications environment reflected in OS/2 Extended Edition's Communications Manager; and a common end-user interface implemented in OS/2 under its Presentation Manager component. The whole of these capabilities will ultimately serve as the vehicle through which a user may access the full range of facilities available on all IBM systems in an IBM complex network.

The Database Manager is a crucial component in OS/2 because mechanisms have to be established to manage, manipulate and store the large data volumes that will be generated in an IBM complex network. . . .

In April, the finishing touches were put to the workstation level of IBM's grand plan with the announcement of OS/2 Extended Edition, which includes a built-in SQL data management function and ECF support. The result is the creation of a multilevel relational DBMS structure with system-transparent user access, support for most key PC software environments and the ability to file and access SQL-format data anywhere within an IBM complex network. . . .

IBM's communications environments have become complex in recent years as the company inserted new systems and applications into an increasingly heterogenous Systems Network Architecture (SNA) line-up . . . IBM built a spider's web of connectivity across diverse and often incompatible systems.

The problem of implementing these various communications features has been quite impressively resolved by rolling almost everything into the Communications Manager component of the OS/2 Extended Edition. . . .

OS/2: Have We Seen the Future?

The end-user interface in OS/2 is based on Microsoft Windows. The interface is implemented in OS/2 Standard Edition as the Presentation Manager, with baseline windowing, pointing device and all-points-addressable graphics. . . .

By now, we are getting close to the Big Blue concept of the Compound Electronic Document (CED). This futuristic concept enables end users to create, edit, store, communicate, receive and play back fully integrated documents incorporating data, text, graphics, image, voice and noncoded or scratch-mark information. As presented by IBM, CED manipulation would include routine data, text and graphics components with some new twists.

The first component of CED is image processing in the form of scanner-inputted material. This material could be expected to consist principally of paper documents that have been entered into an IBM data base and then called up by the workstation user to incorporate a copy of one or more images into a compound document.

The second component is scratch-mark data manipulation. This element allows the possibility of being able to electronically sign a document with a light pen or comparable pointing device, thereby removing the necessity for a separate hard copy of a document in applications in which a personal signature is required.

Thirdly, CED would include voice in the form of a voice-over to a document that could be played back by a recipient as he reviewed the document . . . The CED concept will get closer to becoming a reality with IBM announcements later this year, although it will probably be a few years before CED is feasible. Certainly, the concept will blossom during the life cycle of the PS/2—that is what the PS/2's 3363 internal optical drive is for. The 3363 built into the PS/2 will provide a means for storing and accessing compact electronic documents.

All the talk about integration brings us inevitably to System Application Architecture (SAA), IBM's global scheme for system integration. IBM describes . . . SAA as consisting of four main elements:

- **Common User Access** to the full range of IBM systems via a common menu-based end-user interface.

- **Common Programming Interface** to support Cobol, Fortran, C, a Cross System Product-based application generator, a Rexx-based procedure language, an SQL-based data base interface, a Query Management Facility-based query interface, a GDDM-based presentation interface and an ISPF-based dialogue interface.

- **Common Communications Support** to include 3270 Data Stream, Intelligent Printer Data Stream, Document Interchange Architecture/Document Content Architecture, Systems Network Architecture Distributed Services, Netview, LU6.2, Low-Entry Networking, X.25, Synchronous Data Link Control and the Token-Ring.

- **A set of common applications** based on the above and initially focusing on VM-based office software.

The principle is simple: IBM wants to create a common user environment in which access to systems for business applications and programming can be performed regardless of the actual IBM hardware and software that the user is utilizing.

Behind the interface, a mass of interlinked software applications written to SAA standards handles all of the jobs generated at the interface and looks after connectivity between the various IBM environments. Probably the best analogy for IBM's setup is of an intricate Swiss clock. The clock's machinery consists of a mass of whirring cogs, interlocking wheels, clanking gears and

swinging pendulums. However, all the observer sees is the clock face, which gives him what he needs—the time.

Source: Excerpted from "OS/2: Have we seen the future?" by Brian Jeffery, *Computerworld*, July 8, 1987, pp. 25–6.

Summary and Key Terms

1. **Operating system software** provides a series of programs that manage the hardware and improve the use and performance of a computer system. An **operating system** is a collection of programs that allows a computer to supervise its own internal operations.

2. With **single-tasking** operating systems, only one task can be performed at a time. **Multitasking operating systems** share the CPU among programs and users. Most microcomputer operating systems are single tasking.

3. A microcomputer operating system has **control programs** and **service programs,** both of which are controlled by **supervisor programs.** The basic functions include **input/output management, program execution,** and **memory management.**

4. Important microcomputer operating systems include AppleDOS/ProDOS, MS–DOS/PC–DOS, UNIX, and Macintosh's mouse-driven system.

5. **System utilities** are simple, single-task programs that make computer operations easier or possible.

6. Large computer operating systems perform many of the same functions as microcomputer operating systems. They are more complex, allowing **multiprogramming,** or the handling of many programs at different stages of execution at the same time; **interrupts** temporarily suspend one program to execute another. Multiprogramming is used mostly for batch processing applications like payroll, accounts receivable, and inventory updates.

7. **Time-sharing** permits more than one user to access a system at the same time. The **multiuser environment** allows a number of users to share a single mini or mainframe connected to individual terminals.

8. **Operating system functions** for large computers include **process management, input/output management,** and **memory management. Spooling** is the term used when peripheral devices can do work while the CPU is working on some processing task. **Multitasking** uses one or more small computers to perform partial tasks, such as printing, while the main CPU performs processing tasks.

9. **Large computer memory management** uses a **fixed-partition** scheme, a **variable-partition** scheme, or a **virtual memory** scheme. **Virtual memory** is the most common scheme. It allows a computer to treat memory address space as if it were larger than it is, and all but time-sensitive multiprogramming applications can use it successfully.

Review Questions

Fill-in

1. _____ _____ software makes it possible for the application software being used to run on the computer hardware.

2. Operating system programs which perform tasks such as data input/output, program scheduling, and job management are called _____ programs.

3. The language used to run specific programs is called _____ _____ language.

4. The _____ manager can link printers, disk drives, and other devices to the computer.

5. Allocating sufficient memory to application programs is the job of the _____ manager.

6. A program written in a procedural language is translated into machine language by a _____.

7. System _____ are programs that handle computer operations such as formatting disks, copying files, and listing a disk's directory.

8. A _____ system can handle the concurrent processing of multiple programs.

9. When the operating system wants to switch from executing one program to running another, this is accomplished by issuing an _____.

10. In a multi-user operating system environment, the _____ manager manages communications among the various processes.

Matching I (Microcomputer Operating Systems)

Match the following terms with their definitions:

_____ 1. User-friendly operating system which uses a mouse to invoke commands

_____ 2. An operating system with time-sharing and multi-user capabilities

_____ 3. Standard operating system for IBM microcomputers

_____ 4. Operating system component which keeps track of hardware devices such as disk drives and printers

_____ 5. Operating system component which allocates RAM to various application programs

_____ 6. Operating system component which controls the entire operating system

_____ 7. Operating system component which loads the rest of the operating system into main memory

a. memory component
b. boot loader
c. input/output component
d. PC-DOS
e. executive component
f. Macintosh operating system
g. UNIX
h. Apple DOS
i. file component

Matching II (Large Computer Systems)

Match the following terms with their definitions:

_____ 1. A processor that makes it possible to handle input/output functions, such

a. time-sharing
b. virtual memory

as printing output, at the same time the CPU is continuing its processing operations

_____ 2. A processor that handles multiple devices of the same type (e.g., tape drives)

_____ 3. A program that will transfer data from a disk to a printer while the CPU is busy with the processing of other data

_____ 4. The ability to handle related processes simultaneously by devoting separate processors to separate parts of a task

_____ 5. The ability to process multiple programs concurrently

_____ 6. Allows us to treat physical memory address space as if it were larger than it really is

_____ 7. Makes it possible for more than one user to have access to a computer system and its resources at the same time

c. multiprogramming
d. control unit
e. channel
f. multitasking
g. spooling
h. multiprocessing
i. supervisor

Discussion Questions

1. Explain the comment that the operating system is the interface between the user, the application program, and the hardware.

2. What are the major functions of a microcomputer operating system?

3. Explain how the computer system manages its input/output operations so that the CPU is kept busy processing programs and so that maximum throughput is achieved. In your explanation, describe the functions of channel programs, control units, and spooling.

4. Describe how virtual memory makes it seem like there is unlimited available storage space for programs and data being processed by the computer system.

Thank you for your recent interest in WordPerfect Corporation's software solutions.

WordPerfect Corporation has expanded its popular line of software to include more than just the most distinguished and best selling word processor in the world.

We now bring you a completely compatible and full featured spreadsheet program, MathPlan. If you already know WordPerfect, many of the keystrokes are the same. This will help you cut way down on costly training and flatten the learning curve for your employees.

The newest celebrity in our ongoing development of fine software in the DG world is WordPerfect Library. It incudes electronic mail, phone messenger, calendar, and scheduler all laced together under the intelligence of the shell program. Having made its debut only a few months ago, Library has dazzled many government agencies and major corporations with its 32bit assembly performance, visual appearance, its interrupt and information exchange capabilities via the clipboard. All this, plus keystroke compatibility integrates WordPerfect, MathPlan or other Data General AOS/VS software applications that developers can and have easily prepared to-d

CORP_DG_LTR.GENE   Doc 1 Pg 1 Ln 31 Pos 52

Word Processing and Application Software

Chapter Objectives

After studying this chapter you should be able to

1. Understand the difference between systems software and application software.

2. Understand the value of word processing software and identify important features available in word processing packages.

Paula Sowers directs the Admissions Office at Carr College, a small midwestern school. Using an IBM PC, Paula maintains a computer record of every student who applies to Carr. She uses the WordPerfect word processing program to write letters to applicants about admission requirements, financial aid, and other enrollment matters, as well as for the reports and other written documents connected with running the Admissions Office. Paula is not a trained typist, but her hunt-and-peck method works very well on the computer, where errors are easy to correct. Since replacing her typewriter with a computer two years ago, Paula produces letters, memos, and reports with greater speed and accuracy. And because all documents are stored in computer files, papers are never mislaid or misfiled.

Today, Paula plans to write up a draft of a new admissions policy. She switches on the IBM PC and inserts the WordPerfect system disk in drive A and a data disk in drive B. She opens a new file and jots down some notes and ideas first. Once she has a rough outline, she can begin to expand ideas into paragraphs. Paula's main concern at this point is to put all the necessary information down. She knows that adding and deleting information, and even moving words, sentences, or paragraphs around is easy. Soon she has a rough draft to print out for the next meeting to discuss the new policy. Paula saves her work onto a floppy disk so she'll be able to retrieve and edit it later.

After the meeting, she returns to work on the proposal, editing text, adding and deleting information, and incorporating ideas and suggestions she and the others discussed. When this draft is revised, Paula formats the text so it looks good on the page. She makes several printouts to circulate to the others on the committee.

In Chapter 6 you learned about **systems software,** programs that run such aspects of computer systems as language translation, input/output management, program management, and memory management. We said that systems software allows people who know little or nothing about the

workings of computer systems to use those systems successfully. Application software fulfills that same purpose—allowing computers to be used successfully by people who are not computer programmers. The difference is that application software is sets of programs designed to let computer users accomplish specific tasks such as writing and formatting a report, analyzing a budget proposal, linking into an on-line data base, or turning data into graphic forms. Systems software runs the parts of a computer system so it can provide a user with data converted to information. Application software turns the running computer system to the production of useful work.

Application Software

Partly because of the popularity of microcomputers, application software development is one of the busiest fronts of the computer revolution. Software companies have turned out commercially available packages to help computer users do everything from balancing a checkbook to simulating underground geology to analyzing an automobile engine's performance. Each day, new packages are introduced for entirely new applications. (We use the words *packages* and *programs* interchangeably in discussing application software.)

Business application software is created for mainframes, minis, and microcomputers. The larger the computer and computer system, the more likely it is that the software will be custom-designed (often by in-house programmers) to respond to the specific needs and characteristics of the business.

Some popular business application areas are bookkeeping, budgeting, human resource management, inventory control, payroll, cash flow management, and profit and loss analysis. When custom-designed software is inappropriate, unnecessary, or unavailable, general software packages are usually available that will satisfy the needs of the business. The majority of these packages are for microcomputers, and they include the following types:

- Spreadsheets
- Word processing
- Graphics
- Desktop publishing
- Data base management
- Data communications

This software is often referred to as **personal productivity software** because it helps the user improve productivity by harnessing the power of the microcomputer for everyday business applications. Using this software allows individuals access to information and computing power once available only to computer professionals. It results in better information, better

analysis of information, better presentation of information, and better communication.

Many microcomputer users prefer **integrated packages** (packages that combine several applications) to **stand-alone packages** (individual applications). Appleworks is the most popular integrated package for the Apple II. It includes a word processor, spreadsheet, and data base manager. Obvious advantages of such packages are that users need learn only one set of commands and that it is easier to integrate the results. An integrated package, for example, can produce a report that incorporates spreadsheet, graphics, data base, and word processing applications, something that would be very difficult to accomplish using stand-alone packages.

Integrated packages have a significant disadvantage, however. They rarely perform each of their applications as well as stand-alones, and there is a great deal of debate over whether future microcomputer users will be using them or a collection of more powerful stand-alones.

In the next few chapters, you will see how personal productivity software and microcomputers combine to accomplish many kinds of projects more quickly and easily—and less expensively—than equivalent work can be done "by hand." Personal productivity software replaces pens and pencils, typewriters, copying machines, calculators, drawing boards, T-squares, and many other kinds of equipment, as you will see from the first application we discuss, word processing.

Word Processing

Word processing packages may be the most common application software in use today. The reasons word processing is so popular are simple:

- Word processing saves work.
- Word processing saves time.
- Word processing saves money.

Where once a business had three workers using three typewriters, today a microcomputer and a word processing package lets one person do the work of three to produce documents faster. The specific advantages of word processing are

- Easy correction of errors
- Availability of varied formats
- Automatic or shortcut performance of many tasks, such as moving, deleting, copying, searching, and replacing

A few writing tasks are quicker to do by hand or with a typewriter. To address an envelope or two, for example, or to write a short memo that doesn't have to be copied and kept, writing or typing is quicker than starting the computer, loading the word processing program, entering the text, and printing the work out. But for most tasks involving the production

of text, word processing saves time and work, and in a business environment, those savings mean saving money as well.

Let's look first at three elements important to word processing: the screen, the cursor, and the keyboard.

The Screen

The computer screen is, in effect, the writing area; entered text shows up on it. (**Text** refers to the work you type into computer memory. Text may include numbers and symbols as well as words.) Word processing programs may also show a **format line** on the screen, giving such details as tab stops and the page width in inches or characters. Some word processing programs show frequently used commands on the screen. WordStar, for example, displays several commands, unless they are deliberately turned off. WordPerfect, on the other hand, ordinarily shows nothing on the screen but the text that is being entered.

The Cursor

The **cursor** is either a one-character-wide flashing square or rectangle or a flashing vertical line that looks like the numeral 1. Always present on the screen, the cursor indicates where the next character typed will appear or where a special function will begin or end. The cursor moves one character forward with each character typed. It can also be moved around the screen for editing and other text functions. You might, for instance, want to move a line, delete a word, or copy a paragraph. With many word processing programs, the first step is to select the operation and the second is to highlight the text involved in that operation by moving the cursor from its first character to its last.

The Same Document Being Prepared on WordPerfect, *right*, and Microsoft Word, *left*

The Keyboard

Most computer keyboards resemble the traditional typewriter keyboard, with its three rows of letters and fourth row of numbers and symbols. Although a more efficient arrangement of keys has been designed, the Dvorak keyboard, convention seems to favor the standard, so-called QWERTY, layout. These keys, however they are arranged on the keyboard, produce the letters, numbers, and symbols—called characters—of the text input with a word processing program.

Function Keys   Computer keyboards have keys that do not produce characters at all. Called **function keys,** these keys, used singly or in combinations, perform special tasks like saving, cutting, or restoring text. One set of function keys is labeled F1 through F10 (or on newer IBM keyboards, F12). The specific function each F key performs differs among word processing programs. For example, F10 in WordPerfect is used to save work by recording it on a floppy disk, but F10 in WordStar moves the cursor to the beginning of the file in use.

The SHIFT key is responsible for uppercase letters, as it is on a typewriter. But in conjunction with keys other than the character keys, SHIFT is a function key. CTRL (control) and ALT are function keys as well. These three keys are used in combination with other keys to extend the function range of a word processing program. WordPerfect's function keys, for example, control more than 80 special tasks within the word processing program.

Function keys exemplify the personal productivity aspect of word processing software. They essentially initiate miniprograms that perform complex operations on text with, at most, a few keystrokes. For example, in one word processing program, moving a word, sentence, paragraph, or more requires six keystrokes: hitting F9, highlighting the text to be moved, hitting the RETURN key, moving the cursor to the new position for the text, hitting F10, and hitting the RETURN key. The equivalent operation with a typewriter requires at least some, and perhaps extensive, retyping, perhaps taking thousands of keystrokes to redo work already done once.

Return Key   The return key has two purposes. First, it acts to enter commands. Second, it ends a line in a so-called hard carriage break (in contrast to the soft carriage return that the computer makes when it automatically moves a word to the start of a new line).

Arrow Keys and the Numeric Keypad   The four arrow keys on the right side of the keyboard control the movement of the cursor. With the PAGE UP and PAGE DOWN keys, and in combination with function keys, it is easy to move the cursor quickly by the character, the word, the line, or the screen (or page) throughout a document. Depending on the specific type of computer, arrow keys may appear twice, once in a cluster of keys whose only function is to move the cursor and again in a **numeric keypad** that itself may be involved in special operations of a word processing program. In some programs, the numeric keypad has a role in automatically numbering the pages of a document and in moving around the document by specific page number.

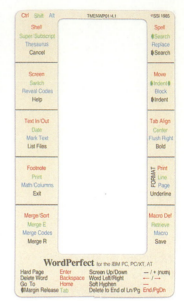

The WordPerfect Keyboard Template, *top,* and the Onscreen Template, *bottom*

Menus and Commands

Word processing programs are either menu driven or command driven. In a **menu-driven program,** such as Microsoft's Word, word "menus" listing various operations or functions are displayed on the screen. A menu is **selected** by highlighting it with the cursor and then hitting the RETURN key. Most word processing programs have a main menu that lists initial choices for creating, naming, opening, editing, saving, and deleting documents as well as exiting the program to return to DOS. Each main menu, in turn, leads to a submenu of choices in the selected category. When the PRINT menu is selected, for example, a submenu appears on the screen from which choices can be made about printing details—number of copies, specific pages to be printed, quality of finished copies, and so on.

WordStar 2000's Opening Menu

Courtesy of Micropro International Corp.

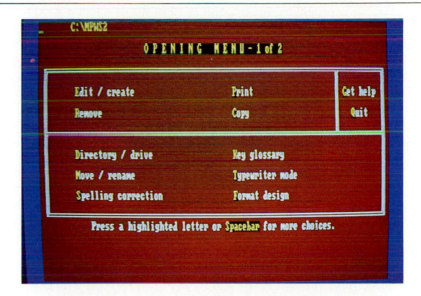

Microsoft Word Screen with Menu at Bottom

```
        A:NEW    PAGE 1 LINE 1 COL 01              INSERT ON
                     < < <    M A I N   M E N U    > > >
      --Cursor Movement--    ! -Delete- !  -Miscellaneous-  !  -Other  Menus-
   ^S char left ^D char right !^G  char  ! ^I Tab   ^B Reform ! (from Main only)
   ^A word left ^F word right !DEL chr lf! ^V INSERT ON/OFF   !^J Help  ^K Block
   ^E line  up  ^X line down  !^T word rt!^L Find/Replce again!^Q Quick ^P Print
      --Scrolling--          !^Y  line  !RETURN End paragraph!^O Onscreen
   ^Z line up   ^W line down  !          ! ^N Insert a RETURN !
   ^C screen up ^R screen down!          ! ^U Stop a command  !
   L-----!-----!-----!-----!-----!-----!-----!-----!-----!-----!--------R
```

WordStar Main Menu

In a **command-driven program,** specific keys must be pressed to carry out commands. In WordStar, a command-driven program, pressing D opens a document, Y deletes a file, and CTRL KX saves the file and exits the program.

Default Settings

All word processing programs are designed with **default settings,** basic format assumptions built into the program that, in effect, create a standard format. For example, software designers who assume that most people using a word processing program want to produce single-spaced documents with a 1-inch left margin and 1-½-inch right margin build these instructions in. These specifications can, of course, be changed, but having a standard format already established saves time in producing any documents for which the standard is appropriate.

Word Wrap and Scrolling

Two other time-saving functions in word processing programs are word wrap and scrolling. All word processing programs automatically wrap text around to the next line. This feature is called **word wrap,** and it automatically begins a new line when the width limit of the preceding line is reached. **Scrolling** is an automatic function that raises the text being entered as it gradually fills the screen. The time- and labor-saving feature implicit in scrolling is that someone using a word processing program is not taking out one sheet of paper and inserting a new one every time a typed

page is filled. With word processing programs, the "new page" aspect doesn't occur until a document is printed out, and then the function is handled automatically, by the hardware, on the basis of a few keystrokes.

Operations on Text

If you compare typing out a page of text on a typewriter to typing that same page with a word processing program, word processing may not seem to offer remarkable advantages. Indeed, for accurate typists who say what they intend the first time, word processing's ease in performing text operations may not be an important feature. But most people find it difficult to produce flawless documents in a single draft. Word processing makes it easy both to correct errors and to revise text.

In typed documents, leaving something out calls for retyping (or handwriting insertions that make the page look amateurish). A word processing program makes **insertions** very easy. You simply position the cursor where you want to insert text. Most programs then require you to press the INSERT key to enter the "insert" mode. Then you type the insertion. All text to the right moves over and down to accommodate the insertion. The insertion and the text after the insertion are reformatted to conform to the dimensions of the document.

Deletions are equally easy. They can be accomplished with the backspace key, which deletes characters to the left of the cursor. They can be accomplished as well by the DELETE key, which deletes characters at the cursor and then from the right. Most word processing programs also have a delete function (often called "cut") that allows the removal of a word, a line, or an entire block of text. In many programs, cut material is temporarily stored in RAM and can thus be recalled with another command. These so-called **cut-and-paste commands** make it easy to move text within a document and, depending on the program, even between files.

The **typeover** (or overtype) mode is the reverse of the insert mode. It is invoked by pressing the INSERT key. When the typeover mode is in effect, you can position the cursor at a character and then type. Instead of creating an insertion, what you type will replace what was there, character by character.

Useful as these basic insert, delete, and move operations are, word processing programs perform more sophisticated operations that can save repetitive work between documents as well as within a given document. **Search and replace** is one such command. Say that you have drafted a paper on your word processor and think you may have used the word *original* too much. You can issue a search command for *original,* and the program will proceed through the entire document, highlighting or marking in some way every occurrence. Perhaps you haven't really used *original* too often, but you decide that *initial* is a more exact word. Not only can you command the program to seach for each *original,* you can instruct it to replace every occurrence of *original* with *initial.*

Think how useful search and replace might be for preparing a standard document in which a little material might change but most of the text would not. A standard contract, for example, might be input to a word

processing program just once. After copying the original document, the search and replace features could be utilized to change specific provisions quickly and easily.

Special Features

The features we have discussed so far are common to all word processing programs. In this section we will look briefly at several special features. Not all word processing programs have these features, and some of the features might not be useful for every word processing application. If you ever have to buy a word processing package, first assess exactly what you want to do with word processing, and then make sure the package you select has the features you want.

Spelling Checkers, Thesauruses, Style Programs One widely useful feature is a spelling checker. Many programs have a dictionary that can check spelling throughout a document. After a document is created, a command invokes the dictionary that resides in the computer's memory. Any words found in the document but not found in the dictionary are highlighted. Many spelling checkers offer substitute words. For example, if the spelling *bous* is encountered, a spelling checker might offer *house* and *hours* as substitutes.

Spelling checkers stop at any word not contained in the program's dictionary. Therefore, proper names, technical words, specialized jargon, and foreign terms may be noted as errors by a spelling checker. Most spelling checkers query whether a word at which they stop should be added to the dictionary. One word of caution: Spelling checkers can be helpful, but they do not identify omitted words or misspellings that are correct spellings of other words. For example, if *hose* is typed for *house*, a spelling

WordPerfect's Spelling Check Finds *kosts*

WordPerfect's Thesaurus Entry for the Word *cost*

checker will not recognize *hose* as an error because it is a word in the spelling checker's dictionary.

Another word-level feature of some word processing packages is a thesaurus. If you want a synonym, you highlight the word in your text, and the thesaurus provides a list of words similar in meaning. If you choose an alternative from the thesaurus list, the program automatically replaces the highlighted word with the new one.

Style programs can provide editorial help by pointing out vague or overused words, slang, and passive verbs. Style programs cannot transform a poorly written document into a well-written one, but they can draw attention to some of the more flagrant stylistic pitfalls.

The value of features like style programs, thesauruses, and spelling checkers is that accessing them through a word processing program is much quicker than searching books for help. Still, not every word can have a synonym in a word processing program's thesaurus, and no spelling checker will point out *hose* as an error for *house*. Features that let you work more efficiently within a program or that let you tailor a program to your specific needs are the real timesavers. Two of these are windows and macros.

Windows Windows are a feature of some of the more advanced word processing programs. Programs that have the window feature can split the screen in two (or even three) parts, or **windows.** Each window shows a different part of a document or parts of separate documents. If you can create windows, you can compare material from different places. You might want to find out how you phrased or formatted something or whether you included an important note. Windows save you the task of scrolling back and forth to find the text you want to compare. With windows between documents, you can see both documents at once rather than having to close one, open another, and then reopen the first, remembering all the while what you saw. When you issue the command to create a window, you are asked to specify what you want to see. Both windows are *dynamic.* That means you can edit the text in both of them.

Macros **Macros** let the user of a word processing program create the equivalent of individualized function keys. They allow you to execute a specified series of commands just by pressing one or two keys. For instance, you might want to create a macro that will invoke a particular format automatically. Say that you have to prepare a weekly report that has a standard format and a standard distribution list, although the actual information in it changes each week. You can create a macro file containing all the standardized information so that whenever you call up that macro —with a keystroke you designate—the standardized parts of the report will be created automatically. Instead of the series of commands and keystrokes and formatting procedures the word processing program requires to invoke these actions, much of the report is already done as soon as you open the macro file.

Other widely used special features include programs to compile tables of contents and indexes, to create and place documentation notes, and to insert superscripts and subscripts. In fact, no matter how complex and unusual a special feature you can think of, someone has probably created a word processing program that performs it.

Using the Windowing
Feature on WordPerfect, *top,*
and Microsoft Word, *center*
& *bottom*

Format Features

Word processing programs make it easy to handle the formatting aspects of producing text documents. **Formatting** means giving shape and style to text by controlling the way it looks on the page. Formatting encompasses such considerations as margins, headers, footers, line spacing, page breaks, page numbering, centering, and other special alignments. In many word processing programs, decisions you make about these items will show up on the screen as you work through a document.

Page Layout

On a typewriter, you set margins before you start to type. With a word processing program, you can set margins before, during, or after typing the text. Some programs make margin choices menu-driven; others have you set up a format line that is applied throughout a document. Most programs allow you to set margins for individual paragraphs as well as for an entire document, so that if you want to, you can indent material from either or both sides.

You can also select various line spacings, often in ½-line increments. Most programs let you vary the spacing within a document, so that if you want to have the body of a paper double-spaced to one measure and the long quotations single-spaced and indented on both sides, you can.

Word processing programs make special alignments easy. You can center text or align all lines evenly (*justify* them) at the left margin or at the right margin. You can set up columns aligned on decimal points. Like other special functions, such choices are selected either with function keys or from menus, and then they are performed automatically.

Page Breaks and Page Numbering

Word processing programs can create page breaks automatically and can place descriptive words and/or page numbers on each page. (Standard lines at the top or bottom of a page are called, respectively, headers or footers.)

Printing

Once a document is complete, its page and spacing formats established, and its text edited, it should be **saved,** or moved from memory to a floppy disk. It can also be printed out. Some format characteristics are invoked only when a document is printed out. These include such things as print quality, number of copies, and style and size of the type in which the document is printed.

Compatibility between a specific word processing program and a specific brand and model of printer is, therefore, an important matter. A printer must be able to execute the special functions a program contains. For example, some word processing programs allow selection of **fonts,** type in a variety of designs and sizes, but not all printers can produce these variations. The information that comes in a word processing package (the program **documentation**) names compatible models of printers.

In most word processing programs, printing is menu-driven. Choices include number of copies wanted; feed commands for printing on computer paper or on single, hand-fed sheets; fonts; print quality (some printers

```
1═[·········1·········2·········3·········4·········5·········6·········7·]···
  1   2P Paragraph 2                          Text paragraph
          Courier (modern a) 12. Flush left.
  2   H1 Paragraph 3                          First level head
          Helvetica (modern i) 12 Bold. Flush left, space before 24 pt, space
          after 12 pt.
  3   1P Paragraph 1                          First paragraph
          Times-Roman (roman i) 12. Justified.
```

```
COMMAND: Copy Delete Exit Format Help
         Insert Name Print Transfer Undo
Edit style sheet or choose Exit to see document
GALLERY  {Paragraph 1 }                          Microsoft Word: NORMAL.STY
```

```
1═[·········1·········2·········3·········4·········5·········6·········7·]···
  MANAGEMENT·INFORMATION·SYSTEMS¶
  →    Robert·McDowell,·vice-president·of·production·and·operations·for·
  Consolidated·Foods,·is·responsible·for·recommending·target·inventory·
  levels·for·each·of·the·products·that·Consolidated·Foods·manufactures·and·
  distributes·to·its·branch·warehouses.··The·firm·manufactures·over·200·
  lines·of·food·products·in·four·plants·and·transports·finished·goods·to·
  its·eight·regional·warehouses.¶
  →    The·"right"·inventories·of·food·products·need·to·be·distributed·to·
  the·various·branch·warehouses·in·order·to·minimize·excess·inventories·
  and·transportation·costs.··For·example,·if·large·inventories·of·Uncle·
  Carl's·Taco·Sauce·are·shipped·to·the·southeastern·branch·warehouse·and·
  much·of·the·demand·for·this·product·is·in·the·midwest,·inventory·will·
  have·to·be·transported·to·midwestern·stores·at·considerably·greater·
  transportation·expense·than·would·be·involved·if·the·midwestern·branch·
  warehouse·had·sufficient·stock·of·taco·sauce·to·accommodate·demand·in·
  the·midwest.¶
  →    Currently,·McDowell·receives·a·monthly·report·listing·inventory·
```

```
FORMAT CHARACTER bold: Yes No        italic: Yes(No)        underline: Yes(No)
        strikethrough: Yes(No)       uppercase: Yes(No)     small caps: Yes(No)
        double underline: Yes(No)    position:(Normal)Superscript Subscript
        font name: Courier           font size: 12          hidden: Yes(No)
Select option
Page 1  {}                                       Microsoft Word: MIS.DOC
```

```
1═[·········1·········2·········3·········4·········5·········6·········7·]···
  MANAGEMENT·INFORMATION·SYSTEMS¶
  →    Robert·McDowell,·vice-president·of·production·and·operations·for·
  Consolidated·Foods,·is·responsible·for·recommending·target·inventory·
  levels·for·each·of·the·products·that·Consolidated·Foods·manufactures·and·
  distributes·to·its·branch·warehouses.··The·firm·manufactures·over·200·
  lines·of·food·products·in·four·plants·and·transports·finished·goods·to·
  its·eight·regional·warehouses.¶
  →    The·"right"·inventories·of·food·products·need·to·be·distributed·to·
  the·various·branch·warehouses·in·order·to·minimize·excess·inventories·
  and·transportation·costs.··For·example,·if·large·inventories·of·Uncle·
  Carl's·Taco·Sauce·are·shipped·to·the·southeastern·branch·warehouse·and·
  much·of·the·demand·for·this·product·is·in·the·midwest,·inventory·will·
  have·to·be·transported·to·midwestern·stores·at·considerably·greater·
  transportation·expense·than·would·be·involved·if·the·midwestern·branch·
  warehouse·had·sufficient·stock·of·taco·sauce·to·accommodate·demand·in·
  the·midwest.¶
  →    Currently,·McDowell·receives·a·monthly·report·listing·inventory·
  data·for·each·of·the·branch·warehouses,·including·the·quantity·on·hand·
  for·each·inventory·item·in·each·warehouse.··Although·this·report·helps·
```

```
COMMAND: Alpha Copy Delete Format Gallery Help Insert Jump Library
         Options Print Quit Replace Search Transfer Undo Window
Select option or type command letter
Page 1  {}                                       Microsoft Word: MIS.DOC
```

Formatting a Document with Microsoft Word, *top* & *center,* and the Partially Formatted Document Onscreen, *bottom*

```
^P        A:NEW    PAGE 1 LINE 1 COL 01              INSERT ON
                   < < <    P R I N T   M E N U    > > >
     ------ Special Effects ------- ! -Printing Changes- ! -Other Menus-
   (begin and end) !  (one time each) ! A Alternate pitch  ! (from Main only)
  B Bold D Double ! H Overprint char  ! N Standard pitch   !^J Help  ^K Block
    S Underscore  ! O Non-break space ! C Printing pause   !^Q Quick ^P Print
    X Strikeout   ! F Phantom space   ! Y Other ribbon color!^O Onscreen
    V Subscript   ! G Phantom rubout  !  --User  Patches-- !Space Bar returns
   T Superscript  ! RET Overprint line! Q(1) W(2) E(3) R(4) !you to Main Menu.
  L----!----!----!----!----!----!----!----!----!----!---------R
```

The WordStar Print Menu

can provide letter quality, near letter quality, or a standard program—the more perfect the quality, the slower the printing); page on which printing should start and page on which printing should stop; and number of columns in which to print.

Another menu selection is **merge print,** which permits the merging of two files into one. You have probably received letters addressed to you, greeting you by name, and perhaps mentioning your name and home town somewhere in the body of the letter. These are form letters computer-tailored to seem like personal letters. The text of the letter is saved in a *primary* file, and a list of names and addresses is saved in a *secondary* file. As the letter is typed, codes can be embedded that will be filled with "personal" information from the secondary file during printing. During printing, the two files are merged.

Ease of Use

Using the simplest word processing program is easier and faster than typing for almost any text-production task. But some programs are easier to use than others, not so much because of the tasks they perform but because of the ways they let a user know what they can do.

Help Screens   **Help screens** are built-in files that can be called up and displayed on the monitor to provide instruction about a command or a key. A strong selection of help screens can keep you from having to search the program documentation (reference guides and other sources of information) for answers to your questions.

```
Move

     Cut/copy/delete specified text or columns.  Depending on whether
     Block is On or Off, one of the following menus is displayed on the
     status line:

     (Block Off)

Move 1 Sentence; 2 Paragraph; 3 Page; Retrieve 4 Column; 5 Text; 6 Rectangle:

   (1)--------------------------!          (2)--------------------------!


     (Block On)

1 Cut Block; 2 Copy Block; 3 Append; 4 Cut/Copy Column; 5 Cut/Copy Rectangle:

(3)----------------------------! (4)----------------------------------!


     Type one of the Parenthesized Numbers for more Help: 0
```

A WordPerfect Help Screen

The WordStar Help Menu, *left,* and the Index of Commands Screen Accessed with ^ JI, *right*

```
^J      A:NEW   PAGE 1 LINE 1 COL 01              INSERT ON
              < < <    H E L P   M E N U    > > >
                                     :        : --Other  Menus--
  H  Display & set the help level   : S  Status line      : (from Main only)
  B  Paragraph reform (CONTROL-B)   : R  Ruler line       : ^J  Help   ^K  Block
  F  Flags in right-most column     : M  Margins & Tabs   : ^Q  Quick  ^P  Print
  D  Dot commands, print controls   : P  Place markers    : ^O  Onscreen
  I  Index of commands             : V  Moving text      : Space Bar returns
                                     :        :   you to Main Menu.
  L----!----!----!----!----!----!----!----!
```

```
^Ji     A:NEW   PAGE 1 LINE 1 COL 01              INSERT ON
       COMMANDS TO --              ARE --
 move cursor                 on main and ^Q menus
 scroll file up or down      on main menu; also find (^QF)
 delete text                 on main and ^Q menus; also ^KY
 move or copy text           on ^K menu
 end edit / save file        ^KD; see ^K menu
 print (while editing)       ^KP
 set tabs and margins        on ^O menu
 reformat text               ^B; ^JB gives info
 find a string; replace      ^QF; ^QA; ^L repeats last
                    press space bar for "entering text":
  L----!----!----!----!----!----!----!----!----!----!--------R
```

Documentation   **Documentation** is information in print form provided by a software manufacturer to explain what a program does and how to use it. It may consist of a user's guide that proceeds step by step through the production of a document. Or it may be a reference manual that lists features in alphabetical or some other order. Excellent documentation is a great asset, but not all documentation is excellent. Sometimes the only way to answer a difficult question is to call the software manufacturer for help. Sometimes documentation lists a phone number for exactly this purpose.

Tutorials   Word processing programs also come with **tutorials,** one or more disks of lessons in particular features of the program. Software manufacturers also provide quick reference cards listing the most often used keys and keyboard templates that lie over the keyboard to identify what given function keys do.

Buying a Word Processing Program

If you are thinking of buying a word processing program, consider first what you want to be able to do. There is no point in spending $500 for a program full of features you will never use. Nor is it wise to buy a cheap program when you are fairly sure that in the future you will be doing a lot of word processing. Before buying a program, see if you can borrow or test it first. Some software dealers have demo (demonstration) disks for this purpose. Remember that if you find a program difficult or the manual unhelpful, it is the program's fault, not yours. Word processors are supposed to make work faster, easier, and less expensive to accomplish. They should be user-friendly and efficient.

Discovering a Common Language

A New Program Allows Many Popular Word Processors to 'Talk' to One Another

The ability to transfer data from 5 ¼-inch to 3 ½-inch disks and vice versa is becoming an important consideration as sales of laptops and I.B.M. PS/2 computers increase. There are various ways to perform this time-consuming nuisance task. One software package specially designed for the purpose, The Brooklyn Bridge from White Crane Systems of Norcross, Ga., was covered in last week's column.

But transferring data to and from disks of different sizes is only half the battle. Increasingly, it is also necessary to translate files, particularly those created through word processing programs, from the format of one program to that of another. Data stored in, say, a WordStar file suddenly needs to be "written" in WordPerfect. This poses a much more complex problem.

Word processing files are essentially composed of two parts: the text itself, and the formatting commands, the instructions that produce such aspects as boldface type, paragraph indentations, centered page numbers and so on. Because of these formatting elements, converting a file from one program to another has always been a tedious task at best.

One way to translate from one word processing program to another was to strip a file of its formatting commands and then to feed the remaining text via ASCII code, which most word processing programs can deal with, to the new word processing program. Then the material would have to be reformatted manually, with the paragraph breaks, page numbers and underlining being reinserted via the keyboard. In the case of tabular material such as tables and lists, however, adding the new formatting commands often would take longer than simply retyping all of the data.

Another solution was to send the disks out to a service bureau specializing in file translations. However, this solution, besides being expensive, was a service of which average individuals could not readily avail themselves.

Enter the conversion utilities, programs that translate files from one program to another. Software publishers are beginning to realize that very few people can be persuaded to buy a new and different word processor—no matter how superior it may be to their current program—unless they will be able to take their previously entered files with them. So, a few publishers have begun to include conversion utilities in their word processing packages.

WordPerfect, for instance, now has an option called Convert that will import and simultaneously translate WordStar and MultiMate files into its own format. It is a good, easily managed translation utility. But if you need access to, say, Microsoft Word or Samna files you are out of luck.

Wherever there's a problem, some software developer is going to try to solve it. A number of independent translation utilities have now reached the market. One that crossed my threshold recently is Software Bridge ($149 for the I.B.M. PC and compatibles with at least 384K of RAM and either two floppy disk drives or a hard disk, from the Systems Compatibility Corporation, Chicago, 60601, (312) 329-0700).

Naturally, a translation program is useful only if it can work with the particular word processors one needs to deal with. Software Bridge handles the following programs: DECdx WPS; Displaya Writer 2, 3, and 4; Microsoft Word; MultiMate; MultiMate Advantage; Samna Word III; Volkswriter 3; Wang PC; WordMARC Composer; WordPerfect; WordStar; and Writing Assistant.

Considering its sophisticated nature, the four-disk Software Bridge is surprisingly easy to use. Someone familiar with word processing will be able to learn the basics fairly quickly. Some of the more intricate features, such as the Edit Character Filter, might take some getting used to. But with the help of the manual, which is reasonably clear, the average user will be able to master them.

In case you're wondering, the Edit Character Filter permits one to replace a character or string characters in the document that is going through the translation process. I have not yet had to use this particular feature, but I suppose if a certain word processor cannot produce, for example, the British pound sign while another can, it could be useful.

Putting Software Bridge into use is a straightforward matter. In the case of a computer equipped with a hard disk, one simply types in ''SB'' to call up the main menu. From there one proceeds to the setup menu and designates the word processor from which a file or files are to be translated, manipulating the up and down arrow keys until the desired name, say WordPerfect, is highlighted. The left arrow key activates the selection.

Personally, I would have preferred the use of the more commonly used Enter key for that purpose, but that's a minor point. Next, the word processor to which the files are to be converted, let's say WordStar, is located on the menu. That selection is made by pressing the right arrow key. Finally, the drive to which the translation is to be sent is indicated before one returns to the main menu.

To translate a number of documents, say half a dozen of my columns, one queues them one at a time from the directory of the disk on which they are stored. The program permits the queuing of 99 documents, which would seem a sufficient number for anyone's purposes.

However, at one point in the course of testing Software Bridge, I looked through a directory of some 300 files only to discover that most of them were missing. It was definitely time to push the panic button!

As it turned out, the files had not been destroyed. Software Bridge's directory function simply cannot show more than 100 file names at a time. An explicit warning concerning this limitation stated in the manual might help to avert heart attacks among users like me who work with very large directories.

Once all the files to be translated have been designated, the F1 key initiates their actual conversion. To convert this column from WordPerfect to WordStar took a little over a minute. Such speed won't exactly set the world on fire. But the conversion was, as I was pleased to discover, free of errors. And it certainly beats re-entry.

Source: Erik Sandberg-Diment, "The Executive Computer," *The New York Times,* Sunday, June 21, 1987.

Summary and Key Terms

1. **Application software** is sets of programs designed to let computer users who are not computer programmers accomplish such specific tasks as word processing, data analyses, creating a spreadsheet, and linking into an on-line data base.
2. **Business application software** is created for mainframes, minicomputers, and microcomputers and may be custom-designed. Business application areas include bookkeeping, budgeting, human resource management, inventory control, payroll, cash flow management, and profit and loss analysis.
3. **Personal productivity software** helps the user improve productivity by harnessing the power of the microcomputer for everyday business applications. It results in better information, better analysis of information, better presentation of information, and better communication.
4. **Integrated packages** combine several applications, in contrast to **stand-alone packages** which provide individual applications.
5. **Word processing packages** help users to produce text documents faster, easier, and less expensively than by other methods.
6. In a word processing program, a computer keyboard's **function keys** help to accomplish specific tasks within programs, which may be **menu-driven, command-driven,** or a combination.
7. A program's **default settings** establish the basic format assumptions the programmer built into the program. Many other automatic features are common to all word processing programs, including word wrap, scrolling, insert, delete, move, copy, and search and replace. Two very useful features not all programs have are macros and windows.
8. Some features of word processing programs are carried out by the printer, so it is necessary to have **compatibility** between the program and the printer. Merge printing is one such feature.

Review Questions

Fill-In

1. _____ software is software that enables the user to perform specific tasks, such as word processing and data base management.

2. Partly because of the popularity of _____, application software development is one of the busiest fronts of the computer revolution.

3. In a word processing program, the _____ line gives such information as tab stops and page width.

4. The _____ is an indicator on the screen that shows where the next character to be typed will appear.

5. The keys that perform such tasks as saving or cutting text are called _____ keys.

6. In a _____-driven system, specific keys must be pressed to carry out certain commands.

7. Basic formatting assumptions that create standard formats are called _____ settings.

8. Most word processing programs can automatically start a new line when text reaches the margin, a feature called _____ _____.

9. _____ are type in a variety of sizes.

10. _____ screens can be called up to find out information about a given command.

Matching

Listed below are a number of functions of word processing programs. Fill in the letter of the correct function at its definition:

a. thesaurus

b. windows

c. search and replace

d. formatting commands

e. style function

f. macros

g. cut and paste

_____ 1. Can recall text that is temporarily stored in main memory.

_____ 2. Can proceed through an entire manuscript, changing one word string to another.

_____ 3. Can be used to find good synonyms.

_____ 4. Provides editorial help by pointing out overused words.

_____ 5. When a screen is split into two parts, it is split into _____ that show the different parts of the document.

_____ 6. Can store a specified series of commands.

_____ 7. Functions such as page numbering and centering are in this general category.

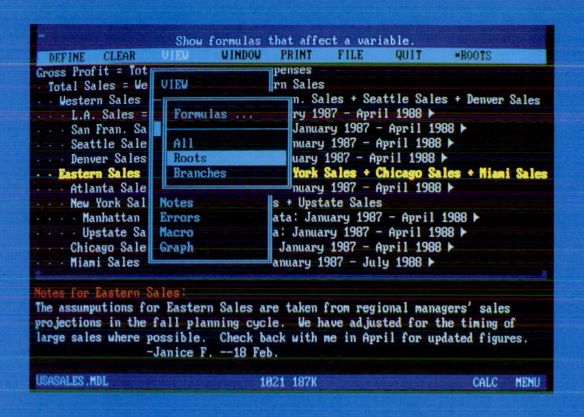

Screen 1:

Show formulas that affect a variable.

| DEFINE | CLEAR | VIEW | WINDOW | PRINT | FILE | QUIT | *ROOTS |

Gross Profit = Tot͟penses
- Total Sales = We͟rn Sales
- - Western Sales͟n. Sales + Seattle Sales + Denver Sales
- - - L.A. Sales =͟ry 1987 - April 1988 ▶
- - - San Fran. Sa͟January 1987 - April 1988 ▶
- - - Seattle Sale͟nuary 1987 - April 1988 ▶
- - - Denver Sales͟uary 1987 - April 1988 ▶
- - **Eastern Sales**͟**York Sales + Chicago Sales + Miami Sales**
- - - Atlanta Sale͟nuary 1987 - April 1988 ▶
- - - New York Sal͟s + Upstate Sales
- - - - Manhattan͟ata: January 1987 - April 1988 ▶
- - - - Upstate Sa͟a: January 1987 - April 1988 ▶
- - - Chicago Sale͟January 1987 - April 1988 ▶
- - - Miami Sales͟anuary 1987 - July 1988 ▶

VIEW menu:
- Formulas ...
  - All
  - **Roots**
  - Branches
- Notes
- Errors
- Macro
- Graph

Notes for Eastern Sales:
The assumptions for Eastern Sales are taken from regional managers' sales
projections in the fall planning cycle. We have adjusted for the timing of
large sales where possible. Check back with me in April for updated figures.
-Janice F. --18 Feb.

USASALES.MDL   1021 187K   CALC MENU

Screen 2:

Denver Sales @ 4 Quarter 1987: Monthly data

Western Region Sales 2

	Jan 1987	Feb 1987	Mar 1987	Apr 1987	May 1987	Jun 1987	Jul 1987
				Sales			
L.A.	3,900	4,850	5,800	5,200	4,800	4,000	3,600
San Fran.	3,900	4,200	4,500	4,850	5,200	5,600	6,000
Seattle	2,900	2,650	2,400	2,150	1,900	1,650	1,900
Denver	3,400	3,650	3,950	4,250	4,600	4,950	4,950
Western	14,100	15,350	16,650	16,450	16,500	16,200	16,450

Quarterly Western Region Sales Report

	1 Q 1987	2 Q 1987	3 Q 1987	4 Q 1987	1987
Sales					
L.A.	14,550	14,000	13,600	20,750	62,900
San Fran.	12,600	15,650	16,650	19,400	64,300
Seattle	7,950	5,700	5,450	8,450	27,550
Denver	11,000	13,800	16,950	15,950	57,700
Western	46,100	49,150	52,650	64,550	212,450

USASALES.MDL   1021 185K   READY

Spreadsheet, Integrated, and Accounting Packages

8

Chapter Objectives

After you have finished studying this chapter, you should be able to

1. Identify typical spreadsheet applications, including "what if" analyses.

2. Describe the basic features of an electronic spreadsheet.

3. Understand what an integrated package is and describe ways integrated packages are used.

4. Understand how accounting modules deal with the five main accounting functions.

A year ago, Dennis would have spent two weeks putting together his department's annual budget. Working with pencil, paper, and a calculator, he would check and recheck his figures before having the draft typed. It would then be carefully proofread (to make sure the typist hadn't introduced errors) before being submitted to his supervisor, Joan. Joan would usually suggest some revisions. These would require additional calculations, typing, and proofing—sometimes several days worth.

A few months ago, Dennis began to use a microcomputer at work. This year, he is using it and TWIN, a popular spreadsheet program, to prepare his budget. Spreadsheets, tools for numerical calculation and analysis, are arranged in rows and columns like an accountant's ledger sheet.

As Dennis enters his figures, the spreadsheet automatically calculates totals. Dennis can also print out the figures directly from the program so no errors are introduced by retyping. Instead of two weeks, it takes him two days to put together a draft for Joan.

Joan asks Dennis to show what would happen if sales increase 6 percent, and if expenses are reduced by 2, 4, 6, 8, and 10 percent. She also suggests using some graphs to illustrate the results so that the board members will understand them better. Before TWIN, this would have taken days. Now, Dennis returns to his microcomputer, loads TWIN, and retrieves his draft. In an hour, he prints out these different versions, with graphs of the results.

As you learned in Chapter 7, application software makes microcomputers indispensable to many people with little computer experience. Word processing software makes producing text documents easy and fast, with savings in time, effort, and money increasing as the complexity of the document increases. Spreadsheet, integrated, and accounting packages also save time, effort, and money for many applications.

Spreadsheets

Microcomputers really came into their own as business computers with the development of electronic spreadsheets. Suddenly, people who worked with figures could create a model, enter and then change the data as desired, and have the new results available almost instantly. In the following section we will look at electronic spreadsheets in some detail—what they can do, features they offer, and how they are used.

A spreadsheet program is designed to perform four basic functions:

1. It allows the user to create a spreadsheet model.
2. It enables the computer to recalculate the model each time data are altered.
3. It allows the model and its contents to be stored for future use, including for the preparation of graphics and for interfacing with other programs (such as accounting, data base management, and word processing).
4. It allows the model and the calculated results to be printed out.

These four functions exist within one program and can usually be invoked from one master menu. (A **menu** lists choices of the operations that the program can perform.)

Empty Spreadsheet Using TWIN

Mosaic Software Inc.

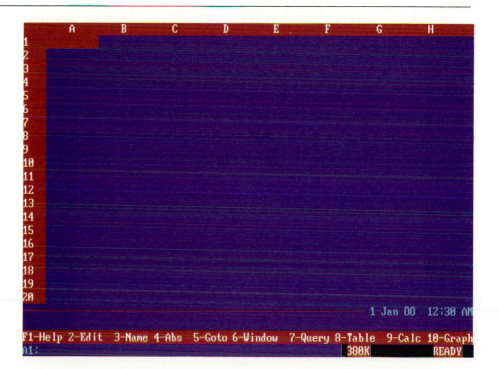

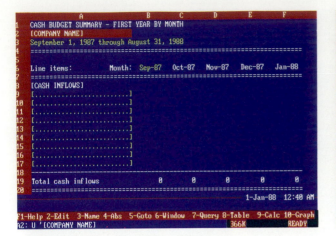

An Empty Cash Flow Analysis Template Using TWIN

Mosaic Software Inc.

A Completed Cash Flow Analysis Using TWIN

Mosaic Software Inc.

Creating the Model

A spreadsheet can be used in any situation where the user would otherwise use a pencil, paper, and a calculator—in other words, in any situation that can be described numerically. A spreadsheet that has been set up for use in a specific situation is called a **model.** Spreadsheet models combine fixed and changeable components. Take, for example, a forecasted budget . . . *any* forecasted budget. Many components in the budget are constant. The headings for each month and the items involved in a budget remain the same. There are usually 12 months in the budget. And although the specific numbers in each budget change, the calculations themselves do not. Sales minus cost of sales is always gross margin, gross margin minus selling costs is always operating profit, and so on.

A spreadsheet lets the user structure the model so that when the variables change, the work does not have to be redone. The headings and calculations will take care of reworking the model with the present data and producing the results of the new calculations instantly. Merely by changing these variables, the structure can be used over and over again.

Data stored on a completed spreadsheet can also be used to create a graphic display of the results. For example, the profit figures generated from the budget can be sent to, or **interfaced** with, a graphics package (often, one is included in the spreadsheet package). The graphics package will then produce a chart of the results, which can be printed out and used in a presentation to management.

The user of a spreadsheet starts by creating a **template** of the model. This template represents the bare bones of a mathematical model. It includes the headings, column and row descriptions, mathematical calculations, and the various formulas that the model requires. Once the model is developed, the empty template can be named and stored on disk to be

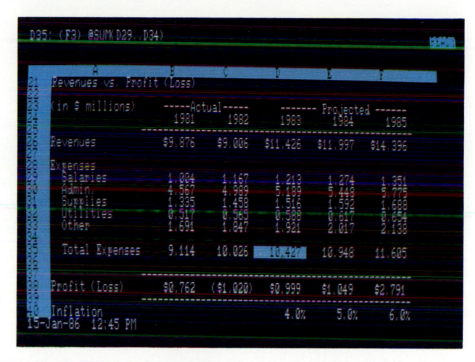

Profit and Loss Analysis
Using 1-2-3 (control panel at
top)

© Lotus Development Corporation,
1987. Used with permission.

reused in the future. Then a clean template—one without actual data entries—will always be available.

The value in a spreadsheet is not in the first-time generation of a template. In fact, the time involved with setting up a template is often no less than the time involved with writing it out by hand. However, a template is seldom used just once. When a budget is being prepared, satisfactory results are rare on the first try, or on the second, or on the third. To change variable data by hand, recalculate the results, and rework the formula wastes time, work, and money. This is where the spreadsheet shines. It recalculates automatically and instantly, and it can be revised as often as necessary to produce the desired results.

Spreadsheet Applications

Many things can be done on a spreadsheet program. A few of them are discussed here, to show you that spreadsheets help users not just to keep track of what has happened but to predict what is likely to happen and to use the information developed from spreadsheets to make decisions.

Financial Analysis   Preparing cost budgets, sales forecasts, production forecasts, and analysis based on speculation (pro forma, or "what if" analyses) are perfect applications for a spreadsheet. Using the spreadsheet, a user can provide information on changing markets and changing price policies. Maintaining current "live" data in relationship to the forecasted data can also help a decision maker to determine whether forecasts are being met and to predict potential problem areas.

Accounting Statements   Preparing and analyzing financial statements is something that most businesses do every month. This repetitive analysis is composed of manipulating the same basic data with the same basic formulas for current ratios, quick ratios, return on assets, return on equity, and so on. Monitoring these ratios can be very useful, but when time is tight, many of these analyses get put off until "a better time." Using a template that automatically calculates these ratios allows for less time in gathering data and more time to analyze information.

Analyzing Performance   Many of the results calculated from accounting data can be used to determine how a business is performing. Comparison of data from month to month can show how a business is faring over time. Many industries and financial organizations publish surveys on industry averages and performance ratios. These can be used to compare a specific business to an industry as a whole.

Investment Costs and Performance   As profit-oriented individuals, we are always interested in the cost of an investment and the performance we are getting on our invested dollar. A spreadsheet can be used to monitor these factors on an ongoing basis. Rate of return on investments, rate of return on equity, and debt to equity ratios can indicate performance in a business. Monitoring stock prices, bond markets, and Dow Jones averages can track the performance of personal investments.

Personal Financial and Tax Planning   In addition to business decisions, spreadsheets can assist in personal financial and tax planning. People often know where they are and where they want to be in a given number of years. Few people however, know exactly whether they will make it until the time actually arrives, but by then it's too late to make any changes. Using a spreadsheet template with present and future value calculations and variable data like the rate of inflation, it is possible to determine whether a given course of action will produce the desired results by retirement. And along with a long-range goal like personal financial planning, short-range goals like paying the least income tax possible can be calculated with a spreadsheet. Simply by filling in known earnings figures and then playing with tax planning tools, it is possible to determine how much tax liability will be and perhaps to take steps to reduce it.

Developing Graphs and Charts   Data from a template can be fed into a graphics program to prepare many different kinds of graphs. Graphs are a powerful tool to show trends and relationships among data. The spreadsheet is a good organizing tool to collect these data, even if they are not going to be used as a mathematical model. Rather than draw the graph by hand, it is better to let the computer do the graphing.

The Spreadsheet Screen

The Work Area   Once a spreadsheet program is loaded into the computer's memory, the screen shows a series of numbered rows down the left-hand

side and lettered columns across the top. (Some spreadsheets use numbers instead of letters to denote columns.) This arrangement creates a series of **cells,** into which data can be entered. Cells can be identified by the row and column coordinates. For example, A1 is the cell in the first row of column A.

Cells can hold alphabetic characters, numerical data, or mathematical formulas. In an expense report spreadsheet, for instance, the first cell in each column might hold the name of a month and the first cell in each row the name of a type of expense. Other cells would hold numeric data: expense amount, in dollars. Some cells would hold formulas. The row labeled *Total Expenses,* for example, would probably contain a formula to automatically add together the expenses entered into the various expense cells.

The Control Panel

A second area on the screen is the **control panel,** or **status area.** Either at the top or the bottom of the work area, depending on the spreadsheet program, the control panel is made up of three horizontal areas: the entry or edit line, the status line, and the prompt line. These three areas are common to all spreadsheets.

The **entry,** or **edit, line** displays commands, prompts, messages, and the contents of the cell to be entered or edited. This line also shows what is being typed into the computer for a specific cell until the return key is pressed. Then the contents or mathematical results are displayed in the cell.

The **status line** includes valuable information such as the present position of the cursor (cell address), the contents of the cell that the cursor is on (including label, numerical, or formula data, the width of the cell, and

TWIN Spreadsheet with Control Panel and Master Menu at Bottom

Mosaic Software Inc.

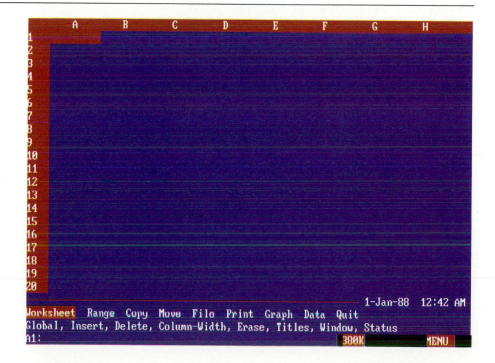

	A	B	C	D	E	F
1	CASH BUDGET SUMMARY - FIRST YEAR BY MONTH					
2	NORMAN KITCHENS					
3	September 1, 1987 through August 31, 1988					
4	==					
5						
6	Line items: Month:	Sep-87	Oct-87	Nov-87	Dec-87	Jan-88
7	==					
8	[CASH INFLOWS]					
9	CUSTOMER P/U	$50,000	$40,000	$15,000	$0	$0
10	SUBCONTRACTED	50,000	50,000	25,000	10,000	15,000
11	INSTALLED	75,000	75,000	40,000	15,000	25,000
12	[......................]					
13	[......................]					
14	[......................]					
15	[......................]					
16	[......................]					
17	[......................]					
18						
19	Total cash inflows	175,000	165,000	80,000	25,000	40,000
20	==					

```
                                          1-Jan-88  12:43 AM
Type X 1 2 3 4 5 6 7 8 Label Options Display Plot Gprint Name Reset Slide Quit
Define the type of graph to display (line, pie, bar)
B6: (D3) @DATE(87,9,1)                       362K              MENU
```

TWIN Spreadsheet with Graphics Menu at Bottom

Mosaic Software Inc.

the format of the data), and the present mode of the program, as discussed below.

The **prompt line** displays messages to the user asking for information necessary to complete a task. For example, when you are going to print, the program will use the prompt line to ask you to enter the coordinates of the area that you wish to print. When you type in the top left and bottom right cell coordinates, the program will mark off the area and print it out.

Some programs also display status indicators, which signal such things as the on or off state of the recalculating feature or that certain kinds of errors have been encountered. Others display the date and time. Still others display the amount of memory remaining for the current worksheet.

Program Modes   Most spreadsheet programs are single-tasking: that is, they can perform only one function at a time. When the program is recalculating data, for example, it cannot accept further data from the keyboard. It is, therefore, important for the user to know what the program is doing at all times, so the current mode is displayed in the status line. Modes are set by the computer program automatically, and although they vary from program to program, all spreadsheets have ready, wait, command, edit, and error modes.

The **ready mode** means the program is waiting for the user to do something: enter data, make up a formula, choose a command, or press a key to start a process. The **wait mode,** on the other hand, tells the user to wait when some process is going on, such as when the program is loading a file from the disk or sending an area to a printer. During this time, the user is signaled to wait, for the process must finish before a different action can take place.

In the **command mode,** the program is expecting some command to happen, such as printing or saving. Commands are set up in menu form, with a number of submenus below the initial master menu. Choosing an item from the master menu will cause a second menu to appear, and so on, until enough selections have been made to allow the desired command to be carried out. For example, from the master menu in Lotus 1-2-3, choosing *W* selects *Worksheet.* A second menu then appears to present the next set of options. From this you might choose *E* for *Erase.* A third menu would then emerge, from which you would choose *Y* for *Yes* if (and only if) you did want to erase the entire worksheet. The command would then be carried out, and the worksheet would be erased.

Edit mode lets the user edit the current data in the entry or edit line. The **error mode** gives a message that an error has occurred and some action is necessary to resolve it.

Spreadsheet Features

Power versus Simplicity   Spreadsheet packages commonly have some sort of tradeoff between power to perform calculations and ease of use, or user friendliness. However, all spreadsheets are designed to be used by people who are not computer experts. Most spreadsheet programs allow even a novice user to prepare fairly sophisticated templates quickly. The more functions it has, the more useful a spreadsheet will become as you become more skilled in using it. Spreadsheets have **macros,** for example, like the macros in word processing programs. Macros seem quite complicated to a novice, but they can be put to productive use after only a few hours of work with the spreadsheet.

TWIN Help Screen

Mosaic Software Inc.

```
GETTING HELP

  To get help at any time, just press F1.  If you need help on a
  specific command, highlight the command name on the menu before asking
  for help.

  You may view information on one of the special topics listed below
  by highlighting the topic or typing the first letter of the desired
  command.

  Use <Esc> to return to where you left off.




Next  Prev  Help  Menus  Keys  Edit  Intro  Application
Next help page
                                                        HELP
```

Help Most spreadsheets have built in HELP functions that act like interactive reference manuals. A good spreadsheet keeps its HELP function accessible at all times, even while a template is being worked on. For example, with Multiplan, help can be accessed at any time. You just press the "?" key after invoking a particular command, and explanations about that command appear on the screen.

Documentation Like word processing programs, most spreadsheets come with three pieces of documentations: a user's manual, a reference guide, and a quick reference chart. The user's manual normally includes a tutorial, which takes the first-time user step by step through the process of creating a spreadsheet. The reference guide describes in detail each command, feature, and function, along with some common trouble-shooting solutions. The quick reference chart is a greatly condensed reference manual that can provide a brief description of the program's commands or functions.

Dimensions of the Spreadsheet In terms of the total number of cells available for a template, most spreadsheet programs are similar in size. (See the box for the sizes of popular spreadsheets.) The overall size of the spreadsheet—the number of rows and columns—does not dictate the size of the template that can be built. Usually, the amount of memory in the computer—RAM—determines the size of the template. For example, if you are using a computer that allows 256K of memory to be addressed, after loading the operating system and the application software there is only enough RAM left for a small template. In comparison, if you are using a 640K computer, which has considerably more RAM available, a much larger template can be developed. Even so, more memory may not be the only limiting factor in determining the size of the template; some electronic spreadsheet programs may be able to access only a certain amount of memory.

Size restriction can be a problem to a user who requires a large template. If you are faced with that situation, check the largest size of template that you will be able to construct. A simple way to do that is to put some dummy data in cell 1 and copy it across and down until you have filled an area approximately the size of the template you are planning to build. If you reach maximum memory capacity (an error message will tell you), it is very likely your template will not fit.

Computational Features Second-generation spreadsheets (Lotus 1-2-3, Multiplan, Twin, and others) have considerably improved computational features over early spreadsheets. Many functions that the user had to develop through mathematical formulas in the early spreadsheets are now built in. For example, if you used an early spreadsheet to calculate a payment schedule for a mortgage, you had to know the formula and enter it into the template. With the newer spreadsheets, you simply enter the formula, preceded by some code to signal that a formula is about to be entered. In Lotus 1-2-3, for example, you would enter @PMT(principal, interest, term) and the payment would be calculated and displayed in the cell. Other financial functions, such as the internal rate of return, net present value, future value, and present value, are also available in the newer generation of spreadsheets.

Using the Spreadsheet

Creating the Template   To start creating a template, the user merely calls up the spreadsheet program so that the blank template described earlier is on the screen. Once executed, the program is ready to accept data for input. It is important to have a detailed idea of how the template should look and of the formulas necessary to complete the task. It can be worthwhile to develop this information on paper and then to create the shell by duplicating the way the model looks on paper.

Formatting   The general format of a spreadsheet is initially set up with **default** settings. (Remember from Chapter 7 that default settings create a basic format that a user can modify to fit his or her particular needs.) For example, most worksheets have columns 9 characters wide, with numbers justified to the right and text justified to the left.

Any cell, group of cells, or even the entire worksheet template can be formatted at once. Two types of formatting are available: alignment and content. In a very general way, alignment formatting refers to the way entered data are positioned in a cell: left justified, right justified, or centered. Content formatting includes using percents, currency, commas, and so on. Once a spreadsheet has been formatted, that format becomes part of the worksheet, and it is saved with the worksheet.

Tips on Building Spreadsheets

Each user will develop his or her own technique in creating and using spreadsheets. Although there is no right way or wrong way, a few tips may help to produce a more usable spreadsheet.

1. Create the outline first. Before you sit down in front of the computer to develop the template, make a paper model. It will show you if everything is logically consistent, whether the formulas reference the proper cells, and whether other errors are present that might be difficult to track down later, when you are actually using the template. You may even want to design a flowchart similar to one you would produce when designing any new system or program. Once the model is complete on paper, plug in some sample data and calculate the results by hand to see if you get the expected results.

Also decide what kind of output you want so you can format the individual cells of the template accordingly. Consider whether you want the output printed on narrow or wide paper, whether on one page or more than one, what the headings and footings should be, and how much detail you want to show. Only when you have developed this outline should you start to create the template on the screen.

2. Separate variables. It is a good idea to section off an area from the work area of the template where all variables can be entered and displayed. This main area will then be known as the data input area. The cells containing these variables can be referenced to the main work section of the template so they can be used in the calculations. For example, when you develop a mortgage payment schedule you can separate an area to input the principle, interest rate, compound rate, and term of the loan. The main body of the

Inputting Data   Once a spreadsheet is visible on the screen, data can be entered. Numerical data are entered by typing numbers into the cell that the cursor is on. Any numerical input is a signal to the machine that the data are likely to be used for calculations. Exceptions make it necessary to tell the machine to treat the numbers as labels, so they are unavailable for calculations.

Most spreadsheets allow alpha data to be entered just by typing the word. The first letter is the identifier. Others require a key letter to be typed in before the program recognizes the alpha nature.

After headings and numerical information are entered into the template, the special power of the electronic spreadsheet becomes available by means of mathematical formulas and the commands resident in the spreadsheet. It is possible to perform any modeling desired and to have the new results available instantly.

Using Mathematical Formulas and Mathematical Functions   Long mathematical formulas can be entered in specific cells to perform calculations automatically. The formulas generally follow recognized mathematical rules, but it is important to be familiar with the specific form that the program requires.

Using formulas in the right way significantly enhances the power of the spreadsheet. For example, suppose you want to calculate the average score

---

template will then use these variables to calculate the amount of the payment and produce the amortization schedule by referring to these amounts. By using a special area for input of new variables you do not have to jump all over the template to find the places to enter new data.

3. Reference where possible. Since errors occur frequently during the data input stage, it is a good idea to reduce this chore as much as possible. Try to set up your spreadsheet so as to input the same data only once and separate the data input area from the rest of the program. The input cells can then be referenced to the main calculation section of the spreadsheet template, where it is used for processing. This procedure prevents the overwriting of formulas with input data that was accidentally placed in the wrong cells, thereby destroying the calculating section of a template.

4. Test the template thoroughly. Never assume that your template is correct until you have tested it with a variety of test data or cases. These tests do not take long and will point out any misreferenced cells, a missed bracket in a lengthy mathematical operation, or errors in a formula. Corrections take only a few seconds when you make them at the startup stage.

5. Always save a blank copy of the template on disk. Save a blank copy of the completed template on disk, and never use this copy for direct data entry. This simple procedure can save hours of time and frustration.

6. Don't be afraid to experiment and have fun. Applications on electronic spreadsheets are limited only by the time you want to spend creating them. Never be afraid to experiment with the spreadsheet program to find new ways of doing things. The more you use it, the more beneficial it will be.

on a test. You can type student names and scores into a template as follows:

```
              A           B          C
   1
   2         Name     Test Score
   3     G. Balmer        85
   4     M. Carpenter     55
   5     D. Laller        90
   6     P. Pushing       72
   7     K. Lantz         77
   8
   9     Average           ?
```

Row 9, column B will contain the average score of the participants. It is possible to get the result in two different ways. You could enter the following into the cell: (85 + 55 + 90 + 72 + 77)/5. This formula will give you the correct answer. However, if you later find that D. Laller actually had a score of 66 instead of 90, you would have to retype or edit the entire formula, which is time consuming and increases the chances of making an error. To avoid changing formulas, it is better to use **cell references** instead of specific numbers in the formula. For row 9, column B (B9), you could type in the following:

```
'(B3 + B4 + B5 + B6 + B7)/5
```

With this new formula, a change in score for D. Laller does not affect the formula in the cell B9. When the score in the appropriate cell next to the student's name is changed, the new average is recalculated immediately.

This formula can be condensed even further by using a **mathematical function** (a preprogrammed mathematical calculation) such as the following:

```
@SUM(B3 .. B7)/5
```

When this function is invoked, the spreadsheet program "sums," or adds up, all the numbers from row 3, column B to row 7, column B inclusive and divides them by 5.

Some spreadsheet programs have specific built-in functions similar to those in a calculator. Mathematical functions are often, although not always, invoked by a special function key. For example, with Multiplan, a *V* (for "value") has to be entered to signal that a mathematical command is about to be entered in a cell.

Using Spreadsheet Commands   Like the extremely helpful mathematical formulas available in a spreadsheet, other capabilities make complex tasks easier. One is the INSERT capability, which allows the addition of rows and/or columns. Another is SORT, which arranges data in a particular order. For example, if you wanted to add two names to the student test score template, an INSERT command could be invoked to create two empty rows for the new data. Then a SORT command could rearrange all the rows into alphabetical order by student last names.

Copying cell contents is another time-saving feature. Working with a calculator and paper, people often find that they are continually making the same calculation or using the same formula. For example, in a 12-month forecast, a user has to add up all revenues and all expenses for each month and then subtract expenses from revenues to come up with net profit for the month. This has to be repeated 12 more times, once for each remaining month and once for the total.

A spreadsheet program has the ability to copy or replicate formulas, values, or any cell contents to any other cells or groups of cells. The ability to copy cell content is extremely useful not only to save time but also for accuracy. The more often data or formulas are typed in, the greater the chance for error. But cell contents typed in correctly once can be copied—correctly—any number of times.

Creating Windows   A spreadsheet template is usually too large for all the key information to show on the screen at one time. In a breakeven analysis, for example, the user will want to know when the breakeven point has been

Using the Window Option to View Two Different Areas of a TWIN Spreadsheet

Mosaic Software Inc.

reached, but this is not easy to do if the net profit number is not shown on the screen. Or in the expense report, the row and column headings are unlikely to show when figures in the second half of the year are being worked on. To solve these problems, most spreadsheet programs allow the user to split the screen into two or more separate **windows.** As in word processing programs, the user can work on the material shown in either of the windows.

A user can choose to have the windows synchronized. If two windows are synchronized, the second window moves along with the first one. Otherwise, only one window moves. In the breakeven analysis, for example, the breakeven figure must stay on the screen at all times, so it should be kept in an unsynchronized window.

Windows can be split horizontally or vertically, and some spreadsheets allow the user to put a fancy border around each window for easier viewing and data entry. As with cell formats, window formats are saved to disk. When the template is recalled, the windows will be there. To cancel them requires only a single command.

Using External Spreadsheets   Some spreadsheet programs permit the connection of separate templates so that data can be transferred between them. With Multiplan this is done by using the command EXTERNAL and the NAME command. For example, you could develop separate monthly income statements for a company and have a summary income statement showing all 12 months on a separate template. You would then update the monthly income statements by entering the revenues and expenses. Each time you loaded the summary template, the individual monthly templates into which new data had been entered would be read. The summary statement is therefore always updated.

Recalculating the Spreadsheet   Calculating results is a basic function of a spreadsheet after data have been entered into the cells. Normally, a spreadsheet is recalculated each time new data are entered into the template. Recalculation can be very time-consuming, and nothing else can go on while it is being done. So, for all but the earliest spreadsheets, the recalculation procedure can be turned off. Whenever you start up a new template, you should always turn this feature off unless you have a short problem using only a few cells. With recalculation turned off, data, formulas, and commands can be entered. Once data entry is completed, simply hitting a special key reinstates the recalculation procedure.

Saving the Spreadsheet   Once a template is developed, it should be stored on disk even before information is entered into it. This creates a clean spreadsheet with all cells formatted appropriately and all formulas and headings entered. The user has to provide a name for the template so that the computer can place it in the directory for future retrieval.

The template contents should also be saved as often as possible, to prevent data loss in case of power failure or a problem with the computer. Remember, computers are powered by electricity, and main memory is volatile. As long as the template is sitting in main memory, a power failure can wipe it out completely.

Printing the Spreadsheet

Before printing out the data in the spreadsheet template on a printer, the data should *always* be saved first as a disk file so that it is not lost if something happens to the computer during the printing process. Once saved, the data can always be recalled from the disk.

Data can be saved to disk as a regular spreadsheet file that can be recalled and worked on again or in a format that can be printed later. This second save format, known as the ASCII file, makes it possible to print the file without calling up the spreadsheet program and reading it into memory. An ASCII file can also be called up with a word processor, for editing or perhaps to be included in a report.

Selecting the Area to Print   The first decision about printing is to decide what part of the template to print. If you need only a part of the template, you can select the area to be printed by entering its coordinates. Alternatively, with some programs areas of the template can be named (via a NAME command) and then specified for printing by name rather than by coordinates.

Formatting the Printed Page   The options in the print menu of a spreadsheet allow the format for the page to be set, including left, right, top, and bottom margins; the print width; and the page length. The characteristics of the paper you are printing on and the printer you are using must be considered here. For example, if you had a template to be printed requiring a width of 132 columns and the printer you are using automatically inputs a carriage return after 132 columns are printed on a page, you must be very careful about the way you set the margins. If you set the left margin at 3 because you do not want to print at the extreme left edge of the paper, then the print width of the document cannot be more than 129 characters. After the 129th character, the printer automatically enters a carriage return, which throws off all subsequent lines as the 130th character is shifted down to the next line.

Depending on the spreadsheet package, a number of other optional set-up features are available. In almost all cases, the user can have the results of the template printed, which is the normal application, or to have the formulas contained in each cell printed instead. A printout of the formulas in the template is useful for error checking and as a backup in case the disk is ever destroyed. Other options include printing the row and column numbers, changing the print font to a wider or narrower style, printing headers and footers on each page, and printing borders around the output.

Integrated Packages

The most popular application software packages tend to be for individual applications. There is, however, a range of software that contains several applications in one program. These are known as **integrated packages.** At

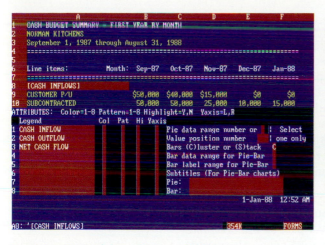

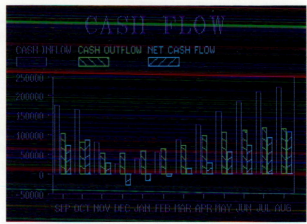

Graphing Spreadsheet Data on TWIN

An attractive feature of the integrated program TWIN is its ability to convert data
into graphic forms.

Mosaic Software Inc.

the beginning of the chapter, we saw how Dennis worked on TWIN to prepare his department's budget. TWIN is an integrated package that contains spreadsheet, graphics, and data management functions. Another example of an integrated program is Javelin, which offers up to 10 views of entered data. Chapter 8's opening photograph shows this feature.

One of the most comprehensive integrated programs is Smart, by Innovative Software, which has a full-function word processor, a very large spreadsheet, and a data base management system. Each can be used separately, and they can be used together in "integrated" fashion. That is, the data created in one application can be exported to another application program for use in another task.

For example, you may want to create a data base of all your employees and then print out a list of the ones who have achieved a sales volume of over $100,000 this month. You could start by making a spreadsheet with all the characteristics about the salespeople. You might want to do this because it is much easier and faster to enter data into a spreadsheet than it is to enter it into a data base management system. By the use of copy replication and mathematical formulas, you can quickly have the list finished.

Once completed, the spreadsheet can be exported to the DBMS, where the data can be manipulated into the proper reporting format, picking only those sales people who meet the given criteria. Once the report has been prepared, it can then be exported to the word processor, which can prepare a report around the data for presentation to management.

Although there are obvious advantages to using integrated programs, they have drawbacks. Rarely do they excel at more than one application: 1-2-3, for example, is primarily known for its spreadsheet; its graphics and data management capabilities do not compare favorably to standalone programs in those areas.

A second drawback is speed and size. Because so much is loaded at one time, integrated packages tend to be rather slow. They also take up so much RAM that in machines below 640K, the amount of space available for files may be too severely limited.

Finally, these programs are often complex and more difficult to learn to use than single-application programs. Still, the basic concept is sound; and with time, integrated packages are likely to become increasingly popular.

Windowing Software

It is possible to create an integrated environment using a windowing program, such as Microsoft Windows. Such software lets the user load into memory two or more single-application programs for simultaneous use. The drawback here is that the data do not always move smoothly between the programs. It may be necessary to go through a special conversion process each time an application is moved. This process can be tedious and even perilous, for the data can be damaged by the movement and thus unusable by any of the applications.

Accounting Packages

Unlike spreadsheets and integrated packages, accounting software is not very flexible. A specific accounting package is designed for a specific application. Custom design is generally limited to the formatting of the output and numbering of the chart of accounts. Although accounting packages are simple to operate, even by novice computer users, setting them up for a particular business requires considerable knowledge about the business and about accounting.

Accounting software packages center around the five main functional areas in accounting: general ledger, accounts receivable, accounts payable, inventory, and payroll. Any of these modules can be used by itself when only one specific function is required. For example, if you have a significant accounts receivable problem and wish to use the accounts receivable module from a particular accounting package, that is all you have to purchase. Most of the larger packages are sold in modular form for this reason.

The better accounting package modules on the market are *integrated,* meaning that a module can transfer its data either individually or in summary form to the other modules. For example, the summary totals from accounts receivable and sales would "integrate" with the general ledger. The control account from accounts receivable, sales, cost of sales, and inventory would be updated, and the individual sales of each inventory item would be transferred to the inventory module in order to update the perpetual inventory accounts.

When modules are not integrated, the user has to manually transfer the summary totals from each module and update the general ledger and any other related accounts with a manual journal entry. Manual updating increases the possibility of errors, and few accounting packages available today require it.

Many of the available accounting packages are in **data base format**—a series of files interrelated to avoid duplication of data. For example, when an item is sold through the accounts receivable system, the customer's name is entered and the program then searches the customer data base to confirm that the customer does exist. Once the name is found, the program checks the accounts data base to confirm that the account is active.

Even though an accounting application uses a data base structure, it should not be confused with what is called a data base management system (DBMS) (discussed in Chapter 10). Unlike a DBMS, accounting packages do not allow any file manipulations by the user, nor can the user extract information from the data base set up in an accounting application by asking a series of questions. The reasons are simple. First, an accounting package is designed to be used by people without any computer knowledge, for the entry of financial and sales data is in general a clerical rather than a managerial function. Second, data that can be easily accessed and changed, as is the case in a DBMS, are subject to being misused. Accounting data contain confidential information about the business or clients that must be kept secure. Finally, errors in the accounts or possible fraudulent use could result if file manipulation were possible.

General Ledger

The general ledger module of an accounting system incorporates the main financial data base of the company. It is comprised of the chart of accounts, their corresponding balances, and all the transactions, in summary form, from any supporting module.

As in any accounting system, the general ledger module of an accounting package is the heart of the system. All other modules are tied together through the general ledger. In the general ledger is kept a summary of all transactions for creating the income statement and balance sheet—the two main reports of any accounting system.

General ledger packages perform some or all of the following functions: They

1. Keep track of accounting periods (up to 13).
2. Keep track of multiple profit centers.
3. Allow maintenance of the chart of accounts.
4. Allow entry, editing, and posting of journal entries.
5. Allow entry, editing, and posting of standard journal entries.
6. Allow printing of the trial balance.
7. Allow general ledger account inquiry.
8. Allow printing of source reference reports.
9. Print the income statement and balance sheet.
10. Maintain transaction details.

11. Interface with other modules, such as accounts receivable, accounts payable, payroll, and inventory.
12. Maintain passwords and data file integrity checks.

Supporting Modules

The supporting modules are somewhat more difficult to operate. They maintain much more accounting detail and are capable of running a multitude of accounting functions. Consequently, before using a supporting module there should be a specific need. A company with only 15 credit customers, all of whom pay on time, does not need an accounts receivable module because it has no billing or collection problems. On the other hand, a firm with 150 credit customers, some of whom do not pay promptly, may have a definite need for such a module. In the second case, close scrutiny of the accounts is required, along with a speeded-up billing process and payment reminders. Before implementing a supporting module, however, it may be wise to get professional help.

It is not necessary to implement a supporting module when the general ledger module is implemented. It is much easier to become proficient with one module at a time, and the logical one to start with is the general ledger. On the other hand, if another area is a source of major problems, its module can be started up first. With a computer, the primary function of an accounting package is to help managers with their tasks. No computer application should ever be implemented merely to add up numbers and produce fancy reports. Priorities are determined by the problem areas.

Accounts Receivable   The accounts receivable module is primarily for tracking customer receivables, but it may also provide for invoicing and statement printing. Businesses that rely primarily on credit sales or that find a significant problem with large amounts outstanding in their accounts receivable can benefit greatly from the use of the accounts receivable module. Most accounts receivable modules perform some or all of the following functions: They

1. Produce open item or balance forward reconciliations for each customer.
2. Provide a list of all customers, with names, addresses, contact, credit limit, and assigned salesperson.
3. Process and post transaction entries for sales and cash receipts.
4. Print aged trial balances.
5. Print invoices and statements for sales.
6. Allow on-line inquiry in customer accounts.
7. Automatically calculate and post finance charges to designated accounts.
8. Control commissions due and print commission reports.
9. Interface with the general ledger module.

Accounts Payable   The accounts payable module is designed to track purchases on credit (other than inventory) from initial order through to receipt and to the final payment. Of course, one company's accounts

receivable is another company's account payable. Proper handling of payables may seem like a rather time-consuming and bothersome task. Some companies state publicly that they do not bother to keep track of their payables, because their creditors do it for them. But when one business controls its payable well, the receivables problems of other businesses decrease, and likely so do some of the receivables problems of the first business. Still, payables, along with payroll, are usually the last modules to be installed. Particularly in smaller companies, they are often of lesser importance than accounts receivable and inventory modules.

Most accounts payable modules perform some or all of the following functions: They

1. Maintain a listing of all creditors with name, address, person to contact, and telephone number.
2. Process and post transactions for purchases and cash disbursements.
3. Print journals.
4. Print the payables trial balance.
5. Produce the cash requirement report.
6. Allow on-line inquiry of creditors.
7. Prepare payment analysis for invoices due to be paid.
8. Prepare checks to be sent to creditors.
9. Print an accounts payable distribution report.
10. Interface with the general ledger module.
11. Carry out period end closing.

Inventory and Order Entry   An inventory, or order entry, system is designed to track inventory items until they are actually sold. It is important to keep track of inventory because there is a cost of carrying items in stock. Furthermore, by holding inventory, working capital is tied up that could be used for other purposes. Most successful businesses have some form of inventory control and very often the system is computerized.

The application of order entry represents the front end of the accounts receivable module. In some cases, the order entry system integrates directly with accounts receivable. In other cases, the accounts receivable systems take over at the point of sale. In either case, both modules likely share a common data base.

Inventory systems modules perform some or all of the following functions: They

1. Maintain an item file of all inventory items with quantity, location, and other details.
2. Handle the receiving transaction entry.
3. Edit and post all receiving entries.
4. Provide inventory costing on the basis of average cost, LIFO, or FIFO.
5. Allow on-line order status inquiry.
6. Print invoices for orders billed.
7. Print packing slips and order picking tickets.
8. Print the stock status report.
9. Print the backorder report.

10. Interface with the accounts receivable module and/or with the general ledger module.

Payroll Payroll is generally the least-used of the major accounting modules. It has not gained much popularity with microcomputer users for two reasons. First, it is the only module in accounting software that requires yearly changes; as tax rates and tax laws change, this module must be updated. Most business people are not experienced enough to make these changes each year and most software manufacturers do not want inexperienced programmers to be changing their programs.

A second, and probably more decisive, reason for limited use is the assistance of the banking industry in the United States in the preparation of payroll for clients. Some of the major banks perform this service for clients, using a professional group of computer people and a large mainframe system. The cost of bank-managed payroll service is so reasonable that running one's own system is often not worth it. Even some large companies with mainframes of their own have discontinued using their own payroll programs to use the banks' systems.

Payroll systems modules perform some or all of the following functions: They

1. Maintain listings of all employees, with name, address, taxpayer identification number, pay rate, earnings to date, pension payments to date, insurance to date, and insurable earnings.
2. Allow for maintenance of standard costing of payroll to various departments or profit centers.
3. Allow for on-line inquiry status of employees.
4. Produce the edit listing of payroll distribution.
5. Maintain employee totals for preparation of year-end government reporting forms and printout forms.
6. Prepare an analysis of monthly government remittances.
7. Interface with the general ledger module by posting period totals and producing audit trail reports.

Accounting Package Features

Accounting packages for a microcomputer can be expensive: $120 to $3,000. It is important to know what they can—and cannot—do. The first step is to do enough systems analysis work to determine the conditions that an accounting package must meet. All packages have various constraints, such as the number of accounts in the general ledger and the number of transactions per month. It is important to be sure that these constraints do not inhibit a specific accounting process.

Second, it is important to determine how much **expansion** is possible if the business grows. If expansion is not possible, then the package should be able to handle from the start as many accounts as the business is likely to have *including* future growth.

A third factor is **flexibility,** which is sometimes accompanied by complexity. One must be weighed against the other. A more complex

system, though requiring more experienced and knowledgeable people to operate, may in turn provide greater flexibility. This may be a good tradeoff.

Documentation for the accounting packages is, for the most part, well done. But purchasing a computerized accounting system is *not* purchasing any systems training. Indeed, those who sell these packages are often not capable of training the user. Therefore, good documentation is critical for successful implementation of the system.

Unlike other computer application packages, accounting packages generally do not offer **tutorials.** The user's own data become the tutorial. The user-friendly nature of accounting packages allows their users to become familiar with the package by using the most familiar data. As long as a user is aware that he or she cannot hurt the machine or the software and is sufficiently adventurous to try each module, the learning process can be a quick one.

A feature of significant importance in an accounting package is the software **support** afforded by the developer. Direct phone contact with the company should be provided for quick access to correct answers when problems are encountered. Talking with other users of the software soon reveals whether good support is available. In most cases, software developers are very approachable because their continued existence depends on the service they provide. Since users are paying for this support, they should use it.

Numbers and Words

Wags say the reason Lotus 1-2-3 has no real word-processing capabilities is that spreadsheet jocks cannot put a sentence together unless at least half of it consists of numbers. Hyperbolic or even envious as this may be, it is true that, for years, if you wanted to provide explanatory wrapping for a spreadsheet, you had to exit the spreadsheet program and call forth a separate word processor.

This switching is clumsy, requiring the transfer of sometimes commodious files between the two programs. And it means learning another program as well. But now at last there are add-in word processors for Lotus users.

Software sectarians, in coining the term "add-in," meant by it something quite distinct from the more familiar "add-on," which is used to denote independent, memory-resident software like Sidekick. An add-on can be summoned by the press of a key any time you are working at the computer, no matter what program you are running. An add-in, on the other hand, becomes an integral part of the program for which it is produced. It is grafted onto the host software, and in this instance it is as if the Lotus Development Corporation had released an entirely new version of Lotus 1-2-3, complete with a functional word processor.

Two Lotus add-ins I have been looking into are 4Word ($99.95 from Turner-Hall Publishing, Cupertino, Calif. 95014, telephone 408-253-9607) and Write In ($99.95 from Blossom Software Corporation, Cambridge, Mass. 02142, telephone 617-577-8879). These programs at first appear quite similar, right down to their matching price and their ability to work only with Lotus Release 2 or later versions. But there are some distinctive differences between them, and the decision on which one to buy will be largely a matter of personal preference based on a sum of small details.

The biggest difference between the two programs probably lies in the way they store their documents. Write In documents are stored as separate, independent files, while the 4Word documents are stored right in the 1-2-3 worksheet files.

One of the advantages of the Write In approach is that there is no way that entering text can inadvertently disrupt important Lotus worksheet files. This danger can be avoided with 4Word as well, by invoking the Lotus range commands. With those commands you can lock in the text area, preventing any overwriting of other material. But you have to remember to do it. The Write In storage tactic, then, is fail-safe, at least when it comes to disrupting other entries, while the 4Word approach leaves an opening for human error.

Another advantage of Write In is that it hides its formatting codes from view unless they are specifically called forth, while 4Word routinely displays all those chicken scratches right on screen. People accustomed to working with programs like WordStar are used to this kind of video clutter in their text, so for them it presumably poses no real problem. But I find formatting symbols a great distraction. Once again, personal taste will decide.

It is true that 4Word offers a preview mode, allowing you to view the results of your word processing stripped of its formatting codes. But the preview presented is not complete, since it does not display headers, page breaks and other print format variations.

Because Write In documents are stored separately from the Lotus worksheet, the program need not rely on Lotus for its printing output. It can therefore produce copy that is more sophisticated in its appearance. Write In also readily accepts data from a number of different documents, permitting the quick consolidation of information for reports that are to include material from more than one spreadsheet.

On the other hand, because these various documents are separate entities, the data from them are not available to other Lotus enhancers, which work only with Lotus files. Power users whose machines are loaded with such Lotus utilities as Hal, SQZ and Note It!, will then probably find 4Word more to their liking, because its document storage method accommodates all those other enhancements.

Another large plus for 4Word is that because its files are stored in Lotus, it is very easy to tie in live data from the spreadsheet. Whenever data are changed in the worksheet, they are changed in the word processing segment as well. Such a link saves a great amount of time when it is necessary to make frequent revisions or updating of the material.

A final point on avoiding human error that is in Write In's favor, however, is that it saves documents automatically. Lotus does not automatically save the material you have been working on when you exit the program, as many users have discovered to their distress. This means that any 4Word document in the works at the same time will also be lost unless you specifically instruct the program to save.

Apart from their different approaches to where data are to be kept, with the different operating consequences that divergence involves, Write In and 4Word are fairly similar. Both offer the basic word-processing functions of word wrap, paragraph reformatting, tab settings, block moves, mail merge and the like. Either is well suited to the task of turning the numerical data of a spreadsheet into a readable report with reasonable ease or otherwise wrapping it in text. Neither program is a full-power heavy-duty word processor, of course. Then again, no one would set out to use Lotus to write the Great American Novel.

Source: Erik Sandberg-Diment, "Personal Computers," *The New York Times,* June 30, 1987.

Summary and Key Terms

1. An **electronic spreadsheet program** lets the user create a spreadsheet model; it lets the computer recalculate the model whenever data are changed; it lets the model be saved and stored for later use; and it lets the model and the calculated results be printed out. An electronic spreadsheet can be used for any situation that can be described numerically.

2. A spreadsheet that has been set up for use in a specific situation is called a **model.** The **template** of a model is its basic format exclusive of (or before) data entry.

3. Spreadsheets are invaluable for many kinds of business and personal financial **applications** that keep track of what has happened, predict what may happen, and/or develop information to assist decision makers.

4. Most spreadsheet programs are single-tasking. The current **mode** is always displayed on the screen, which is divided into the **work area** and the **control panel,** with its **entry line, status line,** and **prompt line.** The work area is arranged in **columns** and **rows** that create cells, into which **numerical** or **alphabetic data** or **mathematical formulas** are entered. Cells can be identified by coordinates. A cell coordinate consists of that cell's column letter and row number.

5. Important considerations in choosing a spreadsheet are a given package's tradeoffs between power and simplicity and its help features, documentation, spreadsheet dimensions, and built-in computational abilities.

6. Like word processing packages, spreadsheet packages have special features, functions, and **menu-driven commands,** such as save, copy, insert, and delete. **Windows** and **macros** are other time- and work-saving features of good spreadsheet programs.

7. **Integrated packages** contain more than one application in one software program. Word processing, data base management, a spreadsheet, and graphics are the applications most likely to be in integrated packages. **Windowing software** can create some of the convenience of an integrated package from separate application software programs.

8. Microcomputer **accounting packages** have a separate **module** for each of the five main functional areas of accounting: **general ledger, accounts receivable, accounts payable, inventory,** and **payroll.** An **integrated module** can transfer its data individually or in summary form to the other modules. Many accounting packages are in **data base format,** but the data files cannot be manipulated as those in a data base management system can, for reasons of utility and security.

Review Questions

Fill-In

1. A _____ represents the bare bones of the mathematical model used in a spreadsheet application.

2. Cells in a spreadsheet can include _____ data, _____ data, and formulas.

3. In a spreadsheet, the _____ line displays commands, prompts, and the contents of cells being edited.

4. The _____ line includes the present cell address and the contents of the cell.

5. Two of the four possible modes of a spreadsheet program are the _____ mode and the _____ mode.

6. The _____ function in a spreadsheet program enables you to gain access to an interactive reference manual.

7. The command you would use if you want to replicate formulas, values, or cell contents is called the _____ command.

8. The function you would use in order to store a template on a disk is the _____ function.

9. Certain areas of a spreadsheet can be specified by printing a _____ instead of specifying its coordinates.

10. Two factors to be taken into account when evaluating a spreadsheet package are its _____ and _____.

Matching

Listed below are a number of functions of various modules of accounting packages. Fill in the letter of the correct module at the following functions:

a. Accounts receivable

b. Accounts payable

c. Payroll

d. General ledger

e. Inventory

_____ 1. Prints a stock status report.

_____ 2. Is the heart of an accounting system.

_____ 3. A program that includes the printing of statements and invoices.

_____ 4. Maintains a listing of all creditors, including names, addresses, and phone numbers.

_____ 5. Prints a backorder report.

_____ 6. Maintains a listing of all employees, including names, addresses, and taxpayer ID numbers.

_____ 7. Is the least frequently used module of an accounting system.

_____ 8. Prints the income statement and the balance sheet.

_____ 9. Calculates and posts finance charges to designated accounts.

_____ 10. Produces the cash requirement report.

Discussion Questions

1. What are several applications of a spreadsheet program?

2. What factors should be taken into account in selecting an accounting package?

3. What are the advantages and disadvantages of an integrated software package?

Computer Graphics and Desktop Publishing

9

Chapter Objectives

After studying this chapter, you should be able to

1. Describe the applications of computer graphics, including presentation graphics, computer-assisted design and manufacturing, and desktop publishing.

2. Recognize how business graphics is used in preparing charts, maps, and presentation materials.

3. Understand the characteristics of desktop publishing software.

Dennis, the manager you read about in Chapter 8, who uses TWIN spreadsheet software to prepare his department's annual budget, has to present a five-year forecast to division management. The black-and-white graphs he can produce with TWIN and the Epson dot matrix printer in his personal-computer-based system are fine for inclusion in the ordinary quarterly and annual budget reports. But for this presentation—to upper management, many of whom are unfamiliar with the specifics of his operation—Dennis needs a different level of graphics support. He wants color versions of the charts and graphs, not only as part of a summary report he will hand out but as transparencies, to use in overhead projections during the presentation.

Not long ago, the kinds of graphics Dennis wants would have been too time-consuming and costly to produce to be considered for an in-house presentation. But personal computers, graphics software, color printers and plotters, and related equipment and services are helping to make sophisticated graphics available to businesses and individuals. Used thoughtfully, these visual aids—called presentation graphics—add impact to many kinds of business reports.

The term *computer graphics* is used to cover a huge range of applications, from a simple one-color bar graph created with an integrated package at a personal computer to an aircraft design created at and tested within a supercomputer. This chapter will introduce you to three application areas: presentation graphics, computer-assisted design and computer-assisted manufacturing, and desktop publishing.

What Is Computer Graphics

Forty years ago, the only way for computers to share data with users was through lists of numbers printed out on paper. In 1950, the U.S. Air Force hired MIT's Digital Computer Lab to come up with a new way to display and interpret information. MIT's solution was cathode-ray tube (CRT) monitors.

During the 1950s, the Air Force had MIT adapt the Whirlwind computer into a system that could compute and display the courses of aircraft. MIT researchers developed the Semiautomatic Ground Environment (SAGE), a system that introduced a feature taken for granted in computers today: Data were displayed as pictures and text on televisionlike monitors. The monitors showed the radar-detected paths of airplanes over images that looked much like weather maps. Each single SAGE computer weighed 250 tons,

Visual Thinking

Professor Bill Benzon of Rensselaer Polytechnic Institute of Troy, New York, theorizes that expressing ideas in a visual form is an aid to thinking. For this reason, Benzon believes that the Apple Macintosh is a highly significant development in microcomputing, as it makes expressing ideas visually easy, even for people with no artistic ability. Benzon points to highly creative mathematicians such as Einstein, whose ideas first took shape as visual images before he was even able to express them as words or in mathematical symbols. Benzon contends that in order to hold the image of an idea in mind while developing it, it is beneficial to create some kind of representation of it in the form of a model or drawing. This is what James Watson and Francis Crick did when they discovered the structure of DNA: They built a three-dimensional model of it in order to be able to both understand and work with their idea, as well as to demonstrate it to others. "Writing and drawing provide external support for thought" (p. 114), Benzon contends. But while writing is relatively easy to learn, drawing and building three-dimensional structures are not. With its easily mastered graphics capabilities, Benzon says, the Macintosh can be a tool to facilitate thinking.

As an example of how images help us to think, Benzon cites the phenomenon psychologists call the **gestalt switch,** or moving back and forth from one interpretation of an image to another. At one moment a particular image looks like a white vase centered on a black background. In another glance, you see the silhouettes of two faces in profile looking at one another. According to Benzon, images like these that convey an idea are similar to proverbs and fables, which of course are communicated verbally. But images are more difficult to pass on to others. And this is where the Macintosh comes in. By making visual expression almost as easy as writing, the computer and its software enable people to create images of their ideas, work with them, and pass them on to others in the form of printouts.

Benzon discusses the method of loci as an illustration of the fact that integrating visual and verbal information is important in thought processes. The method of loci is a system for remembering verbal material by visualizing it in a particular location. In ancient Greece, young people trained in public

had 55,000 tubes, and was connected to 50 display monitors. Interestingly, these computers were considerably less powerful than the average personal computer today.

MIT made another landmark contribution to graphics display in the early 1960s, when faculty member and graphics pioneer Ivan Sutherland demonstrated a computer system, called Sketchpad, that used a light pen to sketch lines on the computer screen. It was an **interactive** graphics device, for it allowed someone to use a computer to create and revise an image as an artist would, instead of by programming and reprogramming.

Computer graphics, the visual display of information by computer, has developed in impressive ways in 40 years. Today, computer graphics has important applications in business, medicine, science and engineering, and the arts, ranging from the most practical—such as package design—to the most esoteric—such as wind-shear simulation.

Engineers, designers, and architects use **computer-aided design (CAD)** to electronically sketch and test their ideas. Manufacturers can

speaking used this technique of visualizing the ideas of the speech as situated in various parts of a particular place. The Greeks might have used a temple and pictured themselves walking around it to retrieve this idea from the first column on the left and that idea from the statue in the corner. On a memorized mental walk through the temple, the speaker goes from idea to idea, the images of each place in the temple activating each subsequent idea of the talk. In a sense, Benzon points out, this kind of memory-retrieval system works in a way that is similar to that of a computer. Whereas the computer assigns codes to information stored in memory, the human mind assigns a place to each piece of data. Both systems later use their own particular indexing system to retrieve stored information.

Today we use illustrations to make our ideas more understandable. Columns of numbers showing profits of a particular company over the last three decades are easier to grasp when presented as a bar graph. People studying grammar often draw diagrams of sentences as an aid to understanding grammatical structure and the way a sentence's various parts work together. More complex images, the double helix that Watson and Crick worked with, for example, while highly informative and useful in communicating concepts, are quite difficult for most people to draw. For this reason, many ideas that would be simple to grasp visually must be described verbally, a method that is ill-suited to them.

The Macintosh allows users to access images that have already been drawn by others and to employ them in their own representations. Without any artistic skill whatsoever, Benzon points out, MacPaint can help users create not only recognizable images of, say, a horse but also abstract images representing concepts. In addition, users can create completely new images to work with to help in the development of an idea or to pass it along to someone else. Benzon believes that in this way the Macintosh can be used as a tool for better, more productive thinking.

Source: Bill Benzon, "The Visual Mind and the Macintosh," *Byte,* January 1985, pp. 113–130.

convert such computerized designs into instructions for **computer-aided manufacturing (CAM)** systems. Cars, sneakers, even spacecraft have been designed this way.

Businesses use **presentation graphics** to create charts and graphs and other kinds of illustrations derived from standard business tools such as statistical analysis programs and spreadsheets. Graphics of this kind can be displayed on the screen, printed out in black and white or color, made into slides for group presentations, or included in reports.

Computer-aided publishing uses graphics to visualize the pages of books, magazines, and newspapers as they are being made up. Different elements of text and illustrations can be moved around on screen until a satisfactory page layout is created. Businesses and individuals alike use similar programs on personal computers to give a professional look to reports, memos, newsletters, and other publications in what has come to be known as **desktop publishing.**

Computer Graphics: Image of a Wireframe Model of a Rotary Turbine Engine

Precision Visuals International, Science Photo Library/Photo Researchers

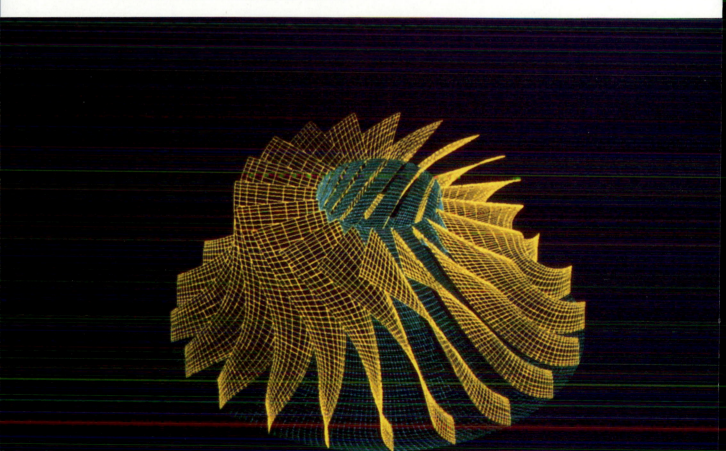

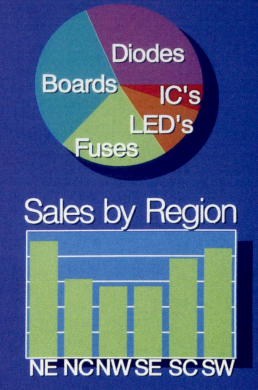

Presentation Graphics: An Example of Pie, Bar, and Area Charts

Magi Corp.

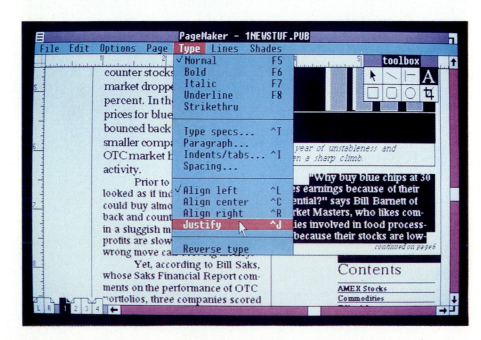

Desktop Publishing: A
Screen from PageMaker
Software

Courtesy of Aldus Corporation

The Influence of Personal Computers

The development and increasing popularity of personal computers was largely responsible for the development of presentation graphics and desktop publishing. Graphics capabilities were important in the first widely available small computers—those meant for home video games. Inside each of these units were microprocessors and stored programs that created screen images. In fact, the 1977 Apple II was originally intended for home video games. The Macintosh (1984) produced much more sophisticated graphics and offered the user **icons**—small screen symbols—rather than word command menus. For instance, the icon command for drawing a line on-screen might be represented as a small pencil.

The use of icons had been the subject of several years' research at Xerox's Palo Alto Research Center (PARC) but hadn't yet resulted in a mass-produced product when Apple Computer cofounder Steven Jobs toured PARC in 1979. Deeply impressed with the use of icons, Jobs made them part of the interfaces in the Apple's Lisa and Macintosh computers. The Macintosh family of computers deserves credit for popularizing the icon interface in personal and technical computing. In a sense, the icon interface also helped users to think of computers not just as number crunchers but as tools with integral graphics aspects.

The Role of Larger Computers

Although personal computers have put graphics capabilities into millions of homes, offices, schools, and small businesses, PCs represent the lower end

A MacWrite Screen

Courtesy of Apple Computer Inc.

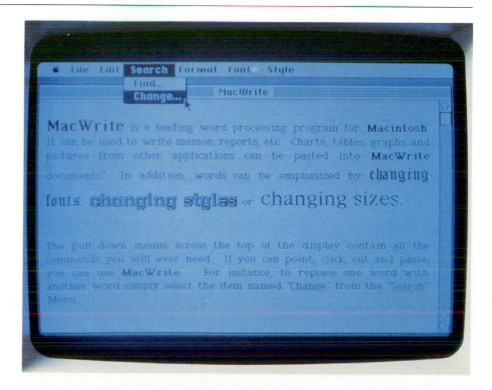

of hardware. Many companies have graphics terminals that are hooked up to mainframes. Tektronix, Megatek, Ramtek, DEC, and IBM all make popular equipment in this category. These terminals can create extremely fine-grained, high-resolution images and have some of their own (local) computing ability.

Personal computers that are connected into so-called networks with other computing resources are becoming common graphics terminals as well. Some of them can serve as "front ends," or operator consoles, to mainframe applications. Others can merge data from remote sources into PC programs, as, for example linking on-line data from the New York Stock Exchange directly into a Lotus 1-2-3 program for ongoing stockmarket analyses with accompanying charts.

Engineering **workstations** are powerful computers made by Apollo Computer, Sun Microsystems, Hewlett-Packard, and Digital Equipment Corp., among others. They are designed for use by scientists and engineers. These systems are made for computer networks as well as for stand-alone computing.

Computer Graphics Standards

Many individuals and organizations use a variety of hardware and software from different manufacturers for graphics applications. This is possible because developers of graphics-related products honor certain computing standards that allow files to be exchanged between different programs and entered and displayed on different hardware devices. The Computer Graphics Metafile standard, for example, applies to graphics software. Many other standards exist, and new graphics products must honor or work with some of these as well.

CAD/CAM and Design Arts

Engineers, architects, cartographers, technical illustrators, and advertising agencies, among others, rely on CAD, or computer-assisted design. The tremendous usefulness of these systems is reflected in the fact that in 1986 sales of CAD/CAM equipment reached $3.3 billion.

Engineers were the first to harness graphics as a design tool. Companies were willing to make the investment in expensive CAD equipment because such systems shaved time and dollars off product design cycles.

An engineer using CAD can easily view an object from any angle, copy it, change dimensions, or perform other manipulations. (The ability to render an image that looks like the final product is called "what you see is what you get" or WYSIWYG.) The engineer can submit the final design to computerized simulations of real-world conditions that might affect the behavior of the part or system, such as simulating extreme heat and air-pressure variations on automobile tires.

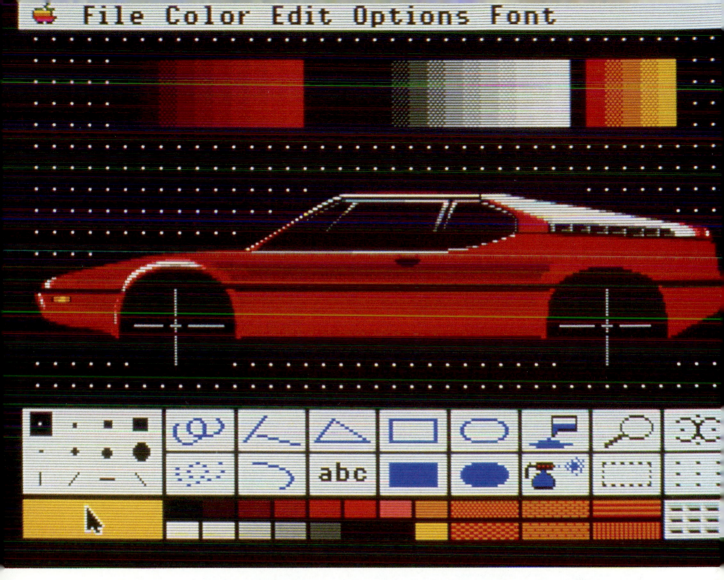

Graphics Software Is an Important Design Tool

Courtesy of Baudville Co.

In architecture, computers are equally important. Before a shovelful of earth is moved, an architect can merge a computerized building design into a captured videotape scene of the future construction site. That building design contains everything from staircases to electrical and piping systems. Along the way, the computer keeps exact records of what materials will be needed reducing waste and benefiting the schedule.

Computer-integrated manufacturing (CIM) is the process of graphically creating and then electronically transferring designs to the manufacturing process. CAD files are converted by computer into instructions for robots, milling and machining tools, and automated inspection of the finished product.

CIM also permits the engineer to monitor the assembly line via computer. True CIM requires that different types of computers be able to

218

A CAD Drawing, *left,* Being Turned into Milling Instructions, *right*

SDRC, I-DEAS Software

"talk" with each other, something that is more easily said than done; and perhaps this requirement is the most important reason for agreed-upon standards for both hardware and software, as mentioned above.

Two-dimensional Programs

Engineering designs are based on geometry. CAD designs thus begin with basic entities called **primitives,** which include lines, arcs, splines, points, polygons, rectangles, and other geometric forms. Primitives may be selected through icons or word menus, depending on the program. They are arranged on-screen to create skeletal or **wireframe** models.

Solid Models

The initial wireframe is composed of dimensions (length, width, and height) of the different geometries. The next step in mechanical design is modeling the object's actual mass. This means that the computer regards the model as a solid, not just an empty wireframe.

Once a three-dimensional model is established, the computer can rotate it or display different views of the model. The computer can quickly remove lines that the designer wouldn't ordinarily see (this operation is called hidden-line removal) and then shade the surfaces. Besides three-dimensional wireframe and surface shading, the computer can actually compute and present a solid model with a true interior. Some software also contains routines for effects such as different light sources and surface textures. (Many iullustration and graphics animation packages use similar techniques.)

Output and Display

CAD designs are displayed in many ways. Hard copy on paper, plastic, film, or vellum are all common. Most CAD hard copy is created on a plotter (pen or electrostatic) or a printer (dot matrix, ink jet, or laser).

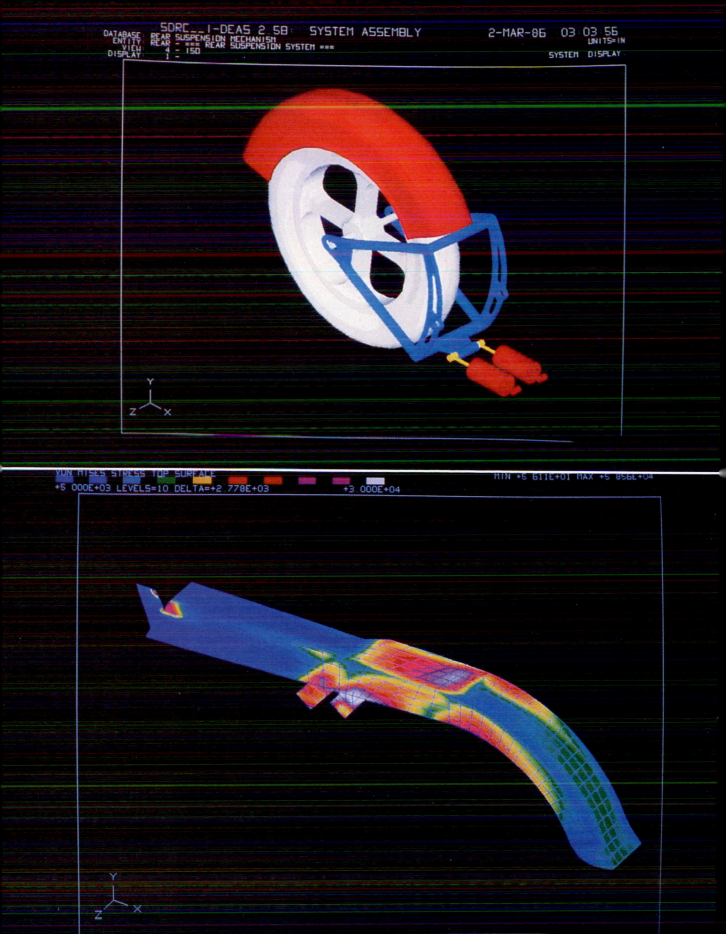

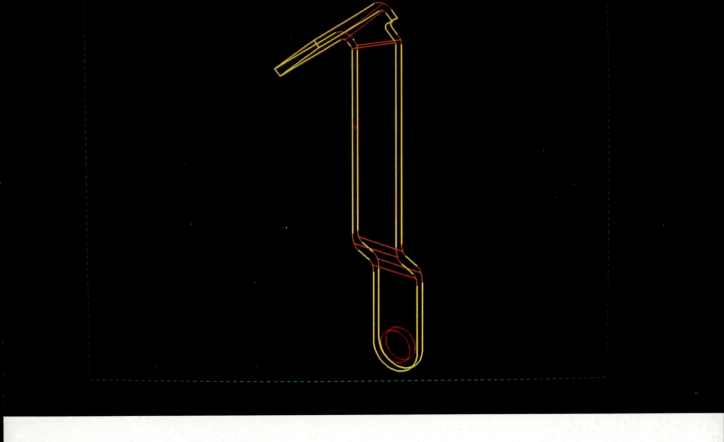

These graphics images and the images in the chapter-opening photo come from a single graphics data base for a computer-assisted engineering, design, and manufacturing system. Says its producer, GE Calma Company, "With this single data base, the product development cycle flows smoothly from a solid model to a 3-D wireframe to engineering analysis and finally to manufacturing applications." *Top left,* the screen shows a study of motorcycle rear wheel assembly; *bottom,* graphic output of finite element analysis of a motorcycle chain guard; *above,* a sheet metal design and manufacturing program is used to fabricate a brake pedal.

Specialized terminals can also create soft copy, a quickly computed, high-resolution screen image of the CAD file. These screen images are practical in cases where the engineer wants to display a design but has neither the time nor need to print it out.

Finally, the CAD image or images of a part or product can be incorporated into the user's manual and into materials for marketing staff and distributors, as well. Frequently, a manual is prepared concurrently with a product, so that both are ready for release at the same time.

Any product is subject to considerable review and revision, and any related change in the manual must be reviewed and approved. Thus,

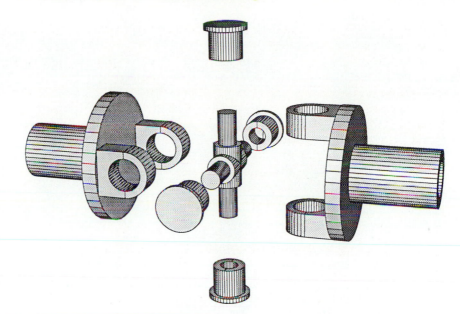

Shaded CAD Output from a Laser Printer

VERSACAD Designer

computerized systems for preparing graphics and text for manuals and other documentation save valuable time and ensures accuracy of printed materials.

Business Graphics

The role of business graphics is to enhance communication both within and outside the office. No consensus exists on how often this goal is actually achieved. Nevertheless, in the last few years all sorts of graphics have become common in the corporate workplace. Like other applications for personal computers (word processing, spreadsheets, and data bases, for example) graphics reinforce the usefulness of office desktop computing.

In certain applications, such as the production of presentation-quality slides, computer graphics have allowed companies to reduce their audio-visual staffs while increasing that department's output. Graphics have also created roles for individuals who can use, and can help others to use, these systems.

Uses for Business Graphics

Business graphics allow charts, plots, and maps to be generated directly from spreadsheet and data base files in order to study statistics, spot relationships among items, and trace emerging trends. Products exist

allowing many ways to enter data and perform modeling, forecasting, project management, optimization and quality control.

Most of these programs begin by having the user "import" information (via a file interchange standard) directly from a spreadsheet or data base, or enter information directly. The system prompts choices as to format (say, chart or text), or the kind of chart (such as pie, bar, or area). Many programs offer templates or basic patterns to follow (or customize) for creating a graphics presentation.

Word charts are frequently combined with graphics for presentations. A word chart might contain titles, introductory information, and a chart of how a company is organized.

Peer and Presentation Graphics

Business graphics systems may be divided into the two categories of peer or desktop graphics and presentation graphics. As the name implies, peer or desktop graphics are for small groups. Dennis, the manager you read about at the start of this chapter, might use such graphics within his department. Such graphics take little time to produce and help to convey ideas with relatively plain visuals.

Presentation graphics are both higher quality and more complex. At one time, presentation graphics were limited to slides and overhead transparencies. But now, software accommodates illustrations, freehand drawing, and combined text and graphics. Further, many graphics packages can create graphics for use in an office publication.

Graphics utilities let the user enhance a basic graphic beyond a particular software package's programmed abilities, in order to achieve presentation quality. In the case of a pie chart, a utility might give you more choices in text types (fonts) or sizes, or add color and a three-dimensional

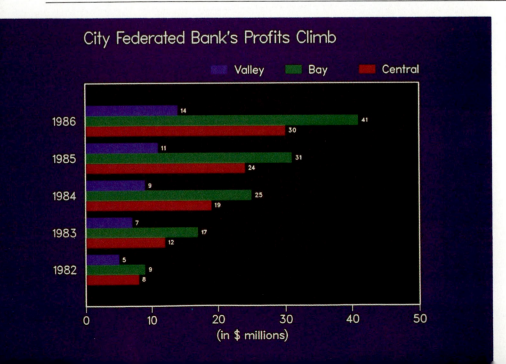

Presentation Graphics Give Impact to Statistical Data

Courtesy of Computer Associates International

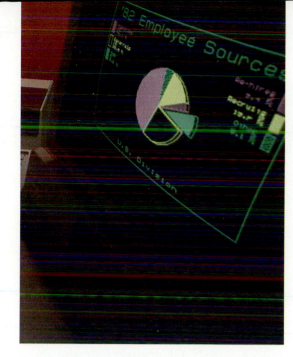

WYSIWYG: Hard Copy of
this Graph Would Look Like
The Screen Display

Management Science America, Inc.

effect to the chart. The utility might allow a series of visuals to be combined from different and otherwise incompatible computing resources in other departments.

Seeing the Results Thanks to WYSIWYG, the first place the resulting graph can be seen is on the computer screen. After that, there are many more options. Suppose you've created a pie chart. It can be sent to a dot matrix or laser printer for a quick printout. To print color, it must be output on a plotter, electrostatic printer, or thermal transfer printer. With a telecommunications set-up, it can be transferred by modem to a remote location for printout.

Presentation Graphics Can Be in Slide Form

Courtesy of Bell & Howell

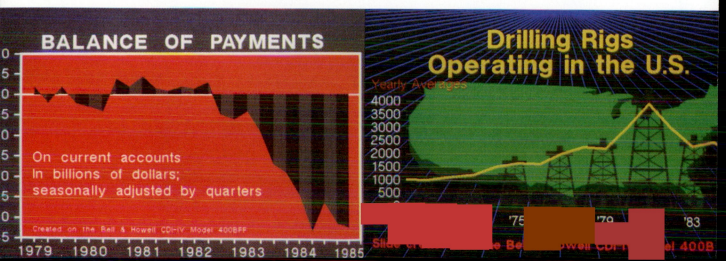

Presentation Graphics Can Be in Transparency Form

Courtesy of Eastman Kodak Company

Film Recorders and Slide Service Bureaus   But perhaps you need the pie chart for a group presentation and want to create a sharp-looking 35mm slide or transparency. Two types of film recorders will give you a professional looking result. One is basically a specialized camera; the other produces the slides directly from computer data.

What if neither is available? In that case, you can send the graphics files via modem to one of the many service companies that convert personal computer graphics into slides or overhead transparencies. Many graphics software packages come with directions on how to do this. Using such a service over and over eventually equals the cost of a film recorder. Nevertheless, overnight services can make up in convenience what they lack in cost effectiveness.

Large Screen and Overhead Projection   Another option is to use the graphics terminal itself as a slide projector. Many graphics software packages allow you to organize a series of graphics and text charts in the order you desire. Then, the image can be sent to a high-resolution large-screen video monitor. This image can also be sent to a computerized overhead projector that uses a liquid crystal shutter (LCS). The LCS is attached to the computer and produces the image in monochrome on an otherwise clear screen.

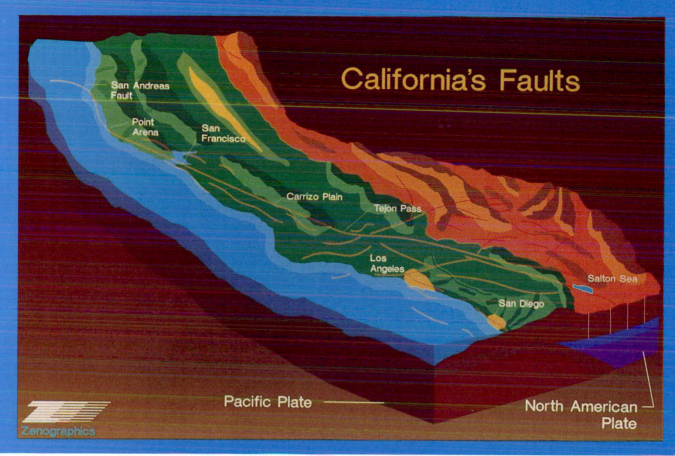

California's Faults

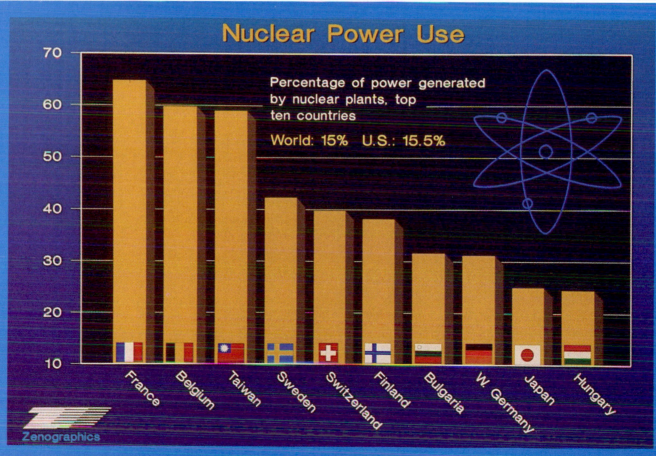

Nuclear Power Use

Desktop and Corporate Publishing

The newest development in corporate graphics has the title of "desktop publishing." This application is making word processing and business graphics more productive as they combine with desktop publishing software to turn out well-designed documents that would once have been professionally typeset and printed.

For years, electronic publishing required the use of a computer-based typesetting system designed to produce documents with complex page layouts, different print styles, and integrated graphics. Today, with the use of PC-based software, users can create, edit, make up page layouts for, and produce high-quality printed documents. Applications include calendars, brochures, letterheads, invitations, invoices, newsletters, and financial reports. The many PC-based software packages under $1000 have created "desktop publishing."

The components of a desktop publishing system include:

1. *Page composition software,* which pulls together text and graphics and provides the on-screen formatting tools to make it possible to lay out the content, columns, headings, and so forth.

2. *The computer,* which must be powerful because desktop publishing not only involves putting a graphic image on the screen but also requires such processing tasks as keeping track of word position on multiple pages and re-hyphenating.

3. *System software,* the operating system and its environment, which should enforce some standards on data types and formats as well as provide the ability to display graphics and text fonts in a consistent fashion.

Ventura Desktop Publishing Software

Courtesy of Xerox Corporation

Presentation Graphics, *left page*

Courtesy of Zenographics

An In-depth Look at PAGEMAKER

Aldus Corporation's PageMaker, originally designed for the Macintosh and Apple LaserWriter printer, was the first major desktop publishing software program incorporating WYSIWYG (What you see is what you get—in other words, a screen display that shows the layout the printed page will have) page displays, integration of text and graphics, and laser printer output. Today, PageMaker is also available on the PC.

Pages are laid out by creating columns on a page and inputting text or graphics. Text can also be imported from word processing programs. PageMaker supports multiple fonts and type styles (e.g. bold, italic, underline, etc.), automatic hyphenation, and control over·interword spacing. Other features include running headers and footers, automatic page numbering, the ability to wrap text around graphics.

Graphics, including lines, rectangles, circles and ovals, can be created, changed, and stored using PageMaker. Graphics and text can be positioned directly on the page or stored in a work area on the streen. One of the major strengths of PageMaker is its ease of use. With only an hour of training, a user can produce simple documents.

Source: Diane Burns and S. Venit, "Muscling in on the Mac," *PC Magazine,* February 10, 1987, pp. 143–150 (about PageMaker).

4. *Display,* which makes it possible to see how your document will be printed.

5. *Input devices,* making it possible to create text separated by lines and boxes and formatted with different type styles and sizes. In addition, most of the graphic images used in desktop publishing are clip art —images produced specifically for use in page composition programs.

6. *Output* is the formatted, printed document, usually printed out at a laser printer with high resolution and quality.

Desktop publishing requires that the skills of writing, editing, and page layout be combined with the knowledge of running the computer application. Traditionally, these two sets of skills have been separated, but today, there is a demand for people who can combine them.

Design

In desktop publishing (as in business graphics) the impact of the final product is partly determined by its basic design. That means you need to know more than just how to type in the command that executes the software. You need to know a little something about designing a document.

Fortunately, many packages allow the user to set up a style sheet, which allows certain standard design features to be stored and reused. Codes for such features can be entered into the original word processing files. The style sheet translates these into the actual element. What appears on screen once the page design program is initiated is more or less how the publication will appear when printed.

Once a style sheet is developed, and you are ready to prepare your document, you "flow" text from a word processor file into pages and

WYSIWYG: Seeing a Layout on the Screen Makes Good Design Easier to Achieve

Courtesy of Aldus Corporation

around pre-masked areas where illustrations, graphics or advertising will appear. Some desktop page design programs let you edit the text interactively in the WYSIWYG format.

Fonts   The word **font** refers to type and means a set of characters in a particular design: Times Roman, Helvetica, and San Francisco, for example. Fonts also come in **sizes**—generally in increments of two—10, 12, 14, 18,

On the following two pages you will see examples of real printed materials created with PageMaker software, as assembled in an Aldus Corporation brochure.

Courtesy of Aldus Corporation © 1986, Aldus Corporation.

A Selection of Fonts

σ ισ Σψμβολ
Symbol 30)

This is Geneva 14

Palatino 72

This is Athens 2·

i.ce 72

is is Zapf Chancery

This is Times 12

❊▲ ❊▲
f Dingbats)

This is San Francisco 36

This is Helvetica 18

his is New York 30

This is Ava

······ 48

Garde 60

Here's What You
Desktop

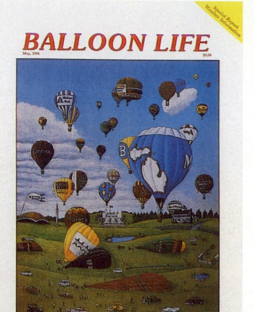

Magazine by Tom Hamilton, Balloon Life Magazine, Inc.

Catalog by Judith Baldwin, Ceramic Supply of New York and New Jersey.

Brochure by Kristen Ransom, Communique, for the Duck Inn.

Letterhead, Business Card by Kristen Ransom, Communique, for Cooks Headquarters.

Tabloid by Bill Bosler, FDR Publications, for Thorek Hospital and Medical Center.

Small Business Communications by Lisa Menders for Frank's Nursery and Crafts, Inc.

Can Do With Publishing.

A LAKEWOOD PUBLICATION

TRAINING DIRECTORS' FORUM
NEWSLETTER
A Forum for Leaders and Managers of Training

Volume 2, Number 4   April, 1986

Protecting a training budget when finances are tight requires timing, sales skills and corporate perspective

Is top management swinging the budget ax in your organization? If so, it's probably too late to prevent deep cuts in your department's spending unless you've already invested a large percentage of your time selling the importance of training.

Robert Schull, chief of operational air crew training at Scott Air Force Base, led a group discussion, How to Keep Training the #1 Priority, at Training Directors' Day at TRAINING '85 in New York. The main idea the group agreed upon, Schull says, is that training managers must keep alive the perception that vital organizations must continually nurture their people and therefore training must be unencumbered and the last entry to be cut when trimming budgets.

"The group had a variety of experiences. Basically what we came up with is that to make training a top priority chief trainers need to keep the impetus alive at staff meetings, through memos to CEOs, and through reports on the numbers and needs of people to be trained. Every department director in an organization has a view of what the department cannot afford to lose. But the only common thread throughout any organization has to be the training program. You must have commitment," Schull says.

Schull presents a variety of data in statistical formats to make his case for the training he provides to all military airlift aircraft personnel. The percent of personnel totally qualified for particular jobs; list of people who are not fully trained; projections about how many people must be trained in each of the next five years,

based on attrition and promotions.

"If a training officer sits back and says nothing, training will be pushed aside. You have to understand how people get into power positions in organizations; it's the top sales people or the top production people who move up. And those people don't always have the management skills or the knowledge of what it takes to make the whole corporation work. Either a top manager has a brainchild of his own and will support a training program, or you have to put him through the program sp

If management isn't sold on training you might as well stay home to bake cookies.

front to get the support. You have to get the support from the top down.

"If training is going to succeed we need to be vibrant, aggressive and action oriented. We've got to make people understand why these things are important and why anything less than the ideal might not have the desired impact." Schull spends about 33 percent of his time selling the importance of training. "It's all the time I have. The majority of it is involved in protecting my budget."

Often, Schull says, training directors say no to new concepts suggested by

training due to a lack of funds. He suggests, however, that reevaluating how training dollars are spent can lead to restructuring that might satisfy the need for the new concept while retaining the integrity of existing training.

"The hardest thing for a training chief is to see what could be deleted, if necessary, to add something new. Often times it becomes a matter of restructuring a training system in order to in-

continued on page 2

INSIDE STORIES...
• The Editors' Forum...p.2
• Hiring Consultants...p.3
• How to Select a CBT Authoring Program...p.4
• Problem Column...p. 5
• Profile—Melinda Bickerstaff American Express...p.6
• Eye on Training—a column by Ron Zemke...p.7
• Directors' Notebook...p.8

—Contributors to this issue...p.5

An Alternative View

Newsletter by Brian McDermott, Lakewood Publications.

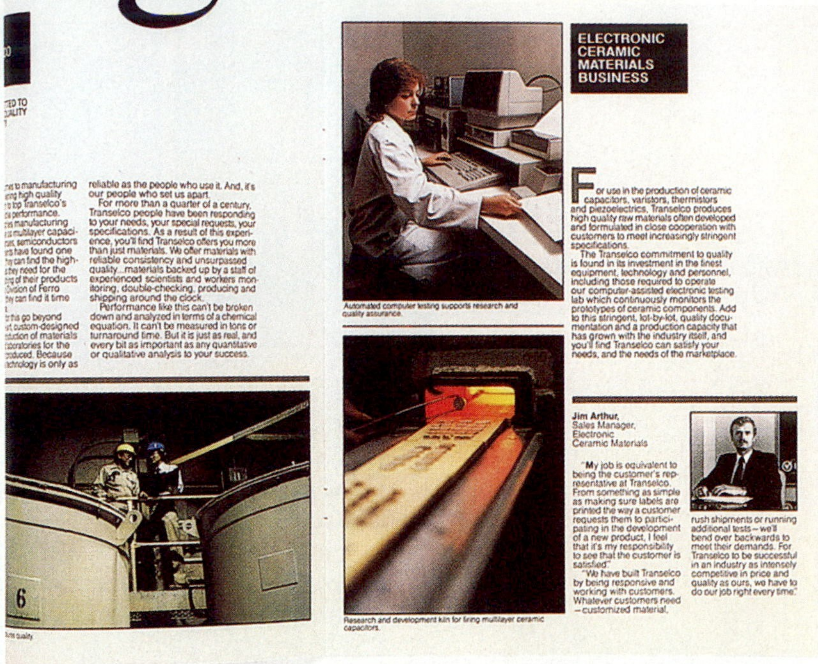

ELECTRONIC CERAMIC MATERIALS BUSINESS

to manufacturing ... high quality ... performance. ... top Transelco's ... manufacturing ... multilayer capacitors, semiconductors ... have found one ... can find the high-... need for the ... of their products ... of Ferro ... can find it time

... go beyond ... custom-designed ... of materials ... laboratories for the ... Because ... technology is only as

reliable as the people who use it. And, it's our people who set us apart.

For more than a quarter of a century, Transelco people have been responding to your needs, your special requests, your specifications. As a result of this experience, you'll find Transelco offers you more than just materials. We offer materials with reliable consistency and unsurpassed quality...materials backed up by a staff of experienced scientists and workers monitoring, double-checking, producing and shipping around the clock.

Performance like this can't be broken down and analyzed in terms of a chemical equation. It can't be measured in tons or turnaround time. But it is just as real, and every bit as important as any quantitative or qualitative analysis to your success.

Automated computer testing supports research and quality assurance.

For use in the production of ceramic capacitors, varistors, thermistors and piezoelectrics, Transelco produces high quality raw materials often developed and formulated in close cooperation with customers to meet increasingly stringent specifications.

The Transelco commitment to quality is found in its investment in the finest equipment, technology and personnel, including those required to operate our computer-assisted electronic testing lab which continuously monitors the prototypes of ceramic components. Add to this stringent, lot-by-lot, quality documentation and a production capacity that has grown with the industry itself, and you'll find Transelco can satisfy your needs, and the needs of the marketplace.

Jim Arthur, Sales Manager, Electronic Ceramic Materials

"My job is equivalent to being the customer's representative at Transelco. From something as simple as making sure labels are printed the way a customer requests them to participating in the development of a new product, I feel that it's my responsibility to see that the customer is satisfied.

"We have built Transelco by being responsive and working with customers. Whatever customers need —customized material,

rush shipments or running additional tests—we'll bend over backwards to meet their demands. For Transelco to be successful in an industry as intensely competitive in price and quality as ours, we have to do our job right every time."

Research and development kiln for firing multilayer ceramic capacitors.

Brochure by Joanne and David Lenweaver, Lenweaver Design, for Transelco Division, Ferro Corporation.

Chapter 5 Fabrication

Wooden Signs

Various materials and techniques are available for making signs. In the following pages, a selection of sign fabrication methods for each type of sign making material are briefly described and commented on.

Painted or printed: Exterior grade plywood, made with waterproof glues, is a good inexpensive material for painted or printed exterior signs. Duraply or Permashield plywoods are covered with a fibreboard face, with a smooth surface for painting. In all cases, when plywood is used the edges should be protected and sealed from moisture.

Carved: Redwood, cedar, cypress or special grades of pine can be used to produce carved wooden signs. The design to be reproduced is transferred at actual size to the solid wood block, and the craftsman will then carve the letter forms and image by hand. The elements in the sign are then painted by hand, often in a number of colours, and sometimes the finished sign is sealed with special protective sealant to guard it from the elements.

Routed: Routing machines (routers) can be used to inscribe letterforms into the face of wooden signs. These machines can be either hand held or controlled to follow the contours of a stencil guide. Painting and finishing is the same as for other wooden signs.

Cut-out: Shaped letters or symbols can be sawn from wood, sanded and then finished by painting or with metallic finishes such as gold or aluminum leaf. Cut-out wooden letters painted with gold leaf are extremely durable and some have been known to survive over twenty years of exposure to the elements.

Sandblasted: Woods like redwood, with very even grain, can be sandblasted. The wooden sign block is covered with a rubber stencil from which the letterforms have been cut. A fine sand is then propelled against the exposed areas of the sign face, thereby etching a channel into the wood. A softer wood will provide a deeper cut. The sign can then be painted or sealed to protect it from the effects of the weather.

Metal Signs

Cut-out: Individual letters or symbols, as well as logotypes and other signatures can be cut in one piece from large sheets of metal. A pattern at full size is laid over a metal plate and a band saw is used to cut along the edges of the pattern. The rough edges are finished by filing or sanding. Most metals can be used to make this type of sign, including aluminum, stainless steel, bronze and brass and the result is a durable, prestige, low maintenance sign. To achieve alternate finishes, the metal can be plated, enamelled or anodized.

Cast: This process can be used to produce high quality, durable, prestige signs, either as individual letters or entire signs. It is often used to create plaques commemorating heritage or historic sites. The casting process involves making a pattern out of plastic, metal or wood; packing the pattern with molding sand to create a mold; and pouring molten metal into the mold. The cooled metal is removed from the mold and cleaned. It can be finished by machining, polishing, plating, anodizing, enamelling or painting.

Fabricated sheet metal: Many separate pieces of sheet metal (stainless steel, copper or aluminum) are assembled by hand into large three-dimensional signs. The face and sides of the sign are fused together either by welding (aluminum), soldering (steel) or brazing (copper). Finishes include polishing, plating, anodizing or enamelling.

Engraved: Metal signs made shallowly cut into the face of the sign. A metal or plastic pattern is made and a tracing device is used to transfer the pattern onto the metal plate using a rotating needle which engraves the plate. The engraved letters are sometimes filled with enamel (available in a variety of colours) to make them more prominent.

Etched: The lettering on this type of sign is in low relief. A precise artwork of the sign is photographed and used to create a film positive. A light sensitive gel when exposed through the film positive transfers the image to the plate. Areas not exposed to light remain unprotected and are etched when the plate is put into an acid bath. The etched letterforms are sometimes coloured or filled with enamels to make them more visible.

Wrought iron: Although this is not a common material for signs, it is possible to use wrought iron to make letterforms. Using a full size plan of the letters, a wrought iron craftsman can form the metal to the desired shape. Wrought iron needs to be painted to protect it for exterior use.

36   37

Book by Denise Saulnier, Communication Design Group Ltd., for the City of Halifax, Nova Scotia, Canada.

1986·87 SEASON

Pegasus Players

Your Ticket to Magic and Excitement!

Program by Eda Warren, Eda Warren Design, for The Pegasus Players.

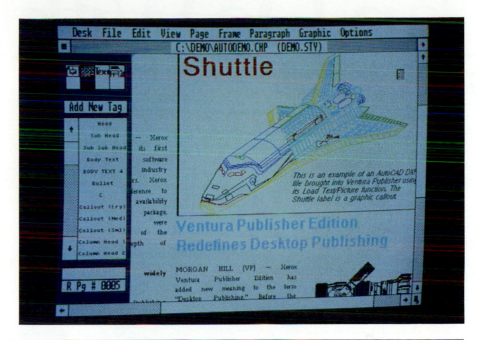

Graphics Can Be Imported with Desktop Publishing Software

Courtesy of Xerox Corporation

20, and then in larger increments. One popular software package, Pagemaker, can give a font size up to 172 points, or a letter several inches high.

Some programs provide lettering with a certain kind of emphasis, such as boldface, underline, or outline. These character attributes can be combined for special effects. Each program has a maximum font size, and its own particular fonts. Many programs carry up to 20 different fonts. The more there are to choose from, the more design flexibility a user has.

Importing Drawings, Graphics, Pictures

It is possible to import drawings or graphics or pictures that have been composed using another application, such as a spreadsheet or a graphics program. Compatability between the page make-up program and the graphics program is essential. It is possible to magnify or reduce imported drawings or graphics that you import because most programs have a Reduce/Enlarge choice on the menu. Photographs can be read with an optical scanner and then imported.

Editing

Pagemaker, the most popular page make-up program, allows the user to move pieces of text around on the page. In general, though, the page make-up software does not permit much text editing.

Output

Many desktop publishing programs allow drafts to be printed out on a dot matrix printer. The result isn't ''camera ready'' (that is, good enough to print from) but it is good enough to proofread and to check the layout.

Some desktop publishing products allow files to be sent directly to a typesetting machine to produce a finer-grained, professional image than a laser printer. Because many companies already have typesetting equipment, bought before desktop publishing was available, the ability to continue to use corporate typesetters can be important.

Faster and Lower-Cost 3-D Imaging Machines Will Transform Product Design

Computer Graphics Are Animating Another Market

Call it the Thousand Island problem. It's a sticky one for product designers at one major food company, who are trying to figure out what the optimal shape is for the salad dressing bottle of tomorrow. How slender can the neck be and still dispense the salmon-colored condiment at a constant rate? How should the lettering appear on the label? What will the bottle look like on a store shelf next to its rivals?

Package designers used to answer these questions by experimenting with dozens of physical models or renderings. But now they're getting a hand from a new generation of special graphics computers. These "super-workstations" let designers create a three-dimensional image of a bottle on the screen, then change it into a hundred different shapes in a stunning spectrum of colors —all on a machine about the size of a large personal computer. This method of simulating a new product in apparent 3-D promises such a competitive edge that the food company now puzzling out the Thousand Island problem won't let its name be used.

Simulated Shopping

Sophisticated computer animation used to be the province of the film industry. For instance, George Lucas developed one of the first super-workstations to depict the floating planets and exploding space ships of movies such as *Star Wars*. Now the number of uses for computerized modeling is soaring. Soon, says Carl Machover, a consultant to Frost & Sullivan Inc. in New York, modeling systems will become commonplace. This year, he says, the systems will account for $500 million to $1 billion of the $4.1 billion computer-aided design (CAD) and manufacturing market.

The key is lower costs. The 3-D systems that aerospace companies and the military used for years to train pilots on flight simulators cost up to $6 million because they included both sophisticated software and special hardware such as multiple processors and a large memory. Because of advances in technology, the new graphics workstations cost only $20,000 to $100,000. For this relatively low price, they can create images on a screen 100 times faster than could be done using early computer-aided design machines.

One leader in the graphics business is Pixar, a year-old spinoff of Lucasfilm Ltd. in San Rafael, Calif. Its largest shareholder is Apple Computer Inc. founder Steven P. Jobs. The company sells its Pixar Image Computer system, which performs 400 million instructions per second, for $79,000. A Pixar is 200 times faster than a typical minicomputer and for some graphics jobs is six times faster than a low-end supercomputer.

Another leader in the field, Silicon Graphics Inc. in Mountain View, Calif., sells its Iris workstation for about $50,000. Silicon Graphics, whose annual revenues have grown to more than $70 million since it was founded in 1981, excels at illustrating moving objects on a computer screen, displaying changing perspectives. For example, to help companies design more eye-catching

packaging, the system can simulate what a shopper would see when strolling down the aisle of a supermarket.

But the uses of computerized imaging go far beyond designing bottles. Aerospace companies are using it to simulate airplane interiors, experimenting with the look of various fabrics and new ways of arranging seats. Radiologists now routinely "Pixar" CAT-scans of fractures to detect hidden problems before the bones are set. The Defense Mapping Agency in Washington is experimenting with a 3-D system to generate maps, charts, and navigational data. And oil companies are finding graphics computers faster than super-minicomputers for analyzing seismic soundings. "The time has come when technology is cheap enough that people can start affording instruments they couldn't touch before," says Pixar Vice-President Alvy Ray Smith.

This is changing the way some people work. Automobile designers, who typically have used graphics terminals linked to multimillion-dollar supercomputers, generally have had to create many costly clay models before moving to a computerized model because supercomputer time is so expensive. Now, with super-workstations, they can test their ideas on computer models first, cutting down on the use of clay models and broadening design opportunities. Chrysler Corp. is now shopping for several hundred powerful workstations, evaluating models from Silicon Graphics, Pixar, Hewlett-Packard, and others. "With our previous system, the turn-around time for generating images of a wheel model was 30 minutes to an hour," says Gregory J. Avesian, a test and development engineer at Chrysler. "With a workstation, you can generate a similar image in a minute."

Stitch In Time

The fashion industry is snapping up the new technology, too. Designers at Levi Strauss & Co. and Limited Stores Inc. are using computers to try out different fabric textures and patterns on 3-D images of dress designs. All this is done before the first prototype is sewn. "It's a whole new industrial revolution based on computers," asserts Roe VanFossen, president of Computer Design Inc. in Grand Rapids, Mich., which sells a computerized fashion-design system. "It's putting American manufacturers in a much better position to compete" internationally.

The success of Pixar and Silicon Graphics hasn't gone unnoticed. Nipping at their heels are well-backed startups Dana Computer Inc. in Sunnyvale, Calif., and Steller Computer In. in Newton, Mass., whose $75,000-to-$125,000 "graphics supercomputers" are due on the market by yearend. Powerful workstations from Sun Microsystems, Digital Equipment, and Hewlett-Packard can already generate sophisticated two-dimensional pictures and are likely to go 3-D eventually. Some companies, such as graphics terminal maker Tektronix, Inc. in Beaverton, Ore., are working on add-on circuit boards to turn a personal computer into a 3-D graphics machine. Noting that even $50,000 is still prohibitively expensive for some customers, Silicon Graphics is readying a version of its Iris that might cost less than $20,000.

Many industry players predict that in the next five years graphics workstations will become part of automated manufacturing. In this scenario, a display of the prototype salad dressing bottle will become the pattern for manufacturing the product. If that indeed happens, many products will never take actual physical shape until they roll off the assembly line. And that could eliminate a lot of bottlenecks.

Source: Katherine M. Hafner, "Information Processing," *Business Week,* March 16, 1987, pp. 88, 92.

Summary and Key Terms

1. **Computer graphics** covers a range of applications. Three important ones are **computer-assisted design (CAD)** and **computer-assisted manufacturing (CAM), presentation graphics,** and **desktop publishing**

2. **Interactive** graphics devices allow people to create and revise graphics images without programming and reprogramming the computer.

3. **Icons,** or small screen symbols signifying selections a user can make, were an innovative graphics aid introduced with the Macintosh (Apple) computer.

4. Many companies have graphics terminals hooked up to mainframes or networks of personal computers that undertake graphics applications. Engineering **workstations** are powerful computers used for scientific or engineering applications. They have high-resolution screens and may be used to simulate real-world conditions as well as for design.

5. Presentation graphics are graphics used in business environments. They include the one-color graphs and charts available in many application packages as well as considerably more sophisticated graphics created with special graphics software and printed out in color or turned into slides, overhead transparencies, or film.

6. Desktop publishing involves the use of PC-based software to create and produce high-quality printed documents. Desktop publishing systems can create documents that combine text and graphics in complex page layouts, various print styles, and reproduction-quality printing.

Review Questions

Fill-in

1. _____ graphics is used to create charts, graphs, and illustrations derived from spreadsheets and statistical analysis.

2. Reports, newsletters, and other publications can be generated using _____ _____ software.

3. Small screen symbols used with the Macintosh are called _____.

4. _____ (abbreviation) is the process of graphically creating and transferring designs to the manufacturing process.

5. A quickly computed, high-resolution screen image of a CAD file is known as _____ _____.

6. _____ or desktop graphics refers to business graphics designed for small groups.

7. WYSIWYG means _____

8. A _____ _____ is used to transfer a graph to a 35-mm slide or transparency.

9. In a desktop publishing system, _____ _____ software provides formats for headings, columns, and content.

10. _____ means a set of characters in a particular design.

Discussion Questions

1. What are some of the benefits of computer graphics in business?

2. Identify two applications of desktop publishing.

Data Base Management

10

Chapter Objectives

After you have finished studying this chapter, you should be able to

1. Recognize the problems with traditional file organization and identify the advantages of data base management systems.

2. Describe the advantages and disadvantages of file managers and data base management systems for microcomputers.

3. Understand the objectives of and procedures for defining a data dictionary.

4. Identify the queries that are possible using a data base.

5. Understand the differences between hierarchical, network, and relational data models.

Jean Gabel is the office manager at a small company that manufactures machine parts. Several years ago, she began to automate the office with a computer system based on a 512K microcomputer. Eventually, Jean became involved in payroll, accounting, billing, employee benefits administration, and other applications, and she appreciated how much time and work the microcomputer saved her. But a change in postal regulations showed her that her computer system was not as useful as it might be.

When the four-digit ZIP code extensions were assigned for the southeastern states, Jean faced the prospect of having to change the numbers in hundreds of records in every computer file that contained addresses. The job seemed especially tiresome because employee addresses were part of the data in four files, and customer addresses were part of the data in three files.

"Having to make the same change over and over in all those different files is the worst part," Jean explained to the dealer who had advised her about the microcomputer.

"Actually, Jean, that's a signal somthing's wrong. Either your files are set up wrong, or, more likely, over time you've developed more complex data needs than the software you're using now can handle efficiently. You're facing a major data update anyway, with those ZIP codes. You might be better off switching right now to a data base management system. You'll have a bigger data entry job than just changing the ZIP codes, but once you design your data base and set up the DBMS, you won't have all that duplicate data. And besides, if ZIP codes ever change again, when you're using a

237

DBMS you just have to type in a command that causes the program to search for the ZIP codes and then change them automatically."

What Is a Data Base?

To fully understand this chapter about systems for organizing and managing data, recall from Chapter 3 the terms *field, record,* and *file.*

- A **field** is an item of data.
- A **record** is a group of related fields.
- A **file** is a group of related records.

Suppose that one of the data requirements at the parts manufacturing company is for information about every part the company makes. This "parts file" has 4,977 records, one for each part. Each record might consist of four fields: the name of the part, the number of the part, the size of the part, and the price of the part. (You should be aware that a field can be any meaningful collection of characters. In the examples here, we talk about items of data made up of words and/or numbers. But in reality, as they apply to electronic data processing, fields can be comprised of symbols, formulas, or any other purposeful collection of characters.)

In Chapter 3, we named a data base as a fourth, more complex level into which data can be organized. A **data base** can be defined as a collection of related data items that are stored together for use in multiple applications. This means that the data need to be physically stored only once in the computer system. The individual data items are related in a logical way and can be accessed by different application programs, as needed.

Defined in this way, a data base may sound fairly simple and straightforward—nothing more than a lot of stored data. But the kind of direct access to data that characterizes a data base is made possible only by the introduction of a "layer of software" between an application program and the stored data. This software layer is known as a **data base management system (DBMS).** The DBMS handles the logistics of storing data in and retrieving it from a data base. To understand why a DBMS is valuable, you must first understand something about traditional file organization.

Traditional File Organization

When a computer system is set up, no matter what size of computer it is based on, all the data the system needs in order to function must be organized and stored in files. These files are used to prepare lists, reports,

summaries, and a variety of other documents. If the demands on a computer system remain static and if the master files are set up carefully at the start, traditional file organization should remain efficient.

But demands on a computer system almost never remain static. When an organization uses a computer system, it tends to develop additional applications. New applications usually require new master files, and when such files are set up at different times for different purposes, data **redundancy**—the repetition in two or more master files of a given data field—eventually occurs. Redundant data create problems in four important aspects of data use: updating, integrity, storage, and accessibility.

An item of data that is repeated in multiple files must be **updated** in each file in which it occurs. It was exactly this problem that sent Jean Gabel to her microcomputer dealer for help. Sooner or later, redundant data will be updated in one file and not another. **Data integrity** is lost as soon as this happens, for the user of data may not know of the discrepancy and may not be able to determine which files contain correct data.

Duplicated data require duplicated **storage.** On a larger scale, duplication can be very expensive, not just because it uses auxiliary storage media but because it makes greater demands on the CPU and may increase accessing and processing times.

But perhaps the greatest drawback of traditional file organization is that it does not provide easy **access** to all the data a computer system actually contains. This system of data organization does not ordinarily permit accessing data in more than one file at a time. Consequently, although some or all the data required for a new application may already exist in various master files, an individual may end up starting a new master file, into which redundant data are entered, perpetuating and even increasing the problems of data update, integrity, storage, and accessibility.

Data base management systems were developed to solve these data problems. We will look first at systems used with microcomputer data bases.

Microcomputer Data Base Management

Many individuals and businesses whose computer systems are based on microcomputers never have to proceed beyond file managers.

File Managers

A file manager stores pieces of information in independent records, as the parts file mentioned early in this chapter stores 4,799 records of part name, number, size, and price. The data stored in these records can also be **sorted,** or put into some specified, usable order. One way to do this is to sort on the basis of a key. **Key** is the term for any data field by which a file can be sorted. A **primary key** is a field that differentiates one record from every other record. Each part would have a part number different from

every other part's, and so in this file, part number would be a good primary key. In the parts file, we might want to know which parts have the same name or price or size. We could set up the fields NAME, PRICE, and SIZE as secondary keys. **Secondary keys** permit us to obtain access to all records that share common nonkey fields, such as all the records of parts that cost $10.00.

We can also sort the records in our data base. For inventory, a sort organized in ascending sequence by part number might be needed. For compiling a parts catalog, on the other hand, a sort organized by part name in alphabetical order might be more useful.

Indexing is different from sorting. When a file is sorted in ascending sequence by part name, for example, the records are physically rearranged in alphabetical order by part name. Indexing makes it possible to obtain access to part name records in alphabetical order without the records being physically rearranged in the data base. An indexed file would consist of a listing of keys of part name records organized in part name sequence instead of part number sequence. The physical records in the data base, however, would still be organized in the order in which they were originally created.

File managers also enable the user to generate reports by specifying the fields to be printed, the column headings, and the report's title. Report formats can be stored in special disk files to be reused.

With a file manager, data are entered in a set format, identical for each record. Setting up a **template,** or a general framework, assures that the data are entered in a standardized way. With a file manager, data in each record can be changed easily when necessary. Certainly a great deal of data about employees can be stored in a file set up this way.

File management systems are usually menu-driven, with choices for setting up files, entering data, searching files, updating or deleting records, sorting and printing files, and formatting reports. If file managers have such strengths, why do microcomputer users turn to more powerful systems for managing data?

The main disadvantage of file managers is that most of them can access the data within only one file. All the data a user needs for a specific application must be in one file.

Say, for example, that a manufacturer wants to set up an employee file. The taxpayer identification number would serve as a unique primary key to the file and the non-key fields would be employee name, employee street, employee city, employee state, job starting date, employee job title, and employee salary.

```
TAXNUM
NAME
STREET
CITY
STATE
JOB-START-DATE
JOB-TITLE
SALARY
```

The problem with organizing a file in this way is that an employee could have many jobs. Let us say that Jim Smith, an employee, has had four different jobs within the company, recorded as shown:

TAXNUM	NAME	STREET	CITY	STATE	JOB-DATE	JOB-TITLE	SALARY
334-565-8811	Smith	24 Pine	Oneonta	NY	01/01/79	Mail clerk	$ 8,700
334-565-8811	Smith	24 Pine	Oneonta	NY	01/01/80	Mgr., mail	$11,200
334-565-8811	Smith	24 Pine	Oneonta	NY	01/01/81	Mgr., adm. serv.	$15,800
334-565-8811	Smith	24 Pine	Oneonta	NY	01/01/82	Dir., adm. serv.	$18,500

If a file management system is used to house the employee records, the entire record has to be repeated every time an employee has a job change. In this case, Jim Smith's name and address information is repeated four times, or every time he makes a job change, because the job change information is in the same record as the employee name and address information. As you can see, in this way redundant data can build up in files, creating the problems discussed above related to data updating, integrity, and storage.

Although file managers are considerably less expensive than so-called relational data base management systems for microcomputers, the latter manage data in much more flexible ways.

Relational Data Base Management Systems

The principal advantage of a relational DBMS is that data entered once can be used for any applications. (Relational structures are used for large-computer DBMSs, as well. Technical aspects of data base structures are discussed later in this chapter.)

In a relational data base, the employee record discussed above could be broken into two records, a main employee record containing employee name and address information, and a job change record containing information on each job change:

Employee Record

TAXNUM	NAME	STREET	CITY	STATE
334-565-8811	Smith	24 Pine	Oneonta	NY

Employee-job-change Record

TAXNUM	JOB-DATE	JOB-TITLE	SALARY
334-565-8811	01/01/79	Mail clerk	$ 8,700
334-565-8811	01/01/80	Mgr., mail	$11,200
334-565-8811	01/01/81	Mgr., adm serv	$15,800
334-565-8811	01/01/82	Dir., adm serv	$18,500

The advantage of this relational data base is that information in the employee record can be stored once but can be used in multiple ways. For

example, suppose that management needs a report of the job changes for all employees. The report should list each employee's full name, date of each job change, and salary figures for each job change. Because the employee number is in both the employee record and in the employee-job-change record files, the employee job-change records can be matched with each employee's name and address information when needed.

In addition, other files can be constructed giving further information about employees. Another such file could be an employee-skills inventory file:

Employee-skills-inventory Record

```
TAX-ID-NUM      SKILL 1   SKILL 2   SKILL 3

334-565-8811   Spanish   Typing   Chess
```

Using this skills-inventory file, management could obtain a report of the names and addresses of all employees who speak Spanish. Because the taxpayer ID number is in both the employee file and the employee skills-inventory file, the number could be used to find the name and address information for each employee with Spanish listed as a skill in the skills inventory file. Without the ability to set up several files using a data base management system, employee name and address information would have to be added to each employee-skills-inventory record. This would create a problem in updating information. If Jim Smith changed his address, for example, this change would then have to be recorded in both the employee file and in the employee-skills-inventory file

As you can see, data base management software makes it possible to use data in flexible ways. Data can be entered once and used in multiple applications. In our example, employee name and address information was entered once in the central employee record but could be used in reports combining information about such things as job changes and skills. This was possible because the key to the employee record, the taxpayer ID number, was also in both the employee-job-change record as well as in the employee-skills inventory record.

Plainly, a DBMS can be much more flexible, and therefore much more useful, than a file manager. Let's run through the process of setting up a data base and using a DBMS. The first step in taking advantage of a DBMS's power is to build the right data base.

Building the Data Base

Three stages are involved in building the data base correctly: making a plan, defining the data dictionary, and entering data.

Making a Plan   Building a data base is like building a house in the sense that to undertake either project without a careful plan is almost certain to produce a flawed final product. Before starting on the project of building a data base, it is important to map out on paper the users' expectations for output from the system.

The layout of the final output, as well as of any interim or related output, must be developed. Imagine, for example, that Jean Gabel decides to convert to a DBMS. She wants to be able to produce a yearly report, the related invoice, the monthly statement, and several other useful reports. Once she decides that this is output she wants, she sketches out each final report. After defining all the data elements required in the output, Jean will know what fields to include in the data base.

Let's look at one of the reports Jean must be able to create, a monthly report showing total customer billings (see Figure 10.1). Such a report has three kinds of data. First, there are **constant data,** which will appear in the body of every report, such as the headings CUSTOMER NAME, PHONE #, CONTACT, and so on, in Figure 10.1. These standard headings appear on every page of the report, regardless of any other information.

In addition to constant data, DBMSs distinguish between primary data and secondary data. Data derived from other data, such as totals computed mathematically from other data elements, are considered to be **secondary data.** In the monthly report, secondary data include the monthly total for each customer and the running total for each customer. Both are computed data, the former calculated from the cost data times the quantity data and the latter from summing the monthly totals.

Data elements that cannot be computed are **primary data.** This category of variable data makes up the fields of the data base and is entered manually (at the keyboard). In the monthly billing report, primary data include the customer names, phone numbers, contacts, part numbers, part costs, and quantities. These data are different for each client, as are any secondary data derived from these primary data.

The expectations a report is meant to fulfill must be analyzed to determine the elements of the data base necessary to create that particular

FIGURE 10.1
Constant, Primary, and Secondary Data in a Monthly Billing Report

02/02/90						PAGE 03
		MONTHLY BILLING				
CUSTOMER NAME	PHONE #	CONTACT	PART #	COST	QUANTITY	AMOUNT
XYZ COMPANY	200–789–4567	SIMON	7037	$3.40	144	$921.60
						$3801.60

report. Once this analysis is complete, it is possible to define the data dictionary.

Defining the Data Dictionary   Defining the data dictionary is a simple task to perform. Entering a one-word command, followed by the name the user chooses for a data base file, begins the definition process. In the monthly billing data base, all that is required in DBase III, a popular microcomputer DBMS, is to type the following:

```
create b:billing
```

This command simply means:

```
create      (start the data dictionary
            definition)
b:          (for a file to be stored on the
            disk in drive B)
billing     (the name of the data base file)
```

After naming the file, the definition process has four parts: naming each field, determining the width of each field, stating the type of data in each field, and setting the number of decimal places in numeric fields.

Describing each field generically   A descriptive name must be chosen for each field. The field name should be easy to remember, for it will be used as a key in sorting data and preparing reports.

Determining the maximum width of each field   A maximum field width must be assigned to each field within the data base. Field width is determined by counting the characters of the longest data item, adding 1 character for each necessary space or punctuation mark, and then using that total as the maximum width. If a data item longer than a field's maximum width is entered, it will be truncated, or cut off, after the last space is filled. Therefore, it is important to allow a great enough maximum width so that alphabetic data entered are unambiguous even if some characters are truncated. Numeric data must be entered completely, so the maximum width of a numeric field must be the length of the longest item of data possible in that field.

Defining the type of data in each field   The next step in defining the data dictionary is to indicate the type of data in each field. Various DBMSs recognize different categories of data, but the following ones are standard:

- **Character**   Any character, number, punctuation, or symbol that will be used strictly for naming or labeling (not mathematical) purposes
- **Numeric**   Any number or symbol that will be used in a mathematical sense, for performing calculations or in a formula
- **Logical**   Any single characters that will be used to represent the answer to a true-false statement

Each of these categories is explained in more detail after the next section.

Defining the number of decimal places for numeric fields   It is necessary to define decimal places for numeric fields. For example, a user setting up a field of salaries stated in dollars and cents will need two decimal places to represent the cents. Setting decimal places usually requires defining a space in the field for the decimal point as well as a space for each decimal place. Cents, therefore, require three places. A field that will accept dollar amounts up to 999.99, for example, is defined as 6 characters wide.

Jean Gabel's monthly billing file is defined as follows:

```
1. name,c,20
2. phone,c,12
3. contact,c,10
4. partno,c,5
5. cost,n,5,2
6. quantity,n,4,0
```

There are six fields in each record. The generic name of the first field is name, for customer name. The c denotes that it will be treated as character information even if it contains numbers. For this field, 123 Corp will be recognized as a valid name, just as John Smith or A1 Auto Repair will be. The 20 designates that entries in the name field can be a maximum of 20 characters long. Any name longer than 20 characters will stop being entered once the 20-character field width is filled.

The second field contains the phone number of the customer. The numbers entered in this field are defined as alpha characters (c) because they will not be used in mathematical computations. (Addresses, box numbers, house numbers, ZIP codes, and the like are treated this way.) The field has a maximum of 12 characters, allowing for area codes and hyphens to separate parts.

Field 3 contains the name of the contact person at the customer's place of business, presumably the one who pays the bills. Here we allot only 10 spaces, as the first name is sufficient.

Field 4 is the part number, which will be treated as character information (c). Five spaces are allotted for the number.

Part cost will be entered into the fifth field. This field allows for a maximum cost of $99.99 per part (5, 2).

The sixth field is quantity bought, a numeric field (n), but one that is not carried to decimal places (since it's impossible to buy a part of a part). The maximum quantity allowed is 9999, and the 0 shows that decimal places are not wanted.

In this example, we do not use a field containing logical data. Logical data are either "true" or "false." For example, this billing report could contain a seventh field, to indicate whether the client has paid the bill:

```
7. paid,1,1
```

The 1 denotes that field 7 is a logic field, and the 1 denotes that the record length is only one character, to contain either T or F.

It is important to understand the data base structure thoroughly in order to use a DBMS effectively, especially during data entry or when a new report is being developed. It helps to keep a printout of the data dictionary handy. The structure, as defined by the data dictionary, can be changed if necessary. But because restructuring a data base that contains records is somewhat tricky, a DBMS user should feel confident that the structure is correct before starting to enter data.

Entering the Data

Once the data dictionary is defined, data can be entered into each field. For some data bases, data entry can be a major task. Consider a library wanting to create a data base of all books by author, number, title, publisher, and subject. Several microcomputer DBMSs are big and powerful enough to handle such a project. Creating the data dictionary would take only a few minutes. But entering the actual data could take thousands of hours. The scope of data entry is an important consideration in deciding whether to convert from a manual system to a computerized system. Since the conversion process can be expensive, the benefits of the new system must be weighed against its costs.

Data can be entered with or without screen **prompts.** Prompts give the user a menu, and the cursor positions itself at the beginning of the first field. The length of the field is usually shown in reverse video or in a contrasting color, to make field width obvious. The prompt option can be turned off, and once a user is very familiar with a DBMS and its structure, the prompts are unnecessary.

DBMS programs automatically keep track of record numbers, assigning a new number to each record as it is begun. Record numbers are not important in the operation of the DBMS; they simply show how many records in total are in the data base.

It is also possible to enter data into a data base from a file created with any standard text editor, such as a word processor. This method of data entry requires the person entering data to indicate the beginning and end of each field, to ensure that the fields are the proper length and that the DBMS understands the fields. When data entry is completed, a special command loads the file into the data base.

Editing the Data

Because incorrect data may be entered into a data base and once-correct data may require revision, there must be some method of editing the raw data. DBMSs allow for editing not only to change the contents of one field of one record at a time but also to change a field throughout the entire data base. Suppose that the parts manufacturer decides to raise part prices by 15 percent. It is very easy to make that change in the data base. Jean Gabel just types in the following instruction:

```
For all fields cost replace with cost x 1.15
```

All contents of the cost field will be replaced with the new prices, 15 percent higher than the old prices.

Displaying the Data

Once all the data have been entered, the contents of the data base can be reviewed. Typing ''display all'' or ''select all'' sends to

Viewing a Record to Edit the
Data

Courtesy of MicroPro International
Corp.

the screen or to the printer a tabular arrangement of the data base contents
just as they were entered.

```
. display all

00001   ABC Company Ltd.        100-234-8907   George   926     2.30    144    331.20
00002   Anderson, Wayne         100-234-8907   Wayne    1491    3.00    144    432.00
00003   XYZ Company Ltd.        200-789-4567   Simon    7037    3.40    144    921.60
00004   Lincoln String Inc.     200-345-5656   Sarah    10256   3.00    1440   4320.00
00005   Long Board Inc.         400-454-9909   Kim      3330    12.80   24     307.20
00006   Trunk Packaging Inc.    600-676-8888   Ralph    519     34.00   144    4896.00
00007   Kelly's Wire Rope       100-565-6655   Kelly    19914   23.00   72     1656.00
00008   Simeon, Cathy           200-343-7767   Cathy    1076    2.00    1440   2880.00
00009   George, Linda           100-232-0090   Linda    202     12.00   24     288.00
00010   Carmen, Greg            100-232-3333   Greg     83      1.00    1440   1440.00
```

The user can then scan the contents for completeness and accuracy.

Using the Data Base

Up to this point, the DBMS has done little that a manual system could not
do. What we describe from here on, though, could not easily be done with a
manual system. The DBMS solves one of management's major problems
—supplying immediate responses to relevant questions. A DBMS uses a
system of qualifiers to allow selection of particular items. Instead of wading
through a long list of items and records to pick out only those required, the
DBMS user can have the computer do the work.

Selective Query

You can think about selective query in a general way as posing and getting answers to "if-then" questions. The qualifiers "less than," "greater than," "not equal to," and "equal to" are required in an "if-then" situation. Although you may be used to seeing these qualifiers only in terms of numerics, they also work with alpha fields.

Suppose, for example, that the parts manufacturer wants a report listing all the customers who purchased a particular part last year. In essence, he needs the DBMS to fulfill this request: "*If* part number is 19914, *then* list certain data I specify." The actual command might be

```
list for partno = 19914

00007  Kelly's Wire Rope  100-565-6655  Kelly  19914  23.00  72  1656.00
```

Suppose the parts manufacturer decides that he wants customers who buy at least a minimum dollar amount of parts each month. Because he must therefore notify his smaller customers about this new policy, he can query the data base this way:

```
list name, phone number and contact for
clients with monthly total less than 1000.00
```

This query is selective not just for the customers it requests—those whose monthly bill is less than $1000.00—but for the fields requested—name, phone number, and contact. It is unnecessary in this case to print out all

A Menu-Based Query System

Courtesy of Ashton-Tate

data in each selected record, for the parts manufacturer needs only the data that will allow him to contact the customers that the computer lists in response to the "less than" query.

With this listing process, a user can choose any combination of fields in any order. "List name, phone, contact," "List cost, name, phone," "List part, quantity, name. The DBMS will then search every record in the data base in the order in which the records were originally set up.

Qualifiers also work with alpha characters, or strings. A **string** is any group of alpha characters recognized by a computer program as an item of data. To list all customer names beginning with *S,* for example, Jean would select the required fields for names beginning with *S.* (Here, the alpha character is enclosed in quotation marks to denote that it is part of a string.)

```
list for name = "S"

00008  Simeon,Cathy  200-343-7767  Cathy  1076  2.00  1440  2880.00
```

Most microcomputer DBMSs do not have the capability of searching for a substring (a set of characters within a string). They search for a particular string of characters starting with the first character and moving to the right. To find the client ANDERSON, the user could search for "A," "AN," "AND," and so on, but not for the substring "SON." With their greater main memory capacity, large computers can search for substrings.

Sorting Data

All the listings we have discussed so far have been arranged in the order in which the records were originally entered. If Jean requests a listing of all client names starting with *S,* she'll get them in their order of entry, not in alphabetical order. But DBMS users often want listings in alpha or numeric order. Such arrangements are accomplished by **sorting** the data in specified ways. Say, for example, that Jean wants a data listing arranged alphabetically by customer name:

```
. sort on name to b:name

SORT COMPLETE
. use b:name
. list

00001  ABC Company Ltd.      100-234-8907  George  926    2.30   144   331.20
00002  Anderson,Wayne        100-234-8907  Wayne   1491   3.00   144   432.00
00010  Carmen,Greg           100-232-3333  Greg    83     1.00  1440  1440.00
00009  George,Linda          100-232-0090  Linda   202   12.00    24   288.00
00007  Kelly's Wire Rope     100-565-6655  Kelly  19914  23.00    72  1656.00
00004  Lincoln String Inc.   200-345-5656  Sarah  10256   3.00  1440  4320.00
00005  Long Board Inc.       400-454-9909  Kim     3330  12.80    24   307.20
00008  Simeon,Cathy          200-343-7767  Cathy   1076   2.00  1440  2880.00
00006  Trunk Packaging Inc.  600-676-8888  Ralph   519   34.00   144  4896.00
00003  XYZ Company Ltd.      200-789-4567  Simon   7037   3.40   144   921.60
```

Jean Gabel can also request a listing for all customers from *D* to *Z*.

```
. list for name > 'C'

00003  XYZ Company Ltd.        200-789-4567  Simon   7037    3.40   144   921.60
00004  Lincoln String Inc.     200-345-5656  Sarah  10256    3.00  1440  4320.00
00005  Long Board Inc.         400-454-9909  Kim     3330   12.80    24   307.20
00006  Trunk Packaging Inc.    600-676-8888  Ralph    519   34.00   144  4896.00
00007  Kelly's Wire Rope       100-565-6655  Kelly  19914   23.00    72  1656.00
00008  Simeon, Cathy           200-343-7767  Cathy   1076    2.00  1440  2880.00
00009  George, Linda           100-232-0090  Linda    202   12.00    24   288.00
```

Or she can request a listing of all customers from *D* to *Z* whose monthly charge is less than $1800.00.

```
. list for name > 'C' .and. amount > 0 .and. amount < 1800.00


00009  George, Linda           100-232-0090  Linda    202   12.00    24   288.00
00007  Kelly's Wire Rope       100-566-6655  Kelly  19914   23.00    72  1656.00
00005  Long Board Inc.         400-454-9909  Kim     3330   12.80    24   307.20
00003  XYZ Company Ltd.        200-789-4567  Simon   7037    3.40   144   921.60
```

A DBMS can sort on any field in the data base, whether numeric or alpha, in either ascending or descending order. This sorting has one primary sort field and with some DBMSs can have up to nine secondary sorting fields.

In some cases, a sorted file becomes a separate data base with its own identity. In other cases, the sorted file created becomes a subfile of the original data base. The difference between the two is quite critical. A sorted file that is a subfile is still linked to the original data base. Records added to the original file will show up in the subfile as well. Records edited in the original are edited in the subfile also. Thus the subfile is as up-to-date as the main data base. A sorted file created as a separate data base is not linked and therefore must be updated or rebuilt separately from the original. In DBMSs that offer a file handling choice, sorting the files in the subfile manner is preferable.

Creating Reports and Forms

Creating professional-looking reports and forms is an important capability of a microcomputer DBMS. With only a few key strokes, the DBMS user can create a specified format. Report and form specifications are saved automatically as a disk file by the DBMS, and they can be reused even if the contents of the data base change.

Combining Existing Files

Many DBMSs can join two separate files to create a new one. The savings in data entry time can be immense. Here are a few possibilities:

As you increase your use of data bases for various applications, you will start to develop your own methods of creating them. Here are a few tips that may help you produce more useful databases.

Tips on Building Data Bases

1. **Start with output.** Develop a clear idea of what you want output to look like. Once you are sure of what you need for output, whether one report or many, you can determine what data must be collected.

2. **Collect only primary data.** Once you are aware of what data are needed, make sure your data base collects only primary data—data that cannot be calculated or picked up from current sources.

3. **Avoid redundancy.** Do not collect data that have been collected elsewhere in another data base or data that you will never use. Redundant data take up time for entering the data and space to store the data.

4. **Allow for data integrity checks.** A data integrity check is a check done by the program to ensure that the data entered make sense or are at least within the sphere of possibility. For example, using the date structure field will ensure that dates entered are in the proper format and are realistic. (Naturally, a data integrity check cannot detect data that are wrong as long as they are realistic.)

5. **Review data after input.** Always check to make sure that entered data are correct. Reviewing each record (a BROWSE or DISPLAY ALL command makes this easy to do) usually reveals major errors. Remember, most errors in computer operations occur at the human-machine interface, so take the time to make sure that what you make available to the machine is correct.

6. **Back up your files.** Once created, make back-up copies of your data bases. Each time they change, make a second back-up. Most data base programs save the file each time onto the disk (either hard or floppy), and you can use the COPY command, either in DOS or in the DBMS, to make the back-up copy.

- Two files can be joined in some order relationship (i.e., alphabetical or numerical).
- A new file can be created from selected fields.
- All the records of one file can be followed by all the records of a second file.
- A new file can be created consisting of all the records in one file that exactly match records in a second file.
- A new file can be created consisting of all the records in one file that do not match records in a second file.
- A new file can be created that deletes all duplicate records.

Interfacing with Other Applications

The data in a data base can often be extremely useful in other operations, so the ability to transfer files between other data bases or between a DBMS and another type of application can be very useful. For example, a data base used for accounts receivable and collection might be transferred to a word processing application and used to send out a mass mailing of sales specials.

A data base of employees on the payroll can be transferred to a spreadsheet to calculate the effects of a 5 percent pay increase.

Choosing a Microcomputer DBMS

Size and Strength   Software producers are constantly striving to make microcomputer DBMSs easier to use. As each company incorporates the good points of the other programs on the market, data base programs are becoming more and more similar. Still, some differences do exist, as the comparison of four popular DBMS packages in the box shows. A potential purchaser of a DBMS should think about each of the following areas so that his or her needs can be best met.

- Maximum number of files (relations) per data base
- Maximum number of fields per record
- Maximum number of characters per record
- Acceptable characters per field
- Maximum number of records per file
- Maximum number of records per data base
- Numeric precision of fields
- Largest calculated number
- Time required to sort and index
- Total number of bytes for memory

It can be difficult for an inexperienced user to evaluate all these facets of a DBMS. A package that allows a large number of records may not be better than one allowing a smaller number, for the sort and query time of the former may be slow. The advice of a DBMS user, a software dealer, or a professional consultant can help in determining size and strength requirements and how best to meet them.

A Comparison of Popular DBMS Software Packages

	DBaseIII÷	PFS:File	RBase 5000	VPInfo
Operating system	MS-DOS, CP/M	MS-DOS	MS-DOS CTOS	MS-DOS
Memory (RAM)	256K	128K	256K	140K
Disk drives required	2	1	2	1
Command structure	Multilevel	Menu	Multilevel	Multilevel
Programmable	Yes	Yes	Yes	Yes
Maximum number of files	10	1	40	6
Maximum number of records per file	1 billion	2,200	2.5 billion	65,535
Maximum number of fields per record	128	3,100	400	512
Maximum number of characters per record	4.000	Unlimited	1,530	1,000
Maximum precision for numeric fields	16 digits	Unlimited	16 digits	16 digits

Help Features   As with word processors and spreadsheets, many DBMSs are equipped with interactive HELP functions, screens explaining the use of commands and other features. A person who does not know how to set up a data base, for example, could type "help create," and the program would respond with instructions on the screen about how to create the data base.

Unlike other application programs discussed in this book, DBMSs can be difficult to master. **Tutorials,** with their step by step introduction to the capabilities of the program, are essential. Most manufacturers include a tutorial with the program documentation. Many also provide books containing tutorials tailored to the DBMS's use in various business operations.

Large Computer Data Base Management

Many of the general topics covered in the discussion of microcomputer data base management apply to large computer data base management as well. Perhaps the most important difference is that a large computer data base is almost certain to have more data used by a greater number of people for a greater number of applications. Both technically and within an organization, creating, using, and managing a large computer data base is likely to be more complex than creating, using, and managing a microcomputer data base.

The Pros and Cons of a Large Computer DBMS

One of the disadvantages of a DBMS is the increased complexity of the software. People responsible for the DBMS will need to develop specialized technical skills, and additional training costs will be incurred. DBMS software and ancillaries, such as query languages and application generators, are very expensive. Their acquisition must be justified in terms of increased productivity as well as increased data accessibility and control of information.

From a practical point of view, DBMSs provide many advantages: They minimize data redundancy, increase data integrity, and make the development of new applications faster and easier. They accomplish this by, in effect, putting all the data in one place, in the data base, where it is easier to watch and control. As we have seen, data distributed and repeated in various files are more vulnerable to error and inconsistency. (Remember that every failure to update an item represents an error in the data.)

When a DBMS is installed, the responsibility for maintaining and updating the data base can be assigned to a data base administrator, someone (or more than one person) who can modify the contents of the data base without having to change any application program. In organizations that use constantly changing information, this is a very important advantage.

Data Bases for All Reasons

What do Horse, Potato, and Matrix have in common? If you answered that each belongs to a guessing-game category (animal, vegetable, and mineral), you are wrong. All three are data bases!

Horse can provide horse breeders with a thoroughbred's pedigree through five generations, its track record, and information about its ability to produce winning offspring. Potato can be called up by fast-food chains and other heavy users of this vegetable for the latest information on plantings, harvests, and stockpiles. And Matrix was developed to help improve patient care while reducing its costs.

Horse, Potato, and Matrix are only three examples in one of the fastest growing areas of data processing—data base information services. These services range in size from the small and highly specialized to the huge and somewhat less specialized. For example, BAMBAM (Bookline Alert: Missing Books and Manuscripts) has 1000 subscribers interested in recovering rare books. Sludge informs sewage engineers of developments in their field.

Then there is INQUIRE, which is used by the National Library of Medicine (NLM) to maintain and develop the world's largest collection of research materials in a single field. It consists of some 2.5 million books, journals, theses, and other documents. Through INQUIRE, the NLM provides computerized information resources to more than 1500 hospitals, medical schools, and

Data security is also a concern of the data base administrator. By **security,** we mean the protection of data against unauthorized use. Data security is commonly enforced by the use of a password. Again, it is much easier to prevent unauthorized access when all the data are in one place, the data base, than when multiple copies of data are distributed in files that are themselves difficult to keep track of.

How a Large Computer DBMS Works

A DBMS for a large computer usually works with a large number of application programs that perform specific tasks. The program indicates the data items or elements required and their identifying key(s) or index(es). (This aspect of accessing data elements will be discussed below.) The DBMS then accesses and retrieves data items required by the application program.

1. An application program initiates the process of obtaining data from the data base by means of a DML command. DML stands for Data Manipulation Language, which the DBMS uses in performing its functions.

2. Whenever the control unit of the computer encounters a DML command during execution of an application program, it transfers control from the program to the DBMS.

3. The DBMS verifies that the data element required has been defined as part of the data base and then determines the address of its location in the storage device.

4. The DBMS next turns control over to the operating system, giving it a command to access and retrieve the data element.

other organizations. The resources include SERLINE (SERials On-Line), which is a file of 34,000 journal titles available through the NLM's public network system. In addition, INQUIRE is designed to enable subscribers to build and maintain their own files.

The range of information available from different data bases is very broad—from advice for wine connoisseurs to the full contents of the *Encyclopaedia Britannica*. In the past few years, the number of data bases has increased rapidly. In 1983 there were more than 1500 available to interested subscribers, an increase of more than 50 percent in two years. And the trend seems likely to continue. The more than 4.5 million home computers now in use provide a market waiting to be tapped. All that the user needs is a modem and the necessary software for dialing into a service, which can be bought for a few hundred dollars. An annual subscription to an informational data base averages about $50; the hourly rates for on-line time vary from a few dollars to several hundred, depending on the time of day and the degree of specialization.

Producers of data base information services (the largest has over 150 on the market) are concentrating on making them very easy for subscribers to access. Perhaps a sign of things to come is the publication last year by *Omni* magazine of a directory of 1200 on-line data bases.

The data base information service being used here is LEXIS, which consists of federal and state codes and court opinions for lawyers all over the country.

Courtesy of Mead Data Control

5. The operating system transfers the requested data element to a special storage area (or buffer) in the DBMS and then gives control back to the DBMS.

6. The DBMS now transfers the data element to the buffer used by the application program. The program takes back control from the DBMS and processes the data element.

Data Dictionaries

In a large computer DBMS, the **data dictionary** not only contains definitions or descriptions of every data element in the data base, it also usually stores information about groups of data elements and cross-references between elements and groups of elements. The data dictionary also lists the elements that are used by each program.

A data dictionary is valuable because it increases the efficiency and effectiveness of data collection and the management of data resources. In particular, a properly designed data dictionary should make it easier for database users to:

1. Communicate with other users (in part by helping to reduce data redundancy and inconsistency).

2. Determine the effect that changes in data elements will have on the data base.

3. Design and expand the data base by centralizing control of data elements.

But is it really necessary to define every data element in a data base, not to mention adding all that other information? A simple example will illustrate just how valuable a data dictionary can be.

It frequently happens that a data item is duplicated because different names and definitions for it were assigned by different systems analysts. For instance, the data item "student number" in a university's data base could appear under a variety of names, including:

```
STUD-NUMBER
STU-NUM
ST-NO
IN-STU#NO
STU-ID
```

These names may all refer to exactly the same information and should be defined using one standard data name and data definition.

```
STU-NUMBER     9 numeric digits
```

Aliases for this data element, or other names by which this data element is known in other programs, should be identified in the data dictionary. Obviously, consistency is desirable. To see why, look at what would happen if we wanted to make a change in how a data element is defined in existing programs. Say that the data element STU-NUMBER changed from 9 numeric digits to 11 alphanumeric digits. In other words, the old student numbers would look like 456-45-6897 and the new student numbers would look like MO456-45-6897. If this change were made, then the data element STU-NUMBER would have to be redefined in all programs and in all records in which that data element was being used. We would have to find every single occurrence of that data element and make the change in its definition.

The task would be easy if everyone who had ever written a program using the data element student-number had named the data element STU-NUMBER, but that is not the case. There are probably lots of other names by which that data element is known. This is where the data dictionary becomes useful.

The data dictionary can help find all the programs using the data element STU-NUMBER and also can identify all programs using aliases, or other names, for this same data element, such as STUD-NUMBER, STU-NUM, ST-NO, IN-STU-NUM, and so on. Now we can search for all occurrences of these other data element names and make the change in the data definition (from 9 numeric to 11 alphanumeric characters) in the programs using it. It would be very time-consuming to try to do this without a data dictionary defining the aliases. So the data dictionary helps to maintain consistent data definitions throughout programs.

In addition, to use the data element, student-number, in a new program, all we have to do is to look it up in the data dictionary and learn the data element name (STU-NUMBER) and data element definition (11 alphanumeric) that we should use.

What Can a Data Dictionary Do? If a data dictionary could do nothing more than enable a user to find out how a data element is defined, it would still be a useful tool. But on-line data dictionaries can do much more. What follows is a summary of three kinds of information that an on-line data dictionary is able to produce:

1. **Ordered Listings.** An on-line data dictionary can produce a full alphabetical listing and relevant information about the data elements in the dictionary. The listing will include data elements and their data defininitions (characteristics of the data).

2. **Cross-references.** It is often necessary to locate data elements in the various files in which they occur. This task is greatly simplified by asking the dictionary, "Where is the data element 'department' used?" The dictionary will produce a listing of all the files or all the programs in which that particular element occurs. Figure 10.2 shows a portion of such a listing as DATAMANAGER, an automated data dictionary package, would produce it.

3. **Machine-Readable Data Definitions.** Programmers must define the data they use in their programs. If their data base has an associated data dictionary, they will want to use the dictionary definitions if possible. But the process of copying definitions from a listing and then coding them is both error-prone and time-consuming. Instead, the data dictionary can be instructed to produce definitions in machine-readable form.

Basic Terminology of Large Computer DBMSs

A **primary key** is a unique data element in a record, an element that can be used to select a single record from all the other records in a file. An example of a primary key in a student record would be the social security number. While more than one student can have the same birth date or even name, no

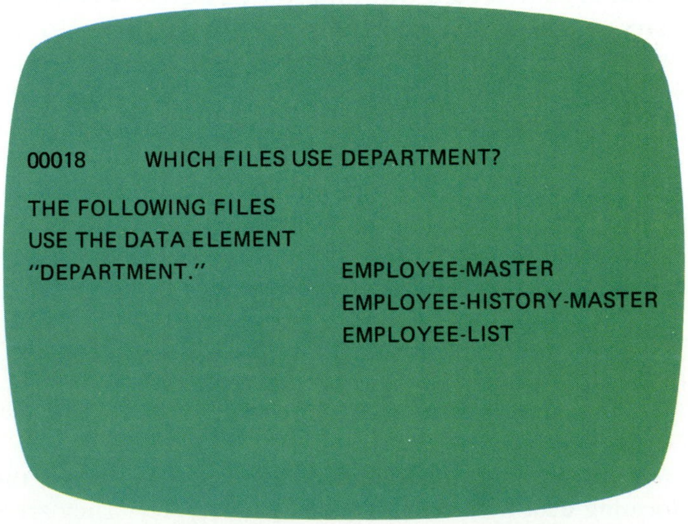

FIGURE 10.2
The user keys in an inquiry to the data dictionary asking for all the names of data files which use the data element "department." In response, the print-out indicates that the data element is used in three different files, the employee-master file, the employee-history-master file, and the employee-list file.

Source: Chris Gane and Trish Sarson, *Structured Systems Analysis: Tools and Techniques.* (Englewood Cliffs, NJ: Prentice-Hall, 1979). P. 71

two people can have the same social security number. An **entity** is the subject of a record—a person, place, or thing or a set of any of these. For example, a student is an entity. An **attribute** is a data element that identifies a characteristic of a particular entity. For example, name and birth date in a student record would both be attributes of a student. Now consider the following file of student records:

Stu-num	Stu-name	Major code	Advisor
53467	Jabonski Carter	03	Thompson
63772	Rockart Matt	05	Williams
76441	Ripley Mary	03	Thompson
88225	Spencer Mark	03	Thompson
99882	Sokol Richard	05	Williams
99934	Wilson Betty	14	Trainer

In this example, the entity is "student," the primary key is "student number," and the attributes of "student" are "name," "major code," and "advisor."

The primary key will identify a single record, but in many cases the user will want to access a group of records about entities that share a particular attribute. For that purpose they will use a **secondary key.** For instance, suppose we need a list of all students majoring in business administration (major code 03). Using the major code as a secondary key, we can access and list all students by major code:

Major code	Stu-num
03	53467, 76441, 88225
05	63772, 99882
14	99934

Inverted Files

The use of secondary keys can be extended to produce what is known as an **inverted file.** An inverted file is created by making all the attributes in a record serve as secondary keys. This means that each attribute field can be used to access the primary key that identifies every record having the attribute in question.

In our student master file, "student name," "major-code," and "advisor" could all be used as secondary keys to access records containing those attributes. If "advisor" were used as the key, the inverted file might look something like this:

Advisor	Student number
Thompson	53467, 76441, 88225
Williams	63772, 99882
Trainer	99934

Inverted files are so called because they invert or reverse the normal order of locating data by first finding the primary key. They are set up to facilitate certain types of data search. For example, frequent demands for a

list of students listed by major-code and by advisor could be met by setting up the inverted files shown on the preceding page. Inverted files enable a data base to answer requests for types of information that might otherwise be difficult to process.

Designing a Data Base for Queries

A request for information from a data base is known as a query. For example, a university needs information in order to operate. A representative set of requests might include the following:

- A list of all students majoring in finance.
- The balance owed on student 53467's account.
- A listing of students with a New York State loan who are either juniors or seniors and have a grade-point average (GPA) of 3.5 or better.
- A list of students who have Robertson as an advisor.

As stated here, these requests may sound pretty much alike, either asking for one data item or several. But logically—from the viewpoint of a programmer—they are quite different. The information a data base can provide to its users (that is, the queries it can answer) depends on how its data have been logically organized.

How can the designers of a data base know how to organize the data for maximum usefulness? When a data base is being designed and developed, it is important to know from the very start what kinds of queries the data base will have to answer. The systems analyst must ask potential users what kinds of information they will need. Then the analyst can determine the logical organization of the data base—how to arrange data elements to answer users' queries.

But what is meant by "logical"? This word, along with "physical," frequently crops up in discussions of data organization. This is not surprising. To understand how data bases deal with information, we must first understand the meanings of these two terms.

Physical versus Logical Data Organization

The relationships of data items to one another can be viewed as physical or logical. Physical data relationships refer to the actual arrangement of the data in a storage device (for example, on the tracks of a hard disk). Logical data relationships refer to how a programmer or user "sees" the data or wants it organized to best meet specific information needs. Logical data relationships involve the meanings of the data elements in relation to one another as opposed to their physical or location relationships to one another.

For example, suppose that each record in a set of student files contains name, birth date, identification number, and so on, but nothing about permanent residence. A programmer could write a program to extract information about age and other attributes listed in the record, and it would not matter whether the data were stored together or in widely separated parts of the disk. However, any attempt to determine which students come

from a particular state would be impossible with this set of files: The data they contain cannot be organized by state.

With a data base, then, the user needs to know what data elements are stored in what records; the data dictionary is of help here. The user also needs to know what kinds of queries (program requests for information) will produce the desired results. What the user does not need to know is how or where data are physically stored; the user is usually more concerned with the logical organization of the data. The next section discusses how data bases may be logically organized according to one of several data models.

Data Models

A data model defines the most important logical relationships among the entities in the data base. There are three main types of data modes: *hierarchical, network,* and the type used in microcomputer DBMSs, *relational.* These three models organize data in distinctly different ways. But they all use a fundamental set of logical relationships that must be defined before the data model can be implemented. These basic relationships consist of a *schema* and one or (usually) more *subschemas.*

Schemas and Subschemas   A **schema** is a broad category that describes all of the data elements in a data base. The schema specifies the names of the data entities, their several attributes, and the logical relationships among them.

Different users are often interested in different information, and therefore in different groups or subsets of data elements. Each data subset is a **subschema.** In data base terminology, different users are said to have different ''views'' of the data and thus to focus on different subschemas within the same schema.

For example, a university's data base will usually include files about classes, containing such information as the name of the instructor, enrollments, and when and where they are held. (Figure 10.3 illustrates a schema.) But the head of a department may be interested only in the instructors in various sections. In contrast, the administrator responsible for the allocation of room space would probably be interested in the number of students enrolled in various courses. The two of them view the same data differently. These views, which focus on subsets of data, are described by subschemas.

Deriving subschemas from a schema, of course, requires that the relevant data be logically related or associated in some way. There are three major relationships that relate data components to one another in a schema: *one-to-one, one-to-many,* and *many-to-many.* An example of a one-to-one relationship is that of *instructor* to *class:* a particular instructor teaching a particular class. A one-to-many relationship is *instructor* to *classes:* a particular instructor teaching two or more classes. An example of a many-to-many relationship is *instructors* to *classes:* two or more instructors team-teaching two or more classes. With this background, we can now look at the different types of data models used for organizing data.

DEPARTMENT

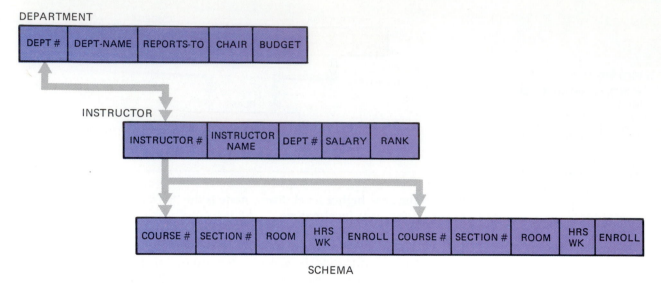

INSTRUCTOR

SCHEMA

FIGURE 10.3
A Schema

Source: James Martin, *Principles of Data Base Management*. Englewood Cliffs: Prentice-Hall, 1976,
Figure 9–3, p. 101.

Hierarchical Data Model   The **hierarchical data model** organizes data in
a ranked or graded series of levels. Because a diagram of this model
resembles an upside-down tree, it is often called a tree model. A hierarchical data structure, like a tree, consists of nodes connected by branches. (See
Figure 10.4.)

A **node** contains an entity and one or more of its attributes. The highest
node in the inverted tree (the single node at the top) is called a **root.** Nodes
at a lower level are said to be "dependent" on the higher node to which
they are connected. Every node below the root node is the "child" of a

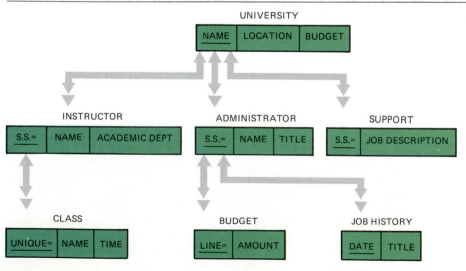

FIGURE 10.4
A Hierarchical Data Model
(Tree Structure).

Source: Burch and Strater, *Information
Systems: Theory and Practice.* John
Wiley & Sons, Inc., 1979. Figure 8–4,
p. 217.

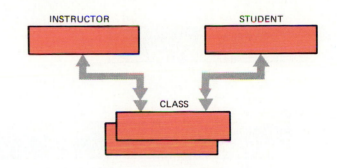

FIGURE 10.5
A Simple Network Data Model

Source: Burch and Strater, *Information Systems: Theory and Practice.* John Wiley & Sons, Inc., 1979. Figure 8–6, p. 218.

node in the next higher level. Every node is the "parent" of any dependent nodes on the next level below.

Network Data Model   In the **network data model,** unlike the hierarchical model, a child node in a data relationship can have more than one parent. This means that data elements can be related in any number of ways. For example, in the network model shown in Figure 10.5, "class" is said to be "owned" by both "instructor" and "student." This double ownership is what makes the structure a network instead of a hierarchy.

The logical relationship between levels determines whether a network is classified as *simple* or *complex.* If the relationship is one-to-many, the network is simple. If it is many-to-many, the network is complex. Figure 10.7 shows a simple network. The network would be complex, however, if two or more classes were taught by a team of instructors.

Relational Data Model   The hierarchical and network data models shown here look relatively uncomplicated. They can, however, easily develop into a confusing web of interrelationships as new data categories are added. This problem does not arise when the relational data model is used. A **relational data model** organizes data as a set of *relations,* or two-dimensional tables. In a relational data model, the logical associations among data elements are shown by reorganizing the data into columns and rows. This reorganization is a step-by-step process known as **normalization.**

Let's look at one example of how logical relationships between data are normalized. Consider a record from a student master file that contains the following data:

STUDENT

Stu #	Stu-name	Stu-address	Stu-major	Stu-advisor	Stu-GPA	Course #	Course-sem	Course-title	Course-credits	Course-grade
43444	Hopkins	43 Evergreen	Physics	Campbell	3.8	MIS 281	Spring	Info Sys Analysis	4	A
						BIO 102	Spring	Intro to Zoology	4	B
						FIN 483	Spring	Investments	4	B
44568	Clarke	11 Pine Lane	Chemistry	So	2.4	HIS 201	Spring	Western Civ	4	B
						GER 101	Spring	Intro to German	4	C
						MAT 101	Spring	Calculus I	4	A
44666	Wilson	33 Northmoor	English	Harper	3.4	BIO 102	Spring	Intro to Zoology	4	A
						MAT 101	Spring	Calculus I	4	B
						HIS 201	Spring	Western Civ	4	A

All these data are in each and every record. When the student takes other courses, the entire record will be repeated. This creates what is known as a *repeating group*. The course information is considered a repeating group because students take a number of courses during their college careers. Since course data is included in each student record, identical course data will appear in the record of every student taking the same course. If 50 students take a particular course, there will be 50 student records with the identical information on that course.

This unwieldy method of keeping data on students and courses can be simplified by separating out the repeating group. The result will be two tables, or relations. One relation will contain data describing the student; the other will describe the courses. A third relation can be created to describe a course taken by a particular student.

What will these relations look like? In the record we started with, STUDENT is the entity, *student* # is the primary key, and all the remaining items are attributes. Separating out the student information will produce the following record:

STUDENT

Student #	Stu-name	Stu-address	Stu-major	Stu-advisor	Stu-GPA
43444	Hopkins	43 Evergreen	Physics	Campbell	3.8
44568	Clarke	11 Pine Lane	Chemistry	So	2.4
44666	Wilson	33 Northmoor	English	Harper	3.4

where again STUDENT is the entity and *student* # is the primary key, associated with five attributes.

Separating out the repeating group of course information will produce the following record:

COURSE

Course #	Course-sem	Course-title
MIS 281	Spring	Info Sys Analysis
BIO 102	Spring	Intro to Zoology
FIN 483	Spring	Investments
HIS 201	Spring	Western Civ
GER 101	Spring	Intro to German

where the entity is COURSE and the primary key consists of two attributes (course # and course-sem) instead of one. Both are necessary for uniquely identifying the particular occurrence involved (some courses are given in several semesters).

Third, we will want to be able to access a record that tells us how well a particular student performed in a particular course. The record shown below would supply the desired information:

STUDENT + COURSE + SEMESTER

Stu #	Course #	Course-sem	Course-credits	Course-grade
43444	MIS 281	Spring	4	A
43444	BIO 102	Spring	4	B
43444	FIN 483	Spring	4	B
44568	HIS 201	Spring	4	B

Because this record must provide the grade earned by a particular student in a particular course in a particular semester, the primary key must include all three of these attributes. Note that the relation is named by the three entities listed above the data headings.

In the process of breaking the student-master-file record into three logical records, we have created three distinct and separate associations of data. Repeating this process for all the records in the student master file would result in three separate tables or relations. This, essentially, is the process of normalization.

To better understand how normalization works we will look at one more example. The following data structure is unnormalized:

EMPLOYEE MASTER FILE

EMPLOYEE

Emp #	Emp-name	Emp-address	Date-of-change	Job-title	Salary
485627456	Robertson	11 King Dr.	01/01/83	WP Supervisor	$24,500
485627456	Robertson	11 King Dr.	01/01/82	Lead Operator	$19,200
497528647	Swanson	44 Alamo	01/01/83	Fin. Plan. Mgr.	$38,200
497528647	Swanson	44 Alamo	01/01/82	Sr. Fin. Analyst	$32,800
497528647	Swanson	44 Alamo	01/01/81	Fin. Analyst	$28,000

This record contains a repeating group—the informtion about job changes. Every time an employee changes jobs within the company, there will be new data for date-of-change, job-title, and salary. To normalize this record requires separating out the repeating group, thereby producing two relations. The first relation lists the employee's number, name, and address:

EMPLOYEE

Emp #	Emp-name	Emp-address
485627656	Robertson	11 King Drive
497528647	Swanson	44 Alamo

The second relation contains the job-change information. The employee number is repeated in order to uniquely identify the record:

SALARY JOB HISTORY

Emp #	Date-of-change	Job-title	Salary
485627456	01/01/83	WP Supervisor	$24,500
485627456	01/01/82	Lead Operator	$19,200
497528647	01/01/83	Fin. Plan. Mgr.	$38,200
497528647	01/01/82	Sr. Fin. Analyst	$32,800
497528647	01/01/81	Fin. Analyst	$28,000

The relational data model has two advantages over the hierarchical and the network models: it is more convenient for the end-user of the data base, and it allows greater data independence than the other data models. All three types are currently used in large computer DBMSs.

Getting the Rhino into the Computer

Is the gorilla in Seattle related to the one in San Antonio?

Until recently, that question could only be answered with a stack of pedigree charts and the time to study them.

Now it can be gathered in seconds—along with other valuable information—with a new computer program in use at more than 90 zoos around the world.

"Most every zoological park on the North American continent is very much into computers now," said Robert O. Wagner of the American Association of Zoological Parks and Aquariums.

The Animal Records Keeping System—which zookeepers call ARKS—allows zoos to tap into information about their animal collections, ranging from how inbred an animal is to how much it cost and the number of times it has been on loan. Each program is tailored specifically to the zoo using it, covering only the animals in each particular collection.

But zoos are not just tracking animals on their computers. "Computers are being used for recording all kinds of information so you can do a better job of marketing the institution," Mr. Wagner said.

For example, he added, "if you look back and see that 10,000 people attended your zoo on the first Saturday of June in 1985, but only 6,000 attended the first Saturday of June in 1986, you can see whether it was raining, whether there was another community event."

ARKS was first marketed in December 1985 by the International Species Inventory System (ISIS). The 13-year-old organization, which is based in Apple Valley, Minn., and keeps track of exotic animals in captivity, is now working to develop a second program. Called MedARKS, that program is being designed to store medical information.

Not surprisingly, the big institutions—the San Diego Zoo and the Bronx Zoo—were the first to be computerized.

And they are still on the leading edge with the sophisticated—and expensive—I.B.M. System 38, which keeps track of animal histories, medical records, employees, and visitors to the zoo.

According to officials at the San Diego Zoo, that system can cost between $300,000 and $500,000.

But now even the smaller zoos are investing in personal computers, which allow them to use ARKS. The software costs $750 and a zoo pays an additional $1.40 each year for each living animal it has entered in the data base.

With thousands of specimens, that could prove costly. But zoos have told ISIS they believe it's worth while.

"An annual report for a zoo would typically have taken several weeks," said Nate Flesness, the director of ISIS. "With ARKS it only takes a couple of hours."

Its very success, however, may result in some new competition. Frank Slavens, who is the curator of reptiles at the Woodland Park Zoo in Seattle, says he can provide similar information about reptiles and amphibians, at least, for a lot less money.

In 1976, he mailed out questionnaires to zoos and, with pen and paper, inventoried all the reptiles and amphibians in captivity. In 1977 he did it again. And in 1980, he updated those records and has continued to do so every year since, now by computer.

For $30 a year, he sends out a book of his inventory to any zoo that wants it. Now he and his brother are trying to write their own animal inventory computer program, which they hope to market to zoos for about $500.

Source: By Hilary Stout, *The New York Times*, Sunday, July 12, 1987.

Summary and Key Terms

1. A **field** is an item of data. A **record** is a group of related fields. A **file** is a group of related records. A **data base** is any collection of related data.

2. All organizations store data which they use to produce information needed to perform their various functions. Traditionally, data have been stored in *master files* created for specific applications. Such files often contain duplicated items; this duplication is known as *data redundancy*. Data redundancy can be avoided by combining data files in an organized way in a data base. A data base is a collection of related data items or elements stored together for use in multiple applications. The functions of assessing and retrieving information from a data base are handled by a **data base management system,** or **DBMS.** A DBMS reduces redundancy, increases data integrity, and makes applications faster and easier to develop.

3. **File managers** and **data base management systems** are two kinds of application software used to help microcomputer users organize and use data in data bases. A file manager stores pieces of information in independent records in files generally separate from one another. Data in a file can be **sorted,** or put into a specified, usable order. The advantages of file managers are that they organize data efficiently, they can handle large amounts of data, and they are relatively inexpensive. The primary disadvantage of file managers is that generally they do not allow communication between files. That is, data stored in one file cannot be called up to be used with data stored in another file.

4. A microcomputer DBMS uses a **relational structure** to organize and store data so that data entered to form the data base can be used in many different applications.

5. Defining the **data dictionary** for a microcomputer DBMS involves giving a name to each field, determining the maximum width of each field, and defining the type of data in each field. **Character data** include any character, number, punctuation, or symbol that is used strictly for naming or labeling purposes. **Numeric data** include any number of symbol used in a mathematical formula or to perform calculations. **Logical data** are single characters used to represent the answer to true-false statements.

6. A DBMS responds to **selective queries,** which are essentially "if-then" statements answerable with the data in the data base. Alphabetic and numeric data alike respond to "if-then" queries. **Qualifiers,** such as "less than" and "not equal to" are required in "if-then" statements. A **string** is any group of alpha characters recognized by a computer program as an item of data.

7. A DBMS responds to selective queries by listing pertinent data in record-number order. Some mathematical calculations can also take place within the listing process. A DBMS can also sort data, by putting a field, alpha or numeric, called a **primary sort field,** into ascending or descending order.

8. Data organization can be described as *physical* or *logical.* Physical organization refers to the actual placement of data in a storage device. Logical organization refers to how the individual data items are related to each other from the programmer's or user's point of view.

9. Four important concepts in describing the logical organization of data are:
   primary key—uniquely identifies a record
   entity—a person, place, or thing that is the subject of a record
   secondary key—identifies an entity by one of its attributes
   inverted file—a file whose attributes all serve as secondary keys
   query—a request for particular data from a data base
   A common query asks for all the records that have a certain attribute, charactristic, or value.

10. The basic organization of a data base is described by its **schema** and **subschemas.** The schema description includes the names of all data entities, their attributes, and their relation to each other. A subschema describes a subset of data entities.

11. The schema and subschemas are the basis for the *data model* used to organize the data base.

12. In the **hierarchical data model,** a "tree" structure organizes data in a ranked series of levels.

13. In the **network data model,** data can be dependent on two or more parents.

14. The **relational data model** relates data elements to each other in two-dimensional tables, or *relations.* The creation of a relational model involves the process of normalization, which creates new relations by separating out *repeating groups* of data items from a file. The relational model is more convenient for the end-user and provides greater data independence.

Review Questions

Matching I

Match the following terms to their meanings:

a. secondary data

b. data base

c. template

d. file

e. primary data

f. primary key

g. record

h. constant data

i. relational structure

_____ 1. A group of related fields

_____ 2. Data is arranged in columns and rows

_____ 3. A general framework for entering data

_____ 4. A collection of related data that can be used for many applications

_____ 5. Differentiates one record from every other record

_____ 6. Headings on a record are _____ _____

_____ 7. Data derived from other data

Fill-In

1. Three types of data that can be entered into a data base are alphabetic, _____, and _____ data.

2. Listing data in alphabetic or numeric order sequence is known as _____ the data.

3. If/then statements that can be answered by the data in the data base are called _____ _____.

4. A _____ is a group of characters recognized by a computer program as an item of data.

5. A _____ _____ defines the characteristics of each field in the data base.

6. The _____ operation makes it possible to create a new file from two existing files in a data base.

7. _____ provide step by step instructions about the capabilities of a program.

Matching II

Match the following terms to their meanings:

a. data base management system
b. data dictionary
c. primary key
d. secondary key
e. inverted file
f. subschema
g. hierarchical
h. normalization
i. query
j. physical

____ 1. A _____ is a layer of software which makes it possible to access stored data to be used in multiple applications.

____ 2. A centralized collection of information about all data elements needed by the organization is known as a _____.

____ 3. A data element is a record which uniquely defines it from all the other records in a file is a _____.

____ 4. Setting up a _____ enables us to identify all records in a file that have a common attribute characteristic.

____ 5. When all attributes of a record serve as secondary keys to the file, this is known as an _____.

____ 6. A user's view of data requirements in a data base is known as a _____.

____ 7. The type of data model constructed from a series of parent and dependent nodes is called a _____ data model.

____ 8. The process for simplifying data into two dimensional tables is known as _____.

____ 9. When a user requests specific data from the data base, this is known as making a _____.

____ 10. _____ organization of data relates to the way in which data are stored on a storage device.

Discussion Questions and Exercises

1. What are the differences between a microcomputer-based file management system and a microcomputer-based data base management system?

2. What factors should be considered in selecting a microcomputer data base package?

3. Explain how the data dictionary makes it easier to assess the impact of changes in the characteristics of data elements on the maintenance of application programs and systems in which these data elements are used?

4. Why are queries so important in serving managers' information needs?

5. Study each of the following data structures. Break each of them into two simpler data structures by taking out the repeating groups and reorganizing the data into the form of two-dimensional tables.

Example 1: PART-ORDER

PART-ORDER(Customer-name, Order-date, Part-#, Part-description, Part-price, Quantity, Order-total).

Example 2: CLASS-ROSTER

CLASS-ROSTER (Class-#, Class-name, Class-credits, Class-room, Class-time, Class-instructor, Class-enrollment, Student-#, Student-name, Student-level).

Example 3: BOOK-ORDER

BOOK-ORDER (Order-#, Order-date, Book-#, Title, Author, Price, Quantity, Publisher).

Data Communications

Chapter Objectives

After studying this chapter, you should be able to:

1. Understand what kinds of data-processing applications depend on data communications facilities.

2. Describe the components of a data communications system.

3. Explain the characteristics of various data communications network configurations, network line-control procedures, and local area networks.

4. Identify data communications services provided by common carriers and telephone companies.

5. Describe emerging data communications facilities supporting electronic mail, videoconferencing, and microcomputers.

It is 9:00 when marketing manager Jim Edwards arrives at work. The first thing he does is sit down at his personal computer to review the electronic-mail messages that have been sent to his mailbox address. As he reviews these messages on the CRT screen, he marks those that require replies and then keys in replies and transmits then over the electronic-mail network to the terminals of the individuals who are to receive them. At the same time, he forwards some of the messages to appropriate departments for further action.

At 10:00 Jim attends a videoconference in the company's teleconferencing facility. During this "electronic meeting," the images of participants in a remote conferencing facility are displayed on the facility's screen. The two groups talk with each other interactively. Before teleconferencing, Jim would have had to go to Chicago to accomplish this hour's work.

At 11:00 he prepares a five-page summary report to be keyed in at the word-processing work station. Jim will review it on his own CRT and then have the word processing department transmit the document over communications lines to each of the fifteen district sales offices, where it will be printed out at remote printers. Managers in those offices will have access to the report within hours, instead of the days it used to take.

Next, Jim signs on to the corporate data-processing system and retrieves data on the sales activity of new products in the different sales territories. Using his personal computer as a terminal, he can obtain the data directly. Finally, before going to lunch, he takes a minute to check the latest financial news provided by a data base service that his company subscribes to.

What do all these applications have in common? They all involve the use of a telecommunications network, the one here tying the manager's personal computer to other terminals, to a corporate data-processing system, to a financial data base, and to printers in remote offices. Such communications technologies grow more important—and more sophisticated—every day.

What Is Data Communications?

Data communications is the transfer of encoded information from one location to another by means of a communications channel. It involves three basic elements: (1) a *sending unit* (the source), (2) a *transmission channel* (the medium), and (3) a *receiving unit* (the destination, sometimes called a "sink"). The sending and receiving units are usually computers or terminals. The transmission channel is commonly a telephone line, though data can also be transmitted in the form of radio waves, microwaves, or laser beams. Data communications systems make the following possible.

Data Capture at the Information Source

Using data communications makes it possible to capture data at the point of origin. That is, data can be entered directly into a system at their source instead of being sent to some other location for data entry and processing. In a business environment, for example, if a company's district sales offices have terminals connected to a data communications network, data entry personnel can enter sales orders directly at the terminals. The order information is directly transmitted to a central office, where it will be used to update inventory records, issue a shipping order to the warehouse nearest the customer, and generate an invoice to be sent to that customer.

Rapid Dissemination of Information

A data communications network provides immediate access to information when it is needed. For example, consider a company that has several regional distribution centers for shipping its products to customers. A warehouse clerk might find that the local stock is insufficient to fill a large new order. If the company's distribution centers are connected by a data communications network, the clerk can use a terminal to find out the current inventory of the requested item in the other centers—and therefore how best to fill the order.

Dispersed Operations

Data communications networks create an efficient way to operate over a wide geographical area. For example, consider a department-store chain that has in each of its retail outlets a minicomputer connected to a central computer by means of a data communications network. Using the local minicomputers, store personnel can process orders and update local inventories; summaries of sales and inventory data can be sent over the network to the central office for analysis and review. Local processing by minicomputers is more economical and quicker than having all the processing done by a central computer. At the same time, data transmitted to the central system become the basis for data on total sales, order, and inventories throughout the firm.

Data Communications Applications

The use of data communications systems in the business environment has grown rapidly. This section describes the data-processing applications that depend on data communications facilities. They are listed below roughly in order of increasing complexity, starting with source-data collection and ending with networks involving data communications between two or more computers.

Source Data Collection

As its name indicates, source data collection involves the acquisition of data at its point of origin. Information is entered at a remote terminal and stored (commonly on floppy disks) for later transmission to a central computer, where it can be processed (see Figure 11.1). This application permits the collection of large amounts of data during those hours most convenient for capturing it (usually daytime) and transmission during hours when the transmission costs are lowest (after the workday or overnight).

Remote Job Entry

Remote job entry is a batch-processing application. The job is entered into the system at a remote terminal or card reader, and the output is returned to a remote printer at some later time. Routing instructions that specify the output destination are submitted along with the job. Remote job entry usually involves medium-sized volumes of data and a response time of one to two hours. This application tends to be vulnerable to error because the input is difficult to check and errors show up only in the output.

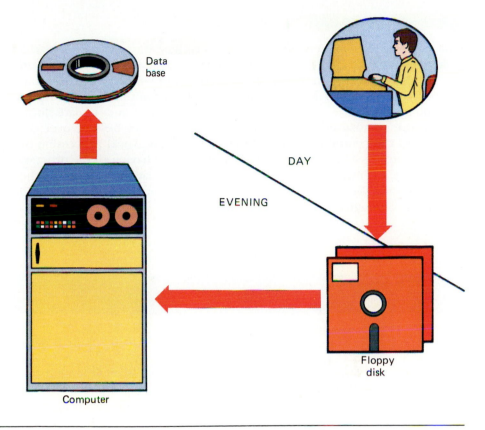

Data
base

DAY

EVENING

Floppy
disk

Computer

FIGURE 11.1
Source Data Collection

To cite only one of its many uses, remote job entry is often employed in computer programming courses at colleges and universities. For instance, a student might submit a program from any of several terminals or card readers on campus. The job is then processed centrally and routed to any of several remote printers. Thus input can be done at one location and output collected at another. (See Figure 11.2)

Message Switching

Message switching permits the sending of a message from one terminal to another on a data communications network. All the sender needs to know is the recipient's mailbox ID, or identification code. Message switching also makes it possible to send a single message to a mailing list consisting of two or more mailbox IDs. The volume of data involved in any one transmission tends to be low, while the response time (the time the receiver responds to his or her messages) may vary from minutes to hours. Electronic mail is an application of message switching in computerized office environments using companywide networks.

On-Line Inquiry

On-line inquiry makes information available to a user who has keyed in a request or inquiry at a terminal connected by a communications line to a

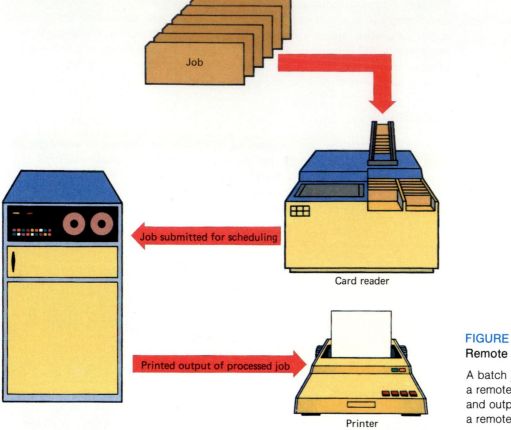

Job

Job submitted for scheduling

Card reader

Printed output of processed job

Printer

FIGURE 11.2
Remote Job Entry

A batch job is submitted from
a remote site, is processed,
and output is later returned to
a remote printer.

host computer. The volume of data transmitted per inquiry is usually quite
low, and response time is measured in seconds. This application is
extensively used by retailers to check the credit status of customers making
credit-card purchases.

But the usefulness and value of on-line inquiry is not limited to making
business transactions more convenient. To cite just one instance, the Baptist
Hospitals of Louisville, Kentucky, have used their own Hospital Data
Network for more than ten years. This network provides the hospitals'
doctors, nurses, administrators, and other staff with access to clinical data,
patients' records, and other health-care-related information. The network
also has a communications link to Blue Cross/Blue Shield for the processing
of insurance claims.

On-line inquiry can be combined with updating procedures. In *on-line
inquiry with overnight update* users can enter update transactions, and
these transactions are used to update the appropriate master files once a day
or less often.

In *on-line inquiry with immediate update* the user can use transac-
tions to update master files as soon as new information becomes available.
The best-known application of this type is the airline reservations system.
The oldest and largest commercial data network using on-line inquiry with
immediate update is SABRE, which was jointly developed by American
Airlines and IBM. SABRE, which became operational in the early 1960s,

features a central computer linked to terminals nationwide. Using SABRE, any reservations clerk can obtain immediate and up-to-date information about available space on a particular flight. When a clerk keys in a reservation, the reduction in available space is immediately recorded in the central computer. The next inquiry—which may come a fraction of a second later—will receive the updated figure.

Time-Sharing

As its name indicates, **time-sharing** refers to the sharing of a computer's time by multiple users. In its most popular form, conversational time sharing, this application allows the user to communicate interactively with the computer, keying in data and instructions at a terminal, and receiving a response in a few seconds, and often faster (see Figure 11.3).

FIGURE 11.3
A Time Sharing System

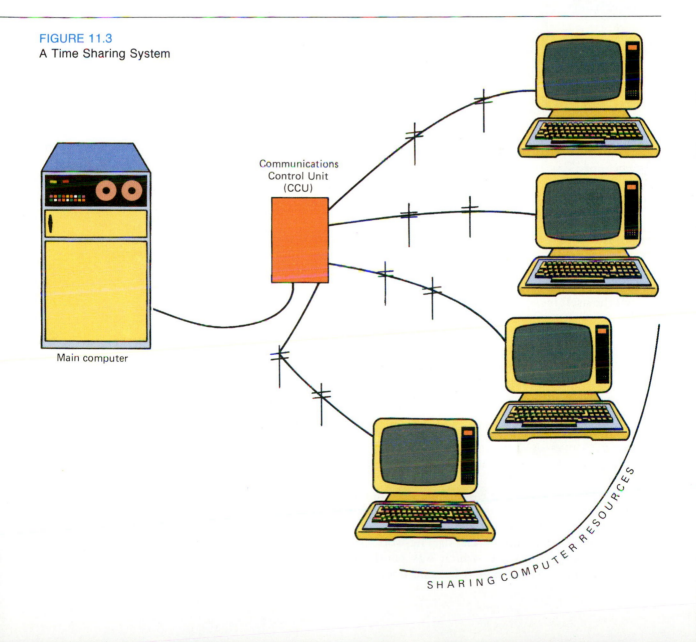

Communications Control Unit (CCU)

Main computer

SHARING COMPUTER RESOURCES

Because of this quick response time, the user has the impression that no one else is using the computer. In fact, the computer is dividing its time among many users, giving each a tiny slice of its time before going on to the next. This process, appropriately called *time slicing,* is so fast that the computer often executes an instruction from one user, makes the rounds of the other users, and returns in time to execute the first user's next instruction.

Computer-to-Computer Networks

The most complex data communications networks consist of distributed computers linked together. Such a network provides users at many different locations with the advantages of having access to all the files, programs, and processing capabilities of the network. Figure 11.4 illustrates this type of network.

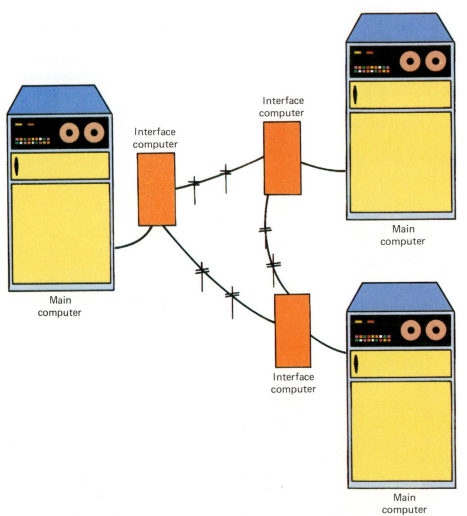

FIGURE 11.4
Computer-to-Computer Networks

Computer-to-computer networks are created by first connecting two computers in the same room. Then control devices, similar to front-end computers, are used to control the link. The link is then extended over communication facilities in order to connect more than two computers.

The first large-scale computer-to-computer network for heterogeneous users is ARPANET. This network, which became operational in 1969, links various government and university computer systems. Needless to say, the on-line library available to users is truly massive. Because the main computers in the network have different characteristics, they are connected by special interface computers. Data enters the system through these interface computers, which in turn distribute the data to the intended destinations.

Distributed Data Processing

Another environment in which data communications is used is in **distributed data processing** networks, which link centralized computer systems to decentralized mini- and microcomputers with local processing ability (see Figure 11.5). The Veterans Administration operates one of the largest distributed processing systems in the world: Five Honeywell mainframes are connected to over 100 Honeywell minicomputers, 3000 terminals, and 900 printers distributed in VA offices around the United States. The network handles in the neighborhood of 250,000 transactions a day, using data bases containing the records of some 30 million veterans and twice that number of dependents.

Now let's examine the components and capabilities of data communications systems in more detail. We will begin with the main components of such a system and then go on to the types of channels and networks, communications services currently available, and new developments in data communications.

FIGURE 11.5
Distributed Data Processing

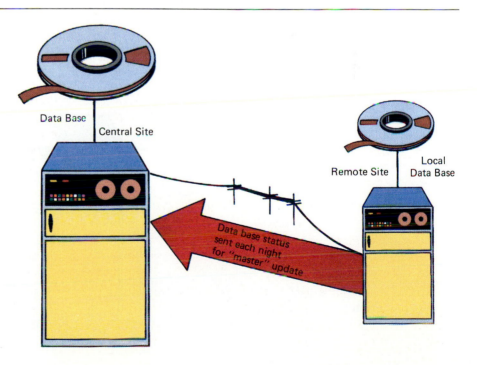

Data Base

Central Site

Remote Site

Local Data Base

Data base status sent each night for "master" update

An Overview of the Components

The structure of a data communications network is more easily understood if it is first compared with a traditional data-processing system. Recall that the CPU issues instructions to the I/O channel by means of a channel program, which in turn instructs the control unit that governs a particular peripheral device that a certain data file is needed by an application program.

In a data communications system, a communications channel links a communications control unit to one or more devices on the network. The communication control unit handles the input/output processing required by dozens of hundreds of terminals trying to send data to or to receive data from the computer system.

To understand how a data communications system functions, we need to concentrate on three main types of components: the controller, the devices, and the communications lines.

1. The **communications control unit (CCU)** is the device controller, which controls the input and output of data from and to the various devices in the network.
2. *Devices* are the input/output devices connected to the communications control unit and include a variety of terminals and printers.
3. *Communications lines* or channels connect the communications control unit not only to input/output devices but also to intermediate devices that facilitate the transmission of data in electronic form—modems, multiplexers, and concentrators. Figure 11.6 shows a generalized data-processing system that uses a data communications network.

Communications Control Unit   A large central computer is seldom the ideal instrument for handling data communications, which involve short bursts of activity in sending and receiving single messages. To make central computers effective in data communications, additional hardware has been developed in the form of *front end* modules. These modules, or CCUs, control data transmission between the central computer and remote devices. They are designed to perform as many communications functions as possible, freeing the computer to perform the data-processing operations for which it is better equipped.

The important functions of the CCU include the following:

- connecting up to several hundred communications lines to the central computer;
- adapting the main computer to a data network by converting the transmissions from remote sites into a form that the computer can accept;
- polling (or monitoring) remote devices to determine their status —ready to send a message or receive one;
- storing and holding data intended for a device that is busy or temporarily out of service;

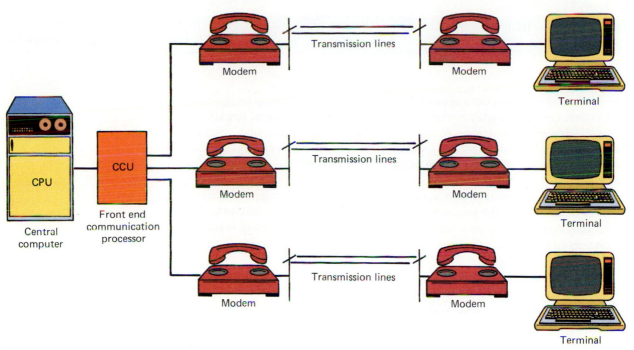

FIGURE 11.6
Components of a Data Communications System

- providing data protection and accountability by maintaining a message log of all transmissions;

- detecting errors in messages, and either connecting them or ordering a retransmission;

- adding communications-control codes to outgoing transmissions and deleting them from incoming ones;

- determining which devices are to receive a transmission (one, some, or all); and

- controlling the message-priority system (if the network has one) so that the more important transmissions are processed ahead of less important ones.

Terminals   In the context of data communications, the terminal used may be any one of several types of input/output devices. *Teletypewriter terminals* have a keyboard for input and can print hard-copy output. *Video terminals* have a CRT screen for displaying input from the keyboard and output from the computer. *Remote-job-entry terminals* are "stations" consisting of a card reader, line printer, often some kind of storage capacity for the local user, and an operator console that has a CRT screen, all of which are connected to a control unit (see Figure 11.2). *Transactions terminals,* such as point-of-sale terminals in retail stores, are linked to a controller or minicomputer in the transaction environment itself. *Intelli-*

gent terminals have a built-in microcomputer that enables them to perform such functions as transaction editing, verification, and even data base inquiry or data processing.

Modem   The term **modem** is an abbreviation for *modulator/dem*ulator. It is easier to understand what a modem does if you think of it as a two-way adapter between a transmissional channel and either a CCU or a terminal. The modem *converts* a digital (that is, binary, or bit-coded) signal received from a CCU or terminal into an analog signal that can be transmitted over a telephone line. (A digital signal is an on-off signal. In contrast, analog signals are continuous but vary in some physical characteristic such as frequency. It is the variations in the analog signal that contain the information.) The modem *converts* an analog signal received over a communications channel back into a digital signal, which is the kind that computers and terminals understand (see Figure 11.7).

Communications Lines   As you will learn in a later section, a communications line or channel that links terminals to the CCU and the central computer can be one of several kinds. For the time being, however, it is necessary to note only that there are two types of arrangement of lines in a network: *point-to-point* and *multipoint.*

In **point-to-point** configurations a single terminal is linked to the central computer. In **multipoint** configurations the line to the computer is shared among several terminals. These *network configurations,* as they are often called, are described in more detail in a later section.

Multiplexers   A communications device is designed to carry only one message at a time; that is, it cannot carry two or more messages simultaneously. However, this limitation can in effect be bypassed with the use of a **multiplexer.** A multiplexer enables a single communications device to carry several combined signals. It does so by converting several low-speed signals and transmitting them over a high-speed line. Given the costs of transmission, it is clearly cheaper to send several signals at high speed over a single line than to send them at low speed over separate lines (or over the same line). Thus multiplexing uses channels more efficiently and reduces

FIGURE 11.7
Modems in a Data Communications Network

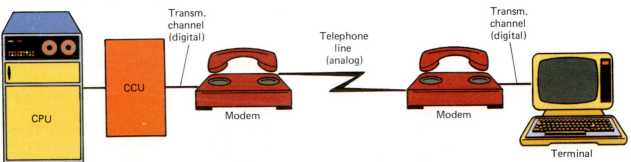

Before multiplexing   After multiplexing

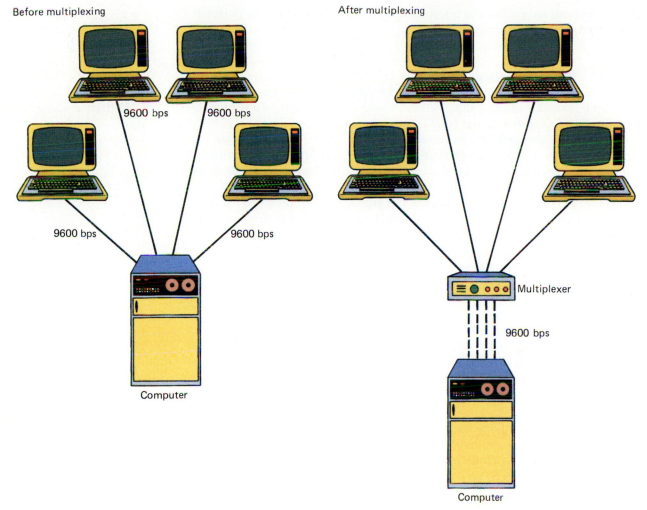

9600 bps   9600 bps

9600 bps   9600 bps

9600 bps

Multiplexer

Computer

Computer

FIGURE 11.8

Multiplexing allows a single communications device to carry several combined signals. (Note: bps stands for bits per second.)

the per-message cost. Figure 11.8 illustrates the use of a multiplexer in a data communications system.

Concentrators **Concentrators** serve much the same basic function as multiplexers, but they have additional capabilities. In effect, they are intelligent multiplexers. Besides combining (or pooling) messages, they can check for errors, change message codes and formats, delete extraneous characters, and temporarily store messages or parts of messages (see Figure 11.9).

The ability of concentrators to pool messages makes it possible to use the full capacity of a transmission line. For instance, in transatlantic transmission, the concentrator would accumulate messages from separate domestic lines before transmitting them together on a single overseas line.

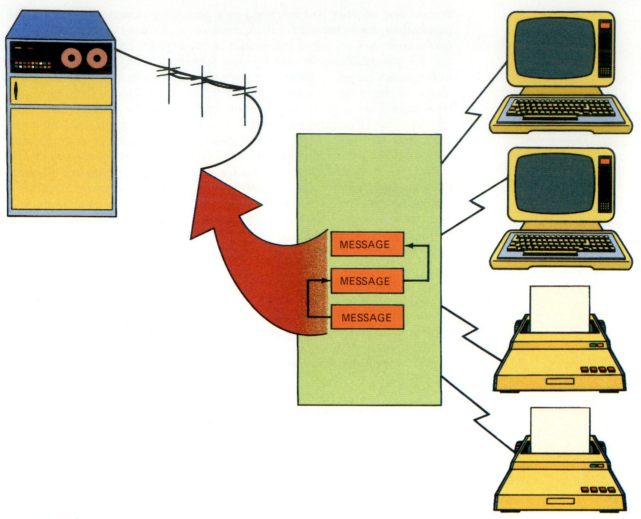

FIGURE 11.9

Concentrators

A concentrator is a programmable device that is not directly attached to a host computer and whose purpose is to more efficiently utilize lines. Messages from the concentrator network are lined up and sent one at a time over a single line to another location.

Data Communications Channels

In the simplest terms, a communications channel can be defined as a path for the transmission of a signal (usually electrical) between two points. A channel is also referred to as a line, circuit, or link. Six types of channels are discussed here.

Telephone Wire Pairs **Telephone wire pairs** are the oldest type of communications channel. Telephone lines contain many such pairs twisted

around one another and wrapped in a protective covering. A single wire pair constitutes a channel for the transmission of voice communication. For that reason they are often referred to as *voice grade* channels.

Telephone channels used for data communications have a bandwidth, or frequency range, of 3000 cycles per second. Transmission is measured in terms of the wave frequency of the transmitted signal. One Hertz—1 Hz—represents a frequency of one cycle, or one complete wave, per second. The larger the bandwidth, the higher the frequency, the more waves are transmitted per unit of time (more cycles per second) and, therefore, the more information can be carried by a transmission. Consequently, even though transmissions travel at the same speed over the same lines, a high-frequency transmission can be said to be *faster* because it carries more information in the same unit of time than does a low-frequency transmission. By the same token, a line that can carry a greater number of frequencies can be said to be faster than one that can carry fewer frequencies.

Wire Cables

Wire cables also contain wire pairs, usually numbering in the hundreds. However, insulation and special twisting methods minimize the interference, or cross talk, between individual pairs. The resulting improvement in the quality of transmission has led to the replacement of earlier, open-wire pairs by cable wires. Today the latter are the type used in most data transmission channels.

Coaxial Cables

A **coaxial cable** provides a much higher quality of transmission than do wire pairs and transmits at much higher frequencies. A coaxial cable consists of a cylinder (usually copper) with a single wire conductor running down its center (see Figure 11.10). Insulation separates the conductor from the cylinder. A large cable can hold twenty operating coaxial cables. Often used for underground transmission lines, a single large cable can carry more than 100,000 telephone calls at one time.

Microwave Links

Microwave links are the chief competition of coaxial cables for transmitting large volumes of data. A microwave link typically consists of several *microwave towers* spaced twenty-five to thirty miles apart. Signals are transmitted on a line-of-sight path from one tower to the next. The path between towers must be clear of any obstruction, because microwaves are easily reflected by solid objects. Towers cannot be spaced more than thirty miles apart, because microwaves travel in a straight line and will not bend with the curvature of the earth.

FIGURE 11.10
Coaxial Cable

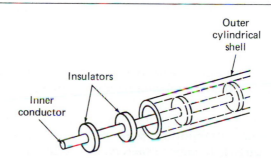

Outer cylindrical shell

Insulators

Inner conductor

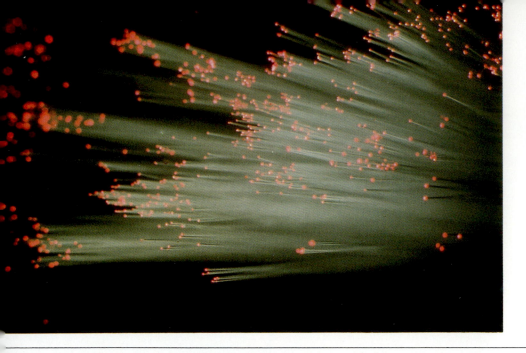

Optical Fibers

Courtesy of AT&T Bell Labs

When a tower receives a signal, it amplifies the signal and retransmits it to the next tower. One hundred towers can carry a signal from coast to coast. Coaxial links are at a disadvantage in this respect, since a coast-to-coast coaxial link requires about 1000 amplifications and retransmissions. Microwave links can carry thousands of voice channels and are widely used for television transmission.

Communications Satellites **Communications satellites** can be thought of as microwave towers placed many miles above the earth. Because of their height, satellite links can transmit microwave signals over great distances, unhampered by the earth's curvature or by mountains and other objects that limit microwave links.

In practice, a communications satellite hangs in stationary orbit over a given geographic area. Signals sent from one station in this area are bounced off the satellite to distant receivers in the same area. The bouncing is done by a combination receiver/transmitter called a *transponder*. This device receives a signal from earth and retransmits it at a different frequency. The change of frequency is necessary to prevent incoming and outgoing signals from interfering with each other.

If the intended receiver lies outside the geographic area covered by a satellite, a second satellite can be used. The original signal is simply bounced back to an intermediate station, which transmits it to the second satellite, which in turn sends it to the intended destination. Three such satellites are sufficient to enable a signal to ''hop'' to almost any part of the world.

Lasers and Optical Fibers Lasers and optical fibers are the products of new technologies that are now being studied for possible applications to data communications.

A **laser** generates a beam of light that is almost perfectly monochromatic, which means that almost all the light rays in the beam have exactly the same frequency. Laser light is also *coherent*. Generally speaking, this means

A Microwave Tower

Courtesy of Sperry Corporation

that all the light waves in the beam are "in step" and therefore interference between waves is minimal. In practical terms, coherence means a minimum of distortion in the information transmitted by a laser beam. These characteristics make a laser beam capable of carrying 100,000 times as much information as a microwave link.

Optical fibers are extremely fine filaments that act as a kind of pipe for the transmission of light. Made of glass or glasslike materials, optical fibers are particularly effective in transmitting laser light with minimum distortion or loss of light. Consequently, the possibility of combining the two is of great interest to researchers in data transmission.

Transmission Fundamentals

In order to understand the basic functioning of data communications networks, we need to know more about how a message is sent over a communications link: modes of transmission, types of transmission, and protocols.

Modes of Transmission

The mode of transmission refers to the manner in which the characters of a message are transmitted. The problem for the receiving unit is to separate one character from the next. There are three ways, or modes, for this kind of decoding: synchronous, asynchronous, and isochronous.

Synchronous Transmission   **Synchronous** transmission sends characters in groups, or *blocks*. A block of data may contain thousands of bits. Each

block begins with a set of bits that enables the receiver to synchronize itself with the transmission. In effect, the receiver times or measures the transmission as it is received and separates the individual characters. In other words, the receiver sets itself to divide the transmitted message into time intervals, or characters. Timing is clearly important.

Asynchronous Transmission   **Asynchronous** transmission sends characters one at a time. Each character is identified by a *start bit* and a *stop bit*. This type of transmission is said to be asynchronous (unsynchronized) because the receiver can identify a character by its start and stop bits regardless of when it arrives; that is, characters can be sent at irregular intervals. Asynchronous transmission is much slower than the synchronous type, being limited to about 1800 bits a second. Figure 11.11 illustrates synchronous and asynchronous transmission.

Isochronous Transmissions   **Isochronous** transmission combines features of the other two. Characters have identifying start and stop bits, and the sender and receiver are synchronized. Rates of isochronous transmission go as high as 9600 bits a second—slower than synchronous but faster than asynchronous.

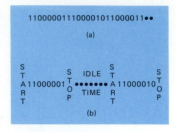

FIGURE 11.11
(a) Asynchronous Transmission
(b) Synchronous Transmission

Data Codes

Characters are the basic information unit of data communications transmission. In data transmission, characters are represented, or *coded,* as bytes. (Remember, a byte is a group of bits treated as a single unit of information. Bytes are usually 8 bits long, but they vary from 5 to 11 bits, depending on the code used.) The two main codes used in data communications are ASCII and EBCDIC.

ASCII   **ASCII** (*A*merican *S*tandard *C*ode for *I*nformation *I*nterchange) is an 8-bit code. It allows for 2^7 (128) bit combinations, or characters. ASCII was originally developed to standardize the code used for data transmission in the United States. ASCII first appeared in 1963 and was later revised. The 1968 version became the U.S. standard and has been very widely adopted. Although it is an 8-bit code, ASCII uses 10 or 11 bits for asynchronous transmission: 1 start bit, 7 data bits, 1 parity bit, and 1 or 2 stop bits. Figure 11.12 shows the transmission of an 8-bit ASCII code. EBCDIC (*E*xtended *B*inary *C*oded *D*ecimal *I*nterchange *C*ode) is discussed in Appendix A.

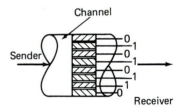

FIGURE 11.12
Transmission of an 8-bit ASCII Code

Types of Transmission

Communications between units of a network obviously require that at least some units be able to both receive and send messages. In this context, we can define three types of transmission: simplex, half duplex, and full duplex.

Simplex Transmission   **Simplex** transmission is one-way. The sending unit always sends and the receiving unit always receives. For example, a printer

at a distribution center may be restricted solely to receiving input for printing hard-copy documents. It cannot be used to transmit messages to the sending unit. For that reason, simplex channels are not used for conventional data communications.

Half Duplex Transmission **Half duplex (HDX)** transmission permits transmission in both directions, but in only one direction at a time. That is, one unit can send a message to another, but the receiving unit must wait until the reception is completed before transmitting a message of its own.

Full Duplex Transmission **Full duplex (FDX)** transmission allows a unit to send and receive messages simultaneously.

Protocols

A **protocol** is a predetermined procedure or routine used by sending and receiving units to ensure that they communicate properly. Protocols are a feature of the hardware equipment and are usually decided on at the design stage by the manufacturer. The protocol chosen may be that of the manufacturer or one previously established by a standards committee.

Protocols define the correct procedure and rules for executing transmissions and related operations. Specifically, they are used to define:

- the proper steps for beginning and terminating a transmission;
- the control characters to be used and how to use them in "laying out" a message;
- the procedure to be followed for on-line dialogue; and
- the procedure for detecting errors and the corrective action to be taken.

To use a simple analogy of a protocol for starting a transmission, consider the start of a telephone conversation. The person receiving the call responds to a ring or buzz by picking up the telephone and making some kind of sound ("Hello" or "Smith here"). The caller then usually gives some kind of identification and the conversation begins.

Data Communications Networks

Given the variety of components and communications links that can be used in networks, it is to be expected that they will differ in other respects as well. Two important features that characterize a network are its *network configuration* and what might be called its *layout configuration*. The second feature will be discussed in the context of local area networks.

Network Configurations

The **configuration** of a network refers to the path by which information is routed through the network; that is, whether the path is fixed or variable.

Networks that use fixed pathways are said to be *nonswitched*. Those that can change the route by which information is sent are said to be *switched*. The two types of nonswitched linkage used in data networks are point-to-point and multipoint. Switched networks, on the other hand, employ two types of *line control* in transmitting data: contention and central control.

Point-to-Point and Multipoint

As described earlier in this chapter, point-to-point lines connect a single terminal to a computer. In a multipoint (or multidrop) configuration, more than one terminal is attached to a single communications line. Obviously it is a relatively simple matter to send a message to the "right" terminal in a point-to-point configuration. The message has nowhere else to go. But how will a message get to the right terminal in a multipoint configuration? And how can a multipoint terminal transmit messages when other terminals are using the same line?

The answer to the first question is that each terminal has an "address" and will accept any message labeled with that address while ignoring other messages with different addresses. For example, when a communications control unit sends a message to, say, terminal Z, it first adds the address of Z to the message before transmitting it. Terminals X and Y, therefore, will ignore the message and Z will accept it. To answer the second question, messages from different terminals carry different identifying codes that enable the communications control unit to distinguish it from other terminals and thus respond to only one particular terminal. In a multipoint configuration, the CCU can also *broadcast* a message to several terminals at the same time. Figure 11.13 shows point-to-point and multipoint configurations.

A variant of the multipoint configuration is the *loop configuration*. Here a message is transmitted at high speed around a loop line to which several terminals are attached. Again, a terminal will accept any message carrying its address and will ignore others.

Note that in every case, the transmission path is always the same. It is the terminal that accepts or ignores a message.

Network Line Control

Network line control involves the use of operating procedures and signals to control the transmission of messages. Its main function is to ensure that all terminals can use the network as needed. The main types of line control are contention and central control.

As the name clearly indicates, terminals in a network that uses **contention line control** actually *contend* for the use of the network's lines on a first-come, first-served basis. When a terminal has a message to send, it first requests the use of the line. Then, if the line is free, it transmits the message. If the line is busy, however, it must wait and repeat the request as often as necessary.

In a central control system, the terminals have no say as to when they can send a message. Instead, a central computer or a CCU controls all transmissions to and from terminals. The central unit uses a process called polling to give each terminal the opportunity to transmit a message. It polls the terminals by "asking" each of them, in turn, if it has a message to send. A terminal responds with the digital equivalent of yes or no. If yes, the terminal is given use of the line. If no, the central unit polls the next terminal (see Figure 11.14).

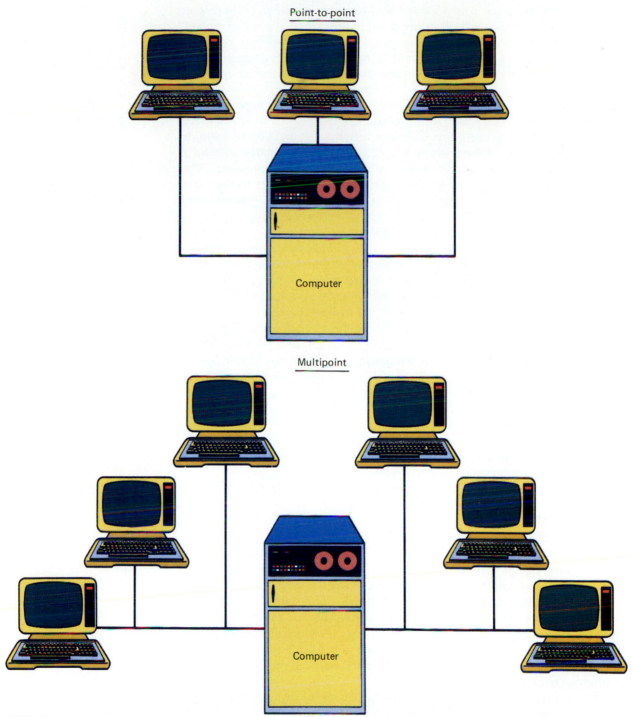

FIGURE 11.13
**Point-to-Point and Multipoint
Lines**

In point-to-point lines, each terminal is connected directly to the central computer. In multipoint lines, several terminals share a single line, although only one terminal can transmit at a time.

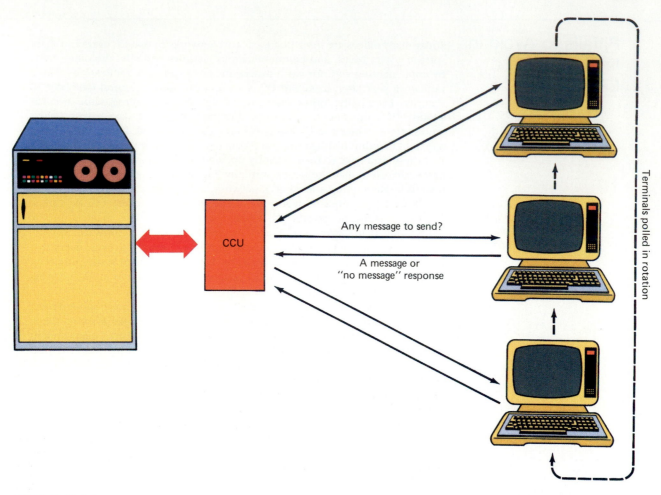

FIGURE 11.14
The Polling Process
In polling, the front-end processor "polls" each terminal in rotation to see if a message is ready to be sent.

In the most common form of polling, the central system "calls the roll" of terminals, using a polling list. In the less common *hub-go-ahead* polling, the polling message is passed to one terminal, which may or may not transmit before passing the polling message on to the next terminal, and so on down the line.

Local Area Networks

In general terms, a **local area network (LAN)** is an electronic communications network that uses private branch exchanges (PBXs) or other local communications channels for transmission instead of public communications facilities such as long-distance links or satellite communications. Perhaps its greatest advantage is that it permits the linking up of a variety of devices—word processors, desk-top computers, printers, and storage

Pitfalls to Avoid in Implementing a LAN:

Today many offices are installing local area networks so that PC users can share software, data bases, and communications facilities. Usually, the office starts by implementing a PC for word processing or spreadsheet applications. Then, perhaps a year later, a second PC is acquired to store a central data base of records. Eventually, other users requiring access to these same records acquire PC's but find they have to duplicate the entire data base on their workstations in order to have access to the data they need. It becomes readily apparent that duplicating the central data base becomes unworkable, especially if these data have to be constantly updated. Making sure that all of the data bases are up-to-date becomes virtually impossible. Soon the office looks toward implementing a local area network.

With a local area network, all of the PC's in the office can be linked together, making it possible to share a central data base located on the workstation that serves as a central file server. Sharing of software, spreadsheets, and documents on the network is also possible. However, users that have begun to implement such networks have experienced some pitfalls. A number of issues must be addressed by thorough planning to make sure that the network is successful.

A local area network creates a multi-user environment, even though most of the applications on the PC's are written for single-user systems. Each workstation on the network may currently have data base management software that is used to access records and to generate reports from the data base. However, just because an application runs on a single workstation on the network doesn't mean that it can run on the entire network and be used by all of its workstations. Network versions of word processing, data base, and other application software packages must be purchased for the network.

Another problem can occur when more than one user tries to access and update the same data file on the file server simultaneously. The network operating systems should provide utilities for file and record locking, so that the first user can successfully update a record in the data base before the

devices—in a small area such as a business office. The importance of this advantage is made clear by a single statistic: 60 percent of office communications involves individuals in the local organization.

Specifically, a small personal or office computer in a local area network is able to:

- gain access to data stored in central disk-storage devices and store data in those devices;
- transmit documents prepared on the computer to an electronic printer;
- transmit electronic messages to other computers in the network; and
- send information to and receive information from a CPU in the network.

To understand the functioning of LANs better, let's now look at the three types of configuration, or layout, of these networks. (These three network configurations are shown in Figure 11.15.)

The Star   The **star** configuration links each device in the network to a central control unit. Star networks represent the traditional approach to network linkage. Most star networks use PBX links (telephone lines). This type of link has advantages and disadvantages. The main advantage is that

second user is given access to this record. Network operating systems and network data base software must be specifically written for the network.

Network access to data bases places increasing demands on the file server, the hard disk system that holds common applications and data bases shared by the users. As a result, one workstation with a hard disk system should be used as a dedicated file server for the network. This means that the file server should not be used as a workstation when the network is running or else severe performance problems can occur.

The personnel cost for system administration is often overlooked. A system administrator should be responsible for user administration, training, backup, and support. Protecting the security of shared data bases on the file server is another important responsibility. A secretary can't be expected to handle these responsibilities in her spare time.

A LAN may include workstations, a hard disk system, a tape backup unit, software, and printers. Each of these devices must be compatible with each other. When configuring a LAN, planning should be done to determine what applications need to be supported. Do the users want to share a common data base, to share software, or to share a printer? Do users want to use the central network system as a gateway to external data bases housed on branch minicomputers or mainframes? Does the system provide control over data security? Can the LAN be interfaced to other departmental LAN's within the organization for file transfer and for electronic mail purposes?

Planning to implement a successful local area network requires an understanding of user requirements, technical knowledge, and personnel administration.

Sources: Alan Hald and Bruce Grant, "LAN Mines for the Unwary," *Information Center,* V. II, No. 12, December, 1986, pp. 38–39; "The Information Center Institute Checklist for Local Area Networks," *Information Center,* December, 1986, pp. 47–48.

telephone lines already exist. The main disadvantage is the limited capacity of such lines.

The Ring   **Ring** networks link devices by cable in a loop or circle. The central controller or computer is part of the loop. Data is transmitted around the ring, with the attached devices picking out from the information stream those messages addressed to them. The ring's disadvantage is that if one computer in the ring fails, the network breaks down.

The particular type of line control used by ring networks is known as *token passing,* which is similar to the hub go-ahead procedure described earlier. Each device is allowed to transmit only when it holds a logical token. The token is passed from device to device. The function of token passing is to prevent multiple devices from transmitting at the same time, a condition that can result in data *collisions.*

The Bus   **Bus** networks consist of a cable to which devices are connected by a cable-interface unit. The network has no central controller, and data can be passed from one device to another through the bus.

Because there is no central controller, the prevention of collisions between messages is a major concern. Bus networks use a form of line

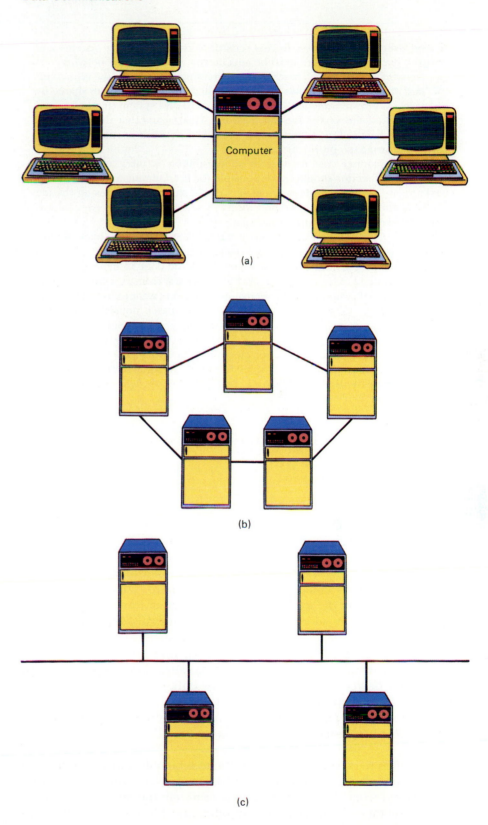

(a)

(b)

(c)

FIGURE 11.15

Network Configurations

(a) star; (b) ring; (c) bus.

control that requires a device to first check the transmission line for traffic before it sends a message. If the line is free, the device transmits. If a collision occurs, the device retransmits its message at the next opportunity.

Broadband and Baseband

A controversial issue in local network design is whether to use broadband or baseband cable for data transmission. **Broadband transmission** uses frequency-division multiplexing, which divides the cable capacity into three channels. This kind of network could transmit, for example, text, data, and video signals at the same time.

In contrast, **baseband transmissions** are sent over a single high-speed channel at a rate of 10 million bits a second (compared to the 64,000 bits a second available on a standard telephone line). A baseband network assigns all its transmission capacity to a single device for a very short period of time. A document of ten to fifteen pages, for instance, could be transmitted through the network in a matter of seconds. Baseband transmission, therefore, would be well suited to the text- and data-transmission requirements of many users.

Communications Services

Up to this point we have concentrated mainly on the technical aspects of data communications networks. But other factors are at least as important to a network's market appeal and its performance value in different environments. Communications-lines costs, for example, must be carefully considered by both the system's designer and the potential customer. Similarly, management must weigh the costs of using a network against its effectiveness in meeting the needs of the organization and furthering its objectives.

Common Carriers and Telephone-Based Services

By definition, a **common carrier** provides a transport service for a fee. A company providing such a service is called "common" because the service is available to anyone who will pay the fee; that is, to the public. A number of companies offer communications services to the public. The best-known include American Telephone & Telegraph (AT&T), ITT World Communications, RCA Global Communications, and Western Union. The types of service provided fall into four main categories: WATS lines, switched lines, leased lines, and value-added networks.

WATS lines provide what is known as a "metered" service. The carrier (in this case AT&T) offers a special bulk rate for station-to-station telephone calls that are directly dialed. WATS lines are voice grade and can be used for data transmission as well as for voice communication.

Switched lines differ from the standard telephone hookup only in being used for data transmission instead of conversation. The user simply direct-dials the intended destination (a computer), the connection is made, and the data sent. The advantage is that the user pays only for the time interval during which the sending unit is connected to the receiving unit.

Leased lines are in effect permanent communications between a sending and a receiving unit. A leased line becomes more economical with increased use. Several hours of transmission a day will make it less expensive than a switched line.

Value-added networks (VANs) employ a transmission technique known as *packet switching*. The supplier of VAN services leases lines from a common carrier and adds to the lines' value by using packet switching to transmit data over the lines.

Packet switching involves first dividing the block of data to be transmitted into packets of about 1024 K. The packets are then transmitted individually over the network and the original block of data is reconstructed at the destination intended.

The advantage of this technique is that individual packets can be sent by different routes to the same destination. Thus the network can transmit data by the fastest, most convenient—and least costly—route or routes.

The Changing Communications Environment

Electronic Mail and Teleconferencing

The use of electronic mail is increasing as more and more desktop computers are linked together in local area networks. Important in moving the business in the direction of electronic mail is the factor of cost. According to one estimate, the average business letter costs more than $8.00 to generate, and that cost is rising. The cost of transmitting the same letter on an intercompany electronic-mail network would be about 10 cents. (This figure does not include the cost of the terminal, the sender's time, and the data line.)

But the real savings come with the elimination of telephone tag. The typical manager makes 10 calls a day and receives 14, for a total of 24. Only about one quarter of all calls that are made result in the call reaching the recipient on the first try. Assuming that all 24 calls are completed at some time (today's unanswered call will be backlogged and added to tomorrow's load), the typical manager will have 24 phone conversations on a typical day. With an average call lasting about 4 minutes, this manager spends 96 minutes on the phone every workday. Now if the same calls were transmit-

ted as messages by electronic mail, each would take about 1½ minutes (to create or to read a message)—a total of about 36 minutes. Thus the time saved could be as much as 60 minutes.

Electronically mediated meetings, or **teleconferencing,** can be a cost-effective substitute for business travel. In fact, some companies have found that they can substitute teleconferences for about 40 percent of their meetings that would otherwise require travel. **Audioconferencing** is more familiar to many people as the conference call, which commonly employs PBX lines. Some communications-service companies provide a dial-up facility for initiating conference calls. **Computer conferencing** enables computer users to exchange information. Among the services provided are shared files and on-line *bulletin boards.* A user signing on at a terminal might be shown a list of the bulletin board items for that day. **Broadcast videoconferencing** provides two-way video by satellite link. It is the most commonly used form of videoconferencing. Major users include tele-conferenced courses in universities as well as transoceanic business conferences in multinational corporations.

The World at Your Keyboard: Communicating by Microcomputer

With a microcomputer, a modem, communications software, and a telephone line, the world of telecomputing is open to the microcomputer user. This means the ability to search on-line data bases for information on hundreds of subjects, to get up-to-date information on news, travel, and stock prices, and even to shop and bank at home. These services are offered by information utilities such as CompuServe, the Source, and Dow Jones. In order to use the applications the service provides, you need to subscribe to the information service and to pay hourly connect-time fees. The applications of telecomputing that you will have an opportunity to use include electronic mail, on-line data bases, computer conferencing, and bulletin boards.

Electronic mail offers the ability to send memos and messages to other subscribers of an electronic mail service. Each subscriber has an "electronic mailbox" and an "address." You need to know the addresses of users on the network with whom you want to communicate.

With a microcomputer, you have access to **on-line data bases** covering the news, legislative records, governmental reports, and laws. National information services provide on-line encyclopedias, up-to-the-minute stock quotes, and national news wires. Specialized information, such as abstracts of scientific papers, market studies, and lists of patents, is available in data banks.

If you want to compare notes with other parents, discuss local politics, or get tips on playing adventure games, participation in a **computer conference** may be a good application for you. The two types of on-line conferences available are delayed-time and real-time conferences. To

CompuServe   Page HOM-40
HOME SHOPPING/BANKING
1 Comp-U-Store
2 Electronic Banking
3 The Athlete's Outfitter
4 Music Information Service
5 Fifth Avenue Shopper
6 Primetime Radio Classics
7 AutoNet/AutoBase
8 Savings–Scan
Last menu page. Key digit
or M for previous menu.
!

Information utilities like CompuServe enable users to access external data bases and to participate in electronic shopping.

Courtesy of CompuServe

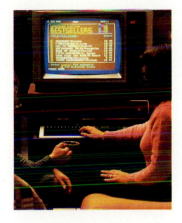

A local bulletin board system makes it possible for users to exchange ideas and opinions about current issues and events.

Courtesy of Bell Laboratories

participate in a delayed-time conference, you send your ideas to a shared mailbox, where others can read your opinions and you can read theirs. This shared mailbox is either on a **bulletin-board system (BBS),** a free service accessible with a phone call, or an information service devoted to conferences. Delayed-time conferences can go on for months, as participants join in and add new ideas. An example of delayed-time conferences is The Source's Participate section, where subscribers share ideas on topics such as "telecomputing in the classroom" and "Apple stock." Another information service, Electronic Information Exchange System, EIES, provides delayed-time conferences on literary, scientific, and philosophical issues for the academically inclined.

Real-time conferences, available through information services, need to be arranged in advance. Information services like CompuServe often schedule real-time conferences for members of special-interest groups (SIGs), such as the IBM PC Special Interest Group.

Bulletin Boards and Business

Abstract

Personal computer bulletin boards can be cheap shortcuts to some of the benefits of electronic mail. Despite raffish publicity about some bulletin boards, mainstream users find that they can solve business problems in the real world. Bulletin boards are used as message exchange centers, billboards, and as a means of distributing software and support to dispersed pc users. Organizations that have set up personal computer bulletin boards tout the speed, accuracy, and efficiency of such systems, as well as the low cost. Software required to operate a personal computer bulletin board can be bought for $100; some systems in the public domain are free.

Most of the publicity inspired by pc-based bulletin boards has focused on techno-vandals trading hot gossip and stolen access codes, but the personal computer bulletin board system (BBS) can also be an economical communications medium for mainstream users. In particular, a BBS can provide some of the features of expensive electronic mail systems for a minimal cost.

The first bulletin board was apparently, and appropriately, a California product. Almost 15 years ago, Resource One, a San Francisco-based nonprofit outfit of computer pros, had a bulletin board called Community Memory running on a donated XDS computer. Terminals were in the San Francisco Public Library and in a health food store near the University of California, Berkeley campus. Today, Ken Goosens, a senior information center analyst who runs a bulletin board at the Federal National Mortgage Association in Washington, D.C., estimates that there are 400 bulletin boards in the nation's capital alone, and over 100,000 in the U.S. . . .

Put to a Variety of Uses

Some boards can act as message exchange centers. Some business BBSs are designed to permit remote communication, say, between people in different offices or on the road. Others can distribute software and support to dispersed

pc users. Some bulletin boards act as billboards, making information easily available to outside users. To reduce telephone tag, a BBS can act as a central message repository for a project team. Not only can the BBS make it easier for team members to stay in touch, but it also can provide a log to track the history of a project. Most of the available bulletin board software supports any or all of these functions, and BBS operators can configure their systems to include, omit, or restrict features to meet organizations' differing needs.

Some BBSS can participate in store-and-forward communications networks wherein correspondents send and receive mail through local participating BBSS. Bulletins from the BBS operator can be posted for all to read. Files—text, data, and program—can be uploaded and downloaded with communications protocols elminating transmission errors.

The user community can be restricted or open to all. Security features found on BBSS include passwords, encryption, multiple security levels for users, the logging of attempted security violations, and automatic disconnect for too many violations.

One company that uses a BBS for electronic communications is Coca-Cola Foods, Houston. The board supports electronic mail between regional sales offices and Houston, and in addition, serves as a document distribution center. About two years ago, Coca-Cola Foods installed its BBS, thinking at the time that it would be an interim solution, according to Cheryl Currid, manager of sales sytems planning and information. The need for electronic mail was recognized, but not well defined, and the BBS approach appealed to Coca-Cola Foods because of its low cost. The investment? A personal computer system that could later be reused for something else. The software was free. At that time the system was expected to be in use for no more than six months.

"We knew we needed something like this, but we really didn't know exactly how we'd use it—things like volume of traffic and use patterns," explains Currid. "That's probably why we went around and around with the MIS staff. We couldn't answer their questions well enough for them to offer a solution."

Now Coca-Cola Foods can better identify its needs for electronic mail. "We know how many calls we have and what the traffic patterns are," says Currid. Statistics gathered from May through October tally up more than 15,000 calls into the BBS, 4,000 messages posted, and 6,000 file transfers.

One use Coca-Cola Foods makes of its BBS is the distribution of Lotus 1-2-3 spreadsheets to regional offices. The regions fill in the spreadsheets and return them to Houston. Error detecting and correcting protocols ensure accurate transmission of the forms in both directions. . . .

A Business in Itself

Distributing public domain software has even become a business in itself for some BBS operators. There are for-profit BBSS that make large software libraries accessible to users for as little as $15 a quarter, while some other BBSS solicit contributions to offset operating expenses. Businesses with large or widely dispersed pcs use BBSS to distribute public domain software and userware. This makes useful software available throughout the organization, and it gives a point of centralized control and support. Additionally, it saves money by letting users try a variety of free (or at least inexpensive) packages before spending hundreds or thousands of dollars on commercial packages or custom code.

The Federal National Mortgage Association, more commonly called Fannie Mae, uses a BBS to provide public domain software to users of its 500 or

so personal computers. Fannie Mae also allows access to its BBS via two listed telephone numbers. A third, unlisted line is reserved for Fannie Mae personnel. . . .

While Fannie Mae operates its BBS as a two-way street, the U.S. Department of Commerce Economic Bulletin Board operates its BBS primarily as a read-only system. This board, supported by users paying a small annual fee, is an attempt to provide a single distribution point for current economic information developed by several federal agencies, including the Bureau of Labor Statistics. Bulletins provide general news, guides to different agency contacts, and a calendar of release dates for pending announcements. The board also offers information on new data and products offered by Commerce agencies, and executive summaries of larger studies available through the Government Printing Office.

Acts as Billing Agent

NTIS, the National Technical Information Service, acts as the billing agent between Commerce and its users. Many users of the Economic Bulletin Board are from the New York financial community, but others are located throughout the world. In fact, to better serve subscribers in the U.K., the board recently included a bulletin explaining how a caller in Britain can make sure his connection is via the transatlantic undersea cable; when the choice is left to the phone system, users routed over satellite can experience awkward transmission delays.

By putting the information onto the BBS, dissemination is faster, more accurate, and requires less labor, explains Ken Rogers, chief of the statistical staff in the Office of Business Analysis at the Department of Commerce. There are eight lines into the BBS, and the system runs at capacity several days a month, according to Rogers, when eagerly awaited data or announcements, such as the Gross National Product, are posted.

This is not the only BBS operated by the Commerce Department. For example, the Bureau of the Census uses a BBS to post job vacancies ranging from entry level to senior management. Another BBS offers pc information to Census Bureau staffers; software and hardware reviews, training programs for Census and Commerce personnel, and support for individual personal computer users.

The National Weather Service operates a number of boards, each targeted to a specific group. Among the users are analysts needing historical meteorological data, and others that seek marine weather and nautical information.

As users come to recognize the potential, bulletin boards may become as common in software as they are on walls.

Source: Excerpted from "Bulletin Boards and Business" by Bill Musgrave, *Datamation*, January 15, 1987, pp. 61–3.

Summary and Key Terms

1. **Data communications** is the transfer of encoded data from one location to another. The advantages of using data communications include data capture at the source, rapid dissemination of information, dispersed operations, and centralized control of business data.

2. The seven main types of applications that employ data communications are

source data collection, **remote job entry, message switching, on-line inquiry, time-sharing,** computer-to-computer networks, and **distributed data processing.**

3. The components of a data communications network include: terminals; a communications **control unit** (CCU), which connects transmission lines to a central computer; **modems,** which serve as two-way adapters between transmission channels and a CCU or a terminal; communications lines, which are connected in point-to-point network configurations or multipoint (multidrop); multiplexers, which enable a single line to carry multiple messages at the same time; and concentrators, which serve the same basic function as multiplexers but are also able to perform other functions.

4. A communications channel is a path for the transmission of a signal between two points. There are six types of communications channels.

5. **Telephone wire pairs** are voice-grade channels (one channel per wire pair). Those used for data communications have a bandwidth of 3000 Hz.

6. **Wire cables** contain hundreds of insulated wire pairs. They are the type of line used in most data transmission channels.

7. **Coaxial cables** give a much higher quality of transmission than do wire pairs and also carry much more information (more than 100,000 telephone calls at a time). Large cables containing twenty coaxial cables are used for underground transmission.

8. Microwave links can carry thousands of voice channels and are widely used for video transmission. Transmissions are sent over a series of microwave towers.

9. **Satellite links** use transponders to "bounce" microwave signals from one station to another. They are capable of carrying very large volumes of information.

10. Lasers and **optical fibers** may be combined in the transmission channels of the future. Laser beams can carry 100,000 times as much information as a microwave link; optical fibers are fine filaments capable of transmitting laser light with minimal loss or distortion.

11. Data communications networks use two types of network configuration—point to point and multipoint. Network line control is of two types—**contention** and central control. The second uses **polling** to monitor the status of the terminal.

12. **Local area networks** use PBX lines as well as other communications channels for transmissions over short distances. The three main types are **star, ring,** and **bus.** LANs may use **baseband** (single channel, high speed) or **broadband** (multi-channel, high speed) transmission.

13. The three modes of transmitting characters of a message are **synchronous** (block transmission at high speed between synchronized units), **asynchronous** (lower speed at irregular intervals; characters identified by start and stop bits), and **isochronous** (synchronized transmission with start and stop bits to identify characters; speed is midway between that of synchronous and asynchronous transmission).

14. Characters are coded for transmission as bytes. The two character codes most often used for transmission are **ASCII** (American Standard Code for Information Interchange) and **EBCDIC.** (Extended Binary Coded Decimal Interchange Code). ASCII uses 11 bits for asynchronous transmission, and has 7 data bits.

15. The three ways of transmitting data between sending and receiving units are **simplex** (one way only), **half duplex** (two way but only one direction at a time), and **full duplex** (sending and receiving at the same time).

16. **Protocols** are predetermined procedures that sending and receiving units use to ensure that transmissions are executed correctly.

17. **Common carriers** offer several kinds of transmission-line service; **WATS lines**

(metered service), **switched lines, leased lines,** and **value-added networks** (which provide packet switching on leased lines). Packet switching divides a transmission into packets, which are sent individually by the most efficient route and then recombined at the receiving end.

18. Every communications service has certain advantages according to the type of link used. Most services use switched telephone lines and leased lines. Microwave links offer high-capacity transmission, but the transmission must be line of sight between towers. Coaxial cable is being used increasingly for local area networks. Satellite links are used mainly for high-capacity communications.

19. Three data communications applications that can be expected to grow rapidly over the next decade are **electronic mail, teleconferencing,** and **videoconferencing.**

Review Questions

Fill-in

1. The device that can connect several hundred communications lines to the central computers is the _____.

2. A _____ converts a digital signal from the computer to an analog signal to be transmitted over telephone lines.

3. A _____ converts several slow-speed signals into a high-speed signal for transmission over a communication line.

4. _____ channels transmit data from tower to tower, roughly thirty miles apart.

5. _____ transmissions send data in blocks, which may consist of thousands of characters.

6. The type of transmission in which data can be sent in both directions, but only in one direction at a time, is called _____.

7. A _____ is a predetermined procedure or routine used by sending and receiving units to ensure that they communicate properly.

8. A _____ line connects more than one terminal to a communication line.

9. Using the process called _____, terminals on a multipoint network have an opportunity to transmit messages.

10. The local area network configuration, _____, links devices together using a central PBX.

11. In a line-control procedure known as _____, each device is allowed to transmit only when it holds a logical token.

12. A _____ connects devices to a coaxial cable on a bus network.

13. A type of bus network in which the communications channel can accommodate text, data, and video transmissions on multiple channels is called a _____ network.

Matching

Match the following terms with their proper definitions:

a. concentrator

b. full duplex

_____ 1. type of line that connects a single terminal to the computer.

c. coaxial cable

d. asynchronrous

e. point to point

f. contention

g. ring

h. bus

i. baseband

j. common carrier

—— 2. local-area-network configuration that links devices in a loop.

—— 3. a type of bus local area network with a single high-speed data transmission channel.

—— 4. offers transmission services to anyone for a fee.

—— 5. "intelligent" multiplexer that can perform such functions as error detection, temporary storage, and changing message formats.

—— 6. a local-area-network configuration with no central controller that uses a contention procedure for transmission.

—— 7. a transmission mode in which characters are identified by start and stop bits.

—— 8. a type of transmission in which data can be sent and received simultaneously.

—— 9. a communications channel offering large capacity for local area networks.

—— 10. a network line-control procedure in which terminals have an opportunity to transmit on a first-come, first-served basis.

Discussion Questions

1. What type of communications channel would support the following applications? Choose from:
   1. telephone lines
   2. coaxial cable
   3. satellite link
   4. microwave link

   Explain the reasons for your answer.

   —— a. A videoconferencing application, between New York and Los Angeles.

   —— b. An application requiring transmission of voice and data between two office buildings in a major corporate complex. The buildings are approximately five miles apart.

   —— c. An application using a local area network linking personal computers and word processors to a hard-disk storage device and an electronic printer in an office environment.

   —— d. A nationwide electronic-mail network.

2. Which of the following data-processing applications using data communications facilities and networks are described in the following situations? Choose from:
   1. source data collection
   2. remote job entry
   3. message switching
   4. on-line inquiry
   5. time-sharing
   6. computer-to-computer networks
   7. distributed data processing

   —— a. transmitting loan payment information from microcomputers in branch offices to the home office's mainframe.

   —— b. using a nationwide electronic-mail system.

   —— c. requesting the credit status of a customer.

   —— d. submitting a computer program to be processed at a central site with output to be distributed to a remote printer.

   —— e. using statistical-analysis tools on a mainframe during a twenty-to-thirty-minute period each day.

Systems Analysis and Design

Chapter Objectives

After studying this chapter, you should be able to

1. Explain the characteristics of a system and subsystems.

2. Identify the stages of the systems development process, including systems analysis, design, and implementation.

3. Understand the tools and techniques of structured systems analysis, including logical data flow diagrams, the data dictionary, decision tables and trees, and data immediate access diagrams.

4. Identify the characteristics of structured design, as well as the physical design of the new system.

5. Explain steps in the implementation process, including testing, training, conversion, and documentation.

Downhill Racer is a busy sporting goods store. The owner and four salespeople work in the store itself. Two clerks operate the office located behind the shop. They order the stock and special items requested by the customers. This small "order department" has been using a typewriter and preprinted forms to order about 35 items a day, ranging from ski masks to tents. For each item requested, the clerks first check to see if it is in stock, then check the customer's credit rating for special orders, and then fill out a purchase order if needed.

As in many small businesses, such procedures work well until the clerks become overwhelmed. The business has grown so rapidly in the last six months that it now must process about 60 orders a day. The order clerks simply can't handle it. Orders pile up; errors are made as the clerks try to handle several orders at the same time; and customers are beginning to complain about delivery delays and that they don't receive what they asked for.

One way out of this dilemma might be to hire an additional order-processing clerk and perhaps obtain a second typewriter. The owner realizes, however, that more growth could soon overload even a three-clerk manual system. Should he anticipate future expansion and join the increasing number of businesses, large and small, that use computers? He has heard of businesses with similar problems where a microcomputer made all the difference. But he has also heard horror stories of companies that plugged in a machine and lost a week's orders or mixed up customer records. He

knows that to benefit from its advantages, a computer must be planned as a working component in the everyday operation of the business. That is, it must become part of a total system, the system by which Downhill Racer is operated. Just how that might be done is the topic of this chapter.

What Is a System?

What do a living cell, an automobile, NASA's Mission Control Center, and a university have in common? The answer is that they are all *systems*.

These systems are, of course, very different. A cell is made up of cytoplasm, membranes, and DNA, while an automobile contains metal, plastic, lubricants, and glass. But both automobiles and cells contain a variety of parts that work together. The university and Mission Control also contain a variety of parts—in these cases, people, equipment, and buildings. But these systems also have specific goals: A university educates people; Mission Control directs space flights. In other words, these systems are more than a set of parts that interact. They exist to achieve a goal.

For our purposes, we can define a system as a set of parts or elements that interact to achieve a specific goal. For instance, a health-care delivery system consists of doctors, nurses, equipment, and facilities that interact to deliver health care. This *goal-oriented* system is the kind that computers deal with and that we will explore in this chapter.

The goal of a system usually involves transforming various kinds of input into a desired output (see Figure 12.1). In a university, the inputs are teaching and related services; the output is educated people and research. In a computerized business system, inputs are raw data, and the output is

FIGURE 12.1

In a system, inputs are transformed into a desired output.

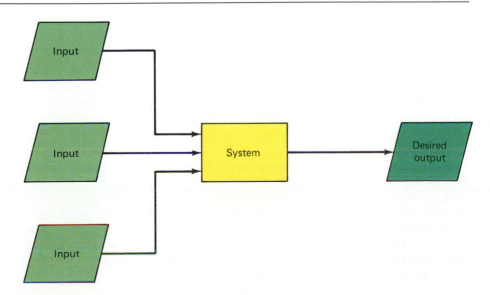

likely to consist of information in a form needed by management for planning and decision making. Let's look at an example.

A Sample System

The Greeting Card Company has met with great success and would like to meet with even more. It already has several useful systems: billing, inventory, and payroll, among others. It wants to add a new system to find out what types of cards have sold best, so that the company can design and market more cards of those types. Although management has an idea of how the cards are selling, it wants to be certain.

The input to the new system will be the sales figures for each card the company makes. The cards have been assigned to categories developed for that purpose: humorous, traditional, risqué, oversized, religious, and so on. The output will be a report that compares the sales figures for these different categories. And the goal of the new system will be to analyze the input to determine the types of cards that are sales leaders.

Several things are worth noting about this example. First, the information that management wants is already contained in the input, but it is not in usable form. (The Greeting Card Company knows how many of each *individual* card it sells, but it has never sorted out the information by *type* of card.) The system will transform or process the raw information into a precise report. Second, several steps may be necessary to achieve this transformation; that is, the system contains a variety of parts that must interact to transform input into output. Figure 12.2 is therefore a more accurate way to look at a system than is Figure 12.1

Feedback

Once a system has been put into operation, it should do the job management wants it to do. If it doesn't, the people who use it will probably complain and the system will be either modified or scrapped. The evalua-

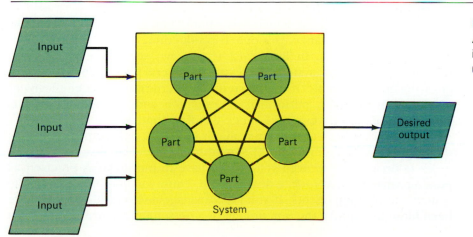

FIGURE 12.2
A system consists of several interacting parts or components.

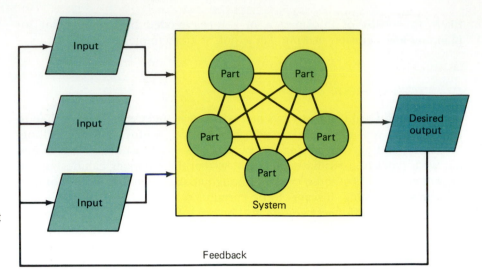

FIGURE 12.3
Feedback is information about a system's output that is used to maintain or correct the operation of the system.

tions of users—"it works, keep it" or "it doesn't work, throw it out"—are a primitive form of feedback. **Feedback** is information about how well a system works; it is used to maintain or improve the system (see Figure 12.3).

A simple example of feedback is a thermostat that controls a heating system. The inputs to the system are the thermostat setting and fuel for the heating unit. The output is the actual heating required to reach that setting. The thermostat continually records the temperature of the room as the output modifies it, it reports this temperature to the system as feedback. When the temperature matches the thermostat setting, the system modifies itself by ceasing its output, that is, turning off the heat.

Systems and Subsystems

You may have noticed that the computer itself is a system and that the organization within which a system operates is also a system. Systems that are part of a larger system are called **subsystems.**

A modern corporation, which meets our definition of a system, contains such subsystems as finance, personnel, production, research and development, and advertising. In Figure 12.4, you can see that each of these subsystems is itself a system made up of several parts. The personnel department, for example, has subsystems for recruiting, equal employment opportunity programs, performance evaluation and promotion, benefits administration, job training, grievance handling, and so on.

A natural reaction at this point might be to ask, "What does it matter that everything is a subsystem of something else?" The answer is that in order to design an improved system you have to pin down as precisely as possible what it is that you are dealing with. Thus, you must first analyze the system and its components. If you are a management consultant and have been hired to improve the functioning of a personnel department, taking a

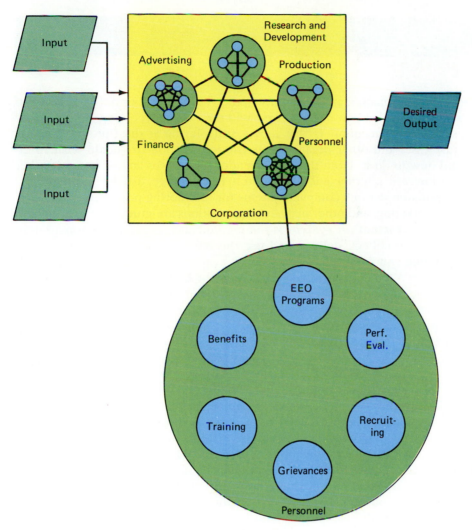

FIGURE 12.4
A subsystem is itself a system composed of several parts.

systems approach will tell you two things: First, you will see how the personnel department, which is a subsystem, fits into the larger system of which it is a part, that is, the corporation (the rectangle in Figure 12.4). Second, you will see how the tasks of the personnel department break down into sub-subsystems (the smallest circles, labeled Benefits, Training, and so on). Only then will you be able to study the interactions among them to find out which interactions can be improved. For instance, are the results of the performance evaluation subsystem being fed back to the recruiting subsystem so that the company can hire people who work harder and don't quit after six weeks? Your ability to look at the corporation as a set of systems and subsystems is probably one of the reasons you were hired as a consultant in the first place.

The feedback loop (Figure 12.3) can itself be viewed as a subsystem —a vital one. Let's take a look at the feedback systems found in organizations, where they are known as information systems.

Information Systems

We use information all the time, whether we realize it or not. Is it going to rain today? What part of the course will the exam cover? How much money is left in my account? Is that movie still playing at the Uptown Cinema? Businesses and other organizations use information to decide what to do and how to do it. From the street vendor who keeps an eye on what other vendors are offering and how much they charge, to the multinational corporation with its complex systems for monitoring production, accounting, marketing, and other matters, organizations are guided by information.

An **information system** is the method and resources an organization employs to collect, deliver, and use the information it needs for efficient operation. An information systems is a subsystem of an organization. It serves as a feedback mechanism to monitor both internal operations (the workings of the organization itself) and the external environment (the world outside with which the organization must interact). At a higher level, the purpose of an information system is to provide managers with data used for long-range and strategic planning.

Figure 12.5 shows how an information subsystem fits into a typical organization. This information subsystem plays a supporting role (implied by the dashed lines in the figure). It doesn't manage the organization, produce goods, or sell them; but by gathering and reporting data it provides a vital source of input to decision making in all these areas.

The information subsystem of the manufacturing firm shown in Figure 12.5 provides information about sales, markets, costs, and other matters to the management subsystem to aid managers in planning and decision making. The same information goes to the marketing subsystem for use in evaluation and regulation of its operations. The production department relies on the information system to keep track of orders and inventories, as well as to supply information that affects the manufacturing process itself, such as routine maintenance and the supply of parts. In all these cases, information flows in both directions: The information subsystem receives raw data from the other subsystems; it reorganizes the raw data into information that it sends back to those subsystems.

FIGURE 12.5
The Information Subsystem in an Organization

Source: J. G. Burch et al., *Information Systems: Theory and Practice*, 3rd ed. New York: Wiley, 1979.

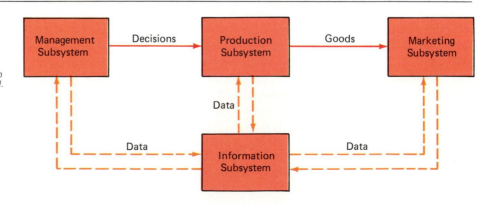

An information system may or may not be computerized. Organizations have been keeping track of their vital data since long before computers existed. However, as a business expands and as the amount of information necessary to run it increases, manual systems may become overloaded with data. When that happens, information gets to managers too slowly to be useful. A production manager may learn, for example, that the supply of paint is low when there is almost no paint left. Managers then find that they need a faster, more efficient information system.

The introduction of computerized information systems has created a need for ways of integrating these complex and versatile machines into ongoing business operations. *Systems development* is the result of this need. In the rest of this chapter we'll take a closer look at the key stages of systems development.

The Stages of Systems Development

The definition of **systems development** includes both the creation of a system where none existed before and the modification of an old system to meet new requirements. Systems development takes place in three stages: analysis, design, and implementation. Figure 12.6 shows that systems development is really a cyclical process. Analysis starts at the top of the circle and proceeds down the right; then design takes over. The left half of the circle is entirely implementation, which leads us back to the top of the circle, which involves analysis of new problems and modifications of the

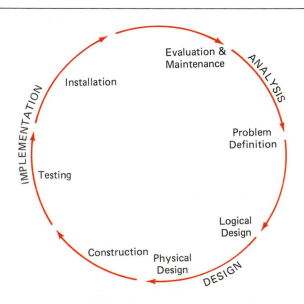

FIGURE 12.6
The Life Cycle of a Computer System

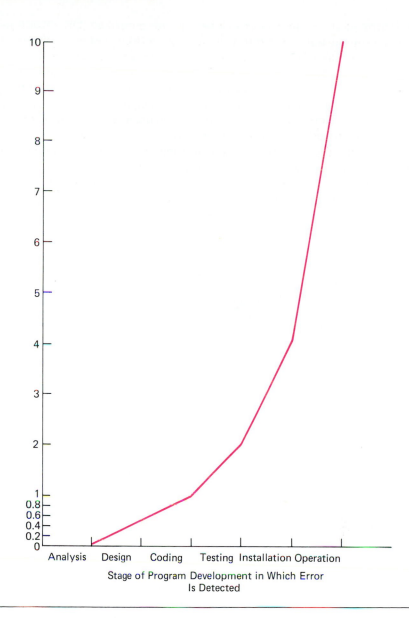

FIGURE 12.7
The Relative Cost of
Correcting an Error in
Systems Design

Source: E. Boehm, "Software Engineering," *IEEE Transactions on Computers,* December 1976.

system or the design of another system to replace it. This is sometimes compared to a life cycle, in which a new system is born, reaches maturity through use and maintenance, and finally dies when it no longer functions effectively.

Mistakes in systems design can come at any point in the process. A user's problem can be overlooked in analysis; a vendor's product can be configured inaccurately in design; a programming error can creep in during implementation. Although implementation can be said to be the "real work" of systems design, the early stages are very important. The later in the process a mistake is found, the more costly it will be in terms of money, time, and efficiency to correct (see Figure 12.7).

Systems Analysis

Now that we have had an overview of systems development, we will examine some of the stages more closely. The stages in systems development correspond to frequently encountered job titles: systems analyst, systems designer, programmer. In this section we'll take a closer look at what systems analysts do.

Systems analysis is the first stage of systems development. It consists of defining a problem to be solved or an opportunity to be taken and identifying the objectives for a new system. Systems analysts seek to study the problem in depth and to understand all the factors involved before suggesting solutions.

Systems analysis was an important business function before the advent of computerized business systems. Systems and procedures analysts were involved with improving manual systems, using techniques such as work simplification, work distribution analysis, and information flow analysis, long before computers were introduced into many organizations.

Analyzing a Manual System

As an example of the use of systems analysis in a manual system, let's use the sporting goods store described at the beginning of this chapter. If you recall, two clerks with a typewriter and some preprinted forms made up the

Systems analysis defines problems or opportunities and identifies objectives for a new system.

Courtesy of Hewlett-Packard

"order department," but they had become overloaded by the volume of work. This manual system could be improved in at least two different ways *without* using a computer.

First, more clerks could be hired to process the additional orders. Second, and probably better, the principles of systems analysis could be applied. Studying how work is done in this small organization, we would see that each clerk is performing all order-processing procedures. Each is checking stock, checking customer credit, and filling out orders. We would also see that it is very time-consuming for both to use just one typewriter. The jobs could be specialized and the work redistributed to make the work flow more efficient. One clerk could be responsible for checking credit and the other for checking stock. Both clerks might then share the order-entry procedure, using individual typewriters. It's possible that work flow improvements of this sort might improve the efficiency of the current manual system without requiring a computer.

Analyzing a Computerized System

Now let's examine a computerized system in an automobile insurance company. Systems analysts have been asked to put an end to some serious problems that have been encountered by the company. Policyholders have complained of being billed incorrect amounts because changes of address have not been recorded promptly. In one case, a subscriber who moved from a central city to a distant suburb continued to be billed at the old address at the higher rates applicable to the central city. Customers who wrote letters and telephoned the insurance company received polite, apologetic answers saying that the address and the premium would be changed promptly. Yet no changes were made and eventually the customers canceled their insurance policies. When top management had accumulated a small but troubling file of such horror stories, a team of systems analysts was called in to find out what was wrong. The analysts studied the complaints and then stated the problem. They found that there were really two problems:

1. Why do address changes take so long to be entered (a study of the records revealed that the *average* response time was three weeks)?
2. Why do some communications from customers never reach the computer system?

The analysts spent some time talking with the people responsible for changing addresses and also with those who deal with customer communications. They learned that address changes were performed by a program that was so crudely coded that it had a reputation for tying up computer resources for a long time; therefore, the computer operations department ran that program as seldom as possible—about once every three weeks. The additional delay in response time was due to bottlenecks in the flow of paper between departments.

The analysts then tried to identify some of the objectives for the new system, a system that would remedy these problems. They realized that solving the first problem would mean designing a new computer-based information system to handle address changes or hiring better maintenance

programmers to modify the existing system. Each alternative would be evaluated by the users on the basis of its effectiveness in enabling the firm to achieve the objectives, and the best alternative would be selected.

Steps in Systems Analysis

Systems analysis proceeds in a series of steps:

1. Define the problem or opportunity
2. Collect data
3. Analyze existing methods and procedures
4. Identify objectives and opportunities
5. Present a proposal to management

Define the Problem or Opportunity Once a problem or opportunity has been pointed out to the systems analyst, the first task is to draw the boundaries of the system involved: Who are the users? What is the activity? How complex is the system? A systems approach will often make it clear that the problem given to the analyst isn't the *real* problem. For instance, in a big corporation, some department managers may complain about having to leave their desks and take an elevator to another floor each time they want to use a company computer. They find this both inconvenient and time-consuming. However, their real complaint might be that, once they get there, they find the data processing facilities inadequate, overcrowded, and poorly organized.

The result of the first step in systems analysis is usually a preliminary report outlining the scope of the problem and making a recommendation, which may be that a more detailed study is needed, or that it is (or isn't) feasible to proceed with the next stage of analysis.

Collect Data Users and management have given the analysts the green light. The next step is to collect data. Just as a detective collects clues, the systems analyst must collect samples of records, documents, or usage patterns. The analyst doesn't collect data about some hypothetical future system; the need is for data about the present system, with all its problems and shortcomings. These data are used to document all the relevant activities of the system under study.

Systems analysts usually collect data by observation, interviews, and questionnaries. Observation can take the form of "walking through" the system—for instance, following a single change-of-address request through the insurance company we discussed earlier. Observations can also be stated in numerical terms; for example, in the insurance company, three weeks was the average time for processing address changes. The results can be recorded in tabular and graphic form, as well as in narrative form.

Interviews with the people who use or run the system can be of great value. Early interviews may be "just talking" so that the analyst can get a free flow of ideas. Once the analyst has a clearer idea of the kinds of information needed, interviews become more structured, possibly with a specific set of questions to be asked. It is important, however, not to word questions so that the answers will confirm the interviewer's own biased

ideas. To the department managers we discussed above, the question, "How much time do you lose each week going to another floor in order to use the computer?" assumes that this trip is a waste of time. However, a manager might regard it as something other than lost time; he or she might encounter business associates along the way and engage in useful conversations. A more specific and neutral series of questions would be better. Open-ended questions will draw more informative answers.

- Do you use the computer?
- How often?
- Are you satisfied with the facilities?
- Can you think of anything that might need improvement?

Questionnaires ask such questions on paper, making it possible to reach larger numbers of people more economically than is possible with interviews. But, like interviews, questionnaires can include questions that force a particular response, as well as questions that are so poorly worded that the responses reveal nothing. The design of a questionnaire is thus an important part of the data collection process.

Analyze Existing Methods and Procedures   After defining the problem and collecting data, the systems analyst must figure out exactly how the current system works in order to see what, if anything, is going wrong. In the case of the insurance company, a look at methods and procedures showed that one bottleneck—the computer operations department's reluctance to run a time-consuming program—was responsible for half of the delay time. This in turn suggested a solution: Change the program.

For many problems, it is necessary to analyze all the jobs contained in the system. Are there inconsistencies? Is there a duplication of tasks? Is the work load poorly distributed? Can the work be simplified? In the case of the insurance company, an illogical flow of paper work accounted for part of the delay. Two parts of a five-part form were being processed but not used, and therefore could be eliminated. Responsibility for actually entering address changes was included in different job descriptions, so no one felt (or was) really responsible. The analysis of carefully collected data in terms of a clearly stated problem brings results at this stage of analysis.

Identify Goals and Opportunities   At this point the analyst must outline, in measurable terms, what the system *should* be able to do. It is important to state the goal clearly and strongly. Do you think that, for our insurance company and department manager examples, respectively, the following goals are stated clearly enough to be readily measurable?

- Improve response time on address changes.
- Reduce time wasted by corporate department managers in traveling to the data-processing center and competing for computer facilities.

The answer, of course, is no. What does "improve" mean? Change the average response time from three weeks to two weeks? Here is a measurable set of goals:

- Reduce the maximum time between the receipt of an address change by

the customer service department and the update of the address in the data base to five workdays.

■ Install computer resources sufficient to assure any department manager access to computer facilities with no more than two minutes of "wait" or "setup" time.

In stating goals, it is important to think not only in terms of improving the present system but also in terms of related benefits or opportunities. For example, there's no reason that the goal of improved response time for the insurance company should not include substantially reduced costs as well.

Present a Proposal to Management   The last step in systems analysis is to make a formal presentation of findings and recommendations to management. The report should contain a menu of alternatives—a list of possible solutions to the problem. The alternatives all solve the problem, or take advantage of the opportunity, that was stated in the problem definition, but they differ in significant ways. Users and management select what they think is the best alternative on the basis of the trade-off between costs and benefits. For our department managers, the systems analysts might offer the following menu of alternatives:

1. Extend present computer facilities to department managers by installing remote terminals. Time required to implement: two months. Total cost: $5000 initial investment, minor maintenance additional. Benefits: (a) Achieves objective of not having to take an elevator to another floor to use facilities by 100 percent. (b) Does not achieve objective of immediate access, since central computer facilities are overloaded.

2. Create satellite computer center in department by installing terminals and a printer for input and output. Time required to implement: five months. Total cost: $10,000 initial investment, extensive maintenance additional. Benefits: (a) Achieves objective of not traveling to another floor to use facilities by 100 percent. (b) Achieves objectives of immediate access by 50 percent, since jobs that are extensive in their input/output processing can do this processing within each department.

3. Install stand-alone micrcomputers in offices of user-managers. Time required to implement: 1½ months. Total cost: $15,000 initial investment, minor maintenance additonal. Benefits: (a) Achieves objective of managers not having to take an elevator to another floor to use facilities by 100 percent. (b) Achieves objective of immediate access by 100 percent. (c) Offers additional benefit of making computer time available to other employees nearby.

To aid users and management in choosing the system that they feel best suits their needs, systems analysts need to be thorough in their descriptions of key factors, such as development costs, development time, benefits, hardware requirements, and personnel changes. Care should be taken in this final presentation, as in earlier ones, to communicate clearly with users. And, of course, since it has been intimately involved in the analysis of the system, the systems analysis team should indicate which alternative it favors.

Structured Systems Analysis

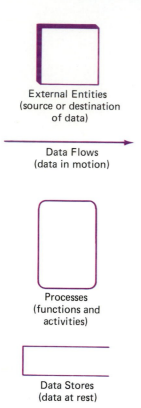

External Entities
(source or destination
of data)

Data Flows
(data in motion)

Processes
(functions and
activities)

Data Stores
(data at rest)

FIGURE 12.8
Symbols Used in Logical
Data Flow Diagrams

Users and systems analysts often don't speak the same language. In the past, designers have often produced elegant systems that didn't match user needs, provoking such comments as "We built a technically excellent system, but it wasn't what the users wanted." Organizations have found that after spending a great deal of money they have come up with systems that failed to meet their needs, didn't work at all, broke down frequently, or soon became obsolete.

Such problems have led to the emergence of what is called **structured systems analysis.** Structured systems analysis produces a step-by-step diagram or model of the proposed system. It involves close interaction between analysts and users at all stages in the design and implementation of a system.

Communication with users is especially important in the analysis phase of systems development. Good communication makes sure the resulting system will really meet the needs of users and management. The analyst's logical model of the system aids communication with users. The tools of structured analysis are both sophisticated enough to capture the complexities of a system and clear enough to be understood by users. We will briefly demonstrate four tools that can be used in building a logical model: logical data flow diagrams, data dictionaries, decision tables, and decision trees.

Logical Data Flow Diagram

Graphics are an effective means of communication, and one of the most easily understood graphic tools for systems analysis is the **logical data flow diagram.** It uses only four symbols (see Figure 12.8). These symbols are *logical.* They allow us to disregard details in order to get the clearest

**A Logical Flow Diagram
from the Excelerator
Software Program**

Courtesy of Index Technology Corporation

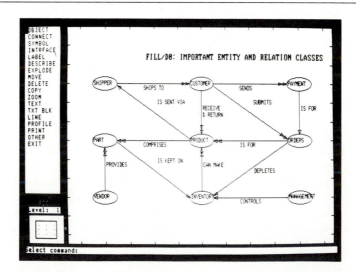

possible picture or "roadmap" of the source and the direction of the data, or the "flow of data." This data flow might be by telephone, six-part form, or computer; the process might consist of seventeen computer programs run in succession or the paper work performed by two clerks; the data might be stored on index cards, computer disk packs, or in a filing cabinet. At this stage of system design, we don't care about details; it is the logical model that counts.

Figure 12.9 is a logical data flow diagram for an order entry and inventory control system for a distributorship of office products. When a customer phones in an order, an order-entry person completes the sales order and verifies the credit, using a customer data store. This data store has information on the current credit status of the customer.

Sales orders with good credit proceed to the next process, where the sales order is edited to assure that the item number correctly matches the item number in inventory. Then, in the next process, the current stock of the item in inventory is checked to see if there is sufficient stock to cover the sales order, and the inventory level is adjusted to reflect the amount of the sale.

For items that are in stock and shippable, a shipping note and invoice are generated. The invoice amount is used to update the customer account balance in the accounts receivable file, and the shipping note and invoice are sent to the customer, along with the merchandise. When the customer pays the invoice, the payment is used to update the accounts receivable balance.

For items that are not shippable and have to be back-ordered, a back-order requisition is produced and a copy placed in a back-order file. Then a purchase requisition to the supplier is created and a copy of the requisition is placed in a purchase requisition data store.

When the supplier sends the shipment in response to the order, the contents of the shipment are checked against the purchase order data store to make sure that what was shipped was what was ordered. Then the shipment contents are matched against the back-order data store so that all back orders can be filled as soon as possible. The inventory levels are also updated to reflect all merchandise that has been received into stock. Then the order is shipped to the customer, along with the invoice. When the customer pays the invoice, the accounts receivable data store is updated to reflect the payment.

The data flow diagram provides the user with a simplified but clear understanding of the activities going on in a system. During systems analysis, the logical data flow diagram of the existing system is developed and analyzed. Then problems in the existing system are identified and objectives for the new system are defined. With these objectives as guidelines, a logical data flow diagram of the proposed system is developed and becomes a blueprint for the design of the new system.

Each of the data flows, data stores, and processes on the new logical data flow diagram is now analyzed in greater depth to determine the data elements for the new system, the logic of various processes, and the tools required to access the data housed in various data stores. These tools can also be readily understood by the user. They include the logical data dictionary, decision tables and decision trees, and data immediate access diagrams. These tools will be explained in the next sections.

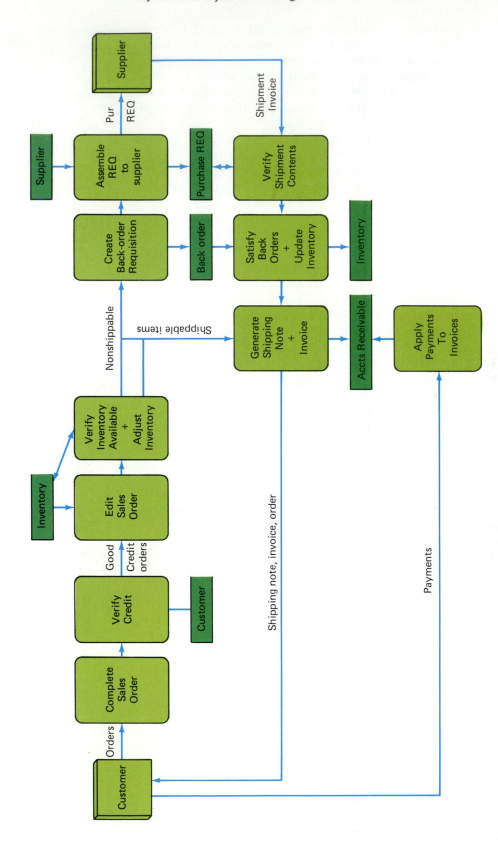

Data Dictionary

Each data store and data flow in a system consists of a data *structure*. Such data structures contain the individual data elements that system processes will require. For instance, the data flow "inventory data" from Figure 12.9 might contain the following data elements: inventory date, item number, item description, quantity, stock location, and shipping address.

A **data dictionary** is used to list and define each data element. One purpose of the data dictionary is to give analysts and users a chance to define the characteristics of all data elements in the data flows and data stores. Figure 12.10 is a data dictionary entry for the data flow "inventory data" taken from Figure 12.9. At the analysis phase, the data dictionary remains at a logical level; no reference is made to the physical medium or the range of possible values of the data. Later, at the physical design stage, data elements can be defined more specifically.

```
INVENTORY-RECORD
ITEM-NUMBER
ITEM-DESCRIPTION
REORDER QUANTITY
PRICE
PRIMARY SUPPLIER
SECONDARY SUPPLIER
STOCK-ON-HAND
REORDER POINT
```

FIGURE 12.10
A Data Dictionary Entry

Decision Trees and Decision Tables

Throughout our system, many processes involve the order entry, inventory control, shipping, and invoicing procedures. These processes actually have a logic of their own. Most businesses have policies on discount terms, shipping terms, and invoicing terms. These policies usually take into account a series of conditions and result in a series of alternative actions.

For example, a policy may say that all orders for over 100 items receive a 10-percent discount, all order for between 50 and 100 items receive a 5-percent discount, and the rest receive no discount. In this case, based on a certain condition, the number of items ordered, various actions (various discounts or no discount) may result. Many business policies involve multiple conditions and multiple actions. A decision tree or table is a particularly useful tool in specifying the logic of business processes.

A **decision tree** for one aspect of order processing is shown in Figure 12.11a. The branches of the tree follow, from left to right, different logical possibilities. (We can see, for instance, that seasonal items—for example, Halloween costumes—in quantities of 100 or more are shipped by normal freight.) A decision tree provides a clear description of the logic of a process so that users and analysts can spot errors. It allows everyone concerned to agree on the procedures to be followed. Once the procedures have been agreed on, decision trees are an excellent starting point for the actual design or programming of the procedure. A **decision table** depicting the logic of this *same* procedure is shown in Figure 12.11b.

A Dictionary Menu from the Excelerator Software Program

Courtesy of Index Technology Corporation

A Dictionary Entry for a Data Element in Excelerator

Courtesy of Index Technology Corporation

Data Immediate Access Diagrams (DIADS)

A **data immediate access diagram,** or DIAD, enables an analyst to identify how a file of records can be accessed. A DIAD expresses in a diagram the immediate accesses to the records in a file. (A primary key is simply the field in a record that uniquely identifies that record; the primary key is the main

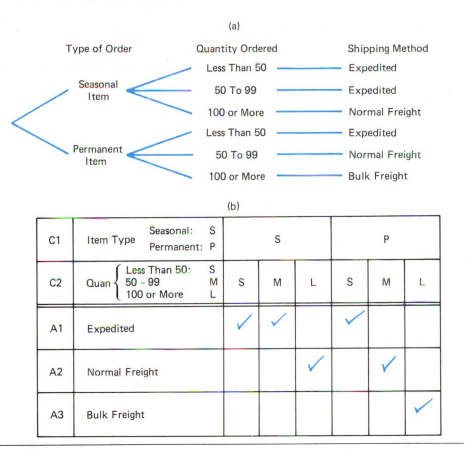

FIGURE 12.11
(a) A Decision Tree for One
Aspect of Order Processing
(b) A Decision Table for the
Same Aspect of Order
Processing Shown in (a)

key.) In a university's student file, each record might contain the following fields:

Student Number	Student Name	Student Address	Major	Advisor
477-65-8765	Hopkins, Joan	67 Ridgemoor	History	Baker

For each student in the file, there will be one student record containing the information shown above. "Student number" is the *primary key*. If we want any information about a particular student, we can use that student's number, for example, student number 477-65-8765, to obtain the record for the student, thereby obtaining all the other information in the record as well.

The primary key to a record is not always known. It might, for example, be necessary to find out the name of a student's adviser when all we know is the student's name. What is needed is a *secondary key* to the record, that is, another field in the record that also identifies it. In our example, the student name is such a field. Using the student name as a secondary key, we can gain access to the student record and to the information it contains.

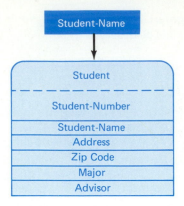

FIGURE 12.12
A DIAD for a Student File, Showing That Student-Name Provides Immediate Access to the Data in the Student Record.

A DIAD for our student file is given in Figure 12.12. This diagram shows that, by using the secondary key of student name, we can access all the other information contained in a student record. When it comes time to actually set up a file, DIADs tell the analyst what immediate accesses are necessary to the records within the file.

Questions like those we have addressed in setting up data flow diagrams, data dictionaries, decision trees, and DIADs bring us nearer to the next stage of systems development (and our next topic of discussion): systems design.

Systems Design

In **systems design,** the first step is to consider a logical model for the proposed system and the set of objectives the proposed system should meet. Then specifications are produced for a physical system to meet those objectives. In other words, in this stage of systems development the processes are designed that are needed to convert the input of the system into output that achieves the system's goals.

Systems design can begin only after systems analysis has been completed, since it is the analysis that creates the model and set of objectives that users, analysts, and management agree on. However, systems design must come before implementation. Programmers sometimes think they can work out the design while coding their programs, but like authors who think they can write a book without making an outline in advance, they generally turn out results that are less than ideal.

An objective of a good design is to produce a flexible system, one that can be modified easily. A system that is easy to modify need not be thrown out in its entirety when something goes wrong. A flexible system can also be adapted and built on more readily than an inflexible one. Another important part of structured system design is to design the system at the *logical* level (what the system must do) before committing oneself to a *physical*

solution. A logical design is easy to understand, since it uses graphics, omits technical details, and aims at brevity.

Structured Design

The purpose of structured design is to take the logical model of the system and to produce the specifications for a physical system that will achieve the objectives of the new system. A key task in logical design is to create a changeable system. The reason for this is that maintenance, or making changes or enhancements to existing systems, still accounts for about 70 to 80 percent of the time spent in data-processing shops. Thus more time is spent modifying existing systems than is spent in creating new ones.

Maintenance and the Ripple Effect   Maintenance involves several tasks, including finding out where to make a change in a program or system, making the change, and being sure that the change has worked. One of the biggest problems in maintenance is the *ripple effect,* which often occurs when such a change is made. An example of the ripple effect is when a programmer makes a change in a part of a program, and this change produces a "bug" in another part. Fixing the second bug introduces a third bug, and fixing the third bug creates a fourth, and so on.

Designs Without Ripples   Structured design has provided tools for avoiding this type of problem. In structured design, the logical model of the new system is used to derive a design that consists of a hierarchy of modular functions. This process involves taking a detailed data flow diagram and organizing it into modules that perform input functions, modules that transform input into output, and modules that perform output functions. Examples of input functions are reading and editing input data. Transform modules transform good input data into output by performing calculations or logical operations, and output modules usually format and print output data in various ways. In Figures 12.13a and 12.13b, you can see how a simple logical data flow diagram is converted into a hierarchy of logical modules that transform data into output. This type of system is known as a transform-centered hierarchy.

The Independent Module   Each module in the system has a name that explains its function, such as "Edit Input." Modules in a system are functionally independent, so a change in one module doesn't affect the inner workings of other modules. This independence prevents the ripple effect from occurring. Finally, each module should perform only one distinct function, and not try to take on other functions. In the hierarchy of modules, there are what are called manager and subordinate modules. Managers "call up" subordinates, and these subordinates are responsible for certain single tasks.

A Payroll System as a Hierarchical Structure   In the example of the payroll system shown in Figure 12.14, you can see the hierarchy of manager and subordinate modules that is necessary to process the payroll and produce

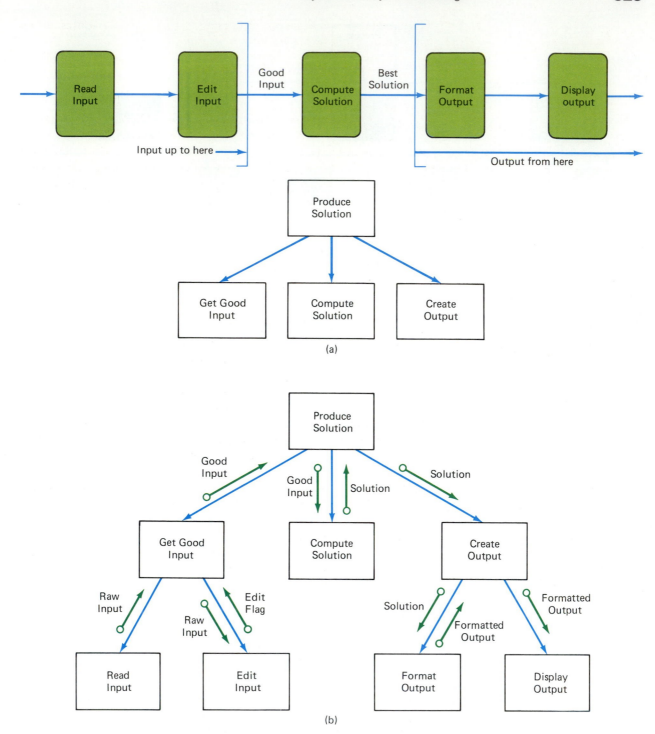

FIGURE 12.13
(a) Data Flow Diagram and the Resulting Hierarchical Structure
(b) Hierarchy Chart for a Simple Transform-Centered System

Source: Chris Gane and Trish Sarson, *Structured Systems Analysis: Tools and Techniques*.
Englewood Cliffs, NJ: Prentice-Hall, Inc. 1979.

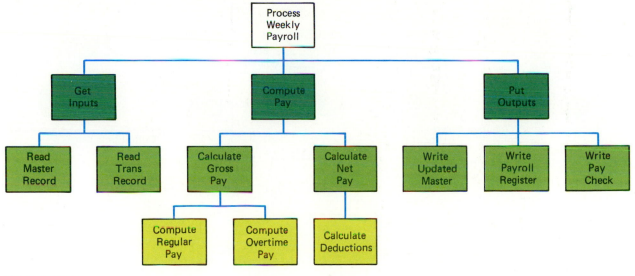

FIGURE 12.14
Hierarchy Chart for Payroll Program

Source: Marilyn Bohl, *Tools for Structured Design.* Chicago: SRA, Inc. 1978.

paychecks. The input manager, or module, is responsible for reading the employee master records and transactions records. The compute pay data module delegates functions such as calculating gross and net pay to its subordinates. In turn, the output manager delegates the responsibilities for creating outputs, including an updated employee master file, a payroll register, and paychecks.

As you can see, structured design is the process of creating a changeable system consisting of a hierarchy of changeable modules, each of which is manageably small and performs its own function without interfering with the other modules. In the next chapter, you will learn how the hierarchy chart can be a valuable tool in program design.

Physical Design

Let's take a look at the steps in a specific example of good system design. Suppose we want to design a simple payroll system that calculates the weekly payroll for a company and updates the employee master file. In this instance, the system will consist of a single program. Our system design will specify the input and output needed and the provisions for handling errors and for recovery in the event that the system fails.

A system flowchart provides a "master blueprint" of this (or any other) system. The system flowchart for our payroll system is given in Figure 12.15.

Input   The input to the payroll program is the sorted transaction file tape, which consists of records specifying the number of hours worked by each employee. These records have been sorted on the transaction file so that

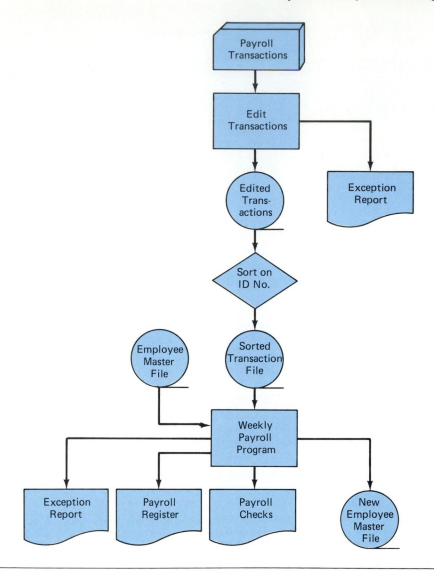

Figure 12.15
Systems Flowchart
for a Payroll Program

they can be read in the sequence established by the employee numbers.

The second source of input to the payroll program is the employee master file tape, which has information on each employee, including hourly rate of pay, year-to-date gross pay, and year-to-date net pay. Figure 12.16 shows the format of records in the employee master file. These records too are sorted in advance so that the employee numbers are in the same sequence as those being read in from the transaction file.

Output   The main goals of the payroll program are to produce employee paychecks and update the employee master file to show the addition of weekly pay in the year-to-date gross and net pay fields. The employee paychecks tape goes to a paycheck-generating program that will print the actual checks. Other outputs are the exception and control totals report and the payroll register, which records earnings and deductions for each employee.

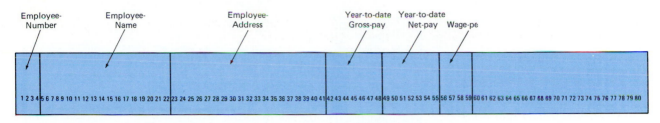

Figure 12.16
Employee Master File

Processing   The payroll program reads in each employee master record and each transaction record. When a master record matches a transaction record, the hourly rate from the master record is multiplied by the number of hours worked from the transaction record to give the weekly gross pay. Deductions are calculated and subtraced from the weekly gross pay to provide the weekly net pay.

Systems Designers

Philip Edwards, a Toronto-based independent designer of large-scale computer systems has analyzed what makes a good systems designer. Drawing on his own experience and that of colleagues involved in designing or hiring designers, Edwards presents a description of the necessary attributes for people working in this area.

One quality that Edwards sees as essential to systems designers is the ability to visualize a number of alternatives simultaneously. Designers should be able to look at a variety of possible solutions to a problem, mentally changing components of these solutions while keeping track of the effects of these changes on other parts. Mentally testing a number of solutions to the design problem involves making use of all technology currently available and finally reaching a state of harmony when the correct solutions are found. A colleague of Edwards's sees lateral thinking—viewing a problem in a unique or unconventional way—and brainstorming—quickly generating large numbers of new ideas—as essential to the designing process. Although these kinds of thinking may be more usually associated with the arts than with computer specialties, Edwards stresses that creativity and imagination are critical to the systems designer.

Another key part of successful designing, Edwards says, is the ability to understand users' needs as they really are, instead of as users themselves describe them. Many end-users of the system are not computer experts. Therefore, their descriptions of their needs may very well be incorrect. Good designers are able to see the system from the perspective of the user who will benefit without becoming side-tracked by the users' own, possibly mistaken descriptions of the desired system. One colleague Edwards spoke to stressed that in job interview situations, designers will describe their successful systems in terms of the user requirements they have satisfied rather than in terms of inputs and outputs. Designers focus on user needs, while those concerned with inputs and outputs are probably programmers or systems analysts, he says.

Another requirement that resembles those of an artistic field is the ability

Controls   Our payroll system has two different procedures to locate errors and correct them. First, all input fields are *key verified*. This means that the program checks for obvious errors, such as alphabetic characters (letters) placed in numeric (number) positions.

Second, *batch control totals* make sure that the numeric amounts have been entered correctly. One batch control total is the sum of the number of hours worked by all employees. Before the transaction file (the input to our program) is prepared from employee time sheets, control totals can be calculated. Later those control totals can be compared with the totals that result when the file is read into the computer. If they don't match, the incorrect transaction records must be corrected before the payroll program can be run.

Backup   In addition to error controls, we should create some kind of *audit trail* for our system so that transactions can be traced through from input to output in the event that the system malfunctions. In our payroll example, which is a batch system, the old master file and the record of employee transactions provide backup and security. If anything happens to the new

to communicate via visual images and not just words. Good designers can usually show the essence of their system in simple drawings, diagrams, or just doodles. In addition, they are usually articulate, often having both good speaking and writing skills.

Others Edwards spoke to emphasized that designers need to be able to break down the larger problem into smaller, more manageable parts. Each problem of system design is made up of simpler ones, so that an important part of the designers's task is to be able to analyze what those components are, come up with solutions for them, and make those solutions work together as an integrated whole.

Flexibility is also important. Edwards stresses that designers have to be able to recognize when to drop an idea that isn't working and move on to something else. In other words, designers should not be so faithful to a favorite idea that they overlook its failings.

Edwards points out that some computer systems research and development departments emphasize teamwork. As an example, he cites Applied Research of Dallas, where the company tries to assemble a group with complementary skills to solve design problems. In small groups of people with varying talents, designers need to be able to make use of the abilities of others in the creation of the system. One person working alone is less likely to see—and have all the necessary skills to solve—all aspects of a problem.

According to Edwards, then, good systems designers can visualize a number of possible solutions simultaneously; can think about problems in a unique way; can see the requirements of the system from the user's point of view; have the ability to communicate through drawings, writing, and speaking; know how to break down a problem into small, manageable parts; are flexible; and can work well with others.

But can they cook and sew?

Source: Philip Edwards, "The Designing Mind," *Datamation,* September 15, 1985, pp. 105–110.

master file, we can recreate it by reprocessing the old master file along with the transaction records, both of which are retained for a period that we must specify.

When the system design is complete, we must seek approval from management and users. This should not be a problem, since we've been working with them all along. Once the design has been approved, we can start implementing it—our next topic.

System Implementation

Implementation is the final phase of system development. In this phase the system is actually created, tested, and documented. The outcome of this stage is the successful placement of the system within the organization's day-to-day operations.

There are five distinct steps in system implementation: programmming, testing, training, conversion, and documentation. Programming is itself a complex step and a major topic, and we will devote all of Chapter 13 to it. In the remainder of this chapter we will explore the other five steps in system implementation.

Testing

A computer system consists of one or more interacting programs. We test a system by running each component program in succession. We want to be sure that each program's input and output fit into the total system in the way the system's designers intended. This is when the "bugs"—unintended errors or problems—should be found and removed.

Artificial Data

Artificial data are usually created expressly for running the first tests. The data should contain all possible combinations of formats and values that we want the system to handle. Such data will force the system through all its possible "paths," that is, really put the system through its paces. Artificial data should include deliberate mistakes, such as numbers occurring in an alphabetic input field where a program expects a name. The mistakes help us check the system's editing, error checking, and error correction procedures.

Live Data

Once the system performs flawlessly on artificial data, we switch to "live" data, or real data taken from the organization. These data probably won't contain as great a variety of combinations of formats and values as our test data did. Instead, they will probably contain more typical values and fewer errors. This underscores the importance of first doing a rigorous test with artificial data.

A system is generally tested in a hierarchical fashion, starting at the bottom and working up. First each program module (a working part of a

program) is tested; next a series of modules is tested; then each individual program, with all its modules; finally, the entire system, consisting of a series of programs, is tested. In this way, problems at the module level can be corrected before programs are tested, and problems at the program level can be corrected before the entire system is tested.

Testing Manual Procedures   Manual procedures contained in the system must also be checked. Users have to integrate the system into their normal work schedule. Therefore, the procedures for using the system must be reviewed and modified, if necessary, to make sure the users can accept the system easily.

As an example of the importance of testing manual procedures, consider a student registration system that required college students to key in their own course registration data at terminals located in each department. A system test found that the programs worked perfectly. However, it was discovered that it took at least 15 minutes to teach each student how to use the terminal correctly. With hundreds of students registering at the same time during busy periods, the system would have brought the registration procedure to a standstill. Systems analysts and designers therefore recommended that one administrative clerk in each department be thoroughly trained in the use of the terminal, and that this individual be responsible for inputting registration data from forms prepared by the students. Thus, a change in the manual procedures of a system made the difference in the system's ultimate effectiveness. And the need for this change was determined during the testing period, instead of when the system was already in operation.

Training

The example described in the box titled "The System Nobody Liked" touches on the importance of training. A system might be flawlessly designed and tuned to perfection, like a fine car, but in the hands of a user who can't get it into reverse gear or panics at the sight of a traffic light, it is useless. All the users who will be affected by the new system should be trained in its use. Training includes an overview of how the system functions, how it will affect their jobs, and how it will relate to current manual procedures.

This is the point where structured systems analysis pays off, since many users will have already been intimately involved in the creation of the system from the start. These users will not feel threatened by the new system; it is *their* system. Inevitably, however, some users will not have been involved, and they need to be reassured that the system isn't a threat to their jobs and that they also have something to gain from it.

Separate and Planned Sessions   Separate training sessions should be designed and held for different user groups as needed. For instance, clerical users and managers will use a new system in different ways; therefore, training sessions specifically aimed at each of these two groups should be held. Clerical training would provide instruction in processing the input to the system, which might include teaching users how to operate new

equipment, such as a terminal. Managerial training would explain the capabilities of the system for generating reports that managers need, answering inquiries, and, in general, providing managers with information to aid them in making informed decisions.

Training should be planned in advance, and the plans should be approved by management. Common sense would dictate that training sessions not be scheduled during high-pressure periods, such as when the system itself is being tested or during the busiest time of the day. Since the system is meant to be used, training for all users should include ''hands-on'' practice with the actual equipment, forms, and output. Training should be supplemented with procedure manuals that users can take away from the sessions, study at their leisure, and have handy for reference when they actually begin to run the system.

Conversion

Once a system has been tested successfully and users have been trained in its use, the old system can be converted to the new one. System conversion can be approached in several ways. We will discuss three of them: the

The System Nobody Liked

Systems are never deliberately designed to fail, but sometimes it seems as though they were. Instead of experiencing the anticipated boons of efficiency, costs savings, and new potential that the system was designed to offer, the organization loses hundreds of thousands of dollars invested in system development and hardware. One way to make this happen is to keep the users from understanding the system, and thus make them resist it.

Take the actual case of a new word-processing system installed at the headquarters of a Fortune-500 corporation. User training about the purpose of the system—and the career futures of the users—was conducted primarily by rumor. When the system was introduced, secretaries feared that it would eventually put an end to their jobs. This was wrong: The system was meant to produce only a single change in their jobs—it automated their repetitive typing chores.

Some of the secretaries were chosen to learn to operate the new system and asked to report to the corporation's Word Processing Center. There they would type all day using the word-processing system. The rest of the secretaries remained in their old offices, where they did only administrative work. They no longer did any typing, which was all being directed to the Word Processing Center. Indeed, typewriters were actually removed from the desks of these office secretaries. When managers needed something to be typed quickly, they found that, although they could still get it done quickly, they had to route it to the Word Processing Center instead of bringing it to a nearby secretary.

The secretaries who stayed in the offices were unsure exactly what they were supposed to do. They opened and routed mail, answered the phones, filed documents, and scheduled appointments. But without typewriters—or typing—they suspected that it was time to update their résumés and look for new jobs; they felt sure that their present jobs would soon be eliminated. Accordingly, some secretaries found new jobs and left the corporation. Others

parallel-systems method, the dual-system method, and the inventory method.

The Parallel-Systems Method

In the *parallel-systems method,* the new system is set to work alongside the old one. Data are input to both simultaneously, until the new system has demonstrated that it functions effectively. At that time, and not until then, the old system can be discarded and the new one used exclusively.

This technique has the advantage of keeping the risk of starting out with a new system at a minimum. Its chief disadvantage, as you might suspect, is cost. Overtime wages may have to be paid to existing personnel, or temporary personnel hired, to keep both systems going at the same time. Additional equipment or duplicate sets of data may also be required. A further drawback of this method is that, in measuring how well the new system performs by comparison to the old one, we are evaluating it on the basis of a system that did not do the job adequately. (If the results produced by the old system were so good, why would we be replacing it?)

The Dual-System Method

Another conversion technique is the *dual-system method* in which the old system is gradually phased out while the

---

actually smuggled in their own typewriters and began typing for their bosses as they had in the past.

As for the managers, there was no way they could regard the new system as an improvement. Instead of having an individual secretary, several managers now had to share one among them. And getting something typed required the cumbersome extra step of routing it to and from the Word Processing Center.

Was the system benefiting the secretaries who now worked full time in the Word Processing Center? Hardly: Without any administrative tasks to do, they felt they were in a slightly glorified typing pool. They hated having to type all day. Removed from direct interaction with managers, they felt they were also removed from the functioning of the organization.

In other words, the system not only failed to please everyone; it failed to please *anyone.* After six months of this all-around agony, the system was scrapped. The hardware was discarded; the Word Processing Center closed down, and those secretaries who remained were returned to their old jobs and old duties. All the time and money invested in designing the new system and trying to make it work were lost. Moreover, even returning to the old setup involved the expense of hiring and training new people to replace those who had left in despair.

System mistakes can be costly. This system failed because of the fear and resentment that resulted from the lack of user orientation, training, and understanding of the new system. Its planners failed: They did not analyze the advantages of the earlier manual system, but saw only its disadvantages. They did not consult the managers and users about the goals and tasks of the system. They provided no orientation or training to users. They looked only at the technical aspects of the system—the hardware, paper flow, and productivity. They did not consider the *human* aspects at any level.

new one is being phased in. This has several advantages over the parallel-systems method: The cost is lower; there is little duplication of work or data; and direct comparisons between the old and new systems need not be made. Drawbacks are that the gradual change can be confusing to users. The extent to which the old system (for example, 80 percent) and the new one (for example, 20 percent) are used can change week by week or even day by day. Moreover, partial use of two systems makes it difficult during the phase-in period for management to obtain information that presents a total picture, since the systems process and output data in different ways. And for some procedures, dual conversion is not possible.

The Inventory Method   A third option is called the *inventory method*. This is a complete, "cold turkey" changeover from the old system to the new one. The advantages of this technique are that it is easy for users to understand, not too expensive, and fast. The considerable disadvantage is that the conversion might not work unless it has been planned thoroughly.

Documentation

Anything that is written about how a system is designed or functions—from whatever viewpoint—is documentation. Documentation can be defined according to the stage of the design process it is intended for.

Design documentation evolves during the system design phase; indeed, it is the end result of system design. It describes the overall system design and includes the system flowchart, all input/output formats, file descriptions, control requirements, and report specifications.

Programming documentation includes the programming specifications; descriptions of program logic, including graphic aids such as program flowcharts; and input/output formats and lists. Design and programming documentation are intended for use by technical personnel. They are used when evaluating the system, making changes in it, or learning from the system when developing others.

Training documentation includes user training manuals and materials to be used in the conversion and installation of the new system. Users must understand how to fill out forms, how to correct errors, and how to interpret output.

Operations documentation is for those who will keep the system running from day to day, such as computer room operators. It contains instructions for normal operations, as well as directions for handling problems and breakdowns. When the system is tested, the operations documentation should also be tested for thoroughness and intelligibility to users.

User reference documentation carries on after training is over and the system is installed and operating. Although by this time users basically know what to do with the new system, questions always arise. User reference documentation should provide quick, clear answers. Using such documents is analogous to using a dictionary to occasionally check the spelling or meaning of a word.

Some of these types of documentation may be combined. Whatever type of documentation is used, it should accomplish the following goals:

1. *The documentation should be adequate.* An undocumented or inadequately documented system is a white elephant; it becomes unusable. A system documented as an afterthought is inferior to one with documentation planned and created while the system is being created.

2. *The documentation should be clear and intelligible to its audience.* Documentation that is incomplete, too technical, or directed to the wrong audience cannot be used effectively by those who must use and operate the system. The effectiveness of the system will deteriorate as a result.

3. *The documentation should be current.* As changes are made to the system, documentation must be updated. Ancient documentation can do more harm than good.

Evaluation

Once a system is installed and running and all the "bugs" have been removed, it should be evaluated to see how well it does its job. This might be done, for instance, within a year after implementation and once every three years thereafter. Evaluation considers such factors as these:

- Does the system meet the objectives originally set for it?
- Was the system developed within the time and budget limits that were set?
- How much does it cost to run the system?
- How effectively is the system performing?
- How beneficial is the system to its users?
- Are any changes needed at this time?

Evaluation is similar to the analysis that gave birth to the system in the first place. The pulse of the system must be taken and the effects that the system has on the users must be monitored. The findings of the evaluation team should be documented and presented to management.

The benefits of the evaluation process are twofold: First, we learn what changes or refinements the present system may need. Second, we find out what changes we should make in our approach when we undertake to develop other systems. Ultimately, there will come a time when the organization's needs or methods of operating change. The next periodic evaluation will tell us that the life cycle of that system is nearing an end. The time will have come to begin the analysis that will lead to the birth of a new system.

Case: Cranking Out Productivity

The backlog of computer applications, which stretches out as far as 30 months at some companies, stands as testimony to the software industry's inability to catch up with itself. Now, a new technology called CASE (computer aided software engineering) promises relief for systems analysts and programmers.

CASE is the generic acronym for a slew of software programs, mostly written for micros, that automate parts of the applications development process. Enthusiasm for CASE from users and vendors suggests it could be the tool that breaks through the applications logjam.

Although the 1987 Datamation/Cowen & Co. Computer and Telecommunications Survey shows that for most large systems users, the applications backlog is down somewhat for the third consecutive year, the survey also indicates that 30% of customers' applications are more than two years away from implementation. And that may be just the paper or visible backlog.

Some MIS professionals speak of an invisible backlog—made up of applications that never get formally requested because users are unable to wait two years. As the window of opportunity for strategic new applications narrows, this invisible backlog is likely to swell.

Measuring the productivity of applications developers is such a nebulous job that most companies don't attempt it. "We don't keep figures on our backlog anymore," says Denny Reiter, a data planning analyst at Deere & Co., Moline, Ill. "We just know development takes too long and costs too much money."

Bruce Holt, manager of technical systems at Babcock & Wilcox Co.'s Naval Nuclear Fuel Division in Lynchburg, Va., also has stopped keeping tabs on the unfinished applications. "Some of our larger projects take six to 12 months," he explains. "We know we need to be able to do twice the work in half the time. You don't need a yardstick to measure that."

He isn't surprised that management may not be eager to shell out $6,000 a shot for a CASE tool on the gut feeling that productivity will improve. "Management is going to want to have a pretty warm feeling in terms of the return on investment," he says. "That probably means that information systems will have to install some measurement tools. It's hard to allocate resources to do measurement when you don't have time to do what has to be done."

Although CASE faces something of a catch-22 in that no one has devised an accepted means of measuring the productivity of programmers and systems analysts, some users already testing the CASE waters cite impressive gains. Du Pont, headquartered in Wilmington, Del., was pleasantly surprised when a CASE product generated 90% of the code directly from design specifications for one application, a finishing area system for production of nylon stretch-wrap.

"Amazing" Productivity Increase   Using a product called Application Factory from Cortex Corp. of Waltham, Mass., Du Pont realized tremendous savings in cost, time, and people power. The application, which was originally expected to cost $268,000, was completed for a mere $30,000. Scheduled to take nine months with three full-time people the application was finished in record time, reports Scott Shultz, Du Pont's manager of information engineering.

"We elected to use Application Factory for a 60-day trial and see what effect that would have on the overall project," explains Shultz. "We were surprised to find we could get the whole project done in the 60-day trial with just two people."

Du Pont has Application Factory installed at 11 sites and has used it on over 40 applications. "We found we can achieve a 600% productivity increase," says Shultz. Ironically, however, he believes the rate of systems development may be too fast. "At an increase rate of six to one, you end up with an implementation backlog," he says. . . .

How to Think of CASE   The broadest definition of CASE—as the automation of anything a human does to software—includes products that impose order on old programs. This may be the right way to go since maintenance is currently chewing up as much as 70% of the total time spent on an application.

It may be helpful to think of CASE as CAD/CAM for code smiths. Early CAD was computer aided drafting more than computer aided design. Only today is CAD fulfilling its design potential by linking the geometric shapes on a workstation screen to the rules of engineering and physics that determine whether a part will survive testing as a prototype.

The scenario is similar for CASE. Three years ago, CASE products did little more than allow systems designers to create dataflow diagrams on a pc screen using computer graphics squares and ovals. Now, CASE tools are starting to link those squares and ovals to the logic of structured design methodologies. Not only can designers speed up the rote job of drawing diagrams, but they also can use CASE tools to perform basic error checking. Some of the more sophisticated CASE wares can check details, right down through tree diagrams in which each function is decomposed into more detailed elements.

Another evolutionary development in CASE is that most products now offer a central repository or data dictionary that stores the various functional elements of a design. Just as CAD/CAM data describing a machine part can now be transmitted to numerically controlled machine tools that cut the part out of metal, some CASE products—such as Cortex/s Application Factory and Information Engineering Workbench from Atlanta-based Knowledge-Ware Inc.—can generate machine-readable code directly from the design elements and specifications in the data encyclopedia. (A data encyclopedia is a data dictionary with more design rules and more relationships between design elements.)

Chris Grejtak, vp of sales and marketing at Index Technology Corp., Cambridge, Mass., believes the future success of CASE hinges upon this seamless interface between design and code generation. "The question we get from customers," Grejtak explains, "most often centers on interfaces—how to interface from analysis and design to other tools. The key will be the data repository. It must be able to share data with a number of tools."

Vendor promises of a flexible data repository tomorrow are winning some customers today. According to Deere's Reiter, the tractor manufacturer chose KnowledgeWare's Information Engineering Workbench not because the company offered all the tools he wanted, but because "we like their long-term direction. We like what they have said about the tools they will develop to integrate into their data encyclopedia."

Tailor-Made Tools   Other companies may not be content to wait for any one CASE vendor to develop all the tools that interface to a central design dictionary. American Management Systems (AMS), a systems development shop in Arlington, Va., began looking into the CASE market several years ago. "Having done several hundred major systems in the last 14 years, we knew what sorts of tools we wanted," says Jerrold Grochow, vp of AMS's corporate

technology group. "We figured if we found a good set, we'd buy it."

Instead, AMS developed a CASE product of its own, called the Life-cycle Productivity System, which combines Index Technology's pc-based workbench Excelerator with other CASE products and a raft of tools and interfaces that AMS developed itself. Writing a program that allows Excelerator to produce a business systems planning matrix, AMS added a COBOL record definition to allow Excelerator to produce complete COBOL code.

Undertaking this sort of integration and tool development is probably more than a dp shop at a typical user company is going to want to do. But the scenario does demonstrate what is needed to carry CASE technology through to what AMS's Grochow calls a "a full-cycle product—one that takes a system from strategic planning to implementation to maintenance and offers every possible interface along the way.

"The best of everything today gets you to the level of a junior analyst," declares Grochow. "No CASE products have the ability to analyze a design and tell you where the holes are. None has experiential capability. They can't look at a design and say, 'The last 400 designs were done such and such a way, why are you departing from that method?' These capabilities are coming, but they are at least five years away."

Source: Excerpted from "CASE: Cranking Out Productivity," by David Stamps, *Datamation,* July 1, 1987, 55-58.

Summary and Key Terms

1. A **system** is a set of elements or parts that interact to achieve a specific goal. Systems can be very different, but the goal of any system usually involves transforming the information fed into it into the desired output. Systems can and should be broken down into **subsystems** to analyze more precisely the different aspects of a problem and how they are interrelated. A vital subsystem is the one that provides **feedback**—information about how well a system works.

2. In organizations, feedback systems are called **information systems.** Information systems comprise the method and resources an organization employs to collect, deliver, and use the information it needs for efficient operation. No decisions are made by information systems, but vital data are provided for those who do make the decisions. Information systems may be computerized, manual, or a combination of the two.

3. **Systems development** takes place in three stages: systems analysis, systems design, and implementation. **Systems analysis** involves defining the problem to be solved or the opportunity to be seized and identifying the objectives of the new system.

4. **Systems design** involves identifying options and selecting the best one.

5. **Implementation,** the final stage of systems development, actually brings the system into being—programming it (if it's a computerized system), installing it, testing it, and developing documentation.

6. In the past, systems were often developed in relative isolation from users and their needs, resulting in systems that didn't meet those needs. Such problems led to the emergence of **structured systems analysis,** which encourages constant interaction between analysts and users at all stages.

7. Certain tools are of great help in structured systems analysis. Among them are

observation, interviews, and questionnaires in the data collection stage; and **logical data flow diagrams, data dictionaries, decision tables** and **trees,** and **data immediate access diagrams (DIADs).**

8. A key principle of structured analysis is the involvement of users. The graphic tools of structured analysis are particularly helpful in communicating with users.

9. Physical design for the new system includes output definition, input definition, specification of a detailed data dictionary, and above all the system flowchart, which specifies the data-processing procedures.

10. In the implementation stage of systems development, the system design approved by users, management, and analysts is transformed into an actual working system. Implementation proceeds in five distinct stages: programming, testing, training, conversion, and documentation.

11. The user involvement inherent in the structured approach to systems development pays off at the time of implementation, when users will act as partisans, rather than opponents, of the system they have helped to create.

Review Questions

1. Business Application

The following case describes the activities of a nationwide financial services company with several hundred branch offices. Read the description of the firm's application, loan processing, and payment processing procedures, and answer the questions given at the end of the case.

When a customer comes into Mutual Finance Company, he or she completes a loan application form. The application is screened at the local branch office, and the local bank and employment references of the applicant are checked. If the loan is approved by the branch, the paper work is forwarded to the headquarters office of the firm, where an additional screening takes place to determine if the applicant has a bad credit history or has defaulted on a loan previously. The entire loan screening process takes about 7 to 10 days. Because of the time it takes, some applicants get approval on their loans from local banks before Mutual Finance has an opportunity to approve their loans.

If a loan is approved, the headquarters office sets up the loan account in a central file, which includes the customer number and the account balance, and then sends the notification of approval, the check, and a voucher booklet to the customer. The local branch also sets up a record for the approved loan, which includes information about the customer, including name, address, and occupation, as well as loan information.

Loan payments are usually made to the branch office. When a customer sends in a payment, the branch office checks to see that the customer account is valid and then updates the branch loan accounts file to reflect the payment. All payments are deposited at a local bank at the end of each day. Then the branch records the payment transaction on a transmittal record that is sent to the headquarters office, which uses payment information to update the records in the central loan file.

Sometimes customers pay the headquarters office directly. When this happens, the central office applies the payment amount to update the central loan file, deposits the payment, and sends a transmittal record to the branch so that the branch can use the payment information to update its file.

At the end of each week, the branch staff search through local files to detect overdue accounts and send notices to those customers whose accounts are 30 days overdue. In addition, the headquarters office uses a computer system to generate reminders on overdue account balances to customers at 30-, 60-, and 90-day intervals.

Answer the following questions about this case.

a. Identify the problems you see with the loan application and payment processing procedures as described.

b. Develop at least two objectives for a new system that would improve the current situation.

c. Determine at least two alternative solutions to the problems, and select the one you feel is best. Give reasons for your answer.

2. Logical Data Flow Diagram

Design a logical data flow diagram for the following case describing the registration procedures of a university office responsible for handling workshops and seminars:

When a person calls up to register for a workshop, the receptionist records the person's name, address, telephone number, and workshop selection on a registration form. One copy of the form is filed in a central file, by workshop, and used to prepare a letter of acknowledgment to the registrant. Another copy is sent to the billing clerk who creates an invoice record for the registrant in a central file and sends a copy of the invoice to the registrant.

One week before a workshop is to be offered, the administrative assistant takes the file with registrations for that workshop and uses the records to prepare a class roster, name tags, and workshop materials.

Registrants are expected to pay in advance of the workshop. When a check comes in, the billing clerk verifies that the registration is valid against the registration record and applies the payment to the balance on the invoice record. Any registrants who do not pay in advance of the program are listed on a special notice, which is given to the instructor on the first day of the program.

All registration records are maintained in a file used to generate mailings publicizing future programs on an ongoing basis.

3. Decision Table or Decision Tree

Draw a decision table or a decision tree to depict the logic of the following admissions policy of a college:

Admit a student who has a high school grade point average of B or better, has SAT scores of over 500, and has knowledge of a foreign language. Also admit if the high school grade point average is less than B but the student has SAT scores over 500 and has knowledge of a foreign language. Admit on probation if the high school grade point average is B or better and if the student has knowledge of a foreign language but the SAT score is 500 or less. Admit on probation if the high school grade point average is B or better and the SAT score is above 500 but the student doesn't know a foreign language. Also admit on probation if the high school grade point average is less than a B and the SAT score is 500 or less, but the student has knowledge of a foreign language. Refuse to admit all others.

4. Systems Flowchart

Draw a systems flowchart depicting the following procedure: Sales order transactions are keyed in at a terminal and stored on a disk storage device. These transactions are sorted in ascending sequence by item number and are used to update the old inventory master file. The outputs of the inventory update procedure are an updated inventory master file and a priced transaction file, showing the prices of all items listed on the sales transactions. Both of these items are disk files.

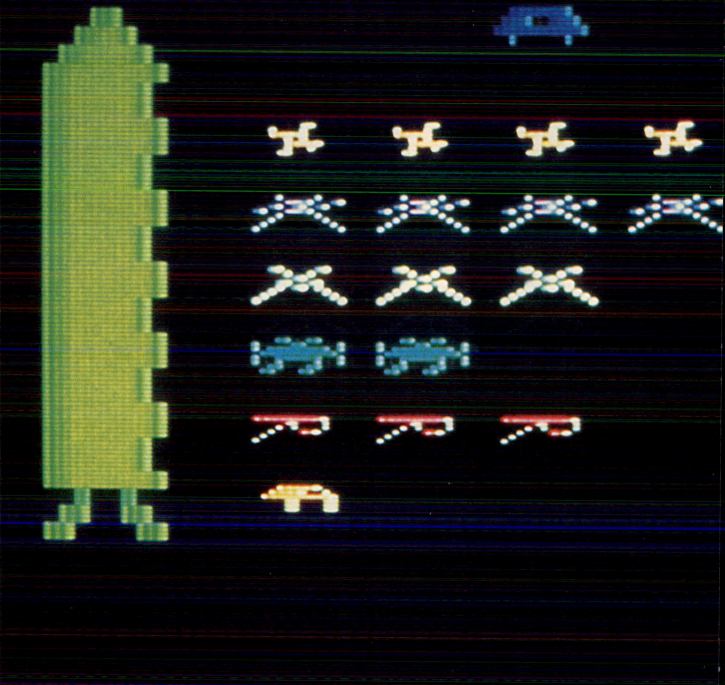

Program Design 13

Chapter Objectives

After studying this chapter, you should be able to

1. Explain how to construct flowcharts.

2. Describe how structured programming differs from unstructured programming.

3. Describe the three control structures that govern the logic of structured programs.

4. Use the program design methods described here (hierarchy charts, traditional flowcharts, N-S charts) in actual programs.

Star cruisers maneuver through dense asteroid belts in search of the enemy. When a sighting is made, deadly lasers are fired. On land, Indianapolis-style racers swirl around curves and dodge oil slicks. Candy-colored spheres emitting strange noises display a huge appetite for gobbling up the opposition. Adults, teen-agers, children, and even preschoolers spend hours in front of video display screens, eyes glued to the constant progression of events. They pull joysticks to speed up or slow down; they punch keys to fire missiles. The spaceships, creatures, chess figures —whatever appears on the screen—respond immediately to a flick of the controls; passing clouds cast realistic shadows on the video landscape; and at the same time a running score is kept. How does all this happen?

A video game is the product of a sequence of words and numbers—a program—stored in the memory of a computer. Those games that measure skill in other things besides trigger-response time nearly give this secret away: "Which difficulty level would you prefer?" the game asks. "Which suspect will you interview first?" "Would you rather take on an additional ton of fuel for the journey to Alpha Centauri, or more medical supplies?" "Do you want to continue?"

Such questions correspond to the logical decision points of a computer program. Without programs, the video game screens would be dark. Without programs, the sophisticated computers in businesses, in universities, and government offices would be only collections of useless electronic components, as would the computers that guide real spaceships.

What Is a Program?

A **computer program** is a set of instructions, written in a language the computer can understand, that tells the computer how to accomplish a task. As we have seen throughout this book, the tasks can be enormously varied: running a video game in an arcade or placing a satellite in orbit around the earth; reserving airline seats or controlling a business inventory; providing surgeons with vital information during an operation or logging students' majors and grades. The languages in which programs can be written also vary, although the general principles remain the same. In this chapter we will not discuss specific programming languages (that is the subject of the next chapter). We will discuss the characteristics of a well-designed computer program. In particular, we'll take a look at the major tools and methods used by programmers when they translate a system design into an effective program.

Algorithms and Flowcharts

When there is something to be done, it is first necessary to understand what is to be done. Human intelligence is able to interpret vague or incomplete directions and figure out what is really wanted. "Get me the file folder on the desk" and "Send her a copy of my last letter" are typically vague instructions. We are able to follow them because we know, from the overall situation, exactly which desk or letter is meant. Computers are not able to judge a situation or context: They can do only what they are told. To write a program, therefore, we must begin with a clear, unambiguous statement of the task the computer is to carry out.

Once we have the problem statement, we must state the rule or rules to follow in solving the problem. For instance, if a fund-raising committee wants to reduce its mailing list, it might set a rule that the names of people who have not contributed in the last five years are to be removed from the list.

Finally, a program needs a procedure, or set of steps, to be followed in carrying out the rule or rules. In the case of a program to reduce a fundraising mailing list, we would first have to get the list and then determine the date of the last contribution made by each person on the list. We could then delete names according to our rule.

The *logic* of what we instruct the computer to do consists of the clear-cut problem definition, rules, and set of steps to be followed. This logic must be unambiguous and must fit all situations that might be found. Algorithms and flowcharts are two tools that help programmers present their computers with first-rate logic.

An **algorithm** is a statement of the steps to be followed in performing a task or solving a problem. Each step advances toward the solution by one small but relentless degree. "Algorithm" really means the same thing as "program," except that in a program the steps of an algorithm are

translated into a specific computer language. Here is an algorithm for a familiar process, getting up in the morning.

> If the alarm goes off and it isn't a workday, turn the alarm off, make a mental note to remember not to set the alarm on weekends, and go back to sleep. If it is a workday, get up, get dressed, and eat breakfast. Then look to see if it's raining. If it isn't, put on your coat and go to work; if it is, take your umbrella and put on your coat and go to work.

Instructions phrased like this are precise, but they require several readings. To make algorithms easier to understand, programmers use flowcharts. A program flowchart is a diagram of an algorithm that uses a set of agreed-upon symbols connected by lines. The five major flow-charting symbols that will be used in this book are shown in Figure 13.1.

The lines on a flowchart that join the symbols indicate the direction or sequence of the separate steps, or the flow. This is generally from top to bottom. Exceptions to the top-to-bottom flow are the decision symbol, which routes one decision out to the side, and the occasional need to return to a symbol higher on the chart in order to start a process over again. A

The Origin of the Flowchart

In the spring of [1946] that year [John] von Neumann and I evolved an exceedingly crude sort of geometric drawing to indicate in rough fashion the iterative nature of an induction. At first this was intended as a sort of tentative aid to us in programming. Then that summer I became convinced that this type of *flow diagram,* as we named it, could be used as a logically complete and precise notation for expressing a mathematical problem and that indeed this was essential to the task of programming. Accordingly, I developed a first, incomplete version and began work on the paper called *Planning and Coding.* . . . Von Neumann and I worked on this material with valuable help from [Arthur Walter] Burks and my wife [Adele Katz Goldstine]. Out of this was to grow not just a geometrical notation but a carefully thought out analysis of programming as a discipline. This was done in part by thinking things through logically, but also and perhaps more importantly by coding a large number of problems. Through this procedure real difficulties emerged and helped illustrate general problems that were then solved.

The purpose of the flow diagram is to give a picture of the motion of the control organ as it moves through the memory picking up and executing the instructions it finds there. The flow diagram also shows the states of the variables at various key points in the course of the computation. Further, it indicates the formulas being evaluated. . . .

Von Neumann was away frequently in Los Alamos and there are a few letters extant from the period which show the genesis of these flow diagrams from crude scrawls into a highly-sophisticated notation still in use today.[1] Finally by April 1947 the paper on *Planning and Coding* was completed and published.[2]

[1] Letters, von Neumann to Goldstine, 16 September 1946, 2 March 1947, 9 July 1947, 19 July 1947.

[2] Herman H. Goldstine and John von Neumann, *Planning and Coding Problems for an Electronic Computing Instrument,* Part II, vol. 1, April 1, 1947; vol. 2, April 15, 1948; vol. 3, August 16, 1948.

Source: Herman H. Goldstine, *The Computer from Pascal to von Neumann.* Princeton, N.J.: Princeton University Press, 1972, 1980, pp. 266–267.

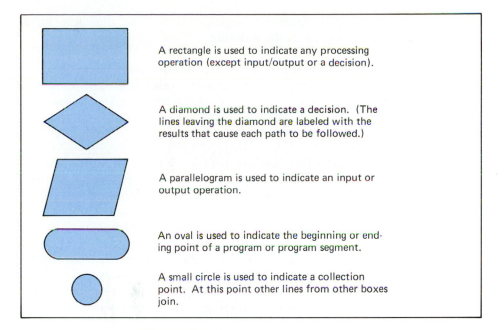

A rectangle is used to indicate any processing operation (except input/output or a decision).

A diamond is used to indicate a decision. (The lines leaving the diamond are labeled with the results that cause each path to be followed.)

A parallelogram is used to indicate an input or output operation.

An oval is used to indicate the beginning or ending point of a program or program segment.

A small circle is used to indicate a collection point. At this point other lines from other boxes join.

FIGURE 13.1
Five Major Flowcharting Symbols

reverse flow direction such as this is generally indicated by an arrow. Figure 13.2 shows a flowchart for the algorithm just described.

Since you have already encountered charts in this book, you may be wondering how program flowcharts differ from them. In the last chapter we took a look at logical data flow diagrams and system flowcharts. These graphic aids provide an overview of an entire system. The logical data flow diagram presents a picture of what takes place in a system by focusing on the data that flow through the system. The system flowchart, although it uses the same symbols as a program flowchart, operates on a much higher level. One "process" box on a *system* flowchart might stand for an entire program, which in turn might have its own complete *program* flowchart. Program flowcharts are *not* concerned with the total functioning of a system. They remain at a logical level. Their concern is with showing the actual algorithm that will carry out the task in question.

Thus, to design programs we need to know how to understand the logic of a particular problem and to express that logic in a flowchart. Let's go through a simple example to sharpen our skill in program design.

Making a Flowchart: Selecting an Employee

Assume that, as the director of personnel of Datatech Industries, you are looking for experienced candidates to fill a position in your new West Coast office. The person you need must have a college degree in business and must have been employed by Datatech for more than five years.

The flowchart should show the logic for selecting qualified candidates from among the company's employees, counting them, and printing their names. Figure 13.3 is such a flowchart. "Start" is clear. The first process box will "set eligible-employee counter to zero." This means that, since we

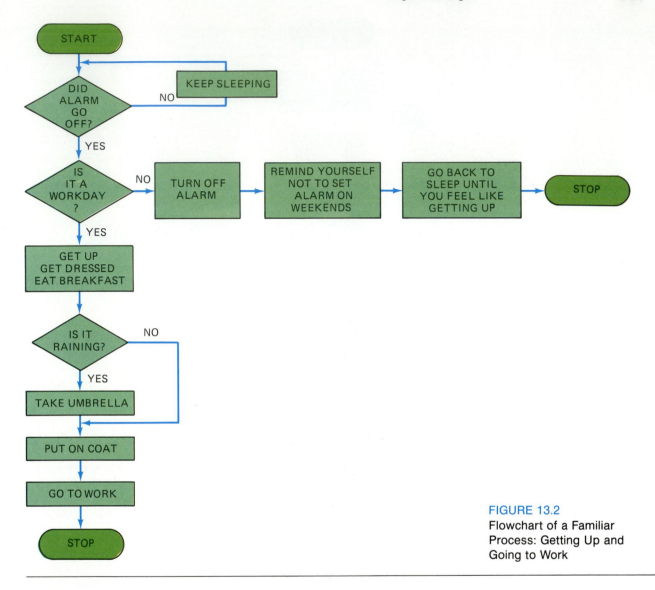

FIGURE 13.2
Flowchart of a Familiar
Process: Getting Up and
Going to Work

intend to count each eligible employee by, in effect, making a mark on a
scratch pad, we want to be sure the pad is blank before we start. Scratch
pads (memory locations) in a computer aren't blank at the start of a
program unless we make them so.

The next step, using the input/output symbol, is to read an employee
record. Then we have to see what the record is. In a computer file, the last
record is always an end-of-file (EOF) record. Thus, the next symbol asks the
comptuer to decide whether we have reached the end of the file. If our
program had already read all the employee records, the next record would
be an end-of-file (EOF) record. Then we would follow the "yes" direction
out of the EOF decision symbol.

But the last record has not yet been processed. We then follow the "no"
path out of the EOF decision symbol and go on to another decision symbol.
This time we test for a college degree. If the employee doesn't have one, our

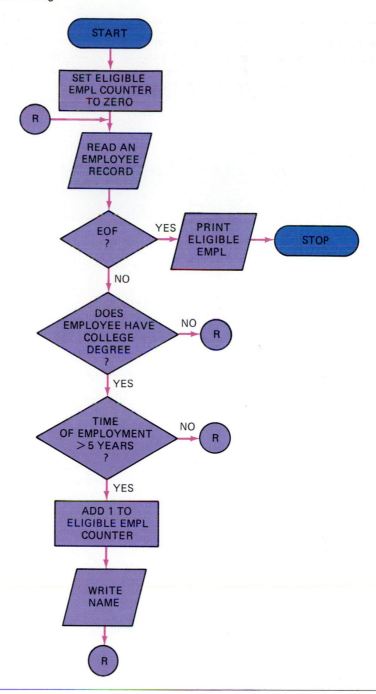

FIGURE 13.3
Selecting an Employee

interest in this person ceases and program control goes to a point called R, which is a connector symbol. (Flowcharts use connector symbols to avoid cluttering up the page with crisscrossing lines.) In this case, R means that the program returns to "read an employee record."

If the employee does have a college degree, a test is then made for our other item of concern, length of time employed by Datatech. If the employee has been with the company longer than five years (the "yes"

Let's make a flowchart to illustrate a simple mathematical problem. We want to find out if a given integer (a whole number) can be expressed as the sum of three consecutive odd integers. We will call those integers x, y, and z. Below you can see the flowchart for a program that will determine this. We start by reading a number, say 75. Then we divide the number by 3, giving us, in this case, $y = 25$. We then test to see if y is an integer. If y is an integer, this means that our input number was successfully divided by 3 without a fraction left over (75 would be successfully so divided; 76 would not). If y is not an integer, we output the message "no solution" and stop the program.

If y is an integer, we check to see if it is odd. If so, we add 2 to y to give us the next higher odd number, $z = 27$. Then we subtract 2 from y to yield $x = 23$. Then we write x, y, and z—that is, 23, 25, and 27—the three consecutive odd integers that form the sum of 75.

Finding Three Consecutive Odd Numbers

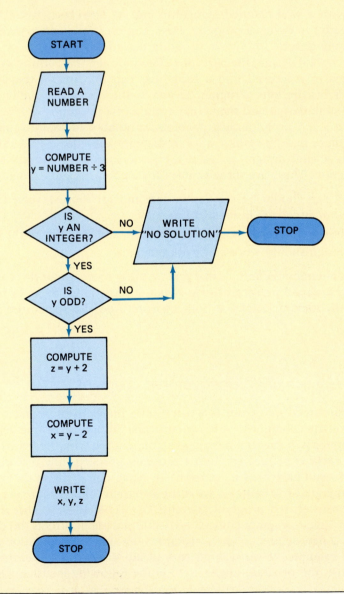

route from the decision symbol), we add "1" to the eligible-employee counter. That is, we put a mark on our scratch pad. Then we output the name. Finally, we use our connector symbol, R, to get back up the chart to start the whole process over again for another employee record. The process is repeated for every employee until an EOF record is encountered.

Structured Program Design

Armed with a well-planned algorithm and its flowchart, we're ready (or nearly ready) to design a program. First, however, we need to take a look at some of the general options in program design.

In program design, the parts of a system design that require a computer program are structured into a form that can be directly translated into computer instructions. Program design is the necessary middle step between system design and the actual coding of a program.

For a given programming problem, a number of solutions may work. That is, there may be several ways to diagram and code a given algorithm. Although several designs arrive at the same solution, they may not all be equally good. There are three criteria for a good program design:

1. The design should be easy to understand for those involved, *and for those not involved,* in its creation.
2. The design should allow easy modification and updating of the program.
3. The design should work and work efficiently.

The programming technique that most readily meets these three criteria is called **structured programming.** What exactly do we mean by that? Let's find out by looking briefly at both unstructured and structured programming.

Characteristics of an Unstructured Program

An **unstructured program** is written on a linear basis: It starts with the instruction the computer will execute first, followed by the instruction the computer will execute next, and so on, ending with the instruction the computer will execute last. Such a program proceeds one instruction at a time. It doesn't have a main "portion" or paragraph to direct the remainder of the program or to indicate what the program functions are.

An unstructured program contains GO TO statements that divert the otherwise linear program control. A GO TO statement directs the computer to follow a new sequence for instructions if a specified condition has been met. For example, if we wanted to find all Massachusetts addresses in a mailing list, the program might include the following instructions:

```
READ ADDRESS CITY, STATE, ZIP
IF STATE MA GO TO LINE 510
READ NEXT ADDRESS
```

And at line 510 there would be another sequence of instructions for making a new list of Massachusetts addresses. The last line in that sequence would also contain a GO TO statement sending the computer back to the original instruction sequence.

Disadvantages of Unstructured Programming

While one or two GO TO statements may not present any problem, a 500-statement program full of them would be difficult for humans to interpret. A mass of such GO TO statements has been described as "spaghetti code," since the logic paths for different situations in the program crisscrosses in a tangle.

Unstructured programming was expensive. A programmer often had to start from scratch in order to modify a program (once the original programmer had departed it was often impossible to understand what he or she had done). Thus, data-processing management was eager to try new techniques to make programming more affordable. After some large and successful applications in the early 1970s, structured programming was born.

Characteristics of a Structured Program

Structured programming allows a changeable, flexible system to be built. Studies have shown that programmers spend somewhere between 40 and 70 percent of their time on maintenance, or making changes in existing programs. These changes are often made in response to user requests for modifications in existing reports or in response to changing business needs (new product lines) that require additional data elements and new program logic. To make a change, the programmer must first find out where to make it; then actually make it; and then determine if the change has worked. Structured programming makes each of these steps less of an art and more of a science.

A structured program is made up of logically independent instruction sequences of modules. Each module is a group of statements that can be referred to as a single unit. Each module handles a specific function, and is given a name that describes its function. For example, the READ-MASTER module would read the master file; the PRINT-TOTAL-LINE module would direct the printing of a total at the end of a report.

Three control structures (and only three) govern the logic of a structured program:

1. **Sequence** is the traditional linear flow, with instructions executed in sequence from the beginning to the end of a program.

2. **Selection** (IF-THEN-ELSE) is a division in the flow based on a test in the program. In effect, it is a fork in the road. For instance, in the program to find three consecutive odd numbers, we took one branch if *y* was an integer and another branch if it was not.

3. **Iteration** (DO . . . WHILE or DO . . . UNTIL) is a loop that will be repeated within a program until a specified condition is met, for instance, until all the employee records have been read.

Figure 13.4 illustrates each of these control structures. Note that there are two kinds of iteration loops. In a DO . . . WHILE loop the specified condition must be met before the loop is executed; if the condition is not met the program will move out of the loop. In a DO . . . UNTIL loop the condition must be met each time after the loop is executed in order for the loop to be repeated; the program moves out of the loop when the condition is no longer met.

Five main tools are used in program design: (1) hierarchy charts, (2) traditional and structured flowcharts, (3) Nassi-Schneiderman structured flowcharts, (4) pseudocode, and (5) decision tables and decision trees. We will dicuss each in turn.

Hierarchy Charts

A chart can be used to depict the design of a structured program. The chart shows all the modules that make up the program and indicates which modules are subordinate to which other modules. The result is similar to the organization chart of a business.

Figure 13.5 shows the organization chart of people in a company. The person on top, the president, is in charge, with the next level down subordinate to the president, and the third level down subordinate to the second level.

FIGURE 13.4
Control Structures Governing Program Logic

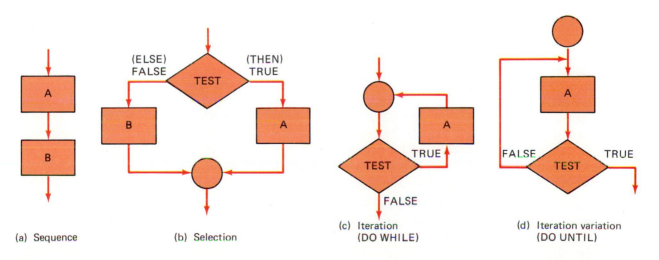

(a) Sequence   (b) Selection   (c) Iteration (DO WHILE)   (d) Iteration variation (DO UNTIL)

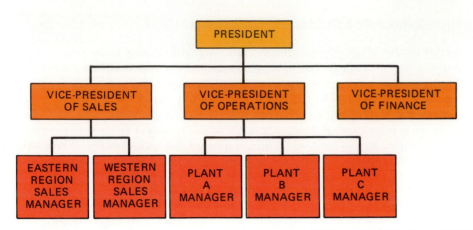

FIGURE 13.5
An Organization Chart Showing the Hierarchy of Management in a Business Organization

Structured programs use a similar design, which is represented by a hierarchy chart. A hierarchy chart is the organization chart of a program. It shows the relationships between modules in the program, just as an organization chart shows the relationships between people in a company. Each box in the hierarchy chart corresponds to a module in the program.

Figure 13.6 is a hierarchy chart of a structured program to select students. The topmost module is in charge. Every other module has a specific job, which it performs only when a higher module directs it to do so. Like a unit in a military organization, a module performs its job only when it gets orders from above, and gives orders only to its subordinates.

When a program is made up of manageably small modules organized in a top-down design, changes can be readily made when necessary. Since each module has a defined function and is largely independent of the other modules in the program, a module can be replaced without affecting other modules in the program. In contrast, when changes must be made in an unstructured program, there is usually a ripple effect in which unexpected problems appear in another part of the program.

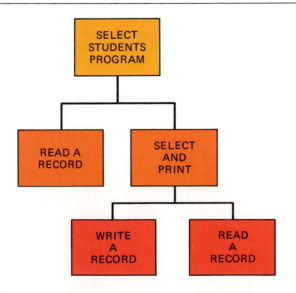

FIGURE 13.6
Hierarchy Chart of a Structural Program to Select Students

Note that each module controls those modules at the next lower level of the hierarchy.

Traditional and Structured Flowcharts

Earlier in this chapter (see the section "Algorithms and Flowcharts"), we showed how the algorithm of a program can be expressed in a traditional flowchart. For a program, one flowchart can show the overall program as outlined in the hierarchy chart. For the program input, we have a group of student records. Each record contains the student's name, age, sex, and score on a physics test. The program's job is to select from this group of records the names of students who are over 15, are male, and have received a score of 80 or better on the physics test. Figure 13.7 shows how to express

FIGURE 13.7
Traditional Flowchart
Showing Select Student
Program

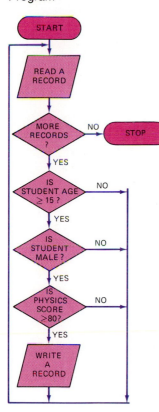

FIGURE 13.8
Structural Flowchart for
Select Student Program

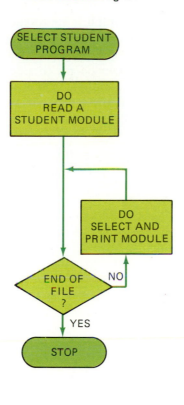

FIGURE 13.9
Select-and-Print Module

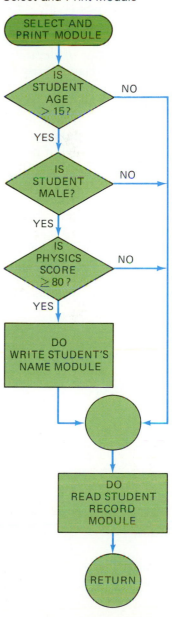

the logic of this program using a traditional flowchart. This chart is for the entire program.

There are some problems with traditional flowcharts, however. First, they are not popular with some programmers, because it takes time to draw them, and they generally have to be completely redrawn when a change is made. Flowcharts also create a tendency to use the GO TO statement, which is not correct in structured programming.

For these reasons, the logic of a program can also be depicted using a *structured flowchart*. In this case, we represent the logic of an entire program in a flowchart and the logic of each module in separate flowcharts. Figure 13.8 shows the logic of the entire select-student program, and Figure 13.9 represents the logic of just the select-and-print module of this program.

Other graphic devices have also been created as replacements for traditional flowcharts. Two such devices are Nassi-Schneiderman structured flowcharts and pseudocode.

Nassi-Schneiderman Structured Flowcharts

Nassi-Schneiderman structured flowcharts—or N-S charts—are an increasingly popular tool. N-S charts are more compact, easier to draw, and in some ways more effective than traditional flowcharts.

Like traditional flowcharts, N-S charts have specific graphic conventions. Recall the three basic control structures used in a structured program: sequence, selection, and iteration. Figure 13.10 shows how N-S charts depict each of these structures.

The great advantage of an N-S chart is that the flow of an entire module or program can be viewed at a glance, without having to follow arrows as in the traditional flowchart. A particular advantage of the N-S chart is the clarity with which it shows the selection structure. It is elegantly simple. See, for instance, Figure 13.11, an N-S chart showing the logic of the select-and-print module of our student selection program. The entire student selection program also looks brief and concise when rendered in an N-S chart, as shown in Figure 13.12.

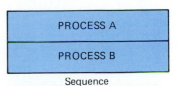
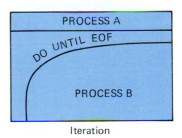
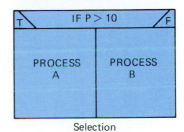

FIGURE 13.10
Nassi-Schneiderman Structured Flowcharts Showing the Three Basic Control Structures of a Program

FIGURE 13.11
An N-S Chart of the Select-and-Print Module

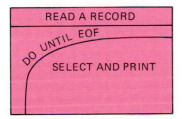

FIGURE 13.12
An N-S Chart of the Select Student Program

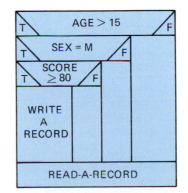

Pseudocode

Pseudocode, also called structured English, expresses the logic of a program in a language quite similar to actual computer languages. Pseudocode is a brief format for writing program statements. It is general enough not to be tied to any specific computer language, yet is easy to use in coding a program.

Two of the three basic program control structures—selection and iteration—are expressed with the terms DO-UNTIL and IF-THEN-ELSE. These always appear in capital letters. All other words are in lowercase letters.

Here's an example of pseudocode that represents the logic of the select-and-print module of our student selection program:

```
IF student age is more than 15
  IF student sex is male
    IF student score is greater or equal to 80
      THEN perform write-out-record routine
    ELSE perform read-a-record routine
  ELSE perform read-a-record routine
Else perform read-a-record routine.
Perform read-a-record routine.
```

Pseudocode makes it easy to understand the program's function at a glance, and it translates well into actual structured code.

Decision Tables and Decision Trees

In the last chapter we saw that decision tables and trees are useful tools for *system* design. They are also useful in *program* design. They make clear what actions a program should take for each given situation. Such clarity becomes especially valuable when a program contains several interacting situations.

Decision tables and **decision trees** have some similarity to pseudocode. We can understand their similarities and differences by comparing their use in a single program. Assume that we want to write a program to grant (or refuse) credit to customers. We can state the algorithm for the program in regular English like this:

> Applicants who have been employed for two years and, in addition, either own their own home or earn more than $20,000 per year are to receive credit. Otherwise, credit will not be given.

You will probably have to read this a second time to understand it fully. It would be even more difficult to develop a program from it. However, a decision table would express the policy clearly (see Figure 13.13).

C1: EMPLOYMENT > 2 YRS?		T				F		
C2: OWN HOME		T		F		T		F
C3: EARNINGS > $20,000	T	F	T	F	T	F	T	F
A1: GRANT CREDIT	X	X	X					
A2: DO NOT GRANT CREDIT				X	X	X	X	X

C = condition to be met
A = action to be taken

FIGURE 13.13
A Decision Table for a Program to Grant or Refuse Credit

Decision trees differ slightly from decision tables. Figure 13.14 shows a decision tree for the same logic. The branches of the tree follow, from left to right, the different logical possibilities. For instance, by running a finger along the tree, we can see that someone who has been employed more than two years but doesn't own a home and earns less than $20,000 per year will be denied credit.

What are some advantages of using decision tables and trees to represent program logic?

1. They provide a procedure for naming conditions and actions within a given operation.
2. They show relationships between conditions and actions.
3. They make it easier to examine all the alternatives within a given problem.
4. The process of preparing the table or tree forces the program writer to think logically.
5. They are easy to prepare and to update.

Like pseudocode, decision tables and trees can readily be translated into actual structured code. The pseudocode for the credit program would read:

```
IF applicant is employed more than 2 years
  and IF applicant owns home
     THEN grant credit
    ELSE (applicant doesn't own home)
     IF applicant has earnings equal to or over
       $20,000 per year
       THEN grant credit
    ELSE deny credit
ELSE (applicant employed less than 2 years)
  deny credit
```

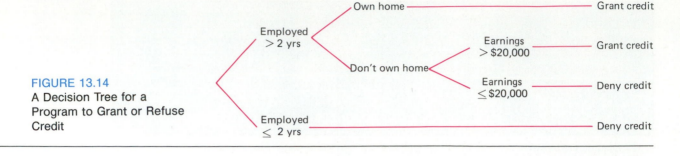

Own home ——————— Grant credit
Employed > 2 yrs
Don't own home — Earnings > $20,000 ——— Grant credit
Earnings ≤ $20,000 ——— Deny credit
Employed ≤ 2 yrs ——————— Deny credit

FIGURE 13.14
A Decision Tree for a
Program to Grant or Refuse
Credit

Implementation of Structured Programming

For some people, programming is fun. An inspired programmer can sit down with a coding pad and pencil and devise a set of instructions, or program, that will direct the computer to do exactly what the programmer says. This provides a sense of power, considerable room for creativity, and the prospect of recognition for doing a difficult job well—maybe even better than anyone else could. Hence, at least partly because of its requirements for concentration, programming was originally viewed as a reclusive occupation. The programmer would come to work and write thousands of lines of code that were technically efficient. However, if the programmer found another job, a new programmer would often have difficulty figuring out what the programs written by the first programmer were all about. If the original program developed problems or needed changes, it often was necessary to throw it out and start from scratch. The program wasn't the only thing thrown out—so was all the money spent to develop it, and develop it all over again, and again. Egoless programming changed all this.

Egoless Programming

As the use of computers and computer programming has mushroomed since the 1950s, programmers and those who use and pay for programs have realized that every program must be accompanied by a written document explaining what that program does. Not only that, *the program itself* must *communicate* what it does, as in structured programming. Programming is still fun and the programmer may still, at least in private, think of himself or herself as an expert. These days, however, programming is more of a group effort. It is **egoless programming**.

Programs are no longer regarded as personal property, and in fact programmers frequently help each other debug their programs. In other words, the programmer's ego trip has been slowed down (but not destroyed) by the need to work with others to detect errors, produce programs that will be long-lived, and create effective structured programs. Some of these group efforts are described below.

The Chief Programmer Team   A chief programmer team consists of a chief programmer, one or more senior programmers, some junior programmers as needed, and a technical secretary to keep track of files, directories, charts, and the like. Together, the team tackles a programming project.

As you can see, such a group effort must use egoless programming. Just as systems analysis and design teams provide a high-powered approach to a problem by pooling the analytical and managerial skills of several qualified people, so the chief programmer team represents a stride forward in program implementation. The chief programmer team has been likened to a surgical team. Each member of a surgical team has a specialized role, permitting a division of work and resources. This results in maximum efficiency and effectiveness from the interactive efforts of the group. In the same way, programming teams can bring more resources to bear on a problem than can the solitary but inspired expert.

Structured Walkthroughs

A **structured walkthrough** is a group review of a program. The purpose is to detect errors and make changes in program design *before* the implementation stage, in order to avoid costly errors. Especially when only one person has been responsible for a program or program module, that person may be too close to the work to see any potential problems. A structured walkthrough, then, allows all group members to review and improve on the independent work done by any member.

Walkthrough procedures vary, but one way of performing a walkthrough is as follows:

- A day or more before the walkthrough the programmer distributes copies of the work to reviewers whom he or she has selected.
- The walkthrough begins. First, roles are divided among the participants. Someone assumes the role of moderator or coordinator, someone else that of secretary; the remainder listen, think, and make comments. The coordinator keeps things on an even keel and resolves disputes. The secretary records any problems that are uncovered.
- The reviewers offer constructive suggestions.

Although programmers have sometimes described walkthroughs as stompthroughs, they need not be unpleasant. Walkthroughs are fast becoming the rule, which means that *everyone's* work, regardless of the person's rank or experience, gets reviewed. In addition, effective moderation, together with suggestions kindly offered and open-mindedly received, should make it clear that it is the *program,* not the programmer, that is being reviewed. An academic analogy to the program walkthrough is reading one's work in a creative-writing workshop, in which peers reflect on content and direction and offer friendly tips.

We have discussed algorithms, structured versus unstructured programing, design tools such as hierarchy charts and pseudocode, and implementation. Now we will attempt to integrate these ideas into a more complete picture by means of some examples.

Program Design: Four Examples

In the remainder of this chapter we will walk through four programs. These programs have been selected because they represent frequently encountered types of problems. For most of these programs we will show a traditional flowchart, a hierarchy chart, a structured flowchart, and a Nassi-Schneiderman structured flowchart. These examples will make the concepts of program design clearer, and also will enable you to see how both the traditional flowcharts and structured program design tools can be used in designing programs.

For the first two programs we need a set of records, each containing information about a particular student. Here is the set of records:

Student Number	Student Name	Student Age	Student Sex	Quiz 1	Quiz 2	Quiz 3	Quiz 4	Quiz 5
0449	Roberts M	35	F	97	78	89	67	88
1334	Harper A	43	M	78	89	99	65	73
2357	Benson R	39	M	87	88	77	98	74
2557	Janacek L	30	F	85	89	92	90	96
2601	Reese I	36	M	91	84	83	95	80
2918	Stone M	32	F	73	79	86	81	90
3459	Phelps K	34	F	99	86	93	80	89
3480	Mills E	29	F	71	62	80	77	79
4195	Flores R	32	M	90	79	87	83	93
4866	Blumenthal J	41	M	69	77	84	90	95

Now let's look at the programs that will read and process these records.

Program One: Listing

Our first program will simply read each record and print it on a list. Figure 13.15 shows a traditional flowchart for the entire program. The hierarchy chart (Figure 13.16) for the program shows five modules on two levels. The mainline module directs the others, which read a record, process a record, and write a record or read the next record. A Nassi-Schneiderman structured flowchart for the entire program is shown in Figure 13.17.

As you have probably noticed, each of the different ways of representing the program logic is quite brief and makes it easy to grasp what the program is all about. Differences among these techniques will emerge more clearly when we deal with more complicated programs. It's worth noting that, although this is a simple program, it is not a simple-minded one: Reading a file and listing its contents neatly on a printout is one of the standard jobs routinely performed in any computer center. Indeed, files contained on any storage medium (except the all-but-obsolete punched cards) *cannot* be read by the human eye until a computer lists (or displays) the contents.

FIGURE 13.15
Traditional Flowchart for Listing Program

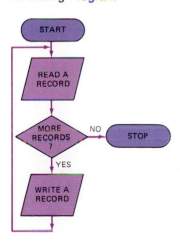

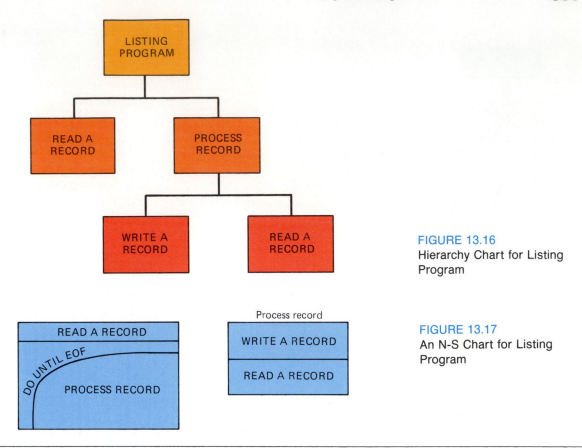

FIGURE 13.16
Hierarchy Chart for Listing Program

FIGURE 13.17
An N-S Chart for Listing Program

Program Two: Calculations and Printed Output

This program performs some further calculations on our student file. In this program, five scores for each student are added together to give the total points scored by each student. This figure is then divided by 5 to give each student's average score. Finally, a grade is calculated. The total score, average score, and grade are then printed out. The grading scale used by the program is:

Grade	Average Score
A	90–100
B	80–89
C	70–79
D	60–69
F	Below 60

The traditional program flowchart for the Student Grade Report program is shown in Figure 13.18. The hierarchy chart is shown in Figure 13.19. As you may have noticed by now, each hierarchy chart is small enough to be read quickly and is ironclad in its logic. Hierarchy charts are not much use for determining what the program actually *does*, which is why we go to flowcharts, pseudocode, or N-S charts.

Structured flowcharts are given in Figure 13.20 for the complete

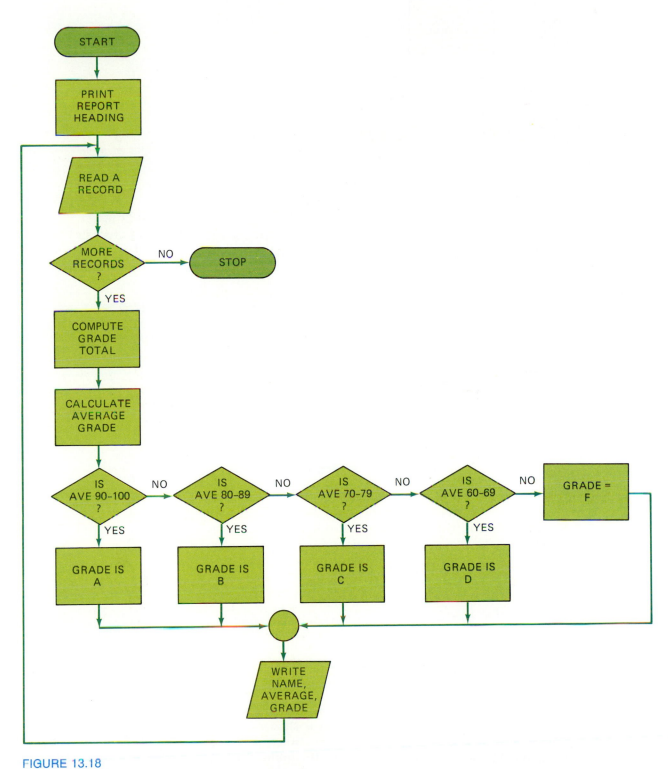

FIGURE 13.18
Traditional Flowchart
for Student Grade Report
Program

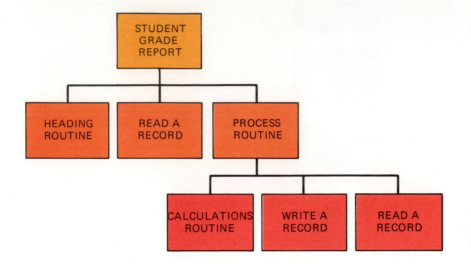

FIGURE 13.19
Hierarchy Chart for Student
Grade Report Program

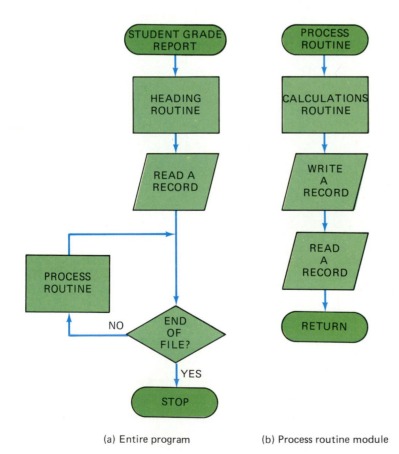

FIGURE 13.20
Structured Flowcharts
for Student Grade Report
Program

(a) Entire program   (b) Process routine module

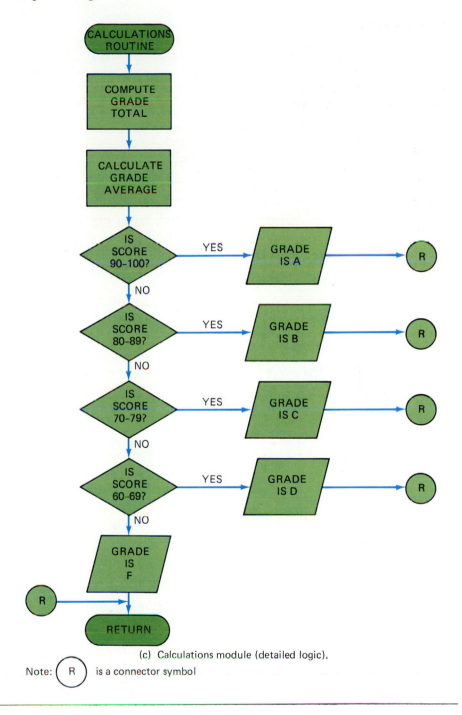

(c) Calculations module (detailed logic).

Note: (R) is a connector symbol

FIGURE 13.20 continued

program, the process-record module, and for the calculations module, which includes the logic for determining a grade. In Figure 13.21, the N-S charts are shown for the entire program and for the grade-determination logic. Figure 13.22 provides the output for the program.

For the next two programs, a control break and a master file update, we will use a different set of records that pertain to business problems.

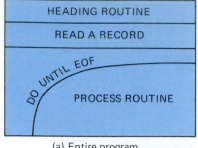

(a) Entire program

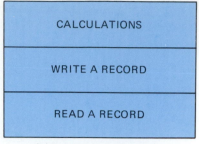

(b) Process routine module

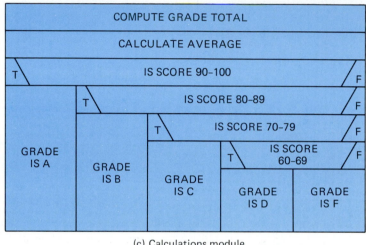

(c) Calculations module

FIGURE 13.21
The N-S Charts for Student
Grade Report Program

Student Number	Student Name	Quiz 1	Quiz 2	Quiz 3	Quiz 4	Quiz 5	Total Score	Ave. Score	Grade
0449	Roberts	97	78	89	67	88	419	83.8	B
1334	Harper	78	89	99	65	73	404	80.8	B
2357	Benson	87	88	77	98	74	424	84.8	B
2557	Janacek	85	89	92	90	96	452	90.4	A
2601	Reese	91	84	83	95	80	433	86.6	B
2918	Stone	73	79	86	81	90	404	80.8	B
3459	Phelps	99	86	93	80	89	447	89.4	B
3480	Mills	71	62	80	77	79	369	73.8	C
4195	Flores	90	79	87	83	93	432	86.4	B
4866	Blumenthal	69	77	84	90	95	415	83	B

FIGURE 13.22
The Output for the Student
Grade Report Program

Program Three: Control Break

A control break is simply a break in the output—such as a space on a printed report—that occurs when a given item changes. In program four, the given item will be a customer. Whenever we finish with one customer's data, we want to print the total amount of sales made to that customer

before going on to the next. There will be a control break at that point. Here is a short input file for this program:

Customer Number	Customer Name	Sales Amount
0817	Hawkins	615
0817	Hawkins	312
0912	Branson	987
0912	Branson	777
0912	Branson	134
1132	Clarke	578

We want to program a control break so that the following report will result:

Customer Number	Customer Name	Sales Amount
0817	Hawkins	615
0817	Hawkins	312
	Subtotal	927
0912	Branson	987
0912	Branson	777
0912	Branson	134
	Subtotal	1898
1132	Clarke	578
	Subtotal	578
	Grand total	3403

A control break is to occur whenever there is a change in the customer number. When this happens, the subtotal for the previous customer is printed out. Figure 13.23 shows the traditional flowchart for the customer report program. The logic of a control break can be described by walking through this program, step by step.

At the beginning of the program, the fields that will be used to add up the sales totals must be initialized (zeros are moved to them). Then, after the first record has been read, the first customer number must be moved into the compare field so that all subsequent records being read in can be compared with this customer number. If the customer number of the second record is the same as that of the first record, the sales amount recorded in the second record is simply added to the sales amount accumulator and to the grand-sales accumulator. Then a line on the report is written, and another record is read.

According to our input file for this program, the third record in the file is 0912. When this number is compared to the previous customer number (0817), a control break occurs. Now the subtotal line with the sales amount accumulated for the previous customer must be printed out. Next,

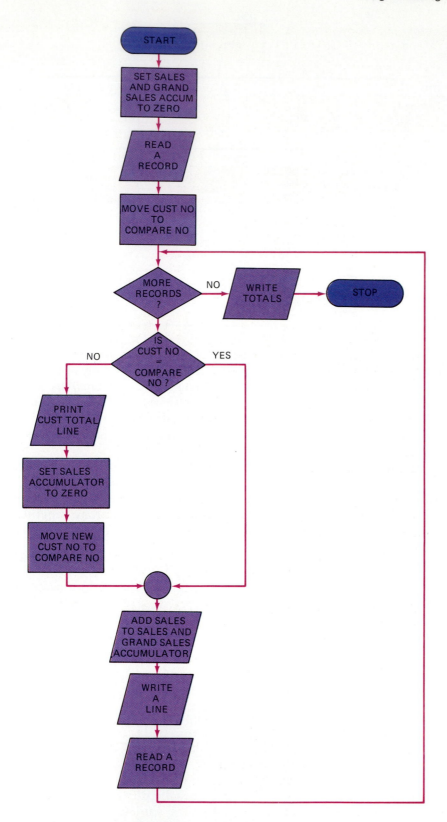

FIGURE 13.23
Traditional Flowchart for
Customer Report Program
(Control Break)

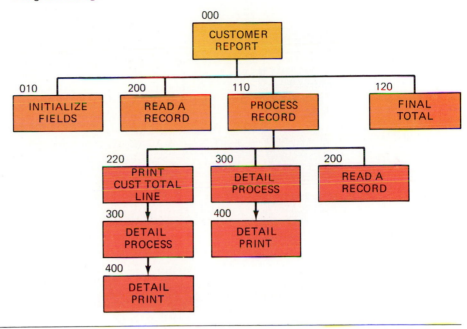

FIGURE 13.24
The Hierarchy Chart for
Customer Report Program

the sales amount accumulator must be set back to zero so that sales amounts for the next customer can be recorded from scratch. Finally, the customer number on the third record (0912) becomes the *new compare field;* all subsequent records will be compared with this number until another control break occurs. At the end of the program, after the last record has been processed, the last subtotal is written, the grand total printed, and the file closed.

Figure 13.24 shows the hierarchy chart for the program. This chart contains a sufficient number of modules for us to number them as well as name them, a common practice. When a given module (for example, detail-process) is used at more than one point in the hierarchy, repetition of both the number and the name helps make it clear that the same module is referred to.

Figure 13.25 shows the structured flowcharts for the conrol break program.

Program Four: Master File Update

Our last program illustrates a master file update procedure that is part of a payroll program. For this program there are two input files: a transaction file and a master file. The *transaction file* contains the employee number and the number of hours worked for the week:

TRANSACTION FILE	
Employee Number	Hours Worked
0317	40
0320	40
0321	23
0325	40

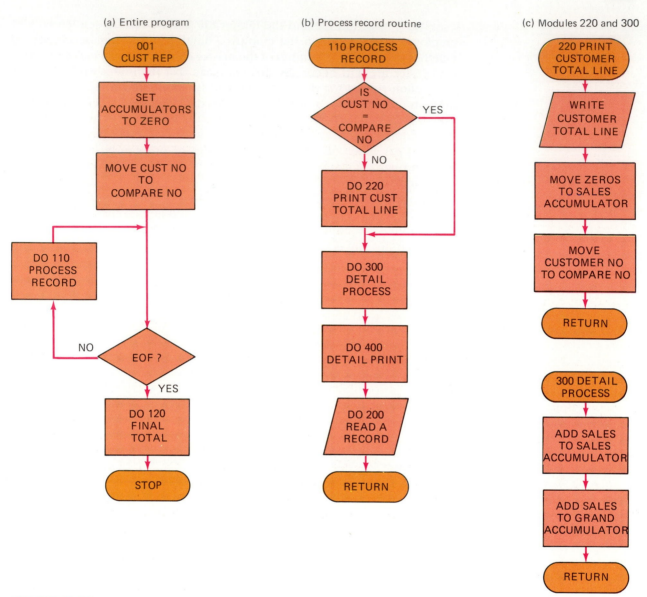

FIGURE 13.25
Structured Flowcharts for Customer Report Program

The *master file* contains the employee number, employee name, hourly rate of pay, year-to-date gross pay, and year-to-date net pay.

MASTER FILE

Employee Number	Employee Name	Hourly Rate	Year-to-Date Gross Pay	Year-to-Date Net Pay
0317	Brockart	3.50	560.00	504.00
0318	Clarkson	9.80	1568.00	1411.20
0320	Chandler	15.80	2528.00	2275.00
0325	Thompson	7.40	1184.00	1065.60

The transaction file and the master file will be read in sequentially by employee number. When the employee number of the transaction record matches the employee number of the master record, the process of updating the master file will occur. By this we mean that the hours worked on the transaction record for the employee will be multiplied by the hourly-rate field on the employee's master record to determine the weekly gross pay. The net pay will be 0.9 × gross pay. Once the weekly gross and net pay for the employee has been calculated, the year-to-date gross-pay and year-to-date net-pay fields on the employee master record can be updated. Let's walk through each step of the processing of the four records just listed.

The first record in the transaction file (0317) matches the first record in the master file (0317). Both have the same key field, employee number 0317. Since we have a match, the hours-worked field in the transaction file is multiplied by the hourly-rate field in the master file to determine gross pay. Then net pay is calculated.

Hours Worked		Hourly Rate		Gross Pay
40	×	3.50	=	140.00

Gross Pay		Net Pay
140.00 × 0.9	=	126.00

Now the year-to-date gross-pay and year-to-date net-pay fields can be updated to reflect the weekly earnings.

Previous Year-to-Date Gross Pay		Current Gross Pay		Updated Year-to-Date Gross Pay
560.00	+	140.00	=	700.00

Previous Year-to-Date Net Pay		Current Net Pay		Updated Year-to-Date Net Pay
504.00	+	126.00	=	630.00

The updated master file now reflects the new year-to-date gross- and net-pay fields:

Emp. No.	Employee Name	Hourly Rate	Year-to-Date Gross Pay	Year-to-Date Net Pay
0317	Brockart	3.50	700.00	630.00

The next record in the transaction file (0320) does not match the next record in the master file (0318). In fact, there is no corresponding record in the master file that does match this record in the transaction file. This might mean that employee 0318 did not work during this pay period. In

such a situation the old master record is written without any changes to the new master file.

The second record in the transaction file (0320) does match the third record in the master file (0320), so the weekly gross and net earnings are calculated for employee 0320 and the master file is updated to reflect the new year-to-date gross and net pay values.

The next record in the transaction file (0321) does not match the next record in the master file (0325). This could mean that employee 0321 has submitted a time card with the number of hours worked, but his or her name is not yet in the employee master file. It could be a new employee, or it could represent some type of error in the transaction file. In our program, any transaction records without matching master records will be listed on an error report.

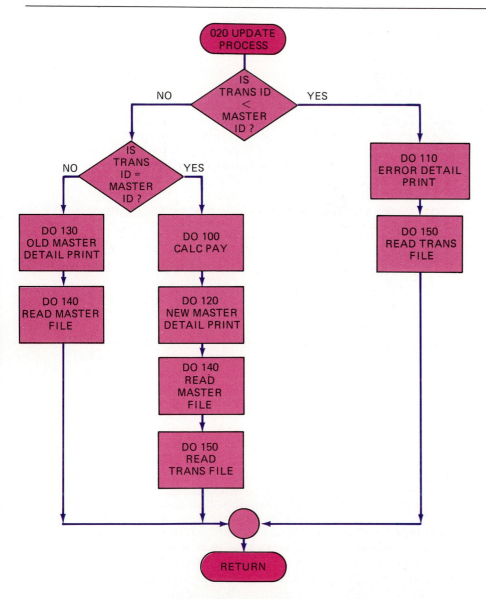

FIGURE 13.26
Structured Flowcharts for Master File Update Process

Finally, we read record 0325 of the transaction file, which matches record 0325 of the master file. We then calculate the weekly gross and net earnings for this employee and update the master file for the new year-to-date gross and net pay figures. Our walkthrough is now complete.

The master file update problem provides us with an opportunity to see how various program design techniques can be used to depict the logic of the main process routine that occurs when a master record and a transaction record have been read.

Figure 13.26 is a structured flowchart depicting the logic of the master file update procedure. Each module on the flowchart has its own function. For example, module 130, Old Master Detail Print, simply takes the old master record and writes it to the new master file. When a master record matches a transaction record, module 100 calculates gross and net pay and updates the year-to-date gross and net pay figures on the master record. Then module 120 writes the new master record using these updated figures. Module 110 prints transaction records that have no matching master and that are errors.

It's a Dirty Job but . . .

Someone's Got to Do Maintenance

Few of us really enjoy performing software maintenance. Just as "I don't do windows" became an infamous cry of housekeepers everywhere, software maintenance tops the list of programmers' least favorite duties. But with an increasing supply of products requiring corrective changes, modifications and enhancements to keep up with user demands and tight budgets, software maintenance is not going to go away. . . .

The statistics are staggering: 50% of MIS/DP budgets are said to be allocated to software maintenance every year. Programmers reportedly spend 50% and, in some cases, 80% of their time on ongoing maintenance. Software maintenance is said to be a multibillion-dollar industry. Industry watchers contend that more than $30 billion is spent annually worldwide on maintenance. The U.S. alone spends more than $10 billion annually.

Recent work at MIT indicates that for every dollar invested in new system development, an additional $9 must be earmarked for maintenance during the system's life cycle. . . .

The keys to increasing productivity in almost any endeavor are the "three Ts"—techniques, tools and training. The three Ts are required for increasing programmer and manager productivity in both development and maintenance.

A collection of maintenance programming and management techniques is the essential base for increasing software maintenance productivity. The techniques can either be generic, such as problem-solving procedures, or be internal to the program or consist of external documentation. Some techniques can be specific to a particular software package or a programming language. A company should also put forth its own techniques for the effective use of software tools in a maintenance environment.

Without ongoing formal training of both programmers and managers in the use of maintenance techniques and tools, a company cannot achieve improvements in maintenance productivity.

It seems that the world of software maintenance tools is about to explode. Tools abound for Cobol; the most widely talked about Cobol tools are the

restructuring products that convert unstructured programs into structured programs automatically. . . .

Standard documentation techniques and automated tools can help boost maintenance programming productivity. There should be a standardized method of communicating information about code and system to the community of programmers.

What companies need is a standard, graphics documentation technique and an automated, preferably interactive, tool to support it. The tool should be integrated in the infrastructure of a maintenance programmer's workbench.

However, all the technological tools and fixes in the world won't help your organization's software if the people performing the function don't know how to use them. Believe it or not, not many MIS/DP professionals are formally trained for a job that accounts for more than one-half of their job responsibilities—that of software maintenance!

This situation must change. The mass education of MIS/DP professionals in software maintenance is in order. Education and training can tie together the materials on maintenance technologies and tools and prepare professionals for performing the vital function of maintenance.

Professionals may pursue specialized training when appropriate. Also, general maintenance training should be ongoing. Companies need to develop education and training materials.

The programming profession is very demanding but at the same time exciting and sometimes frustrating. While meeting day-to-day demands—some requiring overtime—it is very difficult to think of anything else. But MIS/DP professionals should take some time off occasionally and try to look at their professional and personal goals. Some self-analysis can be revealing. Also, set up your own productivity improvement program. Such a self-improvement program can include studying articles and reading selected professional books regularly.

Multiskilled programmers are in demand, which puts a burden on programmers who want to specialize in one or two areas while having a working knowledge of other areas.

In addition to technical know-how, interpersonal skills are also required for an employee to survive and even flourish in DP/MIS environments. Verbal as well as written communication skills are necessary.

Proficiency in system/program design methods, data/data base design techniques and, last but not least, maintenance programming tools and techniques are also important, but in most environments, these skills take the back seat. Mastering all of these topics while designing and maintaining programs is a formidable, if not downright impossible, task.

However, just because you are keeping the software up and running, you are not indispensible. Job security is a myth. The key to real security is in becoming a productive professional.

Management should develop a positive maintenance attitude and motivate programmers. It should also provide the necessary tools and training to the programmers. With support from above and a positive outlook, MIS/DP professionals can make the most of the opportunity to solve the problems of software maintenance, rather than avoid this necessary chore.

Source: Excerpted from "It's a Dirty Job, but . . ." by Girish Parikh, "Focus," *Computerworld,* July 8, 1987, pp. 47–48.

Summary and Key Terms

1. A **computer program** is a sequenced set of instructions, written in a language the computer can understand, that tells the computer how to accomplish a task. Although both tasks and languages can vary substantially, the general principles of programming do not. An effective computer program must have an unambiguous problem statement, a set of rules for the program to apply, and a procedure for the program to follow.

2. An **algorithm** is a statement of the steps to be followed in accomplishing a task or solving a problem. To make algorithms easier to understand, programmers use flowcharts. A program **flowchart** is a diagram that visually presents an algorithm, using a set of agreed-upon symbols connected by lines.

3. **Program design** takes those parts of a system design that require a computer and structures them into a form that can be directly translated into computer code. In other words, program design is an intermediate step between system design and the actual coding of a program.

4. The criteria for a good program design are:
   - The design should be easy to understand for those involved, *and for those not involved,* in its creation.
   - The design should permit easy modification and updating of the program.
   - The design should work.

5. **Structured programming** meets all criteria for good design. An **unstructured program** is written on a linear basis, with no main portion to direct and indicate the functions of the remainder, and includes numerous GO TO statements. In contrast, a structured program is made up of logically independent modules, each of which is a series of statements grouped together as a unit.

6. Three control structures govern the logic of a structured program: **sequence, selection,** and **iteration.**

7. **Traditional flowcharts** are often used to show the algorithm of a structured program. One flowchart can show the overall program.

8. Structured programs are designed in a hierarchical manner. The module on top of the hierarchy controls the modules in the next lower level of the hierarchy, which in turn control modules still lower, and so on.

9. Each module performs its job only when it gets orders from above, and gives orders only to its subordinates. Thus, each module has only one entry and one exit point. The relationships between modules in a structured program are shown in a **hierarchy chart.**

10. Gaining in popularity are **Nassi-Schneiderman structured flowcharts,** which are more compact, easier to draw, and in some ways more effective than traditional flowcharts.

11. **Pseudocode** is another technique for expressing the logic of a program. It uses a language quite similar to actual computer languages but not so similar as to be language specific. **Decision tables** and **decision trees** are also useful techniques for summarizing the logic behind program decisions, and are not hard to translate into actual code.

12. Just as program design techniques have evolved from less structured to more structured, so have program implementation strategies. **Egoless programming** means that programs are no longer regarded as the personal property of a single programmer. The chief programmer team develops a program cooperatively. **Structured walkthroughs** of programs encourage constructive criticism and peer participation in the design process.

Review Questions

Fill In

1. A _____ is a set of instructions, written in a language the computer can understand.
2. A statement of the steps to be followed in performing a task or solving a problem is an _____ .
3. A _____ is a diagram of an algorithm that uses a set of agreed-on symbols.
4. A program using a GO TO statement is probably an _____ program.
5. The control structure that makes a test and then goes to one procedure or another depending on the outcome of the test is _____ .
6. During a _____ programmers work with each other to detect errors in a program.
7. A technique used to represent program logic in English-like language is called _____ .
8. A structured program is made of logically independent _____ , each of which is a series of statements grouped together as a unit.

Program Design Exercises

1. Develop a flowchart to take student records listing grade point average (GPA), major, and age and to select students who have a GPA of over 3.2, are majoring in biology, and who are over 22 years of age.

2. You are to design a program that provides student fees. Your input is student records, consisting of student number, student name, and the number of credits for which each student is registered:
Sample Input Record:

Student #	Stu-Name	Credits
4812	Allen L	6

Student fees are calculated as follows, based on the number of credits taken:

No. of Credits	Student-fee
1-9	$25
10-15	$50
over 15	$60

Design a program that will provide a report listing the student number, student name, number of credits, and appropriate student fee for each student. Also, create a final total number of students registered.

3. Design a flowchart to represent the logic of a program that will take input records that list salesperson number, salesperson name, and sales transactions and provide a report that lists the total sales (sum of transactions) for each salesperson as a subtotal.

Input Records Salesperson #	Salesperson Name	Sales Transaction
1001	Jones K	34
1001	Jones K	95
1001	Jones K	56
1005	Baker D	33
1005	Baker D	88
1007	Johnson A	11

Output Report

1001	Jones K	34
1001	Jones K	95
1001	Jones K	56
	Subtotal	185
1005	Baker D	33
1005	Baker D	88
	Subtotal	121
1007	Johnson A	11
	Subtotal	11

Programming Languages

14

Chapter Objectives

After studying this chapter, you should be able to

1. Identify the characteristics of machine language, assembly language, and higher-level languages.

2. Identify the characteristics, major features, and applications of FORTRAN, COBOL, and BASIC.

3. Recognize the characteristics of fourth-generation programming languages and very high-level programming languages.

4. Understand the impact of fourth-generation languages on improving the development and the ease of use of applications.

Marcia Alvers is an instructor at a business school. Each term she gives five quizzes and uses the averaged scores on these quizzes to determine student grades for the course. In a term she has approximately 40 students in each of three sections, for a total of 120 students. That means Marcia has to make the same set of calculations—adding up five numbers and then dividing the sum by the number 5—120 times.

Marcia owns a personal computer and knows the BASIC programming language. She has reasoned that an hour spent writing a program plus a half-hour checking it with some data to make sure it functions properly would save a couple of hours a term.

In effect, Marcia will be using the computer interactively; that is, she and the computer will conduct a "dialog." She will enter the data, which are the five scores for each student, and direct the computer to run the program. The computer will then perform the calculations according to the program and print out the students' average scores. Not only is this much faster than doing it by hand, but Marcia will immediately see the results of the computer activity. After she has verified that the program works properly, she will not have to repeat each calculation, as she has been doing, to be sure that she hasn't made a mistake.

Some computer programming languages *invite* use for a task like this. Marcia does not call herself a programmer, but she does know BASIC, which was easy to learn. She could not write a program to simulate a complex model in particle physics or to pay dividends to 10,000 stockholders, but she can get her personal computer to do useful work for her through her fluency in a programming language.

```
05 REM this programs reads series of numbers and calculates average of such
06 REM S = the quiz score
07 REM T = the total of the quiz scores
08 REM A = the average of the quiz scores
09 REM C = the number of quizzes read by the machine
10 INPUT S
20 IF S = 999 GOTO 60
30 LET T = T + S
40 LET C = C + 1
50 GOTO 10
60 LET A = T / C
70 PRINT "TOTAL", "NUMBER", "AVERAGE"
80 PRINT     T,         C,         A
90 END
```

FIGURE 14.1
BASIC Program to Sum Quiz Scores and Print Average

Figure 14.1 shows the BASIC program Marcia wrote. With this program, the computer will give her the average she needs for each student in order to calculate a grade. Then, the computer will wait while Marcia decides what grade this score should actually translate into.

Perhaps you can figure out what all the statements of Marcia's program mean. After reading this chapter, you will be able to translate the program. You will understand what each of the main computer languages is designed for and how they all work. Although you will not yet be able to code a program in a particular language, you will be well on your way to reading a program-language instruction manual or pamphlet for that language. When you do, or if you study the BASIC Appendix in this book, you will be able to write a simple program, too. You will also know about machine language and assembly language, and understand what is meant by the term *fourth-generation languages*.

The Four Levels of Programming Languages

In this chapter we will come closer to the nuts and bolts of computer programs by examining what they are made of—programming languages. This is a different, and complementary, look at programs from that of Chapter 13, where we discussed the principles of program design. Once a program has been designed, it has to be written or coded, and it is written in a programming language.

You might wonder how a computer can understand a language. Computers are made up of silicon chips, wires, plastic, and metal. How can people "talk" to these inanimate materials?

The answer is that, although it may seem that people are talking to a computer, the languages used actually have to be translated before any computer can understand. The CPU understands only whether a given location in its memory is "on" or "off"; this is a straightforward kind of electrical notation. "On," you will remember, corresponds to a binary 1 and "off" to a binary 0. Following the principles of the binary number system (discussed in Appendix A), it is possible to express any number, letter, or character by combinations of 1 and 0. Not only can a computer understand such combinations, but it can perform computations using them.

The computer circuitry that performs computations employs this same "on/off" notation. It is possible, in other words, to give instructions to a computer by stringing together 1s and 0s. Early computers could be programmed only by using the 0/1 combinations that corresponded to the operations their circuitry could perform. These elementary programming languages are called machine languages.

As you might imagine, it is tedious figuring out the combinations of 1s and 0s to write for a series of instructions. People do not normally think, speak, and write in 1s and 0s. Mistakes could easily occur in writing the instructions of a program that involved hundreds or thousands of 1s and 0s. To improve on machine language in these respects, assembly languages were invented.

Assembly languages are still very close to instructions for the actual computer circuitry. Their advantage to humans is that they use mnemonic codes in alphabetic letters—such as "DC" for "definite constant," or "MR" for "multiply registers"—instead of strings of 1s and 0s. Assembly languages thus work on the next "higher" level from machine language. (In the conventions of computer terminology, "higher" always means further away from the machine level.)

The language you saw in Figure 14.1, BASIC, is a representative of the third level of languages. These are known as *high-level* or *procedural languages,* and they include COBOL, FORTRAN, PL/I, and Pascal. All use terms that either *are* English (PRINT, GOTO, END, and so on) or are Englishlike. This makes them much easier for people to understand than either strings of 1s and 0s or curt mnemonic codes. We will be taking a closer look at each of these languages later in this chapter.

Finally, a new series of languages, known as fourth-generation languages, has recently appeared. These include data base query languages, report generators, and application generators.

The four layers of programming languages can be represented by their proximity to the machine's level or orientation, as shown in Figure 14.2. The further from the center, the further the language is from a CPU's way of looking at things and the closer it is to the way people actually think and write. The ease of use of the higher-level languages, however, comes at some expense. These costs include slower computer run time and reduced efficiency in programming some of the more exotic things computers can do. However, the improved efficiency in programming most applications vastly outweighs these concerns.

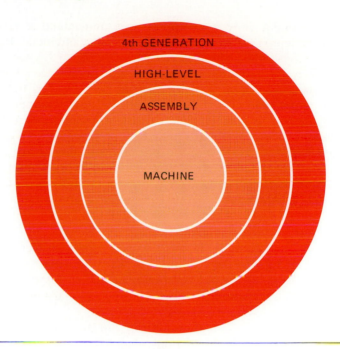

FIGURE 14.2
The Four Levels of
Programming Languages

In this chapter we will start at the lowest level of programming languages—machine language—and work our way out to the fourth generation. We will give some brief examples in each language group and discuss its drawbacks and merits in relation to the others.

Machine Language

Computers are actually quite adamant about understanding only one thing: machine language. Consisting of instructions expressed as binary numbers, **machine language** is the only language a computer understands. Programs written in any other language must be translated (by other programs) into machine language in order to run. This means that even when we use a higher-level language, it is still machine language that is getting the computer to do the work.

A machine-language instruction consists of two parts:

1. An **operation code.** This identifies what the computer is to do.
2. An **operand.** This gives the address in the computer's working storage to be used in the operation.

Let's look at a machine-language instruction. We will write it in decimal numbers rather than in binary to make it easier to discuss. Here is the instruction:

In this instruction the operation code is 2. Codes are specific to a given machine; for this (hypothetical) machine, 2 means "read input." The

operand, 51, designates the memory location in the computer's main storage having 51 as its address. Taken as a whole, then, the machine-language instruction means "read input data into main storage location 51"—a lot of content compressed into three numbers.

Each particular computer has its own machine language. Operation code 2, for instance, on another computer might mean "write output." Machine-language instructions usually occupy one word. An example of a computer word would be a 32-bit word, consisting of 4 bytes of 8 bits each. A machine-language instruction fills a 32-bit word in the following way (see Figure 14.3):

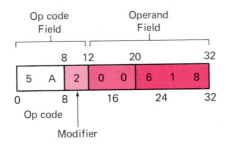

FIGURE 14.3
A Machine-Language
Instruction

■ Bits 0 through 7 (the first byte) contain the operation code, which tells the computer what operation is to be performed.

■ Bits 8 through 11 contain a modifier, which may tell the computer which register in the CPU is being used as the accumulator.

■ Bits 12 through 31 contain the operand.

A machine-language instruction written in binary in this format would look like the one in Figure 14.4:

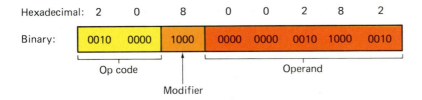

FIGURE 14.4
A Machine-Language
Instruction Written in Binary

Programmers usually write machine-language instructions in **hexadecimal notation,** a shorthand for binary, which is then translated to the actual binary. Hexadecimal is easier than binary to understand, and each hexadecimal digit is equivalent to 4 binary digits. Figure 14.5 shows how the machine-language instruction just given in binary would appear in hexadecimal:

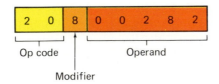

FIGURE 14.5
A Machine-Language
Instruction Written
in Hexadecimal

This instruction means the following: Clear the accumulator and add (specified by operation code 20) the contents of computer memory

location 282 (specified by the address 282) to the accumulator, which is register 8 (represented by the modifier). This brief overview should give you the flavor of writing in machine language.

Disadvantages of Machine Languages One of the main disadvantages of machine language is that it is time-consuming to code. The programmer must keep track of all the different addresses into which data go, the addresses where each instruction is placed, the different operation codes and operand and modifer requirements for each, and so on. A second disadvantage is that it is very hard to change a machine-language program after it has been implemented. Frequently the addition of just one instruction in a program would require the programmer to change almost every other instruction because the addresses are different. A third disadvantage of machine language is that it is machine specific. A program written for one computer system can only be used on that system. Writing machine language requires the programmer to have high-level knowledge of the specific machine. For these reasons, higher-level languages were invented. Today very few programs are written in machine language.

Assembly Language

Assembly language uses mnemonic codes in place of numeric operation codes used by machine language. It also uses symbolic addresses (that is, symbols used as addresses) for memory locations instead of operands with address locations in machine language. Although one step further away from the CPU than machine language, assembly language is still considered a low-level language because its coding closely resembles machine language in the type of information that is supplied.

Instructions in assembly language are translated into machine language by a program called an **assembler.** As the assembler program reads each instruction, it converts the mnemonic operation code into a binary operation code and the symbolic address into a binary address.

Uses, Advantages, and Disadvantages of Assembly Language Programming in assembly language, because it uses mnemonic codes and symbolic addresses, is not quite so tedious and time-comsuming as programming in machine language. The mnemonic codes bear some similarity to the real words intended, remembering them is easier. There is no need to keep track of the addresses of everything, since the symbolic name alone suffices. An actual assembly language command (such as LD HL, MEMLOC), which means load register HL with the value of the variable MEMLOC, is easier to understand than its machine language counterpart (00100001 10001111 00001000). As a result, programmers can work more accurately and effectively with assembly language. But although assembly language is some improvement over machine language, it is still time-consuming to use compared with the languages we are going to study.

Assembly language also has other strengths—everything that a computer can do can be programmed in assembly language. Although it is not as widely used as the higher-level languages, most large computer centers have some programmers who can code in assembly language, because at

some point or other an application—or part of an application—will arise that is best or more efficiently programmed in assembly language. Because knowledge of assembly language increases one's knowledge of the machine, most programmers at some time will wish to code in it to sharpen their skills. Doing so, however, remains a challenge.

A disadvantage of assembly language is that, like machine language, it is machine-specific. Some machine groups by one manufacturer will employ a common assembly language, such as IBM Assembly Language; but even in such cases, there will be differences from model to model that must be observed, and a program written for one computer system will not necessarily run on another.

High-Level Languages

High-level languages move still nearer to the programmer and further away from the machine's orientation. High-level languages make it possible to write programs without knowing the computer's repertoire of instructions or how the computer handles addresses. High-level languages are designed to work with the particular type of problem to be solved or procedure to be used.

Features of High-Level Languages

Before we examine some individual high-level languages, we will look at some features they have in common. First, all must be translated into machine language in order to run on computers. Second, high-level languages share some structural features, which we will also examine.

Compilers and Interpreters
Translation of a program written in a high-level programming language into the computer's machine language is done by a special program known as a **compiler.** This program replaces each instruction in the entire high-level language program with an appropriate series of machine-language instructions to carry out the requested operation. The compiler translates the entire program into machine language all at once before execution.

In contrast, an interpreter translates one instruction at a time into machine language. This means that the interpreter performs the operations in the program as it reads them—line by line, using a built-in dictionary that gives machine-language equivalents of high-level commands. An interpreted language enables the inexperienced programmer to make changes and improvements to the program during its execution. Using a compiler, an entire program must be translated over again if changes are required. However, the interpreter is slower because each statement must be translated every time it occurs, whereas a compiler can repeat statements without translating them each time. About half the available translators for BASIC, a

FIGURE 14.6
The Function of a Compiler

programming language for beginners, are interpreters and about half are compilers.

An illustration of how the compiler works is given in Figure 14.6. The high-level language program that a compiler translates is known as a **source program.** The machine-language program that the compiler produces as output is called an **object program.** The first compilers translated source programs into assembly-language programs and then called on an assembler to do the final translation into machine language. Today most compilers translate directly from source program to object program.

High-level languages were developed to give more people access to the computer—they were, in fact, one of the first key steps in the ''democratization'' of the computer. Programs written in a high-level language are not as time-consuming to code; they can easily be changed; and a program written for one computer can generally be run on another.

But the use of high-level languages necessitates compilers—which cost money, occupy computer storage, and take time to run. The machine language of the object program produced by a compiler may not be as efficient and to the point as a program originally coded in machine language. Even if a large program is run only once, it may include a subroutine that has to be executed 50,000 times during that one run. In this case, the less efficiently coded object program produced by a compiler may take much longer to run.

Language Characteristics

Although the parallel between human languages and computer languages should not be belabored, it is worth making. Each human language has its specific vocabulary, rules of grammar and syntax for making up sentences, and conventions for writing. This is true of computer languages as well: Each has a vocabulary of possible operations (READ, GET, GOTO, and so on); their grammar and syntax rules tell how variable names and instructions are written; and each has specific coding conventions (such as where blank spaces may be used and what abbreviations are permitted).

In human languages, words are put together to make sentences. In a high-level computer language, basic vocabulary items (ADD, PRINT, RETURN) are combined with other elements to make up **statements.** For any language, there are five different categories of statements:

1. **Statements to Describe Variables.** Each language must have a way to identify variables that will be read by a program, used in computations in the program, or written by the program. Statements that identify variables also indicate how much storage should be allowed in the computer for the variable.

2. **Input/Output Statements.** Each language has statements specifying that input should be read from an input device and that output should be written to an output device. The variables to be read or written must be identified, and in some cases the specific device must also be identified. (When it is not identified, it is specified by information outside the program that describes the devices in the system.)

3. **Control Statements.** Control statements are used by each language to skip from one part of a program to another without executing every statement in between. Often a variable is tested for a specific value first; then, depending on the value, a control statement is used to transfer control to the appropriate part of the program.

4. **Arithmetic Statements.** The end purpose of most computer programs is to compute; consequently, each language has a set of statements that perform basic arithmetic operations, mainly addition, subtraction, multiplication, and division. More complex mathematical operations can also be done, by combining sequences of basic arithmetic statements or by using special statements the compiler may be programmed to understand, such as for finding a square root.

5. **Termination Statements.** Each language has one or more statements to indicate that no more program statements follow, and thus that the program is finished.

Now that we know the general types of statements in most high-level computer languages, we will look at six actual languages: BASIC, FORTRAN, COBOL, PL/I, Pascal, and RPG. For each language, we will see what specific statements it uses to define variables, for input/output, and so on, in the sequence listed above; we will examine the advantages and disadvantages; and we will show a sample program.

BASIC

BASIC is an acronymn for **B**eginner's **A**ll-Purpose **S**ymbolic **I**nstruction **C**ode. It was developed in 1963 as an easy way to teach a programming language to Dartmouth College students. When microcomputers began to appear in the following decade, BASIC was available as a "natural" easy-to-learn computer language. Today BASIC is the main language used by private individuals and businesses to program their microcomputers.

Another important feature of BASIC is that it is an **interactive** language. This means that the user can communicate directly with the computer when programs are being typed in and run. If you type in an incorrect line, you get an error message and you have a chance to correct the error immediately. This feature makes it possible to learn how to program through a process of trial and error and to modify programs in the process of writing them.

Statements to Describe Variables   In most programs it is often necessary to store values in memory. These values, obtained as input data or as the results of calculations, are assigned by the program to variable names, which correspond to specific memory locations. READ and DATA statements may be used in conjunction with one another to give values to variables. For example, the following statements would give values for five quiz scores:

```
READ Q1, Q2  Q3, Q4, Q5
DATA 86, 77, 92, 79, 90
```

The READ statement makes use of the data created by the DATA statement. When a READ statement is encountered, values from the DATA statement are assigned to variable names in the order that the names are written in the READ statement. Thus, after the execution of these two statements, the memory location now named Q1 holds the value 86; Q2 holds the value 77; and so on.

Input/Output Statements   INPUT statements are placed in a BASIC program whenever the program needs some data. When the program reaches an INPUT statement, it stops; the person using the computer can then enter the data needed. Thus, an INPUT statement could allow a user, during the execution of the program, to type in five quiz scores of 86, 77, 92, 79, and 90.

    The PRINT statement allows us to transfer data from the computer memory to an output device. An example is the statement PRINT "THE RESULT IS" 6 * X. If we assume a value of 3 for X in this example, the following would be printed: THE RESULT IS 18.

Control Statements   In BASIC, the GOTO statement transfers control to the program location specified. GOTO 99 would cause the computer to next execute the program statement labeled 99.

    IF/THEN is a conditional control statement. Control is transferred only if a specified condition exists. For example, the statement 140 IF C = 20 THEN 60 would make the computer next execute the program's statement number 60 if the variable C equals 20.

Arithmetic Statements   The LET statement is used to assign values to variables. For example, the statement LET X = C + D assigns the sum of C + D to X. When the LET statement is used for calculations, arithmetic operators such as +, −, *, and /, are used to represent addition, subtraction, multiplication, and division. For example, LET Y = (4 + D) / C will cause the computer to add 4 to the variable D, divide the result by C, and store the result of the division in the location labeled Y.

Termination Statement   The termination statement in BASIC has to qualify as the easiest statement in the language. It is simply: END.

Uses and Advantages/Disadvantages   BASIC is easy to learn, easy to use, and easy to debug. A disadvantage of using BASIC is that a simple program that is repeatedly extended might become unwieldy and difficult to understand. This problem can be overcome by using good structuring,

which means organizing the program in a logical way, and by using extensive comments.

FORTRAN

FORTRAN is an acronym for **FOR**mula **TRAN**slation. Created in the mid-1950s by a group of IBM employees and users of IBM computers, FORTRAN was the first high-level computer language to become widely available. Because it could be used on different types of computers and because many programs were written in it, standardization became a concern. The American National Standards Institute (ANSI) has developed FORTRAN specifications to be followed by FORTRAN compilers.

FORTRAN is specifically designed to solve problems in science, engineering, and mathematics. Scientific applications involve less input/output data than business applications, but the data are usually processed using complex mathematical and logical operations. One type of scientific application is statistical analysis. To assess the impact of drinking on traffic accidents, researchers may gather data on traffic accidents and compute statistics such as the correlation of drinking and accidents. The amount of data used in the program may be relatively small but the data will be analyzed in complex ways.

Scientists and engineers use FORTRAN to solve technical and mathematical problems in their fields and analyze data in complex ways.

Courtesty of AT&T Technologies, Inc.

A FORTRAN program hs a number of types of statements, including input/output statements, control statements, and arithmetic statements.

Input/Output Statements Input and output statements require a specific format for reading and printing data. The format of the data to be read or written is specified in the FORMAT statement. For example:

```
READ  (9,1) N
1 FORMAT (12)
```

The FORMAT statement says that the data item to be read from an input record is an integer value that is two digits long (12). The 1 in the READ statement corresponds to the statement number of the format statement describing the input record.

Control Statements FORTRAN has three different control statements: the GO TO statement, the IF statement, and the DO statement.

The GO TO statement transfers control to the program location specified. GO TO 99 would cause the program to next execute the program statement labeled 99.

The IF statement is a conditional control statement. A test is made, and control is transferred depending on the result of the test. For example, the statement IF (C.EQ.20) GO TO 60 would make the computer next execute the program's statement number 60 if the variable C equals 20.

The DO statment is one of the more complex statements in any high-level language. It causes a set of statements within a program to be repeated. The DO statement also tells how many times to repeat them. For example:

```
DO 20 I = 1,15
READ (9,2) GRADE
2 FORMAT (F10,2)
SUM = SUM + GRADE
20 CONTINUE
```

Here, the DO statement says to repeat all the instructions up to and including the one labeled 20 (the CONTINUE statement) 15 times, using an index variable named I that will start with the value 1 the first time through the instructions. The index variable increases by 1 on each subsequent repeat, finally reaching 15. At that point the DO loop is finished and the program goes on to whatever statement follows the CONTINUE statement.

Arithmetic Statements Arithmetic is FORTRAN's forte. It is specified by algebralike statements using variables and arithmetic operators such as $+$, $-$, $*$ (multiplication), and $**$ (exponentiation). For example, the single statement $X = B + ((A + B) * C) + A ** 2$ causes the computer to perform the following operations:

```
1. Add A + B          Call the result M   B + (M * C) + A ** 2
2. Multiply M × C     Call the result N   B + N + A ** 2
3. Compute A ** 2     Call the result O   B + N + O
4. Add B + N          Call the result P   P + O
5. Add P + O          Final operation
                      (Answer is X)
```

Termination Statements   FORTRAN uses two different termination statements, STOP and END. STOP is used anywhere in the program to halt execution if, for instance, the results of a test are so far off that there is no need to run the program further. END is the termination that is the last statement in a program.

Uses and Advantages/Disadvantages   FORTRAN is extensively used for scientific, engineering, and mathematical operations. It continues to be used for a handful of commercial applications.

The advantages of FORTRAN are that it expresses mathematical formulas easily and is thus a powerful tool in the hands of scientists, engineers, and mathematicians. Its modular structure lends itself to using library routines that have already been developed for a wide range of mathematical functions and statistical calculations. Its disadvantages are its limited file processing capabilities, its limited usefulness in business applications, and its rigid formatting requirements. Its strict column alignment and formatting conventions date back to a time when programs were entered statement by statement, onto 80 column punched cards. Another problem is that many FORTRAN programs are written in an unstructured, poorly organized way, and are difficult to read and to understand. Figure 14.7 gives an example of a complete FORTRAN program to compute and print out an average for quiz scores.

COBOL

COBOL is an acronym for **CO**mmon **B**usiness **O**riented **L**anguage. Like FORTRAN, COBOL was developed as a committee effort by a group representing government, business, and the academic world. In the case of COBOL, one of the users was the U.S. Department of Defense, which was concerned about the proliferation of business languages then being developed by different computer makers. The group concluded that a common language which could be used to produce machine-independent applications would save effort all around. As with FORTRAN, an ANSI standard has developed specifications for COBOL compilers.

COBOL was specifically designed as a commercial language, and thus its strength is in business applications. Business applications involve processing large amounts of data, such as thousands of sales-order transactions used to update an inventory master file. However, processing these data usually involves simple arithmetic operations, such as subtracting a quantity ordered from the existing, on-hand quantity of a particular inventory item.

COBOL is an extremely successful business programming language for a number of reasons. COBOL's Englishlike syntax, including data names and procedure names that are clear and concise, enables nontechnical users to understand COBOL programs. COBOL programs are also maintainable, which means that they can be modified or changed easily. Since about 65 percent of all code used in data processing departments is written in COBOL code and since programmers spend close to 60 to 70 percent of their time maintaining existing application programs, this ease of maintenance is critical.

One reason why COBOL programs are so easily modified is they are structured programs, and most business data processing organizations have

```
C*******************************************************************/
C*    THIS PROGRAM CALCULATES THE AVERAGE OF N GRADES.              */
C*    INPUT:   N     THE NUMBER OF GRADES                           */
C*             GRADE    EACH INDIVIDUAL GRADE AS IT IS READ         */
C*                                                                  */
C*    OUTPUT: AVERAGE    THE SUM OF GRADES DIVIDED BY N             */
C*                                                                  */
C*******************************************************************/
      REAL GRADE,SUM,AVRAGE
      INTEGER N
      WRITE(6,10)
10    FORMAT('ENTER NUMBER OF GRADES..5 IS ENTERED 05')
      READ(9,1) N
1     FORMAT(I2)
      SUM = 0
      WRITE(6,11)
11    FORMAT('ENTER EACH GRADE AFTER   ?-INCLUDE DECIMAL POINT')
      DO 20 I = 1,N
         READ(9,2) GRADE
2        FORMAT(F10.2)
         SUM = SUM + GRADE
20    CONTINUE
      AVRAGE = SUM/N
      WRITE(6,3) N,AVRAGE
3     FORMAT('FOR',I4,' GRADES, THE AVERAGE IS',F5.0)
      END
```

FIGURE 14.7
FORTRAN Program to Sum Quiz Scores and Print Out Average

supported the development of structured programs. A COBOL program is said to be well-structured if it is composed of modules that are complete, logical functions and if its modules are hierarchically organized, so that within each module there are subordinate functional modules that are themselves structured and can contain further subunits. COBOL programs are also maintainable because their straightforward, readable code makes them self-documenting.

COBOL is designed to support business applications because its strengths include
file processing and table processing.

COBOL is unlike the other languages that we have described in that
each program written in it is organized into four distinct areas or "divisions." These are:

- Identification division, which identifies the program.
- Environment division, which identifies specific features of the computer
  system and assigns files to peripheral devices.
- Data division, which describes input and output files and provides
  detailed descriptions of all data items.
- Procedure division, which contains the program's major functions.

The procedure division has a "driver" or "main line" routine that provides
an outline of the major procedures of the program. Each major procedure
branches to lower-level procedures, which in turn call on other lower-level
procedures.

Statements to Describe Variables   COBOL gives information about files in
the data division, where the programmer also names variables. The PIC-
TURE clause for each variable specifies its length and characteristics
(alphabetic or numeric). For example, a picture clause of PIC 9(7)
represents a numeric, seven-digit data item. Variables can also be set up in
working storage, rather than as input or output. The following statements
would set up a variable named TOTAL-GRADE-A as a two-digit number in
working storage with an initial value of 0:

```
WORKING-STORAGE SECTION
01    TOTAL-GRADE-A    PICTURE 9(2)    VALUE 0.
```

Input/Output Statements   READ statements in the procedure division read
input data into the variables set up in the data division. WRITE statements
output data in the form specified in the data division.

Control Statements   The control structures governing the logic of COBOL programs are implemented using the control statements, PERFORM . . . UNTIL and IF . . . ELSE.

The PERFORM . . . UNTIL statement passes control to a given procedure, which is executed a number of times until a specified test condition is met. This statement is commonly used to read input data until an end-of-file condition is met.

The IF . . . ELSE statement is a conditional control statement. A test is made, and control is transferred depending upon the results of the test. For example, the statements below would add 20 to the student fee for students older than 27, and add 15 to the student fee for those students 27 or younger:

```
IF STUDENT AGE IS GREATER THAN 27
  ADD 20 TO STUDENT FEE
ELSE
  ADD 15 TO STUDENT FEE.
```

Arithmetic Statements   As you have probably already noticed in the example, COBOL appears very much like English when written. This is especially true of the arithmetic. Variables and arithmetic operators such as plus and minus are used to construct statements that explain themselves: MULTIPLY CREDITS-TAKEN BY 250 GIVING TUITION.

Termination Statement   COBOL ends with the statement STOP RUN.

Uses and Advantages/Disadvantages   COBOL became the most popular business language because it was the first computer language that could be practically applied to business needs. It could edit and process input files and print reports in various formats. The data-division statements that specify all the details of a printed report are time-consuming to set up in COBOL, yet not as tedious as writing the great number of FORMAT statements that this would require in FORTRAN. The powerful file-handling abilities of COBOL make it fairly easy to set up procedures that meet most business needs, such as matching a transaction file with a master file or sorting the records of a file into a desired sequence for processing. COBOL can handle sequential, direct access and indexed sequential files.

The advantages of COBOL are that it is Englishlike and thus easy both to write and to understand once written. In addition, COBOL was the first fully supported standard language, allowing both programs and programmers' skills to be easily transported from system to system. Disadvantages are that the rules for writing a COBOL program are quite rigid, that COBOL programs are wordy compared to those of other languages, and that COBOL does not lend itself to nonbusiness applications, because its handling of complex calculations is cumbersome. Figure 14.8 gives an example of a partial COBOL program to sum five grades and calculate their averages.

PL/I

PL/I is an acronym for Programming Language I. In some ways, PL/I is a blend of COBOL and FORTRAN. IBM representatives and users developed

```
00220    ************************************************************
00221    *   DETAIL RECORD COMPUTATIONS AND PROCESSING              *
00222    ************************************************************
00223    DETAIL-PROCESSING.
00224        COMPUTE TOTAL-POINTS = CARD-ALGEBRA-SCORE +
00225                               CARD-GEOMETRY-SCORE +
00226                               CARD-ENGLISH-SCORE +
00227                               CARD-PHYSICS-SCORE +
00228                               CARD-CHEMISTRY-SCORE.
00229        DIVIDE TOTAL-POINTS BY 5 GIVING TOTAL-AVERAGE.
00230        IF GRADE-A
00231            ADD 1 TO TOTAL-GRADE-A
00232            MOVE 'A' TO STUDENT-GRADE
00233        ELSE
00234        IF GRADE-B
00235            ADD 1 TO TOTAL-GRADE-B
00236            MOVE 'B' TO STUDENT-GRADE
00237        ELSE
00238        IF GRADE-C
00239            ADD 1 TO TOTAL-GRADE-C
00240            MOVE 'C' TO STUDENT-GRADE
00241        ELSE
00242        IF GRADE-D
00243            ADD 1 TO TOTAL-GRADE-D
00244            MOVE 'D' TO STUDENT-GRADE
00245        ELSE
00246            ADD 1 TO TOTAL-GRADE-F
00247            MOVE 'F' TO STUDENT-GRADE.
00248    DETAIL-PROCESSING-EXIT.  EXIT.
00249    ************************************************************

00250    ************************************************************
00251    *   DETAIL RECORD PRINT ROUTINE                            *
00252    ************************************************************
00253    DETAIL-PRINT.
00254        MOVE CARD-STUDENT-NO TO PRINT-STUDENT-NO.
00255        MOVE CARD-STUDENT-NAME TO PRINT-STUDENT-NAME.
00256        MOVE CARD-SEX TO PRINT-SEX.
00257        MOVE CARD-AGE TO PRINT-AGE.
00258        MOVE CARD-ALGEBRA-SCORE TO PRINT-ALGEBRA.
00259        MOVE CARD-GEOMETRY-SCORE TO PRINT-GEOMETRY.
00260        MOVE CARD-ENGLISH-SCORE TO PRINT-ENGLISH.
00261        MOVE CARD-PHYSICS-SCORE TO PRINT-PHYSICS.
00262        MOVE CARD-CHEMISTRY-SCORE TO PRINT-CHEMISTRY.
00263        MOVE TOTAL-POINTS TO PRINT-TOTAL.
00264        MOVE TOTAL-AVERAGE TO PRINT-AVERAGE.
00265        MOVE STUDENT-GRADE TO PRINT-GRADE.
00266        MOVE SPACES TO PRINT-REC.
00267        WRITE PRINT-REC FROM DETAIL-LINE
00268            AFTER ADVANCING 2 LINES.
00269        MOVE SPACES TO PRINT-FLAG.
00270    DETAIL-PRINT-EXIT.        EXIT.
00271    ************************************************************

00272    ************************************************************
00273    *   TOTAL LINE PRINT ROUTINE                               *
00274    ************************************************************
00275    TOTAL-PRINT.
00276        MOVE TOTAL-COUNT TO TOTAL-STUDENT-COUNT.
00277        MOVE TOTAL-GRADE-A TO PRINT-GRADE-A.
00278        MOVE TOTAL-GRADE-B TO PRINT-GRADE-B.
00279        MOVE TOTAL-GRADE-C TO PRINT-GRADE-C.
00280        MOVE TOTAL-GRADE-D TO PRINT-GRADE-D.
00281        MOVE TOTAL-GRADE-F TO PRINT-GRADE-F.
00282        MOVE SPACES TO PRINT-REC.
00283        WRITE PRINT-REC FROM TOTAL-LINE
00284            AFTER ADVANCING 2 LINES.
00285    TOTAL-PRINT-EXIT.        EXIT.
00286    ************************************************************
```

FIGURE 14.8
Part of a COBOL Program to Compute the Average of Five Test Scores and to
Assign a Grade

PL/I in the mid-1960s in an attempt to simplify the increasingly confused
and crowded world of computer languages by replacing both FORTRAN and
COBOL with a single language. Although that replacement attempt failed,
PL/I is a rich language with many useful features—more than either

COBOL or FORTRAN alone—and is well suited for both business and scientific applications.

Uses and Advantages/Disadvantages PL/I has a large repertoire of statements that can be used in different ways. For a computer system seeking the power of a language that can deal with both business and scientific applications, it is an excellent choice. The fact that COBOL is much more frequently used in business settings, however, does give COBOL the edge because more people know it, and are used to reading it and

FIGURE 14.9
PL/I Program to Sum Quiz Scores and Print Out Average

```
/**********************************************************************/
/*    THIS PROGRAM CALCULATES THE AVERAGE OF N GRADES.             */
/*    INPUT:    N    THE NUMBER OF GRADES                          */
/*              GRADE   EACH INDIVIDUAL GRADE AS IT IS READ        */
/*                                                                 */
/*    OUTPUT:  AVERAGE    THE SUM OF GRADES DIVIDED BY N           */
/*                                                                 */
/**********************************************************************/
AVGR: PROC OPTIONS(MAIN);
    DECLARE GRADE,SUM,AVERAGE DECIMAL FIXED REAL (5,1);
    DECLARE N DECIMAL FIXED REAL (5,0);
    PUT SKIP  FILE(SYSTERM) LIST( 'ENTER NUMBER OF GRADES');
    PUT SKIP FILE(SYSTERM);
    GET FILE(CONSOLE) LIST(N);
    PUT FILE(SYSTERM) LIST('ENTER EACH GRADE AFTER ?');
    PUT SKIP FILE(SYSTERM);
    SUM = 0;
    DO COUNT = 1 TO N;
        GET FILE(CONSOLE) LIST(G);
        SUM = SUM + G;
        END;
    AVERAGE = SUM/N;
    PUT FILE(SYSTERM) LIST('FOR',N,'  GRADES, THE AVERAGE IS ',AVERAGE);
END AVGR;
```

programming in it. Figure 14.9 gives an example of a complete PL/I program that computes and prints out an average for quiz scores.

Pascal

Pascal is named for the mathematician Blaise Pascal, a pioneer of computing devices. Pascal was written in Switzerland by Niklaus Wirth as an aid in teaching structured programming. Every Pascal program is composed of smaller subprograms, each of which is a structured program. Pascal programs are easy to read and to maintain because variables and subprograms can be named with a high degree of flexibility.

In addition, Pascal's large variety of data types makes the language useful in a wide variety of applications. In addition to simple data types such as character, integer, and real, Pascal includes records (groupings of logically related information); files (groups of records of some type); arrays (tables of identical kinds of data types); and pointers (links between data structures).

Statements to Describe Variables Pascal has a special section at the beginning of each program that declares all variables and data types used in the program. For example, VAR GRADE, SUM, AVERAGE: REAL sets up the real variables GRADE, SUM, and AVERAGE in storage.

Input/Output Statements READLN is used to read data and WRITELN to write data. For example, READLN (NAME, PAYRATE, HOURS) reads one instance each of the variables NAME, PAYRATE, and HOURS.

Control Statements Pascal has a block structure, and related statements are grouped into blocks. These blocks are procedures that are given names and are invoked by name from other parts of the program. Pascal uses several control statements to implement control structures governing program logic, including the IF statement, the REPEAT UNTIL, and the WHILE DO statements.

The IF . . . THEN . . . ELSE statement is a conditional statement that carries out different actions depending upon the results of a test. For instance, the following statements cause one of three messages to be printed:

```
BEGIN
  IF WEALTHY
    THEN IF VENTURESOME
      THEN WRITELN ('I'LL START MY OWN BUSINESS.')
    ELSE WRITELN ('I'M WEALTHY BUT I'M NOT VENTURSOME');
  WRITELN ('SO I'LL INVEST MY MONEY WISELY.')
END;
```

The REPEAT . . . UNTIL statement repeats a set of statements until a certain condition is true. The WHILE . . . DO statement repeats a set of statements while a particular condition continues to be true.

Arithmetic Statements   Computations are done in Pascal using arithmetic operators such as plus and minus and variables in the following way: AVERAGE:=SUM/N. This divides SUM by N, and stores the result in AVERAGE.

Termination Statement   END is used to terminate a Pascal program.

Uses and Advantages/Disadvantages   Pascal is a language well suited to scientific and engineering programming as well as to computer-science instruction. Its advantages are that it is expressly devised to be consistent with the principles of structured programming and that it is fairly easy to program in. Disadvantages are that it has not yet been standardized (as FORTRAN, COBOL, and PL/I have been) and that it is not yet well known by business programmers. Figure 14.10 shows a Pascal program to compute and print out an average for quiz scores.

APL

A popular programming language is **APL** (which is an acronym for **A** **P**rogramming **L**anguage). It was first developed at IBM for internal use and then released in the 1960s. APL is used for scientific applications on mainframe computers and is available on some mini- and microcomputers as well.

Although APL has considerable power, it can be used without much programming knowledge. Basic APL conventions can be quickly learned. For instance, if you type 6 + 6 at a terminal (and hit the RETURN key), APL responds immediately with the answer 12. It is designed to be an interactive, conversational language.

A language that gives such immediate answers invites more complex use, and APL can do calculations of any complexity in the same manner as the addition of 6 + 6. Moreover, it does not just calculate. It can perform involved mathematical operations. It can set up complicated tables of numbers and then manipulate them as the input data are changed. APL compilers are available that offer data base query and update, application generators, and report generators. It is a language that opens up the world of programming to the nonexpert.

RPG—A Precursor of Fourth-Generation Languages

RPG is an acronymn for **R**eport **P**rogram **G**enerator. RPG I was invented in the mid-1950s to meet a specific need and has continued in use even after the context of that need has changed. Specifically, RPG II was developed by IBM in 1964 to process sequential files, tabulate the information contained in them, and produce printed reports as output. Designed to handle data, RPG was really a precursor of fourth-generation languages. (Fourth-generation languages will be discussed in the next section.)

The conventions for coding RPG are different enough that we cannot present it in the same statement-by-statement form we have used with the other languages. Programming in RPG means first describing the type of

```
(*****************************************************************)
(*    THIS PROGRAM CALCULATES THE AVERAGE OF N GRADES.          *)
(*    INPUT:    N      THE NUMBER OF GRADES                     *)
(*              GRADE    EACH INDIVIDUAL GRADE AS IT IS READ    *)
(*                                                              *)
(*    OUTPUT:  AVERAGE    THE SUM OF GRADES DIVIDED BY N        *)
(*                                                              *)
(*****************************************************************)
PROGRAM AVRAGE(OUTPUT);
VAR GRADE,SUM,AVERAGE: REAL;N,COUNTER:INTEGER;
BEGIN
WRITELN('ENTER NUMBER OF GRADES');
WRITELN;
RESET(INPUT);
READ(N);
SUM := 0;
WRITELN('ENTER GRADES...');WRITELN;
FOR COUNTER := 1 TO N DO
   BEGIN
    READLN;
    READ(GRADE);
    SUM := SUM + GRADE;
   END;
AVERAGE := SUM/N;
WRITELN('FOR', N,  '  GRADES, THE AVERAGE IS',AVERAGE);
END.
```

FIGURE 14.10
Pascal Program to Sum Quiz Scores and Print Out Average

report to be generated. The RPG compiler itself then generates the program and logic to produce the report you request. The algebralike programming we have seen in other languages simply does not exist in RPG.

RPG programs contain four different kinds of specifications: input specifications, file-description specifications, calculation specifications, and output specifications (see Figure 14.11a). Since every RPG program does

RPG programs define input, file, and output specifications that are used to generate reports.

Photos courtesy Grumman Data Systems Corporation

the same basic thing, the same kinds of information have to be supplied for any program. Figure 14.11b shows an RPG program to calculate averages.

The advantage of RPG is that it does superbly what it was designed to do: generate reports. The completeness of its program specifications reduces the opportunity for errors. In addition, RPG has copy commands and the ability to call subprograms written in different languages. Although RPG is an efficient report-generating language, a general-purpose language such as COBOL is usually used when complex programming logic is involved.

FIGURE 14.11a File Description Specifications

FILE DESCRIPTION SPECIFICATIONS

Line	Form Type	Filename	I/O/U/C/D	P/S/C/R/T/D	E	A/D — F/V	Block Length	Record Length	L/R	A/K/I	I/D/T or 19	Key Field Starting Location	Extension Code E/L	Device	Symbolic Device	Lables (S, N, or E)
3 4 5	6	7 8 9 10 11 12 13 14	15	16	17	18 19	20 21 22 23	24 25 26 27	28	29 30	31	32 33 34 36 36 37 38	39	40 41 42 43 44 45 46	47 48 49 50 51 52	53
0 2	F															
0 3	F															
0 4	F															

File Type
File Designation
End of File
Sequence
File Format

Mode of Processing
Length of Key Field or of Record Address Field
Record Address Type
Type of File Organization or Additional Area
Overflow Indicator

```
01010H
01020H***********************************************************
01030H*                                                         *
01040H*    THIS PROGRAMS READS A SERIES OF QUIZ SCORES AND       *
01050H*         CALCULATES THE AVERAGE TO BE PRINTED             *
01060H*                                                         *
01070H***********************************************************
01080FINPUT-F IP  F      80              WORKSTN
01090FOUTPUT-FO   F      132             PRINTERSYSLST
02010IINPUT-F AA  99
02020I                                        1   25 NAME
02030I                                       26   30 SCORE
03010C          TOTAL    ADD  SCORE      TOTAL    90
03020C          NUM      ADD  1          NUM      40
03030CLR        TOTAL    DIV  NUM        AVE      42
0401000UTPUT-FH  201   1P
040200     OR          OF
040300                          UDATE Y    9
040400                                     30 'GRADE AVERAGES'
040500                                     38 'PAGE '
040600                          PAGE       42
040700     T   1    LR
040800                          TOTAL Z    10
040900                          NUM   Z    15
041000                          AVE   Z    20
041100     T   1    LR
041200                                     30 'END OF REPORT'
```

FIGURE 14.11b
A Sample RPG Program

Fourth-Generation Languages

Fourth-generation languages are languages that are on a level above high-level languages, and thus even nearer to the user. They can also be called "very high-level languages." Since much software "insulates" or lies between a person using a fourth-generation language and the machine, it hardly seems like a programming language at all. Users might actually feel as if they are "talking" to a computer.

Fourth-generation languages are *nonprocedural*. In the procedural languages such as COBOL, FORTRAN, BASIC, PL/I, or Pascal, you specify to the computer *how* something is to be done. With a nonprocedural language, you don't tell the computer how to do something, just *what* to do. If you want a report, you don't instruct the computer how to produce it, you just specify what report you want. RPG, as we saw, was an early example of this kind of language. There is no need to tell RPG that you want a report—it already knows that. You just tell it what kind.

A second characteristic of fourth-generation languages is that they are generally linked to a data base. (In fact, the terms *fourth-generation language* and *data base language* are sometimes used interchangeably.) This is significant. Being linked to a data base gives users access to predefined data. Someone else (or you at an earlier time) has already set up the data, which frees you from doing so when defining your application.

Improving Application Development Productivity Without Programming

Many organizations have begun to use fourth-generation tools, data base management systems, and software packages to improve application development productivity. Fourth-generation languages, or 4GLs, are nonprocedural languages that can be used to make queries and to generate reports from existing data bases. Fourth-generation tools support a prototyping approach, in which a systems analyst works with a user to generate a model of a system and then modifies and enhances the system until a version that meets the user's requirements is achieved. Another method of improving application development productivity is to purchase software packages instead of coding programs from scratch. Software packages can be modified to meet the user's needs, but if over 50 percent of a package has to be modified, the system should probably be developed in-house.

The use of fourth-generation tools, prototyping, and software packages makes it possible to develop information systems without programming. The following case studies provide some insight into how these tools are being used.

Morgan Stanley. At Morgan Stanley, an investment bank, a 4GL named NATURAL and a data base management system called ADABAS combine to build major transactions systems as well as to generate quick reports from databases. NATURAL was used to reduce the backlog of systems that were needed to make money for the firm. When existing programmers resisted the change from traditional methods, the firm began recruiting non-MIS graduates who were willing to learn to use the new tools. As a result, productivity increased and old-fashioned documentation techniques were no longer required.

Environmental Research Lab of the National Oceanic and Atmospheric Administration. At the Environmental Research Lab prototyping was used to develop a property accounting system to keep track of the National Oceanic and Atmospheric Administration's (NOAA's) inventory of scientific instruments and equipment. Under pressure by the General Accounting Office to develop a new system with 31 different reports, the Environmental Research Lab used a 4GL, Control Data's Information Management facility, and an information analysis methodology combining prototyping and data modeling. End-user involvement helped to identify problems up front and made it possible to make changes before implementing the system.

Pratt Institute. At Pratt Institute, a private college, a 4GL called LINC was used to design and implement several on-line college administrative systems. With the help of LINC, a prototyping approach was used to involve the users directly in specifying system requirements. A report generator called LIRC was used to speed the development of most of the reporting programs.

These case studies illustrate that a prototyping methodology and fourth-generation tools can be used to involve users in specifying their requirements and to speed development. By automating many of the coding and maintenance tasks of the past, these tools make it possible for analysts to spend more time working with users. As a result, systems can be built more quickly and can last longer because changes and enhancements are less likely. Using the prototyping approach requires the programmer/analyst to have communications skills as well as technical skills.

Source: Jesse Green, "Productivity in the Fourth Generation: Six Case Studies," *Journal of Management Information Systems*, Winter 1984–85, pp. 49–63.

There are three different kinds of fourth-generation software:

1. Data base query languages
2. Report generators
3. Application generators

We will discuss each of these groups in turn.

Data Base Query Languages

Simple **data base query languages** make it possible for a record stored in a data base to be displayed or printed out in response to a query. Complex query languages are designed in such a way that the user can ask questions about multiple records using commands very similar to written English. For instance, a user might enter on a terminal the following query:

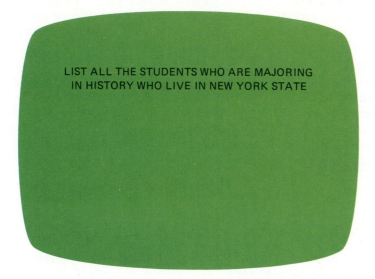

LIST ALL THE STUDENTS WHO ARE MAJORING
IN HISTORY WHO LIVE IN NEW YORK STATE

This query causes the system to search its data base using two different search fields: state (or zip code) and major. Queries that are even more complex than this can be made to existing data bases, giving users access to much valuable information on demand.

Report Generators

If you can imagine RPG with access to a data base system, you understand the fourth-generation **report generators.** They make it possible to extract data from a data base and create the kind of report from this data that a user requests. There are a number of report generators, and the better ones not only extract data and print it out but also allow some calculations to be performed on the data.

Some report generators act in combination with a data base query language. This enables an end user such as a manager to make a query and

then, based on the displayed response (which might, for instance, indicate an alarming situation), request a report on the matter. All of this could be done with no knowledge of programming beyond the conventions of the data base query language and report generator.

Application Generators

Some software is available to enable a programmer to generate an application program by providing additional functions such as editing input, specifying program logic, and creating output formats. Creating a complex application program requires some individualized programming even with an **application generator;** but automatic generation of routine functions can save a lot of time in application development.

As with all of the fourth-generation software, fourth-generation languages are at a very high level. With these languages, "programming" may be done by an end user who has little or no knowledge of programming. One statement in such a language can do the work of twenty or more statements in a high-level language such as COBOL.

How is this possible? Recall that a compiler translates a COBOL program into machine language. In this way each COBOL statement generates a number of machine-language statements. A fourth-generation language can, in the same way, generate a number of COBOL statements. Or it can skip the intermediate high-level language routine and generate machine-language instructions directly. The advantage of using a fourth-generation language is that programming can be done much faster, saving time and money.

A Closer Look at a Fourth-Generation Language

For a better understanding of what a fourth-generation language can do, we will take a closer look at one.

Query by Example   One currently available data base query language is IBM's Query by Example. Let's see how it compares to the COBOL program that produced the report shown in Figure 14.12. This report lists patients in a number of hospitals who are in quarantine wards and who have also had another hospital stay within the preceding year.

The COBOL program for this application is quite lengthy—364 lines of code (too lengthy to reproduce here). Its creation took a substantial amount of time for an experienced COBOL programmer.

Using Query by Example, an end user rather than programmer easily produced the same report. Query by Example takes about half a day to learn. Once learned, an end user can produce the report in about ten minutes. The user requests "skeletons" of records for the different files containing the pertinent information. In response, the computer produces a display such as that in Figure 14.13. The user then proceeds to "fill in" the skeleton by, for instance, entering QUARANTINE under WARD TYPE in the WARD skeleton. This specifies that only patients in quarantine are of

PREVIOUS STAY REPORT

PAGE 1

HOSPITAL NAME   HOSPITAL ADDRESS   HOSP PHONE

MAC NEAL   1234 MAIN STREET, CHICAGO, IL   3125554376

WARD NO	TOT ROOMS	TOT BEDS	BEDS AVAIL	WARD TYPE
01	34	112	018	QUARANTINE

PATIENT NAME	BED	ADMIT DATE	PREV DATE	PREVIOUS HOSPITAL	PREVIOUS REASON
O'HARA	0050	062377	1176	MAC NEAL	BUBONIC PLAGUE
OZIER	0051	052177	1176	ST JOSEPH	BUBONIC PLAGUE
PARELLA	0056	052777	1076	MAC NEAL	BUBONIC PLAGUE
WRIGHT	0057	052677	1176	MAC NEAL	BUBONIC PLAGUE
YANCEY	0058	052977	0976	RIVEREDGE	BUBONIC PLAGUE
ERIN	0059	051277	1176	MAC NEAL	BUBONIC PLAGUE
KAPP	0060	061777	1076	MAC NEAL	BUBONIC PLAGUE
CLAPPER	0070	071877	1176	MAC NEAL	BUBONIC PLAGUE
LEBEN	0071	080177	1076	ST JOSEPH	BUBONIC PLAGUE
CAROL	0072	080177	1176	MAC NEAL	BUBONIC PLAGUE
JOE	0074	071777	1076	RIVEREDGE	BUBONIC PLAGUE
KATIE	0077	080177	1176	MAC NEAL	BUBONIC PLAGUE
PAT	0078	072677	1076	ST JOSEPH	BUBONIC PLAGUE
LANOU	0079	072677	1076	MAC NEAL	BUBONIC PLAGUE
ELLGLASS	0080	072277	1176	MAC NEAL	BUBONIC PLAGUE
CARLSON	0082	072177	1176	MAC NEAL	BUBONIC PLAGUE
BUHL	0090	072477	1076	MAC NEAL	BUBONIC PLAGUE

FIGURE 14.12

A Sample Page from a Report Produced by a COBOL Program

Source: James Martin, *Application Development Without Programmers* (Englewood Cliffs, NJ: Prentice-Hall, Inc. 1982), p. 31.

interest. Once the user has filled in the skeleton, the user presses the enter key and obtains the same report as that shown in Figure 14.12.

Using such a system requires learning its conventions, and practicing, but makes it possible for people who actually need the information—a physician or admissions manager, for example—to obtain it without the intervention of a programmer and without programming knowledge. Moreover, it is not necessary to go through a lengthy software-development process first.

Two Important Fourth-Generation Languages

C Language: A Portable Assembly Language   C language is a relatively new programming language one of the major strengths of which is its transportability. Programs written in C can be easily transferred to computers with different processors. This is critical in today's competitive software

FIGURE 14.13
A Query-by-Example Screen Display
By calling up "skeletons" of the records HOSPITAL, WARD, and PATIENT, the user can enter all categories of interest within the spaces and receive a report. Thus, to get the report shown in Figure 14.11b, all the user needs to do is to indicate the items desired, such as BED, ADMIT. DATE, PREV. DATE, and so on.

Source: James Martin, *Application Development Without Programmers* (Englewood Cliffs, NJ: Prentice-Hall, Inc. 1982), p. 36.

HOSPITAL	HOSPITAL NAME	HOSPITAL ADDRESS	HOSPITAL PHONE

WARD	HOSPITAL NAME	WARD NO.	TOTAL ROOMS	TOTAL BEDS	BEDS AVAIL.	WARD TYPE

PATIENT	PATIENT NAME	HOS- PITAL NAME	WARD NO.	BED	ADMIT. DATE	PREV. DATE	PREV. HOS- PITAL	PREV. REASON

industry, which requires programs (including application software) to be adaptable to three or four of the leading microprocessors.

C language has some of the characteristics of assembly language and some of the characteristics of a high-level language. Its high-level language characteristics include program organization based upon functional modules that can be called by name, and use of control structures such as IF, ELSE, and WHILE. Its use of flexible program and variable names makes C programs easy to design, read, and debug. In addition, like assembly language, C provides dozens of low-level operations that correspond to the

Program Translator

The variety of available computer languages can present almost as many communication problems as the large number of human languages. Just as people who speak only Chinese can't say much to people who speak only Dutch, neither can computers that run on Cobol do much with software written in Pascal. When the Pentagon announced in 1983 that all Defense Department software must be written in the new language Ada, it meant that the many companies who do business with the Pentagon would have to switch all their programs to Ada. At the time, Pentagon estimates stated that by the year 1990 they would be spending $11 billion per year on Ada software.

Changing software from one language to another was, until recently, tedious and time-consuming. Programmers had to look at each line of software in one language and then translate it into another. This process is also expensive. It can cost between three and ten dollars per line of translation. Software manufacturers have seen a need here for a new kind of product. A few have developed programs that translate programs in one language, say Basic, into another, like Fortran. But one company, Pittsburgh's Lexeme Corp., seems to be a step or two ahead of the others. Lexeme's product can translate any of eight programming languages into any of three others. Programming languages including Fortran, Cobol, Basic, and Pascal can be

machine language operations of various microprocessors. This mix of assets makes it possible for C programs to be transported to new computers with 80 percent or more of the original code unchanged. Because C is highly structured, routines and subroutines that are frequently used can be stored in standard libraries and can just be inserted, or "plugged in" when needed, to other C programs. Many of the input/output functions that vary between different computers are already available in these libraries and can be easily borrowed when other programs that are being developed need them.

The eventual standardization of C will ensure compatability among various operating systems and compilers written in C. The flexibility and transportability of software written in C during the 1980s will virtually assure that it will have a predominant role in software development and systems programming.

Ada: The Defensive Language   Ada is a programming language originally commissioned in 1974 by the Department of Defense (DOD) for use on military projects, and ten years later adopted by the DOD as *the* standard language for all their major programming projects.

One characteristic that sets Ada apart from other languages is a concept called a "package." A package enables a user to define a structure, such as a matrix, that was not originally a part of the language. A programmer, using Ada, can define what a matrix is and what it does, and use the structure without making any changes in the compiler (the element of the computer systems that translates programming instructions into machine language). This characteristic, combined with the modular structure of the language, means that Ada can be used over and over again in a variety of specialized applications with only minor modifications, and without needing new compilers.

automatically translated into Ada, for example, using Lexeme's new software. The cost can be as low as ten to twenty-five cents per line if users license the software to do the work themselves and fifty cents to two dollars if the company does it for them. The time it takes for the Lexeme software to translate a program can be as little as one one-hundredth the time it would take to do the job manually.

The way Lexeme's product works is to break down a language into its smallest units, called lexemes, from which the company takes its name. These are used to build a parse tree, or diagram, of the information, which is then converted to an intermediate language. From this intermediate translation, the software converts the information once more, this time into the final language.

Lowering the price of software translation, Lexeme Corp. founder Michael Shamos believes, will open an enormous market for potential business. Programs in older languages become worth salvaging, users may feel, if the cost is low enough. And for companies dealing with a new standard language, such as the Pentagon's Ada, software like Lexeme's may become indispensible.

Sources: Edward C. Baig, "Bilingual Software," *Fortune*, July 21, 1986, p. 74; "A Berlitz Course in the Pentagon's Computer Language," *Businessweek*, November 4, 1985, p. 107.

Intellect

Natural-language processing systems are like expert systems because they are used to interpret the meaning of English-like sentences. Like other expert systems they contain rules (e.g. rules about grammar) and facts (e.g. a dictonary of words and their meanings).

Using INTELLECT, a natural language processing system, the user can type in an English-language query such as "Give me the names of students who are majoring in geology." The system will analyze the sentence structure, determine the meanings of words, and retrieve the desired information. If ambiguities occur, the system can explain the problem and ask the user for clarification. For example, if the user asks "Give me the names of stock brokers in New York," the system may respond: "Is New York a city or a state?"

INTELLECT is being used by managers in business and industry. At Pet, Inc., marketing managers can analyze sales trends using INTELLECT. Home Owners Warranty, an organization that provides a warranty program for home builders, has set up a data base listing builders, disputes, claims, and regional offices. INTELLECT is used to make queries such as "How many builders in New Jersey have open claims?" The ease of learning to use and of using a natural language processing system will enable many managers to use such systems on a day-to-day basis.

Source: "Database System Understands English," *High Technology*, April 1987, p. 27.

Portability, the result of standardization, was seen as Ada's second major strength. The Department of Defense set up a series of stringent tests that involved running over 2,000 Ada programs. It used these tests to validate Ada compilers and hoped thereby to produce such a degree of standardization that, at least in theory, any Ada program could run on any Ada compiler. The reality, however, has turned out to be somewhat different, as the Focus section in this chapter explains.

User-Driven Computing

As we have seen in our excursion through computer languages, the development of each successively higher level of language made it possible to produce application programs more quickly and with less knowledge of machine details. For most applications this is desirable because of the time and money it saves and the greater access to computers that it allows.

In particular, fourth-generation languages can increase the productivity of individual users. They can also end the domination of users by specialists. Because application generators and report generators make it possible for users to create their own programs, we are able to talk about user-driven computing. Now, program changes can be made by the user as needed. When a user had to request a program or program modification from a programmer, there was a long wait before the first output from that program was in hand. Now users can have the information they need more quickly, and presumably improve the operation for which they need the information in the first place.

Computer professionals are still needed, of course. They can help users become more productive by:

- Developing ever-more-user-friendly application generation software.
- Developing training techniques and documentation that motivates the user, provides hands-on experience, and eliminates jargon and mystique.
- Dividing training into distinct stages so that users learn simple functions first and—encouraged by results and success—gradually move on to more complex ones.
- Creating information centers to solve users' problems, motivating them to learn to use the new tools at their disposal, and following through to see that the tools are used efficiently and that user objectives are met.

On the Battlefield of the Future It Would Undoubtedly Help if the Computers Could All Talk to One Another.

Name, Rank, and Computer Log-on

Outgunned and outmanned by a militaristic Soviet Union, the Pentagon for years has pursued a strategy of counting on technology to help it overcome what would otherwise be the crushing weight of that country in a major conventional war. But the strategy has lately run into an obstacle any computer nerd can appreciate—getting the computers that are now integral to everything from the M-1 tank to the F-16 fighter to communicate effectively with one another, as well as with "command control" centers far removed from the battlefield.

At the heart of the problem is the so-called Ada computer language, named after Lord Byron's daughter, programmer of Charles Babbage's analytical engine, thought to be the first digital computer.

First proposed by Defense Department planners in the early 1970s, Ada was to be the operative electronic language for all computerized military operations in the 1990s and beyond. Its mission is to reduce the burgeoning costs of developing and maintaining separate and often incompatible computer software languages in individual weapons systems, an undertaking that currently costs more than $3 billion annually.

Yet after a decade of effort involving 27 different contractors and a reported $1 billion in taxpayer treasure, Ada has become an electronic tower of babble. One reason is that the Defense Department never provided complete performance specifications to the contractors.

Planners wanted a language that would, among other things, be smart enough to recognize errors being input by everyone from programmers to battlefield users, be compact enough to be stored on memory devices a foot soldier might backpack into battle and be ready to use by the early 1990s. Such basic decisions as how data would be structured, stored and manipulated were never specified.

William Suydam, editor of the *Ada-Data* newsletter, likens the problem to trying to build a house without a blueprint. Says he, "Someone has to decide on standards. Leaving it to the contractors means inviting everyone to solve problems his own way. Thus, you get a lot of different solutions."

In fact, although Ada was supposed to serve as a single, all-embracing language for global warfare, there are already at least five ways of implementing it. Complains David Quigley, Ada product manager for Digital Equipment

Corp., "We took Ada real seriously and built a product that the government apparently doesn't need. Now we have to recoup that investment some other way."

Undoubtedly the military could benefit from an all-purpose language. Glitches in the welter of more than 70 different—and often incompatible—computer tongues the military currently uses regularly produce major and costly foul-ups. One reason it costs $250 million annually (three times the originally projected cost) to maintain and upgrade the software for the F-16 is that some of the planes use different versions of a language while the ground-control computers for the planes use yet another.

In some instances, lives can be at risk. During the 1983 Grenada invasion, the radios of Naval commandos could not communicate with those of Army Rangers because the transmissions had to be relayed through incompatible computer-controlled shipboard facilities. In one memorable instance, an Army lieutenant attempted to report potential ground targets to Air Force bombers overhead but was not able to get through on his radio. Finally, he was forced to run to a pay phone and use his personal AT&T credit card to telephone the target coordinates into Fort Bragg, N.C., some 1,500 miles away.

Though Ada's present state of development is not encouraging, the Pentagon is pressing ahead with a plan to have soldiers in the trenches begin using laptop computers in battle as early as 1991. For what purpose? According to the Army, one man in each infantry platoon, a so-called forward observer, would send data about the condition of the battlefield and the location of the enemy up the ranks to the company and battalion levels. There, powerful minicomputers would quickly digest the data and evaluate scenarios for troop movements and artillery targets. Battlefield commanders would theoretically be able to make sounder tactical decisions more rapidly.

This is a preposterous idea on its face, maintains a former military commander, now retired to a West Coast defense contracting firm. "Lap-top computers are almost useless in battle. The first thing that happens is you become overwhelmed with fear. War is full of signals, sounds and information. The last thing you need is even more information."

Nonetheless, the military is forging ahead. The Defense Department spent an estimated $10 billion last year on computerized battle systems and is likely to continue such spending, Ada or no Ada. Yet, unless the Pentagon gets a firmer grasp on the project quickly, the day may not be far off when America marches off to war armed with keyboards, terminals and floppy disks—and nothing much to do with the gadgets except throw them at the enemy.

Source: Kathleen Healy, "Science & Technology," *Forbes*, April 20, 1987, pp. 87. 90.

Summary and Key Terms

1. Computers operate using **machine language**—binary strings of 0s and 1s—and programming can be done in machine language as well. This is, however, time-consuming, difficult to modify, and machine specific.

2. **Assembly language** improves on machine language by substituting mnemonic codes and symbols for the binary numbers of machine language, while retaining the command of the computer that machine language offers. It is subject to the same drawbacks, although to a slightly lesser degree. Instructions in assembly language can be translated into machine language by a program called an **assembler.**

3. **High-level languages** move nearer to the programmer and farther away from the workings of the machine. A program written in a high-level language, called the **source program,** must be translated into the computer's machine language, called the **object program;** this is done by a **compiler** or by an **interpreter.** Programs in a high-level language are not time-consuming to code; modification is fairly easy; and a program written for one computer can generally be run on another.

4. High-level computer languages share different **statement** functions: statements to describe variables, input/output statements, control statements, arithmetic statements, and termination statements.

5. **BASIC** is a high-level language supplied with most microcomputers and small business computers. It is easy to learn and use, but not appropriate for sophisticated computer applications.

6. **FORTRAN,** the first high-level language to become widely available, is suited to scientific and engineering applications but not commercial applications.

7. The opposite can be said of **COBOL,** the most widely used business language. COBOL is well-suited to commercial applications.

8. **PL/I** incorporates features of both FORTRAN and COBOL, and is suitable for any application. Moreover, it lends itself to structured programming.

9. **Pascal,** an elegant scientific language also consistent with structured programming principles, was developed for teaching purposes. It has not yet been widely used in business applications.

10. **APL** is a popular programming language with considerable power that is basically used for scientific applications on mainframe computers.

11. **RPG** is a high-level language that generates reports without describing program logic; it was an early forerunner of fourth-generation languages.

12. The **fourth-generation languages** include **data base query languages, report generators,** and **application generators.** The fourth-generation language is called "very high level" because it enables users to obtain information or to create applications or reports with little or no knowledge of programming. **ADA** and **C** are both fourth-generation languages.

13. **User-driven computing** means that, with fourth-generation application generators and report generators, users can create their own programs and reports, ending their dependence on programmers and speeding up the application-development process.

Review Questions

Fill-in

1. The most fundamental programming language, consisting of binary digits, is called _____.

2. A _____ translates programming-language instructions into machine-language instructions and executes each instruction—one at a time.

3. A program that has not been translated yet into machine language is known as a _____ program.

4. Two factors to be taken into consideration in selecting a programming language are _____ and _____.

5. A tool that enables a manager to extract data from existing data bases in response to queries is called a _____.

Multiple Choice Questions

_____ 1. A language best suited to solving problems in science, engineering, and mathematics.
   a. BASIC
   b. FORTRAN
   c. RPG
   d. COBOL

_____ 2. The language that was developed at Dartmouth College to teach students how to program.
   a. BASIC
   b. FORTRAN
   c. PL/I
   d. RPG

_____ 3. In this language, the DO statement is used to create a loop, or repetition of statements within the program.
   a. BASIC
   b. FORTRAN
   c. COBOL
   d. APL

_____ 4. Programs written in this language are organized into four sections.
   a. BASIC
   b. FORTRAN
   c. COBOL
   d. APL

_____ 5. The first standarized programming language, which was developed primarily to support business applications.
   a. BASIC
   b. FORTRAN
   c. COBOL
   d. RPG

_____ 6. The language developed by IBM for mainframe computers that can be used for both scientific and business applications:
   a. BASIC
   b. FORTRAN
   c. PL/I
   d. COBOL

_____ 7. Commonly used structured-programming language that is widely used in computer-science courses.
   a. BASIC
   b. FORTRAN
   c. PL/I
   d. Pascal

_____ 8. A language that was a precursor to today's fourth generation-languages and is useful in reading data files and in producing reports.
   a. BASIC
   b. COBOL
   c. RPG
   d. Pascal

____ 9. An interactive language that is easy to learn and is similar to using a calculator.
   a. BASIC
   b. Pascal
   c. APL
   d. RPG

____ 10. The type of fourth-generation languages that enables the user to edit input data, perform calculations, and format output data, much in the same way as in traditional programming.
   a. data base query language
   b. report generator
   c. application generator

Discussion Questions

1. Identify the programming language we have studied that would be most appropriate for each of the following applications, and give the reasons for your choice:
   a. Calculating salesmen's commissions, using a microcomputer.
   b. Extracting data records of all students with over a 3.5 average and majoring in Spanish from an existing data base.
   c. Performing a statistical analysis to determine the relationship between age, socioeconomic status, educational background, and achievement motivation.
   d. Updating an accounts-receivable file to reflect payments to these accounts.
   e. Learning to use structured concepts in a programming class in school.
   f. Generating reports from existing data records along with creating the necessary programming documentation for these reports.

2. What do you feel were some of the underlying factors in creating a standarized language like COBOL? Why was it important that a standardized language be developed?

3. Fourth-generation languages have made it possible for users to obtain access to data in existing data bases and to generate reports using these data on demand, rather than waiting for a programmer to program these applications. What do you feel will be the impact of these fourth-generation languages on a traditional business-application programming language like COBOL?

Management Information Systems

15

Chapter Objectives

After studying this chapter, you should be able to

1. Understand the frameworks for information systems, including operational, control, and planning systems.

2. Recognize how an organization defines its information needs and designs computer-based information systems to meet these needs.

3. Describe how individual managers can determine their own information needs using critical success factors.

4. Describe the characteristics of centralized, decentralized, and distributed data processing.

5. Understand the characteristics of end-user computing and its organization and management.

Robert McDowell, vice-president of production and operations for Consolidated Foods, is responsible for recommending target inventory levels for each of the products that Consolidated Foods manufactures and distributes to its branch warehouses. The firm manufactures over 200 lines of food products in four plants and transports finished goods to its eight regional warehouses.

The "right" inventories of food products need to be distributed to the various branch warehouses in order to minimize excess inventories and transportation costs. For example, if large inventories of Uncle Carl's Taco Sauce are shipped to the Southeastern branch warehouse and much of the demand for this product is in the Midwest, inventory will have to be transported to Midwestern stores at considerably greater transportation expense than would be involved if the Midwestern branch warehouse had sufficient stock of taco sauce to accommodate demand in the Midwest.

Currently, Robert receives a monthly report listing inventory data for each of the branch warehouses, including the quantity on hand for each inventory item in each warehouse. Although this report helps him identify where excess inventories exist, it does not assist him in planning for future inventory requirements in various regions.

Robert McDowell has looked to the information systems department for help in obtaining information on sales history for various product lines in various regions. With this information, he feels, he can develop a sales forecast for each product line and estimate the target ending inventory

413

levels that need to be maintained in each warehouse to meet demand on a monthly basis. He has heard about "decision support systems," microcomputers, and other technologies that help the manager obtain and analyze the information needed to make decisions.

In this chapter, you will learn about the information systems that have been designed to help managers obtain information to manage day-to-day operations, to control resources, and to develop business plans. You will learn how MIS professionals and users work together to identify the application development projects that can provide useful information for managers throughout the business.

What Is a Management Information System?

A management information system, or MIS, is an integrated human- and computer-based process for providing all of the information needed to support the activities, management, and decision making of an organization. This definition emphasizes that information is needed by the organization to support specific functions and that data can be collected and organized in different ways to meet those needs. The information provided by an MIS is used to plan, operate, and control all of the organization's activities.

A corporate management information system is the sum of several individual information systems, each devoted to a specific business function. Thus, there are management information systems that serve marketing, manufacturing, accounting, shipping, and so on. But in order to understand how management information systems work, we first need to understand some basic facts that are common to most organizations.

Frameworks for Information Systems

The Activities of an Organization

The levels of activities of an organization are of three kinds: operations, control, and strategic planning (see Figure 15.1). *Operations* are the day-to-day activities of the firm. In the course of its operational activities the firm acquires and consumes various resources: land, labor, capital, and so on. Operations managers must identify, collect, and register all transactions that result from acquiring or expending these resources. These kinds of activities take place daily. Whenever a sale is made or goods are shipped, the event is recorded. These day-to-day transactions produce data that form the basis for operational systems.

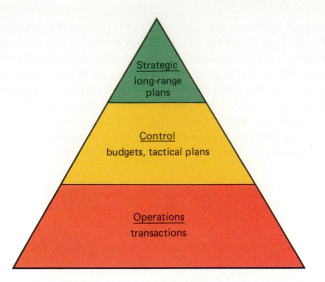

FIGURE 15.1
The Anthony Model
The Anthony Model provides
a structure for understanding
information systems and how
they are used.

The **control** function of an organization reviews operational activities to make sure that the organization is meeting its goals and not wasting its resources. The time frame for control activities may be month to month, quarter to quarter, or year to year. For example, orders of raw materials might be monitored monthly, productivity might be tallied quarterly, and department budgets reviewed annually. Problems faced by department managers at the control level, therefore, may occur within various time frames and are ongoing. Control management is also concerned about measuring performance against a plan or a standard, such as projected versus actual sales.

Strategic planning is carried out by the chief operating officers of the organization. While operational and control managers are primarily interested in reviewing internal data, planning managers are also interested in external data. They need to know such things as competing firms' activities, interest rates, consumer behavior trends, and proposed changes in governmental regulations. Problems addressed by strategic planners involve long-range analysis and prediction—a time frame of three to five years. Typically, the problems addressed at this level take from a few months to a few years to be solved.

Each of these organizational levels—operational, control, and strategic planning—will need different information systems, the subject of the next sections.

MIS Needs at the Operational Level

At the operational level the primary concern is to collect, validate, and record the data of day-to-day transactions. The operational level is also concerned with the control of errors in the input, processing, and output of these data.

These data generally describe the acquisition or expenditure of corporate resources. For instance, transactions in accounts receivable, accounts

payable, payroll, and cash receipts need to be recorded as they occur. These transactions include keeping track of accounts to receive money due, paying out what is owed to suppliers and employees, and processing orders to customers. When a sale is made, the stock inventory level for that item must be adjusted, a shipping label and packing slip must be prepared in the warehouse, and an invoice must be generated in the billing section. Thus, a single transaction, the sale of an item, in turn creates numerous transactions that need to be recorded. Every time a sale is transacted, these same kinds of data are generated.

MIS Needs at the Control Level

Transactional data must also be presented in an appropriate format so that middle managers can review and control current operations. For example, a control system can be designed to summarize (or collect) all the sales of a particular product for six months, January through June, 1989, and compare it with the sales of that product for the six months January through June, 1988. Such a summary of transaction data (data generated from original sales of tennis rackets, for example) provides information that can be used for the control and the better use of resources within the organization.

As an illustration, let's say the sales of a product (for instance, a $75 tennis racket) are down 50 percent in a six-month span in 1989 as compared with the 1988 figures. The manager will then want to study the situation to find a way to increase sales. Perhaps he interprets the decline in sales as due to decreased interest in tennis. He might then decide to concentrate the efforts of the sales force on other sports products, as shown by more current trends in sports interests. Or he may interpret the figures as a reflection of competitors' success with the introduction of large-face rackets. As a result, he may encourage the product development department to come up with a marketable line of large-face rackets. Or he may conclude that in some regions the sales force is selling tennis rackets below quota and that both training and support of regional product managers should be stepped up.

Another example shows a slightly different use of the same data: The sales manager reviews sales analysis figures for 1989 as compared with 1988. He finds that sales of tennis rackets (product line) to large department store accounts (customer) within Southern California (geographic region) are up 24 percent. However, sales to specialty stores in this same region are down 50 percent. He may conclude from this that more customers are buying sporting goods at department stores and that the sales reps handling large accounts should try to expand sporting goods sales to department stores. On the other hand, from this same information the sales manager could conclude that the marketing department is failing to place its products in the sporting goods specialty stores. Our sales manager may then plan some specific strategies to gain marketing success in these segments of the marketplace.

Our national sales manager needs an information system that summarizes sales by product line, by salesperson, by customer and customer type, and by geographic region to manage the sales organization more effectively.

Transactional data obtained from this bicycle shop (such as sales figures for a six-month period) can be used by bicycle manufacturers to predict sales trends for the coming year.

Courtesy of Hewlett-Packard

This is how he can learn of trends that reflect changes in consumer behavior, in sales reps' performance, and in product success. The sales manager will want to focus on products that enjoy considerable success in the marketplace, and at the same time minimize losses due to continued promotion of products with declining sales.

Also, the sales manager will want to identify those customers whose interest is waning, or where sales-force strategies have not been effective. Training and improved management of the selling staff may renew some of these accounts.

Finally, the sales manager needs to be sensitive to regional and geographic trends. A product that is "hot" in the Midwest may be "cold" in another region.

All these types of information come from summarized data created in day-to-day transactions. The sales manager depends upon this summarized information to make decisions: how to allocate the time and energies of the sales force, what products to push and what products to withdraw from the market, what customer accounts demand immediate attention, and which salespersons need training and support. In this way, information is used for effective control of organizational resources toward the achievement of organizational goals.

Control also involves setting a standard for performance, measuring performance, comparing performance to the standard, and taking corrective action. For example, a control system may be designed to compare projected versus actual sales for tennis rackets, both on a monthly and on a yearly basis. A report could be designed to compare projected versus actual sales for certain types of rackets to certain types of customers (department store versus specialty store) and by certain salespersons. This information could be used by sales managers to identify problems, to take corrective action, and to allocate existing resources more effectively.

MIS Needs at the Strategic-Planning Level

The third type of information system is designed for strategic management. The real purpose of strategic planning is to devise effective strategies for accomplishing the organization's goals. Senior managers need to identify new promotion and advertising strategies, come up with ideas for new products, and develop plans for business expansion.

Information needed at this level may include data about the industry, competitors, governmental regulations, and data on the constituencies that the firm serves (customers, labor pool, investors). Much of this information comes from sources outside the firm. New product development ideas, for example, may come from demographic data identifying new population trends. Suppose projections suggest that women's participation in tennis will grow from 50 to 70 percent of the total number of adults who participate in the sport. A sporting-goods manufacturer might then see a growing market and decide to expand the line of light-weight tennis rackets to meet anticipated demand. New product lines may also come from actions being taken by competitors or from opportunities to pursue an entirely new market segment.

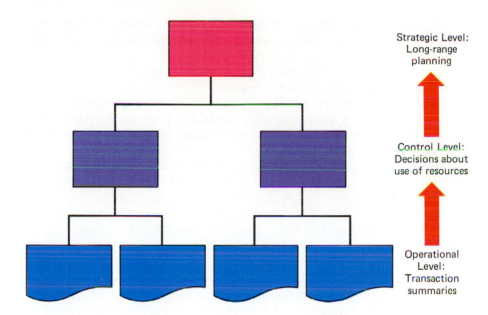

Strategic Level:
Long-range
planning

Control Level:
Decisions about
use of resources

Operational
Level:
Transaction
summaries

FIGURE 15.2
The Levels of Activities of
an Organization

Sequence of Development for MIS

Now that we have examined the ways in which information is used in an
organization, we can refine our definitions of data and information. Data are
the individual elements in a transaction. In a sales order, for example, the
data elements are: customer, quantity, price, and so on. Information, on the
other hand, is data that have been summarized or arranged in some way so
that management can use them for decision making. Thus, transaction data
are collected at the operational level to provide information to both the
control and strategic-planning systems. In turn, these higher-level systems
generate further information. When we speak of an integrated management
information system, we speak of those control and planning systems that
provide information for decision making on more than one level of
management (see Figure 15.2).

How Organizations Define Their Information Systems Needs

In this section we will see how companies define their own information
needs and design information systems to meet those needs. One theory that
attempts to describe this process is Richard Nolan's theory of data processing development. It describes the stages through which organizations
generally progress as they use computer technology and develop computer-
based information systems. Then we will learn about a formal planning
methodology that helps users and information managers define their infor-

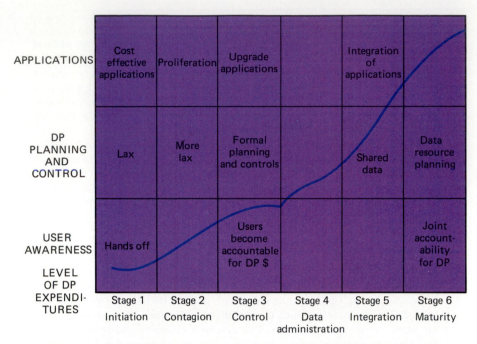

FIGURE 15.3
Nolan's Stage Theory

Adapted from Richard L. Nolan, "Managing the Crises in Data Processing," *Harvard Business Review*, March-April 1979, p. 117.

mation requirements and the application development priorities of the organization. Finally, we will learn about the role of a systems development methodology in the development of computer-based information systems and the responsibilities of those who manage the organization's computing resources. The corporate Management Information Systems plan spells out the portfolio of application projects and technology resources that will meet the needs of the firm.

Nolan's Stage Theory of Data Processing Development

Richard Nolan and Chuck Gibson were the first to identify the stages through which a firm moves as it begins and expands its use of computer-based technology. Nolan's stage theory describes the evolution of computing within an organization[1] (see Figure 15.3). According to this theory, companies go through a learning curve as computing technology evolves within the organization. The first stage is *initiation,* when firms introduce cost-effective accounting applications such as accounts payable, accounts receivable, and general ledger.

Initial success in using the computer to automate accounting operations leads to stage two, *contagion.* In this stage a number of computer-based information systems are enthusiastically introduced in rapid succession. Little attention is given to costs or to whether the information systems that are being developed are absolutely necessary. People think that the computer is the solution to all kinds of problems, and many applications

[1] Richard Nolan, "Managing the Crises in Data Processing," *Harvard Business Review*, March/April 1979.

The Management Information Systems at Farm Chemicals, Incorporated

Farm Chemicals, Incorporated (FCI), is a manufacturer and marketer of farm chemicals: pesticides, herbicides, fertilizers, and so on. The company has a highly regarded research and development laboratory that has produced several new products in the last two decades that have given FCI a distinct competitive advantage in the business. FCI carries out an aggressive marketing effort to maintain contact with its customers and to carefully watch the evolution of its own products and the products of competitors.

FCI began using computers in the early 1960s, and it has a rather mature management information system. FCI uses sophisticated, state-of-the-art technology to implement its MIS. However, what we are interested in studying are the following information systems that give FCI its ability to remain competitive in an ever-changing business: research and development, marketing, and manufacturing.

Research and Development Systems

Research and development at FCI is carried out at a large laboratory in Lincoln, Nebraska. The research and development (R&D) laboratory has the responsibility for new product development, screening, FDA approval, and pilot plant design and operation. The research chemists and biologists rely heavily on information systems to scan scientific literature for the development of new chemicals. This access to up-to-date information hastens product development and saves substantial costs by minimizing any duplication of effort.

Once a product has been approved and FCI has decided to manufacture it, engineers within R&D design pilot plants. These pilot plants are used to define the manufacturing process before a new chemical goes into large-scale production. Computer-aided engineering and computer-aided design are used to define the specifications for the pilot plant and to speed the analysis of pilot plant results. Computer-aided design has sharply reduced the cost of developing new engineering specifications; this, in turn, has held down manufacturing costs once production has begun. (The research and development systems network is illustrated in Figure 15.A).

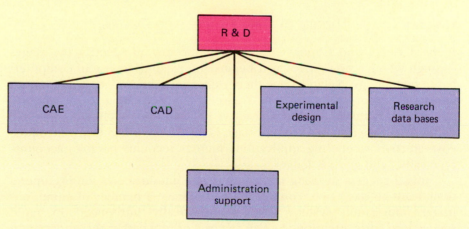

FIGURE 15.A
Research and Development
Information Systems

Marketing

FCI's market is complicated by the seasonal nature of the agricultural business and the dealer network through which products are sold to the farmer.

Dealers in general buy bulk chemicals from FCI and its competitors. Sales are made in late fall for delivery in January and February. Sales are made on the quality of the product, the perceived effectiveness of the product in local geographic areas, sales promotions, the vendor's willingness to negotiate flexible payment plans, and product support for the sales force and technical field representatives.

Obviously, marketing at FCI goes substantially beyond taking orders for chemical products. Salesmen are organized by geographic region, in order to establish long-term relationships with dealers and farmers. They need the latest information on agricultural and weather conditions and crop-planting patterns in order to serve their geographic areas effectively. The sales force, along with technical field representatives, gather local intelligence about the effectiveness of various chemicals—both those manufactured by FCI and those of competitors. They also monitor the effectiveness of various promotions. During the annual planning process, they continually meet with dealers and farmers and gather feedback for research and development and for marketing. They play the key role in supporting the product, such as investigating misapplications, product quality, and product availability.

Next to product acceptance and market surveillance, perhaps the most important role that the sales force plays is to gather information about next year's planting. Natural crop rotations, a crop's popularity, and the farmer's perception of the market for a crop a year hence—all this is important information that marketing management must use to prepare annual sales projections, which are due by August 1.

Information systems support the marketing effort across the board (see Figure 15.B). In addition to handling the actual ordering process, including the negotiation of financial arrangements that are part of the dealer relationship, data-entry systems provide information about product location and shipping dates. They also support the county-by-county reporting of chemical usage. In addition, regional management is able to monitor the sales-call patterns of individual sales representatives and redirect those patterns through counseling on a weekly basis. This has permitted regional management to make sure that the right dealers are being offered the right products at the right time. It has also permitted the sales force to understand where they need to spend the majority of their time and effort.

FIGURE 15.B
Marketing Information Systems

Manufacturing Systems

The manufacture of chemicals is a high-technology business at FCI. The latest in process control equipment allows the firm to "tune" the production of chemical products carefully. Much of this monitoring of temperatures, pressures, and flow rates is accomplished with the aid of computer-aided manufacturing (CAM) systems that permit the plant to run largely from

electronic rooms. FCI's manufacturing plants are scattered throughout the country; each plant can produce several of FCI's products. Hence it becomes a major scheduling problem to determine which plant should produce what volume of a product. Many factors go into the decision, including the efficiency of each plant, the marginal cost of shipping the raw materials to each plant, the demand for a product, the geographic region served by a plant, the cost of "setting up" a plant to produce a product, and the availability of raw materials at the plant site. This complex scheduling is accomplished with an MRP (material requirement planning) system; the MRP is an automated process for collecting and analyzing production requirements, plant capacities, and raw material costs and availability. The result of material requirement planning is an ongoing schedule of production and raw materials requirements for each plant. This is most helpful to FCI because plant management can plan ahead to have materials and people available to carry out the production required. CAM and MRP provide FCI with a competitive advantage (see Figure 15.C).

FIGURE 15.C
Manufacturing Information Systems

are developed quickly. However, by the end of stage two, the company realizes that it has lost control over data-processing costs.

In the third stage, *control,* senior management's concern over mushrooming costs leads them to force the data processing department to operate in a more cost-efficient, businesslike fashion. Formalized planning and control mechanisms are introduced. Generally, users and the data processing staff both are held accountable for the development of information systems projects. The foundation is laid for the future development of data processing systems. Formal processes are set up to identify those systems that need to be developed and to describe how these systems are to be designed. In addition, top management recognizes the need to plan MIS as an integral part of the corporation.

At stage three, time is taken to design more effective information systems. Applications that were rapidly developed during stage two often lack sufficient documentation. Structured programming methods were probably not used in their design; thus they are difficult to maintain and modify. For this reason, control and planning systems cannot be developed on the foundation of operational systems that was laid in stage two.

Thus, at stage three, it is often necessary to rebuild some operational systems (as opposed to designing new systems from scratch). When sound operational systems are in place, then it is possible to build the control and planning systems which use the transactional data that are captured and initially processed at the operational level. As you recall from the previous

section, these operational-level systems provide the data that can be collected for use in control and planning systems.

At stage three, also, new technologies are used to upgrade some systems. For example, a bank may have automated systems to handle checking and savings accounts. It is a relatively small step to add automated teller machines to provide teller services twenty-four hours a day. The next step might be to offer bank customers who have personal computers the opportunity to bank at home.

In stage three, then, companies begin to design information systems that are relevant to their business objectives. This requires a formal planning process to define the company's application requirements. As the organization develops its portfolio and applications, there is a gradual move from stage three. The transition from stage three to four involves a change from management of the computer technology to management of the data.

Generally, information systems were developed independently of one another during stages one through three. Now, beginning at stage four, there is an effort to integrate existing management information systems. This integration process uses advanced data base and communications technologies. Efforts are made to design data bases that support many applications instead of just one at a time. In this new environment the corporate MIS staff becomes responsible for managing the data resource, a function that is called data administration. At the same time, users have become aware of their own information needs. They can even begin to develop their own information systems, using desk-top computers and end-user application development tools.

In the following section we will look at enterprise analysis, a formal planning technique used to eliminate confusion in the early stages of setting up MISs in a company. In the last section we will look at some of the reasons for end users' involvement in developing their own information systems, and some of the technologies that support this development.

Enterprise Analysis

In many companies, in the early stages of system development, numerous transaction-processing systems are set up. Each of these applications requires the creation of a new file of the records needed for that particular application. Eventually dozens of applications are developed, and data on customers becomes duplicated in many files, all of which must be updated regularly.

Enterprise analysis is a formal planning technique used by managers to define the information requirements of an organization before systems are developed. This planning approach was developed to end the confusion over duplicate systems and to prevent the designing of files that store the same data. If data requirements are established during the planning phase, these data can be stored once and the logical interrelationships among these data elements identified. Using a data base management system (see Chapter 8), both programmers and users can obtain access to these data for multiple applications. However, for enterprise analysis to work, the data elements that support business requirements and shared application systems must be defined first.

This is how the approach works: A project team selects a sample of the organization's managers and interviews them to determine the major processes involved in the enterprise. During these interviews managers are given an opportunity to define the data needed to support these business processes. All of the company's activities (such as personnel management, marketing, business planning, shipping, and distribution) are reviewed.

With this information, project team members can classify the data needed to support business activities, including data on customers, orders, inventory, and facilities. Once the data classes are itemized, the team analyzes the relationships between various processes in order to determine which data classes are shared. For example, manufacturing processes such as purchase of raw materials, work in progress, scheduling, and capacity planning are all supported by the same data classes.

After the study is complete, management reviews it to set up priorities for the development of business applications. For example, should the production scheduling system or the inventory control system be developed first? The decision may depend on management's views of which system will best help the organization realize its goals within a given time.

Enterprise analysis allows a company to plan for and construct the management information system that it needs. Haphazard development and the extra costs of duplicated efforts are eliminated. This type of study gets many managers involved in defining their information needs and makes them recognize the importance of designing a well-integrated management information system.

Once these application development priorities are established, the next step is the systems development process, which involves the analysis of user requirements and the design of a computer-based information system. This process, like the planning process, requires a formal methodology that spells out activities and goals along the way. This process is known as the systems development methodology, and we will study it in the next section.

Systems Development Methodology

When the concept of an information system was first developed, the method of designing the system was left to experienced systems analysts. At that early stage, each analyst had an individual approach to the problem. Thus there was little consistency in the methods used to design systems. This led to confusion and in some cases time and cost overruns.

As applications proliferated and information needs grew, it became obvious that the data processing department would have to be reorganized. Some people began to specialize in systems design, while others concentrated on delivery of data processing and MIS services. In this section we will look at methods used in developing information systems. In the next section we will look at MIS delivery systems.

We have seen that systems development includes system analysis, system design, and system implementation. We are concerned here with the development not of individual applications, but of the system to produce information needed by the company's various managers. The definition and practice of a rigorous **systems development methodology** has been a major change in MIS development.

The need for more precise systems development methods grew out of the problems that arose when less rigorous methods were used. Errors made in the analysis and design phases of a project often were not caught until the implementation phase, when corrections had to be made at a cost many times greater than if such changes had been made earlier. Furthermore, a lack of communication with end users at the analysis and general design phases often led to the development of systems that did not meet users' needs. As a result, major modifications and enhancements had to be designed after the system was implemented, causing substantial time and cost overruns. Generally, users were frustrated with data processing and with the inability of data processing professionals to solve their problems.

These problems influenced the growth of a more precise systems development process as shown in Figure 15.4. The major activities of the systems development process are now well defined, as are management checkpoints and the "deliverables" that should result from each activity. Usually, a user's request calls attention to the opportunity being proposed for automating an activity and sets this process in motion. At the very outset, both data processing and end-user managers view the automation proposal and make a commitment to go on to the next phase—detailed analysis and design. This represents a preliminary commitment to the project based on an acquaintance with its scope, costs, and potential benefits.

During detailed systems analysis and design, the "blueprints" for the new system are drawn. These blueprints include procedures, program specifications, and design of the data base, as well as a plan for the next phase, implementation. After each phase of the project, management has an opportunity to review the quality of the effort and to see whether or not the "deliverables" of that phase meet expectations.

If the implementation plan is approved, then the actual development of the system, its programs, data bases, and procedures can begin. Program specifications and programs are designed according to a predetermined set of standards. The systems development methodology also includes maintenance. Maintenance is the ongoing effort to keep the information system up to date with new technologies, and to serve changing corporate requirements.

Finally, the system is subjected to periodic review and auditing to make sure it continues performing as desired. Feedback from this type of periodic review provides management with the opportunity to improve the system if necessary. Management must determine whether the system is creating too many reports or not enough reports; whether information requirements have changed; and whether the technology currently in use needs to be modified. The periodic review also tells the systems development staff what changes and enhancements need to be made in the future.

Systems, development professionals, including systems analysts, programmers, documentation specialists, and project managers, are responsible for the set of activities and outcomes we have just described.

The MIS Delivery System

Managing the information systems function also includes managing the MIS delivery system. The delivery system, in essence, manages the organization's computing resources. It is concerned with the kinds of computers

Technical support specialists are responsible for maintaining the hardware, software, and the operating system environment.

Courtesy Honeywell, Inc.

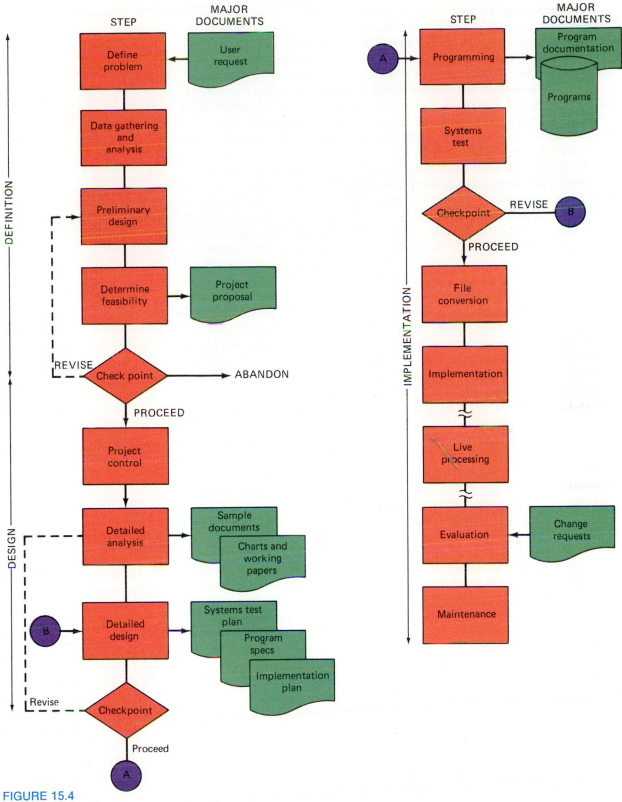

STEP   MAJOR DOCUMENTS

DEFINITION

- Define problem ← User request
- Data gathering and analysis
- Preliminary design
- Determine feasibility → Project proposal
- Check point — REVISE / ABANDON
- PROCEED
- Project control
- Detailed analysis → Sample documents / Charts and working papers

DESIGN

- Detailed design → Systems test plan / Program specs / Implementation plan
- B
- Checkpoint — Revise / Proceed
- A

STEP   MAJOR DOCUMENTS

IMPLEMENTATION

- A → Programming → Program documentation / Programs
- Systems test
- Checkpoint — REVISE → B
- PROCEED
- File conversion
- Implementation
- Live processing
- Evaluation ← Change requests
- Maintenance

FIGURE 15.4
Systems Development Methodology

and peripheral equipment used, the selection of support software for data bases and programming languages, and the design of telecommunications networks. Persons in this function are responsible for computer hardware performance and capacity planning, for data security, and for backup and recovery procedures.

The organization of data processing into systems development groups and delivery system groups has raised a major issue: Should the computing function be decentralized? Increasingly, systems development—analysis, design, and implementation of business applications—is being decentralized. This means that systems analysts and programmers are being assigned to operating groups within the organization, rather than being a centralized corporate staff group. In other words, a programmer/analyst may work within the marketing division and be responsible for developing and maintaining information systems for marketing.

The delivery system side, in contrast, generally remains centralized in a corporate data center. Fewer people are involved in delivery systems work than in application systems development, and the delivery systems individuals are more highly trained.

With the dispersal of computing throughout the firm, the question of how to charge for computing services has arisen. Traditionally, in stages one and two (initiation and contagion), corporate overhead swallows most computing-related expenses. But as stage two draws to a close and stage three (control) begins, the cost of developing systems and operating hardware is too great to be absorbed by the central corporate budget. As a result, at stage three, operating units of the firm begin paying directly for their own application development costs, as well as for their use of the computing resource.

There are two different methods of charging for computing. In one case the corporate data center acts as a break-even cost center. Its costs are allocated according to some agreed-upon plan to the operating units and charged back to them as overhead. The second approach to charging is a price delivery system services as they would be priced in a free market environment. In this situation, operating units can either pay for computing resources provided by the central corporate data center or else can spend their computing dollars externally if they find a better deal. In the latter approach, the internal computer department acts as a service bureau, and can earn a profit if the services can be delivered at a cost that beats the market.

Meeting Information Needs for Individual Managers

So far this chapter has dealt with defining the information needs of the corporation as a whole. However, individual managers may require information that is not part of the corporate information system in order to make some decisions. Individual managers need a method for defining their own information needs.

Using Intellect in Business

Everything from personnel records to billing accounts are filed away in corporate computer systems, but much of this information cannot be accessed easily without learning the computer's language. However, programs have been developed to teach the computer enough English words and grammar to understand questions being posed to computerized records. One such program is INTELLECT, produced by Artificial Intelligence Corporation. Using INTELLECT, a manager can get answers to questions such as: "How many salespersons do we have?" or "How does the average salary of women compare to that of men?"

Some queries are slightly more complex. For example, someone may ask "How many Fords do we have?" To answer, the computer must know if 'Ford' is an automobile or an employee name. If 'Ford' appears in both the employee and the auto files, then INTELLECT asks:

```
YOUR REQUEST IS AMBIGUOUS TO ME. DO YOU WANT:
1. MANUFACTURER = FORD
2. LAST NAME = FORD
PLEASE ENTER THE NUMBER OF THE INTERPRETATION
YOU INTENDED.
```

User-friendly systems can now catch mistakes and question ambiguities that would confound a traditional computer. For example, a hurried executive might accidentally request information on the RATION OF SALES TO EARNINGS. A program would come back with: DIDN'T YOU REALLY MEAN RATIO? In another case, a sales manager might tell the computer: "List all the

Critical Success Factors

A strategy to enable managers to define their information needs, using critical success factors, was developed by John Rockart.[2] In the course of his or her work, every manager uses certain indicators to tell whether or not those things that are critical to the success of the business are going successfully. A critical success factor defines what must go right for the business or manager to be successful.

In the automobile industry, for example, a critical success factor is good product styling. Without good styling, an automobile manufacturer will risk losing its competitive edge in the marketplace. In contrast, in the insurance business, the development of effective agency management personnel and creation of new types of policies spell the difference between success and failure. These are the critical success factors most relevant to the insurance business.

Once the critical success factors have been identified, measures can be defined to determine whether things are going well. These measures may be "hard" information produced by computer-based information systems, or they may be "soft" data, such as opinions from interviews. For example, an

[2]John F. Rockart, "Chief Executives Define Their Own Data Needs," *Harvard Business Review*, March/April 1979.

salesmen in LA." Artificial Intelligence Corporation's program would respond: I AM A LITTLE UNCERTAIN ABOUT WHAT YOU MEAN. I THINK YOU MEAN PRINT 'LAST NAME, FIRST NAME' OF ALL SALESMEN IN THE LOS ANGELES AREA. IS THAT CORRECT? If the manager answers yes, the computer goes ahead. If the response is no, the computer is prepared to list the salesmen in Louisiana, the other possibility.

Natural Language Programs and Microcomputers

Natural language programs are now available for microcomputers. One such program, called NaturalLink, has been released by Texas Instruments. NaturalLink allows users to access the Dow Jones News/Retrieval Service, a subscription database with information ranging from stock market prices to weather reports. NaturalLink provides the user with several lists of words and phrases which are used to construct sentences. For example, the first list may show beginnings, such as "What is the current stock price . . .", or "What are the headlines. . . ." In this way, one can easily form sentences such as "What is the current stock price for General Dynamics stock," or "What are the headlines concerning U.S. Steel Company." The use of a predefined vocabulary the computer understands simplifies the computer's tasks and enables users to recognize the limits of the database.

Sources: James Hassett, "Hacking in Plain English," *Psychology Today,* June 1984; Libby Rosenthal, "Friendly Interface: Building Computers with Hearts," *Science Digest,* January 1983.

emerging company in the electronics industry may indentify the following critical success factors:

- Reputation for state-of-the-art technology
- Market success of new products.
- Performance within cost and time constraints for development of new products.

For each of these critical success factors, an appropriate measure can be defined. "Reputation for state-of-the-art technology" is important, because the ability to get contracts depends upon customers' confidence in the firm's technical ability, which must be considered to be state-of-the-art. One measure of "reputation" might be a "hard" data measure: the order/bid ratio on contracts. For example, if ten orders were generated from fifteen bids for contracts, then this could be considered to reflect high customer confidence in the company's technological expertise. However, if only two orders were generated from twenty bids, then customer confidence could be considered to be quite low.

On the other hand, a "soft" measure could also be developed for this same critical success factor. Through person-to-person interviews, for example, the firm could obtain direct views about its current reputation in the marketplace.

Measures of critical success factors don't have to be computer-generated data; soft measures may be effective in many cases. Table 15.1 summarizes some measures of the critical success factors for our hypothetical electronics organization.

Table 15.1   Measures of Critical Success Factors for an Emerging Electronics Company

Critical Success Factor	Measure
Reputation for state-of-the-art technology	Order/bid ratio on contracts (hard) Opinions solicited during interviews (soft)
Market success of products	Change in market share, by product line (hard) Advance reports by sales reps (soft)
Performance within cost and time constraints for new product development projects	Job cost and time statistics—planned verus actual (hard)

Market success of products can be measured using data generated from a control system that describes sales by product line, comparing this year's figures with those of last year. However, even before this year's figures are in, the sales reps will be reporting back from the field, telling the sales manager in general terms about the reception the products are receiving. Performance within cost and time constraints on new product development projects can also be determined; a computer-based project management system will track budgeted and actual costs and time requirements.

When the computing needs of an organization are being planned, it is important to make room for the development of individual information systems. First, managers should define their critical success factors. Then, the measure that will best enable managers to track the success of these critical factors should be developed. Only then can the information system to support these information requirements be developed.

How Is Data Processing Organized?

Data Processing operations in a corporate or other institutional setting can be organized in one of several ways: centralized, decentralized, and distributed. We will review the characteristics of each of these methods. We will also study alternative ways of organizing these operations, in terms of data processing *functions*—systems development, operations, and technical support. While many types of personnel are required to run the data processing organization, in this chapter we will focus our attention on organizing and managing the data processing functions. We will look more closely at data processing careers in Chapter 17.

Centralized Data Processing

Hardware and Software   The hardware for a centralized data processing installation generally consists of a large central processing unit supporting a variety of peripheral devices (see Figure 15.5). The system can process more than one application program, often simultaneously, and can handle various kinds of input and output.

A centralized computer system may support remote terminals scattered about a business, school, or city. Although this gives the appearance of decentralized data processing—and is, in reality, decentralized in terms of *access* to computer resources—*control* of those resources, their priorities, the charges for them, and so on, are still determined by the central facility that does the actual computing.

A centralized system can support many business applications, such as basic accounting systems, sales and marketing information systems, and personnel information systems. The operating-system software that manages the processing of multiple applications, and the application software, tends to be complex.

Personnel   Centralized data processing organizations maintain a permanent staff of highly trained specialists. These individuals select the hardware, manage the operating-system environment, set up and manage data bases, arrange telecommunication facilities, run the computer and its

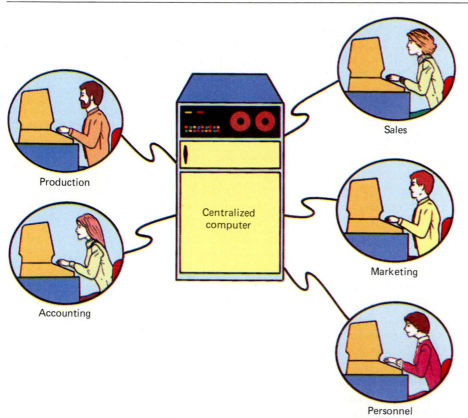

FIGURE 15.5
Central Data Processing

Production

Accounting

Centralized computer

Sales

Marketing

Personnel

peripheral devices, perform systems analysis and design, and do the actual
programming. The larger the central facility, the more specialized its staff,
which may include documentation specialists, network communications
consultants, and data base specialists.

Advantages of Centralized Data Processing

Centralized facilities came
about because they had—and have—certain advantages. First is "economics of scale"—that is, they aim to satisfy the diverse computing needs of
an entire organization with a single facility, thereby saving the costs of
multiple facilities. Decentralized small computers may have unused capacity, whereas central facilities eliminate the cost of such capacity. Second,
centralized data processing centers can keep all the files needed by an
organization in one place, which can increase the consistency and standardization of the data. Let's look at an example of what might happen if data
were decentralized, or part of the data were decentralized. The example is
that of a centralized corporate information system. Let us say that a company
keeps records of all its customers stored in a central information system.
This system is used to generate billing, service, and new product announcements. At the same time, one of the divisions of the company decides to set
up and maintain its own customer information system. They create records
for customers of that particular division, in order to generate letters and
announcements to these people.

There are several problems that could come from this situation. The
first is the redundancy of the data. The same data are stored on both a
centralized system and on a decentralized system. The second problem is
the possible lack of consistency of the data. The data may be updated on the
decentralized system, and not on the centralized system, when customers
report changes in address. However, if all the data were centrally maintained, and access to these data was provided to decentralized users, these
inconsistencies would not occur.

Closely tied to this advantage is the great security and tight controls on
access to the data that housing it in a central facility permits. In a large data
processing center, a data base administrator is responsible for keeping
backup copies of data files, so that data are not lost, and also for distributing
passwords and providing other security precautions, so that sensitive data
are not accessible to persons not permitted to use them.

The advantage of any sort of "center" is that users of many types,
including those in remote divisions of a firm, can have access to important
data and the use of computing power without having to set up such facilities
themselves. Moreover, centers attract computer personnel more readily
because the applications that are designed and maintained are more
sophisticated and because they offer multiple career paths, in-house training, and upward mobility. In contrast, a programmer hired to maintain
applications supported by a department's minicomputer may find that
opportunities to gain specialized technical knowledge are limited.

Centralization makes it possible to use systems development and
project control techniques, such as the use of a data dictionary defining all
data elements and their characteristics. Systems documentation standards
that help to insure maintenance of programs and systems in the future can
be enforced. Proper structured design and programming techniques can be
used to develop more changeable systems. Effective project control meth-

ods that help to insure that projects are completed on time and within estimated cost can readily be implemented in centralized organizations.

Another point in favor of centralization is its ability to control the overall cost of data processing on an organization-wide basis. Decentralized installations are difficult to audit and control, and total data processing costs may be obscured or recorded in other organizational components (for instance, manufacturing or accounting). Upper management can more easily monitor the data processing costs of a central operation. The costs of systems development, equipment maintenance, and training can be readily presented, and management can respond accordingly.

Disadvantages of Centralized Data Processing Naturally, centralized data processing has its drawbacks. First, forcing all systems development to flow through a central facility can lead to backlogs when the existing staff is overloaded. It is not uncommon in large corporations to find projects that management approved for development as long as two years ago still waiting for the centralized facility to *get started* on development.

Closely related to this first advantage is the next—small projects may not get done at all. A systems development project that is important only to an individual department—as opposed to a corporation-wide information-systems development project—may be placed on hold indefinitely.

The third main drawback is the lack of user control over the development of computer-based information systems and also over their day-to-day operations. Computers are meant to serve their users, but in trying to serve a great number of users—as in a center—responsiveness to individual application areas may be lessened. The ever-lower costs of buying new hardware, and the widespread availability of customized software, have given users an alternative to the frustrations that they may meet at their center.

Many different functions are required to keep a centralized data-processing facility running. These same functions are generally not required by a decentralized facility, as we will see in the next section, although a complex decentralized setup may contain some of them—such as programming, systems analysis, and operations. In a simple decentralized setup it could be said that the computer's sole proprietor has all of these functions under his or her single hat. Let's take a brief look at what they are.

The Functions of a Centralized Data Processing Facility

The functions of a centralized data processing facility have traditionally been grouped into three categories that apply to most installations: systems development, operations, and technical support. The purpose of the *systems development* function is to analyze the application area, determine its requirements, and design and program the actual computer-based information system. The goal of *operations* is to keep the computer and its programs running on a day-to-day basis. The *technical-support* function is to tune hardware and software to peak efficiency, to maintain a data base meeting the organization's needs, and to handle such matters as data communication links between facilities. All three functions are needed to keep a centralized computer installation humming. In the next chapter we

will discuss how each of these three functional areas breaks down into specific jobs. Now we will discuss in some detail an alternative to centralized data processing, decentralized data processing.

Decentralized Data Processing

Hardware and Software For a decentralized data processing installation, the hardware generally consists of a single minicomputer or microcomputer and its associated peripheral devices (see Figure 15.6). The system usually processes only programs for a specific application area, although the computers themselves are capable of handling a wide variety of applications. For instance, a minicomputer might run a production scheduling system for a local production plant, or a microcomputer might be used to process accounting data from only one department.

A decentralized installation is self-contained, with its own operating system and data base management system. The data files kept by the decentralized installation will be used only by that computer, and may not be compatible with the organization's central mainframe computer or with other decentralized installations in the organization. The software used by a decentralized installation may be simple, not offering many options outside the application's specific needs. Packaged software is often used in whole or in part; if the installation lacks programming expertise altogether, packaged software can be customized to an application's requirements for a charge by an outside consultant or firm.

Personnel Decentralized computers usually need at least one person to handle the day-to-day operations of the computer. This person would, for instance, enter data files, keep the printer supplied with paper and distribute printouts, make backup files in case the originals get lost or damaged, and so on. This person might be a computer professional, or a secretary or clerk. If packaged software is used—which is purchased ready to run from outside vendors and can be tailored to individual requirements by outside firms as well—then a programmer is not necessary. Depending on the sophistication of the application, however, one or more programmers may be desirable.

Advantages of Decentralized Data Processing Local autonomy, of course, is the prime advantage of decentralized data processing. With a machine on hand, and the availability of appropriate software assured, users are freed from dependence on a centralized facility that may not be responsive to their particular needs. Moreover, once the computer has effectively taken over the processing of the particular application for which it was intended, it probably has the capacity and ability to take on new tasks the department or user can devise. This responsiveness to new and changing user application needs is frequently missed in centralized processing situations.

Cost used to be a factor that argued against decentralized facilities, but this is no longer the case. Whether or not a mini or micro costs less to use than a mainframe computer in a given situation depends on the specific features of that situation. In their favor, minicomputers and microcomput-

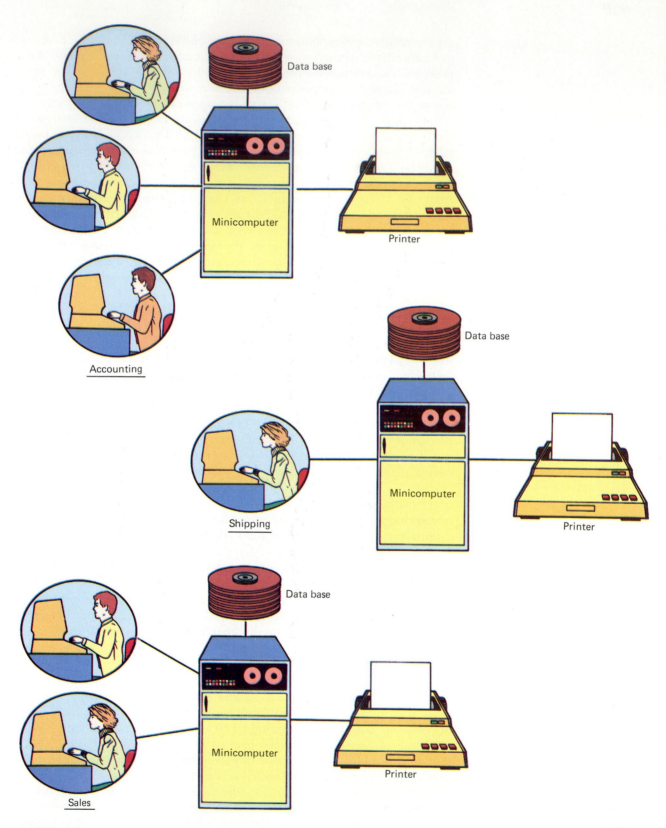

Data base

Minicomputer

Printer

Accounting

Data base

Shipping

Minicomputer

Printer

Data base

Minicomputer

Printer

Sales

FIGURE 15.6
Decentralized Data Processing

crs are relatively inexpensive to purchase and do not require the personnel of a centralized facility; thus they cut out a major overhead expense. There is no analyst, perhaps no programmer, and in the simplest cases the operator can supervise computer operations. A single-purpose mini- or microcomputer programmed for a specific application can be cost-effective.

In cases where local systems analysts are needed, these analysts are more attuned to local needs. They are able to acquire an in-depth knowledge of division operations, management preferences, and organizational needs. As a result, local analysts are able to establish user requirements and design systems that are best suited for the local user. In addition, local analysts can respond more quickly to changing priorities, avoiding the long lead times required to get projects approved and designed by a centralized group. The close association between analysts and users in the decentralized environment enables users to become knowledgeable about the benefits and limitations of data processing and to avoid seeking technical solutions to problems that are actually business or organizational problems.

Disadvantages of Decentralized Data Processing   Decentralized data processing has its drawbacks, not so much for the specific department or application area, but for the organization as a whole. One disadvantage is loss of control of the organization's data processing operations by centralized management. Users may see this as an advantage, but the corporation can take a different view. One feature of loss of centralized control is that users may do an efficient job of meeting their own needs but may fail to perceive where data from their operation fit into the larger, corporate picture for the benefit of the organization.

A proliferation of decentralized facilities is, in a sense, a step in the wrong direction when it comes to providing access to data for various corporate users. As with mainframes, there are many mini- and microcomputer manufacturers, each with their own operating systems and data base management systems. With incompatible systems scattered about an organization, the machines cannot share data or be hooked together into a network.

From a computer professional's standpoint, decentralized installations may be inefficiently run. The application systems may be designed without adequate standards, data security, backup files, or documentation. Security may consist of duplicate diskettes, and whatever access protection the packaged software provides. A lot that the data processing industry has learned in terms of planning and control will not even be known—let alone utilized—in a decentralized setup.

Decentralized computers may also lead to an inefficient use of personnel. Whether more programming and operations personnel are actually used by a number of decentralized installations, or by a centralized facility of comparable power to the group taken as a whole, is a topic of debate. The purchase of identical software packages, and even the development of identical programs in different departments, is a more obvious type of inefficiency. A centralized facility is aware of all the software that is in existence and under development, and can not only preclude such duplication but can inform users about what other programs are already available that might be of use to them. The next alternative, distributed processing, combines many features of both the centralized and decentralized systems.

Distributed Data Processing

Hardware and Software

In distributed data processing, a communications network connects centralized and decentralized computers, which are compatible with each other. Local mini- or microcomputers, with local data files and local processing ability, can interact with a central computer system to obtain access to central data files or to transmit information to the central system. Figure 15.7 depicts a distributed data processing system.

For example, local point-of-sale systems in branch stores of a large retailing chain are used to record local sales transactions and to update local store inventory levels. Summary sales and inventory data can be batched and transmitted to a central computer system each night over communications channels in a distributed data processing situation. In another case, local processors can validate and edit transactions and transmit good data to the central computer system to be processed.

Personnel

Responsibilities for data processing systems development and operations in distributed data processing are shared between centralized and decentralized personnel. In most cases, centralized personnel set the standards for the communications network and establish interface requirements to the central system, including methods of accessing centralized data bases. In addition, central systems development professionals may define standards for project selection, project control, and management.

Data processing personnel in decentralized sites have responsibility for determining local application development priorities, for managing local data processing operations, and for maintaining local hardware and software. Local management also selects employees and develops budgets.

Advantages of Distributed Data Processing

One of the benefits of distributed data processing is the ability to offload work from the central computer system and in this way reduce processing costs. If data can be validated locally, or if transactions can be recorded and files updated locally, the costs of communications to the central system, as well as the costs of processing, are substantially reduced.

Distributed data processing not only decentralizes some processing but also decentralizes some of the responsibility for data processing activities, including systems development and operations. Local systems analysts, who are familiar with local problems and priorities, are more likely to be responsive to user needs. Local operations personnel can make sure that computer-generated reports are distributed on time and can provide users with the training and support they need.

Most importantly, in distributed data processing, local management can directly control data processing costs. In the case of centralized data processing, the division manager may feel little control over salaries paid to central personnel, overhead rates, the choice of equipment, and time spent on projects. In contrast, if data processing resources are local, the division manager can better understand and control data processing costs.

Disadvantages of Distributed Data Processing

The problems with distributed data processing are similar to some of the problems with decentralized data processing. For example, users in remote sites may reinvent the

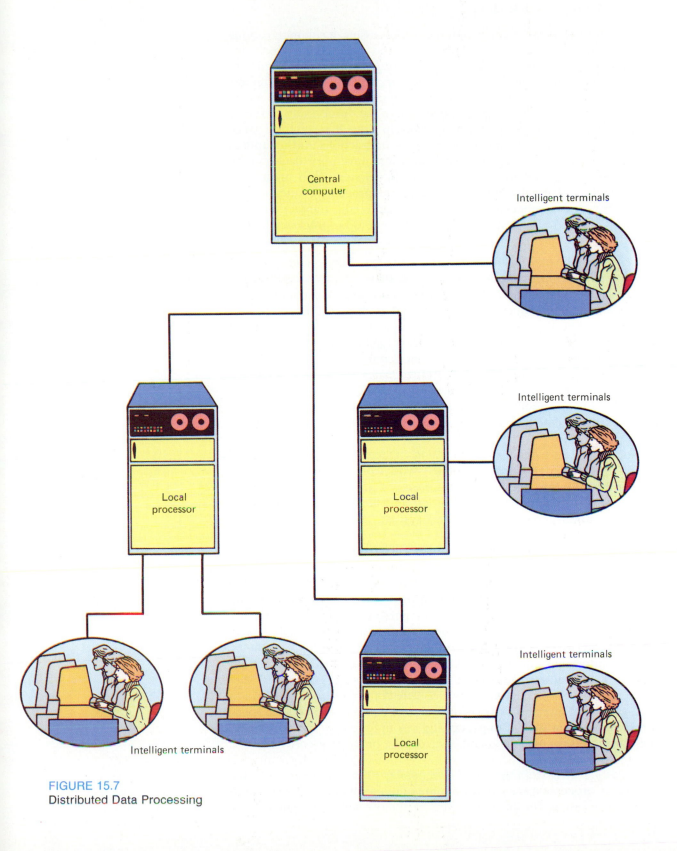

FIGURE 15.7
Distributed Data Processing

wheel by approving systems projects that already exist and in this way actually add to overall corporate data processing expense. Central data processing personnel may feel a lack of control over locally approved projects and may question their justification. Systems projects that are completed may not conform to central systems and programming and documentation standards, making more locally developed applications difficult to maintain.

In addition, central data processing professionals express concerns about computer-operations management in local sites. For one thing, they feel a lack of control over computer utilization. Local procedures for data security and contingency planning may be inadequate compared with central plans.

However, distributed data processing has great advantages and can work if certain guidelines are developed to overcome some of these problems. In the area of systems development, representatives of the corporate staff and operating divisions can work together on steering committees to set application development priorities. In some cases, central personnel may review systems design activities to be sure that locally developed systems have adequate documentation.

In the area of operations, centralized design and management of large-scale telecommunications networks is necessary to assure that local processors can interface with central systems. Central data base management must assure the integrity of central data as well as provide access to these data to remote users. Local users need to select hardware and software that conform with central guidelines in a distributed data processing environment. However, local control over such things as type of terminals, languages, and day-to-day operations is possible.

How to Organize   One factor that affects the decision of how to organize data processing is *how the organization is structured.* A conglomerate of decentralized divisions will likely place considerable computing power in the hands of these divisions. However, the central corporation will maintain some control over *operations,* as a way of monitoring and controlling EDP expenses.

Another factor is the stage that data processing has reached within an organization. According to Nolan's stage theory, data processing begins with cost-effective accounting applications in user departments. Initial success generates a proliferation of applications, and data-processing budgets for both hardware and personnel go out of control as users contract for services. Management concern over data processing expense leads to the development of central MIS plans and priorities, as well as to the establishment of formal procedures and standards for systems development in stage three. In later stages, the design of on-line systems and increasing user involvement in planning and systems design leads to the selection of organizational arrangements—centralized, decentralized, or distributed—that conform with business requirements.

Other considerations, of course, play a large role as well. Control of computing operations is a form of *power,* and people have seldom shown a reluctance to acquire it or to prevent others from doing so. In the case of centralization versus decentralization, this may mean that large divisions

will prefer a decentralized approach because this enhances their own power. Smaller divisions may favor centralization because they can benefit more from the expertise of the central facility.

The Organization of Data Processing Personnel

The organization of a data processing installation includes three functional divisions: systems development, operations, and technical support.

Systems Development

The purpose of the systems development function is to analyze the application area, to determine its requirements, and to design and program the actual computer-based information system. The systems development function of any data processing organization can be organized in one of two ways. The first is *by skill*. Developing a system entails the two main skills of systems analysis and design, and programming. The fundamental organizational split would then be into these two areas, which may be further subdivided as shown in Figure 15.8.

A different view of systems development is *by type of system*. Figure 15.9 shows an example of this kind of organization. The analysis design and programming functions are still kept distinct from one another, but are duplicated for each of the various types of systems that are under development or are being maintained. This type of organization may be more appropriate when the members of a development team need to be thor-

FIGURE 15.8
Systems Development
Organized by Skills

Source: *Management & Administration,*
Oct. 1976, p. 113.

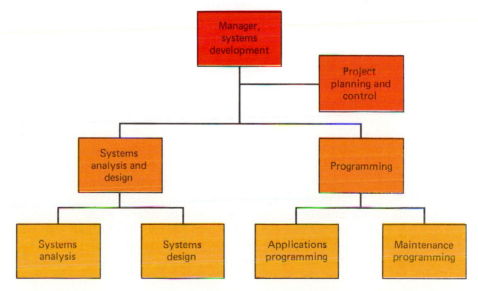

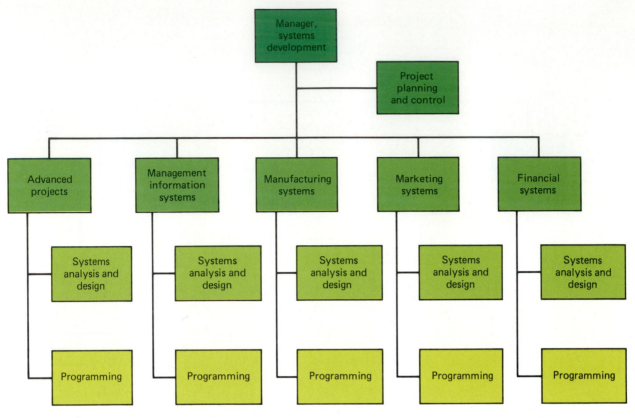

FIGURE 15.9
Systems Development Organized by Types of Systems

Source: *Management & Administration*, Oct. 1976, p. 114.

oughly versed in the nature and requirements of a user's operation. For instance, systems analysts in an ongoing marketing information systems project would view themselves both as professional systems analysts and as experts in the organization's marketing information needs, with the requisite knowledge in each.

Operations

There is less abstraction involved when organizing the operational function of a data-processing installation. The computer and associated machines must be run, and someone must schedule this; essentially, that is the mission of operations. Figure 15.10 breaks down these two functions into somewhat more detail.

Production support schedules the running of the computer center and controls jobs (programs) in terms of priorities, based upon when output is required. In these respects the manager of computer operations will be implementing the policies set by the data processing installation manager.

Equipment operation means running the machine and its peripheral equipment, keeping the printer supplied with paper, mounting magnetic

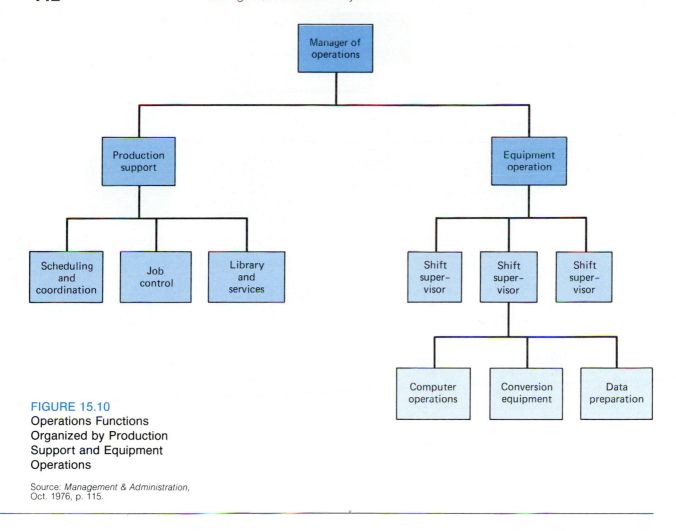

FIGURE 15.10
Operations Functions
Organized by Production
Support and Equipment
Operations

Source: *Management & Administration*,
Oct. 1976, p. 115.

tape onto magnetic tape drives, and monitoring the computer's console. In most installations data preparation is also one of the responsibilities of operations. Since computer operations often run two or three shifts, organization into these shifts is a key feature.

Technical Support

This part of a computer center is meant to "support" both the systems development and operations functions. Technical support is divided into these key areas:

■ *Systems programming group.* Here personnel install the computer's operating system, tailor it and maintain it, and improve the efficiency of application programs.

■ *Documentation support.* Although project documentation is generally produced by the systems development team, it must be maintained in a central library by technical support. Specific documentation telling

how to run programs will be provided to operations by systems development and/or technical support.

- *Systems evaluation.* This group monitors how well the computer itself and its operating system perform. In multiprocessing and time-sharing installations, this is a vital and continuous function. Suggesting new hardware and software alternatives is part of this group's mission.
- *User services.* Personnel in this group help users gain access to computer-center facilities, conduct training courses, and troubleshoot when users have problems with their computer support.
- *Data base administration.* The skill of setting up and administering the organization's data base falls to this group. It is a multifaceted assignment, which includes establishing the logical data requirements of the enterprise; setting up the data base; controlling security and providing backup to the data; and helping the systems development staff use the data in designing computer-based information systems.

The Role of MIS Management

Developing the Corporate MIS Plan A key responsibility of the MIS manager is to develop the corporate MIS plan. This plan sets down the strategies for developing information systems to meet the needs of the firm. It spells out the application development projects that will support the organization's business goals and that have the highest return, based upon the judgment of the corporate steering committee. The activities and resources that are requirements for the development of new applications and for the operation of existing systems are included in the MIS plan. In addition, the MIS plan identifies the new opportunities that changing information technologies provide.

Selecting the Organizational Structure The organizational structures that an MIS manager is responsible for designing as needs shift are centralized, decentralized, and distributed. The choice of whether to centralize systems development and operations or whether to decentralize responsibility for these activities in operating divisions of the firm should be determined with input from a corporate steering group. Other organizational concerns are whether to group programmers and analysts within the systems development department by skill or by type of system and where such functions as user services and telecommunications should be housed.

Identifying Application Priorities Identifying application priorities is a joint undertaking between MIS management and user executives. The two groups sit together on a high-level corporate steering committee to identify new applications and to review MIS plans. In addition, functional managers in areas where computer-based information systems are being developed should have an opportunity to evaluate alternative systems-design options —batch versus on-line systems, packaged software versus in-house software development, and a range of input, processing, and output options. Their feedback on the success of data-processing projects should be continually sought and used to redesign applications.

A Profile of the DP Professional

Data processing professionals have been described as independent self-starters and as different from other professionals. Perhaps this idea is best expressed by Gerald Weinberg in his book *Psychology of Computer Programming*. "If asked," Weinberg says, "most programmers would probably say they preferred to work alone in a place where they wouldn't be disturbed by other people." Other characterizations of data processing people are:

- they are technical, detail-oriented people, many of whom possess superior analytical skills;
- they are creative and intelligent.

Two professors from the University of Colorado, J. Daniel Cougar and Robert Zawacki, have written a book entitled *Motivating and Managing Computer Personnel,* which describes the findings of a study that proved statistically that DP people are different from other professionals, especially in terms of their needs and how they are motivated to satisfy those needs on the job.

Their study looked at three variables:

1. *Social Need Strength*. How much social interaction is needed to make individuals happy in their work.
2. *Growth Need Strength*. How much growth the job should provide to make individuals happy in their work.
3. *Motivation Potential Score*. The potential of the job for providing individuals with the level of professional growth needed in their work.

The survey of more than 600 DP professionals showed that they had the lowest social need and the highest growth need of all the professionals studied.

Social Need

One possible reason for the low social need score (see Figure 15.D) may be the fact that many DP jobs provide an unusually large amount of feedback. Programming, for example, gives the worker a sense of completion and accomplishment without the involvement of others.

However, the fact that many DP professionals feel little need for social interaction at work and see little value in meetings, walk-throughs, and feedback sessions may have adverse effects on their productivity, since productivity depends heavily upon interaction and communication among persons involved in planning and controlling projects—including peers, subordinates, superiors, and users. Lack of effective communication about job performance and progress on projects leads to missed deadlines and budget overruns. The persistent problems of relations between users and systems analysts can be largely attributed to poor communications.

Solving these problems means that DP professionals need to develop their communications skills, particularly their listening, questioning, and interviewing skills. These skills are vital in such activities as defining a user's problem or discussing project status with a subordinate. In addition, DP supervisors need to learn how to provide their subordinates with feedback about their work performance, since feedback is essential for high morale and job satisfaction.

"Up Until Now I Didn't Believe There Was Life Outside of High Tech."

Computerworld, Dec. 12, 1983. p. 42. Used by permission.

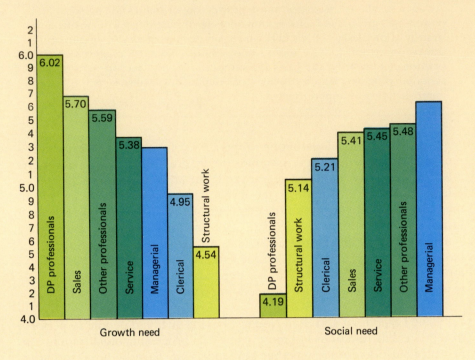

FIGURE 15.D
The results seem to confirm that programmers, analysts, and programmer/analysts are "loners." They are also unusual in their need for individual growth. (Responses are on a scale of 1 to 7.)

Source: J. Daniel Cougar and Robert A. Zawack, "What Motivates Data-Processing Professionals." *Datamation*, Sept. 1978.

Growth Need and Job Motivating Potential

Cougar and Zawacki's findings also indicate that DP professionals have the highest growth need score of the professionals studied. This means that their jobs must provide them with an opportunity to grow. DP professionals view their profession as providing a high potential for meeting these growth needs. (see Table 15.A).

However, high turnover rates in many DP organizations may indicate that many employers either don't offer sufficient opportunities for DP professionals to grow, or else maintain a set of policies and procedures that stymie the growth of highly motivated people.

Table 15.A
The Growth Needs and Motivating Potential of Data Processing Professionals*

Job Category	Growth Need	Motivating Potential
DP professions	6.02	157.5
Other professions	5.59	153.7
Sales	5.70	146.0
Service	5.38	151.7
Managerial	5.30	155.9
Clerical	4.95	105.9
Machine trades	4.82	135.8
Bench work	4.88	109.8
Processing	4.57	105.1
Structural work	4.54	140.6

*The scale for growth need is again 1 to 7; the "motivating potential" scores are derived numbers and are not relative to any scale.

As a result, DP managers must provide opportunities for personal and professional growth and must re-think policies that deter growth. An effective strategy is the design of job enrichment programs that enable employees to achieve more and to have more responsibility. In any DP organization, job performance must be the basis for advancement. An effective performance appraisal program, which provides counseling and feedback, is the key to improving employee performance.

Managing Computer Operations   Operations may be the MIS manager's most visible exposure. If the system is down, everyone knows it. If reports are distributed late, the word gets around. The MIS manager must be able to establish performance and service levels for computer operations and to measure the effectiveness and the efficiency of the operations function. Full utilization of equipment, adequate capacity for processing, and timely scheduling of all operations activities. Although the overall success or failure of an MIS plan depends on the extent to which corporate needs and MIS resources are balanced, it also depends on how well the computers work and how effectively users' needs are met.

Handling Equipment and Staff Needs   Having qualified people to perform data processing functions is a must in any data processing organization. The manager must determine whether new specialists must be hired to undertake new assignments, whether training is adequate, and how to improve productivity. He or she must identify a way of handling the overwhelming requests for development work—by hiring more programmers, by using contract staff, by buying packaged programs, or by putting application development tools such as report generators in the hands of the users. This latter decision would mean the development of information center specialists to train and to consult with end users.

Equipment, too, must be continually evaluated. As new information technologies emerge, these new technologies must be evaluated. What different vendors offer, how efficient they are in upgrading and servicing equipment, and what future developments will be offered are an ongoing topic of research and debate. In addition, standards for equipment acquisition must be set to assure compatibility.

The Next Steps

Today many organizations are finding that information systems cannot be developed fast enough to meet the growing demand of enlightened managers who understand their uses. The result has been a five- to seven-year backlog of systems waiting to be developed. Indeed, by the time a system is about to be developed, analysts find that the information needs of the

appropriate department have changed. At the same time, the tools and techniques to make information systems professionals more productive exist, but they have not yet effectively lessened this application development backlog.

To speed up the process and to give managers the advantages of information systems when they are needed, new approaches have been devised. Organizations as a whole are planning for and adapting strategies to more rapidly implement systems development throughout the business. These strategies include end-user computing and the information center.

Microcomputers and End-User Computing

End-user computing—computing done by employees themselves usually with microcomputers rather than computing done by a data processing department—is growing by leaps and bounds. In many companies there is as much as a 15 percent increase per month in the number of end users who are doing their own computer work. By 1990, it is anticipated, end users will directly utilize 70 to 80 percent of all computing power.

There is a growing awareness on the part of managers that by using computers they can expand productivity. For example, with application prototypes end users can use a system before it is "set in concrete." Also, personal computing applications such as electronic spreadsheets can significantly improve the individual's professional productivity on tasks such as budget analysis, sales forecasting, and marketing analysis.

End-user computing is not without its problems, however. When end users design information systems they often provide inadequate documentation and insufficient data security and backup/recovery precautions. Also, data files created by end users are often isolated from the integrated data base management systems that support corporate data processing applications. Finally, there is the issue of how much time a manager should spend developing his or her own personal information systems. An occasional manager may use application development tools to generate literally hundreds of reports. Is it really productive for a financial analyst or research chemist to spend that much time developing computer-based information systems? In some cases, of course, the answer will be yes. Too often, however, the time spent on technology is disproportionate to the value of the output. But this is the user's decision; it is he or she who has to live with the results.

To make end-user computing work, corporate MIS must establish policy guidelines for the company's hardware acquisition and data base requirements. Data housed in corporate data base management systems should be accessible to end users. At the same time there should be security safeguards against end users changing the "live data" present in the corporate data base. The company must also be able to set adequate controls over the development of end-user computing. While it is important to encourage end-user computing, it is also necessary for such computing to evolve along corporate-defined lines. In other words, an end user may need to acquire the type of computer that is compatible with the corporate information system. This makes it possible to access data from the central corporate computer for use in designing local applications.

The Information Center

An information center is designed to support end-user computing within the organization. End-user computing is valuable because computing tools can substantially improve the productivity of individual managers and professionals.

Often the information center begins with a few personal or microcomputers, and then moves to time-sharing terminals tied to the corporate central computing systems and data bases. Ultimately, a combination of microcomputers and mainframe data bases is possible, as managers begin to use micros not only to support local applications but also as terminals to interact with the central computer system. The evolution of end-user computing within an organization is a process that should be guided by the personnel responsible for the information center.

The purpose of the information center is to provide decision support for managers and professionals. For example, decision makers may need to

One of the uses of an information center is to train end-users on software that creates presentation graphics.
Courtesy of IBM Corp.

analyze or collect existing corporate data to satisfy their own information requirements. Software tools such as financial planning packages, electronic spreadsheet programs, graphics, and word processing systems are all useful in supporting professional information requirements.

Another important role of the information center is to serve as a liaison between corporate data processing and the end user of the company's computing systems. These information centers are staffed by information systems professionals, familiar with standard systems development methodologies and responsible for assuring that user-developed systems adhere to corporate standards. In this way, high-quality corporate information systems can be designed effectively and within guidelines that will make them usable throughout the firm.

One of the major goals of the information center is to provide users with the tools—both hardware and software—they need to develop their own information systems. These tools may include personal computers, data base query languages, and end-user application development tools. Such tools can be used to develop either prototypes of information systems or an entire information system.

However, none of these tools can be used by managers unless these managers know how to use them. As a result, training and support are two of the most important functions of the information center. If a manager needs a question answered or has a problem, it is essential that assistance be provided quickly. If managers have nowhere to go to get questions answered, then they are unlikely to learn how to use the tools necessary to enhance their own productivity. Figure 15.11 summarizes the functions of the information center.

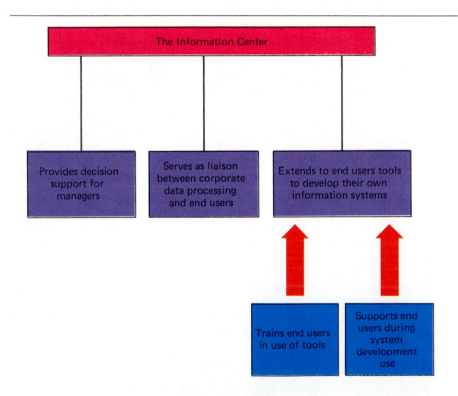

FIGURE 15.11
The Functions of the
Information Center

A job created by the information center is the **information center consultant.** Although large computer centers have always supplied consultants to help users, the information center consultant will work closely with the user to determine application requirements and provide the user with tools to design and generate reports from existing data bases without having to rely on traditional systems development methods and programming. The tools supported by the information center include data base query languages, report generators, and application generators. With guidance on how to use these tools, interested users can either design their own applications or provide models or prototypes of applications to be developed later by data processing professionals.

The explosion of information technologies has also created the need for a new breed of systems analyst who can identify applications of office automation systems, review alternative design options, and conduct training programs for new users of office systems. One of the responsibilities of the office-systems analyst will be to study the traditional office—the nature and volume of work, work flow, office procedures, work distribution, and organization—in order to spot bottlenecks, inequitable use of resources, and duplication of effort. Another responsibility will be to identify situations in which new office technologies will support both secretarial and managerial productivity. Typical among office technologies are word processors, microcomputers, intelligent copiers, and electronic mail systems —all tools which can make the creation, storage, retrieval, and distribution of administrative information more efficient and more productive. Because new office technologies change the way in which work is organized, the relationships between secretaries and managers, and the ways in which managers communicate with each other, the office analyst must understand and manage the process of change in the office. Finally, the office analyst must provide ongoing training and support to users learning to apply new tools to their work. Training programs—both small group sessions and individualized consulting—will require hands-on learning activities and practice on realistic job-related applications. The development of instructional programs and materials will draw upon the teaching skills of the analyst.

Tracking America's Health

How the Centers for Disease Control in Atlanta Is Getting Control of Its Data.

To the American public, the Centers for Disease Control (CDC) has become known as something akin to a health department CIA. Its "shoe-leather" epidemiologists scour the country, tracking outbreaks of often deadly illnesses much the way intelligence agents go after other deadly forces. Legionnaires Disease, Toxic Shock Syndrome, and AIDS (Acquired Immune Deficiency Syndrome) are among the ailments that "agents" of the Atlanta-based CDC have helped investigate and identify.

The CDC is much more than a medical intelligence unit. Its mission under law is, simply put, to help prevent the preventable. To accomplish that task, the decentralized cluster of five centers and one institute tracks not only communicable diseases but also chronic, environmental, and occupational

diseases; it designs programs to counter those ailments; and, finally, it monitors the programs' effectiveness.

The organizational chart for the CDC shows it operates something like a corporate conglomerate, with virtually autonomous "subsidiaries." But unlike a corporation—whose divisions can produce such diverse products as toothpaste, financial services, and footwear—each CDC entity deals in the same product: information. "Our widget is data—information," explains Howard W. Ory, information systems director. "We produce incredible quantities of data."

As you might expect, CDC employs a considerable amount of computer technology to produce its information widgets. But it hasn't always been so. Like those of many of its counterparts in private industry, CDC's computer operations have grown "from the ground up," as Ory puts it. Scattered throughout scientific offices at the surburban Atlanta complex is a mishmash of Apples, Kaypros, Compaqs, and IBM personal computers. Secretaries and administrators use a separate Wang network for word processing, and keypunched batch jobs are run on a mainframe, an IBM 3083 (model J–32).

That's much the way Dr. James O. Mason found the system when he took over the directorship of CDC in November 1983. Mason felt it was time to give the decentralized computer operation some direction from the top, and he quickly put together a high-level task force of top scientists, executives, and technicians to study the centers' technology needs. One of the task force's many recommendations was that a central information office be established to oversee the computer, data processing, and telecommunications functions that had previously been organized into separate divisions. In March 1985, Ory was named the first director of the new office, called the Information Resources Management Office (IRMO).

That Ory, who previously had been research chief of the Epidemiology Program Office, was named to direct the new information management effort is an indication of how the CDC views computer technology. "They've put a really key person in the job," explains one CDC researcher. "It's indicative of the kind of importance the CDC is giving to the new operation." Ory's staff currently numbers about 80; his annual budget is $5 million.

The CDC's computer operations are highly decentralized: a central office maintains the mainframe, but each center, division, and project is responsible for assessing its own computer needs and buying its own terminals. This is a structure that is increasingly popular among private companies—and one Ory says he has no intention of changing. "I'm not out to create an empire," he maintains. "My job is to put computing power in the hands of the creative."

Ory describes his mandate as having four parts:

- updating and maintaining the centers' "hard iron" equipment;
- helping scientists learn to use computing equipment and to design data processing programs of their own;
- encouraging the sharing of data; and
- automating the myriad administrative and managerial tasks involved in scientific research.

Perhaps Ory's most pressing and difficult challenge is to develop a network that will link the center's dp, personal computing, and word processing functions. Under the current system, many researchers must have their data keypunched and fed into the mainframe; they download the data to their pcs to massage it; they write reports on their pcs and print them out; their secretaries rekey the material into their Wang terminals (powered by

Wang's Office Information System central processing units) for word processing. If the scientists want to send messages or material to each other, they must send it via the mainframe.

One of the major roadblocks to creating a single, centerwide computer system is compatibility—or, rather, the lack thereof. Because CDC's $10 million investment in Wang word processing equipment currently precludes it from purchasing new IBM-compatible hardware, it must jury-rig compatibility. Ory's office is now experimenting with new Wang word processing software designed to run on the IBM PCs. It's also investigating a fledgling Wang product, the 3270 protocol converter, designed to allow Wang terminals to communicate with IBM mainframes, and it is looking into buying disk converters that can translate IBM disks to Wangese.

Also standing in the way of a unified computer network is the dynamic nature of CDC, which employs some 4,300 medical doctors, scientists, administrators, and other workers nationwide. As Debbie Jones, IRMO's assistant director for office systems, notes, CDC researchers move every eight months or so as they take up new areas of study—making it "virtually impossible" to wire the complex of buildings for computers. Computing needs also vary widely from project to project. "We go through tremendous trauma to gear up every time a new health problem crops up," Jones says.

Another of IRMO's immediate concerns is meeting a pent-up demand for computer power and assistance. When terminals first appeared on CDC desks, Jones reports, there was "tremendous resistance" to the new technology. "But now we are facing tremendous demand instead. Everybody wants his own pc." While each individual center or research project is required to buy its own equipment, IRMO is charged with approving each purchase order and providing users with general technical assistance.

That support effort is headed by Jerry Sanders, a 20-year veteran who helped program the first IBM 371/45 installed at CDC in 1975. Sanders and his staff of 21 troubleshoot calls from researchers whose latest reports have just disappeared in the system or who can't get their printers to work. At the same time, they must maintain the IBM mainframe—which processes between 1,200 and 1,500 batch jobs each day—and also design new applications for the system, such as on-line graphics programs.

Filtering Out Easy Questions

Under study by Ory's office is a new plan that would help filter out the easy questions from among the hundreds of calls for assistance that barrage IRMO every day. Aided by two policymaking boards staffed by managers and executives from every department of CDC, Ory hopes to create two more layers of computer assistance at the center and division level: lead users and IRM coordinators. Selected from regular CDC employees, lead users and IRM coordinators would receive special training and support from IRMO to help them distribute computer expertise and aid users at the local level.

Just as Sanders and his team provide technical support for the CDC system, Al Barber, who heads the database administration branch, is charged with responding to the data needs of the agency's many users. One of his first assignments since IRMO was organized has been to develop a small-purchases system that would streamline the laborious process of requisitioning supplies and equipment under $25,000. The database office also is creating a spreadsheet program to permit project heads to track each expenditure and run what-if projections for budgeting.

For CDC's contingent of 600-odd scientists working on their studies of birth control pills, Agent Orange contamination, or the latest strain of flu, Barber's branch has designed a separate system that works like this: an IRMA board connects IBM ATs or XTs to the IBM mainframe through Software AG's communications software product, Natural Connection. ADABAS, written in Natural, is the mainframe data management program. A different program —the Statistical Analysis System (SAS), from Statistical Analysis System Institute, Cary, N.C.—is used for number crunching. ROSCOE is the language that allows researchers to access SAS.

System security and backup is yet another of Barber's responsibilities. Because CDC operates with one mainframe computer, thorough backup measures are necessary to ensure that data aren't lost if the system crashes. Currently, tapes are backed up each evening, but Barber is looking into new simultaneous backup techniques. Strict procedures also are needed to keep confidential data from falling into the wrong hands and to guarantee that they can't be tampered with. "Almost every thing we do is a group effort. It would be very hard for someone to tamper with the data and go unnoticed," Ory says. "Before CDC becomes more dependent on computers, you have to do more and more in the way of security."

IRMO recently assigned a full-time staff member to head its data security effort. It also hired an outside security consultant to conduct a security analysis of the CDC systm. The result: IRMO has purchased a new data security package, Top Secret, from Computer Associates, South Bend, Ind., and is starting a transaction logging procedure that will allow computer technicians to reconstruct a data tape if the system should crash. Farther down the line, IRMO is looking into the use of simultaneous backup technology.

To protect the integrity of the data CDC researchers gather and analyze, IRV data management employees draw up a department security profile and assign security codes to individual users each time a new data file is set up. For instance, a secretary might receive a code and password that prevent her from calling up sensitive data being studied in her department; some researchers might be given access to the data but might not be permitted to enter new data; other scientists might have full run of the database.

Because most of the data—between 90% and 95%—that CDC researchers collect and study are not tagged with personal identifiers, confidentiality is seldom an issue. But in some situations, particularly in AIDS research, great pains are taken to code personal IDs and keep them separate from the data. That means a special program would have to be run to link the files. According to Ory, the procedure is both complicated and secret, making the possibility of invasion of privacy, in his words, pretty remote.

Actual names of the AIDS victims are not on file in the Atlanta offices. The full names are on file with state health departments. Only three CDC staffers have clearance even to the coded names.

Branch Maintains All Data

The branch is also charged with maintaining all the data collected by CDC. Some 135 separate systems currently are run on the main frame—systems as diverse as small purchasing, vaccine inventory, and bibliographic retrieval. Similarly, the office must maintain the 80-odd applications that have been developed by the various centers for specific research projects or administrative needs. "Over the past few years, we've seen some very good development

by our own end users," says Don Rice, chief of database management. But he notes that keeping up with the products of that "good development" can be challenging.

The AIDS research team is among the many end users currently developing special computer applications to assist the 90 different investigations now being conducted into the mysterious and deadly new disease. The AIDS effort—sponsored by the Center for Infectious Diseases—has budgeted funds for pcs for all of its researchers, and has hired a team of technology professionals to help coordinate and support its computing needs.

Under the direction of Meade Morgan, a statistician and computer veteran, the team of seven programming and statistical experts collaborates with investigators as they design their projects and helps them analyze their data once they are collected. Morgan's operation also has set up a personal computer network that allows researchers to share such peripherals as printers. (The system employs a Hewlett-Packard 9000, a Unix-based desktop mini.)

The AIDS project has also placed computing power in the hands of the state health departments that must file weekly AIDS data with the CDC. Using special federal grant funds, Morgan supplies states with IBM ATs and with a homegrown software package called the AIDS Reporting System. State health workers use the system to prepare floppy disks of verified data each week; the disks are mailed to the CDC and filed directly into the computer, rather than being keypunched from printed forms. The system also permits state users to design their own programs to analyze and maintain AIDS data.

The AIDS project has spent between $150,000 and $200,000 to date on computer equipment, Morgan says—a sum that he notes is small in comparison with most equipment employed by scientific researchers. "AIDS is an important public health problem now," he explains. "So far, we haven't had any trouble getting funds for equipment."

The CDC's Statistical Services Branch is another department that is working to deliver computing power to state and local health departments. For years the branch prepared its weekly summary of reportable diseases by telephoning state health workers for the latest count—figures that were then keypunched into the computer. Two years ago, though, the branch began supplying the far-flung health departments with software that permits figures to be recorded locally and sent via a MYNET electronic mailbox into the CDC system. The new computer reporting system not only makes it easier to tabulate the weekly "Mortality and Morbidity Report," but it also allows the CDC access to additional information about those suffering from reportable diseases: age, sex, onset of illness, and other variables now are reported along with the incident of disease.

To date, some 15 states have joined the program, and supervisor Norma Gibbs hopes to have all 50 on-line by 1990. Gibbs sees a day when the new system will eliminate duplicate reporting—AIDS information currently must be reported to several different departments, for instance. She also envisions putting the mortality reporting system and medical examiner reports on-line. "Things are changing pretty fast," says Gibbs.

Computers also have wrought dramatic changes in the operations of the field epidemiologists who are dispatched to investigate unusual outbreaks of illness. Until a few years ago such "detectives" had to wait until they returned to the office to analyze the information they had gathered. Often, the computer would reveal holes in their research that could only be filled by going back to the site. Today, using Compaq portable computers and modems, these investigators can key their data directly into the mainframe in Atlanta and try out their theories while still in the field.

All 50 States Linked

CDC Prevention Service health workers permanently stationed in all 50 states and in U.S. territories have also been linked, via modem, to the Atlanta computer over the past five years. They assist states and localities in running their immunization, dental health and quarantine programs and in developing prevention plans for sexually transmitted diseases, tuberculosis, and diabetes.

Ory says he eventually would like to see a far wider spectrum of data streaming into CDC's workhorse computer. Hospitals, medical schools, and private physicians cumulatively hold a wealth of data that is rarely reviewed or shared with other health professionals.

"Ultimately, every physician is going to have a pc on his desk, just for billing," Ory explains. "Even if you could just pick up what physicians bill for every day, you'd have an incredible disease surveillance program." He notes, though, that such a data-sharing network is unlikely in the near future—in good part because of budget constraints among both government and private health care concerns.

A more immediate challenge will be to help restructure the computer system to conform with the centers' recent shift in focus. After years of concentrating primarily on communicable diseases, CDC's mandate has been broadened to include the prevention of such problems as heart disease, birth defects, cancer, toxic poisoning, and occupational ailments. That means that researchers will need access to a far wider spectrum of data, both from internal and external sources.

"If you're tracking communicable diseases, you're simply counting individual cases," Seligman says. "You can count cases of leukemia, but you can't determine the causes as easily as you can for measles."

Source: Gail Gregg, *Datamation,* June 12, 1986, pp. 136, 138, 140.

Summary and Key Terms

1. A **management information system (MIS)** combines the resources of computers and people to develop a system that will process all of the information needed to support the activities, management, and decision making of an organization.

2. There are three levels of activity in an organization: operations, control, and strategic planning. Operations managers must identify, collect, and register all transactions that result from acquiring or expending resources. These day-to-day transactions produce data that are the basis for operational systems. The control function of an organization reviews operational activities to make sure that the organization is meeting its goals and is not wasting its resources. Strategic planning involves using internal and external data to make long-term plans and solve problems.

3. The three organizational levels in a company use different information systems. **Operational information systems** collect, validate, and record transactional data. **Control information systems** summarize data in different ways so that managers can review trends and allocate resources more effectively. The information generated by a control system is also used to measure and compare performance to a standard, thereby identifying problems and correcting them. **Strategic planning information systems** enable senior managers to devise

long-term strategies that will allow their company to compete in the market-place or achieve other business objectives.

4. Management information systems usually develop in a sequence. The base of operational information systems should exist before effective control information systems can be developed.

5. **Enterprise analysis** is a formal planning technique that managers use to define the information requirements of the organization. A project team interviews managers from all branches of the organization and finds out what data the managers need to support business processes. The project team classifies all the data and determines which data classes are shared by different business processes. Then the organization begins to identify information systems development priorities.

6. A **systems development methodology** assures that end users' needs are satisfied and costly errors are avoided.

7. The MIS delivery system manages an organization's computing resources, which include the computers and peripheral equipment used, the support software for data bases and programming languages, and telecommunications networks. Delivery system personnel are responsible for computer hardware performance and capacity planning, for data security, and for backup and recovery procedures.

8. The **corporate MIS plan** is a comprehensive portfolio of the computer services and applications that will be developed and supported by the corporation in order to accomplish its business goals. The plan notes all the applications to be developed and the technology needed to supply computing resources to the firm.

9. Data-processing operations in a corporate or other institutional setting can be organized in several ways: centralized, decentralized, and distributed.

10. Historically, the first computer operations were centralized. A trend can now be seen in the opposite direction. Some organizations centralize some functions and decentralize others.

11. **Centralized data processing** has advantages in possibly saving costs, securing data more effectively, and offering a high-powered array of staff specialists. Drawbacks include a possible unresponsiveness to user needs.

12. **Decentralized data processing** has the advantage of putting the user in the driver's seat. Not only can users then do the computing they planned to do themselves, but they will likely find new productive uses to apply their computers to. Drawbacks include incompatibility with larger systems and loss of central management control.

13. **Distributed data processing** provides a communications network linking centralized and decentralized computer systems. This arrangement enables local analysts to identify local systems requirements and provides local processing capacity, while at the same time assuring centralized control over the design and management of computer networks and data base management systems.

14. Data processing functions at an installation are split into systems development, operations, and technical support.

15. Systems development personnel analyze the application area, determine its information systems needs, and design and write programs to implement a computer-based system. Systems development personnel include systems analysts, application programmers, maintenance programmers, documentation specialists, user training specialists, and project managers.

16. The operations division of a computer center runs and schedules the computer and associated machines. Production support people schedule machine time and determine job priorities in the computer center.

17. The technical support group is divided into several key areas: (1) systems programming group, (2) documentation support, (3) systems evaluation, (4) user services, and (5) data base administration.

18. End-user computing is computer work that users do themselves. An information center is often organized to support end-user training and consulting.

Review Questions

Fill-in Questions

1. The day-to-day activities of an enterprise (checking credit, filling orders, applying payments to account balances) are known as _____.

2. In general, _____ systems must be developed prior to control systems.

3. Data that are aggregated or summarized to be useful to the manager in making decisions are called _____.

4. Nolan's first stage, during which companies introduce cost-effective accounting application, is called _____.

5. A planning approach in which managers help to define the organization's information needs is _____.

6. The activities that are a part of the systems analysis and design process compose the _____.

7. The plan that identifies applications and technology resources to be utilized by the organization is the _____.

8. Individual managers can define their information needs by identifying their _____.

9. A _____ is a model of an application that can be experimented with, modified, and even discarded when a better model is made.

10. In many organizations, end-user computing resources and services are provided by the _____.

Matching

A. What level of the framework for information systems describes the type of information that is produced in each of the following cases? Select from:

a. Operational

b. Control

c. Strategic planning

_____ 1. Sales, by customer, this year to date versus last year to date.

_____ 2. Amounts due vendors and payment terms.

_____ 3. Net profit, for a particular product line, planned versus actual.

_____ 4. Effectiveness of alternative advertising and promotional strategies.

_____ 5. Credit status of various customers.

_____ 6. Inventory items requiring reorder, and the economic order quantities of these items.

_____ 7. Data depicting socioeconomic status, age, income, and educational background of a given population group this year, compared with five years ago.

_____ 8. Profit potential of alternative store sites.

B. Identify whether the following statements are characteristics of centralized, decentralized, or distributed data processing systems, and indicate your choice as:

1. centralized
2. decentralized
3. distributed

_____ a. Local analysts can develop applications independently.

_____ b. Specialized personnel have an opportunity to develop sophisticated systems.

_____ c. Remote sites adhere to standards of a communications network.

_____ d. Users may feel out of control of data processing costs and data processing project priorities.

_____ e. Remote systems analysts may have to conform with central guidelines for project management and systems documentation.

C. Given the brief descriptions of the following applications, identify the data processing alternative that is most appropriate. Select from:

1. centralized
2. decentralized
3. distributed

Give reasons for your answers.

_____ a. A point-of-sale inventory system in 250 retail stores that are part of a national chain.

_____ b. A data base of all inventory records used by a particular department of a hospital.

Multiple Choice

_____ 1. The data processing professional responsible for making modifications in existing application programs is the:
   a. Application programmer.
   b. Maintenance programmer.
   c. Systems programmer.
   d. User training specialist.

_____ 2. The data processing professional who writes detailed systems design specifications, program design specifications, and user manuals is the:
   a. Project manager.
   b. Systems analyst.
   c. Documentation specialist.
   d. Maintenance programmer.

_____ 3. The data processing professional who provides training and support to end users interested in developing their own applications is the:
   a. Office-systems analyst.
   b. Systems analyst.
   c. Information center consultant.
   d. Data base administrator.

_____ 4. The data processing professional who maintains the operating-system environment, so that hardware and software run at peak efficiency is the:
   a. Maintenance programmer.
   b. Systems programmer.
   c. Application programmer.
   d. Operations manager.

_____ 5. The data processing professional who interviews users to determine their requirements for the development of a computer-based information system is the:
   a. Data base administrator.
   b. Systems analyst.
   c. Project manager.
   d. Operations manager.

Discussion Questions

1. Write critical success factors for each of the following organizations. Explain reasons for your choice.
   a. A retail grocery chain.
   b. A national rental-car company.
   c. A local travel agency.
   d. An express mail delivery service.
   e. A two-year community college specializing in business and vocational training.

2. Determine what type of systems development strategy would be most appropriate for each of the following end-user applications. Choose from:
   1. Traditional systems development process.
   2. Prototyping, using an application generator, followed by traditional development process with COBOL.
   3. Using an application generator to design the entire application.
      Provide reasons for your answers.
   ____ a. A report listing all students in a student data base who are majoring in MIS and who live within a particular zip code area.
   ____ b. An integrated accounting system for international divisions of a consumer products company.
   ____ c. A report listing sales, by product line, and by geographic area, planned versus actual, on a monthly basis.
   ____ d. A mailing list of all customers listed in a customer data base.
   ____ e. A production scheduling system for all the plants of a manufacturing company.

3. What are the advantages of centralized data processing?

4. What are the disadvantages of decentralized data processing?

5. How does distributed data processing help to overcome some of the disadvantages of decentralized data processing, while offering some of the advantages of centralized data processing?

6. Identify five skills that would enable the programmer/analyst to move ahead and assume project-management responsibilities. Explain why you think these skills are important.

7. Of the data processing roles and responsibilities that have been described in this chapter, which one interests you the most? Explain reasons for your answer.

Case Analysis

A major insurance company, Federated Mutual Life, centralized its information-processing activities in the early 1970s, because of economies of scale and the need to develop an expert systems development and technical staff. Also, corporate management was concerned that data processing be kept under control. Competitive contracts for equipment upgrades were available to the firm through a national vendor at this time.

However, the availability of cheap mini- and microcomputers made many user managers want to move toward decentralized data processing in the late 1970s. They argued that the availability of inexpensive hardware and packaged software made traditional arguments for centralization no longer valid. They also stated that eventually it would be possible to tie all of the different minis and micros together. Right now, however, they wanted information systems to be more responsive to their needs, and that meant putting minis in their own departments and hiring analysts and programmers to do the work.

a. What potential problems could occur if the user managers move quickly toward decentralized data processing?

b. Are the centralized data processing arguments still valid?

c. What considerations are important in moving Federated Mutual into an environment in which user managers have more control over information systems?

d. Can user managers get what they want without necessarily having control over their own hardware and computer operations?

Decision Support Systems and Artificial Intelligence

16

Chapter Objectives

After studying this chapter, you should be able to

1. Describe the characteristics of decision support systems.

2. Identify how decision support systems are developed.

3. Describe the characteristics of expert systems.

4. Understand how an expert system works and explain how expert systems are developed.

5. Describe the differences between expert systems and decision support systems.

A small business, like any other organization, needs information systems to support day-to-day operations. At Consolidated Business Products, Inc., information systems made it possible to enter sales order information, to update inventory levels, to generate invoices, and to update accounts-receivable balances when customers sent in their payments. When customer payments were overdue, a report of their overdue balances was printed out and payment reminder notices were also sent to customers. These information systems worked well and streamlined the paperwork involved in processing day-to-day transactions such as orders, bills, and payments.

However, managers at Consolidated Business Products were complaining about the reports they received from data processing. Every morning the sales manager received a report listing the sales orders that had been processed the previous day. This report listed thousands of sales transactions but did not provide any indication of how well certain product lines were doing or what types of customers were most profitable. The sales manager wanted a report that would compare sales results for each product line for the past month with sales results for each of the previous six months. This type of report, he felt, would help him analyze which product lines needed to be expanded or discontinued. He also wanted a sales report that compared sales results for different types of customers (for example, small businesses versus large companies), in different territories (such as the Northeast versus the Midwest). This would enable regional managers to focus on their most profitable accounts or reinforce sales efforts in areas where business was weak.

The inventory manager had similar complaints. Each week he received a stock status report listing inventory on hand and on order for 6,000 different inventory items. However, he wanted to know about which items

had the greatest turnover and the least turnover so that he could more effectively control inventory levels. He also needed information about the seasonal demand for various inventory items so that sufficient quantities of seasonal items could be ordered and so that stock of excess inventory items could be minimized.

What these managers were saying was that the day-to-day information about sales and inventory levels they were receiving did not help them make important decisions. They needed information about sales trends, inventory turnover, and important customer accounts so that they could make decisions about how to allocate their salespersons' efforts, what stock levels should be maintained for various inventory items, and what customers should receive special attention.

In addition, they couldn't anticipate the precise information they needed because the business situation changed all the time. The sales manager might want to obtain customer feedback on a new product line and want to ask a question like "Give me all the names of customers who have purchased one of the new color copiers in the past six months." He might be planning a sales reward program and want to ask "Give me all the names of salespersons who have sold over $50,000 in electronic typewriters in the past two months." Although these queries are important, it would be extremely difficult to obtain the needed information from existing reports. It would also be difficult to design a management reporting system to provide this information because the sales manager's questions would change on a day-to-day basis.

Managers' pent-up demand for useful information has created a new type of information system called a *decision support system*. Decision support systems enable managers to obtain access to the information they need and to develop meaningful reports. In this chapter, the evolution and characteristics of decision support systems are discussed.

Many managers confront problems that are unstructured and that take into account many complex variables. These complex problems require expert knowledge, which in the past has only been available from experts themselves. Tools are available today making it possible to capture expert knowledge and to program computers with this knowledge to support effective decision-making. Expert systems incorporate "expert" knowledge that can be used to solve problems in medicine, engineering, and in business. The field of expert systems is part of the larger field of artificial intelligence, which is concerned with the creation of computer programs to do things in ways more like human patterns of thinking than "traditional" computer programs. In this chapter, the evolution and characteristics of artificial intelligence, and particularly expert systems and robotics, will be covered.

Decision Support Systems

Managers chronically complain that the data-processing reports they receive on a daily, weekly, or monthly basis overload them with information. MIS professionals are not sure what information managers really need and as

a result have developed reports that provide too much information. Managers themselves aren't sure what information they really need because they do not understand their own decision-making processes. The problems they encounter change on a day-to-day basis, and this changes the information they need.

One way of providing managers with information is to develop **exception reports,** which show significant deviations from planned activity. For example, an exception report will show if actual sales of a particular product line are 25 percent greater than expected for a given sales period. Unexpected changes in sales, in inventory turnover, in overdue accounts, and in net income can all be highlighted on exception reports.

The only problem with exception reports is that the exception conditions are fixed. A manager may receive a report that tracks sales, by product line, this year versus last year. However, if the manager would like a breakdown of these sales on a month-to-month basis, the program generating the report would have to be modified by data-processing professionals. With months of work in a backlog, many MIS organizations find it difficult to respond to this type of request.

One study of managers' information needs discovered that many of the exception-reporting systems that had been developed by MIS professionals were not supporting important decision-making needs.[1] They also found that there was a tremendous pent-up demand for inquiry systems. **Inquiry systems** provide a data base with flexible inquiry capability, making it possible for managers to ask questions of a data base. For example, a manager can ask "Give me all the names of customers who did over $10,000 business with us this past year" or "Give me all the names of salespersons with over 20 years of experience with the company." Inquiries can change on a day-to-day basis, and the inquiry systems managers used have been shown to be effective in supporting their information needs.

Managers also wanted information systems that would enable them to analyze data using modeling, simulation, and statistical routines. Although few of these systems existed, managers believed that 97 percent of these systems supported their information needs. The invisible backlog for inquiry and analysis systems exceeded the known backlog by 700 percent. This meant that the pent-up demand for inquiry and analysis systems was seven times greater than the projects that had been approved and that were part of the known backlog.

Characteristics of Decision Support Systems

In describing decision support systems and their characteristics, it is useful to compare their development with the types of information systems that have been developed in the past. John Rockart, in a paper on executive information systems, contrasts decision support systems with accounting and operational control systems, as shown in Table 16.1.

A decision support system can be defined as a computer-based system that helps decision-makers use data and models to solve unstructured

[1]The study cited in this section is "User Managers' System Needs" by Robert Alloway and Judith Quillard, *MIS Quarterly,* June 1983, 27–41.

Table 16.1   Eras of Computer Use

	Era I	Era II	Era III
Sample Applications	Payroll, general ledger	On-line order entry	Decision support systems
Justification	Clerical replacement	Service asset reduction	Better analysis, planning, control
Managerial Involvement in Systems Design	Minimal	Supervisory level only	Significant
Expected Change from Initial Design	None	Minimal	Extensive
Primary Systems Technology	Batch, large central computer	On-line local and central computers	On-line local and central computers
Primary Languages	COBOL	COBOL	Fourth generation like FOCUS, NOMAD
Data Base Used	Separate files for each application	Data base optimized for machine efficiency	Data base designed for ease of use

Source: John Rockart and Michael Treacy, "Executive Information Support Systems," Sloan Working Paper No. 1167–80, Center for Information Systems Research, MIT, April 1981.

problems. Decision support systems are designed to support inquiry and analysis needs. As shown in Table 16.1, a decision support system requires a data base that serves as a repository of data for managers to use in making queries and in generating reports. Englishlike data base query and reporting languages like FOCUS and NOMAD are used by the manager to make queries and to generate reports.

Managers are directly involved in defining their data needs and in developing their own decision support systems. Because the problems they need to solve change from day to day, these systems undergo constant change. Managers usually start by developing simple query and reporting systems that answer requests such as "Give me all the names of customers in the northeastern region who have purchased over $50,000 worth of word processors in the past year." With experience, their decision support systems build in modeling and data analysis capabilities, making it possible to answer more complex questions, such as "Give me the percentage increases and decreases in sales of word processors for various regions for the past 3 years."

Another characteristic that distinguishes decision support systems from information systems is their basis for justification. Accounting and operational control systems have been justified on the basis of hard dollar savings, often achieved by replacing clerical workers with automated procedures. Many information systems enable managers to cut the cost of excess inventory or to minimize bad-debt expense. Other systems are justified on the basis of improvements in customer service.

Decision support systems generally are not justified in these ways. They make it possible for managers to have access to data that will enable them to make better decisions. These decisions may enable them to anticipate market demand, to direct sales efforts to the most profitable buyers, and to

minimize potential losses of a poor financial decision. Decision support systems also make it possible for managers to minimize the time and effort they spend on manual calculations in preparing budget forecasts or in analyzing the cash-flow potential of alternative business decisions.

Decision-Making and Decision-Makers

A good decision support system has to take into account the characteristics of decision-making and decision-makers. A decision support system must support unstructured decisions, must support all phases of the decision-making process, and must support communications between decision-makers. In addition, an effective decision support system must provide memory aids and training facilities that make its tools easy to learn how to use.

Ability to Support Unstructured Decisions
A decision support system must support both structured and unstructured decisions. The chapter on management information systems presented a framework for information systems including operational control, management control, and strategic planning systems. Operational control systems support decisions involving day-to-day activities, such as the processing of accounts receivable or monitoring of inventory. Management control systems enable managers to allocate existing resources to achieve business objectives. Strategic planning systems support senior managers who are responsible for setting organizationwide objectives.

Table 16.2 gives examples of both structured and unstructured decisions that can be supported at each of these three levels.

Table 16.2 Different Types of Decisions

	Operational Control	Management Control	Strategic Planning
Structured	Accounts receivable	Budget analysis	Store site selection
	Production scheduling	Long-term forecasts	Mergers
Unstructured	Cash management	Budget preparation	Product planning

Source: Adapted from Gorry and Scott Morton, "A Framework for Management Information Systems," *Sloan Management Review*, Vol. 13, No. 1, Fall 1971.

At the operational level, an accounts receivable system is a highly structured business application with well-defined procedures and outputs. However, because of the wide range of money management alternatives and judgmental factors, cash management is a much more complex, unstructured problem. The same is true with budget analysis and budget preparation. Analyzing a budget is a fairly straightforward task, but preparing a budget is a much more creative responsibility requiring experience and insight.

At the strategic planning level, an example of a structured task is store site selection. A number of variables, such as traffic flow, competition, and demographic data, might be used to assess the value of alternative store sites. However, developing a product planning strategy is a far more complex, unstructured decision involving many possible variables.

Although decision support systems are developed to support structured decision-making, they are mainly aimed at providing data and models that are relevant to addressing the more unstructured decisions that managers at all levels have to make. More sophisticated data analysis and modeling are needed to address the less structured problems like cash management and budget preparation.

Ability to Support All Phases of the Decision-Making Process   When managers need to make a decision, they often collect tremendous amounts of data, hoping that something they discover will help them make the decision. An example of this approach is described by Russell Ackoff in his article "Management Misinformation Systems." The managers Ackoff described wanted to determine the best location for a gas station. Because they were unsure of the information that would be most relevant to site selection, they collected data on at least 70 different variables related to making a choice. Five or six of these variables, including traffic volume and proximity to major intersections, correlated with successful location. However, a great many data elements were collected for no reason.

A far more productive method of making the decision on where to locate a gas station would involve using a decision-making model. Decision-making can be divided into three phases: intelligence, design, and choice. During the first phase, **intelligence,** a situation requiring a decision is visualized. During the second phase, **design,** the problem is defined and alternative solutions are evaluated. The third phase, **choice,** results in the selection of the proper course of action.

At each phase of the decision-making process, different data are needed and different operations occur, as we can illustrate by applying the decision-making model to the gas station site selection problem. Here are the data that would be relevant to making this decision:

- **Intelligence**   A graph depicting population growth in a particular community and a listing of competitive gas stations in this community
- **Design**   A weighted factor analysis comparing three alternative gas station sites using three variables: traffic volume, access to major highways, and competition in the immediate area
- **Choice**   A report on simulated sales for each alternative site over the next three years

At the intelligence phase, data indicating that a decision needs to be made are collected. A graph depicting population growth in a new community may show that a gas station should be located there. Additional data listing competitive gas stations that have moved into the area would provide further evidence of the need to locate a gas station there. As a result of the intelligence phase, management should move to the next step—evaluating alternative locations.

During the design phase, possible sites could be evaluated using a weighted factor analysis based on several critical variables. Let's say that

traffic volume, access to major highways, and competition are important factors to consider in evaluating a site. A percentage could be assigned to each of these three factors on the basis of its importance in the overall decision:

Factor	Percentage
Traffic volume	40%
Access to major highways	30%
Competition	30%

Then each site could be scored on a scale of 1 to 100 on the extent to which it met each of these factors:

Factor	Site A	Site B	Site C
Traffic volume	98	76	88
Access to major highways	77	85	82
Competition	85	88	90

To complete this analysis, the scores for each site would be multiplied by the percentage importance assigned to each factor to determine the best site selection. The analysis of site A would look like this:

```
Traffic volume              98 × (40%) = 39.2
Access to major highways    77 × (30%) = 23.1
Competition                 85 × (30%) = 25.5
                                TOTAL = 87.8
```

According to this analysis, the weighted factor scores would be calculated for the other sites and the highest total score would determine which alternative scored best on the established criteria. Here are the total scores:

```
Site A    87.8
Site B    82.3
Site C    86.8
```

Although site A seems to be the best choice, further analysis could be done to support the choice phase of the decision-making process. A report of simulated sales for each of the three sites might provide further insight into the decision and lead to the final choice.

At each phase of the decision-making process, different operations are useful. During the intelligence phase, data are used to identify a situation

requiring a decision. Data are manipulated to evaluate alternative design options during the design phase. A simulation of the results of the alternatives provides useful information at the choice phase.

The tools used to support each of these phases vary because the operations that need to be conducted vary. For example, a data base package can be used to generate data needed at the intelligence phase. A spreadsheet package may be more useful in examining a series of alternatives at the design phase. Still other tools, such as a statistical analysis or a graphics package, could be used to demonstrate the results of various alternatives during the choice phase.

Ability to Support Communications Between Decision-Makers

Decision-making involves both individuals and groups. Therefore, decision support systems need to support both individuals and groups. Group decisions involve different processes. Sometimes decisions are made sequentially, which means that one decision-maker makes part of a decision and passes it along to another decision-maker. An example of a sequential decision is the approval of funds for travel to a conference. Preliminary approval by a department chairperson may need to be followed by final approval by the school dean.

Other decisions involve negotiation or interaction among several decision-makers. An example of a group decision might be the choice of a restaurant for a family dinner. Each member of the family might have a specific preference and the decision would need to be reached through a process of negotiation. A group decision support system would need to support interactions among the decisions-makers participating in this process.

Availability of Memory and Control Aids

Decision-makers need memory aids, or information about the results of operations that have been conducted at previous times. Workspaces for storing the intermediate results of operations are very useful. Triggers reminding users to perform certain operations before starting others are also helpful.

Training aids are important, particularly in the early months of system use. Decision support tools should provide menus, help screens, and prompts, which ease the learning process and help users develop language skills. Software with function keys for standard operations and a standard command syntax also eliminates much of the confusion that may result when users are forced to learn new commands when they switch from a spreadsheet to a data base package or from a microcomputer-based data base to a mainframe-based one.

Decision Support Systems in Practice

Decision support systems are generally developed by user managers who decide to use a data base, spreadsheet or other program to support a business need. By learning about case studies of decision support applica-

tions in a number of different functional areas, the benefits and uses of decision support systems are easier to understand.

Decision Support Systems in Accounting and Finance

The first three cases describe DSS projects supporting accounting and financial applications.

A Budget Forecasting System

One of the responsibilities of a marketing analyst in a consumer goods manufacturing company was to determine if budget projections submitted by field sales managers were realistic. Paper and pencil calculations of projected sales were often as much as 20 percent wrong. Past sales history data for the various regions were stored in a mainframe-based data base, but these data were virtually inaccessible for manipulation, reporting, and analysis purposes.

In order to remedy this situation, the marketing analyst acquired a microcomputer equipped with data base and spreadsheet packages. Sales history data were downloaded from the mainframe-based data base to the PC, making it possible to use past sales data to generate field sales forecasts. These sales forecasts were then used to make budget projections.

When the field sales managers submitted their own budget forecasts, the analyst doublechecked his figures to determine if their requests were reasonable and accurate. If their requests were out of line, he could suggest more realistic alternative budget requests. In this way, budget preparation was more consistent with actual performance. Field sales managers with increased sales volumes were able to obtain resources to support their needs.

A Financial Control System for Bank Clients

In a commercial bank serving corporate customers, a decision support system for clients was developed by the product marketing group. Corporate customers were accustomed to receiving printouts of monthly financial statements in the mail. When the product marketing group introduced a system that enabled these customers to download their financial statements from the bank's computer to their personal computers, users not only had more timely access to their data but could also use a spreadsheet program to manipulate these data for cash flow and other types of analyses.

Although the application was originally designed to provide better service to the bank's clients, it became an effective marketing tool because it differentiated the bank's services from the services provided by other banks. Customers felt they were receiving special attention because the bank's product marketing group offered them a spreadsheet program designed to implement the kind of cash flow analysis they needed.

A System to Monitor Existing Loan Portfolios

One of the major responsibilities of a commercial bank is to develop a loan portfolio that will minimize risk and provide good investment opportunities. In the international division of a commercial bank, a manager created a data base of international loan accounts using a microcomputer data base management package. Originally, the data base was set up to provide information such as interest income, loan balances, and credit ratings.

Although the system was originally designed to enable users to query loan data, it evolved into an analysis system. By analyzing current loan balances by obligor and by type of loan rating, the manager could determine the riskiness of the current loan portfolio. For example, the user could query the data base and ask for all the balances of outstanding loans to clients in Latin American countries with credit ratings of BB. High balances in accounts that were considered risky would enable the manager to justify making conservative loan decisions to offset the potential risk of the existing portfolio.

Decision Support Systems in Production and Operations Management

A number of decision support systems are being developed to improve inventory control and to control day-to-day operations, as the following examples show.

A Production Planning System

A company in the food marketing business had 6 plants in which food products were manufactured and 15 branch warehouses from which these products were distributed to grocery stores. The production planning department was responsible for identifying target inventory levels for the branch warehouses in various regions. These target inventory levels were then used to determine the plant production schedules that would be needed to provide an adequate supply to the respective warehouses.

The decision support system developed to address this need used a sales history file consisting of 3.5 million records with data on the past 18 months' sales of all product lines. A mainframe-based data base query language, FOCUS, was used to develop a sales forecast using these sales history data. A PC-based spreadsheet program using these sales forecast data was designed to project sales and to determine target inventory levels. Information on inventory levels was then transmitted directly from the personal computer to branch warehouses where these data were printed out at local printers.

Once production planners had better information on needed inventory levels in the warehouses, they could develop more accurate production plans to fill these inventory needs. Excess inventories were minimized and distribution costs were cut because finished goods inventory was more accurately allocated to the respective branches. This personal-computer-based decision support system was believed to be saving the company thousands of dollars each month in excess inventory and in distribution costs.

A System for Loan Delinquency Reporting

One of the major issues the mortgage loan business faces is possible default on loan contracts. Many companies face bad-debt expense in excess of 5 percent of the balances on the loans they make to consumers. If the existing loan portfolio amounts to $10,000,000, this 5 percent would mean losses of $500,000 per year. At one mortgage loan company, a decision support system was developed to identify the characteristics of delinquent loans. Past loan delinquency data

were used to identify variables associated with delinquent loan accounts. These data helped insurance agents screen applicants who appeared to fit a potential delinquency profile and to focus marketing efforts on the more stable accounts instead. Prior to the development of this system, it was very difficult to tell in advance which loans were in a high-risk category.

Decision Support Systems in Sales and Marketing

Many successful decision support systems address issues in sales and marketing, as illustrated by the following examples.

A Decision Support System to Determine Pricing Strategy

Today, the insurance business is very competitive compared with 10 years ago, when a limited number of product options existed. Many new insurance products, including a variety of financial services, are being offered. A competitive edge can be achieved by announcing a new product on a timely basis or by offering a competitive price. Keeping track of the products and pricing strategies of competitors is a major undertaking.

This problem led two marketing analysts in an insurance company to develop a decision support system. The purpose of the system was to create a data base about competitors' products and the pricing of these products. When new insurance products were announced, the company could analyze their competitors' strategy and develop a pricing strategy that would enable their products to be competitive.

A Sales Analysis System

Marketing efforts were also supported by the development of a sales analysis system. This system used account history data to analyze market penetration and product success. For example, a sales manager could use data on past sales to determine the characteristics of customers desiring certain types of insurance programs. The profitability of various product lines and of various customer groups could also be analyzed as a basis for more effective target marketing. These data could be used to target marketing efforts toward the more profitable customers and to design new insurance programs for these groups. As a result, sales managers could reallocate sales efforts toward selling the most profitable insurance programs possible within various sales regions.

Assessing the Impact of Marketing Efforts

Marketing analysts in a consumer loan company were not sure of the impact of various marketing strategies on sales. In order to get a better understanding of the impact of these strategies, a decision support system was developed. Sales data by region were analyzed and evaluated with regard to various advertising and promotional programs. Eventually, these data were used to identify successful promotional strategies in one region compared with another and to direct marketing efforts accordingly.

Computerized Searching for New Business

The aerospace industry has to be able to react to potential opportunities for government-funded contracts on a timely basis. Identifying these opportunities requires being able to learn about and react to perceived contract development opportuni-

ties. The marketing department of one defense contractor developed a decision support system to make its search for business opportunities more thorough. Using a keyword search facility, marketing analysts were able to search through government publications to identify possible contract openings. Without question, this system minimized manual effort and assured a more thorough search of thousands of pages of detailed information per month.

Implications of DSS Cases

These case studies of decision support systems being developed and used in business and industry point out a number of interesting features. First, many of these systems used mainframe-based data bases such as account history and sales order history data. These data were relatively useless until managers were given the tools to query and generate reports from these data bases using fourth-generation languages and personal computers.

Each of these decision support systems supported important departmental objectives such as production planning, product marketing, sales analysis, and loan application screening. These systems were helpful in cutting the costs of excess inventories, in identifying the most profitable market segments, and in avoiding the potential cost of bad debt expenses.

Another characteristic of many of these decision support systems was their constant evolution. Although many of these systems were originally created to store data and to make these data more accessible, they evolved into information systems that could be used for analytic purposes as well as for query and reporting. A good example is the international loan account analysis system. Originally, this system was put together to keep track of data about international loan accounts, such as loan balances, credit ratings, and industry type. However, the system made it possible to assess the riskiness of the international loan portfolio and to determine the impact of future loan decisons.

The final characteristic of decision support systems is that they are often developed and used by business professionals who have very little formal training in (1) how to use computer hardware and software and (2) how to develop information systems. The major motivation for developing these decision support systems is a business need or a competitive strategy. The tools used to develop decision support systems are microcomputer-based data base and spreadsheet packages and mainframe-based data base query and reporting languages.

The Development of Decision Support Systems

A review of a number of decision support systems has illustrated that these systems are in constant evolution. The strategy used to develop a decision support system involves interaction between a user and a builder. At the

start, the user ordinarily defines a problem area and begins to think about the information needed. However, the user doesn't have a firm idea of what kind of reports he or she needs from the system. The builder works with the user to come up with some "mock-up" versions of reports. The user tries these reports out, and they are continually modified until the correct information has been defined. This approach encourages the development of short-lived, ad hoc systems that can be constantly refined as the user's needs change and discarded when no longer needed.

Figure 16.1 gives a schematic diagram of how the **adaptive design** process works. Continuing user feedback brings about new versions of the system. The adaptive design approach is different from the traditional systems development process. In the traditional development process, the first step is problem definition and requires the user to define the nature and scope of the problem. Problem definition leads to requirements analysis, during which the objectives of the system are established and preliminary blueprints for the system are laid down in the form of a requirements document or specification. Specifications include a description of the major system outputs, files, and inputs as well as a description of the business procedures to be redesigned and automated. During design, various alternative approaches for implementing the systems design project are evaluated and the best approach selected. Then, during implementation, the coding, testing, and conversion from the old system to the new one are accomplished.

In the traditional systems development process, the requirements document that establishes what the specifications of the system will be is frozen. This means that any changes or modifications to the preliminary design will create cost and time overruns that the user will be responsible for supporting. The requirements document is a contract assuring that major changes won't occur once the system is undergoing implementation.

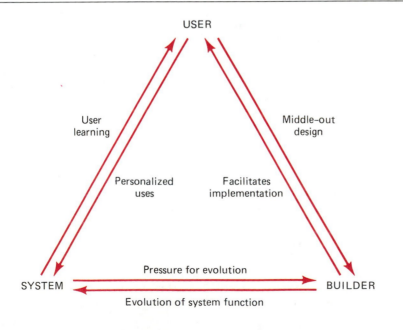

FIGURE 16.1
Adaptive Design Approach

Source: Peter Keen and Thomas Gambino, "The Mythical Man Month Revisited" in R. Sprague and E. Carlson, *Building Effective Decision Support Systems,* Prentice Hall, Inc., Englewood Cliffs, NJ, 1982.

In large projects involving hundreds of programmers and years of effort, the requirements document is necessary. It serves the same purpose as architectural specifications do in a major building project. The document makes sure that users won't change their minds on major features of the system. Changing system specifications would be the same as a prospective home owner insisting that a builder redesign room layouts, ceiling heights, and the dimensions of windows once a house is half built.

Unlike the traditional development process, the DSS development process recommends that the builder produce a mock-up of the desired outputs at the start and continually modify these outputs until the user agrees with the results. The resulting design is likely to differ from its original version. A key element in this process is experimentation, because the new versions that are developed give the user a better understanding of what is needed.

The major steps in the DSS development process are contrasted with the major steps in the traditional development process in Table 16.3. Although the two approaches may seem remarkably similar, the process of developing a decision support system is quite different from the methodology followed in developing a traditional information system. The first phase, **planning,** involves the user in diagnosing a problem that can be solved through the development of a decision support system. Often, the problem occurs because information is not accessible in the form needed for decision-making, such as information available on computer-generated reports that is too highly summarized to be of value. After planning, the user considers what development approaches and tools are appropriate for the project. This phase is called **application research.** The user might want to evaluate whether a system should be developed using a microcomputer-based data base or a mainframe-based data query language during this phase. The decision may depend on the size of the data base, the cost of ongoing data access and maintenance, and the availability of training and technical support.

During **analysis,** the best approach is selected; and during **design,** the detailed specifications for the system, including major reports, files, and inputs are established. **System construction** is the technical implementation of the design. So far, these steps are comparable to the steps taken during the traditional design process. However, the entire effort so far may be considered **prototyping:** The system that is constructed is treated as a model, or prototype, and it may be constantly reevaluated and modified.

Table 16.3   DSS and Traditional Development

DSS Development Process	Traditional Development Process
Planning	Problem definition
Application research	Requirements analysis
Analysis	General design
Design	Detailed design
System construction	Implementation
Evaluation	Maintenance
Adaptation	

Adaptation means the periodic planned recycling of the entire set of tasks that are part of DSS development.

The development of decision support systems means a different role for data processing professionals. Most programmers and systems analysts have developed technical skills in systems design and implementation but are not well-prepared to work with users in a consulting role. In the role of a system builder, the systems analyst needs to have insight into business problems and needs to be able to evaluate and recommend appropriate system building tools. Both business skills and communications ability are needed, along with technical skills. MIS professionals need to provide guidance, training and ongoing support to user-developers.

Existing decision support systems apply analytic techniques with traditional data access and retrieval functions to unstructured problems. The major limitation of this approach is the need to develop an analytical model which structures the problem to be solved. This problem is in part solved by the development of expert systems which take advantage of the strengths of DDS but also expand the flexibility of the problem structure. The topic of expert systems is a part of the field of artificial intelligence which will be covered in the remaining half of this chapter.

Artificial Intelligence

Artificial intelligence refers to the development of computer-based systems that simulate human performance. In other words, a computer system that has some capacity to "analyze" a situation and "act" on the basis of that analysis is "behaving" in a humanlike way. The area of artificial intelligence includes expert systems, natural-language processing, robotics, machine vision, and machine hearing.

This gripper developed at the University of Massachusetts has a sensor pad for detecting objects

© Hank Morgan/Photo Researchers, Inc.

Expert systems are systems that simulate the knowledge of experts on specialized, professional tasks. Expert systems are taught the "rules of thumb," or **heuristics,** that experts use to solve problems. These rules can be continually updated as the situation changes. The expert system integrates the experts' heuristic knowledge with their informal styles of reasoning.

Natural-language processing applications are also part of artificial intelligence. Natural-language queries make it possible for users to ask such questions as "What is my bank balance?" and to retrieve the information they need. Another type of natural-language processor, called ELOISE, has been developed by the Securities and Exchange Commission to analyze financial statements, calculate key ratios, and develop a text data base providing a conceptual view of the financial status of companies relevant to acquisition decisions.

Although natural-language processing is a developing technology, its usefulness is limited to very specific applications. One reason is that computers have difficulty understanding the semantics of the English language. For example, the statement "I saw the hill with a telescope" can

be interpreted in several different ways. A human being understands which meaning is intended in a given situation; a computer does not.

Another application of artificial intelligence is **robotics.** Robots have been taught to cut, drill, weld, and paint as a part of factory automation. They are most effective when they can be programmed to perform a specific task again and again. Adding sensors and capabilities like machine vision to robots helps them to shift their tasks according to the computerized instructions being communicated to them.

One of the issues brought forth by the emergence of artificial intelligence is whether computers will become as smart as humans. Actually, computers cannot learn; they can only be programmed to incorporate the rules they are taught. However, computers have unlimited powers of concentration and unlimited stamina to solve problems, and they can be programmed to provide expert assistance or support for many human tasks. In the future, it might be common to see humans work with the help of intelligent assistants in fields such as medicine, law, and engineering. The major focus of the rest of this chapter will be in describing what expert systems are, how they are being used, and how they are developed.

The Characteristics of Expert Systems

An expert system uses rules of human experience and judgment to solve difficult problems in much the same way an expert consultant would, by asking the user for information and relating this information to general rules. If it needs additional information, it asks more questions until it arrives at conclusions or makes recommendations. An expert system is composed of a knowledge base, an inference engine, an explanation subsystem, a knowledge acquisition subsystem, and a human interface component. Figure 16.2 illustrates the major components of an expert system.

The Knowledge Base

The expert system has a "knowledge base" that stores the factual knowledge and the rules of thumb it needs to make decisions. One of the ways of representing knowledge is to use rules. In a rule-based system, the knowledge base is a collection of facts and inference rules, such as:

```
IF AT & T DROPS BELOW $50
THEN BUY 10,000 SHARES
```

The facts deal with the system's specialized area of expertise and are applied to specific problems as needed. Additional facts can be derived when the rules are applied to a given situation or problem.

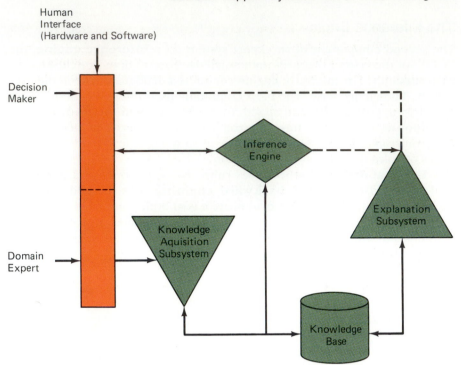

Human
Interface
(Hardware and Software)

Decision
Maker

Domain
Expert

Inference
Engine

Knowledge
Aquisition
Subsystem

Explanation
Subsystem

Knowledge
Base

FIGURE 16.2
The Components of an
Expert System

Source: Robert Keim and Sheila Jacobs, "Expert Systems: The DSS of the Future," *Journal of Systems Management*, December 1986.

Rule-based systems also have **metarules** that may figure in a specific problem. For example, other rules may apply to the decision "If AT & T drops below $50, then buy 10,000 shares." The system may have to explore these metarules, other related questions such as "Do I have enough money?" or "Is financing available at an acceptable interest rate?"

When a computer-based expert system receives input data, it picks the rules that apply to the particular problem. Depending on the nature of the decision, different rules may apply. The system does not proceed through the same rules for every decision in a lockstop manner. An expert system also asks the user additional questions in order to learn more about the situation and the rules that may apply.

For example, a defense contractor has developed an expert system for battlefield repair of equipment. If the user keys in information about a specific problem, the system may generate a series of questions. If the user asks "Can it be repaired within two hours?" the system may have to learn what kind of glue is available and how much time it will take the repair to dry in order to recommend a course of action.

The approach to representing knowledge other than a rule-based system is a frame-based system. A **frame-based system** is designed to deal with objects and classes of objects. Attributes that an object has are arranged in slots. For the object "dog," for instance, there are slots for typical attributes such as breed, owner, and name. There are also procedures to transfer from one frame to another and to attach procedures for computing values. For example, a frame may have an attached procedure for finding out who the owner of a dog is.

The Inference Engine

The second component of an expert system is an **inference engine,** the "CPU" of the system that uses the knowledge base to draw conclusions for each situation. The inference engine conducts a dialogue between the user and the knowledge base. The most commonly used inference methods are data-driven, goal-driven, and mixed. In the **data-driven method,** which is also known as **forward chaining,** the user enters a series of facts and the program responds by asking questions. In so doing, the system explores a series of rules to arrive at its conclusion.

The **goal-driven method** uses rules that apply only to a particular goal. Otherwise known as **backward chaining,** this method proceeds backward through its rules to try to prove a goal. Rules unrelated to the goal are not used. The mixed method combines the data- and goal-driven methods and allows the user to volunteer information relevant to solving the problem.

The Explanation Subsystem

The **explanation subsystem** explains the line of reasoning that has been used in arriving at a point in the decision-making process or at its recommendations. Explanations the system provides can explain the strategies used to solve the problem at hand, can respond to specific questions of the user, and can critique the solutions being proposed.

The Knowledge Acquisition Subsystem

The expert system continues to grow by adding on to its knowledge base new rules and by modifying existing ones. The **knowledge acquisition subsystem** makes it possible for new rules to be added to the knowledge base. Because of this knowledge acquisition component, the expert system can be developed in an ongoing process. Normally, a prototype is developed using a simple problem, and the system is continually modified with new rules as more complex situations are addressed.

The Human Interface

Expert systems are designed to be used by business, engineering, and other professionals—not by technical experts. As a result, these users need to be able to communicate with the system and to understand its feedback. Since most expert systems are designed to deal with a narrow area of knowledge, the vocabulary they use should be familiar to their users.

How an Expert System Works

To learn more about how an expert system works, it is useful to provide an example. This example is of an expert system for automobile ignition system fault diagnosis. An expert system is designed to achieve a **goal,**

which in this case is to avoid ignition system problems. The **domain** identifies the general area of knowledge about the application. In this case, the domain is the mechanics of an ignition system. The expert system is designed to accomplish a **task,** the diagnosis of ignition system faults. **Input** into the system consists of data such as ignition system temperature, air pressure, and engine performance. The **output** of the system should identify the problem or else provide a self-correcting mechanism to fix it.

The **paradigm** refers to the conceptual model the expert system uses to diagnose possible ignition system problems. The model is supported by the **inference engine,** the part of the software environment which uses the knowledge base to implement the procedures necessary to diagnose the problem. The **knowledge base** consists of the data and procedures relevant to the problem.

The expert system for the diagnosis of ignition system faults cycles through the rules in its knowledge base to determine if a problem exists. Its data base consists of information about temperature, air pressure, and voltage being transmitted to the cylinder engine. If the temperature in the ignition system is too high, if gas is vaporizing too soon, if the engine is firing too soon, or if the engine is running too roughly, then the expert system may trigger a self-correcting measure by turning on a fan. If this doesn't work, the expert system will ''learn'' that the self-correcting procedure has failed and will cycle through the ignition data again. It will continue executing more rules until it flashes on a light to warn the driver about insufficient fluid levels. This time the driver has to take corrective action to solve the problem.

Examples of Expert Systems

Many of the earlier expert systems were designed in medical diagnosis and engineering management. In many of these cases, expert knowledge was available and could be organized into rules which were needed. MYCIN was developed to assist physicians in the diagnosis of bacteremia, meningitis, and cystitis infections using knowledge of patient history, symptoms, laboratory test results, and characteristics of the infecting organisms. The system diagnoses the cause of the infection and selects appropriate therapy. There are dozens of other expert systems in the field of medical diagnosis.

In the area of geology, many expert systems have been developed to aid in the exploration and drilling of oil wells. An expert system called DRILLING ADVISOR assists an oil-rig supervisor in resolving problems relating to the drilling mechanism sticking within the borehole during drilling. Another system, MUD, helps engineers maintain optimal drilling fluid properties by diagnosing problems with drilling fluids and by suggesting treatments. PROSPECTOR is an expert system that helps geologists search for ore deposits in various geological regions.

Many successful expert systems have been designed to diagnose faults in electronics systems. A system called ACE identifies trouble spots in telephone networks and recommends appropriate repair and maintenance

work. Once ACE locates faulty telephone cables, it selects the most effective type of maintenance and stores its recommendations in a data base that users can access. Another system, SADD, assists engineers in the design of digital circuits. Engineers provide a functional description of the proposed circuit in English, and the system uses this information to build an internal model of the circuit. Then, the system uses knowledge of the model, component characteristics, and circuit behavior to design and test a plausible circuit.

One of the most successful business-related applications of expert systems helps Digital Equipment Corporation (DEC) configure its VAX 11/780 computers. XCON, the name of this system, uses information on a customer's order to decide what components must be added to produce a complete operational system and determines the relationships among these components. XCON helps make sure that VAX computer systems are successfully configured, and it has been central to DEC's success in the computer business.

The success of XCON has encouraged other businesses to explore the opportunities that expert systems development provides. Expert systems development is no longer just applicable to problems in engineering, medicine, and electronics. There is great potential to develop commercial applications of expert systems. The following examples provide some insight into how expert systems are being used in business and industry.

A Credit Authorization System at American Express

At American Express, an expert system for credit authorization has been developed to minimize fraud and credit losses from incorrect authorizations. Prior to the development of the system, credit card transactions were analyzed using statistical models to determine which charges fell outside of typical credit patterns for cardholders. These charges were then investigated by authorizers, people who searched for clues to determine if the person using the card was the true cardholder and if the person was likely to pay the charge.

The tremendous time and effort involved in the credit authorization process was cut down by the development of an expert system composed of about 800 rules. Since rules for credit authorization could be defined, an expert system was feasible. With the expert system, American Express is able to make more accurate credit authorizations, reduce training time, and stabilize staffing levels.

An Expert Financial Planner

Another type of expert system is an expert financial planner. PlanPower uses its knowledge of interest rates, expected inflation rates, tax laws, and standard investment strategies to develop financial plans for its clients. PlanPower uses clients' objectives, as well as information about their taxes, prior investments, insurance coverage, and real-estate holdings, to recommend appropriate strategies. PlanPower can also do "what if" projections and compare the short- and long-range impact of alternative plans.

An Expert System for Aircraft Design

Another complex problem that expert systems development has addressed is aircraft design and engineering. At Northrop Corporation, military aircraft design involves more than 10,000 parts, each requiring its own process plan describing the manufacturing steps and methods. If design errors aren't discovered until the plane

reaches the shop floor, the required revisions may result in major costs from production delays, the reworking of tools, and the scrapping of parts.

The expert system designed at Northrop makes it possible to convert descriptions of parts into process plans in about five minutes, in contrast to the hours human planners need. The system also establishes knowledge of process planning as a permanent corporate resource. Prior to the development of this system, designers developed plans, and much of the reasoning behind these plans was in their heads. When these people left, the plans and the designers' experience developing them were lost.

In the future, Northrop feels that the development of expert systems to model events happening on the shop floor will help it schedule its manufacturing operations more efficiently. Another expert system could support manufacturing engineers, who determine the feasibility and expense of manufacturing aircraft parts which have been designed.

Prospecting for Direct Mail Buyers An expert system has been designed to identify the hottest products for direct mail campaigns put on by businesses using mail-order catalogs and by fund-raising organizations. MORE/2 software is an expert system that ranks these mailing lists, based upon the results of previous mailings and test mailings. For example, an initial analysis may indicate that the best prospects for a specialty sportswear catalog are single women between 25 and 35 years of age who live in apartments. MORE/2 creates a mailing model based on these key variables, conducts a promotion, and analyzes response rates in order to improve the mailing program model.

The characteristics of these systems projects make them good opportunities for the development of an expert system. In each case, expert knowledge was available and the task at hand was primarily cognitive. These tasks would normally take an expert a few minutes to a few hours to solve, making them appropriate for expert systems development. Finally, and most important, each project had a high payoff in business terms.

The Development of Expert Systems

An expert systems development project is quite different from a traditional data-processing systems project. In the development of data-processing systems, data structures are defined, procedures are specified, and code is written to implement these procedures. In contrast, in expert systems development, data are stored in a data base and the procedures to be executed are expressed in rules. Depending on the problem, the rules can be executed in various sequences.

Characteristics of Expert Systems Development

In order to understand how expert systems are developed, it is important to recognize how knowledge is acquired. First of all, knowledge is inexact, and no one has complete knowledge. Even though the expert's knowledge is often 10 times more complete than the knowledge of amateurs, his or her

answers are still only about 70 to 80 percent certain. An expert auto mechanic, for example, may identify the correct problem only about 75 percent of the time. When he misses, however, he learns from his mistakes. An expert system is no better than an expert and will never be able to offer knowledge that is completely certain.

Secondly, knowledge is incomplete. Knowledge is usually acquired incrementally, through trial and error. For example, an expert baseball player learns his skill from hundreds of hours of practice. College students majoring in chemistry are usually exposed to general principles during their early courses but don't really learn why things happen until they take more advanced courses in later years and develop real expertise. Expert systems are also developed in an incremental way. Requirements are not all defined in advance. Normally a prototype is developed and rules are added as new situations occur.

Expert knowledge usually applies to a very specific area. We know of expert auto mechanics, expert chefs, and expert tennis players. No one is an expert doctor, but a doctor may be an expert in diagnosing infectious blood diseases. No one is an expert lawyer, but a lawyer may have expertise in the area of maritime law. Problems with very few rules (fewer than 10, for example) are not good candidates for expert systems development because they can be handled well by most humans. Problems with too many rules (more than 10,000) are too complex, and knowledge bases relating to them would be too time-consuming to develop.

Some projects are not feasible for expert systems development. Problems so complex that there are no experts or problems where there is substantial disagreement among experts are not good candidates for the design of an expert system. An expert system cannot have common sense, so problems requiring common sense are not good candidates either.

The problems suitable for expert systems development include those requiring analysis and synthesis. Medical diagnosis and electronics fault detection are both analysis problems, in which data describing a situation are entered and analyzed. In a synthesis problem, the expert system must develop a solution that achieves a goal within certain constraints. Computer system configuration and electronics design problems are both synthesis-type problems. These problems sometimes require the solutions to several smaller problems to be synthesized into an overall solution that satisfies overall constraints.

An expert system can serve well as a consultant or specialist in the absence of a human consultant. The expert system can combine the knowledge of several different specialists and actually be superior to the expertise of a single consultant. Expert systems have greater consistency in dealing with problems because they don't forget relevant factors under the constraints of stress and time. They can also arrive at faster solutions and generate a greater number of alternatives. In addition, an expert system can be recorded and used for consultation and training purposes in multiple locations, simply by copying a disk file.

The Development of Expert Systems

The process of designing an expert system is quite different from the traditional systems development process. The process involves knowledge

engineering, which refers to the creation of knowledge bases. Knowledge engineers build the pieces of the knowledge base, and the expert supplies the rules and facts.

The process starts by having the expert write down the variables and the rules that apply to a particular problem. The problem here is that most people have a working memory of only about six seconds. Their long-term memory stores the information on causes and relationships that are needed to design the system. As a result, expert systems projects use a prototyping approach, in which a group of rules are defined up front and applied to about six or seven cases. These cases point out the need for more rules, and more rules are accumulated. Gradually, these rules can be grouped together into "chunks" of knowledge, as shown in Figure 16.3. These chunks of knowledge are normally not identified in sequence but have to be organized after considerable testing. The number of rules may increase from 20 to 100 after a series of cases are explored. Eventually, these rules need to be boiled down to a reasonable number. The ultimate system may end up with 30 to 40 rules. This does not mean that these rules will stay static. Instead, they will constantly evolve as the system is used and refined. Standards of accuracy for expert systems will vary, but a good expert system should be 75 to 80 percent accurate.

The expert systems development process is similar to the decision support systems development process in that it relies heavily on a prototyping approach and the continuing evolution of the system. Revisions are inevitable and involve the reformulation of rules and concepts and a refinement of the system that has been implemented.

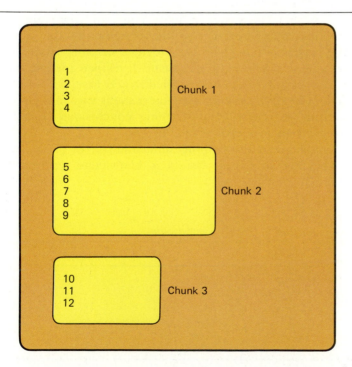

FIGURE 16.3
Rules Organized into Chunks in a Knowledge Base

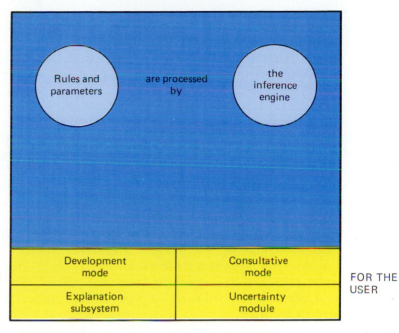

FIGURE 16.4
An Expert System Shell

Software for Building an Expert System

Expert systems can be developed using procedural langauges such as LISP and PROLOG or expert system shells. An **expert system shell,** depicted in Figure 16.4, consists of a **knowledge base,** which includes the rules and parameters, and an **inference engine,** which processes these rules and parameters. These shells also provide an **explanation subsystem,** which tells users how they got to where they are and an **uncertainty module,** which provides advice relevant to the certainty of the system. Some examples of expert system shells are provided in Table 16.4.

Expert system shells have also been developed for use on personal computers. For example, a package called Expert-Ease works on an IBM PC and requires only 128K of memory. Expert shells vary in their approaches in representing knowledge and reaching conclusions. Some are more suitable for certian applications than others.

Expert systems can also be programmed in LISP or PROLOG. The main task in developing an expert system is knowledge representation, and

Table 16.4   Examples of Expert System Shells

Vendor	Shell	Language
Intellicorp	KEE	LISP
Teknowledge	M.2, S.1	C
Inference Corp.	ART	LISP
IBM	ESE, Expert Systems Environment	Pascal
Xerox	LOOPS	InterLISP

languages that offer flexibility and the ability to explore possibilities are needed. Both LISP and PROLOG are interactive so that the programmer can get feedback from the language as programs are being written. Both LISP and PROLOG are Englishlike in syntax.

Expert Systems and Decision Support Systems

Expert systems and decision support systems both support problem-solving in an unstructured environment. Expert systems make it possible to expand the flexibility of the problem structure. They also offer the use of an inference engine, a knowledge base, and a knowledge acquisition subsystem. A DSS provides the user manager with alternatives for consideration, but an expert system can help the user evaluate these alternatives or may even prompt the decision-maker with approaches or choices that have been employed in other situations. The expert system can serve as a consultant, providing rules of thumb for situations that deal with incomplete, uncertain data. In the future, many managers may use expert system shells to augment the decision support systems they have already developed.

Robotics

Another application of artificial intelligence that has been a major part of factory automation is robotics. Most robots handle specialized tasks, such as cutting, drilling, painting or welding. Most are designed to do a single function, following the same pattern of motion day after day. At an IBM typewriter plant, work is passed from robot to robot. Each typewriter's frame and paperfeed structure are passed down a line of robots, each of which does one simple job, such as inserting a screw.

Arc welding using the MetaTorch, a second-generation robot manufactured by Meta Machines Ltd. The robot's sense of sight is provided by a combination of lasers and miniature cameras, which look ahead of the welding torch to locate the precise position of the joint. This information is processed and instructions passed to the robot's arm and welding set.

Sheila Terry, Science Photo Library/Photo Researchers, Inc.

A robot's ability to complete a variety of tasks is one of the factors that differentiates it from automated machinery or androids. This robot at Ford's Wayne, Michigan, Assembly Plant is programmed to perform welding operations on the body of Ford Escorts and EXPs and Mercury Lynxes. Other robots are programmed for spray painting, material handling, and other tasks.

Courtesy of Ford Motor Company

Although most robots are programmed to perform a simple, repetitive task, some robots perform a series of operations. At General Dynamics F–16 aircraft assembly plant in Fort Worth, a robot drills some 6,000 holes and inserts a rivet or other fastener in every hole. To do this, the robot has to move into position, drill each hole, gauge its depth, pick up and insert the proper fastener, and shave off the protruding end.

One problem in robotics is that robots cannot be programmed to move exactly according to the computer's instructions. One way of dealing with this problem is to endow robots with sensors, such as machine vision or tactile feedback. When a sighted robot misses its target, it can see its error and adjust its position accordingly.

Machine vision can help the robot take a snapshot of the object being worked on and to execute a preprogrammed series of motions based on knowing the object's position. In an electronics assembly plant, for example, a vision system is used to check the position of printed circuit boards and enables the robots to know where to reach to insert components.

Vision systems are also used to enable robots to identify objects correctly so that they know what stored programs to use. Ford Motor Company uses robots to rivet parts onto truck chassis. A vision system views a truck, identifies it by the pattern of mounting holes on the chassis, and then directs a robot holding a rivet gun.

Tactile sensing is also an ability of robots. A robot responsible for grinding bumps off the surface of a part will know to keep grinding until the resistance diminishes, indicating that the lump has been worn down.

In the past, robots have been used primarily for jobs in which humans faced safety and health hazards. In general, robots are slower and more expensive than people. They are much better equipped to perform a single task day after day than they are to handle complete operations. They also threaten a highly unionized labor force in many industries.

Robotics is an important part of factory automation. The automation of factory operations will continue to be a critical factor in improving the competitive advantage of American industry. In Japan, a line of 47 robots churns out 100,000 quartz watches a month at the Seiko/Epson plant west of Tokyo. Robots are also at work in assembling copiers, automobiles, and electronic equipment of many types. American industry will continue to introduce robots into its manufacturing operations during the next 10 years and beyond.

Conclusion

The development of decision support systems enables managers to use computer-based information systems as a tool to support their decisions on a day-to-day basis. The tools for decision support are user-friendly microcomputer-based data base and mainframe-based fourth-generation languages that can be learned by people who are not computer professionals. As such, decision support systems have integrated the computer into the working habits of many managers and professionals.

Chrysler's huge computer-controlled robot called the Turnkey Gate does 78 crucial welds at once, setting a vehicle's body dimensions with absolute precision.

Artificial intelligence has brought humans and machines even closer together. Now, computers can capture the knowledge of experts and make it possible for hundreds of doctors, lawyers, science professionals, and business persons to benefit from this expertise. In the future, many professionals will use these "expert assistants" to help them solve their day-to-day problems.

The development of decision support systems and expert systems has directly involved the user in information systems development. No longer are systems designed by technical professionals who write hundreds of lines of code and deliver a finished product to the user. With these new systems, a prototyping approach is used, making it possible for the user to continually revise and refine the systems that are developed. The role of the MIS professional has changed from one of a technical designer to one of a facilitator and consultant to the user.

With the dramatic growth of technology in the artificial intelligence area, we might feel that it will not be very far into the future before fiction becomes fact, and expert systems are able to read a human's thought processes and to do the reasoning for him or her. However, before we begin to think that computers may become intelligent in and of themselves, we need to rethink their potential. Computer technology is only as powerful as we can design it to be. It is only as useful as our requirements dictate. User designers, knowledge engineers, and system builders in the future will have a growing role in business, industry, and the service professions. The need to control the effective use of these technologies so that they can be used productively and successfully to solve business, scientific, and medical problems.

Clever Elevators "Learn" from Experience

Newest Cars Will Even "Learn" from Experience

A new generation of elevator technology is working its way into the world's office buildings, bringing with it a promise that many New Yorkers will find irresistible: the savings of dozens of wasted seconds each day.

The result is, in effect, a thinking elevator—a hybrid of programmable computer chips and high-technology sensors. Advanced versions will appear in new skyscrapers this year and next, and in many existing buildings the technologies are being grafted onto old cars and motors.

Elevator designers hope to save either passengers' waiting time or, by carrying more people with less equipment, building owners' money. Clever programming alone—apart from increases in elevator speed—can serve as many as 1,500 people an hour with elevators that formerly reached their limit at 1,000.

The smart elevator will sense not only how many people are riding but also how many are waiting at each floor. In buildings with just one or two elevators, the microprocessor has little to add, but where banks of multiple elevators handle heavy, complex traffic, the computer comes into its own. Using techniques borrowed from game theory, it makes rapid choices, sending cars to where they can do the most good, considering the system as a whole. The next leap forward will be learning ability, enabling elevators actually to anticipate riding patterns.

The idea is to stamp out the various bug-bears of elevator traffic. There is the phantom pickup, for example—the door of car number two opens to greet a rider who is no longer there, having just boarded car number one. There is car-bunching—elevators all heading upward in packs around the 20th floor while impatient crowds wait at the lobby.

"In today's world an elevator systems gets overloaded and overpopulated, and the elevators tend to bunch together" even when passengers are distributed more or evenly, said William S. Lewis of Jaros, Baum & Bolles, a consulting engineering firm in New York. Any system with many imperfectly coordinated moving parts can fall into an undesireable pattern. To overcome that, the computer has to overrule the tendency of every car to try to answer the nearest call.

In the past, when elevators were controlled by relays, simple electromagnetic switches, complex logic was impossible, and individual cars were mostly on their own. Now the computer lets elevators look at one another and adjust to changing circumstances.

"It can say, 'Skip these calls and run express to the lobby, even though someone is going to wait longer,'" Mr. Lewis said. "That gets to be a very esoteric algorithm."

Elevator as Anthropologist

Over the past few years, some elevator riders have already had to adjust to the first signs of the new technologies, such as graphic color television displays of schematic elevators gliding up and down the screen. Some riders have had to suppress their annoyance at the sound of synthesized voices asking them to "Clear the door" or explaining dolefully, "There is no cause for alarm."

Elevator systems have long been able to adjust somewhat to periods of peak up or down traffic, by automatically sending extra cars to the lobby in the morning, for example. With learning computers, a building's elevator system will act like a sort of anthropologist, studying rider habits until it can anticipate what people are going to do before they do it. This capability allows

a system to adjust when it discovers that the law firm on the 14th floor begins to empty out early Friday afternoons during the summer, say, or to recognize cafeteria-bound traffic at lunch time.

"*React* is the key word here," said Merton Meaker, director of technical marketing for United Technologies Otis Elevators. "The elevator control systems will recognize different traffic patterns in a building, day to day or week to week, and respond accordingly."

Bonuses and Penalties

Mathematical ingenuity is required for banks of cars to make the optimal decisions for moving people around large office buildings. Manufacturers have worked out programs that calculate different hypothetical futures and compare their desirability, just as a chess-playing computer does, using penalties and bonuses to help weigh the alternatives.

Bonuses can be awarded for assigning a call to a car that has a rider who wants to stop at that floor anyway—a seemingly obvious strategy that was beyond the capability of old-fashioned systems. Penalties are awarded for decisions that lead to too many stops.

And, most important, penalties are awarded for keeping people waiting; long waits get extra heavy penalties. The appropriate threshold is a matter of debate. Officials of Fujitec America, for example, cite a psychological study that found "great irritation" after 60 seconds or more.

That study was conducted in Osaka. "Thirty seconds is the rule of thumb in New York," said James J. Mancuso, area manager for Fujitec.

Fujitec hopes to begin installing within the next few months the first infrared sensing devices to detect the body heat of waiting riders, in office buildings at Battery Park City. Other companies, too, are preparing such devices—"people sensors"—to let their computers recognize a nascent mob before it is too late.

In some ways, that information is even more important than it would have been in the era when every elevator was on its own. The new computer strategies can outsmart themselves, programmers have discovered.

For example, suppose 20 people are waiting on the 11th floor. After 29 seconds, one car arrives. Eight people board. The remaining people press the button again. Without people sensors, the computer will start its waiting-time count all over again at zero, giving the floor a low priority.

Many systems already have the ability to estimate how many riders are in a car by weighing it, and that information, too, is being added to computer strategies. Cars that feel full can be instructed to stop trying to pick up new riders. And as an "anti-nuisance feature," when a dozen buttons are pushed in a car that is suspiciously light, the computer can automatically turn them all off.

The first generation of operatorless, automatic elevators is now more than 30 years old, so modernization of old systems forms the largest share of the market. In a new building, however, the potential for saving money is vast. The central elevator space of a building represents a tremendous cost, and allowing 8 elevators to do the work of 12 can mean millions of dollars in rents.

Raw speed alone seems to have reached its useful limit. Said Mr. Meaker of Otis: "There's a physiological restriction that's going to limit us to about 2,000 feet per minute: the comfort level on the human body when you change cabin pressure."

In other words, ears start popping. "If you want to go faster your only alternative is to pressurize the cab," Mr. Meaker said.

Dealing with Randomness

Computer strategies must deal with tremendous variation and randomness in rider behavior. On average, some manufacturers estimate that an office worker will make six trips a day, but that can be much higher when a company extends over several floors.

In a building with 10 floors and 1,000 people, elevators might need to handle 250 rides an hour. In the World Trade Center, more than 200 elevators carry 40,000 people an hour.

The millions of seconds freed by the technologies will not necessarily be distributed democratically. "We do have what is known as executive service," said Joel Tuman of Millar Elevator Industries in New York which has updated elevator systems in many existing buildings.

Certain New York City executives—they know who they are—can press a button at their desk, causing an elevator to speed toward their floor. Or an executive can dial a number from a car telephone to make sure an elevator will be standing by at garage level.

The microchip has made other special services available, as well. In the event of a terrorist attack, for example, an operator can instruct the computer to send all the elevators in a building to a particular floor and open the doors one by one, presumably delivering the occupants into the hands of the waiting security forces.

For now, human operators do control even the computerized systems. Consoles with elaborate color-coded graphic displays have been set up at lobby security desks or in special elevator control centers.

In some buildings, the designers have begun to note an unexpected, and possibly unsettling, phenomenon. The operators develop a tendency to involve themselves in their work.

"Particularly in New York, certain individuals like to play with the system," said Mr. Mancuso of Fujitec. "They make it like a video game."

Source: James Gleick, *The New York Times,* April 28, 1987.

Summary and Key Terms

1. **Decision support systems** are computer-based information systems that help decision-makers use data and models to solve unstructured problems.

2. An effective decision support system must take into account the characteristics of decision-making and of decision-makers. It must be able to support unstructured decisions, to support all phases of the decision-making process, and to support communications between decision-makers.

3. Decision support systems are designed using a **prototyping approach,** during which a system builder works with a user to develop a model of the proposed system and continues to refine the system until the user's requirements are met.

4. **Artificial intelligence** refers to the development of a computer-based system that produces performance that in humans would be associated with intelligence.

5. An **expert system** uses rules of human experience and judgment to solve difficult problems much in the same way an expert would.

6. An expert system consists of a **knowledge base,** an **inference engine,** an **explanation subsystem,** a **knowledge acquisition subsystem,** and a **human interface.**

7. Expert systems have been developed for medical diagnosis, oil well drilling and exploration, electronic systems fault diagnosis, and computer systems configuration, as well as for a number of business applications.

8. In the development of an expert system, a **knowledge engineer** works with an expert to build pieces of the knowledge base that are needed for problem solving.

9. Expert systems can deal with more unstructured problems than decision support systems because the problem structure does not have to be defined in advance.

10. **Robotics** is another application of artificial intelligence in which robots are programmed to handle specialized assembly and manufacturing tasks.

Review Questions

Fill-In

1. Information systems that support day-to-day operations are known as _____ _____ systems.

2. The three phases of decision-making are intelligence, _____, and choice.

3. The design process for support systems is called _____ design.

4. _____ is the development of computer-based systems that simulate human performance.

5. The component of an expert system that uses the knowledge base to draw conclusions for each situation is called the _____ _____.

6. A _____ refers to the conceptual model the expert system uses to diagnose possible problems.

7. An expert system _____ consists of a knowledge base, an inference engine, an explanation subsystem, and in some cases an uncertainty module.

Discussion Questions

1. What are three characteristics of a decision support system?

2. You are supposed to make a decision about what kind of car to purchase. You have a budget of $15,000. Identify the data you would use to support each of these three phases of the decision-making process:
   a. intelligence
   b. design
   c. choice

3. What are the major differences between the traditional systems development process and the decision support systems development process?

4. What are four major characteristics of an expert system?

5. Do you feel that the following projects are good candidates for expert systems development? Explain why or why not.
   a. An expert system to forecast presidential election results.
   b. An expert system to diagnose faults in gas turbine engines.
   c. An expert system to underwrite insurance policies.
   d. An expert system to qualify sales leads.
   e. An expert system to select convention sites.

Careers in Data Processing

17

Chapter Objectives

After studying this chapter, you should be able to

1. Describe the duties of various jobs within data processing.

2. Identify the educational requirements for entry into selected computer positions.

3. Name the kinds of data processing personnel needed by industry.

4. Describe the steps to take if you are considering a career in data processing.

After graduating from college with a bachelor's degree in biology, Steve was unable to find a job in his field. Because he could not afford to continue his studies, and do graduate work, he took a job in the construction industry. After several years, when Steve was 30, construction in his area slowed down and he saw that the field held no future for him. At the same time, Steve was increasingly struck at how computers were present in nearly every phase of life. He wondered about the opportunities for a career in this growing industry. To satisfy his curiosity, Steve enrolled in an introductory computer programming course at a local college. He found the work challenging, and got outstanding grades. Steve met with his instructor to discuss the potential for a career in data processing. His teacher gave Steve the Berger Aptitude for Programming Test, and he scored extremely well, obtaining 28 points out of a possible 30. Next, Steve met with a vocational counselor at the college. With the counselor's guidance, he applied for, and entered, the Computer-Science Business Applications program at North Idaho College. When he completed the program, Steve found a job as a programmer at a local utilities company. He remained there for two years, and then moved to a programmer/analyst position at Transtector Systems, a developer of customized business applications. Steve advanced steadily at Transtector, and has recently been promoted to Systems Manager.

Steve's story is just one example of how people enter computer careers from many avenues and at many ages. For a long time, it was commonly believed that you remained with one job for most of your life, even if you were unhappy there. Because of many changes in our society (such as individual and corporate relocation, more women in the work force, and the transition from a manufacturing to a service economy), there is now a high level of career mobility. It is not unusual to find people who have changed careers several times in their lives.

In order to accurately identify an appropriate career, and to take the steps necessary to pursue that career, you must have adequate information about the field and the opportunities available. In this chapter, we'll examine the recent changes in the data processing industry, and identify those areas where growth is expected. We'll provide descriptions of the positions available, along with educational requirements and salary levels of those positions. We'll present a four-step plan for pursuing a career in data processing.

Changing Needs of the Computer Industry

The Outlook for Computer Professionals

As the computer industry matures and changes, the need for trained and experienced personnel shifts as well. From 1970 to 1985, there was consistently high demand for computer professionals. As the sales of computers grew, the need for programmers and systems analysts grew as well. Employment of programmers grew nearly seven times as fast as the economy as a whole, while the employment of systems analysts grew even more rapidly, almost ten times as fast.

A Long and Distinguished Career in Computers: Grace Hopper

One woman who has had a lifelong involvement with the development of computers is Grace Hopper, who at age 79 recently retired from the U.S. Navy but not from the field. Immediately following her retirement, Hopper took a post as full-time senior consultant for Digital Equipment Corp.

As Hopper tells it, one of the reasons she was attracted to computers in the first place was that she loved gadgets. As a girl, she liked to dismantle alarm clocks to figure out how they worked. Two other reasons she chose computers were her excellent mathematics ability and her interest in ''the future.'' After earning a bachelor's degree from Vassar College in 1928, Hopper went on to get a doctorate in mathematics from Harvard University. While at Harvard she worked with the Mark I, the first large-scale computer in the United States. Hopper describes the 51-foot-long machine as the ''biggest, fanciest gadget'' she had ever seen, and she felt she had to find out how it worked. Working with the Mark I, Hopper developed a reputation for taking on projects that seemed to overwhelm others. It was Hopper who tackled the job of writing the Mark I's manual.

Among Hopper's many contributions, industry historians agree, was her ability to recognize early the potential commercial and industrial applications for computers. Perhaps even more importantly, she was able to bridge the communication gap between managers and programmers, who without her seemed to have trouble understanding one another. Hopper explains that she

However, in 1985 there was a slowdown in the sales of computers, and many programmers and systems analysts faced layoffs. Industry specialists have identified many reasons for this slump, including overall economic conditions, a cautious approach by many businessmen in the purchase of equipment, the rise in the value of the dollar (and a resulting reluctance on the part of foreign buyers to purchase computer equipment), and the glut of computers and computer-related products competing for space in the marketplace. Other factors contributing to the personnel layoffs included a surplus of entry-level applicants, and a shortage of positions.

What does the 1985 slowdown mean for job-seekers of the future? Many industry observers believe that there will be continued growth, and that the job outlook will become more positive. Reasons for these beliefs include the development of newer, more easy-to-operate machines, and the consequent demand for more applications; continued expansion of the kinds of tasks computers can perform; and the increasing necessity to connect microcomputers to mainframes to optimize processing power. It is important, though, for career planners to be aware of the areas in which jobs will be available.

Programmers write the instructions (computer programs) so that computers can perform the desired tasks. In recent years, there has been an ongoing debate as to whether the need for programmers will gradually diminish. Sparking this debate is the growth of various programmer productivity tools. These are aids that perform many of the routine tasks previously done by programmers. Such tools include development workbenches, program generators, and fourth generation languages. The argument is that these tools will soon remove the need for programmers. Other experts cite the presence of packaged software products as also contribut-

promoted computers by simply showing business people how the new technology could benefit them. Many credit Hopper's early marketing efforts with attracting the insurance and aerospace industries to automation.

Her many other accomplishments include working for Eckert-Mauchly, the company that built UNIVAC, and participation in the creation of the programming language COBOL, which has become a standard language for business applications. Hopper is sometimes credited with singlehandedly developing this language: actually, she got the project started and put together a team of people to work on it. She also attended the first meeting of the Committee on Data Systems Languages (CODASYL) and has earned some 30 professional awards and 37 honorary degrees during her career.

Today Hopper continues to look into the future. In her vision, she sees optical computers becoming increasingly important within the next five years (see the FOCUS in Chapter 2). Hopper also sees a general shift away from mainframes as minis become more powerful. She has been discouraging the Pentagon from a continuing dependence on mainframes lately and supports its increased use of networks of minicomputers. One of her continuing frustrations, however, is that people are slow to change and some people insist on clinging to an old familiar tool when a new one can do the job better.

Source: George Leopold, "Beacon for the Future," *Datamation*, October 1, 1986, pp. 109–110.

ing to the gradual obsolescence of programmers. They feel that these packages will not need to be customized, thus eliminating the need for programmers to write client-specific applications. The debate continues, and the general feeling is that the need for programmers will grow, not diminish. Reasons for this anticipated growth include the ever-increasing number of applications that will be needed and developed.

Nevertheless, potential programmers must be better equipped than ever before. Applicants will have a better chance at employment if they are knowledgeable about specific industries. In addition, good communication and problem solving skills are in demand, so that employers will be able to promote programmers when supervisory and management vacancies arise. Knowledge of programming languages beyond COBOL and FORTRAN (including ADA, Pascal, C, and LISP) are an asset to job applicants.

Systems analysts dissect the various applications in terms of procedures, work flow, data flow, and problems. They gather the information to define the requirements for computerized information systems to serve the applications areas. Industry specialists believe that the need for systems analysts will continue to grow at a high rate. Many systems analysts begin as programmers. In addition, knowledge of several computer languages and specialization in particular industries make systems analysts more marketable. The most lucrative opportunities for systems analysts are projected in the transportation, utilities, data processing services, and non-financial banking services fields.

Data base specialists design data bases to meet organizational needs. They also create programs to use those data bases effectively. As more corporations rely on data bases, the need for these professionals grows. Data base specialists must possess excellent design and analysis skills. They must also be familiar with both the particular industry and the specific firm in which they work. They need superior communications skills, in order to work with management to translate the firm's requirements into a functioning system.

In Chapter 15, we spoke of the emergence of the corporate information center. Users turn to the center for assistance in developing applications, and in learning how to use and maintain the data processing resources they possess. The information center specialist works closely with users to define requirements, and to provide them with tools to meet their needs. As the number of corporate information centers expands, so the demand for information center specialists increases.

Data communications specialists develop and design data communications networks and create the installation and operations procedures for data transmission lines. There is great need for personnel who can link the various computers and peripherals within an organization. This "link-up" enables the company's resources to communicate with each other. Sample applications include the downloading of data from a mainframe, the processing of that data on a microcomputer, and then the return (upload) to the mainframe. In some situations, the procedure is reversed: The information is entered on the microcomputer and then moved to the mainframe for more complex processing. As more companies realize the crucial importance of connectivity, the demand for, and salaries of, data communications specialists grows.

What Kinds of Workers Are Needed?

The technological changes of the past 10 years, beginning with the microcomputer explosion, have produced many new jobs. Virtually every industry needs computer-trained employees at all levels of responsibility. In this section, we'll examine just a sampling of the job opportunities available within the major computer industry categories.

Hardware Manufacturers

As the number of software applications increases, computer manufacturers must produce more machines and peripheral devices to execute those applications. In addition, as researchers discover how to build computers that will accomplish more sophisticated tasks in less time, corporations replace old, outdated hardware with more efficient equipment. Hardware manufacturers today face this challenge: how to produce higher-level equipment in greater quantity at lower cost. As the desire to link the various computers expands, computer corporations must also create the peripheral devices that will foster compatibility.

Hardware manufacturers employ a diverse group of specialists to meet the needs of today's computer users. These employees work on all phases of the product cycle: from conception through assembly, and on to sales and service.

Computer designers conceptualize the machines and computer equipment. They begin with an idea of the kinds of tasks they'd like the machine to perform, and develop a computer (or peripheral device) to perform those tasks efficiently. Computer designers must create new machines that fit into the users' lifestyles: for example, laptop computers for the executive who travels frequently but needs access to his department's data; typewriter-sized computers for the college student who lives in a dormitory; and portable computers for the auditor who moves from one client site to another to test the controls for those clients' systems.

Computer engineers are responsible for translating the designer's concepts into the specifications for an actual machine. Engineers design the circuit boards, memory chips, and the inner workings of various peripheral devices.

Computer technicians use the engineers' specifications to assemble the actual computers and peripheral devices. After they build the product, the technicians run prescribed tests to ensure that the machines function properly.

In addition to the technical specialists, many hardware manufacturers employ support personnel to sell, service, document, and market their products. The size of the support staff varies with the size of the manufacturer: generally the larger the manufacturer, the more intricate a support staff is employed. Smaller and more specialized hardware vendors often

employ outside agencies to perform the support functions. Support staff personnel include:

- *Sales representatives.* A sales team is needed to actually sell the hardware product. The representative's clients may range from other hardware companies to corporations and on to the end user. Sales personnel must know the specifications and capabilities of their products, the devices offered by the competition, and the requirements of the market in general. They must also be familiar with their users' needs and environments so that they can assist their clients in making sound choices.

- *Customer systems engineers.* These technicians are responsible for keeping their clients' equipment in good working order. Also called computer service technicians, they install, maintain, and repair the computers and peripheral devices.

- *Technical writers.* Hardware manufacturers produce different kinds of documents to accompany their products. Technical writers produce manuals for technicians that provide information on how to assemble, install, and repair the manufacturer's product. They also write instructions for users who purchase and run the equipment.

- *Educators.* Hardware vendors offer many courses to support their products. These include courses for technicians on new products, classes for sales staff on how to market the equipment, and, sometimes, seminars for end-users on the features and operation of the hardware. Educators design and conduct these sessions.

- *Marketing specialists.* These employees develop strategies to foster awareness of the product. They create the marketing plan, produce materials to support that plan, coordinate trade show participation, and develop press releases. They also might create advertisements for the product, or work with advertising agencies to develop campaigns.

Software Manufacturers

As the amount of, and need for, applications grows, the software industry expands as well. Software manufacturers employ various specialized programmers and systems analysts, as well as support personnel similar to those found in hardware companies.

Application programmers design, code, and test computer programs for applications areas. They might be involved in the creation of new applications, or the maintenance of previously developed software.

Systems programmers maintain the hardware and software operating environment.

Systems analysts, within the software manufacturing environment, break down the various applications into their component parts, in preparation for software design.

Software manufacturers often use contract programmers for special projects, or at particularly busy times. Such programmers, often supplied by temporary help agencies, supplement the in-house staff. They are paid on a contract or per job basis. Software manufacturers employ many of the

Today, computers provide a wide range of careers.

Courtesy of AT&T Information Systems

chard Hutchings/Photo Researchers

Courtesy of Mohawk Data Sciences

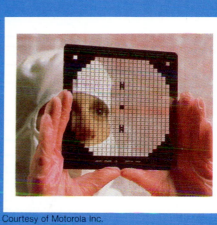

Courtesy of Motorola Inc.

ohn Curtis/Taurus Photos

Courtesy of Computerland

same support personnel as hardware manufacturers, although their responsibilities may vary slightly.

- *Sales representatives.* Like their counterparts in the hardware industry, sales representatives are employed to sell the product. Their clients might be corporations, other software manufacturers, hardware vendors, computer stores, and end users.

- *Technical writers.* It is crucial that software systems be accompanied by clear instructions for use. Technical writers prepare user manuals and other reference aids to support the software. They might be involved in software development, through the design and review of help screens.

- *Educators.* Sales representatives, computer store employees, and, of course, end users, must be properly trained in the use of application packages. Educators design, develop, and conduct training sessions for these groups.

- *Marketing specialists.* With the advent of microcomputers and computer retail stores, software packages often compete for shelf space, like other packaged goods. Marketing specialists are often involved in package design, in addition to the formulation and execution of a marketing program for the product.

Growth Area: Computer Services

One area of expanding job possibilities in the computer field is professional services. In the past, computer companies have emphasized the development and sale of their products. But now that many businesses have already invested in computer systems, the focus has shifted to demonstrating new uses for them as well as working out specific business problems through computer applications. Many hardware and software companies believe that through personalized instruction, demonstrations, and applications analysis, they will sell more of their products. In addition, as businesses are becoming more sophisticated in the use of computers, they want systems that are designed for their own particular needs. Computer consultants are professionals who may work for the computer or software companies, meeting with customers to advise them on the the use of their company's products; within a traditional business consulting firm; in special departments of large companies that use computers; or in independent firms that specialize in computer consulting.

In 1984 Wang Laboratories Inc. started a special computer services unit called WangCare. Consultants work on two- to three-day projects, helping Wang customers to select the right software for their needs, individually tailoring the hardware to fit the customers' applications, and installing and maintaining Wang systems. After a system is in place, WangCare consultants may return periodically to bring the system up to date. For these services WangCare receives about $2,000 to 3,000 for each initial project. Manager Donna L. Cheney expected total revenues to double in its third year of business.

IBM has been involved in the computer services area for thirty years, but lately this segment of its business is expanding dramatically. One division of the company, Federal Systems, employs 5,000 people. While Federal Systems did only government work until recently, today the division is moving into consulting for private businesses, including an extensive project for United

Like hardware manufacturers, software manufacturers employ support staffs according to their size and needs. It is not unusual for small developers to sell their applications to larger corporations, for the purpose of attaining the marketing and support prowess of the larger firm.

Computer Services and Supplies

A significant segment of the computer industry is the service and supply area. Included in this category are repair service companies and businesses, computer retail stores, computer service bureaus and companies, computer publishing companies, and private consulting firms.

Often, hardware manufacturers will offer service contracts for their equipment. Sometimes, the service and maintenance will be handled by a separate repair company. These companies employ computer service technicians to install, maintain, and repair the hardware. They also use technical writers to prepare manuals for the technicians, and sales representatives to sell service contracts. The sales representative would sell to hardware vendors, computer retail stores, and end users. The representa-

Airlines, which will develop an improved computer reservations system.

Recently, North American Philips Consumer Electronics Corp. hired Arthur Andersen & Co., a Big Eight accounting firm that has begun working in the area of computer consulting, to sort out a number of problems in distribution, marketing, and management. Arthur Andersen set up a team of 45 computer consultants to study Philips's operations. The consultants' task was to talk with distributors, salespeople, company executives, and customers in order to analyze problem areas and generate possible solutions. The total project cost to North American Philips was $5 million, and it lasted 18 months. The end result was a reorganization in the company's marketing department and a simplification of the ordering process. More importantly, though, the team designed a new computer system that set up a network of distributors, shippers, salespeople and manufacturers. While the cost of the project was high, Philips executives believe that it will result in a reduction of the business's overall operating costs.

Smaller firms involved in consulting are focusing on areas of industry in which they have specialized knowledge. Management Science America Inc., a software company in Atlanta, concentrates on developing systems for education and manufacturing, while Control Data Corp. consults mainly electric utilities and oil companies and Burroughs Corp. focuses its services on hospital systems.

As this area continues to grow, it will provide increasing opportunities for professionals working in a variety of settings—from computer and software companies, large and small, to consulting companies with broad or narrow focus.

Source: Anne R. Field, "The Next Boom in Computers: Services," *Business Week*, July 7, 1986, pp. 72–73.

tives must be familiar with the hardware configurations possessed by their clients.

Computer stores employ systems consultants to advise customers on how to assemble systems to meet their needs and budgets. The stores also use hardware and software salespersons to assist customers in making appropriate selections. These employees must work together, so that the customer purchases compatible components, and is thus satisfied with the service. The computer retail store might also employ technicians, to provide installation and maintenance on the equipment sold.

Computer service bureaus and companies provide computing power to firms that either possess no data processing capabilities, or those that require applications beyond the scope of their in-house systems. An example of the latter would be the small accounting firm that has a limited computer system, and thus sends tax forms to an outside bureau to be processed.

Service bureaus employ a variety of data processing personnel. Since most of their clients do have some kind of automated system, it becomes desirable to link the client's computer system to the system at the service bureau. This avoids time-consuming and costly duplication of data entry. Thus, data communications specialists are needed by these service bureaus to design and implement the mechanisms for these business-to-business communications.

Systems analysts are employed by the bureaus to determine the clients' needs and to design a system that will enable the bureau to meet those needs efficiently.

Service bureaus also employ data entry and computer operators. Data entry operators enter the information required for particular applications. Operators of computers and peripheral equipment follow instructions to set the controls on the various devices, monitor the computer console, and take action in response to messages generated by the system.

Because many hardware and software companies are not large enough to have regular support staffs, they turn to computer publishers. These publishers employ technical writers to develop both user and technical documentation for hardware devices and software packages. The publishers also use marketing and promotion analysts to devise and execute marketing plans for the products. In addition, they retain sales representatives to sell their services to the manufacturers, and, sometimes, to sell the products to outside clients.

The number of private consulting firms has grown rapidly within recent years, and is expected to continue to grow. These firms assist corporations in determining their computer needs, advise them on the kinds of systems to purchase to meet those needs, and help train corporate personnel so that those systems can be implemented. Consulting firms employ systems analysts to determine and design systems for their clients, application programmers to develop the software for those systems, and customer engineers (trainers) to develop and educate users so that the system is implemented efficiently.

An additional field where computers are in wide use is education. Computers are used from elementary through high school to teach skills in many subject areas, and to foster computer literacy among the student population. As a result, schools need teachers who can implement and use

Table 17.1   Computer-Industry Careers

Hardware Research, Development, and Repair

These employees are directly involved with the research, development, and repair of computer equipment, including CPUs, monitors, disk drives, scanners, printers, and tape drives.

Job Title	Job Description
Electrical Engineer	Designs the circuit boards, memory chips, and other electronic components of the computer and peripheral equipment. *Education*: Bachelor's degree in electrical engineering. *Salary*: $26,000–$76,000
Design Engineer and Mechanical Engineer	Designs the hardware components of the computer and related peripheral devices. *Education*: Bachelor's degree in mechanical engineering. *Salary*: $26,000–$76,000
Computer Service Technician	Installs, maintains, and services computer equipment according to manufacturer's instructions. Also called field engineers or customer engineers. *Education*: Minimum of two-year degree from a community college, vocational school, or the military. Usually obtain on-the-job training from employer for specific equipment. *Salary*: $15,000–$45,000

Software Development

These employees design the systems and develop the software that address the needs of business and scientific users.

Job Title	Job Description
Business Application Programmer	Writes and maintains computer programs that process business applications such as payroll, accounting, and inventory control. *Education*: Bachelor's degree with courses in computer science, accounting, or finance or a two-year degree from a technical or vocational school that specializes in computer programming. *Salary*: $15,000–$33,000
Scientific Application Programmer	Writes and maintains the computer programs that are used in scientific and engineering applications. *Education*: Bachelor's degree with courses in math, computer science, engineering. *Salary*: $18,000–$25,000
Systems Programmer	Installs and maintains operating system programs. Examples include compilers, linkage editors, systems utilities. *Education*: Bachelor's degree with courses in math and computer science. *Salary*: $27,000–$42,000
Contract Programmer	Writes customized application programs on contractual or single program basis. May work at a site other than the firm's data center. *Education*: Bachelor's degree with courses in computer science, accounting, finance (for business applications), and math and engineering (for scientific applications). *Salary*: $15–$50 per hour, or on a "job-finished" basis.
Data Base Designer/ Administrator	Designs and coordinates an organization's data base. Responsible for issues concerning file content, usage and security. *Education*: Bachelor's degree in computer science, with specialization in data base management systems. *Salary*: $26,000–$44,500
Data Communications Specialist	Provides computer communications expertise to clients or employer. *Education*: Bachelor's degree in computer science, specializing in data communications. *Salary*: $26,000–$43,000

Table 17.1   Cont'd

Job Title	Job Description
Programmer/Analyst	Performs the duties of both a systems analyst and application programmer. *Education*: Bachelor's degree in computer science or a two-year degree from a technical or vocational school. Several years of experience and proven ability are additional requirements for this position. *Salary*: $22,000–$33,000
Systems Analyst	Designs complete systems that solve data processing problems for the end user. *Education*: Bachelor's degree in computer science or information systems. Must have skills in design, interpersonal communication, business systems and management concepts and practices. Programmers with analysis skills will sometimes be promoted to systems analysis positions. *Salary*: $27,000–$65,000

Computer Operations

These employees operate the physical computer equipment on a day-to-day basis. They work with devices such as the CPU console, disk and tape drives, printers, plotters, and data entry machines. They might also be responsible for report distribution and activation of modems and other communications hardware. They help the information systems operating environment function as efficiently as possible. Computer operators do not design or write application programs.

Job Title	Job Description
CPU Operator	Monitors and controls the operation of the CPU of a minicomputer or mainframe. Commands the CPU to begin batched jobs, and responds to messages from the CPU for various actions required by application programs. *Education*: High school diploma. Training may be acquired at selected high schools, technical and vocational schools, community colleges, and in the military. Technicians usually obtain on-the-job training from employers for specific equipment. *Salary*: $15,000–$25,000

computers in their classrooms. Technical and vocational schools require instructors to develop and conduct courses for aspiring technicians. Finally, colleges and universities employ teachers who can integrate the computer into their specialized areas, as well as researchers and developers to study and determine future trends in the field, and devise applications to meet future needs.

Educational software vendors often employ teachers as product developers, reviewers, and consultants. In addition, they use marketing specialists to create programs to ensure that their products reach the appropriate educational users.

Table 17.1 gives job descriptions, educational requirements, and salary ranges for some of the positions that we've discussed. The salary ranges refer to salaries for entry level through experienced personnel, and job applicants may encounter salaries below or above the ranges.

Steps to Take if You're Considering a Computer Career

Career planning, regardless of the specific profession or industry, should always be a logical, well-thought-out process. You must first identify the field in which you're interested, and then learn about the positions in that field. It's necessary to gather information about the training required for the positions you've targeted, and then formulate an action plan. In Table 17.2 we present some steps to take if you're planning a career in data processing.

Table 17.2   Four Steps to a Career in Data Processing

1. *Use aptitude tests to identify interests and abilities.*
   Tests such as the Strong-Campbell Interest Inventory and the Berger Aptitude for Programming can help determine your general goals and values, and indicate your potential for a data processing career. Your college counselor can provide information about, and arrange for you to take, these tests.

2. *Research job descriptions.*
   Use publications and people to learn about specific positions. *The Dictionary of Occupational Titles* and *The Occupational Outlook Handbook* contain descriptions of specific jobs. In addition, speak to people currently employed in the position you seek.

3. *Research training requirements.*
   Identify the training requirements for the position you've decided upon, and locate the institutions that offer the courses you need. Use published curriculum guides from various institutions, and speak to college counselors, to obtain this information.

4. *Make the decision.*
   Create a plan to accomplish your goal. Divide your plan into manageable tasks, and set target dates for the completion of each task, as well as a final date by which you will meet your overall objective.

Bill Gates' Challenge Now: Running Miscrosoft

Software's Old Man Is 30

When William Henry Gates, chairman of Microsoft Corp., leaves his Redmond, Wash. office on a business trip, he deliberately sets out for the airport a few minutes later than he should. Says he: "I like pushing things to the edge. That's where you often find high performance." Gates generally makes his planes with only a minute or two to spare. In larger ways, his near-perfect performance in one dazzling decade in business has made him the yuppie Chuck Yeager, pushing the envelope not of space but of software.

Gates, who does so many things so well, is more remarkable than better-known princes of high-tech like Steven Jobs. He is not only a technological visionary who can dream of software applications years ahead but a marketing strategist who prices his products for the mass market, not only a charismatic leader who keeps his 1,200 employees challenged but a tough CEO who fired his first president after 11 months. Beyond that, his overall whiz-kid intelligence puts him at the head of any class. (His math score on his Scholastic Aptitude Test was a perfect 800.)

Microsoft, with sales of $100 million in its 11th year, began as a college boy's bluff. In 1975, Gates was a Harvard sophomore who preferred late-night poker, hard-core hacking and such sentimental reading as *A Separate Peace*

and *The Catcher in the Rye* to his pre-law studies. When his boyhood friend Paul Allen showed him an ad in Popular Electronics for the Altair, a build-it-yourself computer, the pair immediately rang up MITS, its Albuquerque manufacturer. With schoolboy bravado, they announced that Gates had already adapted the computer language BASIC for the machine. He had not, but after four frantic weeks, he did. Says Gates: "One little mistake would have meant the program wouldn't have run. The first time we tried it was at MITS, and it came home without a glitch." It also changed the course of Gates' life: he quit Harvard and with Allen formed Microsoft to create a line of software products.

Growth has been remarkably smooth and steady. In fact, Gates has financed his company's expansion completely out of earnings. The next great risk of Gates' career came when he set out to develop the operating system for IBM's new PC. His MS-DOS has since become the industry standard. "We bet all our resources on that system," he recalls. He also helped design Radio Shack's Model 100, the first truly portable computer; he produced MSX systems software, the soul of a new series of Japanese machines; and more recently, he released Windows, the much delayed program that allows various applications to appear on the screen at once. Last January Miscrosoft launched its most ambitious project, the long-term develooopment of CD-ROM, a compact disk that can hold any kind of computerized information—musical, textual or visual. During all this warp-speed activity, Gates took his company public in March, making his own shares—40% of the outstanding total —worth $390 million as of June 1.

Microsoft's master views nonwork warily. He puts in 65-hour weeks but no longer pulls all-nighters as he did in the early days. In the first five years of Microsoft he took only two vacations, of two to three days each. Now he permits himself seven or eight days off a year plus some weekends. About twice a month he sees a San Francisco friend, Ann Winblad, 35, who also founded her own software company with three partners. She recently sold out for $15.5 million. This spring he took his most extravagant holiday to date, renting a 56-foot sailing vessel with crew for four days off Australia. Says Gates, somewhat apologetically: "We'd just gone public, and I was sort of pampering myself."

Relaxing is not at all Gates' style. He believes that bad habits in one segment of life—say, personal finance—can spill into others. So Microsoft's $175,000-a-year chief executive is a financial conservative. He has no debts and invests only in stocks he knows well. In the early '80s, he ran a $40,000 ante up to $1 million by investing in undervalued technology stocks, including Apple. In 1983 he bought his $780,000, 11-room house with its 30-foot-long indoor swimming pool with those profits. In 1981, the last year of his partnership with Allen, he made more than $1 million and paid $500,000 in taxes. Says Gates, who was too busy running his company to bother about sheltering his income: "I got a letter from Reagan thanking me for paying all that money."

Gates, who grew up the middle child and only son of a prominent Seattle lawyer and his wife, acknowledges a debt for his success that goes way beyond taxes. "The software business is very American," he says. "The original technological advances were all made here. The largest markets are here. And the atmosphere that allowed it all to happen is here. That's how our original customers, including IBM, could be so open-minded about buying from a 25-year-old guy with a small company out in Washington. They may have thought it was crazy at the time, but they said, 'Hey, if he knows so much about software, maybe he knows even more.'" And he did.

Source: *Money,* July 1986, pp. 54, 56.

Summary and Key Terms

1. Careers in computers are among the fastest growing occupations in the United States.
2. The three major sources of career opportunity are hardware manufacturers, software manufacturers, and computer services and supplies.
3. Computer designers and engineers are responsible for the design of all computer hardware.
4. Application programmers design business programs and will generally have a business oriented education.
5. Systems programmers install and monitor operating systems and will generally have a computer science education.
6. Systems analysts are responsible for the design of entire systems. They generally are required to have an information systems or computer science education. This occupation is one of the fastest growing in the economy.
7. Contract programmers work on a contract basis, usually on a per-hour or finished-program basis. They are usually required to have several years of experience.
8. Repair and service occupations are in great demand. They are usually required to have technical training from a technical school, vocational school, or the military, or a college degree in electrical engineering.
9. The steps to take if you're considering a career in computers include (1) take aptitude tests to identify your interests and abilities, (2) research job descriptions, (3) research training requirements and locate institutions that offer the courses you'll need, (4) make the decision.

Review Questions

1. Identify two of the fastest growing data processing jobs.
2. Describe the types of products that are produced by hardware manufacturers.
3. Describe the types of products that are produced by software manufacturers.
4. What is the difference between a business application programmer and a systems programmer?
5. What is the difference between a systems analyst and a programmer/analyst?
6. Describe two positions within the computer services area.
7. Define the term *contract programmer*.
8. Identify the general education requirements for a systems analyst.
9. Identify the general education requirements for a computer service technician.
10. Describe the steps that should be taken if you are considering a computer career.

Representing Data Within the Computer

A

To understand better how the central processing unit functions, let's look more closely at how data and instructions are represented inside the computer. First we'll examine the binary numbering system and see how it is used to code information. Then we will look at the hexadecimal system, which serves as a kind of shorthand for computer programmers.

The Binary Numbering System

The decimal numbering system, so familiar to us, is based on the numeral 10 and uses the ten integers 0–9. The **binary system,** which is based on the numeral 2, uses only two integers, 0 and 1.

Subscripts are used to identify a numbering system. Thus the subscript $_{10}$ denotes a number in the decimal system; 43_{10} refers to the decimal number 43. The subscript $_2$ denotes a number in the binary system; 101_2 denotes the binary number 101.

In both the decimal and the binary systems, the value of a digit varies according to the position it occupies in a number. We can compare the values of some decimal digits and some binary digits. In the decimal system, each digit in a number is expressed as a power of 10. In a decimal number, each successive digit to the left of the decimal point represents a value ten times greater than the digit to its immediate right. Let's illustrate how the power of a number increases by 10 as we move to the left of the decimal point. (The value of any number raised to the 0 power is, by definition, 1.)

Place value:	10,000	1000	100	10	1
Expressed as:	10^4	10^3	10^2	10^1	10^0

As an example of the value of decimal digits, let's look at the decimal number 62,017.

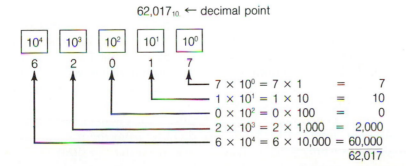

$62{,}017_{10}$ ← decimal point

$$7 \times 10^0 = 7 \times 1 = 7$$
$$1 \times 10^1 = 1 \times 10 = 10$$
$$0 \times 10^2 = 0 \times 100 = 0$$
$$2 \times 10^3 = 2 \times 1{,}000 = 2{,}000$$
$$6 \times 10^4 = 6 \times 10{,}000 = 60{,}000$$
$$62{,}017$$

By comparison, each digit in a binary number is expressed as a power of 2. Each successive position to the left of the binary point has a value two times greater than the digit to its right. We can illustrate how the power of each digit increases by 2 as we move to the left.

Place value:	64	32	16	8	4	2	1
Expressed as:	2^6	2^5	2^4	2^3	2^2	2^1	2^0

Now let's consider, as an example, the binary number 11011 and multiply each digit times its place value.

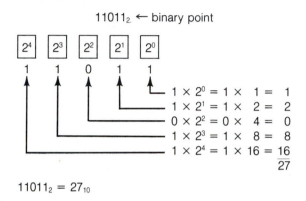

$$11011_2 = 27_{10}$$

Converting Binary Numbers into Decimal Numbers   By multiplying each digit times its place value, we have just seen an example of how a binary number is converted into its decimal equivalent. In this case, we have found that the binary 11011 is equivalent to the decimal 27. Let's look at another example of converting a binary number into a decimal number. This time, we will find the decimal equivalent of 1101_2.

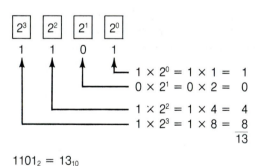

$$1101_2 = 13_{10}$$

Converting Decimal Numbers into Binary Numbers   A decimal number can also be converted into a binary number. The easiest way to accomplish this is to divide the decimal number repeatedly by 2, the base of the binary system, until we reach a quotient of 0. After each division, we will indicate the remainder. The series of remainders will then be the digits in the binary equivalent of the original decimal number.

Let's consider an example. We will convert the decimal number 14 into its binary equivalent. Note that we are dividing from the bottom upward. The digits in our binary equivalent are read from the top down.

14_{10}

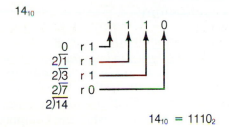

$$14_{10} = 1110_2$$

The binary equivalent of 14_{10} is 1110_2.

As another example, let's convert 43_{10} into its binary equivalent.

43_{10}

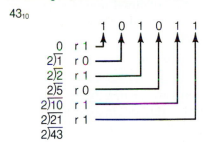

$$43_{10} = 101011_2$$

We see that 43_{10} is equivalent to 101011_2.

Figure A.1 shows some binary and decimal equivalent values.

FIGURE A.1

(a) Place Values of Binary Numerals (b) Equivalent Values of Decimal and Binary Numbers

Note that four digits (bits) are needed to represent one decimal digit.

2^{14}	2^{13}	2^{12}	2^{11}	2^{10}	2^9	2^8	2^7	2^6	2^5	2^4	2^3	2^2	2^1	2^0
16384	8192	4096	2048	1024	512	256	128	64	32	16	8	4	2	1

(a)

Decimal System	Binary System Place (Bit) Values			
	8	4	2	1
0	0	0	0	0
1	0	0	0	1
2	0	0	1	0
3	0	0	1	1
4	0	1	0	0
5	0	1	0	1
6	0	1	1	0
7	0	1	1	1
8	1	0	0	0
9	1	0	0	1

(b)

The Hexadecimal System

Although information is stored in the computer's memory as combinations of binary 0s and 1s, binary numbers become cumbersome when expressing large numbers. For this reason, the internal contents of the computer are not displayed in binary form. Instead, computer programmers often use hexadecimal digits as a condensed or shorthand way of representing the binary digits stored and processed inside the computer.

Just as the decimal system is a base 10 system and the binary system is a base 2 system, the **hexadecimal system** is a base 16 system. Each successive digit to the left in a hexadecimal number represents a value 16 times greater than the digit to its immediate right. Let's look at the place values in the hexadecimal system:

Place value:	65,536	4,096	256	16	1
Expressed as:	16^4	16^3	16^2	16^1	16^0

The hexadecimal system contains sixteen digits. The first ten hexadecimal digits are equivalent to the ten decimal digits 0 through 9. The remaining six hexadecimal digits are represented by the letters A through F. The letter A represents 10, B represents 11, C represents 12, D represents 13, E represents 14, and F represents 15. Figure A.2 shows equivalents for binary, hexadecimal, and decimal values.

Converting Hexadecimal Numbers into Decimal Numbers   Hexadecimal numbers can be converted into decimal numbers. To demonstrate this process, let's convert the hexadecimal 36 into its decimal equivalent:

36_{16}

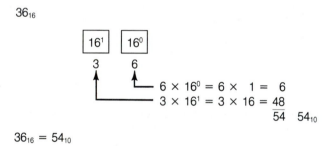

$36_{16} = 54_{10}$

We see that 36_{16} is equivalent to 54_{10}.

Now let's convert the hexadecimal number $B51_{16}$ into its decimal equivalent. (Remember that the hexadecimal B is equal in value to the decimal 11.)

$B51_{16}$

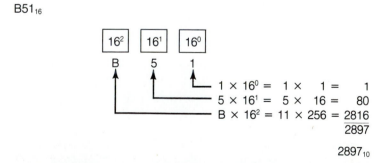

$B51_{16} = 2897_{10}$

Decimal System	Binary System				Hexadecimal System
	Place (Bit) Values				
	8	4	2	1	
0	0	0	0	0	0
1	0	0	0	1	1
2	0	0	1	0	2
3	0	0	1	1	3
4	0	1	0	0	4
5	0	1	0	1	5
6	0	1	1	0	6
7	0	1	1	1	7
8	1	0	0	0	8
9	1	0	0	1	9
10	1	0	1	0	A
11	1	0	1	1	B
12	1	1	0	0	C
13	1	1	0	1	D
14	1	1	1	0	E
15	1	1	1	1	F

FIGURE A.2
Equivalent Values of Decimal, Binary, and Hexadecimal Systems

We see that $B51_{16}$ is equivalent to 2897_{10}.

Converting Decimal Numbers into Hexadecimal Numbers

How do we convert decimal numbers into hexadecimal numbers? Remember that we converted a decimal number into binary form by repeatedly dividing the decimal number by 2 and keeping track of the remainders. Converting a decimal number into its hexadecimal equivalent is a similar process. But because we are converting a decimal (base 10) number into base 16 rather than converting to base 2, we will repeatedly divide the decimal number by 16. The remainders of each quotient will be the digits of the hexadecimal equivalent.

Let's convert 432_{10} into its hexadecimal equivalent. We divide, as before, from the bottom upward; the hexadecimal digits will be read from the top down.

432_{10} $1B0_{16}$

```
                    1   B   0
            0 r  ↑   ↑   ↑
      16)1 r 11 ─────┘   │
      16)27 r 0 ─────────┘
       16)432
```

$432_{10} = 1B0_{16}$

(Remember that the decimal 11 is equivalent to the hexadecimal B.)

Internal Coding Schemes

After this brief introduction to the binary and hexadecimal systems, we will see how characters are actually represented inside the computer. Using pure binary form to represent all the necessary alphanumeric characters

—such as numbers, letters, and punctuation marks—internally would require long strings of 0s and 1s.

Computer designers have over the years tried to develop more convenient ways to represent characters. These efforts have produced a variety of codes that use binary-system terms to represent decimal numbers, alphabetic characters, and commonly used symbols.

Eight-Bit Codes We know that in most computers one byte is one character, and each byte may contain eight bits. It makes sense, then, that the most commonly used binary code system employs eight bits to represent each character. This code uses the four bits representing the four binary place values, 1, 2, 4, and 8. Four zone positions are also added, expanding the size of the potentially codable character set to 256 (2^8).

The structure of an eight-bit code for a character is:

Zone Bits				Numerical Bits			
				8	4	2	1
X	X	X	X	X	X	X	X

One eight-bit code is the **Extended Binary Coded Decimal Interchange Code (EBCDIC,** pronounced eb-suh-dik), which was developed by IBM and is now used in computers produced by many manufacturers. Another is the **American Standard Code for Information Interchange (ASCII,** pronounced as-key), which is widely used in data communications as well as in most microcomputers and some larger machines (see Figure A.3).

FIGURE A.3
Examples of EBCDIC and ASCII Coding

Character	Extended BCD Interchange Code (EBCDIC)	ASCII
0	1111 0000	0101 0000
1	1111 0001	0101 0001
2	1111 0010	0101 0010
3	1111 0011	0101 0011
4	1111 0100	0101 0100
5	1111 0101	0101 0101
A	1100 0001	1000 0001
B	1100 0010	1000 0010
C	1100 0011	1000 0011
D	1100 0100	1000 0100
E	1100 0101	1000 0101

EBCDIC in Action Remember that hexadecimal numbers are a form of shorthand employed by computers to simplify the writing of data in computer programs. Each hexadecimal digit represents four bits. Let's consider the word "auto" as it is represented in EBCDIC:

LETTERS:	A	U	T	0
Hexadecimal:	C1	E4	E3	D6
EBCDIC binary:	1100 0001	1110 0100	1110 0011	1101 0110

Now let's see examples of how numbers are represented in EBCDIC:

Decimal numbers:	7	6	5
Hexadecimal:	F7	F6	F5
EBCDIC binary:	1111 0111	1111 0110	1111 0101

Figure A.4 shows EBCDIC representations of the alphabet and decimal numbers.

Character	EBCDIC Binary	EBCDIC Hexadecimal	Character	EBCDIC Binary	EBCDIC Hexadecimal
A	1100 0001	C1	0	1111 0000	F0
B	1100 0010	C2	1	1111 0001	F1
C	1100 0011	C3	2	1111 0010	F2
D	1100 0100	C4	3	1111 0011	F3
E	1100 0101	C5	4	1111 0100	F4
F	1100 0110	C6	5	1111 0101	F5
G	1100 0111	C7	6	1111 0110	F6
H	1100 1000	C8	7	1111 0111	F7
I	1100 1001	C9	8	1111 1000	F8
J	1101 0001	D1	9	1111 1001	F9
K	1101 0010	D2	Blank	0100 0000	40
L	1101 0011	D3	.	0100 1011	4B
M	1101 0100	D4	(	0100 1101	4D
N	1101 0101	D5	+	0100 1110	4E
O	1101 0110	D6	$	0101 1011	5B
P	1101 0111	D7	*	0101 1100	5C
Q	1101 1000	D8	)	0101 1101	5D
R	1101 1001	D9	—	0110 0000	60
S	1110 0010	E2	/	0110 0001	61
T	1110 0011	E3	'	0110 1011	6B
U	1110 0100	E4	,	0111 1101	7D
V	1110 0101	E5	=	0111 1110	7E
W	1110 0110	E6			
X	1110 0111	E7			
Y	1110 1000	E8			
Z	1110 1001	E9			

FIGURE A.4
EBCDIC Coding of Alphanumeric and Some Special Characters

Six-Bit Codes   We know that in some computers each byte contains six bits. These computers would then require six-bit codes. The structure for a six-bit code is similar to an eight-bit code in that it contains four numeric

bit positions. But there are two, rather than four, zone positions. This is the structure of a code for a character expressed using six bits:

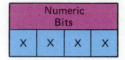

Detecting Coding Errors

Because computers are not infallible, a method for detecting coding errors made in incoming data has been developed. An extra bit—called a *check bit* or a *parity bit*—is added to each byte within the computer. This means that every eight-bit byte actually contains nine bits and that every six-bit byte actually contains seven bits. We can illustrate the check bit position:

8-Bit Byte		
Check Bit	Zone Bits	Numeric Bits
X	XXXX	XXXX

6-Bit Byte		
Check Bit	Zone Bits	Numeric Bits
X	XX	XXXX

Remember that every bit is either a 0 or a 1. Every error-detection code is designed in one of two ways—so that every byte representing a coded character will contain an even number of 1-bits or so that every byte representing a coded character will contain an odd number of 1-bits. These two approaches are known as *even parity* and *odd parity,* respectively.

The value for the check bit in each character code is set at either 0 or 1, depending on whether an extra 1-bit is required in order for the character to be in even or odd parity. Computer manufacturers determine whether the machines they produce will be in even parity or odd parity.

Even Parity   If a computer is designed to use the *even-parity approach,* then the code used inside the computer for each character must contain an even number of 1-bits. If, for example, the internal code for the character A contains an odd number of 1-bits without the check bit, then the value for the check bit will be set at 1.

Even parity provides that any character that is coded with an odd number of 1-bits will contain a 1-bit in the check-bit location. The value in the check-bit position for every character that has a code containing an even number of 1-bits will be set at 0.

Odd Parity   Other computers are designed to use the *odd-parity approach,* which means that the internal code for each character must have an odd number of 1-bits. In such computers, if the letter B were represented by a code containing an even number of 1-bits, then the value for the check bit would be set at 1 to give the code an odd number of bits. If the character code had an odd number of 1-bits, then the value for the check bit would be set at 0. In this way, all characters would be expressed by codes containing an odd number of bits. Examples of parity are shown in Figure A.5.

Check Bit	Zone Bits	Numeric Bits
C	Z Z Z Z	8 4 2 1
1	1 1 0 1	0 1 1 1
0	1 1 1 0	0 0 1 0
0	1 1 0 0	0 0 0 1

} row #1

} row #2

} row #3

No. This character code is invalid because it has an odd number (7) of 1-bits. If the value for the check bit were set at 0, there would be 6 1-bits, making it valid. VALID: 011010111.

Yes. This character code is valid because it has 4 1-bits. It is in even parity.

No. This character code is invalid because it has 3 1-bits. If the check bit were set at 1, there would be 4 1-bits. It would then be valid. VALID: 111000001.

FIGURE A.5
Examples of Parity

Assume that a computer uses even parity, meaning there must be an even number of 1-bits in each character. Are the following EBCDIC characters valid?

Review Questions

Binary-Decimal Conversions

1. Write the decimal numbers equivalent to the following binary numbers:
   _____ 1101
   _____ 100110
   _____ 0101101
   _____ 110011000
2. Write the binary numbers equivalent to the following decimal numbers:
   _____ 7
   _____ 16
   _____ 43
   _____ 62

Parity Checking

Determine whether each of the following characters is in even parity. If not, change the character to even parity by changing the check bit and rewriting the character in the blank at the right:

Example: 1001101111 0001101111
1. 0 11111010 _____
2. 1 10101110 _____
3. 1 01110111 _____
4. 1 01111100 _____

Introduction to BASIC Programming

Michael J. Murphy
Jean Longhurst

Contents

Before beginning the coverage of BASIC, we would like to cover a few of the ground rules under which this section was written.

The programs were written on an IBM PC under DOS. The majority of the programs will run as is on an Apple II. Where this is not the case, the changes will be pointed out in the section "BASIC Language Discussion" following the program.

Meaningful variable names are used rather than just one or two letters. IBM allows the use of up to forty characters for a data name. Apple ignores all but the first two.

The sample programs use LPRINT to direct the output to a printer for the IBM. This should be changed to PRINT for an Apple. With the Apple, output is directed to the printer with a separate command. A person using an IBM who wants screen output should also change LPRINT to PRINT.

Structured programming is introduced in Section 2 and used to the extent possible in all succeeding sections. Emphasis is placed on structure and documentation even though it is recognized that the programs could be written with fewer lines of code.

521

Section 1: A Simple Program

Topics Covered in This Section

BASIC Instructions	LOAD
REM	Other
LET	Line numbers
PRINT	Logic
END	Simple calculation
BASIC Commands	Programming Project
NEW	Entering and running a
LIST	simple program.
RUN	
SAVE	

We are going to start our discussion of BASIC programming with a very simple program. The purpose of this first program is to teach you a little about BASIC and give you the opportunity to try a small program out on your equipment. Some of the anxiety that comes with learning to program is associated with entering the first program into the computer. Once you have entered your first program and find that the machine doesn't disintegrate at your touch, it is easier to relax and concentrate on learning the rules of the programming language.

We will approach the project in the following manner:

1. Present a project to computerize. Under "Problem Analysis" we will describe the output we must produce, and the input and processing required.
2. Provide the actual data.
3. Describe the output, which will always be a printed report in our projects. We will provide a print chart showing the design of the output.
4. Present a flowchart of the logic and a discussion of the logic.
5. Show the program coded in BASIC.
6. Provide the actual output produced by the program.
7. Provide an explanation of the BASIC statements used.

Problem Analysis

Output Required

Input Required

```
QUANTITY
UNITPRICE
```

Processing Required

1. Multiplication of QUANTITY times UNITPRICE to produce AMOUNT.
2. Printing the result.

Input Values   Two items of data are required to arrive at the amount of an order:

■ Quantity
■ Unit price

   We will assign the data names QUANTITY and UNITPRICE to these items. Notice that we left the space out between UNIT and PRICE. We cannot use spaces in the names we assign to data. If we did, the computer would treat the name as two data names rather than one. Rules for the formation of data names are presented in the next section.

Input Data Values

14   (which will be represented by the data name QUANTITY)
 2.11   (which will be represented by the data name UNITPRICE)

Output Format   No print chart is provided here. The answer, which we will call AMOUNT, will be printed at the left margin.

The Flowchart   See Figure B.1.1.

FIGURE B.1.1

Explanation of Logic Used

The flowchart of Figure B.1.1 is a graphic representation of the logic steps we need in our BASIC program. Three different symbols have been used in this flowchart. We will describe the appropriate uses for each symbol as well as the specific step it represents in our flowchart.

This first symbol is called the *terminal* symbol. It has nothing to do with terminals in the sense of a keyboard and a screen. It represents a terminal point in the flowchart, such as the beginning or the end. Every flowchart needs at least two terminal points: one for starting and one for stopping. Later, when we break our flowchart into sections, we will use the terminal symbol to begin and end each section. In this flowchart it represents the beginning and ending of the logic steps.

This symbol is called the *process* symbol. When representing the BASIC language, this symbol is used to represent the assignment of values to variables. In the first process symbol we assign the value of 14 to QUANTITY using a LET statement. Next we assign the value 2.11 to UNITPRICE. The third process symbol contains the calculation of AMOUNT. Notice that this is also done with a LET statement.

This symbol is the *input/output* symbol. We use it to represent the transfer of data into or out of the computer. In this case we are transferring the data to a piece of paper.

In this logic we are processing only one value each for QUANTITY and UNITPRICE. This is not a very powerful program. It will, however, give us the opportunity to introduce you to a number of elements in the BASIC language.

The BASIC Program

```
 10 REM * * * * * * * * * * * * * * * * * * * * * * * * * * *
 20 REM *                                                   *
 30 REM *  PROGRAM NAME: CASE 1A                            *
 40 REM *  AUTHOR:       JEAN LONGHURST                     *
 50 REM *  DATE WRITTEN: 4/15/19--                          *
 60 REM *                                                   *
 70 REM *  PROGRAM FUNCTION: CALCULATES AN ORDER AMOUNT GIVEN *
 80 REM *  THE UNIT PRICE AND QUANTITY AND PRINTS THE ANSWER. *
 90 REM *                                                   *
100 REM * * * * * * * * * * * * * * * * * * * * * * * * * * *
110 REM
120 LET  QUANTITY = 14
130 LET  UNITPRICE = 2.11
140 LET  AMOUNT = QUANTITY * UNITPRICE
150 LPRINT AMOUNT
160 END
```

FIGURE B.1.2

The Actual Output

29.54

BASIC Language Discussion

Line Numbers   In BASIC each line has a number in the integer range of 1 to 99999. The computer selects the next statement to be executed based on its line number. It is possible to enter more than one BASIC statement on a line to conserve memory. However, with the increased availability of micro-computers with 64K memory of more, this practice is used less and less.

REM

```
                                    IBM AND APPLE
FORMAT:
   line # REM any string
```

The REM statement provides a way to place comments and notes about a program in the program listing. REM statements are completely ignored

when the program is running and therefore have no effect on the logic of the program. Their only purpose is to provide explanation of the program to anyone who is looking at the program listing. A statement (like REM) that is ignored during the running of the program is called a nonexecutable instruction.

After the line number and the instruction REM, *any* sequence of characters may follow. It must be remembered, however, that anything in a REM statement is completely ignored when the program is run. If a comment requires more than one line to complete, each line of the comment requires a line number and the instruction REM.

REM statements are not required, and a program will run exactly the same with or without them. However, they should be used to document a program. It is a good idea to begin each program with a block of information in REM statements that includes the program name, the author's name, the date the program was written, and the function of the program. Other information that would be useful in understanding the program should also be included here. The next section describes the purpose of every variable in the program. This section is referred to as the Variable List, Data Dictionary, or some similar term.

```
10  REM  PROGRAM ID: CASE2
20  REM  AUTHOR ID: MURPHY/LONGHURST DATE WRITTEN: 5/26/8X
30  REM
40  REM  THIS PROGRAM DISPLAYS CUSTOMER ORDER INFORMATION
50  REM
60  REM  VARIABLE LIST
70  REM  CUSTNAM$.............CUSTOMER NAME
80  REM  CUSTNO..............CUSTOMER NUMBER
90  REM  PARTNO..............PART NUMBER
100 REM  QUANTITY............QUANTITY
110 REM  UNITPRICE...........UNIT PRICE
120 REM
```

REM statements may also be used to comment on and clarify sections and subroutines within a program. We will provide examples of this as our programs become longer and are broken into sections and subroutines.

A comment can be put on the same line as an executable BASIC statement. In Apple BASIC use a colon to separate the statements and then REM followed by the comment. On the IBM no separator is needed and an apostrophe is used to begin the comment.

```
200 GOSUB 1000: REM INITIALIZATION  (APPLE)
200 GOSUB 1000    'INITIALIZATION    (IBM)
```

LET

```
                                    IBM AND APPLE
FORMAT:
   line # LET variable = expression
```

The LET statement, to give a simple explanation, gives a value to something. The first LET statement in this program gives a value of 14 to QUANTITY. The second LET statement gives UNITPRICE the value of 2.11. The third statement multiplies UNITPRICE by QUANTITY and gives the value that results to AMOUNT. (In BASIC an asterisk (*) represents multiplication.)

We will discuss a more complete set of possibilities for the LET statement in the next section. With the LET statements we used in this programming project, we created three variables (QUANTITY, UNITPRICE, and AMOUNT). In Section 2 we will explain variables in detail. In the meantime, just consider them names we give to a value we want the computer to store. BASIC uses the name to keep track of where it stored the actual value.

PRINT

```
                                    IBM AND APPLE
FORMAT:
   line # PRINT [list of expressions]
```

PRINT allows us to transfer data from the computer memory to an output device. What we want to print must be detailed in the list of expressions that follows the word PRINT. (In describing the syntax, we enclose optional matter within brackets.) One of the things we can print is the value of a variable. In our first case we are asking the computer to transfer the value of AMOUNT from the memory to an output device. On IBM, PRINT will put the output on the screen and LPRINT will send the output to the printer. Apple uses the PR#0 command to send output to the screen and the PR#1 command to send output to the printer. The PRINT statement will also be covered more fully in Section 2.

END

```
                                    IBM AND APPLE
FORMAT:
   line # END
```

The END statement marks the end of a BASIC program. When an END statement is encountered the program stops executing. The END statement should be the last statement in a BASIC program unless there are subroutines (discussed in Section 3).

BASIC Commands

In order to have the computer execute the instructions we have written, the program must be keyed in. If we wish the program to be available after we turn the computer off or give it up to another student, we must store the program on a tape or diskette. The BASIC language provides us with *commands* to assist with the entering and storing of programs. When commands are entered at the terminal for immediate execution, not as program statements, line numbers are not used. The most often used commands are:

```
NEW
LIST
RUN
SAVE
LOAD
```

NEW

```
                                        IBM AND APPLE
FORMAT:
  NEW
```

The NEW statement is used to clear memory. As a student, you should always use the NEW command before you enter your program. Otherwise, you can find yourself with parts of someone else's program mixed in with yours.

LIST

```
                                        IBM AND APPLE
FORMAT:
  LIST [line [-line]]
```

All or part of a program can be listed on the screen. The main reason for listing a program is to view the portion you are working on when making additions, deletions, or corrections. To list the entire program:

```
LIST
```

To list a range of line number (inclusive)

```
LIST 400-600
```

To list beginning at a particular line number until the end of the program:

```
LIST 400-
```

To list from the beginning of a program to a particular line number:

```
LIST -600
```

Remember that your screen will only hold approximately twenty-five lines at one time. Any time your LIST specifies more than the screen will hold, the first lines listed will be lost to view as they roll on by. Pressing CTRL and NUM LOCK simultaneously will pause the scroll; pressing any key will resume scrolling. You can stop the listing by using the CTRL and BREAK keys simultaneously. To transfer this listing to the printer, the IBM user changes the command to LLIST. The Apple user enters PR#1 to transfer output to the printer.

RUN

```
                                    IBM AND APPLE
FORMAT:
   RUN [line number]
   RUN file name
```

This command starts a program executing. When only the word RUN is used, the program currently in memory will be executed. If a line number is specified, execution will begin with that line number. If the name of a program is used the appropriate program will be loaded from the diskette and executed.

SAVE

```
                                              IBM
FORMAT:
   SAVE "program name"
```

```
                                                          APPLE
  FORMAT:
    SAVE program name
```

The SAVE command is used to store a BASIC program on a diskette. When the SAVE command is issued, the BASIC program in memory is stored on the diskette and given the name specified. On the IBM the program name may be up to eight characters long. If a disk drive is not specified, the default drive is used; otherwise, the program name is preceded by drive letter and a colon A:, B:, or C:, for example. After the save operation has been completed, there is a copy of the program on diskette and it is also still in memory. Because a copy remains in memory, you must use the NEW command to clear it out if you wish to work on another program. Also, if you continue to make changes to your program after it has been saved and you wish to retain these changes, you must save the program again. Otherwise, you would lose the changes that were made since the last time you saved the program. When the save is performed, if there is already a program on the diskette with the same program name, the program in memory will be written over the program on disk. The old program will be destroyed. This is useful when you are replacing an old version of a program with a new version of the same program. It can be dangerous, however, if you accidentally try to name two programs with the same name. If you do, you will lose the old program. So, be careful when naming programs to use unique names.

LOAD

```
                                                          IBM
  FORMAT:
    LOAD "program name"
```

```
                                                          APPLE
  FORMAT:
    LOAD program name
```

The LOAD command is used to retrieve a program (that had been previously saved on diskette) from diskette and place it in memory. The program name used in the LOAD command must be the same name that was used when the program was saved. Again, if a disk drive is not specified, the default drive is used. Before issuing the LOAD command, make sure memory is clear by issuing the NEW command. Otherwise you may end up with lines of the old program interspersed with lines of the loaded program.

A Session with the Computer

The instructions for this session assume you are using a microcomputer with a disk drive. (Note ↵ represents the ENTER key.)

1. Be sure that the computer is turned on and that the BASIC language has been loaded. The screen should look like this:

```
    IBM                          APPLE
    _____         _____
        OK                           OK


    _____         _____
```

2. Type in NEW ↵

3. Type in your practice program. You may use the example in this chapter or one assigned by your instructor. Press ↵ as you finish each line of the program. If you make an error and discover the error before you have pressed ↵, you can correct the error by moving the cursor back to the part of the line that needs correcting and redoing it. If you have already pressed ↵, you can

a. delete the line in error by typing in DELETE nn ↵, where nn is the statement number;

b. correct the statement using the same statement number by retyping the entire line (the new version will replace the old); or

c. using the screen editor features, move the cursor back to the statement with the error, correct the error, and press ↵.

As you correct errors you may wish to type in LIST ↵. This will list your program on the screen and allow you to look at a version of it that is not cluttered with already corrected errors.

4. When you have completed the entry of your program, type in RUN ↵. The computer will execute your program and produce any results your program specifies.

5. If your output is not what you expected, correct any errors and continue to LIST ↵ and RUN ↵ until you have the correct output.

6. Place your initialized diskette in the disk drive and close the door. If your machine has more than one drive, your instructor or lab aide will advise you on the drive to use.

7. Type in SAVE "xxxxxxxx" ↵, where the *x*'s represent the name you want to give your program. Do not use quotes around the name for Apple.

8. Check to see if your program has been saved by typing in FILES ↵. You should see the name of the program you just saved listed on the

directory. If the correct name is not there, is there a similar name? We don't always type what we intend.

9. If your computer does not have its own printer or is not connected to a common printer, take your diskette to a unit that is equipped with a printer. Make sure that the printer and the microcomputer are turned on and BASIC is loaded into memory. Insert your diskette in the dirve and close the door.

10. Load your program by typing in LOAD "xxxxxxxx" ↵ (no quotes around the name for Apple).

11. List the program by typing LLIST ↵ on an IBM. Use PR#1 to direct the output to a printer on an Apple.

12. Run your program by typing RUN ↵. Respond to the question about "output on the printer" with a Y ↵.

13. Remove the paper from the printer.

Section 2: Programming a Simple List

Topics Covered in This Section

BASIC Instructions	Logic
READ/DATA	Simple list
PRINT	Programming Project
GOTO	Simple list

In Section 1 the program was so simple that the result could have been arrived at without pencil and paper let alone a computer program. In this section our program will be only slightly more complex so that we can introduce you to the BASIC language in small increments.

Problem Analysis

Output Required

```
CUSTNAM$
CUSTNO
PARTNO
QUANTITY
UNITPRICE
```

Input Required

```
CUSTNAM$
CUSTNO
PARTNO
QUANTITY
UNITPRICE
```

Processing Required   Processing consists of reading the data, represented by the variable names listed above, and printing a list of the same data. The actual data values will be included as a part of the program.

Input Values

```
MACRO LTD, 101, 1234, 11, 1.02
MACRO LTD, 101, 1867, 21, 1.16
ABLE INC,  102, 3491, 12, 2.13
BETA CO,   103, 2209, 15, 3.71
BETA CO,   103, 2019, 19, 1.47
DONE,        9, 9,     9,   9
```

Output Format

FIGURE B.2.1

The Flowchart

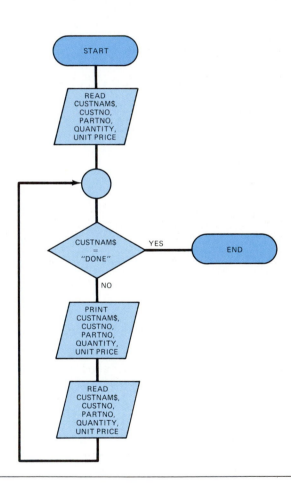

FIGURE B.2.2

Explanation of Logic Used

We begin the program by reading the first set of data. Notice that we use the same input/output symbol to represent READ as we used for PRINT. We are transferring data into the computer with READ. This first READ is referred to as a *priming read*. We will not return to this READ statement. As you can see from the flowchart, this READ statement is above the loop formed by the

flow line. Now the data that we have read is tested to see if the CUSTNAM$ = DONE. This test is made using the *decision* symbol:

This symbol always has one way in and two ways out. In this symbol we test a variable or variables and go one way if the test is true and the other way if the test is false. Here we have asked if CUSTNAM$ = DONE. Yes (true) means we have no more good data and we end the program. No (false) means the data is good and we should continue. Notice that the last line of data given as input values contains DONE, 9, 9, 9, 9. When this set of data is encountered, CUSTNAM$ will equal DONE and the program will end. This data is referred to as the trailer record. If CUSTNAM$ is not equal to DONE, we drop to the next symbol and print a line. Then we read the next set of data and branch upward to a point above the comparison. This process of testing, printing, and reading will continue until we encounter the set of data with the trailer.

The BASIC Program

FIGURE B.2.3

```
10 REM   PROGRAM ID: CASE2
20 REM   AUTHOR ID:  MURPHY/LONGHURST       DATE WRITTEN: 5/26/8X
30 REM
40 REM   THIS PROGRAM DISPLAYS CUSTOMER ORDER INFORMATION
50 REM
60 REM   VARIABLE LIST
70 '        CUSTNAM$..........CUSTOMER NAME
80 '        CUSTNO............CUSTOMER NUMBER
90 '        PARTNO............PART NUMBER
100 '       QUANTITY..........QUANTITY
110 '       UNITPRICE.........UNIT PRICE
120 '
130 '***************PROCESSING ROUTINE***********
140 READ CUSTNAM$, CUSTNO, PARTNO, QUANTITY, UNITPRICE   ' PRIMING READ
150 '
160 LPRINT "COMPANY","COMPANY NO.", "QUANTITY", "PART NO.", "PRICE/UNIT"
170 LPRINT
180 '
190 IF CUSTNAM$ = "DONE" THEN 320
200     LPRINT CUSTNAM$, CUSTNO, QUANTITY, PARTNO, UNITPRICE
210 READ CUSTNAM$, CUSTNO, PARTNO, QUANTITY, UNITPRICE
220 GOTO 190
230 REM ************END OF PROCESSING
240 REM
250 REM **************DATA TO BE PROCESSED
260 DATA MACRO LTD, 101, 1234, 11, 1.02
270 DATA MACRO LTD, 101, 1867, 21, 1.16
280 DATA ABLE INC,  102, 3491, 12, 2.13
290 DATA BETA CO,   103, 2009, 15, 3.71
300 DATA BETA CO,   103, 2019, 19, 1.47
310 DATA DONE,      9,    9,   9,    9
320 END
```

The Actual Output

COMPANY	COMPANY NO.	QUANTITY	PART NO.	PRICE/UNIT
MACRO LTD	101	11	1234	1.02
MACRO LTD	101	21	1867	1.16
ABLE INC	102	12	3491	2.13
BETA CO	103	15	2009	3.71
BETA CO	103	19	2019	1.47

BASIC Language Discussion

In this section you will learn enough about BASIC to write a program of your own similar to the one shown above. We will start with an explanation of variable names and then explain the instructions included in Case 2.

Variables   In all but the simplest of BASIC programs, it is necessary to store values in memory. For example, if we multiply two numbers together, as we did in Case 1, we need a place to store the result. BASIC allows us to store and retrieve values in memory by giving them names. These values that are stored in memory with a name are called *variables*. (They are called variables because their values may be changed during the running of the program, *not* because they are algebraic variables.) Each variable consists of two parts, the name with which the location in memory is referenced and the value that is stored at that location.

Variable Names   Each version of BASIC has different rules about what is acceptable as a varible name and what is not acceptable.

IBM Variable Names Variable names may be any length. However, only the first 40 characters are recognized by BASIC. Therefore, if two variable names are identical through the first 40 characters, they both refer to the same variable regardless of the remainder of the variable name. Since a variable name that is 40 characters long is an extremely long variable name, there is usually no need to use longer variable names.

Each variable name must begin with a letter. The remaining characters may consist of letters, numbers, and periods. Variable names many not be reserved words but they may contain reserved words embedded within them.

IBM Variable Names

Name	Comments
DEPT3	Valid
DEPT.3	Valid
TEND	Valid, may contain embedded reserved words
DEPT 3	Invalid, may not contain spaces
3DEPT	Invalid, may not begin with a number
.DEPT3	Invalid, may not begin with a period
END	Invalid, may not be a reserved word

Apple Variable Names Variable names may be as long as 238 characters. However, *only the first 2* characters are recognized by the computer. Any variable names that begin with the same 2 characters will refer to the same variable. The variable names *IN*COME and *IN*TEREST would refer to the same variable because their first 2 characters are the same. In our program change CUSTNO to CSTNO. When creating variable names for the Apple, you must either stick to variable names of only 1 or 2 characters or you must be careful not to reuse the same first 2 characters.

The first character of the variable name must be a letter. The remaining characters may be letters and/or numbers. Variable names may not be reserved words and they may not contain embedded reserved words.

Apple Variable Names

Name	Comments
D3	Valid
DEPT	Valid*
DEPT3	Valid*
3DEPT	Invalid, may not begin with a number
DEPT.3	Invalid, may not contain a period
DEPT 3	Invalid, may not contain a blank
TEND	Invalid, may not contain embedded reserved words
END	Invalid, may not be a reserved word

*Please note that these names would be considered identical in a BASIC program written for the Apple.

Variable Types Variables are classified by the type of data they can hold.

- **Numeric Variables** A variable that can hold a number is called a *numeric* variable. There are two types of numeric variables: variables capable of holding integers and variables capable of holding real numbers.

- **Integers** In both IBM and Apple an integer variable is capable of holding an integer number in the range -32767 to $+32767$. Any valid variable name with a % tacked on to the end of it is an integer variable (for example, DEPT3%).

- **Reals** A real variable is capable of holding a real number (a number that can include a decimal point). This is the default for variable type in IBM and Apple. Any variable name without a special character tacked on to the end of it is a real variable. (In IBM any variable with a ! attached is also a real variable.)

- **String Variables** A string is a sequence of letters and/or digits and/or special symbols. In order to work with string data in BASIC, the strings, or *literals,* must usually be enclosed in quotation marks.

Examples of Strings:
```
"ACCOUNTING DEPARTMENT"
"!@#$%&*"
"3RD FLOOR"
```

A string variable is capable of holding a string and is indicated by a *$* on the end of a variable name (for example, DEPT$).

Because each type of variable is capable of holding only one type of data, it is important to be aware of the types of variables you need when writing your BASIC programs.

READ/DATA

```
                                          IBM AND APPLE
FORMATS:
  line # READ  list of variables separated by
commas

  line # DATA  list of values separated by
commas
```

The READ and DATA statements are used in conjunction with one another in order to give values to variables. The READ/DATA statement combination is one of three ways to assign values to variables (LET and INPUT are the other two and these will be discussed later). Remember, that *line #* represents line number.

The DATA Statement DATA statements containing values that may be used by the program when it is run. Each DATA statement may contain any number of values and may contain either numeric constants or string constants or both. Before the actual execution of the program begins, the data must be put in a sequence in a specified memory location. This location is called the *data stack*. The data stack is a list of all the values contained in DATA statements in the order in which they occur in the program. The number of values in each DATA statement has no effect on the data stack. Because of this, the following examples of DATA statements all create the same data stack and would function identically if included in a program.

```
Example:  210 DATA 4,9,GEORGE
          220 DATA 3,10,JACK
          230 DATA 9,2,ALAN
          ----
          210 DATA 4,9
          220 DATA GEORGE,3,10
          230 DATA JACK,9,2
          240 DATA ALAN
          ----
          210 DATA 4,9,GEORGE,3,10,JACK,9,2,ALAN
```

String constants, when included in DATA statements, require quotation marks only if the string includes a comma. Numeric expressions such as (4 * 3) are not allowed in DATA statements.

DATA statements are not executed when the program is run (like REM statements they are nonexecutable instructions). Therefore, they are ignored when encountered during the running of the program and may be placed anywhere in the program. For clarity, they are often grouped together and placed at the end of the program.

The READ Statement   The READ statement makes use of the data stack created by the DATA statements. When a READ statement is encountered while a program is being run, values from the data stack are assigned to the variable names in the order in which the names are written in the READ statement. If there are not enough values left in the stack for *all* the variable names in the READ statement, an error message (usually "insufficient data" or "out of data") is displayed and the program terminates.

Example: `10 READ A,B,C,D`
             `  ⋮`
             `100 DATA 100,600,200`
             `999 END`

When the READ statement is encountered, an error message indicating insufficient data will be displayed and processing will be terminated. The data stack created by this program contains only three values (100,600,200) and the READ statement attempts to read values for four variables.

If the READ statement does not use all of the variables in the stack, the next READ statement encountered will pick up where the last one left off in the data stack.

Example: `10 READ A,B$,C,D`
             `  ⋮`
             `100 DATA 3,GEORGE,5,KAREN`
             `999 END`

When this READ statement is encountered, an error message ("type mismatch") indicating a mismatch in data types will be displayed and procesing will be terminated. The string constant KAREN may not be read into the numeric variable D.

The data type of the data from the data stack must match the variable type of the variable name in the READ statement (i.e., a string constant may not be read into a numeric variable).

```
Example:  10 READ A,B,C$
          20 READ L,M,N$
          ⋮
          100 DATA 30,2,JENNIFER
          110 DATA 21,0,KEVIN
          120 DATA 57,3,JIM
          999 END
```

When the first READ statement (line 10) is encountered, the first three values in the data stack are assigned, in order, to the variables listed in the READ statement. A is assigned the value 30, B is assigned the value 2, and C$ is assigned the value JENNIFER. When the next READ statement is encountered (line 20), the next three values in the data stack are assigned to the variables listed in that READ statement. L is assigned the value 21, M is assigned the value 0, and M$ is assigned the value KEVIN. At this point three values remain unused in the data stack (57,3, JIM) and could be assigned to variables by any subsequent READ statements.

Notice in Case 2 how the last set of data contains DONE,9,9,9,9. A DATA statement set up with unlikely values (dummy data) is often called a *trailer*. This set of unlikely values gives us something to compare against to see if we have processed all of the real data. Without this dummy data we would only know we were out of data when an error message occurred.

Print

```
FORMAT:
   line # PRINT [list of expressions] [;]
```

PRINT allows us to transfer data from the computer memory to an output device. It is assumed here that the output device you will be using is the screen. The request to print can include the following:

1. variables   PRINT X
2. numeric literals (constants)   PRINT 6
3. string literals (constants)   PRINT "JUNE"
4. arithmetic expressions   PRINT 2 * X

It is possible to combine any of the items listed above into a single PRINT statement.

```
Example:  PRINT "THE RESULT IS" 6 * X
```

If we assume a value of 2 for X in this example, the following would be printed:

```
THE RESULT IS 12
```

Notice that the arithmetic expression is evaluated and the result is printed.

You can also print a blank line by using the PRINT statement without a list of expressions.

Example: `PRINT`

In order to control the position of the printed item, you may use a semicolon (;) to separate the items; each one will be printed immediately after the previous one.

Example: `PRINT "THE"; X; "TH"; "ITEM IS"; Y`

If we assume that the value 2 has been stored for X and the value 3 has been stored for Y, we will get the following results:

IBM
___

```
THE 2 THITIEM IS 3
```

Apple
___

```
THE2THITEM IS3
```

Notice that IBM reserves spaces around the numbers so that they are separated from the nonnumeric literals by a space. These leading and trailing spaces are for optional use of + or − signs. The two nonnumeric literals that are not separated by variables are printed with no spaces between them (THITEM). Any spaces reserved with a nonnumeric literal remain (ITEM IS).

Apple does not surround the number with blanks. As a result, the only blanks produced by this PRINT statement is the one embedded in the nonnumeric literal. If commas (,) are used to separate the items, the items are assigned to a print zone. Each zone is fourteen characters wide for the IBM (sixteen for the Apple).

IBM
___

| 1 | 15 | 29 | 43 | 57 |

Apple

1	17	33	49	65

Example: `PRINT "A","B","C","D","E"`

IBM

1	15	29	43	57
A	B	C	D	E

Apple

1	17	33	49	65
A	B	C	D	E

Example: `PRINT "STUDENTS","TUITION","REVENUE"`

IBM

1	15	29	43	57
COURSE STUDENTS PER COURSE	NO. OF SECTIONS		STUDENTS PER SECTION	

Apple

1	17	33	49	65
COURSE	NO. OF SECTIONS	STUDENTS PER SECTION		STUDENTS PER COURSE

If an expression is wider than one print zone, it is printed in the adjacent zone. The comma will cause the following expression to be printed in the next available free zone. Thus the STUDENTS PER SECTION expression is printed in the fourth print zone.

A semicolon (;) or a comma (,) at the end of a print statement is a "dangling" printer control which is used to "hook" the printer on the same print line. In this way more than one PRINT statement can be used to print one printed line.

Example: `PRINT "STUDENTS","TUITION",`
`        PRINT "LAB FEES","REVENUE"`

IBM

1	15	29	43	57
STUDENTS	TUITION	LAB FEES	REVENUE	

```
Apple      1           17           33          49          65
          |STUDENTS|TUITION |LAB FEES|REVENUE |           |
          |        |        |        |        |           |
          |        |        |        |        |           |
```

Notice how two print lines created only one line of output. This is not the best approach for the column headings we have been printing. The technique was introduced here because placing a ' or a ; after the last item in the list when no continuation is desired is a common error for beginners. Later we can use the technique when we begin formatting output.

GOTO

```
                                        IBM AND APPLE
FORMAT:
   line # GOTO line
```

The GOTO is used to specify the line number that we want to directly transfer control. This branching of the logic is an unconditional transfer of control. That is, the logic flow is transferred without any questions asked. Refer back to the flowchart and program for the programming project in this section. The flow line goes from the bottom of the program to just above the decision symbol. This represents a repetition, or loop, in our logic. This loop will continue until the IF THEN statement is answered in such a way that the program is completed. The IF THEN is an example of a conditional transfer of control. Structured programming techniques discourage or prohibit the use of GOTO statements. In this text we will follow the convention of only allowing GOTOs to direct the flow of logic downward by only allowing line numbers below the GOTO.

Section 3: Programming More Complex Lists

Topics Covered in This Section

BASIC Instructions	Programming Projects
WHILE	1. Simple listing with column headings and totals
WEND	2. Simple listing with column headings and totals
LET	3. Simple listing with column headings and totals produced using subroutines (suitable for any number of pages)
Hierarchy of operations	
GOSUB	
RETURN	
Logic	
Column headings	
Simple calculations	
Final totals	
Subroutine	

In this section we will make modifications to the program used in section 2. We will introduce a structured loop using WHILE/WEND statements, add column headings to the output, and use subroutines to divide the program logic into manageable chunks.

Problem Analysis—Project 1

Output Required

1. Appropriate column headings (first page only).
2. Detail lines including:

```
CUSTNO
INVNO
PARTNO
QUANTITY
UNITPRICE
AMOUNT
```

Input Required

```
CUSTNAM$
CUSTNO
PARTNO
QUANTITY
UNITPRICE
```

Processing Required

1. Print column headings for each column.
2. Similar to Section 2 except use structured programming techniques.

Input Values   The same as Section 2.

Output Format

FIGURE B.3.1

The Flowchart   See Figure B.3.2.

FIGURE B.3.2

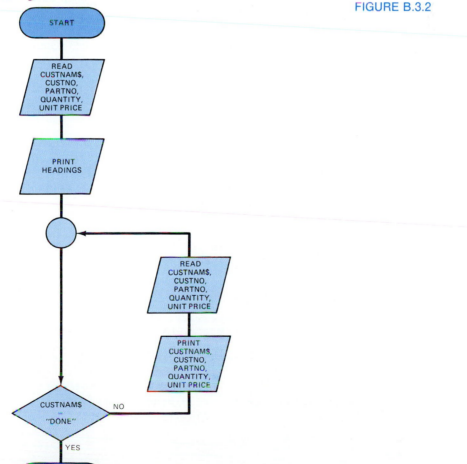

Explanation of Logic Used

The first program in this section is the same as the one in the last section except that WHILE/WEND statements are used for structured loop control. The WHILE indicates the beginning of the loop and WEND the end of the loop. Statements in between the WHILE and WEND are loop statements.

The WHILE also provides loop control and is similar to our use of the IF/THEN. When the expression (question) in the WHILE statement is true the loop statements inside the loop are executed. When the WHILE expression is false looping ceases and control is passed to the line immediately following the WEND.

In our first program the WHILE on line 190 evaluates the CUSTNAM\$. As long as this is not equal (<>) to the string literal "DONE" the loop will continue executing. It produces the same output as the program in Section 2.

It would be useful to have the report have column headings and have the output printed under these headings. Program CASE3A provides this. Line 160 prints the column headings. The string literals are enclosed in quotes and separated by commas. The result is each heading is printed in one of the print zones. Line 170 prints a blank line. The output is shown in Figure B.3.3.

Only one new flowcharting symbol is used here: the small circle called the *connector* symbol. We use it to show a branch from one point in the logic to another. The numbers in the symbols allow us to match them up. The arrowheads let us know whether we are coming or going.

The BASIC Program

FIGURE B.3.3

```
10 REM    PROGRAM ID: CASE3
20 REM    AUTHOR ID:  MURPHY/LONGHURST         DATE WRITTEN: 5/26/8X
30 REM
40 REM    THIS PROGRAM DISPLAYS CUSTOMER ORDER INFORMATION
50 REM     USING WHILE/WEND LOOP CONTROL
60 REM    VARIABLE LIST
70 '      CUSTNAM$...........CUSTOMER NAME
80 '      CUSTNO.............CUSTOMER NUMBER
90 '      PARTNO.............PART NUMBER
100 '     QUANTITY...........QUANTITY
110 '     UNITPRICE..........UNIT PRICE
120 '
130 '***************PROCESSING ROUTINE***********
140 READ CUSTNAM$, CUSTNO, PARTNO, QUANTITY, UNITPRICE   ' PRIMING READ
150 '
160 LPRINT "COMPANY","COMPANY NO.", "QUANTITY", "PART NO.", "PRICE/UNIT"
170 LPRINT
180 '
190 WHILE CUSTNAM$ <> "DONE"
200     LPRINT CUSTNAM$, CUSTNO, QUANTITY, PARTNO, UNITPRICE
210     READ CUSTNAM$, CUSTNO, PARTNO, QUANTITY, UNITPRICE
220 WEND
230 REM *************END OF PROCESSING
240 REM
```

```
250 REM ***************DATA TO BE PROCESSED
260 DATA MACRO LTD, 101, 1234, 11, 1.02
270 DATA MACRO LTD, 101, 1867, 21, 1.16
280 DATA ABLE INC,  102, 3491, 12, 2.13
290 DATA BETA CO,   103, 2009, 15, 3.71
300 DATA BETA CO,   103, 2019, 19, 1.47
310 DATA DONE,        9,    9,  9,    9
320 END
```

The Actual Output

FIGURE B.3.4

COMPANY	COMPANY NO.	QUANTITY	PART NO.	PRICE/UNIT
MACRO LTD	101	11	1234	1.02
MACRO LTD	101	21	1867	1.16
ABLE INC	102	12	3491	2.13
BETA CO	103	15	2009	3.71
BETA CO	103	19	2019	1.47

BASIC Language Discussion

WHILE/WEND   There is an instruction available on the IBM PC that will control a loop in much the same way we controlled Process with a switch (CUSTNAM$). This instruction is called WHILE/WEND. This instruction is not available to Apple users, but it can be simulated using IF/THEN and GOTO instructions.

```
                                            IBM
FORMAT:
   line # WHILE expression
     .
     .
     (loop statements)
     .
     .
   line # WEND
```

This combination of statements allows the repeated execution of statements contained between them as long as the expression in the WHILE statement is true. When the expression in the WHILE statement is no longer true, control is transferred to the statement following the WEND.

Problem Analysis—Project 2

Output Required   The same as Project 1, except QUANTITY and AMOUNT totals will be calculated. Part NUMBER is deleted.

Input Required   The same as Project 1 except PART NUMBER is deleted.

Processing Required   The same as Project 1 except:

1. Multiply QUANTITY by UNITPRICE and print the resulting amount on the same line as the rest of the data for each customer.
2. Accumulate totals for QUANTITY and UNITPRICE and print them when all of the data have been read.

Input Values   The same as Project 1.

Output Format   See Figure B.3.5.

FIGURE B.3.5

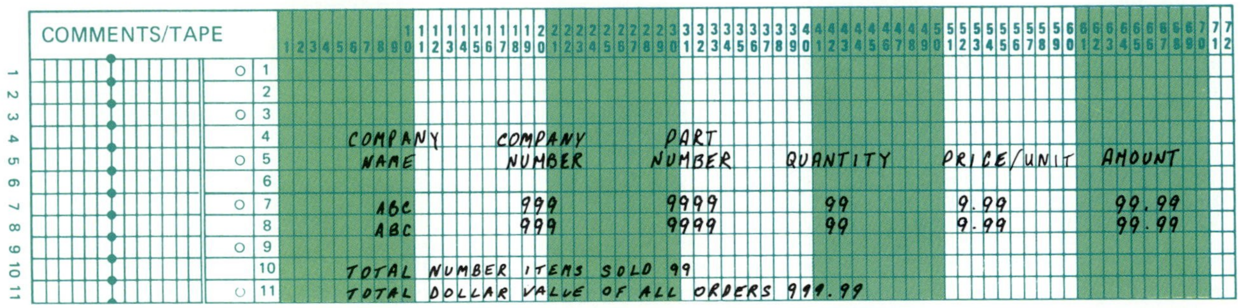

The Flowchart   See Figure B.3.6.

Explanation of Logic Used

The first six steps of the flowchart are initialization of housekeeping functions, which are performed only once. We initialize TAMOUNT and TQUANTITY accumulators to 0 using LET statements. The column heading is printed and a blank line printed after it.

The first or priming read statement is executed. This provides the variables with initial values so that the loop control can be tested. This READ statement is executed only once and will not be used again.

Access to the loop and control of looping is performed by the WHILE statement. As long as CUSTNAM$ is not equal to the literal "DONE" looping will continue and all statements inside the loop will be executed repeatedly. AMOUNT is calculated by multiply QUANTITY by UNITPRICE. The AMOUNT is added to the old value of TAMOUNT (initially 0), giving a new amount to TAMOUNT, which is the total amount at this stage of processing. Similarly, TQUANTITY is calculated by adding QUANTITY to TQUANTITY.

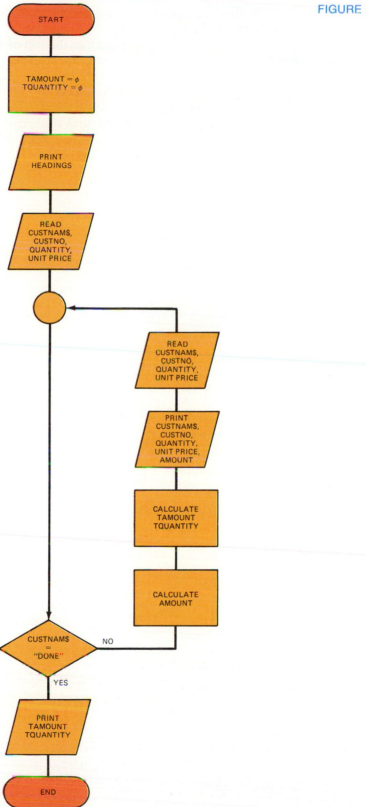

Now that the calculations are complete, the detail line is printed. A second READ statement reads the next record. The WEND statement transfers control back to the WHILE at the top of the loop. Notice that the WEND does not use a line number. The WHILE checks that the customer name is not equal to "DONE" and loop processing is repeated.

When the customer name is equal to "DONE" loop processing is completed and control passed down to the statement immediately following the WEND. The totals are printed, and since the DATA statements are not executable, the program is completed and stops processing when it encounters the END statement.

The BASIC Program

FIGURE B.3.7

```
10 REM    PROGRAM ID: CASE3B
20 REM    AUTHOR ID:  MURPHY/LONGHURST          DATE WRITTEN: 5/26/8X
30 REM
40 REM    THIS PROGRAM DISPLAYS CUSTOMER ORDER INFORMATION
50 REM    AND CALCULATES TOTAL AMOUNT FOR EACH ORDER AND TOTAL
60 REM    QUANTITY AND AMOUNTS AFTER ALL ORDERS HAVE BEEN PROCESSSED
70 REM
80 REM    VARIABLE LIST
90 '      CUSTNAM$..........CUSTOMER NAME
100 '     CUSTNO............CUSTOMER NUMBER
110 '     AMOUNT............DOLLAR VAULE OF ORDER
120 '     QUANTITY..........QUANTITY
130 '     TAMOUNT...........TOTAL DOLLAR VAULE OF ALL ORDERS
140 '     TQUANTITY.........TOTAL QUANTITY OF ALL ORDERS
150 '     UNITPRICE.........UNIT PRICE
160 ' *************INITIALIZATION MODULE**************
170 LET TAMOUNT = O
180 LET TQUANTITY = O
190 '     PRINT HEADINGS
200 LPRINT "COMPANY","COMPANY NO.", "QUANTITY", "PRICE/UNIT", "AMOUNT"
210 LPRINT
220 '***************PROCESSING ROUTINE***********
230 READ CUSTNAM$,CUSTNO,QUANTITY,UNITPRICE                ' PRIMING READ
240 '
250 '
260 WHILE CUSTNAM$ <> "DONE"
270     LET AMOUNT = QUANTITY * UNITPRICE
280     LET TAMOUNT = TAMOUNT + AMOUNT
290     LET TQUANTITY = TQUANTITY + QUANTITY
300     LPRINT CUSTNAM$, CUSTNO, QUANTITY, UNITPRICE, AMOUNT
310     READ CUSTNAM$,CUSTNO,QUANTITY,UNITPRICE
320 WEND
330 REM PRINT TOTALS
340 LPRINT
350 LPRINT "TOTAL NUMBER OF ITEMS SOLD  "; TQUANTITY
360 LPRINT "TOTAL DOLLAR VAULE OF ALL ORDERS  "; TAMOUNT
370 REM *************END OF PROCESSING
380 REM
390 REM **************DATA TO BE PROCESSED
400 DATA MACRO LTD, 101, 11, 1.02
410 DATA MACRO LTD, 101, 21, 1.16
420 DATA ABLE INC,  102, 12, 2.13
430 DATA BETA CO,   103, 15, 3.71
440 DATA BETA CO,   103, 19, 1.47
450 DATA DONE,        9,  9,    9
460 END
```

FIGURE B.3.8

```
COMPANY          COMPANY NO.    QUANTITY       PRICE/UNIT     AMOUNT

MACRO LTD        101            11             1.02           11.22
MACRO LTD        101            21             1.16           24.36
ABLE INC         102            12             2.13           25.56
BETA CO          103            15             3.71           55.65
BETA CO          103            19             1.47           27.93


TOTAL NUMBER OF ITEMS SOLD    78
TOTAL DOLLAR VAULE OF ALL ORDERS     144.72
```

BASIC Language Discussion

LET LET is used to assign values to variables. The assignment always takes the value from the right and assigns it to a variable on the left. This is why there must be one and only one variable on the left of the equal sign. The LET statement can be used with both numeric and string variables. Some examples are shown below.

```
LET X = 0          assigns zero to the variable X
                   (used in initializing
                   counters and accumulators)
LET A$ = "QTY"     assigns a string constant to
                   a string variable.
LET X = A + B      assigns the sum of A and B to
                   X
LET X = X + 1      assigns sum of X + 1 to X
                   (used for counting)
LET A$ = B$        assigns the value of B$ to A$
                   the values are string values
```

In order to write more complex arithmetic expressions on the right side of the equal sign we need to be familar with the hierarchy of operations. The following arithmetic operators are available for calculations:

^   exponentiation (raising to a power)
*   multiplication
/   division
+   addition
−   subtraction

These operators are arranged in a hierarchy, or order of precedence, that governs which operator is evaluated before another. The order is as follows:

^   first
*,/   second
+,−   third

As in algebra, any expression in parentheses ( ) is evaluated first. Multiplication and division have the same precedence and if used in an equation are evaluated left to right. Addition and subtraction are evaluated in a similar manner.

Example: LET X = 2 + 3 * 4

The answer is 14. The multiplication was performed first, giving a result of 12. The addition added 2 to 12, giving the final answer of 14.

Example: LET X = 12 / 2 + 4 * 10

The answer is 46. First the division is evaluated, giving 6. Then the multiplication is evaluated, giving 40. Finally, the addition of 6 + 40 gives the final result, 46.

Example: LET X = (2 + 3) * 4

The answer is 20. The expression in parentheses is evaluated first, giving a result of 5. This is multiplied by 4, giving the final answer of 20.

Example: LET X = (12 / (2 + 4)) * 10

The answer is 20. The expression in the innermost parentheses is evaluated first, giving a result of 6. This then becomes part of the expression in the outer parentheses, which results in 2. The multiplication is performed last, giving the final answer of 20.

Problem Analysis—Project 3

Output Required   The same as Project 2.

Input Required   The same as Project 2.

Processing Required   The output is the same as Project 2 but the logic is divided into three distinct pieces: initialization, detail processing, and printing totals. These three sections are implemented using subroutines.

Input Values   The same as Project 2.

Output Format   The same as Project 2.

The Flowchart   See Figure B.3.9

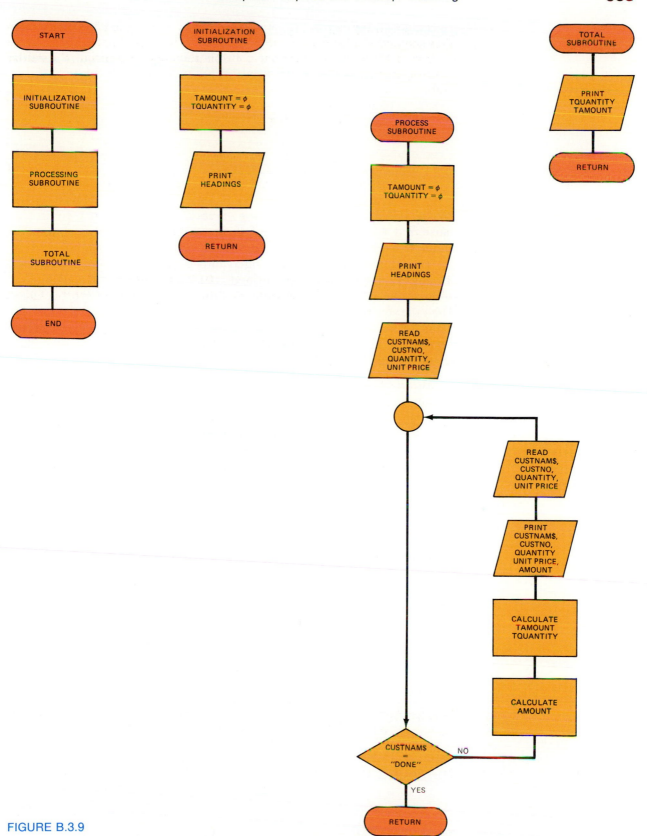

Explanation of Logic Used

We have a Mainline routine that controls the execution of all the other routines. It divides the program into three parts through the use of this symbol:

This is called a *predefined process symbol;* it indicates that control is transferred to the routine named in the symbol. When that routine is complete, control is transferred back to a point below the symbol.

The program is logically divided into initialization, processing, and printing totals. These are performed under the control of a command module. This module directs the logic flow to a subroutine for processing. When the subroutine processing is completed, the logic flow returns to the command module, where it is directed to the next subroutine. When all the subroutines in the command module are completed, the program has performed all its processing.

1. **Initialization**—This subroutine should include everything that must be done only once at the beginning of the program. This could include initializing variables, printing headings, and opening files.

2. **Process**—This module performs detail processing including calculation, printing detail lines and reading the next record. This subroutine should contain the logic for processing each set of data. Since we can enter the routine with good data only, the general order of Process will always be
   a. calculations
   b. print
   c. read

As our program becomes more complicated, we will add steps and call other subroutines from Process.

3. **Totals**—This subroutine should include everything we want to do only once, after all of the data have been processed. This generally includes printing totals and closing files.

Study the Mainline logic until you understand it. It will be the basis for the remainder of the programs.

End of Job   This subroutine prints TQUANTITY and TAMOUNT.

The BASIC Program

See Figure B.3.10.

```
10 REM    PROGRAM ID: CASE3C
20 REM    AUTHOR ID:  MURPHY/LONGHURST          DATE WRITTEN: 5/26/8X
30 REM
40 REM    THIS PROGRAM USE SUBROUTINES AND DISPLAYS CUSTOMER ORDER INFORMATION
50 REM    AND CALCULATES TOTAL AMOUNT FOR EACH ORDER AND TOTAL
60 REM    QUANTITY AND AMOUNTS AFTER ALL ORDERS HAVE BEEN PROCESSED
70 REM
80 REM    VARIABLE LIST
90 '        CUSTNAM$...........CUSTOMER NAME
100 '       CUSTNO.............CUSTOMER NUMBER
110 '       AMOUNT.............DOLLAR VALUE OF ORDER
120 '       QUANTITY...........QUANTITY
130 '       TAMOUNT............TOTAL DOLLAR VALUE OF ALL ORDERS
140 '       TQUANTITY..........TOTAL QUANTITY OF ALL ORDERS
150 '       UNITPRICE..........UNIT PRICE
200 '************ COMMAND MODULE**********
210 '
220 GOSUB 300                    ' INITIALIZATION SUBROUTINE
230 '
240 GOSUB 400                    ' PROCESSING
250 '
260 GOSUB 600                    ' TOTAL SUBROUTINE
270 '
280 ' *****************END OF COMMAND MODULE****************
290 END                    ' END OF JOB
300 ' ************INITIALIZATION MODULE*************
310 LET TAMOUNT = 0
320 LET TQUANTITY = 0
330 '
340 '
350 '   PRINT HEADINGS
360 LPRINT "COMPANY","COMPANY NO.", "QUANTITY", "PRICE/UNIT", "AMOUNT"
370 LPRINT
380 RETURN
390 ' *******************END OF SUBROUTINE**********
400 '
410 '*************PROCESSING ROUTINE**********
420 READ CUSTNAM$,CUSTNO,QUANTITY,UNITPRICE                    ' PRIMING READ
430 '
440 WHILE CUSTNAM$ <> "DONE"
450 '
460    LET AMOUNT = QUANTITY * UNITPRICE
470    LET TAMOUNT = TAMOUNT + AMOUNT
480    LET TQUANTITY = TQUANTITY + QUANTITY
490    LPRINT CUSTNAM$, CUSTNO, QUANTITY,
500    LPRINT UNITPRICE, AMOUNT
510 '
520    READ CUSTNAM$,CUSTNO,QUANTITY,UNITPRICE
530 WEND
540 RETURN
550 ' ******************* END OF PROCESSING SUBROUTINE
560 '
600 REM *******************PRINT TOTALS  SUBROUTINE
610 LPRINT
620 LPRINT "TOTAL NUMBER OF ITEMS SOLD  " TQUANTITY
630 LPRINT "TOTAL DOLLAR VALUE OF ALL ORDERS  " TAMOUNT
640 '
650 RETURN
660 REM ************END OF TOTALS SUBROUTINE
1000 REM *************DATA TO BE PROCESSED
1010 DATA MACRO LTD,  101, 11, 1.02
1020 DATA MACRO LTD,  101, 21, 1.16
1030 DATA ABLE INC,   102, 12, 2.13
1040 DATA BETA CO,    103, 15, 3.71
1050 DATA BETA CO,    103, 19, 1.47
1060 DATA DONE,         9,  9,    9
1070 ' ******************END OF DATA STATEMENTS
```

The Actual Output

See Figure B.3.11.

FIGURE B.3.11

COMPANY	COMPANY NO.	QUANTITY	PRICE/UNIT	AMOUNT
MACRO LTD	101	11	1.02	11.22
MACRO LTD	101	21	1.16	24.36
ABLE INC	102	12	2.13	25.56
BETA CO	103	15	3.71	55.65
BETA CO	103	19	1.47	27.93

```
TOTAL NUMBER OF ITEMS SOLD   78
TOTAL DOLLAR VALUE OF ALL ORDERS   144.72
```

Section 4: A Discount Program

Topics Covered in This Section

BASIC Instructions
  IF/THEN
  IF/THEN/
  ELSE
  AND/OR (logical operators)
  PRINT USING TAB (function)
Logic
  Decision
  Logic

IF/THEN/ELSE logic
Programming Projects

1. Customer report showing discount detail and total discount
2. Same as Project 1 except with formatted output

In a program, logic flow usually comes to a point where a question is asked and a decision is made. Looping is one area where a decision is used to control loop processing. Another type of decision causes the logic flow to go in one of two directions. In this section we will add a module which calculates quantity discounts, totals these discounts and improves the appearance of the printed report.

Problem Analysis—Project 1

We will create the same report as in Section 3 but we will decide if a quantity discount applies. The report will have an additional column for the discount detail and an additional line at the end for total discount.

Output Required

1. Appropriate column headings.
2. Detail lines including:

```
CUSTNAM$
CUSTNO
QUANTITY
UNITPRICE
AMOUNT
TOTALS
```

Input Required

```
CUSTNAM$
CUSTNO
QUANTITY
UNITPRICE
```

Processing Required

1. Print column headings.
2. Decide if a discount applies.
3. Perform discount calculations.
4. Accumulate totals.
5. Print detail line.
6. Print totals.

Input Values   The same as Section 3.

Output Format   The same as Section 3.

The Flowchart   See Figure B.4.1

Explanation of Logic Used

The program logic is very similar to that in the previous section. The difference is that in this program we have to decide if an order qualifies for a quantity discount. We accomplish this by adding a new subroutine in the processing module. This subroutine, using IF/THEN statements, will decide if the discount applies. If the quantity is greater than 15 units, a 10% discount applies. If the quantity is 15 units or less, the discount does not apply. In either situation the price is calculated and the various calculations performed and totals accumulated.

We are printing out the individual discount information in an additional column. Since this will be our sixth column and only five print zones are available, we will introduce the TAB statement to specify the exact position we want this column printed on our report.

The BASIC Program

See Figure B.4.2

The Actual Output

See Figure B.4.3

FIGURE B.4.1

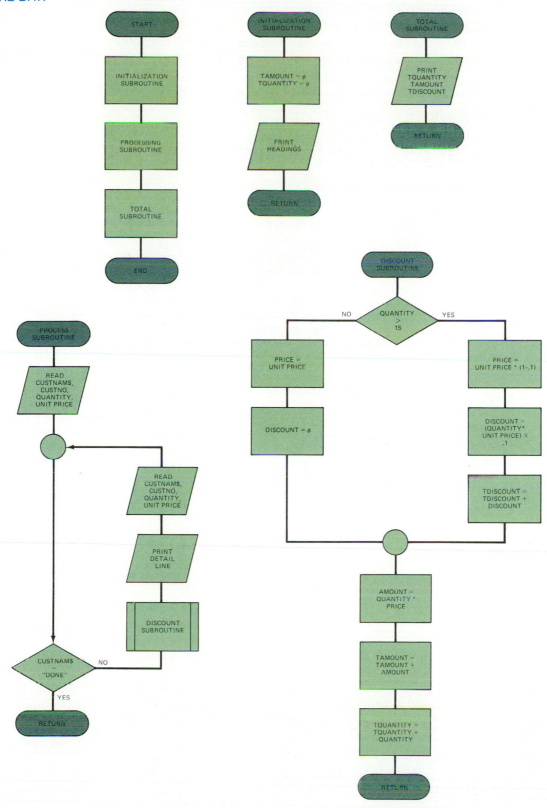

FIGURE B.4.2

```
10 REM    PROGRAM ID: CASE4
20 REM    AUTHOR ID:  MURPHY/LONGHURST        DATE WRITTEN: 5/26/8X
30 REM
40 REM    THIS PROGRAM CALCULATES DISCOUNTS, DISPLAYS CUSTOMER ORDER INFORMATION
50 REM    CALCULATES TOTAL AMOUNT FOR EACH ORDER AND TOTAL
60 REM    QUANTITY AND AMOUNTS AFTER ALL ORDERS HAVE BEEN PROCESSED
70 REM
80 REM    VARIABLE LIST
90 '      CUSTNAM$..........CUSTOMER NAME
100 '     CUSTNO............CUSTOMER NUMBER
110 '     AMOUNT............DOLLAR VALUE OF ORDER
120 '     QUANTITY..........QUANTITY
130 '     UNITPRICE.........UNIT PRICE
140 '     TAMOUNT...........TOTAL DOLLAR VALUE OF ALL ORDERS
150 '     TQUANTITY.........TOTAL QUANTITY OF ALL ORDERS
160 '     TDISCOUNT.........TOTAL DISCOUNTS
200 '*********** COMMAND MODULE**********
210 '
220 GOSUB 300                    ' INITIALIZATION SUBROUTINE
230 '
240 GOSUB 400                    ' PROCESSING
250 '
260 GOSUB 600                    ' TOTAL SUBROUTINE
270 '
280 ' *******************END OF COMMAND MODULE****************
290 END                         ' END OF JOB
300 ' ************INITIALIZATION MODULE*************
310 LET TAMOUNT = 0
320 LET TQUANTITY = 0
330 '
340 '
350 '    PRINT HEADINGS
360 LPRINT "COMPANY","COMPANY NO.", "QUANTITY", "PRICE/UNIT", "AMOUNT"
        TAB(68) "DISCOUNT"
370 LPRINT
380 RETURN
390 ' *******************END OF SUBROUTINE**********
400 '
410 '***************PROCESSING ROUTINE**********
420 READ CUSTNAM$,CUSTNO,QUANTITY,UNITPRICE              ' PRIMING READ
430 '
440 '
450 WHILE CUSTNAM$ <> "DONE"
460      '
470      GOSUB 700                                       ' DISCOUNT ROUTINE
480 '
490      LPRINT CUSTNAM$, TAB(18) CUSTNO, TAB(32) QUANTITY,
500      LPRINT UNITPRICE,AMOUNT;
510      LPRINT TAB(68) DISCOUNT
520      READ CUSTNAM$,CUSTNO,QUANTITY,UNITPRICE
530 WEND
540 RETURN
550 ' ******************* END OF PROCESSING SUBROUTINE
560 '
600 REM ****************PRINT TOTALS  SUBROUTINE
610 LPRINT
620 LPRINT "TOTAL NUMBER OF ITEMS SOLD  " TAB(37) TQUANTITY
630 LPRINT "TOTAL DOLLAR VALUE OF ALL ORDERS  " TAB(37) TAMOUNT
640 LPRINT "TOTAL AMOUNT OF DISCOUNTS " TAB(37) TDISCOUNT
650 RETURN
660 REM ***********END OF TOTALS SUBROUTINE
670 REM
700 ' ***************DISCOUNT SUBROUTINE
710 IF QUANTITY > 15 THEN 750
```

FIGURE B.4.2 cont'd

```
720      LET PRICE = UNITPRICE
730      LET DISCOUNT = 0
740      GOTO 810
750      LET PRICE = UNITPRICE * (1- .1)
760      LET DISCOUNT = (QUANTITY * UNITPRICE) * .1
770      LET TDISCOUNT = TDISCOUNT + DISCOUNT
780 '
800 '
810      LET AMOUNT = QUANTITY * PRICE
820      LET TAMOUNT = TAMOUNT + AMOUNT
830      LET TQUANTITY = TQUANTITY + QUANTITY
840 RETURN
1000 REM **************DATA TO BE PROCESSED
1010 DATA MACRO LTD, 101, 11, 1.02
1020 DATA MACRO LTD, 101, 21, 1.16
1030 DATA ABLE INC,  102, 12, 2.13
1040 DATA BETA CO,   103, 15, 3.71
1050 DATA BETA CO,   103, 19, 1.47
1060 DATA DONE,        9,  9,    9
1070 ' ******************END OF DATA STATEMENTS
```

FIGURE B.4.3

COMPANY	COMPANY NO.	QUANTITY	PRICE/UNIT	AMOUNT	DISCOUNT
MACRO LTD	101	11	1.02	11.22	0
MACRO LTD	101	21	1.16	21.924	2.436
ABLE INC	102	12	2.13	25.56	0
BETA CO	103	15	3.71	55.65	0
BETA CO	103	19	1.47	25.137	2.793

```
TOTAL NUMBER OF ITEMS SOLD        78
TOTAL DOLLAR VALUE OF ALL ORDERS  139.491
TOTAL AMOUNT OF DISCOUNTS         5.229
```

BASIC Language Discussion

In order to write the program to accomplish this, we will need to use new BASIC instructions. These are:

```
IF/THEN/ELSE
AND/OR (logical operators)
TAB (function)
```

IF/THEN/ELSE

```
                                        IBM
FORMAT:
   line # IF expression THEN clause [ELSE
clause]
```

```
                                                    APPLE II
FORMAT:
   line # IF expression THEN clause
```

IF/THEN or IF/THEN/ELSE statements are used in BASIC to test conditions or to ask questions. Relational operators are used to compare values and are represented by the symbols below.

=	is equal to
<>	is not equal to
>	is greater than
>=	is greater than or equal to
<	is less than
<=	is less than or equal to

Numeric or string conditions may be tested. The data in the comparisons may be in variable, constant, or equation form. For example:

```
100  IF CUSTNO = PRMETER THEN...
110  IF CUSTNO > 25 THEN...
100  IF CUSTNO >= X + Y THEN...
100  IF CUSTNAM$ <> "DONE" THEN...
100  IF CUSTNAM$ = LAST$ THEN...
```

Any valid BASIC command can follow the THEN or ELSE of the IF/THEN. However, if more than one command is required, a line number is entered to direct the flow of logic. For example:

```
IF AMOUNT > 75 THEN 345 ELSE 400
```

Once we have established the relationship to be tested, our next concern is what actions we wish to take if the relationship is true and what actions we wish to take if the relationship is false. The planning can be done with a flowchart. We use the decision symbol, below, to represent the IF statement:

Let's suppose a situation where, if the condition is true, we want to print "EVERYTHING IS OKAY"; if the condition is not true, we want to print "EVERYTHING IS NOT OKAY". The logic is drawn in Figure B.4.4.

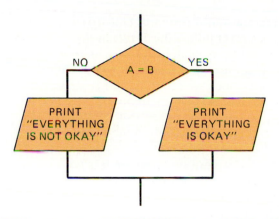

Using a system with an IF/THEN/ELSE (IBM PC), the code could be as follows:

```
4010 IF A = B THEN PRINT "EVERYTHING IS OKAY"
          ELSE PRINT "EVERYTHING IS NOT
          OKAY"
```

Notice that only one line number is involved. We must state the relationship, all actions to be taken if the condition is true (THEN), and all actions to be taken if the condition is false (ELSE), all within the 255 characters allowed for one BASIC statement. If multiple actions follow either the THEN or the ELSE, they should be separated by a colon. Use a CTRL with an ENTER to move to the second line so that the system will not expect a new line number.

If the evaluation of the IF/THEN is true, the line number or BASIC command following the THEN is executed. Otherwise, the statement immediately below the IF/THEN is executed.

```
4010 IF A = B THEN PRINT "EVERYTHING IS OKAY"
          ELSE 4030
4020 GOTO 4040
4030 PRINT "EVERYTHING IS NOT OKAY"
4040 RETURN
```

If A is equal to B, we print the literal "EVERYTHING IS OKAY" and execute the command on the next line, 4020, which instructs us to jump to line 4040. If A is not equal to B, then we would jump to line 4030 and proceed from there. Remember, the line numbers in the IF/THEN can be replaced with BASIC commands.

To accomplish the same thing on a system without an ELSE (APPLE II), we use GOTO to direct the logic flow.

```
4010 IF A=B THEN PRINT "EVERYTHING IS OKAY":
          GOTO 4030
4020 PRINT "EVERYTHING IS NOT OKAY"
4030 RETURN
```

After the relationship is tested in Line 4010, a PRINT ("EVERYTHING IS OKAY") and a GOTO follow the THEN in the same line. Both the PRINT and the GOTO will be executed if A = B is true. Notice that the PRINT statement is first; if they were reversed, we would execute the GOTO and not the PRINT since once we go we do not come back. The GOTO takes us around statement 4020, so that it will not be executed when A = B. If A = B is false, we drop to line 4020 and PRINT ("EVERYTHING IS NOT OKAY"). Either way we end up at line 4030, which could be any BASIC statement.

AND/OR—Logical Operators   Although it is not required in the programming problem for this section, we should consider ways to handle multiple conditions for selection of a record. Suppose we are looking for those customers who have purchased a particular part number in quantities greater than 15. We now have two conditions that must be met. This involves AND logic. It must be a particular part number *and* the quantity must be greater than 15. There is more than one way to accomplish this in BASIC. The first way is called a nested IF. A portion of the flowchart would be as shown in Figure B.4.5.

This flowchart can be coded in BASIC as follows:

```
5010 IF PARTNO=PRMETER THEN
          IF QUANTITY>15 THEN
          GOSUB 5000
```

This nested form of the IF command is available on the IBM PC but not on the APPLE II. In this instruction, only if the first condition is true (yes) will the second condition be tested. If the second condition is also true, then the PRINT routine will be performed. Nested IFs are a form of AND

FIGURE B.4.5

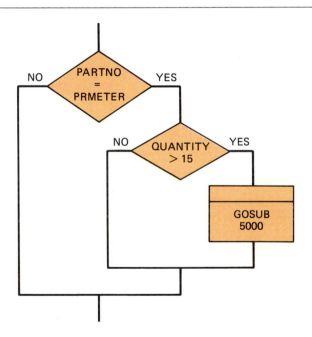

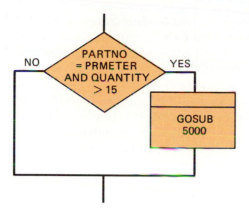

logic; we are saying if the first condition is true and the second condition is true, we will take some action.

On the IBM PC and the APPLE II we can accomplish the same objective using the relational operator AND. AND means that both conditions must be true before we will take the actions specified. The flowchart is shown in Figure B.4.6 and the code follows it.

When we combine IFs using relational operators, we lose the opportunity we would have on a system allowing ELSEs to have a separate ELSE for each IF. We have combined both tests into one IF and therefore are allowing only one ELSE. On a system that allows nested IFs, we choose nested IFs or the relational operator AND depending on whether we need to have separate ELSE conditions for each IF.

OR logic is used when we are willing to settle for one *or* the other condition

```
5010 IF PARTNO=PRMETER AND QUANTITY>15 THEN
     GOSUB 4000
```

being true. If we are interested in customers who buy very small or very large quantities of a part, we could test in the following manner:

```
5010 IF QUANTITY<5 OR QUANTITY>500 THEN GOSUB
     4000
```

In this instance *either* a quantity of less than 5 *or* a quantity of greater than 500 will cause us to GOSUB 4000.

TAB—Function

```
                              IBM AND APPLE II
FORMAT:
   line # PRINT TAB (n)
          (n may range from 1 to 255)
```

The TAB function is used in combination with the PRINT statement in order to control print spacing. The TAB function causes the printer to space over to the column specified by *n*. If the printer is already positioned past column *n*, the printer will tab to that column on the next line. When using the TAB function to print strings, *n* should specify the column number where the first character of the string is to print. The same is true when printing numbers on an Apple system. However, in IBM BASIC one space is automatically left before and after the number to be printed. Because of this, *n* should specify the space just prior to the column in which we expect the first digit to print.

Up to this point we have depended on the use of commas to provide the spacing of the output. As long as you wish to print five columns or fewer, this method is usually satisfactory. When you need more than five columns of information, a new technique is required. One approach is to use the TAB function. Use of the TAB function requires some planning of the output by the programmer. The use of a print chart is strongly recommended.

In Section 4 projects we will print the following fields with the following column positions.

FIELD	COLUMN
CUSTNAM$	1
CUSTNO	18
QUANTITY	32
UNITPRICE	ZONE 4
AMOUNT	ZONE 5
DISCOUNT	68
TQUANTITY	37
TAMOUNT	37
TDISCOUNT	37

Problem Analysis—Project 2

Output Required   The same as Project 1 except we must change the format to include dollar signs ($) and decimal points (.).

Input Required   The same as Project 1.

Processing Required   The same as Project 1 except we will change the initialization module and use PRINT USING statements.

Input Values   The same as Project 1.

Output Format   The same as Project 1 except the output will be formatted.

The Flowchart   The same as Project 1.

Explanation of Logic Used

The same as Project 1 except for one difference: we will use PRINT USING to format the output. We will add format strings to the initialization module and change the appropriate PRINT statements to PRINT USING statements.

The BASIC Program

See Figure B.4.7.

FIGURE B.4.7

```
10 REM   PROGRAM ID: CASE4B
20 REM   AUTHOR ID:  MURPHY/LONGHURST          DATE WRITTEN: 5/26/8X
30 REM
40 REM   THIS PROGRAM DISPLAYS FORMATTED CUSTOMER ORDER INFORMATION
45 REM   CALCULATES QUANTITY DISCOUNTS
50 REM   AND CALCULATES TOTAL AMOUNT FOR EACH ORDER AND TOTAL
60 REM   QUANTITY AND AMOUNTS AFTER ALL ORDERS HAVE BEEN PROCESSED
70 REM
80 REM   VARIABLE LIST
90 '       CUSTNAM$..........CUSTOMER NAME
100 '      CUSTNO............CUSTOMER NUMBER
110 '      AMOUNT............DOLLAR VALUE OF ORDER
120 '      QUANTITY..........QUANTITY
125 '      UNITPRICE.........UNIT PRICE
130 '      DISCOUNT..........AMOUNT OF DISCOUNT
140 '      TAMOUNT...........TOTAL DOLLAR VALUE OF ALL ORDERS
150 '      TQUANTITY.........TOTAL QUANTITY OF ALL ORDERS
160 '      TDISCOUNT.........TOTAL DISCOUNTS
170 '      F1$...............FORMAT VARIABLE
180 '      F2$...............FORMAT VARIABLE
200 '************* COMMAND MODULE**********
210 '
220 GOSUB 300                    ' INITIALIZATION SUBROUTINE
230 '
240 GOSUB 400                    ' PROCESSING
250 '
260 GOSUB 600                    ' TOTAL SUBROUTINE
270 '
280 ' *****************END OF COMMAND MODULE*****************
290 END                         ' END OF JOB
300 ' *************INITIALIZATION MODULE**************
310 LET TAMOUNT = 0
320 LET TQUANTITY = 0
330 LET F1$ = "$$###.##     $$###.##"
340 LET F2$ = "$$####.##"
350 '    PRINT HEADINGS
360 LPRINT "COMPANY","COMPANY NO.", "QUANTITY", "PRICE/UNIT", "AMOUNT"
        TAB(68) "DISCOUNT"
370 LPRINT
380 RETURN
390 ' ********************END OF SUBROUTINE**********
400 '
410 '***************PROCESSING ROUTINE**********
420 READ CUSTNAM$,CUSTNO,QUANTITY,UNITPRICE                  ' PRIMING READ
430 '
440 '
450 WHILE CUSTNAM$ <> "DONE"
460     '
470     GOSUB 700                                      ' DISCOUNT SUBROUTINE
480 '
490     LPRINT CUSTNAM$, TAB(18) CUSTNO, TAB(32) QUANTITY,
500     LPRINT USING F1$;UNITPRICE,AMOUNT;
510     LPRINT TAB(65) USING F2$; DISCOUNT
520     READ CUSTNAM$,CUSTNO,QUANTITY,UNITPRICE
530 WEND
540 RETURN
550 ' ******************* END OF PROCESSING SUBROUTINE
560 '
```

FIGURE B.4.7 cont'd

```
600 REM ********************PRINT TOTALS  SUBROUTINE
610 LPRINT
620 LPRINT "TOTAL NUMBER OF ITEMS SOLD  " TAB(43) TQUANTITY
630 LPRINT "TOTAL DOLLAR VALUE OF ALL ORDERS  " TAB(37) USING F2$; TAMOUNT
640 LPRINT "TOTAL AMOUNT OF DISCOUNTS " TAB(37) USING F2$;TDISCOUNT
650 RETURN
660 REM ************END OF TOTALS SUBROUTINE
670 REM
700 ' ***************DISCOUNT SUBROUTINE
710 IF QUANTITY > 15 THEN 750
720      LET PRICE = UNITPRICE
730      LET DISCOUNT = 0
740      GOTO 810
750      LET PRICE = UNITPRICE * (1- .1)
760      LET DISCOUNT = (QUANTITY * UNITPRICE) * .1
770      LET TDISCOUNT = TDISCOUNT + DISCOUNT
780 '
800 '
810      LET AMOUNT = QUANTITY * PRICE
820      LET TAMOUNT = TAMOUNT + AMOUNT
830      LET TQUANTITY = TQUANTITY + QUANTITY
840 RETURN
1000 REM ***************DATA TO BE PROCESSED
1010 DATA MACRO LTD, 101, 11, 1.02
1020 DATA MACRO LTD, 101, 21, 1.16
1030 DATA ABLE INC,  102, 12, 2.13
1040 DATA BETA CO,   103, 15, 3.71
1050 DATA BETA CO,   103, 19, 1.47
1060 DATA DONE,        9,  9,  9
1070 ' *******************END OF DATA STATEMENTS
```

The Actual Output

See Figure B.4.8.

FIGURE B.4.8

COMPANY	COMPANY NO.	QUANTITY	PRICE/UNIT	AMOUNT	DISCOUNT
MACRO LTD	101	11	$1.02	$11.22	$0.00
MACRO LTD	101	21	$1.16	$21.92	$2.44
ABLE INC	102	12	$2.13	$25.56	$0.00
BETA CO	103	15	$3.71	$55.65	$0.00
BETA CO	103	19	$1.47	$25.14	$2.79

```
TOTAL NUMBER OF ITEMS SOLD            78
TOTAL DOLLAR VALUE OF ALL ORDERS   $139.49
TOTAL AMOUNT OF DISCOUNTS           $5.23
```

Section 5: Programming Tables

Topics Covered in This Chapter

BASIC Instructions
  DIM
  FOR/NEXT
Logic
  Loading a table from input data
  Loading a table from calculations
    Writing out a table

Programming Projects
1. Listing of customer data. The data is to be accessed from a table that was loaded in the program
2. Creation of a two-dimensional table. Contents of the table are to be printed at end of job

In this section we begin to use tables or arrays to assist us in processing data. We will use the term *table* and *array* interchangeably for the discussion in this section. Tables make the handling of large amounts of similar data easier. Everything we can do with tables we can also do without them. However, it would be so tedious that few people would enjoy programming.

Tables allow us to store many similar elements of data under one variable name rather than the 100 or 1000 or 10,000 names we might otherwise have to use. We can still reference any one part (element) we are interested in by using a subscript to indicate which of the elements we want. For example TPART(150) would be a reference to the 150th element of a table named TPART. In this example 150 is the subscript.

As long as the subscript is a constant such as 150, we do not gain a great advantage using tables. If we change the subscript to a variable, then we have the ability to access various elements of the table by just changing the subscript as the program is executing.

Before we deal with the programming projects in this section, let's look at some tables and the vocabulary we use to reference them.

1014	TPART(1)
1015	TPART(2)
1234	TPART(3)
1867	TPART(4)
2008	TPART(5)
2019	TPART(6)

This is a one-dimensional table with six elements. The name of the entire table is TPART. We can reference any single element by placing a subscript after the table name as in TPART(3). This references the third element of TPART, which has a value of 1234. We call this a one-dimensional table, because it has multiple rows but only one column. In order to communicate which element we want, we have to specify only the appropriate row (that is, we need to use only one subscript). In memory these table elements are stored one after another; however, it is easier for us to visualize them if we place the elements in rows and columns.

A two-dimensional table can be drawn as follows:

TINVTOT(1, 1)	184	35.58	TINVTOT(1, 2)
TINVTOT(2, 1)	185	27.44	TINVTOT(2, 2)
TINVTOT(3, 1)	186	14.69	TINVTOT(3, 2)
TINVTOT(4, 1)	549	53.61	TINVTOT(4, 2)
TINVTOT(5, 1)	410	83.58	TINVTOT(5, 2)
TINVTOT(6, 1)	412	60.27	TINVTOT(6, 2)
TINVTOT(7, 1)	414	33.32	tinvtot(7, 2)
TINVTOT(8, 1)	402	44.47	TINVTOT(8, 2)
TINVTOT(9, 1)	0	.00	TINVTOT(9, 2)
TINVTOT(10, 1)	0	.00	TINVTOT(10, 2)
TINVTOT(11, 1)	0	.00	TINVTOT(11, 2)
TINVTOT(12, 1)	0	.00	TINVTOT(12, 2)
TINVTOT(13, 1)	0	.00	TINVTOT(13, 2)
TINVTOT(14, 1)	0	.00	TINVTOT(14, 2)
TINVTOT(15, 1)	0	.00	TINVTOT(15, 2)

The name of this table is TINVTOT. This name is not suitable for Apple because of the embedded reserved word TO. The table has fifteen rows and two columns. The row then has two elements: one represents an invoice number and the other represents a total amount for that invoice. Since this table has both multiple rows *and* multiple columns, it requires two subscripts to identify a table element: one to say which row and one to say which column. Notice that the row subscript is first followed by the column subscript. This is the way it is normally done. The subscripts can be reversed as long as the programmer keeps track of the way the elements are arranged in the table and arranges the data accordingly.

Each time we add a dimension to a table we must also add a subscript when we reference the table. Although it is more than we can put to

practical use, the Apple II allows 88 subscripts and the IBM PC allows 255 subscripts.

Problem Analysis—Project 1

Output Required   The same as Section 4.

Input Required

```
CUSTNAM$(  )
CUSTNO(  )
QUANTITY(  )
UNITPRICE(  )
```

Processing Required   The same as Section 4 except that the data will be loaded in arrays. These arrays will be accessed for the data needed for calculation and printing output.

Input Values   The same as Section 4.

Output Format   The same as Section 4, Project 2.

The Flowchart   See Figure B.5.1. This flowchart is the same as that in Section 4 except FOR/NEXT statements are used for loop control.

Explanation of Logic Used

In our initialization module we have to assign a variable with a value which represents the number of rows in our arrays. In this case the arrays will have 5 rows. Next we allocate space in memory for the arrays using the DIM statement. After the headings are printed, the load arrays subroutine is executed. This routine uses FOR/NEXT loops and READ statements to assign values to the various positions in the different arrays. Processing proceeds in the same manner as the previous section, but now the specific position in the appropriate array is accessed to obtain the data needed for calculation or printing out detail lines.

The BASIC Program

See Figure B.5.2.

The Actual Output

See Figure B.5.3.

FIGURE B.5.1

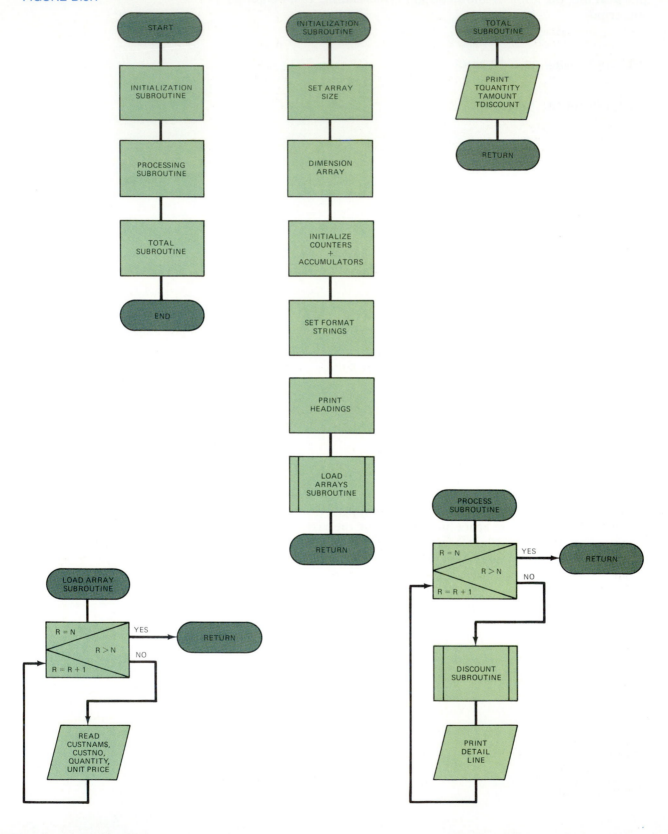

FIGURE B.5.2

```
10 REM    PROGRAM ID: CASE5
20 REM    AUTHOR ID:  MURPHY/LONGHURST        DATE WRITTEN: 5/26/8X
30 REM
40 REM    THIS PROGRAM USES A ONE DIMENSIONAL ARRAY TO
45 REM    LIST CUSTOMER ORDER INFORMATION CALCULATE DISCOUNTS
50 REM    AND CALCULATES TOTAL AMOUNT FOR EACH ORDER AND TOTAL
60 REM    QUANTITY AND AMOUNTS AFTER ALL ORDERS HAVE BEEN PROCESSED
70 REM
80 REM    VARIABLE LIST
90 '        CUSTNAM$( ).............CUSTOMER NAME  ARRAY
100 '       CUSTNO( ).............CUSTOMER NUMBER ARRAY
110 '       AMOUNT( ).............DOLLAR VALUE OF ORDER ARRAY
120 '       QUANTITY( )...........QUANTITY  ARRAY
130 '       TAMOUNT..............TOTAL DOLLAR VALUE OF ALL ORDERS
140 '       TQUANTITY............TOTAL QUANTITY OF ALL ORDERS
150 '       UNITPRICE............UNIT PRICE
200 '************* COMMAND MODULE***********
210 '
220 GOSUB 300                      ' INITIALIZATION SUBROUTINE
230 '
240 GOSUB 500                      ' PROCESSING
250 '
260 GOSUB 700                      ' TOTAL SUBROUTINE
270 '
280 ' *****************END OF COMMAND MODULE*****************
290 END                           ' END OF JOB
300 ' *************INITIALIZATION MODULE*************
305 LET N = 5
310 DIM CUSTNAM$(N), CUSTNO(N), QUANTITY(N), UNITPRICE(N), AMOUNT(N)
320 LET TAMOUNT = 0
330 LET TQUANTITY = 0
340 LET F1$ = "$$###.##      $$###.##"
350 LET F2$ = "$$####.##"
360 '   PRINT HEADINGS
370 LPRINT "COMPANY","COMPANY NO.", "QUANTITY", "PRICE/UNIT", "AMOUNT"

          TAB(68) "DISCOUNT"
380 LPRINT
390 GOSUB 1000                       ' LOAD ARRAYS
400 RETURN
410 ' *********************END OF SUBROUTINE**********
420 '
500 '****************PROCESSING ROUTINE**********
510 '
520 '
530 '
540 FOR R = 1 TO N
550      '
560      GOSUB 800
570 '
580      LPRINT CUSTNAM$(R), TAB(18) CUSTNO(R), TAB(32) QUANTITY(R),
590      LPRINT USING F1$;UNITPRICE(R),AMOUNT(R);
600      LPRINT TAB(65) USING F2$; DISCOUNT
610 '
620 NEXT R
630 RETURN
640 ' ********************* END OF PROCESSING SUBROUTINE
650 '
700 REM *****************PRINT TOTALS  SUBROUTINE
710 LPRINT
720 LPRINT "TOTAL NUMBER OF ITEMS SOLD  " TAB(43) TQUANTITY
730 LPRINT "TOTAL DOLLAR VALUE OF ALL ORDERS  " TAB(37) USING F2$; TAMOUNT
740 LPRINT "TOTAL AMOUNT OF DISCOUNTS " TAB(37) USING F2$;TDISCOUNT
750 RETURN
```

FIGURE B.5.2. cont'd

```
760 REM *************END OF TOTALS SUBROUTINE
770 REM
800 ' ***************DISCOUNT SUBROUTINE
810 IF QUANTITY(R) > 15 THEN 850
820     LET PRICE = UNITPRICE(R)
830     LET DISCOUNT = O
840     GOTO 900
850     LET PRICE = UNITPRICE(R) * (1- .1)
860     LET DISCOUNT = (QUANTITY(R) * UNITPRICE(R)) * .1
870     LET TDISCOUNT = TDISCOUNT + DISCOUNT
880 '
890 '
900     LET AMOUNT = QUANTITY(R) * PRICE
910     LET TAMOUNT = TAMOUNT + AMOUNT
920     LET TQUANTITY = TQUANTITY + QUANTITY(R)
930 RETURN
1000 '*************ARRAY LOADING MODULE
1010 FOR R = 1 TO N
1020     READ CUSTNAM$(R), CUSTNO(R), QUANTITY(R), UNITPRICE(R)
1030 NEXT R
1040 RETURN
1050 '
1100 REM **************DATA TO BE PROCESSED
1110 DATA MACRO LTD, 101, 11, 1.02
1120 DATA MACRO LTD, 101, 21, 1.16
1130 DATA ABLE INC,  102, 12, 2.13
1140 DATA BETA CO,   103, 15, 3.71
1150 DATA BETA CO,   103, 19, 1.47
1170 ' *******************END OF DATA STATEMENTS
1180 '    END OF PROGRAM STATEMENTS
```

FIGURE B.5.3

COMPANY	COMPANY NO.	QUANTITY	PRICE/UNIT	AMOUNT	DISCOUNT
MACRO LTD	101	11	$1.02	$0.00	$0.00
MACRO LTD	101	21	$1.16	$0.00	$2.44
ABLE INC	102	12	$2.13	$0.00	$0.00
BETA CO	103	15	$3.71	$0.00	$0.00
BETA CO	103	19	$1.47	$0.00	$2.79

```
TOTAL NUMBER OF ITEMS SOLD            78
TOTAL DOLLAR VALUE OF ALL ORDERS  $139.49
TOTAL AMOUNT OF DISCOUNTS           $5.23
```

BASIC Language Discussion

DIM

```
                                    IBM AND APPLE
FORMAT:
   line # DIM variable (subscripts)
```

We use the DIM statement to allocate storage for a table or array in a BASIC program. We follow the word DIM with a variable name. The choice of names will depend on the type of array we need, numeric or string (alphanumeric). We use the same naming convention as before a $ on string variables whether they represent a single variable or an array.

After choosing the variable name that indicates the type of array, we must deal with the size of the array. We tell the computer the number of dimensions by the number of subscripts we use. The number we use for each subscript indicates the maximum number of elements for that dimension. When we dimension an array we can allocate more space than we need and it simply will not be used. If we allocate less space than we need, an error message will result when we attempt to exceed the size of the array.

In the examples below we are assuming the subscripts start at 1, although subscripts of 0 are possible on both Apple and IBM.

```
Examples:

  DIM CUST(6)
    A one-dimensional numeric array with 6 rows
    (6 elements)
  DIM BOOKS(20, 4)
    A two-dimensional numeric array with 20
    rows and 4 columns (80 elements).
  DIM EARNINGS (15, 8, 20)
    A three-dimensional numeric array with 15
    planes, 8 rows, and 20 columns (2400
    elements).
  DIM TITLE$(16)
    A one-dimensional string array with 16 rows
    (16 elements)
```

If we do not dimension (DIM) an array before we use it, BASIC will allocate storage for a one-dimensional array with 10 elements. As long as this meets our needs, the program will function. It is recommended, however, that you dimension all arrays to document their existence.

FOR/NEXT

```
                                     IBM AND APPLE
  FORMAT:
    line # FOR variable=x TO y [STEP z]
          - - -
          - - -
    line # NEXT variable
```

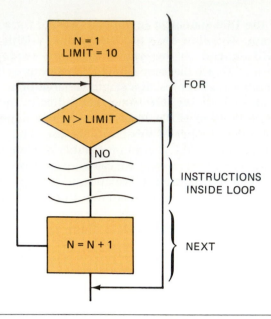

FOR

INSTRUCTIONS
INSIDE LOOP

NEXT

The FOR/NEXT statements in BASIC are used to control a loop. It is easier to understand how the loop is controlled if we show the separate steps in a flowchart (see Figure B.5.4).

```
FOR N=1 TO 10
    --
    --
NEXT N
```

When the FOR statement is encountered, the variable being used as a counter (N) is initialized to 1. The limit is set at 10 and the increment is set at 1. If we wanted the increment to be other than 1, we would use the STEP portion of the statement. The value following STEP may be either positive or negative. If we make it negative, then we must initialize the counter at a high value and the limit at a lower value.

After the counter is initialized, the limit is set, and the increment is established, a test is made to see if the counter is greater than the limit. If it is, control is transferred to the statement below the NEXT statement and the loop is terminated. If the counter is not greater than the limit, the statements between the FOR and NEXT statements are executed and control goes to the NEXT statement. The NEXT statement causes the counter to be incremented and returns control to the FOR statement, which tests the counter. This process continues until the counter is greater than the limit and the loop ends.

Problem Analysis—Project 2

In this program we will focus only on the company name, unit price, and orders for each day of the week. The company name and unit price arrays will be one-dimensional and the quantity arrays will be two-dimensional.

We will increase the number of companies to 10 and will use 5 days in the week. Processing will be similar, but now we will process the data for each company for each day of the week and calculate weekly as well as grand totals.

Output Required   Column headings showing company name, days of the week, weekly amount, and discount totals. Summary lines for grand totals of quantity, amount, and discount.

Input Required

```
CUSTNAM$(  )
UNITPRICE(  )
QUANTITY(  ,  )
```

Processing Required

1. Print headings
2. Load arrays
3. Perform calculation
4. Accumulate totals
5. Print detail lines
6. Print total lines

Input Values

```
MACRO LTD,  1.02,  11,  12,  15,  15,  15
MACRO LTD,  1.16,  21,  20,  20,  25,  25
ABLE INC,   2.13,  12,  15,  15,  20,  22
BETA CO,    3.71,  15,  15,  15,  15,  15
BETA CO,    1.47,  19,  21,  23,  25,  27
CHUNKY,     3.49,  10,  10,  10,  30,  30
POOR INC,   2.50,   2,   2,   3,   4,   5
ZORRO CO,   4.00,  20,  20,  20,  20,  20
HARPO INC,  2.50,  10,  15,  20,  30,  40
ZORPAC,     2.00,  20,  30,  35,  35,  35
```

Output Format   The same as Section 4, Project 2 except output is formatted.

The Flowchart   See Figure B.5.5. This flowchart is the same as that in Project 1 (Figure B.5.1) except nested FOR/NEXT statements are used to load the arrays.

Explanation of Logic Used

The logic is very similar to that used in Project 1 except we have to load a two-dimensional array with the daily orders of the week. We assign a variable with a value which represents the number of companies or rows in the array and a second variable with the number of days in the week or

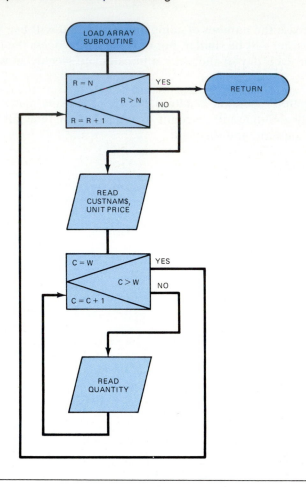

FIGURE B.5.5

columns for the two-dimensional array. The DIM statement is then used to reserve the memory locations. The calculation for AMOUNT, DISCOUNT, TOTALS will be the same as in previous sections, except they will be performed for each day of the week for each company. Nested FOR/NEXT loops will be used to load, calculate, and print information from the two-dimensional array.

The BASIC Program

See Figure B.5.6.

The Actual Output

See Figure B.5.7

BASIC Language Discussion

No new BASIC statements have been introduced.

FIGURE B.5.6

```
10 REM   PROGRAM ID: CASE5B
20 REM   AUTHOR ID: MURPHY/LONGHURST        DATE WRITTEN: 5/26/8X
30 REM
40 REM   THIS PROGRAM USES ARRAYS TO DISPLAY CUSTOMER ORDER INFORMATION
50 REM   AND CALCULATES TOTAL AMOUNT FOR EACH ORDER AND TOTAL
60 REM   QUANTITY AND AMOUNTS AFTER ALL ORDERS HAVE BEEN PROCESSED
70 REM
80 REM   VARIABLE LIST
90 '     CUSTNAM$( )...........CUSTOMER NAME ARRAY
100 '    CUSTNO( )............CUSTOMER NUMBER  ARRAY
110 '    AMOUNT( )............DOLLAR VALUE OF ORDER  ARRAY
120 '    QUANTITY( )..........QUANTITY ARRAY
130 '    TAMOUNT..............TOTAL DOLLAR VALUE OF ALL ORDERS
140 '    TQUANTITY............TOTAL QUANTITY OF ALL ORDERS
150 '    UNITPRICE............UNIT PRICE
200 '*********** COMMAND MODULE**********
210 '
220 GOSUB 300                      ' INITIALIZATION SUBROUTINE
230 '
240 GOSUB 500                      ' PROCESSING
250 '
260 GOSUB 600                      ' TOTAL SUBROUTINE
270 '
280 ' *******************END OF COMMAND MODULE*****************
290 END                           ' END OF JOB
300 ' ************INITIALIZATION MODULE*************
310 LET N= 10
320 LET W= 5
330 DIM CUSTNAM$(N), UNITPRICE(N), QUANTITY(N,W)
340 LET TAMOUNT = 0
350 LET TQUANTITY = 0
360 LET F1$ = " ### "
370 LET F2$ = "$$####.##"
380 '   PRINT HEADINGS
390 LPRINT "COMPANY" TAB(55) "WEEKLY" TAB(65) "WEEKLY"
400 LPRINT " NAME" TAB(20) " M    T    W   TH    F  TOTAL" TAB(55) "SALES"
                TAB(65) "DISCOUNT"
410 LPRINT
420 GOSUB 1000                         ' LOAD ARRAYS
430 RETURN
440 ' **********************END OF SUBROUTINE***********
500 ' **********************PROCESSING ROUTINE
510 '
520 FOR R = 1 TO N
530      '
540     GOSUB 700
550 '
560 '
570 NEXT R
580 RETURN
590 ' ********************** END OF PROCESSING SUBROUTINE
600 '
610 REM *******************PRINT TOTALS  SUBROUTINE
620 LPRINT
630 LPRINT "TOTAL NUMBER OF ITEMS SOLD " TAB(42) TQUANTITY
640 LPRINT "TOTAL DOLLAR VALUE OF ALL ORDERS  " TAB(37) USING F2$; TAMOUNT
650 LPRINT "TOTAL AMOUNT OF DISCOUNTS " TAB(37) USING F2$;TDISCOUNT
660 RETURN
670 REM ***********END OF TOTALS SUBROUTINE
680 REM
700 ' **************DISCOUNT SUBROUTINE
710  FOR C = 1 TO W
720    IF QUANTITY(R,C) > 15 THEN 760
```

FIGURE B.5.6 cont'd

```
730      LET PRICE = UNITPRICE(R)
740      LET DISCOUNT = O
750      GOTO 810
760      LET PRICE = UNITPRICE(R) * (1- .1)
770      LET DISCOUNT = (QUANTITY(R,C) * UNITPRICE(R)) * .1
780      LET RDISCOUNT = RDISCOUNT + DISCOUNT
790 '
800 '
810      LET AMOUNT = QUANTITY(R,C) * PRICE
820      LET RAMOUNT = RAMOUNT + AMOUNT
830      LET RQUANTITY = RQUANTITY + QUANTITY(R,C)
840   NEXT C
850   GOSUB 1110
860      LET TDISCOUNT = TDISCOUNT + RDISCOUNT
870      LET TAMOUNT = TAMOUNT + RAMOUNT
880      LET TQUANTITY = TQUANTITY + RQUANTITY
890      LET RDISCOUNT =O
900      LET RAMOUNT = O
910      LET RQUANTITY = O
920 RETURN
1000 '**************ARRAY LOADING MODULE
1010 FOR R = 1 TO N
1020      READ CUSTNAM$(R), UNITPRICE(R)
1030      FOR C = 1 TO W
1040            READ QUANTITY(R,C)
1050      NEXT C
1060 NEXT R
1070 RETURN
1100 ' ***********PRINT DETAIL LINE
1110      LPRINT CUSTNAM$(R) TAB(18);
1120         FOR C = 1 TO W
1130            LPRINT USING  F1$; QUANTITY(R,C);
1140         NEXT C
1150      LPRINT USING F1$; RQUANTITY;
1160      LPRINT TAB(52) USING F2$; RAMOUNT;
1170      LPRINT TAB(62) USING F2$; RDISCOUNT
1180   RETURN
1200 REM **************DATA TO BE PROCESSED
1210 DATA MACRO LTD,  1.O2,  11,  12,  15,  15,  15
1220 DATA MACRO LTD,  1.16,  21,  20,  20,  25,  25
1230 DATA ABLE INC,   2.13,  12,  15,  15,  20,  22
1240 DATA BETA CO,    3.71,  15,  15,  15,  15,  15
1250 DATA BETA CO,    1.47,  19,  21,  23,  25,  27
1260 DATA CHUNKY,     3.49,  10,  10,  10,  30,  30
1270 DATA POOR INC,   2.50,   2,   2,   3,   4,   5
1280 DATA ZORRO CO,   4.OO,  20,  20,  20,  20,  20
1290 DATA HARPO INC, 2.50,  10,  15,  20,  30,  40
1300 DATA ZORPAC,     2.OO,  20,  30,  35,  35,  35
1310 ' ******************END OF DATA STATEMENTS
1320 '    END OF PROGRAM STATEMENTS
```

FIGURE B.5.7

COMPANY NAME	M	T	W	TH	F	TOTAL	WEEKLY SALES	WEEKLY DISCOUNT
MACRO LTD	11	12	15	15	15	68	$69.36	$0.00
MACRO LTD	21	20	20	25	25	111	$115.88	$12.88
ABLE INC	12	15	15	20	22	84	$169.97	$8.95
BETA CO	15	15	15	15	15	75	$278.25	$0.00
BETA CO	19	21	23	25	27	115	$152.14	$16.91
CHUNKY	10	10	10	30	30	90	$293.16	$20.94
POOR INC	2	2	3	4	5	16	$40.00	$0.00
ZORRO CO	20	20	20	20	20	100	$360.00	$40.00
HARPO INC	10	15	20	30	40	115	$265.00	$22.50
ZORPAC	20	30	35	35	35	155	$279.00	$31.00

```
TOTAL NUMBER OF ITEMS SOLD              929
TOTAL DOLLAR VALUE OF ALL ORDERS    $2022.77
TOTAL AMOUNT OF DISCOUNTS            $153.17
```

Section 6: Advanced Table Manipulation

Topics Covered in This Section

BASIC Instructions	**Programming Project**
SWAP	1. Sort of data from Section
Logic	5 in ascending order on
Sorting in ascending order	customer name
using a bubble sort	2. Control break reports
Control break reporting used	showing subtotals for
to produce subtotal reports	each customer

In this section we will discuss techniques for more complex manipulation of arrays. The first technique will be sorting data and placing the data in a particular order. The second technique is to use CUSTNAM$ as a control field. Every time this field changes a subtotal will be printed out. This output is produced by a control break routine.

Problem Analysis—Project 1

Output Required   Same as Section 5, Project 2 except output will be in ascending alphabetic order based on company name.

Input Required   The same as Section 5, Project 2.

Processing Required   The same as Section 5, Project 2 except after the arrays are loaded they are sorted in alphabetic order.

Input Values   The same as Section 5, Project 2.

Output Format   The same as Section 5, Project 2 except sorted by company name.

The Flowchart   See Figure B.6.1. The flowchart is the same as that in Section 5 except a SORT routine is added.

Explanation of Logic Used

The sorting logic used here is a bubble sort. This type of sorting routine sorts the data by comparing adjacent values. If the values are in incorrect sequence, their positions are switched and comparing continues. If the values are in correct sequence, the next pair is compared and switched if necessary. The comparing and switching process continues until all the data is sorted into the correct sequence.

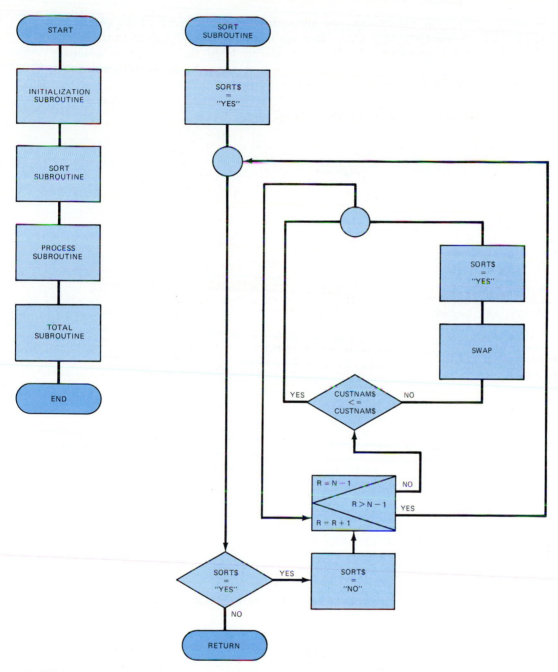

FIGURE B.6.1

Since this usually takes more than one pass through the data, a looping routine is created. The control for this loop is an indicator variable, or *flag*. Any time a switch of data values occurs, the indicator variable is set to "yes". The loop control continues looping through the data as long as the indicator variable is "yes". This indicates that the data is still not sorted. If after a complete pass through the data, the indicator variable is set to "no" then the data is sorted and the looping is finished.

In this example we are sorting on CUSTNAM$. If we switch values in the CUSTNAM$ array, then we must also switch values in the UNITPRICE and QUANTITY arrays in order to keep the individual company data together. Switching is accomplished using the BASIC function SWAP. This function automatically switches the values of the identified variables. Notice that since the QUANTITY array is a two-dimensional array, the SWAP function is used in nested loop.

The BASIC Program

See Figure B.6.2.

FIGURE B.6.2

```
10 REM   PROGRAM ID: CASE6
20 REM   AUTHOR ID:  MURPHY/LONGHURST          DATE WRITTEN: 5/26/8X
30 REM
40 REM   THIS PROGRAM USES ARRAYS TO DISPLAY CUSTOMER INFORMATION IN SORTED
50 REM   ORDER AND CALCULATES TOTAL AMOUNT FOR EACH ORDER AND TOTAL
60 REM   QUANTITY AND AMOUNTS AFTER ALL ORDERS HAVE BEEN PROCESSED
70 REM
80 REM   VARIABLE LIST
90 '        CUSTNAM$( )...........CUSTOMER NAME ARRAY
100 '       CUSTNO( )............CUSTOMER NUMBER  ARRAY
110 '       AMOUNT( )............DOLLAR VALUE OF ORDER  ARRAY
120 '       QUANTITY( )..........QUANTITY ARRAY
130 '       TAMOUNT..............TOTAL DOLLAR VALUE OF ALL ORDERS
140 '       TQUANTITY............TOTAL QUANTITY OF ALL ORDERS
150 '       UNITPRICE............UNIT PRICE
160 '       RAMOUNT()...........WEEKLY TOTAL AMOUNT ARRAY
200 '*********** COMMAND MODULE**********
210 '
220 GOSUB 300                      ' INITIALIZATION SUBROUTINE
230 GOSUB 1200                     ' SORT SUBROUTINE
240 GOSUB 500                      ' PROCESSING
250 '
260 GOSUB 600                      ' TOTAL SUBROUTINE
270 '
280 ' *******************END OF COMMAND MODULE****************
290 END                           ' END OF JOB
300 ' ***********INITIALIZATION MODULE*************
310 LET N= 10
320 LET W= 5
330 DIM CUSTNAM$(N), UNITPRICE(N), QUANTITY(N,W), RAMOUNT(N)
340 LET TAMOUNT = 0
350 LET TQUANTITY = 0
360 LET F1$ = " ### "
370 LET F2$ = "$$####.##"
380 '   PRINT HEADINGS
390 LPRINT "COMPANY" TAB(55) "WEEKLY" TAB(65) "WEEKLY"
400 LPRINT " NAME" TAB(20) " M   T   W   TH   F  TOTAL" TAB(55) "SALES"

                 TAB(65) "DISCOUNT"
410 LPRINT
420 GOSUB 1000                      ' LOAD ARRAYS
430 RETURN
440 ' **********************END OF SUBROUTINE***********
500 ' **********************PROCESSING ROUTINE
510 '
520 FOR R = 1 TO N
530       '
```

FIGURE B.6.2 cont'd

```
540      GOSUB 700
550  '
560  '
570 NEXT R
580 RETURN
590 ' *********************** END OF PROCESSING SUBROUTINE
600  '
610 REM *********************PRINT TOTALS  SUBROUTINE
620 LPRINT
630 LPRINT "TOTAL NUMBER OF ITEMS SOLD " TAB(42) TQUANTITY
640 LPRINT "TOTAL DOLLAR VALUE OF ALL ORDERS  " TAB(37) USING F2$; TAMOUNT
650 LPRINT "TOTAL AMOUNT OF DISCOUNTS " TAB(37) USING F2$;TDISCOUNT
660 RETURN
670 REM ************END OF TOTALS SUBROUTINE
680 REM
700 ' **************DISCOUNT SUBROUTINE
710  FOR C = 1 TO W
720    IF QUANTITY(R,C) > 15 THEN 760
730      LET PRICE = UNITPRICE(R)
740      LET DISCOUNT = 0
750      GOTO 810
760      LET PRICE = UNITPRICE(R) * (1- .1)
770      LET DISCOUNT = (QUANTITY(R,C) * UNITPRICE(R)) * .1
780      LET RDISCOUNT = RDISCOUNT + DISCOUNT
790  '
800  '
810      LET AMOUNT = QUANTITY(R,C) * PRICE
820      LET RAMOUNT(R) = RAMOUNT(R) + AMOUNT
830      LET RQUANTITY = RQUANTITY + QUANTITY(R,C)
840    NEXT C
850    GOSUB 1110
860      LET TDISCOUNT = TDISCOUNT + RDISCOUNT
870      LET TAMOUNT = TAMOUNT + RAMOUNT(R)
880      LET TQUANTITY = TQUANTITY + RQUANTITY
890      LET RDISCOUNT =0
910      LET RQUANTITY = 0
920 RETURN
1000 '**************ARRAY LOADING MODULE
1010 FOR R = 1 TO N
1020      READ CUSTNAM$(R), UNITPRICE(R)
1030      FOR C = 1 TO W
1040              READ QUANTITY(R,C)
1050      NEXT C
1060 NEXT R
1070 RETURN
1100 ' ***********PRINT DETAIL LINE
1110    LPRINT CUSTNAM$(R) TAB(18);
1120      FOR C = 1 TO W
1130            LPRINT USING  F1$; QUANTITY(R,C);
1140      NEXT C
1150    LPRINT USING F1$; RQUANTITY;
1160    LPRINT TAB(52) USING F2$; RAMOUNT(R);
1170    LPRINT TAB(62) USING F2$; RDISCOUNT
1180  RETURN
1200 '**************SORT SUBROUTINE
1210 LET SORT$ = "YES"                        'FORCES 1 PASS THROUGH LOOP
1220 WHILE SORT$ = "YES"
1230    LET SORT$ = "NO"
1240    FOR R = 1 TO N-1
1250        IF CUSTNAM$(R) <= CUSTNAM$(R+1) THEN   1320
1260            SWAP CUSTNAM$(R), CUSTNAM$(R+1)
1270            SWAP UNITPRICE(R), UNITPRICE(R+1)
1280            FOR C = 1 TO W
1290              SWAP QUANTITY (R,C), QUANTITY(R+1,C)
```

FIGURE B.6.2 cont'd

```
1300          NEXT C
1310          LET SORT$ = "YES"
1320     NEXT R
1330 WEND
1340 RETURN
1350 ' ***************END SORT SUBROUTINE
1600 REM ***************DATA TO BE PROCESSED
1610 DATA MACRO LTD, 1.02, 11, 12, 15, 15, 15
1620 DATA MACRO LTD, 1.16, 21, 20, 20, 25, 25
1630 DATA ABLE INC,  2.13, 12, 15, 15, 20, 22
1640 DATA BETA CO,   3.71, 15, 15, 15, 15, 15
1650 DATA BETA CO,   1.47, 19, 21, 23, 25, 27
1660 DATA CHUNKY,    3.49, 10, 10, 10, 30, 30
1670 DATA POOR INC,  2.50,  2,  2,  3,  4,  5
1680 DATA ZORRO CO,  4.00, 20, 20, 20, 20, 20
1690 DATA HARPO INC, 2.50, 10, 15, 20, 30, 40
1700 DATA ZORPAC,    2.00, 20, 30, 35, 35, 35
1710 ' *******************END OF DATA STATEMENTS
1720 '    END OF PROGRAM STATEMENTS
```

The Actual Output

See Figure B.6.3.

FIGURE B.6.3

COMPANY NAME	M	T	W	TH	F	TOTAL	WEEKLY SALES	WEEKLY DISCOUNT
ABLE INC	12	15	15	20	22	84	$169.97	$8.95
BETA CO	15	15	15	15	15	75	$278.25	$0.00
BETA CO	19	21	23	25	27	115	$152.14	$16.91
CHUNKY	10	10	10	30	30	90	$293.16	$20.94
HARPO INC	10	15	20	30	40	115	$265.00	$22.50
MACRO LTD	11	12	15	15	15	68	$69.36	$0.00
MACRO LTD	21	20	20	25	25	111	$115.88	$12.88
POOR INC	2	2	3	4	5	16	$40.00	$0.00
ZORPAC	20	30	35	35	35	155	$279.00	$31.00
ZORRO CO	20	20	20	20	20	100	$360.00	$40.00

```
TOTAL NUMBER OF ITEMS SOLD            929
TOTAL DOLLAR VALUE OF ALL ORDERS   $2022.77
TOTAL AMOUNT OF DISCOUNTS           $153.17
```

BASIC Language Discussion

SWAP

```
                                        IBM

 line # SWAP variable 1, variable 2
```

SWAP automatically switches the values of the two designated variables. The two variables must be of the same type and can be subscripted or nonsubscripted.

The SWAP can be simulated in those systems that do not support it, such as the Apple, by using a temporary variable. For example:

```
10 LET TEMP$ = CUSTNAM$(I)
20 LET CUSTNAM$(I) = CUSTNAM$(I+1)
30 LET CUSTNAME$(I+1) = TEMP$
```

The value for CUSTNAM$(I) is assigned to TEMP$. The value from CUSTNAM$(I+1) is assigned to CUSTNAM$(I). This results in destroying the original value of CUSTNAM$(I) so that CUSTNAM$(I) and CUSTNAM$(I+1) now contain the same values. Last, the value of TEMP$ is assigned to CUSTNAM$(I+1). The result is that the values of CUSTNAM$(I) and CUSTNAM$(I+1) have been switched.

Problem Analysis—Project 2

Output Required

1. Detail line showing:
   CUSTNAM$ once
   RAMOUNT for different weeks for the same CUSTNAM$
2. SUBTOTAL for the different CUSTNAM$.

Input Required   The same as Project 1.

Processing Required   The same as Project 1 except after the sorting and processing routines are completed, a control break routine is processed, which outputs the CUSTNAM$, weekly totals, and final SUBTOTAL when the CUSTNAM$ changes.

Input Values   The same as Project 1.

Output Format   The same as Project 1 except a subtotal is printed.

The Flowchart   See Figure B.6.4. The flowchart is the same as Project 1 except a CONTROL BREAK subroutine is added.

Explanation of Logic Used

CUSTNAM$ is our control field. When it changes a control break has occurred. Until this happens the CUSTNAM$ is printed once and the weekly total, RAMOUNT, is printed for each week and accumulated in a new variable called SUBTOTAL. SUBTOTAL will continue to accumulate

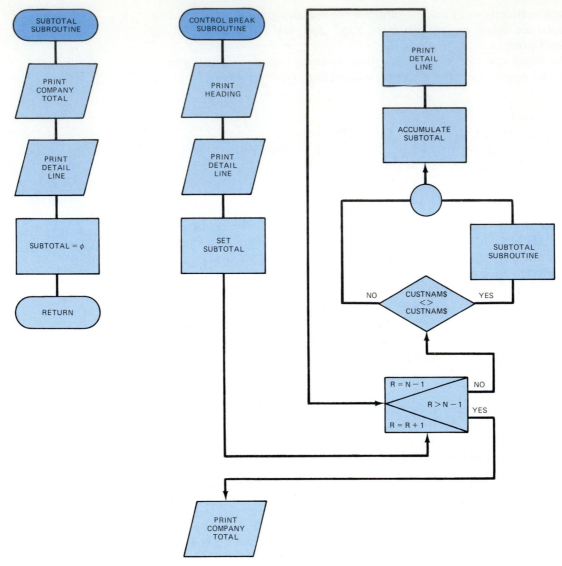

FIGURE B.6.4

RAMOUNT until the CUSTNAM$ changes. When the CUSTNAM$ changes, the previous value of CUSTNAM$ is printed; SUBTOTAL is printed; the new value of CUSTNAM$ is printed once; and SUBTOTAL is reinitialized to zero. This process is repeated until all the data have been compared. The last comparison corresponds to the end of the data. At this point the last value of SUBTOTAL is printed out.

The BASIC Program

See Figure B.6.5.

FIGURE B.6.5

```
10 REM    PROGRAM ID: CASE6B
20 REM    AUTHOR ID:  MURPHY/LONGHURST       DATE WRITTEN: 5/26/8X
30 REM
40 REM    THIS PROGRAM PRODUCES SUBTOTALS, DISPLAYS CUSTOMER ORDER INFORMATION
50 REM    AND CALCULATES TOTAL AMOUNT FOR EACH ORDER AND TOTAL
60 REM    QUANTITY AND AMOUNTS AFTER ALL ORDERS HAVE BEEN PROCESSED
70 REM
80 REM    VARIABLE LIST
90 '        CUSTNAM$( )...........CUSTOMER NAME ARRAY
100 '       CUSTNO( )............CUSTOMER NUMBER  ARRAY
110 '       AMOUNT( )............DOLLAR VALUE OF ORDER  ARRAY
120 '       QUANTITY( )..........QUANTITY ARRAY
130 '       TAMOUNT..............TOTAL DOLLAR VALUE OF ALL ORDERS
140 '       TQUANTITY............TOTAL QUANTITY OF ALL ORDERS
150 '       UNITPRICE............UNIT PRICE
160 '       RAMOUNT()............WEEKLY TOTAL AMOUNT ARRAY
170 '       SUBTOTAL.............SUBTOTAL FOR WEEKLY AMOUNTS
200 '*********** COMMAND MODULE**********
210 '
220 GOSUB 300                       ' INITIALIZATION SUBROUTINE
230 GOSUB 1200                      ' SORT SUBROUTINE
240 GOSUB 500                       ' PROCESSING
250 GOSUB 1400
260 GOSUB 600                       ' TOTAL SUBROUTINE
270 '
280 ' ******************END OF COMMAND MODULE****************
290 END                            ' END OF JOB
300 ' ************INITIALIZATION MODULE*************
310 LET N= 10
320 LET W= 5
330 DIM CUSTNAM$(N), UNITPRICE(N), QUANTITY(N,W), RAMOUNT(N)
340 LET TAMOUNT = 0
350 LET TQUANTITY = 0
360 LET F1$ = " ### "
370 LET F2$ = "$$####.##"
380 '    PRINT HEADINGS
390 LPRINT "COMPANY" TAB(55) "WEEKLY" TAB(65) "WEEKLY"
400 LPRINT " NAME" TAB(20) " M    T    W    TH    F  TOTAL" TAB(55) "SALES"

                   TAB(65) "DISCOUNT"
410 LPRINT
420 GOSUB 1000                          ' LOAD ARRAYS
430 RETURN
440 ' *******************END OF SUBROUTINE**********
500 ' *******************PROCESSING ROUTINE
510 '
520 FOR R = 1 TO N
530     '
540     GOSUB 700
550 '
560 '
570 NEXT R
580 RETURN
590 ' ******************* END OF PROCESSING SUBROUTINE
600 '
610 REM *****************PRINT TOTALS  SUBROUTINE
620 LPRINT
630 LPRINT "TOTAL NUMBER OF ITEMS SOLD " TAB(42) TQUANTITY
640 LPRINT "TOTAL DOLLAR VALUE OF ALL ORDERS  " TAB(37) USING F2$; TAMOUNT
650 LPRINT "TOTAL AMOUNT OF DISCOUNTS " TAB(37) USING F2$;TDISCOUNT
660 RETURN
670 REM ************END OF TOTALS SUBROUTINE
680 REM
700 ' ***************DISCOUNT SUBROUTINE
```

FIGURE B.6.5 cont'd

```
710  FOR C = 1 TO W
720   IF QUANTITY(R,C) > 15 THEN 760
730     LET PRICE = UNITPRICE(R)
740     LET DISCOUNT = 0
750     GOTO 810
760     LET PRICE = UNITPRICE(R) * (1- .1)
770     LET DISCOUNT = (QUANTITY(R,C) * UNITPRICE(R)) * .1
780     LET RDISCOUNT = RDISCOUNT + DISCOUNT
790  '
800  '
810     LET AMOUNT = QUANTITY(R,C) * PRICE
820     LET RAMOUNT(R) = RAMOUNT(R) + AMOUNT
830     LET RQUANTITY = RQUANTITY + QUANTITY(R,C)
840  NEXT C
850  GOSUB 1110
860     LET TDISCOUNT = TDISCOUNT + RDISCOUNT
870     LET TAMOUNT = TAMOUNT + RAMOUNT(R)
880     LET TQUANTITY = TQUANTITY + RQUANTITY
890     LET RDISCOUNT =0
910     LET RQUANTITY = 0
920 RETURN
1000 '**************ARRAY LOADING MODULE
1010 FOR R = 1 TO N
1020    READ CUSTNAM$(R), UNITPRICE(R)
1030    FOR C = 1 TO W
1040         READ QUANTITY(R,C)
1050    NEXT C
1060 NEXT R
1070 RETURN
1100 ' ***********PRINT DETAIL LINE
1110    LPRINT CUSTNAM$(R) TAB(18);
1120     FOR C = 1 TO W
1130          LPRINT USING  F1$; QUANTITY(R,C);
1140     NEXT C
1150    LPRINT USING F1$; RQUANTITY;
1160    LPRINT TAB(52) USING F2$; RAMOUNT(R);
1170    LPRINT TAB(62) USING F2$; RDISCOUNT
1180  RETURN
1200 '***************SORT SUBROUTINE
1210 LET SORT$ = "YES"                          'FORCES 1 PASS THROUGH LOOP
1220 WHILE SORT$ = "YES"
1230    LET SORT$ = "NO"
1240    FOR R = 1 TO N-1
1250       IF CUSTNAM$(R) <= CUSTNAM$(R+1) THEN   1320
1260          SWAP CUSTNAM$(R), CUSTNAM$(R+1)
1270          SWAP UNITPRICE(R), UNITPRICE(R+1)
1280          FOR C = 1 TO W
1290             SWAP QUANTITY (R,C), QUANTITY(R+1,C)
1300          NEXT C
1310          LET SORT$ = "YES"
1320    NEXT R
1330 WEND
1340 RETURN
1350 ' ***************END SORT SUBROUTINE
1400 ' ****************CONTROL BREAK SUBROUTINE
1410 LPRINT
1420 LPRINT TAB(20) "CONTROL BREAK REPORT"
1430 LPRINT
1440 LPRINT CUSTNAM$(1) TAB(30) USING F2$; RAMOUNT(1)
1450 LET SUBTOTAL = RAMOUNT(1)
1460 FOR R = 1 TO N-1
1470    IF CUSTNAM$(R) <> CUSTNAM$(R+1) THEN GOSUB 1570
1480       LET SUBTOTAL = SUBTOTAL + RAMOUNT(R+1)
```

FIGURE B.6.5 cont'd

```
1490        LPRINT TAB(30) USING F2$; RAMOUNT(R+1)
1500 NEXT R
1510 '
1520 LPRINT
1530 LPRINT TAB(5) "TOTAL AMOUNT FOR  " CUSTNAM$(R) TAB(40) USING F2$; SUBTOTAL
1540 LPRINT
1550 LPRINT
1560 RETURN
1570 '**************SUBTOTAL OUTPUT FOR CONTROL BREAK
1580 LPRINT
1590 LPRINT TAB(5) "TOTAL AMOUNT FOR  " CUSTNAM$(R) TAB(40) USING F2$; SUBTOTAL
1600 LPRINT
1610 LPRINT CUSTNAM$(R+1);
1620 LET SUBTOTAL = 0
1630 RETURN
1640 '****************** END CONTROL BREAK ROUTINE
1700 REM **************DATA TO BE PROCESSED
1710 DATA MACRO LTD, 1.02, 11, 12, 15, 15, 15
1720 DATA MACRO LTD, 1.16, 21, 20, 20, 25, 25
1730 DATA ABLE INC,  2.13, 12, 15, 15, 20, 22
1740 DATA BETA CO,   3.71, 15, 15, 15, 15, 15
1750 DATA BETA CO,   1.47, 19, 21, 23, 25, 27
1760 DATA CHUNKY,    3.49, 10, 10, 10, 30, 30
1770 DATA POOR INC,  2.50, 2,  2,  3,  4,  5
1780 DATA ZORRO CO,  4.00, 20, 20, 20, 20, 20
1790 DATA HARPO INC, 2.50, 10, 15, 20, 30, 40
1800 DATA ZORPAC,    2.00, 20, 30, 35, 35, 35
1810 ' ******************END OF DATA STATEMENTS
1820 '    END OF PROGRAM STATEMENTS
```

The Actual Output

See Figure B.6.6.

FIGURE B.6.6

COMPANY NAME	M	T	W	TH	F	TOTAL	WEEKLY SALES	WEEKLY DISCOUNT
ABLE INC	12	15	15	20	22	84	$169.97	$8.95
BETA CO	15	15	15	15	15	75	$278.25	$0.00
BETA CO	19	21	23	25	27	115	$152.14	$16.91
CHUNKY	10	10	10	30	30	90	$293.16	$20.94
HARPO INC	10	15	20	30	40	115	$265.00	$22.50
MACRO LTD	11	12	15	15	15	68	$69.36	$0.00
MACRO LTD	21	20	20	25	25	111	$115.88	$12.88
POOR INC	2	2	3	4	5	16	$40.00	$0.00
ZORPAC	20	30	35	35	35	155	$279.00	$31.00
ZORRO CO	20	20	20	20	20	100	$360.00	$40.00

```
            CONTROL BREAK REPORT

ABLE INC                $169.97

    TOTAL AMOUNT FOR  ABLE INC        $169.97
```

FIGURE B.6.6 cont'd

```
BETA CO                        $278.25
                               $152.14

    TOTAL AMOUNT FOR  BETA CO          $430.40
CHUNKY                         $293.16

    TOTAL AMOUNT FOR  CHUNKY           $293.16
HARPO INC                      $265.00

    TOTAL AMOUNT FOR  HARPO INC        $265.00
MACRO LTD                       $69.36
                               $115.88

    TOTAL AMOUNT FOR  MACRO LTD        $185.24
POOR INC                        $40.00

    TOTAL AMOUNT FOR  POOR INC          $40.00
ZORPAC                         $279.00

    TOTAL AMOUNT FOR  ZORPAC           $279.00

ZORRO CO                       $360.00

    TOTAL AMOUNT FOR  ZORRO CO         $360.00


TOTAL NUMBER OF ITEMS SOLD           929
TOTAL DOLLAR VALUE OF ALL ORDERS   $2022.77
TOTAL AMOUNT OF DISCOUNTS           $153.17
```

BASIC Language Discussion

No new BASIC statements have been introduced.

Section 7: Creating and Accessing Sequential Files

Topics Covered in This Section

BASIC Instructions
  OPEN
  CHR$(4)
  INPUT#
  WRITE#
  EOF
  CLOSE
  WHILE/WEND
Logic
  Creation of a sequential file
  Accessing a sequential file

Programming Projects
1. Create a sequential disk file that could be used in place of DATA statements for some of the previous projects
2. Access the sequential disk file and make a simple listing

To create a sequential file the records must be written to the file in the order in which they are to be stored. Later, when the file is read, it must be read in the same order. Each version of BASIC handles sequential file creation and access in a slightly different manner. The programming projects were run on an IBM PC. Formats are provided for Apple when they differ.

Problem Analysis—Project 1

Output Required

1. A sequential disk file of invoice data.
2. Screen prompts to assist the person entering the data.
3. A printed listing of the data.

```
CUSTNAM$
CUSTNO
QUANTITY
UNITPRICE
```

Input Required

```
CUSTNAM$
CUSTNO
QUANTITY
UNITPRICE
```

Processing Required

1. Include disk file handling statement.
2. Input the data from a keyboard.
3. Confirm that data is correct as entered before writing it on disk.
4. Write the data to a print and a disk file.

Input Values   The same as Section 4, Project 2.

Output Format

FIGURE B.7.1

The Flowchart   See Figure B.7.2.

Explanation of Logic Used

When creating disk files it is necessary to OPEN them prior to writing to them. Since this needs to be done only once, it is done in initialization. Processing is under the control of an inner and outer loop. Each data item is inputted separately with appropriate prompts. This is performed in the inner loop controlled by OK$. This loop allows the user to accept or reenter data. If OK$ is set to NO the user is prompted to reenter the data. If OK$ is set to yes the data is written to the disk file. Processing is now under the control of the outer loop. If FINISHED$ is set to NO the outer loop will continue to add data records. If FINISHED$ is set to yes processing is completed. Control is passed back to the command module, the file is closed, and the program completed.

End of Job   The file is closed. This causes any data left in a buffer to be written to the file and an end-of-file marker to be placed at the end of the file.

The BASIC Program

See Figure B.7.3.

FIGURE B.7.2

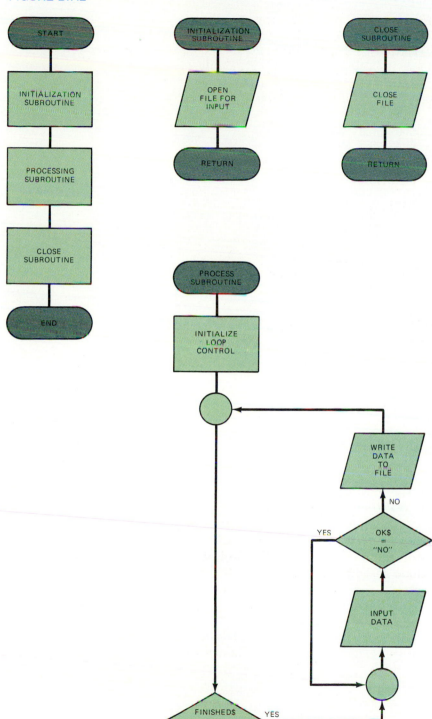

FIGURE B.7.3

```
10 REM   PROGRAM ID: CASE7
20 REM   AUTHOR ID:  MURPHY/LONGHURST        DATE WRITTEN: 5/26/8X
30 REM
40 REM   THIS PROGRAM ALLOWS A USER TO CREATE AND NAME A DATA FILE
50 REM   ENTER RECORDS INTO THIS FILE, AND CLOSE THE FILE
60 REM
70 REM
80 REM   VARIABLE LIST
90 '     CUSTNAM$..........CUSTOMER NAME
100 '    CUSTNO............CUSTOMER NUMBER
110 '    UNITPRICE.........UNIT PRICE
120 '    QUANTITY..........QUANTITY
125 '    OK$...............LOOP CONTROL FOR VALIDATING DATA
130 '    FINISHED$.........LOOP CONTROL FOR ADDING RECORDS
140 '    FILE$.............NAME OF DATA FILE
150 '    OK$...............LOOP CONTROL FOR VALIDATING DATA
200 '*********** COMMAND MODULE**********
210 '
220 '
230 GOSUB 300                    ' INITIALIZE DATA FILE
240 GOSUB 400                    ' PROCESSING
250 '
260 GOSUB 600                    ' CLOSE SUBROUTINE
270 '
280 ' *******************END OF COMMAND MODULE****************
290 END                         ' END OF JOB
300 ' ***********DATA FILE CREATION SUBROUTINE
310 INPUT " ENTER THE NAME OF THE DATA FILE YOU WISH TO MAKE  ",FILE$
320 OPEN FILE$ FOR OUTPUT AS # 1
330 RETURN
400 '***************PROCESSING ROUTINE**********
410 ' ***********DATA FILE CREATION SUBROUTINE
420 LET FINISHED$ = "NO"
430 WHILE FINISHED$ = "NO"
440  LET OK$ = "NO"
450  WHILE OK$ = "NO"
460     LPRINT "ENTER THE CUSTOMER NAME, NUMBER, QUANTITY, AND UNITPRICE"
470     INPUT " CUSTOMER NAME";CUSTNAM$
475     INPUT "CUSTOMER NUMBER";CUSTNO
480     INPUT  "QUANTITY "; QUANTITY
490     INPUT "UNITPRICE"; UNITPRICE
500     LPRINT "THIS IS WHAT YOU ENTERED"
510     LPRINT CUSTNAM$,CUSTNO, QUANTITY,UNITPRICE
520     INPUT "ENTER YES TO CONTINUE OR NO TO REENTER THE DATA";OK$
530  WEND
540  WRITE #1, CUSTNAM$, CUSTNO,QUANTITY, UNITPRICE
550  INPUT "ARE YOU FINISHED ADDING RECORDS?  ENTER NO TO ADD MORE OR YES TO END
             THE PROGRAM";FINISHED$
560 WEND
570  RETURN
600 '***********CLOSE FILE SUBROUTINE
610 CLOSE #1
620 RETURN
```

BASIC Language Discussion

```
                                                    IBM
FORMAT:
   line # OPEN file name [FOR status] AS [#]
   file number
```

In order to use a file in BASIC, it must be opened. The OPEN statement requires

1. File name—In our example, this is a file whose name is DATA7. This file will be placed on the default disk drive, usually referred to as the A drive. If you wish the file to be on another drive, you must include that in the file specification (e.g., "B:DATA7"; the B: directs the file to the B drive).

2. File status—The choices are:
   Input—to read from a file that already exists.
   Output—to create a new file. Opening a file as output destroys any existing with the same name.
   Append—to add records to an existing file.

3. File number ($\#1$ in our example)—DOS automatically sets up buffers for three files for IBM BASIC. If you require more than three, use the /f:n option when you load BASIC (n represents the number of files up to a maximum of fifteen). File numbers can be reused in the same program. If you close $\#1$, then $\#1$ can be opened as a different file in the same program.

```
                                                  APPLE
FORMAT:
   line # PRINT CHR$(4);"OPEN file name"
```

This command is used to open a file as either input or output. If the file does not already exist, a label will be created for it and space will be allocated. A second command, WRITE, is used in addition to the OPEN to indicate that the file is to be used as output.

The OPEN command is a DOS instruction and is therefore handled differently in the Apple BASIC program. It is preceded by PRINT (CHR$(4) (which represents CTRL-D) and it is enclosed in quotes. Although the statement can be used in a program as it is shown in the format, a convention has been developed that replaces the CHR$(4) with a variable name, D$. Many programs use this convention since it is easier to repeat D$ as needed in the program rather than CHR$(4).

```
          LET D$ = CHR$(4)
          PRINT D$;"OPEN DATA7"
```

These statements should go in the Initialization subroutine. We will assume this convention in future Apple file formats. If the file is to be used as output, it needs the following statement:

```
                                          APPLE
FORMAT:
  line # PRINT D$;"WRITE file name"
```

This statement must occur prior to the PRINT statement that lists the variable names to be written on disk. It is used to direct the data in the second PRINT statement to the file specified in this one.

```
          PRINT D$;"WRITE DATA7"
          PRINT CUSTNO;",";INVNO;",";PARTNO
```

This combination will direct the fields CUSTNO, INVNO, and PARTNO to an output file called DATA7. Notice the special punctuation between variable names. Unfortunately this WRITE directs all subsequent PRINT and INPUT statements to that file until the WRITE statement is canceled. If our program has an INPUT statement as a part of the loop and we do not wish the data to go directly to the output disk, we can cancel the WRITE after each PRINT statement has transferred data to the disk using the following combination:

```
          PRINT D$;"WRITE DATA7"
          PRINT CUSTNO;",";INVNO;",";PARTNO
          PRINT D$
```

INPUT

```
                                   IBM AND APPLE
FORMAT:
  line # INPUT ["prompt string";] variable
  [,variable]..
```

This format shows a style of input allowed on both IBM and Apple that includes the screen prompt as a part of the INPUT statement. The characters in the prompt string will appear on the screen followed by a question mark. If you do not want the question mark, use a comma rather than a semicolon. Because the prompt is a part of the INPUT statement, which requests the input of some variable, there will be a pause until you enter that data. Using an INPUT statement in Initialization allows us to follow with our standard process loop, where the data that determines whether we continue or not is entered at the end of the loop and tested at the top of the loop.

In order to show you the use of prompts with the INPUT statement, a portion of the screen display from Project 1 is shown in Figure B.7.4.

FIGURE B.7.4

```
  ENTER THE NAME OF THE DATA FILE YOU WISH TO MAKE   DATA
  ENTER THE CUSTOMER NAME, NUMBER, QUANTITY, AND UNITPRICE
   CUSTOMER NAME? MACRO LTD
  CUSTOMER NUMBER? 101
  QUANTITY ? 11
  UNITPRICE? 1.02
  THIS IS WHAT YOU ENTERED
  MACRO LTD        101              11              1.02
  ENTER YES TO CONTINUE OR NO TO REENTER THE DATA? YES
  ARE YOU FINISHED ADDING RECORDS?  ENTER NO TO ADD MORE OR YES TO END
      THE PROGRAM? NO
  ENTER THE CUSTOMER NAME, NUMBER, QUANTITY, AND UNITPRICE
   CUSTOMER NAME? MACRO LTD
  CUSTOMER NUMBER? 101
  QUANTITY ? 21
  UNITPRICE? 1.16
  THIS IS WHAT YOU ENTERED
  MACRO LTD        101              21              1.16
  ENTER YES TO CONTINUE OR NO TO REENTER THE DATA? YES
  ARE YOU FINISHED ADDING RECORDS?  ENTER NO TO ADD MORE OR YES TO END
      THE PROGRAM? NO
  ENTER THE CUSTOMER NAME, NUMBER, QUANTITY, AND UNITPRICE
   CUSTOMER NAME? ABLE INC
  CUSTOMER NUMBER? 102
  QUANTITY ? 12
  UNITPRICE? 2.13
  THIS IS WHAT YOU ENTERED
  ABLE INC         102              12              2.13
  ENTER YES TO CONTINUE OR NO TO REENTER THE DATA? YES
  ARE YOU FINISHED ADDING RECORDS?  ENTER NO TO ADD MORE OR YES TO END
      THE PROGRAM? NO
  ENTER THE CUSTOMER NAME, NUMBER, QUANTITY, AND UNITPRICE
   CUSTOMER NAME?
  CUSTOMER NUMBER?
  QUANTITY ?
  UNITPRICE?
  THIS IS WHAT YOU ENTERED
                   0              0              0
  ENTER YES TO CONTINUE OR NO TO REENTER THE DATA?
  ARE YOU FINISHED ADDING RECORDS?  ENTER NO TO ADD MORE OR YES TO END
      THE PROGRAM?
```

WRITE#

```
                                                       IBM
  FORMAT:
    line # WRITE #file number, list of
    expressions
```

The WRITE# statement is used to write data to a sequential file. The items in the list of expressions may be separated with either commas or semicolons. When the data is written to the file, the following occur:

1. Commas are placed between data items.
2. Strings are surrounded by quotes.
3. No blank space is placed in front of a positive number.
4. A carriage return is inserted after the last item in the list.

This statement sends data to a file in a manner that can be read using the INPUT# statement.

CLOSE

```
                                                       IBM
  FORMAT:
    line # CLOSE [[#] file number [,[#]file
number]...]
```

When we are finished with a file, we close it so that:

1. the device or file number may be reused
2. any data still in the buffer of a file that has been opened for output will be written to the file.

If no file numbers are used in the CLOSE statement, then all devices and files that are open are closed. If we wish to close specific files, we use the file numbers.

```
                                                     APPLE
  FORMAT:
    line # PRINT D$;"CLOSE file name"
```

The PRINT D$ is used when we close the file just as when we issued the OPEN and WRITE commands. This command causes any data left in a buffer to be written. In the case of an output file, an end-of-file marker is placed at the end of the file. Remember, the D$ is a variable name representing CHR$(4).

Problem Analysis—Project 2

Project 2 is designed to access the sequential file created in Project 1.

Output Required   The same as Section 4, Project 2.

Input Required   The same as Section 4, Project 2.

Processing Required   The same as Section 4, Project 2, except include disk file handling statements.

Input Values   The same as Section 4, Project 2.

Output Format   The same as Section 4, Project 2.

The Flowchart   See Figure B.7.5.

Explanation of Logic Used

The file created in Project 1 is OPENed. The data records will be processed until the loop control detects the end of the data file. The end is detected using the built-in BASIC function EOF(). With detection of the end of file processing is completed. Control is passed back to the command module, the file is closed and the program completed.

End of Job   The disk file is closed.

The BASIC Program

See Figure B.7.6.

The Actual Output

See Figure B.7.7.

BASIC Language Discussion

OPEN   For IBM the file DATA7 is being opened as input with a file number 1 assigned to it. The only change, then, is the word *input* rather than *output*. The OPEN for Apple is the same whether the file is being used for input or output. Apple does require a separate statement to indicate that the file is to be read, however; it is shown below.

```
                                         APPLE
 FORMAT:
    line # PRINT D$;"READ file name"
```

FIGURE B.7.5

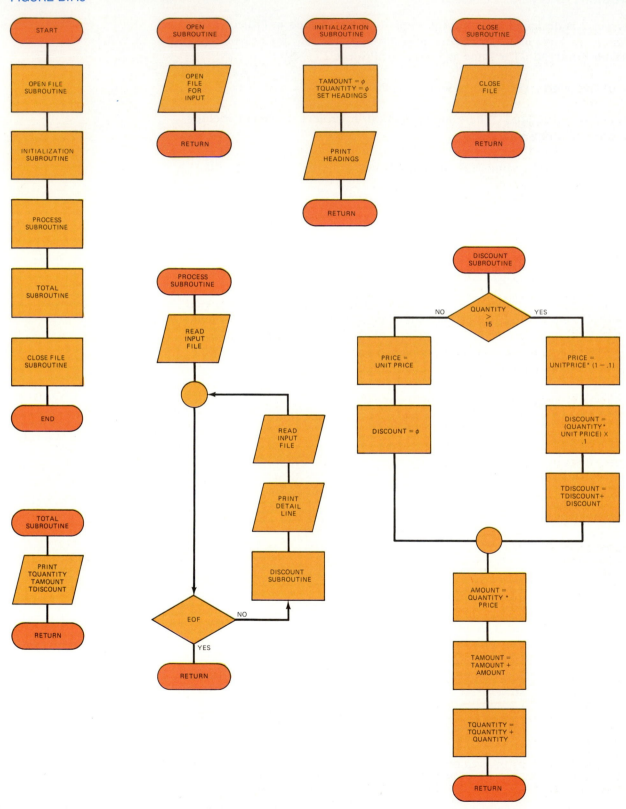

```
10 REM   PROGRAM ID: CASE7B
20 REM   AUTHOR ID:  MURPHY/LONGHURST        DATE WRITTEN: 5/26/8X
30 REM
40 REM   THIS PROGRAM ACCESS A DATA FILE FOR CUSTOMER INFORMATION
50 REM   CALCULATES TOTAL AMOUNT FOR EACH ORDER AND TOTAL
60 REM   QUANTITY AND AMOUNTS AFTER ALL ORDERS HAVE BEEN PROCESSED
70 REM
80 REM VARIABLE LIST
90 '     CUSTNAM$............CUSTOMER NAME
100 '    CUSTNO..............CUSTOMER NUMBER
110 '    AMOUNT..............DOLLAR VALUE OF ORDER
120 '    QUANTITY............QUANTITY
130 '    DISCOUNT............DISCOUNT AMOUNT
140 '    UNITPRICE...........UNIT PRICE
150 '    TAMOUNT.............TOTAL DOLLAR VALUE OF ALL ORDERS
160 '    TDISCOUNT...........TOTAL DISCOUNT OF ALL ORDERS
170 '    TQUANTITY...........TOTAL QUANTITY OF ALL ORDERS
180 '    FILE$.............. NAME OF DATAFILE
200 '
210 '************* COMMAND MODULE***********
220 '
230 GOSUB 1000                    ' OPEN DATA FILE
240 GOSUB 310                     ' INITIALIZATION SUBROUTINE
250 GOSUB 500                     ' PROCESSING
260 '
270 GOSUB 700                     ' TOTAL SUBROUTINE
280 GOSUB 1100                    ' CLOSE DATA FILE
290 ' *******************END OF COMMAND MODULE****************
300 END                          ' END OF JOB
310 ' *************INITIALIZATION MODULE*************
320 CLS
330 LET TAMOUNT = 0
340 LET TQUANTITY = 0
350 LET F1$ = "$$###.##     $$###.##"
360 LET F2$ = "$$####.##"
370 '   PRINT HEADINGS
380 LPRINT "COMPANY","COMPANY NO.", "QUANTITY", "PRICE/UNIT", "AMOUNT"

                TAB(68) "DISCOUNT"
390 LPRINT
400 RETURN
410 ' *********************END OF SUBROUTINE***********
420 '
500 '***************PROCESSING ROUTINE***********
510 INPUT #1,CUSTNAM$, CUSTNO, QUANTITY,UNITPRICE              ' PRIMING READ
520 '
530 '
540 WHILE NOT EOF(1)
550     '
560     GOSUB 780
570     '
580     LPRINT CUSTNAM$, TAB(18) CUSTNO, TAB(32) QUANTITY,
590     LPRINT USING F1$;UNITPRICE,AMOUNT;
600     LPRINT TAB(65) USING F2$; DISCOUNT
610 INPUT #1, CUSTNAM$,CUSTNO, QUANTITY,UNITPRICE              ' NEXT RECORD
620 WEND
630 RETURN
640 ' ********************* END OF PROCESSING SUBROUTINE
650 '
700 REM ******************PRINT TOTALS  SUBROUTINE
710 LPRINT
720 LPRINT "TOTAL NUMBER OF ITEMS SOLD  " TAB(43) TQUANTITY
730 LPRINT "TOTAL DOLLAR VALUE OF ALL ORDERS  " TAB(37) USING F2$; TAMOUNT
740 LPRINT "TOTAL AMOUNT OF DISCOUNTS " TAB(37) USING F2$;TDISCOUNT
```

FIGURE B.7.6. cont'd

```
750 RETURN
760 REM ************END OF TOTALS SUBROUTINE
770 REM
780 ' **************DISCOUNT SUBROUTINE
800 IF QUANTITY > 15 THEN 840
810     LET PRICE = UNITPRICE
820     LET DISCOUNT = O
830     GOTO 900
840     LET PRICE = UNITPRICE * (1- .1)
850     LET DISCOUNT = (QUANTITY * UNITPRICE) * .1
860     LET TDISCOUNT = TDISCOUNT + DISCOUNT
870 '
880 '
890 '
900     LET AMOUNT = QUANTITY * PRICE
910     LET TAMOUNT = TAMOUNT + AMOUNT
920     LET TQUANTITY = TQUANTITY + QUANTITY
930 RETURN
1000 REM ************ACCESS DATA FILE
1010 INPUT "ENTER NAME OF INPUT DATA FILE ";FILE$
1020 OPEN FILE$ FOR INPUT AS #1
1030 RETURN
1100 ' **************CLOSE DATA FILE
1110 CLOSE #1
1120 RETURN
```

FIGURE B.7.7

```
ENTER NAME OF INPUT DATA FILE ? DATA
COMPANY         COMPANY NO.   QUANTITY        PRICE/UNIT    AMOUNT     DISCOUNT

MACRO LTD           101          11              $1.20      $13.20     $0.00

TOTAL NUMBER OF ITEMS SOLD                 11
TOTAL DOLLAR VALUE OF ALL ORDERS       $13.20
TOTAL AMOUNT OF DISCOUNTS              $0.00
Ok
LOAD"CASE3D
Ok

RUN
COMPANY         COMPANY NO.   QUANTITY        PRICE/UNIT    AMOUNT     DISCOUNT

MACRO LTD           101          11              $1.02      $11.22     $0.00
MACRO LTD           101          21              $1.16      $21.92     $2.44
ABLE INC            102          12              $2.13      $25.56     $0.00
BETA CO             103          15              $3.71      $55.65     $0.00
BETA CO             103          19              $1.47      $25.14     $2.79

TOTAL NUMBER OF ITEMS SOLD                 78
TOTAL DOLLAR VALUE OF ALL ORDERS       $139.49
TOTAL AMOUNT OF DISCOUNTS             $5.23
Ok
```

This is a DOS instruction that tells the computer that all INPUT statements should come from disk until another DOS instruction is executed. After this statement a normal INPUT statement may be used to read from the disk.

```
PRINT D$;"READ DATA 7"
INPUT CUSTNO, INVNO, PARTNO
```

EOF

```
                                        IBM
FORMAT:
   line # EOF (file number)
```

The file number should be the same file number that was specified of the input file in the OPEN statement.

The EOF function provides a value that can be tested in a program to determine if end of file has been reached. This test can be made using the IF, ON, or WHILE statements.

```
Examples:
   IF EOF(1) . . .
   WHILE NOT EOF(1) . . .
   ON EOF(1) GOSUB . . .
```

```
                                        APPLE
FORMAT:
   line # ONERR GOTO line number
```

This statement can be used to test for the end of a disk file when using Apple BASIC. The statement should go in the Initialization subroutine. When any error occurs, including attempting to read past end of file, this command transfers control to the line number specified. It can be used to transfer control to the End of Job subroutine.

INPUT#

```
                                                      IBM
FORMAT:
  line # INPUT# file number, variable
  [, variable]
```

The file number must be the same file number used in the OPEN statement when the file was opened as input. The list of variable names should represent the data items in the order they were stored in the file with the WRITE statement.

Glossary

Access Time The time required to read out the contents or to write information into a randomly selected address in memory.

Accounting Programs Application software for performance of accounting functions. *See also* Module.

Accumulator The arithmetic/logic unit (ALU) of the central processing unit of a computer, where the actual data processing takes place.

ADA A fourth-generation language endorsed by the U.S. Department of Defense for use by its suppliers and contractors.

Address Number assigned to a specific memory location.

Algorithm A statement of the steps to be followed in performing a task or solving a problem. In a computer program the steps of an algorithm are specified in a specific computer language.

Analog Computers Computers that respond to infinite variations in electrical current or voltage and thus are the opposite of digital computers, which respond only to the binary digits 1 and 0. Earliest computers were analog computers, and are less accurate than digital computers. Analog technology lends itself easily to voice-wave input.

APL A popular programming language with considerable power that is used primarily for scientific applications on large computers.

Application Automation of business or other procedures by computer to solve a problem or accomplish a task.

Application Programmer Member of the systems development team who designs, codes, and tests computer programs for application areas.

Application Generator Software device enabling a programmer to generate an application program by providing additional functions, specifying program logic, and creating output formats.

Application Software One of the two broad kinds of instructions needed by computers to make them function. Application software tells a computer how to perform a specific task.

Arithmetic/Logic Unit (ALU) The part of the CPU that does the actual computing and performs logical operations such as comparing, guided by a computer program.

Artificial Intelligence A computer-based system producing performance that in humans would be associated with intelligence.

ASCII (American Standard Code for Information Interchange) An 8-bit code, the most common code used for the transmission of text between computers. It differs from the EBCDIC in the bit patterns used to identify zone positions.

Assembler Program through which instructions in assembly language can be translated into machine language. At the same time, the assembler assigns them specific locations in computer memory.

Assembly Language An improvement on machine language, substituting mnemonic codes and symbols for the binary numbers of machine language, while retaining the command of the computer that machine language offers.

Asynchronous Transmission mode in which characters are identified by start and stop bits. Characters can be sent at irregular intervals and the transmission is much slower than synchronized transmission.

Automated Data Processing The manipulation of data in a computer-based system to achieve a desired result. The components of a data processing system include input devices, output devices, auxiliary storage devices, and the central processing unit.

Auxiliary Storage Because only a very limited amount of data or instructions can fit into main memory at one time, auxiliary storage is required to hold the excess. These auxiliary storage units are magnetic disks and magnetic tape, the same media generally used for input and output. When needed, the data and instructions in auxiliary storage can be read into main memory. Also known as secondary storage.

Backup An extra copy of a file or disk, kept in case the original is damaged or destroyed.

607

Bar Code Data encoded by means of lines of varying widths that can be read by an optical reader device.

Baseband Single-channel, high-speed transmission mode used by a LAN. *See also* Broadband.

BASIC A high-level language supplied with most microcomputers and small business computers; easy to learn and use, but not appropriate for sophisticated computer applications.

Batch Processing System by which the computer processes all input for an application at one time to produce the desired output even though input data might be collected periodically.

Binary System Notation based on the number 2, using only two integers, 0 and 1. Most computers use the binary system to store and input information.

Bit Short for **bi**nary di**git**, the smallest possible unit by which data are represented in a computer system.

Black Box Data processing jargon for the computer itself.

Blocking The grouping of several records (known in this context as logical records) together into one block (called a physical record).

Blocking Factor The number of logical records per physical record. The higher the blocking factor, the less wasted space a tape contains. *See* Density and Blocking.

Broadband Multichannel, high-speed transmission mode used by a LAN. *See also* Baseband.

Bus LAN configuration that consists of a cable to which devices are connected by a cable-interface unit. The network has no central controller, and data can be passed from one device to another through the bus.

Business Application Data processing in the context of a business environment.

Business Application Software Application software for such business areas as bookkeeping, human resource management, and inventory control.

Byte A grouping of bits (usually eight) required to define one character.

C A fourth-generation language with some characteristics of assembly language, some characteristics of a high-level language, and the great strength of transportability: programs written in C can be transferred among computers whose processors differ.

CAD/CAM Computer-assisted design and computer-assisted manufacturing, an important use of computer graphics.

Card Reader A device that "reads" the information on punched cards containing data to be entered into the computer. A group of such cards can then be sorted by the computer according to a program.

Cassette Tape Magnetic medium played on cassette recorders. Cassettes work quite slowly because access to them is sequential.

CD-ROM Disk A data-storage device capable of holding huge amounts of data and easily usable with personal computers, but presently capable of read-only memory.

Central Control A type of data communication network control. *See also* Contention.

Centralized Data Processing System in which the functions of operations, technical support, and systems development are centralized.

Central Processing Unit (CPU) The part of the computer that actually handles and processes data. It contains three parts—the arithmetic/logic unit, main memory, and the control unit.

Chain and Train Printers A class of fast impact printers.

Channel Output processors that work concurrently with the main CPU but do not work in total independence. For a channel to operate, the supervisor must issue a channel command accompanied by the necessary information, such as memory location for input or output, device name, file name, etc.

Character A number, a letter, or a special symbol, which is the lowest level of organization by which data are processed and stored by a computer.

Character Data Any character, number, or symbol used in a microcomputer DBMS for naming or labeling purposes in the data base. *See also* Logical Data, Numerical Data.

Coaxial Cable Mode of transmission that gives a much higher quality of transmission than do wire pairs and also carries much more information at one time.

COBOL A high-level language well-suited to commercial applications.

Common Carrier A provider of communication services for a fee.

Communications Control Unit (CCU) A device that can connect several hundred communications lines to the central computers.

Compatability In the most general sense, the ability of various components of a computer system to work with other components in that system and, sometimes, with components of other systems. More specifically, especially concerning PC systems, the ability of an application program to function with a particular computer system's hardware and operating system as well as the ability of a computer system's hardware and operating system to support a particular application program.

Compiler A program that translates a program written in a high-level language into the computer's machine language.

Computer Electronic machine which stores and processes data according to the step-by-step directions of a program in order to produce the desired output.

Computer Graphics Applications involving the production of graphic images by a computer; important

ones include CAD/CAM, presentation graphics, and desktop publishing.

Computer-Assisted Retrieval (CAR) Memory system less expensive than computer memory or magnetic disk storage, CAR has improved the accessibility of files stored on microforms. Documents are indexed in a computer, and when the information is needed, the index is brought to a video display screen. With the aid of a micrographics reader, the user can key in the index and retrieve the wanted document.

Computer-Output Microfilm (COM) A process in which hardcopy computer output to be microfilmed is output on magnetic tape; it can be alphanumeric, graphic, or a combination of both. The tape is then input to an off-line microfilm recorder to create the microfilm.

Computer Program A sequenced set of instructions, written in a language the computer can interpret, that tells the computer how to accomplish a task.

Concentrator Refers to an "intelligent" multiplexer that can perform such functions as error detection, temporary storage, and changing message formats.

Conferencing Teleconferencing involves using computer terminals, a CPU, and a communications network for an ongoing meeting among people in separate geographic locations, who send and receive information at various times. Videoconferencing allows groups in different cities to meet by use of a large screen that projects each group's image and sound to each other and a smaller screen for the display of documents.

Contention A type of data communication network control. *See also* Central Control.

Control Language Software that allows the programmer to request the resources needed to run an application and to provide the operating system with the information it needs to allocate these resources.

Control Programs An operating system's programs for managing tasks and hardware and for scheduling other programs.

Control Information System Branch of an organization whose function is to overview operational activities to make sure that the organization is meeting its goals and not wasting its resources. Control involves setting a standard for performance, measuring performance, comparing performance to a standard, and taking corrective action.

Control Unit That part of the CPU that functions as a sort of traffic manager within the CPU, guiding the transfer of data and instructions to and from main memory and to and from auxiliary storage and input/output devices.

Corporate MIS Plan Sets down the strategies for developing information systems to meet the needs of an organization. The corporate MIS plan is a compre-

hensive portfolio of the services and applications that will be developed and supported by the corporation in order to accomplish its general business goals.

CRT Cathode-ray tube.

Cylinder All of the tracks on a disk that the comblike access mechanism can reach in any one position.

Daisy-Wheel Printer The most popular of the solid-font computer printers, with the capability of delivering letter-quality printouts.

Data Unorganized facts or representations of facts presented to the computer for processing into information.

Data Base Any collection of related data.

Data Base Administrator Member of the technical support system of a computer center whose function is to design and maintain a data base for the organization, establish security and backup procedures for the data base, and assist systems development teams in designing programs that use the data base.

Data Base Management System A layer of software that makes it possible to access stored data to be used in multiple applications.

Data Base Query Language A special language that makes it possible for a record stored in a data base to be displayed or printed out in response to a query. Complex query languages are designed in such a way that the user can ask questions about multiple records using commands very similar to written English.

Data Communications The transfer of encoded data from one location to another by electronic means.

Data Dictionary A centralized collection of information about all the data elements and resources of a particular data base.

Data Immediate Access Diagram (DIAD) Enables an analyst to identify how a file of records can be accessed.

Data Processing System The equipment and procedures by means of which the collection, processing, and distribution of data is achieved.

Data Recording Media Materials such as punched cards, paper tape, magnetic tape, or magnetic disk on which data are recorded and introduced into a computer system.

Deadlock Deadlock is a situation in which two or more processes are blocking each other in such a way that no process can finish its designated activity. This impasse condition is eliminated by introduction of the multiuser system.

Decentralized Data Processing An installation in which the hardware generally consists of a single minicomputer or microcomputer and its associated peripheral devices. The system usually processes only those programs for a specific application area.

Decision Support System (DSS) A computer-based system that helps decision makers use data and models to solve unstructured problems.

Decision Table Useful tool for program design and systems design. Decision tables make clear what actions a program should take for each given situation.

Decision Tree A tool that provides a clear description of the logic of a process so that users and analysts can spot errors.

Default Settings Basic assumptions about fundamental conditions made in many kinds of application programs, such as margin width and page depth in a word-processing program or column width in a spreadsheet program, which have program-specified sizes—default settings—until a user changes them.

Density The number of characters, or bytes per inch (bpi), that a tape upon which data are stored accommodates.

Desktop Publishing The use of PC-based systems and software to create and produce high-quality printed documents that may combine text and graphics.

Digital Computers Computers that respond to the binary digits 1 and 0, or on/off. Most computers today are digital, and they are faster and more accurate than the older analog computers.

Digitizer A device that scans graphic material and transforms it into digital data that can be read on a CRT screen.

Direct Access The capacity of a computer to go directly to any specified item of data stored anywhere on a disk instead of having to read from the beginning of a file until a specific item could be located.

Direct Access File A file from which data can be read and to which data can be written by placing the read/write mechanism directly at the location for this data. It is the opposite of sequential- or serial-access files.

Direct Access Storage Device (DASD) A device, almost always magnetic disks, that must be used for storage of direct access files. Direct access records can be written in changed form back to the storage locations they were read from.

Disk Drive A device that writes information onto—and reads information off—a floppy or hard disk; the most common storage and reading device on microcomputers.

Distributed Data Processing Refers to a data processing system in which a communications network connects centralized and decentralized computers that are compatible with each other.

Documentation Refers to anything that is written about how a system is designed or functions.

Dot-Matrix Plotter Plotting device that works without a pen, operating in the same manner as the dot-matrix printer. These plotters do not produce output in color, but are faster than pen plotters.

Dot-Matrix Printer Printer that forms characters by setting dots end to end. The dots are made by print needles in a matrix, or crisscross pattern.

Drum Printer Printout device shaped like a drum or cylinder with a complete set of characters engraved on it. The drum rotates rapidly against a row of hammers positioned on the opposite side of the paper to produce the printout.

Dumb Terminals Input devices that are used only to input data and instructions into the computer and to receive the processed information from the computer. A dumb terminal consists of a display screen, a keyboard for data entry, and a communication link to the CPU.

EBCDIC (Extended Binary Coded Decimal Interchange Code) One of the most widely used codes, developed to represent information more efficiently inside the computer. An 8-bit code, EBCDIC is also used for data transmission in data communications.

Egoless Programming A programming philosophy in which programs are no longer regarded as the personal property of a single programmer; the chief programmer team develops a program cooperatively.

Electronic Computer A computer which uses vacuum tubes, not mechanical gears or electromechanical relays, as switching devices. The ENIAC was the first completely electronic computer.

Electronic Funds Transfer Systems Computerized systems allowing a purchaser to pay for merchandise by direct transfer of funds, thus eliminating a great deal of paperwork.

Electronic Mail Application of information transfer by which messages are sent first by entering them into computers or other automated office systems and using telephone lines, local networks or satellites, to transmit them to other work stations. Once transmitted, they are stored and retrieved at a later, more convenient time.

Electronic Spreadsheet *See* Spreadsheet Program.

Electrostatic Printer Printout device that electrically charges spots on treated paper that correspond to letters or graphics. After being "charged" the paper is passed through a toner solution that sticks to the charged spots to produce the printed output.

Encoder A key-driven machine used primarily in banking transactions.

Enterprise Analysis The formal planning technique used by managers to define the information requirements of an organization before systems are developed.

Entity Person, place, or thing that is the subject of a data record.

Equipment Operator Member of the operations division of a computer center who runs the computer, including locating and placing magnetic disk and tape files on input devices, keeping output devices supplied with fresh media, and reporting visible problems with the way programs run.

Explanation Subsystem The aspect of an expert system that can explain to a user the line of reasoning that has resulted in a given conclusion.

Expert System A computer-based system that captures the rules of thumb, unwritten procedures, and intuitive judgments of experts in a field. Using algorithms developed from artificial intelligence research, developers of expert systems have created software that can be used to draw on expert knowledge to reach informed conclusions. *See also* Explanation Subsystem, Human Interface, Inference Engine, Knowledge Acquisition Subsystem, Knowledge Base.

Feedback Information about a system's output that is used to maintain or correct the operation of the system.

Field A basic unit of data, such as a person's name, used to organize data for purposes of storage and retrieval. *See also* Record and File.

File A collection of related records and the highest level in the data hierarchy.

File Management System An application software program that enables the user to create forms and to enter data records on these forms. The user can also verify, update, rearrange, retrieve, and print the data.

First Generation of Computers The characteristics of the first generation were (a) the machines were entirely electronic, using vacuum tubes for switches; (b) they employed binary notation; and (c) they used the stored-program concept.

Fixed-Length Record In a fixed-length record, as opposed to a variable-length record, every occurrence of the record has each of the fields present, and a given file is the same length from record to record.

Fixed-Length Word When each word in memory is assigned an address, information is stored and retrieved as words rather than as individual characters.

Fixed Partition Scheme in multiprogramming that tries to handle multiple users with a simple scheme for allocating memory. The system can run a fixed number of programs, and each user gets a fixed memory allocation for his or her program.

Floppy Disk Flexible plastic disk used for auxiliary storage of data on most small computers.

Flowchart A diagram of an algorithm that uses a set of standard symbols connected by lines.

FORTRAN The first high-level language to become widely available, suited to scientific and engineering applications but not commercial applications.

Fourth-Generation Languages (4GL) Very high-level languages enabling users to obtain information or to create applications or reports with little or no knowledge of programming. This group includes data base query languages, report generators, and application generators.

Fourth Generation of Computers In general terms, a generation of decreasing size and increasing power based on LSI and VLSI chips.

Full Duplex One of the three ways of transmitting data; permits data to be transmitted and received at the same time.

Function Key In a PC application program, a key that performs a special task.

Golf-Ball Printer Printing device that uses a movable sphere that rotates to the appropriate position and strikes an inked ribbon against the paper.

Graphic Output Any computer output that consists of line figures or other illustrations in place of or as a supplement to words or numbers. Graphic output, like text, can be either soft or hard.

Half Duplex One of the three ways of sending data between sending and receiving units, half duplex transmits two ways but only one way at a time.

Hard Copy Printed computer output.

Hard Disk *See* Winchester Disk.

Hardware The devices for inputting, processing, and outputting data in a computer system.

Hashing A means of getting at data in a direct access file by use of some type of calculation to convert a key to a disk address.

Hexadecimal Base 16 number system that computer programmers often use as a condensed way to represent the binary digits stored and processed inside the computer.

Hierarchical Data Model Data base in which data is organized in a ranked or graded series of levels. Because a diagram of this model resembles an upside-down tree, it is often called a tree model.

Hierarchy Chart Chart showing the relationships between modules in a computer program; the organization chart of a program.

High-Level Languages Refers to any computer language that is further away from the machine level.

Human Interface The aspect of an expert system that permits users who may not be technical experts to communicate with the system and understand its feedback.

Icon A screen symbol representing a choice available to the user of certain microcomputers. Apple Computers introduced icons, which are the equivalent of the menu- or command-driven systems of other PCs.

Impact Printer Printer that actually comes into contact with a type element in order to print output from a computer.

Implementation The final stage of systems development, bringing the system into being.

Indexed Sequential File File organization technique that permits both sequential and direct access to data. With this technique, indexes are used to divide a sequential file into segments which enable the operator to find a record more quickly from a sequential file.

Inference Engine The component of an expert system that uses the knowledge base to draw conclusions. Inference methods may be data-driven, goal-driven, or a combination of the two.

Information The results from purposeful processing of data.

Information Center Department of an organization designed to support end-user computing and provide decision support for managers and professionals.

Information Processing Processed data in a form that can be used for decision making.

Information System A subsystem of an organization with the method and resources an organization employs to collect, deliver, and use the information it needs for efficient operation. It serves as a feedback mechanism to monitor both internal operations and the external environment.

Information Utility A service that transfers data, text, and programs to any subscriber who owns a computer with a modem and communications software.

Input To introduce data into a computer; also, the data introduced.

Input Device Device that converts data into a computer compatible format.

Inquiry Checking data, using a terminal that the computer maintains on auxiliary storage. With on-line inquiry, a number is entered at the terminal which the computer uses as a key to match against a corresponding record it searches for on an auxiliary storage file. When a computer finds the matching record, it displays the data requested on the terminal screen.

Instruction Specification of how the CPU is to process the data that have been put into the computer. An instruction must tell what kind of operation is to be performed and it must provide the address in main memory of the data to be used in the operation or of another storage location to be referenced during the operation.

Integrated Circuit Commonly called a ''chip,'' an integrated circuit is an electronic circuit that has been greatly miniaturized and put on a chip.

Integrated Program Software combining two or more applications.

Intelligent Terminals Systems that incorporate microprocessors along with the display screen, keyboard, and the communication link to the CPU. They have the ability to edit, manipulate, store, and process data at the data-entry site, thus increasing data entry efficiency.

Interactive Responding directly and immediately to a user's input, as a PC does. Interactive graphics allow the revision of computerized graphic images without reprogramming.

Interpreter A program that translates one instruction at a time into machine language. This means that the interpreter performs the operations in the program as it reads them—line by line, using a built-in dictionary that gives machine-language equivalents of high-level commands.

Iteration One of the three control structures governing the logic of a structured computer program, an iteration is a loop that will be repeated within a program until a specified condition is met.

Inverted File Term used to describe a record in which all data elements serve as secondary keys to the file.

Isosynchronous Transmission mode using start and stop bits to identify characters. Speed is midway between that of synchronous and asynchronous transmission. Both sender and receiver are synchronized.

K A letter representing the number 1024, used to express the number of storage addresses in main memory. It is used to express the capacity of a computer's memory.

Key In computer processing and storage, the field that identifies each record in order to differentiate it from other records. It provides a unique identifier for the record. *See* Secondary Storage.

Keypunch Data entry machine that converts keyboard-entered data into a pattern of punched holes on a card. *See* Card Reader.

Key-to-Disk Auxiliary storage system in which storage disks are magnetic plates that hold much larger volumes of data than other media. Information contained on a disk is indexed by storage address and can be retrieved quickly by address or content. New data can be inserted into an existing file.

Key-to-Floppy Disk Auxiliary storage system in which data are input onto a flexible magnetic plate that can be used in a minicomputer or a microcomputer. This system is especially suitable for tasks involving relatively small volumes of data.

Key-to-Tape Recorder in which data are input by means of a keyboard similar to that of the keypunch machine. Key-to-tape recorders store data on half-inch computer-readable magnetic tape in either ASCII or EBCDIC.

Knowledge Acquisition Subsystem The aspect of an expert system that permits the addition of new rules to the knowledge base.

Knowledge Base The part of an expert system that

stores the factual knowledge and rules of thumb, or heuristics, the system uses for drawing conclusions.

Knowledge Engineer The person who, in the development of an expert system, works with an expert in a given field to develop and build a knowledge base.

Large-Scale Integration (LSI) The technology that can compress large numbers of integrated circuits or transistors on a single silicon chip.

Laser Communication Mode of transmission in which optical fibers are used to transmit laser light with minimal loss or distortion.

Leased Line Service provided by a common carrier that is in effect a permanent communications link between a sending and a receiving unit. A leased line becomes more economical with increased use.

Line Printer A computer output device that prints a whole line at a time, advances the paper, and then prints the next line.

Link Editor Before a program can be run, a compiler translates it into an object module. Then the link editor links together the object module and stored instructions that are already in the computer's memory to create a load module.

Loader A very simple routine of programming that takes each successive instruction in the program and puts it in a successive address in memory.

Load Module The end result of linking in computer programming, the load module is the code that is actually going to be loaded into the computer and executed.

Local Area Network (LAN) An electronic communications network that uses private branch exchanges (PBXs) or other local communication channels for transmission instead of public communications facilities such as a long-distance link or satellite communication. Its greatest advantage is that a LAN permits the linking up of a variety of devices.

Logical Data In a microcomputer DBMS, single characters used to represent the answers to true-false statements.

Logical Data Flow Diagram Easily understood graphic tool for systems analysis. The logical data flow diagram uses only four symbols, which allows the analyst to disregard details in order to get the clearest picture of the source and direction of the data.

Logical Operations The use of a computer to compare one value with another value and take alternative actions based on the outcome of the comparison is called a logical operation, as opposed to an arithmetic operation.

Machine Language Binary strings of 0s and 1s on which computers operate; the only language a computer understands.

Macro A selected series of keystrokes that invokes a particular function of an application program. The user of an application program, rather than the original programmer, creates macros.

Magnetic Bubble Memory A series of small magnetic fields, all magnetized in the same direction, clustered on a chip of garnet crystal. Each magnetic field can function as an on/off switch when the direction of its magnetic force is changed. Each memory chip is surrounded by a permanent magnetic field and thus is protected from dust and other contaminants.

Magnetic Core Memory Used in UNIVAC II, it became the industry standard in the second generation of computers. A magnetic core is a tiny ring of ferromagnetic material only a few hundredths of an inch in diameter. Thousands—sometimes millions—of these rings were strung on ultrathin wires to build a computer memory. They reduced data retrieval time to millionths of a second.

Main Memory The part of the CPU that holds both the data and the instructions needed for processing. Only a limited amount of data or instructions can fit into main memory at one time. Also called primary storage or main storage. *See also* Auxiliary Storage.

Management Information System (MIS) A system using computer and human resources to process all the information needed to support an organization's activities, management, and decision making.

Memory *See* Storage

Menu A list of choices in a software program.

Message Switching Sending messages from one terminal to another in a data communcation network.

MICR Magnetic-ink-character recognition is one of the three major technologies used in source data automation. MICR readers can read and interpret a single line of information printed in a special ink that contains magnetic particles.

Microcomputer A small-sized computer made possible by the invention of the microprocessor. Also known as a personal computer or PC.

Microprocessor A general-purpose computer that could be programmed to do any number of tasks, making it no longer necessary to design circuits specifically for each intended purpose. In the microprocessor a single chip contains all the circuits necessary to perform the basic functions of a whole computer.

Microwave Link Mode of transmission that sends data in microwave form from tower to tower, roughly thirty miles apart. Such links can carry thousands of voice channels and are widely used for video transmission.

Minicomputer A class of computer introduced in 1965 that was smaller and less expensive than the large computers. Many small businesses bought these more affordable computers, resulting in a wide

range of new English-based languages developed for use with them.

Mode A particular operating state of a software program, such as insert mode or print mode. An indication of a program's current mode is very often part of the screen display.

Model A spreadsheet that has been set up for a specific application.

Modem A two-way adapter between a transmission channel and either a CCU or a terminal; *modem* comes from modulator-demodulator.

Module A program for a particular aspect of accounting practice, including general ledger, accounts receivable, accounts payable, inventory, and payroll.

Multiplexer A device that converts several slow-speed signals into high-speed signals for transmission over a communication line.

Multiprogramming A system that has the ability to handle many programs at one time.

Multitasking The use of one or more small computers to perform partial tasks while the main CPU performs processing.

Multitasking Operating System An operating system that enables a CPU to perform more than one task simultaneously.

Multiuser System A system that prevents deadlock, which can occur when two users are trying to gain access to the same file and to update it at the same time.

Nanosecond A billionth of a second.

Nassi-Schneiderman Structured Flowchart (N-S Chart) These flowcharts have traditional specific graphic conventions, but the flow of an entire module in an N-S chart can be viewed at a glance, without having to follow arrows as in traditional flowcharts.

Network Data Model One of the three major types of data base models. In the network data model, data can be related in many ways, including one-to-many and many-to-many.

Nonimpact Printer Usually faster and better quality than an impact printer producing computer output, the nonimpact printer does not come into contact with a type element in order to print. There are four categories of nonimpact printer: thermal, electrostatic, laser, and ink-jet.

Normalization The process for simplifying data into two-dimensional tables.

Numeric Data In a microcomputer DBMS, any number or symbol used in a mathematical formula or used to perform calculations.

Object Program A program written in a high-level language that has been translated into the computer's machine language by the compiler.

OCR Optical character recognition is a technology that reads input characters optically rather than magnetically.

Off-Line DP system in which data are recorded on a computer-readable medium, such as cards, magnetic tapes, or magnetic disks, before entering the computer itself.

On-Line Interactive system in which terminals can be used to enter data into the computer system and also to receive processed data as output.

On-Line Inquiry A request made through a personal computer with access to on-line data bases. On-line inquiries make information available to a user who has keyed in an inquiry at a terminal connected by a communications line to a host computer.

On-Line Processing Data processing alternative in which input is processed when it is entered.

Operating System A collection of programs that allows a computer to supervise its own operations, automatically calling in programs, routines, languages, and data as needed for continuous throughput of jobs. The system controls input and output operations, provides data to programs, and assigns data and programs to storage locations.

Operational Information System The procedure by which all of the data resulting from an organization's day-to-day transactions are acquired, recorded, and stored. It consists of identifying, collecting, and registering all transactions that result from acquiring or expending resources. The data resulting from this activity produce the basis of the operational system.

Operation Code The number assigned to each of the operations a computer is able to do that specifies to the CPU what the computer is to do.

Operations Division Refers to that section of a computer center of an organization that runs and schedules the computer and associated machines. Operations personnel consist of a manager, data entry operators, and equipment operators.

Optical Fibers Used together with laser beams, an extremely high-capacity mode for data communications, capable of carrying 100,000 times more information than microwaves can.

Output Data after they have been processed by a computer. *To output* is to transfer these data to a printer or storage device.

Output Device Translates data from the format used in the computer back into the form that people understand.

Overlay An important feature of a direct access storage device by which a record can be read from direct access storage into the computer's main storage, updated there by a computer program, and then written back into the original direct access storage location.

Page Printer Computer printout device that prints an entire page at a time.

Pascal An elegant programming language used for scientific applications consistent with structured programming principles.

Pen Plotters Plotting technique in which a pen comes into contact with paper, producing hard copy output by drawing graphs, maps, charts, and pictures on paper.

Personal Productivity Software Application software mainly for PCs enhancing the gathering, analysis, presentation, and communication of information.

PL/I A high-level language more useful than either COBOL or FORTRAN alone; well suited for both business and scientific applications; lends itself to structured programming.

Point-of-Sale Terminals Terminals used in a retail setting to act as a cash register. They may be programmable or connected to a central computer.

Polling Process used by the central unit of a communications center in which it "asks" each terminal in turn if it has a message to send.

Presentation Graphics Computer-generated graphics including graphs and charts producible as soft copy and many different kinds of hard copy and used in business environments.

Primary Key A data element in a record that uniquely defines it from all the other records in a file.

Primary Sort Field A field of data arranged by a DBMS in a selected order.

Process Act upon or manipulate data to produce information.

Process Management Computer programming activity ensuring that processes don't get in one another's way; to make sure not only that they do what they are supposed to do, but that they do it when they are supposed to.

Program A series of instructions that direct the computer system to perform a specific operation.

Program Design The middle step between system design and the actual coding of a program; in this step, the parts of a system design that require a computer program are structured into a form that can be directly translated into computer instructions.

Protocol In data communications, a predetermined procedure or routine used by sending and receiving units to ensure that they are communicating properly.

Prototype A model that is developed, experimented with, modified, and discarded when a better model can be made; often used in engineering processes.

Prototyping Approach A strategy characteristic of the design of a decision support system in which a builder works with a system user to develop a model

and to refine the system until the user's requirements are met.

Pseudocode Also called structured English, pseudocode expresses the logic of a program in a language quite similar to actual computer language; a brief format for writing computer program statements, general enough not to be tied to any specific computer language yet easy to use in coding a program.

Punched Card Card on which data is stored by means of punched holes.

Qualifier A limiting condition in an "if-then" statement.

Query The request for specific data made by a user or manager.

RAM (Random Access Memory) Also called main memory or read/write memory, RAM is the place from which the central processing unit of a microcomputer "reads" software instructions and data and to which the CPU "writes" its output. Allows each word held in main memory to be directly retrieved from its address independent of the order in which the words are stored.

Random Access File *See* Direct Access File.

Reader-Sorter Used primarily in banking transactions, a reader/sorter processes a check after it has been encoded on the encoder.

Read-Only Memory *See* ROM

Record A collection of related fields in the processing and storage of data. Records can be fixed or variable in length. *See* Secondary Storage.

Register Temporary storage area for data and instructions within the CPU. A register can receive information, hold it, and transfer it very quickly.

Relational Data Model Relates data elements to each other in two-dimensional tables, or relations. The creation of a relational model involves the process of normalization, which creates new relations by separating out repeating groups of data items from a file.

Relational Structure *See* Relational Data Model.

Remote Job Entry Describes the submission of a computer program to be processed at a central site with output to be distributed to a remote printer.

Remote Terminal Used to collect data at a different location from the computer itself. Some types of remote terminals are point-of-sale terminals, touch-tone devices, data collection devices, graphic-display devices, and voice-input devices.

Report Generators Make it possible to extract data from a data base and create the kind of report from this data that the user requests. Some report generators act in combination with a data base query language.

Resolution Refers to the quality of the computer graphics produced by printout devices, low resolution

being of poor quality and high resolution being of good quality.

Retrieval The recapture of stored data.

Ring LAN configuration that links devices together in a loop or circle. Data are transmitted around the ring with the attached devices picking out the information addressed to them.

Robotics An application of artificial intelligence in which robots are programmed to handle specialized tasks, most often in product manufacture and assembly.

ROM (Read-Only Memory) A memory chip containing instructions that have been permanently stored during the manufacturing process. Such instructions are written into storage locations only once; they can be read repeatedly whenever needed but cannot be changed.

RPG A high-level language invented to generate reports without describing program logic, a forerunner of fourth-generation languages.

Satellite Link Mode of transmission using transponders to "bounce" microwave signals from one station to another; capable of carrying very large volumes of information.

Schema The basic organization of a data base. The schema description includes the names of all data entities, their attributes, and their relation to each other.

Scrolling Moving text up or down, right or left on a CRT screen. Horizontal scrolling lets the screen show lines of text that are wider than the screen itself. Vertical scrolling is the most common form used and provides the capability to change the display by moving text up or down.

Secondary Key Data element in a file that enables the data processor to identify all records in a file that have a common attribute characteristic.

Secondary Storage *See* Auxiliary Storage.

Second-Generation Computers Employed transistors in place of vacuum tubes, greatly increasing the speed and reliability of computers. They also used magnetic-core memory for internal storage and made extensive use of magnetic tape and disks for external storage.

Selection One of the three control structures governing the logic of a structured program, selection is a division in the flow based on a test in the program.

Selective Query An "if-then" question whose answer draws on the data in a DBMS.

Semiconductor Memory Memory type characteristic of most modern computers; in semiconductor memory an electronic current is a memory cell.

Sequence One of the three control structures governing the logic of a structured program, sequence is the traditional linear flow, with instructions executed in

sequence from the beginning to the end of the program.

Sequential File A file containing records ordered in key sequence and typically requires two files, one containing data that must be updated, based on transactions read from the other. Sequential files must be processed in sequence.

Serial Printer Like a typewriter, serial printers can only print one character at a time in delivering computer output.

Service Programs An operating system's programs for preparing and executing application programs.

Simplex One of the three ways of sending data between sending and receiving units, simplex transmits one way only.

Single-Tasking Operating System An operating system that enables a CPU to perform only one task at a time.

Single-User System A system designed to execute one program at a time. Single-user systems handle a number of functions, including link editing and loading, execution, file management, device management, and memory management.

Smart Terminal An alphanumeric terminal that can perform all the tasks of a dumb terminal plus edit and format data for both input and output.

Soft Copy Computer output in a form other than a printed page or object. Both video and audio output are soft copy.

Software Computer programs that can be grouped into two categories: systems software, which directs the operation of a computer system; and application software, which allows the user of a computer system to accomplish specific data-processing tasks.

Sort Process by which files are read and information rearranged according to the listings the operator wants. Sorts can be done in ascending order, which begins with the lowest value and progresses to the highest; and descending order, which begins with the highest value and progresses to the lowest.

Source Data Collection The acquisition of data at its point of origin. Information is entered at a remote location and then stored for eventual transmission to a central computer.

Source Document Any material bearing data for inputting into the computer by means of source data automation.

Source Program The high-level language code that must be translated into a computer's machine language by a compiler or interpreter.

Spooling An acronym for *Simulated Peripheral Operations On-Line.* The term *spooling* indicates the ability to have peripheral (I/O) devices doing work at the same time that the CPU is doing work.

Spreadsheet Program Application program enabling

the arrangement of data in columns and rows, calculation and recalculation of numerical data, and automatic changes in other data based on the calculations.

Star LAN configuration that links devices together using a central PBX.

Storage The holding of data. Within a computer, data can be stored in CPU locations; outside the computer, data can be stored in or on auxiliary storage media.

Stored Program The ability to store programs enabled a computer to perform a variety of tasks without cumbersome rewiring. This innovation was one of a group of typical characteristics of first-generation computers. It was first employed in the EDVAC.

Strategic Planning Information System Activity carried out by the chief operating officers of an organization through which data are collected on such things as competing firms' activities, interest rates, consumer behavior trends, and proposed changes in governmental regulations. Problems addressed by strategic planners involve long-range analysis and prediction.

String Any group of alphabetic characters recognized by a computer program as an item of data.

Structured Programming Technique that most readily meets the three criteria for a good program design: ease of understanding; ease in modifying and updating; and efficiency in execution.

Structured Systems Analysis Encourages constant interaction between systems analysts and users at all stages of systems design to assure a system that meets the needs of the users. Tools of structured systems analysis are logical data flow diagrams, logical data dictionary definition, and decision tables and trees.

Structured Walkthrough A group review of a computer program to detect errors and to make changes in the program design before the implementation stage.

Subschema Along with the schema, subschema are the basis for the data model used to organize the data base. Each data subset is a subschema defining a set of logical relationships that must be defined before the data model can be implemented.

Subsystem A system that is part of a larger system.

Supercomputers Computers, first developed in the second generation of computers, that perform greater numbers of calculations many times faster than other classes of computer.

Supervisor A program that normally resides in main computer storage when the computer is working and whose job it is to direct and control the execution of programs.

Switched Line Type of common-carrier transmission

capable of changing the route by which information is sent.

Synchronous Transmission mode that sends data in blocks, which may consist of thousands of characters.

System A set of parts or elements that interact to achieve a specific goal.

Systems Analysis Definition of a problem to be solved or an opportunity to be seized and determination of the objectives of a new, improved system.

Systems Design Design of the logical functions needed to achieve the goals a systems analysis has set forth.

Systems Programmer Member of the technical support segment of a computer center who maintains the hardware and software operating environment. A systems programmer installs the computer's operating system, tailors it and maintains it, and improves the efficiency of application programs.

Systems Software One of the two kinds of instructions needed by a computer in order for it to function; systems software directs the operations of the computer system, including such functions as controlling the input and output of data, translating input into machine-readable forms, and directing data and instructions to and from various locations.

Systems Utility Programs that enable such computer operations as the copying of data files from one disk to another and the editing or changing of files.

Technical Support That segment of a computer center responsible for the systems programming, documentation support, system evaluation, user services, and data base administration.

Teleconferencing *See* Conferencing.

Telephone Wire Cables Type of lines used in most data transmission channels, usually containing hundreds of wire pairs.

Telephone Wire Pairs Voice-grade channels that in data communications are 3000 Hz.

Template A spreadsheet model set up but with no data entered into it.

Terminal Emulator Software that makes a microcomputer look like a terminal to a mainframe computer.

Terminals Devices through which data are input into a computer and output is received from it. Types of terminals are video terminals, teletypewriter terminals, remote-job-entry terminals, transactions terminals, and intelligent terminals.

Thermal Printer One of four types of nonimpact printers used in computer printout, this type of printer uses a number of small heating elements to construct each character from dots. It requires special heat-sensitive paper.

Third Generation of Computers Computers characterized by the use of integrated circuits, or "chips,"

in place of transistors, increasing computational speed and decreasing computer size.

Time Division Multiplexing (TDM) One of the two types of multiplexing which first merges characters from separate messages into a "frame" and at the receiving end then "demultiplexes" the frame and transmits each individual character to its proper destination.

Time-Sharing The sharing of a computer's time by multiple users.

Touch-Tone Phone Input Data entry system useful when numeric data must be collected from general branch offices or other remote locations.

Track On the recording surface of a magnetic disk, concentric paths for recording data.

Transaction Data items that are input for a business application. A transaction can be a sales order, a name change, a time card, a bank deposit slip, or any of numerous other items. Transactions are used to update master records, such as employee records and inventory records.

Transistor A tiny electric switch that generates electric currents to turn each circuit in a computer's memory to the "on" or "off" position.

Type-Bar Printer Computer output machine in which the type characters that contact the paper are placed at the end of individual rods or bars.

Unstructured Program A linear computer program written so that it starts with the first instruction for the computer to execute, followed by the next instruction for the computer to execute, continuing sequentially to the last instruction for the computer to execute.

User-Driven Computing With fourth-generation application generators and report generators, users can create their own programs and reports, ending their dependence on programmers and speeding up the application-development process.

User-Programmed Terminal Has all the features of a smart terminal but also has a complete set of software for editing and formatting data as well as for compiling programs.

Utilities Specialized programs written to help the programmer perform routine and repetitive activities that are common to many applications, such as sorting and copying files.

Value Added Network Mode of transmission offered by common carriers that provides packet switching on leased lines. Packet switching divides a transmission into packets, which are sent individually by the most efficient route and then recombined at the receiving end.

Variable-Length Record A record in which every occurrence of the record need not have each of the fields present, and a given field need not be the same length from record to record. This means that each

occurrence of a record in a file is not the same—or is of a variable length.

Variable-Length Word When each address in working storage can reference only one byte, each byte is assigned an address and information is stored and retrieved as individual characters. This approach is called variable word length storage.

Variable Partition Scheme for allocating memory in a multiprogramming system that allows a number of variable sized partitions.

Very Large-Scale Integration (VLSI) The state of the art today. It refers to the ability to compress 500,000 or more transistors on a single chip. By the 1990s as many as 10 million transistors may be contained on a chip.

Videoconferencing *See* Conferencing.

Virtual Memory Scheme for expanding memory in a multiprogramming system by creating many small partitions and dividing programs into very small portions.

Voice Output Output available as vocal responses by telephone or "talking" terminal.

Voice Recognition An input technology that requires only the words spoken by the user and does not require keyboard skills or other technical training. Voice waves are directly converted to electrical waves in this input method, and are thus applicable in analog computer technology.

WATS Line Type of transmission-line service offered by common carriers, a WATS line provides what is known as a "metered" service.

Winchester Disk A nonremovable disk offering greater storage capacity and faster access speed than floppy disks. It is made from metal rather than plastic and is not flexible, removable, or exposed at any time to foreign objects such as dust and therefore can be engineered to greater precision. Also known as a hard disk.

Window Feature that enables users to view relevant aspects of different application programs, different parts of a document, or parts of separate files onscreen at the same time.

Wire Cables *See* Telephone Wire Cables.

Word A group of bits or binary digits in each address in main memory.

Word Processing Program Application software that automates processing or manipulation of characters by the computer. It includes editing, moving, deleting, inserting, and other operations on typed documents.

Working Memory *See* RAM.

Workstation A powerful computer used for engineering, scientific, and more recently business applications. Many workstations have very high-level graphics capabilities.

Index